MICHAEL PALIN
HALFWAY TO HOLLYWOOD
DIARIES 1980–1988

MICHAEL PALIN

HALFWAY TO HOLLYWOOD

DIARIES 1980–1988

Weidenfeld & Nicolson

LONDON

First published in Great Britain in 2009
by Weidenfeld & Nicolson

1 3 5 7 9 10 8 6 4 2

© Michael Palin 2009

A CIP catalogue record for this book is available
from the British Library.

ISBN: 978 0 297 84440 2 (hardback)
ISBN: 978 0 297 86018 1 (trade paperback)

Editorial by Linden Lawson and David Atkinson

Index by Douglas Matthews

Typeset by Input Data Services Ltd,
Bridgwater, Somerset

Printed in Great Britain by Clays Ltd, St Ives plc

Weidenfeld & Nicolson
The Orion Publishing Group Ltd
Orion House
5 Upper St Martin's Lane
London WC2H 9EA

An Hachette UK Company

www.orionbooks.co.uk

For Angela

Contents

List of illustrations

Section One:

With Laurel and Hardy in the garden at home[1]
Rachel Palin at Tower Bridge[2]
Tom with Denis the cat[2]
By a pool in Kenya[2]
Tied to a tree with Shelley Duvall, *Time Bandits* 1981[3]
Filming the Giant on Wembley Studio roof, *Time Bandits* 1981[3]
Pythons at the Hollywood Bowl 1980[4]
With George Harrison, Denis O'Brien, John Cleese and Neville Thompson on *Time Bandits* set[2]
John rehearsing Silly Walk, Hollywood Bowl 1982[2]
MP and John in Dead Parrot sketch, Hollywood Bowl 1982[2]
MP disrobing during Camp Judges sketch, Hollywood Bowl 1982[2]
Framed photos from the *Missionary* 1982[2]
MP with Rachel on set, *Missionary* 1982[2]
Bathing in the waterfall at Shava Lodge, June 1982[1]
Richard Loncraine, MP plus executive producers, *Missionary* 1982[2]
Receiving award from Chamrousse Festival, March 1985[5]
MP as The Missionary[6]
MP receives pie in the face, *Missionary* publicity, Dallas October 1982[7]
MP before cameras at same event[7]
MP as TV Presenter for *Comic Roots*, Sheffield 1983[2]

Section Two:

Pythons (sans Eric) at video launch, September 1985[8]
MP and animals supporting City Farm, 1984[2]
MP as Dad in Every Sperm is Sacred, *Meaning of Life* 1982[9]
Eric, Terry Jones, MP with friends, Christmas in Heaven, *Meaning of Life* 1982[9]
Dad with children, *Meaning of Life* 1982[9]
Pythons on location, jungle scene, *Meaning of Life* 1982[9]
MP as Jack Lint, *Brazil* 1984[2]
MP, Terry Gilliam and Jonathan Pryce rehearsing *Brazil* 1984[2]
MP surprised by Jonathan Pryce, Brazil 1983[2]
Terry Gilliam with Ray Cooper[2]
MP's mother in New York, January 1984[10]
MP, sister Angela, Nancy Lewis and his mother, New York January 1984[2]
MP's mother and Angela, *Saturday Night Live* party, January 1984[2]
Tristram Powell and Innes Lloyd, East of Ipswich filming, June 1986[2]

End of filming party, *East of Ipswich*[2]
MP, Terry Gilliam, David Robinson, John Cartwright and interpreter, Moscow 1986[2]
MP's mother and neighbour, at Reydon, Southwold, Suffolk[2]
Launching a rebuilt steam engine, Bluebell Railway[2]
"Mash" Patel, newsagent[2]
Sam Jarvis, painter and decorator[2]

Section Three

Will Palin and Eric Idle, at Eric's cottage in France 1984[2]
Al Levinson and Norman Rosten, Brooklyn, New York[2]

Filming of *Private Function*, 1984
George H and Denis O'Brien, Executive Producers[3]
Alan Bennett and MP on location in Yorkshire[2]
Maggie Smith and MP on location[11]
Trying to kill the pig. MP, Betty (the pig) and Maggie Smith[11]
Alan Bennett, Maggie Smith, MP with large foot, on location[11]
The two Grannies, Helen and MP, Private Function Royal Premiere, November 21st 1984[5]
Denholm Elliott and others in Private Function cast, in the gents toilet, Great Western Hotel
    Paddington[11]
Will, Tom, Rachel and Helen in Majorca, August 1986[2]
MP in cycling publicity shot, March 1986[2]
MP on Joan Rivers Show, 1986[12]

A Fish Called Wanda, Summer 1987
MP with Charlie Crichton[2]
MP with stand-in Gerry Paris[2]
MP with Kevin Kline[2]
John Cleese trying to get information from MP[13]
Ken Pile. Fan photo[13]
Jamie Lee Curtis and MP embrace[13]

The family with Granny outside Sunset House, Southwold 1987[2]
MP on location with Joyce Carey, Number 27, June 1988[2]

1 Brian Moody
2 Author's Collection
3 HandMade Films Partnership
4 Sam Emerson
5 Pic Photos
6 Trevor Jeal
7 Andy Hanson
8 Chris Richardson
9 David Appleby
10 Mark Mullen
11 David Farrell
12 Erik Heinila
13 David James

Acknowledgements

As with the first volume, 1969–1979, *The Python Years*, I have had to reduce over a million words of diary entries to something nearer a quarter of a million. In this task I have, as before, been sagely advised and supervised by Ion Trewin. Michael Dover at Weidenfeld and Nicolson has been a constant encouragement in the completion and collation of the edit, and Steve Abbott and Paul Bird at my office have been, as ever, hugely supportive.

Once again, I must reserve my most special thanks to Katharine Du Prez for her patience and persistence in the Herculean labour of transcribing the contents of twenty-four close-packed, handwritten notebooks.

Who's Who in the Diaries 1980–1988

FAMILY

Mary Palin, mother, living at Reydon, Southwold, Suffolk. Father died in 1977.
Helen, wife
Children:
Tom born 1968
William born 1970
Rachel born 1975

Angela, sister. Married to **Veryan Herbert** and living at Chilton, Sudbury, Suffolk. Died 1987.
Children:
Jeremy born 1960
Camilla born 1962
Marcus born 1963

Helen's family:
Anne Gibbins, mother
Elder sister, **Mary**, married **Edward Burd** in 1964
Daughter, **Catherine**, born 1966
Younger sister, **Cathy**

FRIENDS, NEIGHBOURS AND COLLEAGUES

Richard and Christine Guedalla, and daughters Louise and Helen, neighbours

Clare Latimer, neighbour

Terry Jones and **Alison**

Terry Gilliam and **Maggie**

John Cleese, formerly married to **Connie Booth**, one daughter, **Cynthia**, born 1971, married **Barbara Trentham** 1981, separated 1987

Graham Chapman, partner **David Sherlock**. **John Tomiczek** (adopted)

Eric Idle, married **Tania Kosevich** 1981

Robert Hewison. Contemporary of MP at Brasenose College, Oxford 1962–5, during which time he persuaded MP to perform and write comedy for first time.

Simon and Phillida Albury. Simon met MP after Oxford in 1965. Television journalist, producer and Gospel music fan.

Ian and Anthea Davidson. Met MP at Oxford. Encouraged him to perform in revue and gave him early work at the BBC. A writer and director and occasional Python performer.

Chris Miller and Bill Stotesbury. Chris looked after Eric's son Carey during *Life of Brian*. Bill is a designer and banjo player.

Neil and Yvonne Innes. Neil, Ex-Bonzo Dog Band. Worked closely with the Pythons especially on their stage appearances. Collaborated with Eric to create the Rutles. Sons: Miles and Luke.

Mel Calman, cartoonist and friend

George Harrison. Musician, ex-Beatle. Married to Olivia Arias, son Dhani born 1978.

Derek and Joan Taylor, Beatles' publicist and wife

Chris Orr, artist and printmaker

Charles McKeown, actor, writer and performer in many MP films and TV shows

Geoffrey Strachan. Editor at Methuen who encouraged Python to go into print. Also published the *Ripping Yarns* books.

Tristram and Virginia Powell. Tristram was director/collaborator on *East of Ipswich*, *Number 27* and worked on development of *American Friends*.

André Jacquemin. Recording engineer, Python recordist, composer (with Dave Howman) of some Python songs. Founder of Redwood Studios.

Trevor Jones/John Du Prez, musician and composer (Python songs and *A Fish Called Wanda*)

Ray Cooper, legendary percussionist who became important go-between and general troubleshooter on all the HandMade films

OFFICE

At Mayday Management / Prominent Features:

Anne James, formerly Henshaw, manager. Married to Jonathan James, a barrister

Steve Abbott, accountant/management, also film producer (*A Fish Called Wanda*)

Alison Davies

At EuroAtlantic / HandMade:

Denis O'Brien, Chief Executive, Executive Producer (*Time Bandits*, *The Missionary*, *A Private Function*)

Mark Vere Nicoll, legal expert

FILM REGULARS

Richard Loncraine, Director. First wife Judy. Married Felice 1985.

Neville Thompson, Producer

Mark Shivas, Producer

Julian Doyle. Editor, cameraman, who could turn his hand to any part of the film-making process. Indispensable part of both Python and Gilliam films.

John Goldstone, Producer of Monty Python films – *Holy Grail*, *Life of Brian* and *Meaning of Life*

Sandy Lieberson, Producer and sounding board for many projects, including Terry Gilliam's *Jabberwocky*

Patrick Cassavetti, Producer

IN AMERICA

Al Levinson. After wife Eve's death, married Claudie Calvez in 1979. Gwenola is their daughter.

Nancy Lewis. Publicist for Python in the USA, deserves much credit for getting them on US TV in the first place. Married actor Simon Jones in 1983.

The Films:

MONTY PYTHON LIVE AT THE HOLLYWOOD BOWL

Directors:	Terry Hughes (concert sequences)
	Ian MacNaughton (filmed sequences)
Producers:	Denis O'Brien – Executive Producer
	James Rich Jr – Concert Film Co-producer
	George Harrison – Executive Producer
Cast:	Graham Chapman
	John Cleese
	Terry Gilliam
	Eric Idle
	Terry Jones
	Michael Palin
	Neil Innes
	Carol Cleveland
Writers:	GC, JC, TG, EI, MP, TJ
Additional material:	Tim Brooke-Taylor
	Marty Feldman
	Angus James
	David Lipscomb
Editors:	Julian Doyle (post-production director and editor)
	Jimmy B. Frazier (editor: concert film)

TIME BANDITS

Director:	Terry Gilliam
Producer:	Terry Gilliam
Executive Producers:	George Harrison
	Denis O'Brien
Associate Producer:	Neville C. Thompson
Cast:	John Cleese
	Sean Connery
	Shelley Duvall
	Katherine Helmond
	Ian Holm
	Michael Palin
	Ralph Richardson
	Peter Vaughan
	David Rappaport
	Kenny Baker
	Malcolm Dixon
	Mike Edmonds
	Jack Purvis
	Tiny Ross
	Craig Warnock
Screenplay:	Michael Palin
	Terry Gilliam
Music:	George Harrison
Editor:	Julian Doyle

THE MISSIONARY

Director:	Richard Loncraine
Producers:	Michael Palin
	Neville C. Thompson
Executive Producers:	George Harrison
	Denis O'Brien
Cast:	Michael Palin
	Maggie Smith
	Trevor Howard
	Denholm Elliott
	Michael Hordern
	Phoebe Nicholls
Screenplay:	Michael Palin

Music:	Mike Moran
Editor:	Paul Green

MONTY PYTHON'S THE MEANING OF LIFE

Directors:	Terry Jones
	Terry Gilliam (segment 'The Crimson Permanent Assurance')
Producer:	John Goldstone
Cast:	Graham Chapman
	John Cleese
	Terry Gilliam
	Eric Idle
	Terry Jones
	Michael Palin
	Carol Cleveland
	Simon Jones
	Patricia Quinn
Screenplay:	GC, JC, TG, EI, TJ, MP
Editor:	Julian Doyle

BRAZIL

Director:	Terry Gilliam
Producers:	Patrick Cassavetti (co-producer)
	Arnon Milchan
Cast:	Jonathan Pryce
	Robert De Niro
	Katherine Helmond
	Ian Holm
	Bob Hoskins
	Michael Palin
	Ian Richardson
	Peter Vaughan
Screenplay:	Terry Gilliam
	Tom Stoppard
	Charles McKeown
Editor:	Julian Doyle

A PRIVATE FUNCTION

Director:	Malcolm Mowbray
Producer:	Mark Shivas
Executive Producers:	George Harrison
	Denis O'Brien
Cast:	Michael Palin
	Maggie Smith
	Denholm Elliott
	Richard Griffiths
	Tony Haygarth
	John Normington
	Bill Paterson
	Liz Smith
Screenplay:	Alan Bennett
Original story:	Alan Bennett and Malcolm Mowbray
Music:	John Du Prez
Editor:	Barrie Vince

A FISH CALLED WANDA

Director:	Charles Crichton
Producer:	Michael Shamberg
Executive Producers:	Steve Abbott
	John Cleese
Cast:	John Cleese
	Jamie Lee Curtis
	Kevin Kline
	Michael Palin
	Maria Aitken
	Tom Georgeson
	Patricia Hayes
Screenplay:	John Cleese
Story by:	John Cleese and Charles Crichton
Music:	John Du Prez
Editor:	John Jympson

Timeline

Main work projects during the period January 1980–September 1988

1980:
Writing and acting in *Time Bandits*
Filming 'Confessions of a Trainspotter', one-hour episode for BBC *Great Railway Journeys* series
Acting and filming *Monty Python Live at the Hollywood Bowl*.

1981:
Writing *The Missionary* and *Monty Python's The Meaning of Life*
Time Bandits released
First One-Man Show at Belfast Festival

1982:
Writing and acting in *The Missionary* and *The Meaning of Life*
The Missionary released in USA

1983:
The Missionary released in UK and Australia
The Meaning of Life released in US and UK. Wins Special Jury Prize at Cannes Film Festival
Film *Comic Roots*, one hour autobiographical documentary for BBC
Second Belfast Festival Show
Begin filming *Brazil*

1984:
Complete *Brazil* filming
Filming *A Private Function*
Shoot short film *The Dress*
A Private Function has Royal Premiere in London and opens in UK

1985:
A Private Function opens in USA

British Film Year
Dr Fegg's Encyclopeadia of <u>All</u> World Knowledge published
Write *East of Ipswich* film screenplay for BBC
Third Belfast Festival Show
Limericks published

1986:
Become Chair of Transport 2000
Brazil released.
East of Ipswich filmed in Southwold, Suffolk
Begin writing 'The Victorian screenplay' (later to become *American Friends*)
The Mirrorstone published
Ripping Yarns premieres on US TV

1987:
East of Ipswich shown on BBC2
Start filming 'Troubles' for LWT (cancelled after one week due to union dispute)
Write *American Friends*, first draft
Write *Number 27* film screenplay for BBC
Filming as Ken Pile in *A Fish Called Wanda*
First discussions for *Around the World in 80 Days*
Fourth Belfast Festival Show
Resign Chair of Transport 2000

1988:
Rewriting, financing and casting trips for *American Friends*
Filming of *Number 27*
A Fish Called Wanda opens in America
Begin London filming on *Around the World in 80 Days*
Leave London to circumnavigate the world

Introduction

These diaries cover a period of my life when, briefly, the prospect of international stardom shimmered on the horizon. As the decade began the Monty Python brand was resurgent. *The Life of Brian* was causing a stir, our stage show was about to be revived at the Hollywood Bowl and there was unprecedented financial interest in any new film we cared to write. By the time these extracts end it was all very different. Python, after many premature obituaries, had, in effect ceased to be. So, to all intents and purposes, had my chances of a Hollywood career. The last entry records my anxiety, not about films, but about an eighty-day journey around the world.

It wasn't that I hadn't given a film career a try. Between 1980 and 1988 I either wrote, or appeared in, seven movies. In varying degrees, all of them received support and interest from the major studios. Universal picked up *Monty Python's The Meaning of Life* and, together with 20th Century Fox, picked up Terry Gilliam's *Brazil*, Columbia took *The Missionary*, *A Fish Called Wanda* was made for MGM. The doors of Hollywood were open. Nor was I reluctant to look inside. As the diaries show I was spending more time on the West Coast than the East. I was hobnobbing with studio executives and being flown by Concorde to casting sessions. And yet, in the end, my feet remained firmly on this side of the Atlantic.

I still can't quite work out why all this happened the way it did, and I re-read the diaries with a mixture of curiosity and disbelief. The overall impression is of a kaleidoscope of characters and events, clarity and confusion, of great strides forward and long and rambling cul-de-sacs, from which a pattern emerges, but only briefly, like the moon between clouds on a stormy night. I'm in my late thirties when this volume begins and my mid-forties when it ends, so one might imagine that the course of my life and career would be settling down. But the inescapable conclusion from reading these entries is that this is a man who still doesn't really know what he wants to do, or what he's particularly qualified to do.

If this were a history, or an autobiography written in the future looking back, I feel sure the temptation would be to impose order and reason and logic on this period of my life, to detect themes and trends that led in one direction, in other words to make sense of it all.

But diaries don't allow such luxuries. The events of everyday life are by their nature unpredictable, not at all at ease with the order that we crave as we grow older. Meaning changes, slips, adjusts, evolves. Narrative exists only in its most basic sense.

Which is why I like diaries. The map may be constantly changing, the steering wheel may be spinning all over the place, but diaries are the sound of an engine running, day in and day out.

Michael Palin
London, April 2009

'I did, I think, nothing'
Evelyn Waugh's diary, *26th June 1924*

1980

As a new decade began I was enmeshed in two new projects. One was collaborating on the screenplay of a children's fantasy dreamt up by Terry Gilliam, and the other a proper serious documentary, on railways, for the BBC. Both of these were off my normal patch, which was exciting in a way but a little less predictable than I'd have liked. The bedrock of the family was being quietly and unsensationally strengthened; Helen and I had been married nearly fourteen years. Tom was eleven and Will was nine and Rachel coming up to five. Which meant a lot more responsibilities than the same time ten years earlier. And I still had no regular job. I was an intuitively stable character living in a state of almost permanent flux. Quite a balancing act.

Keeping a diary had, after tentative beginnings in 1969 and 1970, become an ingrained habit, and a discipline too. Like the running I'd recently taken up, it was something consistent, a necessary complement to the mercurial world of work. Something to keep me grounded.

I continued to write up the diary most mornings, aware as ever how selective I had to be and how little time I ever had for honing and shaping. But I kept the story going. Just about.

Unless otherwise indicated, the entries are written in my house in Oak Village in North London.

Sunday, January 6th

With the social and gastronomic excesses of Christmas and New Year over, life this weekend has returned, after many weeks, to something approaching calm. I find I can easily cope with eight hours' sleep a night. I find I enjoy having time to sort my books out or take the children out or sit in front of the fire. I feel my body and my mind adjusting to a new pace and a new rhythm. I've hardly used the car in the last week. I haven't been into town, or shopping, or having business meetings. And I feel the benefits of this pause, this time to take stock of the present instead of endless worryings over the future or the past.

I've become a little self-sufficient, too. Though Gilliam is a regular visitor – like a mother hen having to keep returning to the nest to make sure the eggs are still all right – I'm responsible for the writing pace at the moment. I know that just over the horizon is the full swirl of a dozen different projects, meetings, responsibilities, considerations and demands, but for now the sea is calm.

Monday, January 7th

Denis [O'Brien] was back from the States today. According to TG he has no backers for the film [*Time Bandits*], but intends to go ahead and do it himself – just to 'spite them all'. I think this leaves me feeling as uncomfortable as it does Terry. But I read him some of the opening scenes, which cheer him up.

Pat Casey[1] rings to know my availability. She has a movie part which was written for Dudley Moore. He's now charging one and a half million dollars a picture and wants to do some serious acting, so Pat is asking me if I would be interested in the part. I have to turn it down as I'm occupied this year.

Wednesday, January 9th

At Redwood [Studios] at four. Eric, moderately well laid-back, occasionally strumming guitar. Trevor Jones[2] bustling. André[3] looking tired, but working faithfully. Graham [Chapman], who is getting £5,000 a month from Python as co-producer of this album [Monty Python's Contractual Obligation], sits contentedly, with John [Tomiczek] in attendance. He seems, as usual, not quite in tune with what's going on around him. I record the Headmaster's speech and that's about all.

Up to the Crown at Seven Dials for a drink with Terry Gilliam and Roger Pratt.[4] This is more like the real world for me. I can believe in the three of us and the place and the people around us far more than I can in what's going on at Redwood. Clearly TG feels the same. He's a bit confused by Denis's attitude to his film – on the one hand he is supportive and confident in TG – the next he's suggesting stars and names with almost frantic indiscrimination.

Thursday, January 10th

Rachel's first day at Gospel Oak School. It's a rather glum, hard, cold day with weather from the east. I don't see Rachel leave as I'm at the Mornington Foot Clinic. Mr Owen natters and reminisces as he slices at my foot – removing not only the corn but valuable minutes of screenwriting!

---

[1] Patricia Casey produced Monty Python's first film *And Now For Something Completely Different* in 1970.
[2] Trevor Jones, composer. To avoid confusion with the film composer of the same name he is now known as John Du Prez. Wrote the music for a number of Python songs as well as the film *A Fish Called Wanda* and, with Eric Idle, the musical *Spamalot*.
[3] André Jacquemin, long-time Python sound recordist and composer.
[4] Roger Pratt, camera operator on *Time Bandits*, later, lighting cameraman on *Brazil* and, more recently, two of the *Harry Potter* films.

Home by ten. Rachel seems to have taken to school without any traumas. In fact Helen seems to have been affected more by the experience.

Unplug the phone and get down to the knotty problems of making an adventure serious and funny. Jim Franklin[1] rings to offer me a part in the Goodies and Pat Casey to try and induce me yet again to take a Dudley Moore cast-off.

Friday, January 11th

Up and running early this morning. The temperature is just on freezing and the grass on top of Parliament Hill is covered with frost. Feel immensely refreshed and thoroughly awoken.

Arrive at T Gilliam's just after 10.30.

Progress is steady but not spectacular, though TG is very amused by the Robin Hood sequence.

To Denis O'B's for a meeting at two. Denis looks weary. He was up working on 'structures' for TG's film until 2.30 yesterday morning. But he seems to be as bright and tenaciously thorough about all my affairs as he ever was.

Home by six. Feel encouraged after our meeting. Denis has talked of an India project – and self-financing of it, rather like TG's film – but basically my encouragement stems from the knowledge that with Denis we are in a different league. For the first time we are being offered the prospect of quite considerable financial rewards. Denis clearly identifies money with power – although in our case our 'power', in terms of reputation, was established and created without vast rewards. Now Denis wants the rewards for us and through us for himself.

At the moment he seems to have admirable goals, but I have this nagging feeling that our 'freedom' to do whatever we want may be threatened if Denis is able to build up this juggernaut of Python earning power and influence. A few of the most interesting projects may be rolled flat.

Monday, January 14th

To Anne's [James] for a Python meeting with Denis. JC, fresh returned from Barbados, stands there shivering. Anne, as thoughtful as ever, has provided some lunch. Meeting is basically to discuss Denis's two offers for the next [Monty Python] movie – from Warners and Paramount. Warners want a screenplay before going ahead, Paramount just a treatment. Denis is asking for 6.4 million dollars.

[1] Jim Franklin directed four of the *Ripping Yarns*.

Time is of the essence, as Paramount, who are offering a better financial deal, do require the movie for summer 1981 release. This, I feel, puts pressures on the group which we would rather not have – and thankfully no-one feels any different. But JC suggests that we go along with Paramount at the moment and just see if, after the seven-week March/April writing period, we have enough to give them a treatment – 'In which case we could all go ahead and make a lot of money very quickly.'

Though we all feel the Paramount deal for the next movie is the one to pursue, Denis is proposing to try and place *Grail*, now released from Cinema 5, with Warners, so they can do a *Life of Brian/Holy Grail* re-release in the US next summer. There is no great enthusiasm for selling the Bavaria film as a Python Olympic Special to the US networks in summer of this year. Eric reckons there will be no Olympics anyway. Certainly the Russian invasion of Afghanistan has shaken things up.

TG comes round and we talk over Denis and the movie. But I'm feeling very unsettled about my role in it at the moment. The script is clogged and I've lost a day's writing today. There seems suddenly so much to do and I refuse to give up my railway project [contributing to the BBC's *Great Railway Journeys*], despite reportedly 'generous' financial inducements from Denis to prolong my work on the TG movie.

André arrives very late, bringing a quite beautiful tape of Trevor Jones's arrangement for 'Decomposing Composers'. How the hell I'll sing it, I don't know.

Thursday, January 17th

Go with Tom and Helen to a 'parents' view' at Acland Burghley Comprehensive, one of the three local schools which Tom will have to be selected for, and where he will be well ensconced by this time next year.

A modern school, presenting a forbidding aspect, cloaked as it is in heavy grey concrete. The doors and passageways give the immediate impression of a hard, unpretty, pragmatist mind at work. But the library/reading room, where about 20 of us parents assemble, is warm and bright, the shelves are well-filled. I noticed *Soviet Weekly* alongside *The Economist*.

We were shown into a biology room and given glowing prospects of the future of this school. However I couldn't help noticing a large piece of paper on the front of a cupboard low on the ground near our feet, which bore the simple legend 'Whoever reads this is a cunt'.

Friday, January 18th

The world seems to have started 1980 so badly that I have on occasions this past week questioned the wisdom of working myself to a standstill when all the elements for the start of another global war crowd the newspapers for headline space. Ultimatums are flying around and ultimatums, to me, are synonymous with the outbreak of World War II.

It may in a few years sound rather laughable that Jimmy Carter threatened Russia that he will pull America out of the Olympics if the Russians haven't withdrawn their forces from Afghanistan by mid-February, but combined as this pronouncement is with the volatility of unsettled Iran and the much more threatening stances being taken up in preparation for President Tito's imminent death in Yugoslavia, the potential flashpoints seem sure to light something.

But it all ultimately is unreal and either you panic and sell everything you've got to buy gold, or you just sit down and have breakfast, presuming it won't be the last one. And of course it isn't.

Saturday, January 19th

Denis O'B rings. His proposal for my work on the T Gilliam film is that I be made a partner, along with Terry G, in the production company, so I will be able to share with TG the depreciation on capital which will be worth £60,000 in tax advantages. Don't ask me why, but this is clearly a generous move on the part of George [Harrison] and Denis O'B, who are the providers of the money.

And I can go ahead with the railway documentary – 'If you really want to,' says Denis, unhappily, knowing that there's precious little he can do to squeeze more than £2,400 out of the BBC for what's ostensibly 12 weeks' work!

In the afternoon a two and a half hour visit to Haverstock School. A lived-in, scuffed and battered collection of buildings. Impressed by the straightforwardness of the teachers. Impressed by the lack of waffle about tradition, Latin and prayers and the emphasis on the future and helping all the children of whatever ability equally.

An impossible ideal, some may say, but at least these teachers are confronting the most basic problems of an educational system with great energy and cheeriness. I was encouraged.

Monday, January 21st

The world situation seems to have cooled down, though I see in my *Times* that Paul McCartney is still in jail in Japan after being caught at the airport with naughty substances. How silly. Eric reckons it's a put-up job – part of John Lennon's price, which he's exacting from Paul for being rude to Yoko.

At five I brave the skyscraper-induced blasts of icy wind that whip round the Euston Tower and find myself in Capital Radio, being asked questions on, and reading extracts from, *Decline and Fall*. I find I'm never as lucid when the tape's rolling as I am over a glass of wine at home an hour later and in the course of an hour I get tongue-tied and fail to say even what I meant to say – let alone whether that was worth saying or not. I'm in august company – Denis Norden and Melvyn Bragg are the other two pundits on this particular book. JC has already said his piece about *Twelfth Night* (from which Shakespeare didn't emerge very favourably) and TJ is soon to do *The Spire* by William Golding.

Wednesday, January 23rd

The fine weather's back again. Tito's recovering and the steel strike is still faced with government intransigence. I have either pulled, twisted or bruised some muscle below and to the right of my kneecap, so I rest from running today, despite ideal, dry, cool, bright conditions out there.

Work on with TG script. The end is in sight, but is this writing to order – 6lbs assorted jokes, half a hundredweight of nutty characters and 20 yards of filler dialogue – really going to stand up? I'm encouraged when I think of the general level of movie dialogue – but this movie has to be judged by exceptional, not general level.

Write myself to a standstill by four and drive into the West End to see *Apocalypse Now.* Impressive – there is no other word for it – and the action sequences of the war are rivetingly watchable.

But the last half-hour – the meat, one feels, of Coppola/Milius' message – is a huge con. The action slows, the dialogue and performance become heavy with significance, sluggish with style.

Thursday, January 24th

Stop work at one. A couple of phone calls, then drive down to Neal's Yard for the Grand Unveiling Ceremony of the 14/15 Neal's Yard sign [designed by Terry G]. On one side red lurid lips and teeth bear the legend 'Neal's Yd. Abattoir' (to correct the present unwholesome imbalance in favour of the wholefooders who have proliferated all over the yard) and on the other side 'The British Film Industry Ltd'.

When I arrive it is made clear to me that a few choice words will have to be spoken and yours truly is the man to speak them. So we troop down into the yard and there, on this perfect sunny day, I bewilder all those queuing for non-meat lunches at the bakery by giving a few loud, but brief words, then smashing a champagne bottle against the building. 'God bless her and all who work in her.' It breaks the second time.

Friday, January 25th

To Terry Gilliam's at 10.15 for session on the film. TG likes the Ogre and the Old Ladies scene, but I think feels that the Evil Genius is too much on one level of cod hysteria. I agree, but we still have time to go over the characters again and invest them with a few more quirks.

We go to lunch at the Pizza Express and talk over the more serious problem of the 'content' of the script – the attitude to the characters, to Kevin's adventures – the message which gives the depth to a superficial story of chase and adventure. Really I feel the depth is there anyway, it's a question of how obvious to make it.

Leave for Dr Kieser's[1] surgery, where I have a cut and cover job on one of my front upper teeth – so my dental surgery is in its third decade. At one moment, as he works on the gum and bone, it begins to hurt. 'Is that pressure or pain you're feeling?' asks Kieser urgently. God . . . how on earth do I tell?

Friday, February 1st

A rush for the tape. Began reassembling and rewriting the section from the Spider Women to the end at ten. Lunch at the desk.

TG arrives about 7.30 and I stumble to the 'End' by eight. He will get all this mass of stuck-up, crossed-out, type-and-longhand-jumbled sheets to Alison [Davies, at the office] this weekend. All should be returned by Sunday a.m., so I can then read through and learn the awful truth about this amazingly speedy piece of writing.

I go to bed at midnight with the satisfaction of having completed my self-set task of a TG script in the month of January. It would be marvellous if the script were of a high standard, worked and immeasurably increased the confidence of all working on the project. Or was the rush just at the expense of quality, an exercise in the lowest form of writing to a deadline?

I shall see. For now, I'm just very happy with a job (almost) done.

---

[1] Bernard Kieser, periodontal surgeon extraordinaire, carried on the fight to keep my teeth in my mouth, with increasing success.

Saturday, February 2nd

In the afternoon the sky clouded and heavy rain set in. Took William, Rachel and the Mini down to the Natural History Museum, whilst Tom P and his friend Tom Owen went 'tracking' on the Heath. Rachel is doing dinosaurs at school and met one or two of her friends there. The central area was very full, but as soon as we ventured into the further recesses of the building there was plenty of space amongst endless glassily-staring models and half-dissected bodies.

Willy went off on his own to, among other things, the human biology section. He is very keen on biology, having just begun talking about it at school. To her great credit, his teacher started straight in with human reproduction, etc, rather than frogs or bees. So Willy now knows all the practical details of procreation, whereas Tom, who affects to know, still calls sexual intercourse 'sexual interchange'.

Sunday, February 3rd

Read papers in the morning. Polls taken in January indicate that more people are expecting World War III to break out now than at any time since Korea. Probably a meaningless statistic, but it makes Python's next film subject gruesomely relevant. Actually the sabre-rattling of the Americans over Afghanistan has died down a little, but they still frighten me more than the Russians.

Terry G brings round the script of the movie, fresh from Alison the typist, and after supper I begin to read. I finish late – it's nearly one. My first reaction is that it's paced wrongly – the individual scenes are in some cases too long themselves, or appear too long when placed next to another, fairly static scene. I missed being gripped by the story, too.

Lay in bed remembering points and scribbling down. Tomorrow I've given a day to Terry G that should be spent on railway research, so that we can talk right through the screenplay.

Monday, February 4th

Up to Terry's. The heavens open and it pours for the rest of the day. Against this gloomy background we slog through. TG liked the script more than I did, I think, and is greatly pleased that Irene Lamb, the casting director, for whom TG has much respect, also likes what she has seen so far and feels there will be little problem in getting good actors interested.

It's clear that there is one more day of writing needed to flesh out the end, especially the hastily-written character of the bureaucratic Supreme Being. So I'll have to restructure the week accordingly. Everything else will have to be squeezed.

Still have no title for the TG epic other than 'The Film That Dares Not Speak Its Name'.

Tuesday, February 5th

Talk over scripts for the new Python film with TJ. We read through and apportion who would be responsible for what.

TJ and I have a game of squash, then a pint of Brakspear's at the Nag's Head in Hampstead. TJ, though bemoaning the fact that he hasn't written anything new for months, is suddenly, and healthily, I think, full of ideas and projects of his own – including the possibility of making a film of *Hitchhiker's Guide to the Galaxy* with Douglas Adams.

Terry goes off to meet Douglas. I drive to a rather swish and un-Pythonlike function at Les Ambassadeurs Club. We are invited here by Warner Brothers Chairman Frank Wells – the man who, TG tells me later, did more than anyone else to try and block the *Life of Brian* deal. He was tall, fit, with those peculiar American spectacles that make a man's face look slightly effeminate; mid-forties, or early fifties, with a firm handshake.

Spread out in the scarlet-panelled, sumptuously-carpeted lower room at the Ambassadeurs was a host of men in grey. An impeccably-manicured host too – hardly a hair put of place on any of them. These were the agents and studio heads and accountants – the businessmen of showbiz.

A cameraman was in attendance, which always indicates that the gathering is a little more than just a thank you from Warners. I was photographed with Eric and with Frank Wells and Jarvis Astaire.[1] I was pleased to see Sandy [Lieberson] and his missus, because Sandy was at least not wearing a grey suit and Birgit was one of the only women there.

Gilliam is wonderfully scruffy, I'm pleased to say.

Leave at 8.15. Avoid getting run over by the sea of chauffeur-driven Rolls Royces and Jags and Mercedes littering Hamilton Place.

[1] Wells was President of Warner Brothers, and later, of the Walt Disney Company. He died in a helicopter accident whilst on a heli-skiing trip in 1994.

Jarvis Astaire, businessman and influential sports event promoter. Co-produced the film *Agatha* in 1978.

Wednesday, February 6th

Work through the last few scenes of the TG film until after lunch, then drive to Denis O'B's. Try to be absolutely clear with him that what I want for Redwood is to keep Bob[1] and André. Denis worries that Bob is 'driving a wedge' between myself and André. Really he is accusing Bob of all the things that Bob is accusing Denis of doing. Denis will not hear a good word said for Bob – but I've made my decision. I'm not prepared to lose André, and if Bob goes, André goes. So Denis talks business and I talk people and that's that.

Drive back in a rain-sodden rush-hour to Abraxas [sports club in Belsize Park gardens]. Am soundly beaten by Richard [Guedalla, my neighbour] at squash. Makes me very depressed. But recover over a bottle of champagne, which I open to mark my last day on, or delivery of, the TG film script. Read TG the new Supreme Being scenes, which he likes.

Tom arrives back from another disco. Not just 'slow dancing' this time, but girls sitting on boys' laps. Reminds me of Eric's wonderful song for the *Contractual Obligation* album, 'Sit On My Face and Tell Me that you Love Me'.

Monday, February 18th

Springlike weather, with daytime temperatures around 50°F, now into its second week. I cycle up to Terry G's in sunshine. From 9.30 till lunchtime we work through the script – still tentatively, but not very enthusiastically, called 'The Time Bandits'. Fortunately we both agree on the major area for cuts and every little rewrite helps. TG is very unhappy about the vast amounts of money the crew are demanding – inflated by commercials. It doesn't help the 'British' film industry at all.

Down to Redwood Studios, where Eric, TJ and myself record 'Shopping Sketch' and 'All Things Dull and Ugly', plus one or two other snippets for the album.

From Redwood round to Anne J's to take in some more Python scripts from last autumn's writing session to be typed up in preparation for Wednesday's meeting. What is rapidly becoming apparent about *Brian* is that Denis's forecast of earnings from it in 1980 was drastically over-optimistic. The £250,000 figure he mentioned in November now looks likely to be nearer £40,000.

Although the distributor's gross in the US was over nine million dollars, over four million was spent on publicity and advertising – and this was where Warners were weakest. Their posters and their slogans were constantly changed

[1] Bob Salmon was André Jacquemin's accountant and helped to set up Redwood Studios.

and we never approved any of them – now they present a bill for this fiasco which is equal to the entire production budget of the film. It is a scandal, but there seems to be nothing Denis can do. They won't even supply him with figures.

The upshot is that not only will there be not a penny profit from America from a movie which was one of the top 40 grossers of the year in the US, but the earnings will hardly cover half the production cost. So the chance of making any more money – beyond our £72,000 fee for writing and acting – depends on the rest of the world. Fortunately the UK is looking very strong, Australia is holding up well and France and Germany remain to be seen.

Wednesday, February, 20th

Python enters the 80's! Pick up Eric on the way to JC's. Arrive at 10.30. Everyone there and chortling over the latest and looniest batch of selected press cuttings about *Brian*. It's noted that Swansea has banned the film totally. Four hundred people in Watford are petitioning because the local council have recommended the film be an 'X'.

Coffees are poured and we settle round JC's ex-prison table, which now seems to be Python's favourite writing venue. Our ages are checked around the table. I'm still the youngest. No-one wants to spend time on business, we all want to write and make each other laugh, but business has to be done, so it's decided that we will make a clean sweep of it today. So Anne stays with us and Denis is summoned at three.

The disillusion with Hollywood and all things to do with Warners and *Brian* lead us into thinking how nice it would be to do a small-budget film just for the fun of it – keeping our own control and making money in the way *Grail*, with its modest budget, did, and *Brian*, with its Hollywood campaign, didn't. Denis is anxious to set up all sorts of production and syndication deals in the US, and he's talked to CBS about two Python TV specials, for which we would be paid 700,000 dollars each.

No-one wants to do specials for the US, but there is still the German material. Suddenly it all gels. We will use the German material, plus some old sketches, plus anything we wrote in October/November and reshoot as a quick, cheap movie. The mood of the group is unanimous. Fuck Hollywood. Fuck CBS. Let's do something we enjoy in the way we want to do it – and so economically that no-one gets their fingers burned if a Hollywood major *does* turn it down.

DO'B seems unable to respond at our level and talks business jargon for a while. I like Denis, and I think he likes us, but he is only in the early stages of finding out what everyone who's ever dealt with Python has eventually found out – that there is no logic or consistency or even realism behind much of our behaviour. No patterns can be imposed on the group from outside. Or at least they can, but they never stick; they crack up and the internal resolutions of Python are the only ones that last.

From international film business to the waiting room of the Mornington Foot Clinic. Mr Owen uses a 'coagulator' on my corn today. I have to have injections around my little toe, which are rather painful, then a sharp, electrified needle burns up the capillaries. All this counterpointed by Mr Owen's extraordinary views about the evils of the world and socialism in particular. I'm getting worried – I think that he is a character I've invented.

Monday, February 25th

Spent much of the weekend, unsuccessfully, trying to finish *Smiley's People*. Also trying to find time to organise the house, spend time with the children and other worthy hopes doomed to failure!

Rachel pottered around me with her Junior Doctor's Kit, taking my blood, giving me blood, thrusting toy thermometers in my mouth, whilst I tried, hopelessly, to assimilate the mass of opinions, facts, thoughts, figures and ramblings which make up the insidiously attractive substitute for experience that is the Sunday papers.

Collected Eric from Carlton Hill and we drove on to JC's. A talk through material. Eric and John have searched the archives, Terry J has been away, GC doesn't appear to have done much, but I saved my bacon by writing an extension to 'Penis Apology',[1] which produced an outstandingly good reaction. Near hysteria. I think Python is definitely working out all the repressions of childhood – and loving it!

Lunch with the French translator of *Holy Grail* and *Brian* at the Trattoo. A wonderful-looking Frenchman with a very special face which could not belong to any other nation. White hair, eyes droopy with a sort of permanent look of apology, a long, curved nose which never goes far from his face at any point. A lovely, squashed, humorous, used feel to the face like a Gauloise butt in an ashtray.

Home by six. Have promised TG that I will read the new, shorter version of 'Time Bandits/The Film That Dares Not Speak Its Name', so I spend most of the evening on that. Poor Terry is being given a hard ride by the doubters

---

[1] 'Penis Apology' was a very long-drawn-out health advisory at the beginning of the film warning the audience that there may be a penis in shot later on. The apology became longer and more complex, including discussions from Bishops for the Church's view etc. It was never used.

and the pessimists. On reading I feel that the movie, which is, after all, an act of faith in TG, is, on balance, do-able by May. But only just!

Tuesday, February 26th

The weather has sharpened a little, but most of February has now gone, with no weather that wouldn't have graced an average April. In short, no winter at all here. But I don't feel any benefits. Wake up feeling like a piece of chewed rag. I have a sore throat, a mild coolness of the blood and a general enervation. There are so many loose ends to be tied up. I feel old for a few minutes.

Some work after breakfast, then round to Eric's. That's very cheering – mainly because all of us are happy to be together at the moment and the tapes that André's prepared of the sketches and songs for the LP assembled by Eric, with a certain amount of gentle bullying over the last two months, are a great boost.

To lunch at a nearby French, where Eric chides Graham for not being totally opposed to nuclear power. Eric deals only in certainties. His views, like his lifestyle at any one time, are very positive.

The talk veers to desultory discussion of bizarre sexual exploits. GC caps all, as he puffs at his pipe and declares that he once had an Indian in an aeroplane. JC is quite skittish too and suggests that perhaps the Pythons should set each other a sexual task. I agree to try and seduce the Queen!

I have a brief script chat with T Gilliam (cheering him up, I hope). Then I drive both of us round to a rendezvous with J Cleese, who was given TG's script and wants to, or 'is prepared to', talk to us about it. John is looking after Cynthia at the moment, on his own as far as I can tell, since Connie's in New York for 11 days.

Cynthia answers the door. With her long blonde hair, tastefully ribboned back, and her neat school uniform she looks, at nine years old, like an Estée Lauder model. Very New York, somehow. She chats confidently and behaves quite like a young lady 10 or 15 years older than she is, but she's humorous with it, which keeps her on this side of precociousness.

She comes out to eat with us. No room at the Japanese, so we go on to Mama San – a clean, smart, soulless Chinese in Holland Park Avenue. Cynthia won't really let John get a word in, but after half an hour she settles to sleep beside an unoccupied table and the three of us talk about the script.

JC speaks with a slight, elder statesman of comedy air, as if he really *does* know how, why and when comedy will work, and we feel a little like naughty boys being told what's good for us. But this is rather unfair to John. I think he went out of the way to try *not* to sound too paternal, and he did give us some sound, unselfish advice, much of which will help in the rewrites. But I couldn't accept his final judgement – that we should postpone the movie on the basis that one day it could be a marvellous film, but if we rush it and go on the present script, it will be just a good-natured mess,

Mind you, JC had a piece of gossip that rather undermined his chances of 'stopping' the movie. He'd heard that Sean Connery was interested and Denis O'B has flown to California to see him!

Friday, February 29th

To Gospel Oak School to see Ron Lendon [the headmaster] about Tom's future.

Ron's report is glowing. Tom, it seems, is regarded very highly indeed. He is in Verbal Reasoning Group 1 – which is the comprehensive system's acknowledgement that abilities have to be tested at some point. There is less chance of him going to William Ellis [school in Highgate Road] if he's Group 1 – the idea is to spread them around the local schools. But Lendon, whose manner is chatty, informal, direct and quite unpatronising, feels that William Ellis is the best place for Tom. His closest friends – Lendon makes much reference to 'peer' groups – will be going there, he's keen on music and Lendon admits that he thinks the academic standards are higher at William E.

An interesting sign of the times is that Tom is one of only three boys amongst 15 in his class who does not come from a broken home.

So we come out greatly heartened and I feel once again the great relief that our children – all of them – will have started out at a school as caring and sympathetic as Gospel Oak.

Work on Python material for a couple of hours, then meet TJ at the Pizza Express in Hampstead. TJ has written something which he cheerfully acknowledges as the ultimate in bad taste – it's all about people throwing up – very childish, but rather well controlled, dare I say – it had me in as prolonged and hysterical a bout of laughter as I can remember.

Saturday, March 1st

Always feel that March is the end of the winter, but this year there has been no winter to speak of and this mild, orderly March morning is only different from much of January and February because the sun isn't shining.

Have to go and talk over script details with TG. The advantage of living within walking distance of your collaborator. Stroll up with my script over the Heath. Up to Terry's mighty attic. Listen to a couple of tracks of the new Elvis Costello.

The good news is that Ian Holm wants to be our Napoleon and loves the script. No further news from Denis who is, much to TG's irritation, still star-searching in Hollywood.

Walk back at 8.15, past South End Green where *Life of Brian* is in '5th Fantastic Week' at the Classic.

Sunday, March 2nd

A most relaxed and happy day. Sun shone – a very springlike Sunday. I cleared my desk prior to beginning the railway script.

Found lots of excuses to talk, drink coffee and generally indulge in what's called a writer's 'negative capability', but eventually was ready to start. Notes assembled, clean sheet of foolscap in the typewriter (I still use a typewriter for the serious stuff!). Then a strange tension gripped me – a tightening of the stomach, a light sweating of the palms just as if I were about to go on stage.

Do all writers, or any writers, suffer this 'typewriter fright', or is it just because I'm a writer/actor and I know that anything I put down now I will have to enact at some future time? Anyway, it's a very difficult task to start the documentary. To actually set this huge and daunting mass of facts and accumulated knowledge in motion.

Monday, March 3rd

Woken by bright sunshine. Rachel unhappy about school. I take her. She tries to be very brave, but bolts back towards the house when we get to the end of Oak Village, and I have to carry her most of the rest of the way. When we arrive at the school, her class are already sitting quietly, waiting for the register.

On the way back up Oak Village, an old lady leans out of her window. She looks distraught. Her gas supply has failed, and she's had no tea or heating. She's asked the gas people to come round, but she's concerned that they're not here. This all takes my mind off Rachel's predicament as I go home, phone up the gas, and Helen goes round to see her and make her tea and fill her hot water bottle.

Set to writing Python stuff. Rachel arrives back from school, a lot happier than when she went, but she *did* cry – 'Only one big tear,' she told me.

Tuesday, March 4th

Another sparkling day. Clear blue skies and a brisk chill giving an edge of freshness to the air. Write more Python material – it's flowing easily and I'm enjoying the chance to write some fairly direct satirical stuff again. Jury vetting was on the list today. And the courts generally.

From two until half past three, TJ and I read. TJ has a good idea for the RAF Pipe-Smokers – extending into wives. I've written huge amounts, as usual, but this time it seems to stand up – and almost nil failure rate over the last two days, which is encouraging. See what the others think on Thursday.

TG has been hearing from Denis O'B in Los Angeles.

Denis, who had sent me a telegram saying the script was 'sensational', is voicing doubts over the quality of writing – especially in the 'Napoleon' and 'Robin Hood' scenes. He even suggested to TG that they could 'get some writers in'. He still hurls out casting suggestions which bear all the hallmarks of a man more desperate about a bank loan than about anything to do with quality of script or trust of the writers – Burt Reynolds for the Evil Genius, Art Carney for the Ogre. All the qualities these actors have are blinded for me by Denis's heavy-handed Hollywood approach. It's killing T Gilliam and may kill the film.

I go to bed trying to put it all out of my mind. But a nagging corner can't be forgotten – I *did* write the script in a month. Denis is right – it *could* be better. Am I just now beginning to get some inklings that I really made a wrong decision to get involved in this project at all? Wrong not because I couldn't do it, but because I couldn't do my best.

I know I'm funnier writing unrestricted Python material. I know I could contribute more as a writer if it had been a 'Ripping Yarn' sort of story. But it wasn't. Will it ever be what everyone wants it to be? Or just a jumble of different ideas and preconceptions? Is it comedy or adventure? Why should it have to be either?

Because that's how Hollywood wants it to be, and Denis wants Hollywood.

Wednesday, March 5th

No brooding today. Up at eight. Buy *The Times* and read of Mugabe's victory in Rhodesia. The Brits have been patting themselves on the back for organising such an orderly election – in best British fashion – so they can hardly grumble at a Marxist getting 62% of the vote. It seems one of the most hopeful transitions from white to black power. But it's taken a guerrilla war to make the point and that must give great heart to guerrilla movements in other countries.

Thursday, March 6th

Rain, most of the day. To Eric's for a Python read-through. Neil [Innes] is staying there. He looks cheery and already his new life in the Suffolk countryside seems to have made him physically different. As though the land has moulded our ex-Lewisham lad. He's rounder. His hair, arranged in a neat coronal around his bald pate, is much fuller and frizzier than I remember before. He looks . . . He looks rather like a Hulme Beaman[1] creation.

Terry J looks tired and harassed and throughout the day there are odd phone calls for him which give one the feeling that his life is a box which is far too full. John C is grumbling about his health again – doing a perfect imitation of the Ogre in *Time Bandits* which he didn't like!

Eric is being very friendly, warm and accommodating. Terry Gilliam isn't there (which provokes some rumblings of discontent from Eric, who, I think, being unaligned to either of the main writing groups, feels that TG's absence deprives him of an ally). GC is as avuncular and benign as ever. And arrives easily last. Eric is trying to get GC to stop smoking his pipe so much. He's the only Python who still smokes.

JC reads out an outrageously funny schoolmaster sex demonstration sketch. Our stuff doesn't go quite as well as expected this morning. Eric has a chilling ending for the film, when the outbreak of nuclear war is announced. He's been reading about the dangers of, and plans in the event of, nuclear war happening.

We talk for a while on this subject, which is so macabre and disturbing because the weapons for our destruction exist – they're pointing at us now – and our response is to build more.

Friday, March 7th

Tried to write a startlingly new and original, brilliantly funny and thought-provoking piece for Python. Did this by staring out of the window, playing with paper clips and shutting my eyes for long periods.

Monday, March 10th

Pressing on. Endless days of writing. They seem to have been going on forever and are stretching on forever. Not that I mind *that* much. I quite enjoy not having to drive across London, not having to go down rain-spattered motorways

---

[1] S.G. Hulme Beaman created the Toytown stories, some of the earliest children's books and radio programmes I remember.

to locations, not having to make meetings and business lunches, not going out to dinners or buying clothes.

Yes, I'm afraid this monastic existence suits me rather well. I shall keep it up this week, hoping for a breakthrough on Python and a completion of the railway script – then I shall take Concorde to New York at the expense of NBC and 'party' for 24 hours.

Work on Python until it's dark outside, then break and work on the railways until midnight. Impossible. I'm beginning to sink under a mass of names, lines, distances, facts, details, anecdotes, diversions, sidings . . .

Tuesday, March 11th

Denis O'B rings – he's returned from the States and positively glowing with enthusiasm for the TG/MP movie. He has Sean Connery absolutely 'mentally committed' (which means he hasn't enough money for him) and George H, who at first was not at all sure why Denis O'B was putting his money into it, has now re-read the script twice, feels it has great potential and is trying to hustle Jack Nicholson into letting us have his name on the credits!

Paramount have agreed a distribution deal with Denis in the US and are seeing it as a new *Wizard of Oz*! However, they are very keen to get the hottest name in Hollywood – Gilda Radner – onto the credits too. Denis, who knows nothing of Gilda, has promptly turned several circles and is now homing in on Gilda as the Ogre's Wife instead of Ruth Gordon. 'Apparently she does a really good old lady on *Saturday Night Live*.'

I have to puncture Denis's epic enthusiasm here. She may do a great old lady, but Ruth Gordon *is* a great old lady, and would easily be my choice (if we need names) for the part.

Wednesday, March 12th

Schizophrenic weather. Today almost continuous rain – yesterday bright sunshine.

To Eric's for a Python meeting.

Over lunch we discuss the general balance of material, which seems to fall into School, War/Army and North-West Frontier. Lists are made in the p.m. and a putative running order worked out. This is the stage when there is much talk of 'What is the film about?' and how we can relate the various themes – whether we should start conventionally or with an apology for what's to be seen. Quite good progress.

Thursday, March 13th

Revision of the railway script proceeds rather slowly. I think one reason is that I have become so steeped in the material over the last three or four weeks that I've lost a lot of the initial enthusiasm. Also concerned about how funny to make the start. In short, I don't think I've found the right tone yet.

Run off my uncertainties at lunchtime. Back to a phone call from Denis. He has just received a mortal blow to his pride from Edna Jones at BBC Contracts. Denis, international financier and deal-maker extraordinary, cannot get the BBC to budge from a max of £2,400 plus £1,800 once and for all foreign sales on the railway programme. Denis, who believes in the success ethic even more than the work ethic, says he's contemplating throwing himself off his balcony!

Saturday, March 15th: London and New York

A dull morning, but no rain, fog or snow to threaten departure. With only a couple of light bags, a book – *Moviola* by Garson Kanin – and a *Time Bandits* script for Ruth Gordon (Garson Kanin's wife!), drive the Mini to Heathrow and park it, as I'm only away for one night.

Board the 11.15 Concorde, a few minutes late – some problem with the earlier flight. But we're airborne, with thunderous noise, by twelve, and there are no more problems. I'm VIP listed and this means it's impossible to quietly stew in a mixture of champagne, relief and a good book without being hauled out to sign an autograph for the crew and visit the flight deck.

The pilot and co-pilot seem more anxious to ask me about Python than to tell me about Concorde, but I do ascertain that they use five tons of fuel every hour and that the fastest Atlantic crossing so far has been two hours 56 minutes.

Well, they catch up half an hour and I'm at Kennedy and through customs and into bright sunshine and crisp snow cover just after 10.30 NY time.

Arrive at NBC at four. Rehearse the moves cold. See Lorne,[1] the cast, Belushi, who is back to do a special appearance. Of *1941* he says 'I was bad, the film was bad', but he's very pleased with the state of the *Blues Brothers* – his soon to be released picture with Aykroyd.

As usual Belushi's presence does not please everybody. He's very rude about the present state of '*SNL*' – and seems disgruntled that he's come back to do so little. Both points are understandable. The material on this 100th show

---

[1] Lorne Michaels produced the ground-breaking, talent-spinning NBS *Saturday Night Live* show. And still does.

reflects age rather than quality and Belushi isn't given much funny stuff. He's smarting because he's been cut out of 'Update' to accommodate one of the 'star guests', Ralph Nader.

After an hour of reacquainting myself with everybody and rehearsing in a darkened set, a dull, persistent headache has set in. So I take an hour off before the dress rehearsal, go back to the Berkshire Place and lie down. Don't sleep, but at least I'm not working or talking.

Shower and leave the hotel at seven, US time – which means it's midnight UK time. I have somehow to try and pace myself to perform live in front of the watching millions at what will be, for me, about 5.30 in the morning at the end of a very crowded day.

When 11.30 finally arrived and the signature tune blared out I knew that I would be alright as the adrenaline started working to clear my befuddled system of the combined effects of too much food, alcohol and fatigue.

The sketch went better than ever and I got a gratifying round of recognition applause when the audience saw me for the first time. I also over-acted happily and shamelessly. John Cleese would have been proud of the way I killed the tarantula.

Thursday, March 20th

Spring starts either today or tomorrow, I'm never sure. The rain's stopped, but there was a frost last night. It's cold, clear and clean.

At a quarter to ten Helen, Tom and I drive up in the Mini to William Ellis School for our interview with Mr Perry [the headmaster]. Talk to one of the senior boys – wearing a gown. Will they still keep gowns in the comprehensive era? He was very well-spoken and presentable and surprised me by saying, quite undefensively, that he wanted to become an accountant.

Into Mr Perry's bland but unintimidating study. Tom is asked most of the questions. What he likes about Gospel Oak – Tom, seriously, 'Well, it's very spacious, but quite small.' His hobbies, interests, friends, preferences (Tom declared for science). Tom answered quite unprecociously and at greater length than I expected. Mr Perry said that it was almost an accepted fact that children from Gospel Oak were more articulate than the norm.

Drive over to EuroAtlantic for a meeting with Denis and T Gilliam. Main subject is whether or not we think J Cleese is right for the Evil Genius. Apparently Denis took the bull by the horns and met the disgruntled Cleese, who's not so far forgiven Denis for promising us a quarter of a million pounds each for *Brian*.

Denis has so successfully charmed JC with soft words and capital allowance schemes, that JC can now see the advantage of being in TG's movie after all –

as a partner. Denis is keen, but both TG and I are unconvinced. Other names hang in the air. Connery still isn't fixed. Ruth Gordon neither. Denis is disappointed that John cannot be easily fitted in.

Watch the BAFTA awards at 9.30 with a glimmer of hope, but little more than that. The Light Entertainment Award is the first. Bruce Forsyth comes on to present it and does an annoyingly unnecessary and lengthy preamble, whilst Anna Ford, Edward Fox and Princess Anne watch lugubriously.

My first pleasure is to hear the laughter in the hall as they show the shooting scene from 'Roger of the Raj', but I can't believe it when Forsyth announces 'The winner is ... the winners are: Alan Bell and Jim Franklin for ... *Ripping Yarns*.' I just leap up and give a few lusty yells. Its like Wednesday scoring twice against Everton in the '66 Cup Final.

The boys come downstairs and stare at me.

Monday, March 24th

TG and I drive down to the King's Road in pouring rain to dine with executives from Paramount and Denis O'B at the Casserole Restaurant.

There were three Paramount people. A young, bright little man, with a combative heckling approach which settled down as one got to know him. He was called Jeffrey Katzenberg, was 29 years old and admitted that he was paid a lot because it was a very high-risk job — the turnover of Hollywood execs is spectacularly fast. His bluffer, less devious, funnier friend was also younger than TG or I and was called David.

They joked heavily as we arrived. Probably to cover their embarrassment at the fact that an hour earlier Paramount HQ had telexed Denis O'B to say that if he stalls on the next Python deal (which he has) then they will stall on the *Time Bandits*. So Paramount in LA are playing Denis's game.

But these two were at pains to deny any close association with their colleagues. These two were interested purely in talent and were keen to know more about the *Time Bandits*. They particularly wanted to be reassured about the dwarves (I mean, just how odd would they look?).

Wednesday, March 26th

At my desk at 9.30 to confront the formidable task of rewriting two scenes for the *Time Bandits* before leaving for the Python promotion in Paris at 3.30. But the muse is helpful and by one I have rewritten the 'Future' and, even more satisfactorily, I hope, the 'Titanic' scene.

Leave for the airport at a quarter past three. Onto an airbus for Paris. Packed solid – must be two or three hundred people. Read my book on the Greeks by H D F Kitto. Most inspirational. In the air only briefly, but on the plane for over an hour.

Python Sacré Graal is in its 71st week of its third reissue in Paris! So clearly there is a cult here, and it's based on only one movie.

A rather dreadful evening at a Sofitel in the 15th Arrondissement. Up to a bleak room on the 16th floor of this French Holiday Inn, where we ate. No-one knew why we were here, or who all the guests were, but it turned out to be some sort of special viewing for Avis, who are renting us the cars for the three days.

Python spirit was high, despite this debacle, though, and much enjoyment was derived from trying to find how many things on the table we could assemble around John before he noticed. Huge numbers of plates, glasses, bread baskets and even an ornamental bowl of flowers were discreetly manoeuvred in front of him, but he never noticed.

Thursdays, March 27th: Paris

Interviews – for *Le Figaro*, *La Revue de Cinéma* and finally a cartoonist called Gottlib, who has a Gumby fascination and gets me to enunciate clearly and slowly the *exact* words for 'Gumby Flower Arranging' into a small tape recorder. The more seriously I try to oblige, the more ridiculous the situation becomes. Eric doesn't help by constantly cracking up and, when I finally make it through to the moment of flower arranging the doors of the room open to reveal an enormous bunch of flowers being carried through. The interviews draw to a close by seven. Terry J and I go off to eat at La Coupole. I have ears and tail – and TJ is most impressed. We talk, for the first time, about the *Time Bandits* script, which TJ has half-read. He wasn't impressed with it until the Greek scene!

Saturday, March 29th: Paris and London

Woken from a very deep sleep in the Hotel Lotti by the soft clinking of a breakfast tray. It's half past seven. Pull myself out of bed and wander across to meet the breakfast, wearing only my underpants, when I'm suddenly aware of the nervous, twitching, apologetic presence of the Very Naughty Valet in my room.

Terry had warned me that there was a man who very lasciviously enquired whether he wanted his shoes cleaned, and here he was, in my room, having caught me with literally everything, apart from my pants, down! He wasn't at all phased by my appearance, but came on in and started to arrange my chair for breakfast in a most epicene manner.

Finally I fled to the bathroom and made loud and hopefully quite unromantic sounds of ablution until I knew he'd gone. Then I crept out again and got to grips with two fried eggs, coffee out of a swimming pool cup and croissants which were pale imitations of Patisserie Valerie's.

The door I never heard open. But I was aware of the presence of the lustful valet even before he said 'I have something for you, sir . . .'. With virgin-like caution I extended my hand to his and he dropped two small bars of soap into it as if they were ripe grapes.

Sunday, March 30th

No work – for the first time in many weeks. The weather back in London is crisp, with high white clouds and breaks of sunshine – and the city looks a lot less grey than Paris.

William and I go for a lunch picnic in St James's Park and walk up the traffic-free Mall. Gentle Sunday strolling in the heart of the city. We eat our lunch on the deckchairs, then improvise a quick game of cricket. Afterwards we drive on to the London Dungeon – William is doing the plague at school, so this *can* be called an educational visit.

This evening Helen – who has bought a £150 dress for the occasion! – and I dine out at Leith's with Denis and Inge [Denis's wife], Terry G, Maggie, George H and Sean Connery – our latest casting coup for *Time Bandits*. Connery is as he seems on screen – big, physically powerful, humorous, relaxed and very attentive to women. He talks with the unaffected ease of a man who is used to having an audience. His main love is clearly golf, but he has some good and sensible suggestions to make on his part as King Agamemnon.

Thursday, April 3rd

Arrive at JC's by ten.

Some progress, but nothing sweeps the gathering off its feet. JC reaches a peak of frustration. 'Nine weeks of writing,' he practically sobs in anguish, 'and we haven't got a *film*.'

But we make lists and from the best elements – mainly 'Kashmir' – I suggest that we play six members of a family – a sort of Python saga, set in the *Ripping Yarns* period of 1900–1930. The idea of telling the story of a family seems to appeal and quite suddenly unblocks the sticky cul-de-sac we appeared to have written ourselves into. It suits me, a *Yarns* film with all the team in it – something I've often been attracted to.

So, quite unexpectedly, the day turns around. At the eleventh hour we have a style, a subject and a framework for the new film.

Ride back with Eric, who becomes very angry when I tell him that John Cleese is doing something in the TG film. He feels this is a plot on Denis's part to make TG's into a new Python film. Eric seems to be able to take *Ripping Yarns* and *Fawlty Towers*, but Gilliam's extra-Python work he has no tolerance for, feeling that it just copies Python and isn't original.

A half-hour phone call with a researcher from the *Dick Cavett Show*, who's doing a pre-interview interview. He says he thought my remark about showbiz being 'a branch of American patriotism' was brilliant, but I can never remember saying it.

Friday, April 4th: Good Friday

The sheer pleasure of having a morning to myself – even though I have to spend it reading the *Time Bandits* latest revised script – is incredibly healing to my creaking system. Clear the desk, write the diary, pull down the blinds against the strong sunlight, brew up strong coffee, and settle down to reading.

To my relief, the *Time Bandits*, as of April 4th, is not in bad shape at all, and most of last week's rapid rewrites, though in many cases the result of writer's cowardice, do seem to improve the shape and pace of the story. So by the time I've completed a thorough read-through I'm feeling very positive.

Up to T Gilliam's to discuss with him. Find him in a house of illness. Amy puffy with mumps, Maggie, newly pregnant, looking very tired, and TG crumpled and dressing-gowned. His temperature returned to 101 last night and he was thrown into a sweating turmoil after a phone call from Denis O'B in Los Angeles. TG thinks he has 'brain fever'.

We talk through for four hours. And by the end I'm exhausted by the effort of keeping concentration and a sense of proportion and not succumbing to Gilliam's periodic moments of eyeball-widening realisation ... 'We only have seven *weeks* ... ' 'I haven't even ... ', etc, etc.

Look forward with glorious anticipation of relief relaxation to my two days off in Southwold this weekend with Rachel.

Sunday, April 6th: Easter, Southwold

Slept a welcome eight hours. Woken by chirpy Rachel at eight and up and eating croissants on Easter morning by 8.30.

Brian appears to have had some effect on Granny – she confessed that she didn't go to church on Good Friday ... 'Thinking of you and your film, I just couldn't.' Has it shaken her faith constructively or destructively? She *did* say she couldn't take Pontius Pilate seriously any more!

Tuesday, April 8th

Drive over to Eric's for a Python meeting about the next album, which we have to deliver under the terms of our Arista/Charisma contract.

Eric suggests we call the album 'Monty Python's Legal Obligation Album' and I suggest that we have it introduced by some legal man explaining why we have to deliver it and the penalties if we don't. This replaces the tentative 'Scratch and Sniff' title.

So we are all going back to our notebooks to cull material and have it typed up, and we reassemble on my 37th birthday to record.

Thursday, April 17th

Gilliam has had positive chats with Jonathan Pryce to play the Evil Genius. Pryce is apparently tremendous in *Hamlet* at the Royal Court and if we get him I think it will add to the extraordinarily confusing richness of the cast.

Bike up to Belsize Park then spend an hour sorting out mounds of unanswered fan mail (well, about 40 letters!) to give to the Python office to dispose of. This is quite a milestone as up till now I've always replied myself – even short, scruffy notes – but such is the amount of work behind and before me that I really can't manage the time any more.

Tuesday, April 22nd

A fine drizzle as I cycle round to Mr Owen the Feet at a quarter to nine. Start of Rachel's second term at Gospel Oak today and she doesn't show any sign of nerves.

Mr Owen talks for 40 minutes and cuts away at my corn for five. 'I would have been a professional violinist if it hadn't been for the war ... '. A cat wanders through the surgery.

Thursday, April 24th

Jonathan Pryce cannot do *Time Bandits* – he's holding out for a part in the new Steven Spielberg – so we discuss alternatives. David Warner top of the list. Denis O'B still wreaking awful havoc with TG's peace of mind. Airily suggesting we try to get Sellers to play the Supreme Being. TG sounds tired and heavily pressured.

Friday, April 25th

Train to Manchester. Although I spend most of the journey bent over my books, I can't help overhearing that there has been some sort of US raid on Iran during the night. About one man in the whole restaurant car seems to have heard the early morning news – and says that the Americans launched an Entebbe-style commando attack in Iran which ended with two US aircraft smashing into each other in the dark and killing eight men.

It really does sound like a most perilous affair and makes me aware of that where-I-was-when-I-heard-the-news sort of feeling – here I am speeding towards Manchester on the day the war broke out!

Arrive at twenty to twelve. Met by Roger Laughton, Ken Stephinson's boss at BBC Features.[1] He's a chattery, eloquent, rather macho head of department, who went to Birkdale School, supports Sheffield Wednesday and also went briefly to the same Crusader class[2] as myself! 'Then why weren't we best friends?' he asked, jokingly but quite significantly.

He drives me out of Manchester to Ken's quite extraordinary converted station cottage at Saddleworth. Extraordinary, not just because expresses thunder past not ten feet from his windows, but because the stretch of railway line is magnificent – coming from the south over Saddleworth Viaduct then curving in an impressive long bend to disappear then reappear in the shadow of massive slabs of moorland.

Marjorie cooks us a very tasty, delicate meal, which we eat in the Ladies' Waiting Room, whilst listening solemnly to President Carter's live message to the US people at one o'clock our time, seven o'clock a.m. their time – describing, quite straightforwardly, his own personal responsibility for the immense cock-up.

---

[1] Ken Stephinson, BBC Manchester producer who recruited me to present an episode of *Great Railway Journeys*.
[2] The Crusaders' Union was an evangelical Bible Class for boys and girls.

Monday, April 28th

At Park Square West to meet Ron Devillier,[1] who is on his way back to the US after a TV sales fair in France. Ron is anxious to market the Python TV shows in the US and, in view of his pioneering work in awakening the US to MPFC [Monty Python's Flying Circus], we listen to him with interest.

Cleese, who had not met Ron before, clearly warmed to him and at the end of an hour's discussion (Ron emphasising the extraordinary audience ratings which Python still picks up whenever it's shown in the US), John proposed that we should meet in a week's time, when all of us reassemble for the recording of *Python's Contractual Obligation Album*, and we should agree to approach Ron formally and ask him to set out his terms for distributing Python tapes.

Denis is quite actively pursuing a company called Telepictures Inc, who he hopes can be persuaded to handle *all* Python product (in and out of the series).

Again the big business approach of Denis confronts and seems to conflict with the decentralised Python plans, which are born of mistrust of big American companies and trust in individuals whom we like instead. I foresee the Telepictures v Ron Devillier situation becoming a head-on battle between Denis's 'philosophy' and our own.

Tuesday, April 29th

As I drive from Wardour Street up to TG's I'm quite forcibly struck by the inadequacy of the title *Time Bandits*. It just won't create much of a stir on the hoardings, marquees and billboards. My favourite new title is 'Terry Gilliam's Greed'.

Saturday, May 3rd

The post brings a very cheering letter from the headmaster of William Ellis to say that Tom has a place at the school from next September. So do most of his best friends, so this is good news indeed, especially as Willy will now automatically be offered a sibling's place.

As a reward I take Tom out for lunch and a trip to the South Ken museums. But the reward turns into quite an effort – for I take Louise and Helen [Guedalla], Rachel and Willy as well as Tom.

---

[1] Ron Devillier ran Dallas Public Broadcasting station, the first place in America to show a series of Monty Python uncut and in its entirety, back in 1972.

Buy the children McDonald's fast food, then drive on down to the Geology Museum. Have to detour as Kensington Gore is cordoned off because of the Iranian Embassy siege at Prince's Gate. Now in its fourth day – and deadlines and threats have passed. There is massive police presence, but a remarkable calm now as the siege becomes a London institution.

Rachel and Helen haul me round the various exhibits and we in fact visit three museums. My mind is a mass of surrealist images from a score of exhibition stands and I am quite exhausted by the time we get home at six.

Wednesday, May 7th

After a poor night's sleep, up in good time and down to Euston by 9.30. Myself and the film crew catch the 9.55 to Manchester. I'm supposed to be an ordinary traveller in an ordinary second-class coach, but will viewers think it entirely coincidental that the only other occupants of the 9.55 today seem to be Orthodox Rabbis?

Monday, May 12th: Grosmont, North Yorkshire

We drive over to Grosmont to interview Kim Mallion about restoring railway engines. It's a strange process trying to appear natural whilst having to do unnatural things like stand in an unusual relationship in order to keep the interviewee's face to camera, having to cut him off in mid-sentence because we have to move casually to another pre-set position and at the same time trying to mentally edit his remarks and your questions, knowing that this whole encounter will probably take up no more than one minute's film. I began to realise why TV interviewers and presenters develop their aggressive pushiness. They're doing their job. Well, I'm glad I'm in comedy.

Tuesday, May 13th: Grosmont

Woke at four to the silence of the countryside.

For a moment or two, lying there in the pre-dawn in the isolation of this tiny North Yorkshire village, I was seized with a crisis of confidence. What I was doing all seemed so unreal. I am not a documentary presenter – I have no special knowledge or authority to talk about railways, or even a special skill in getting people to talk. I have been chosen mainly because of what I have done in the past, which has made me into a reasonably well-known TV figure, but more precisely I've been chosen because Ken senses in my personality something which the viewer will like and identify with.

So there I am, lying, listening to a cuckoo which has just started up in a nearby wood as the grey gives way to the gold creeping light of another hot day, trying to bring into sharp and positive focus this ephemeral 'personality' of mine, which is my chief qualification for this job. How I wish I were dealing in something much more finite – like the skill of an engine driver or a cameraman. Something which you can see, feel, touch, switch on and off. But no, for an hour on national TV I am to be everyone's friend – the traveller that millions are happy to travel with.

Up at a quarter to eight, resolved to treat my predicament in the classic existentialist way – not to worry, just to do. The weather is perfect for our idyllic shots of Egton Station and the Esk Valley Line. I lie in the grass by the track reading Paul Theroux's terrible adventures in La Paz [in *The Old Patagonian Express*] and thinking myself in paradise here, with the hot sun shining from a cloudless sky and wind in the thin line of pines above my head.

Wednesday, May 14th: Teesside

Interviewed a man who knew some details of Stockton–Darlington, the world's first public passenger railway. Only after the interview do I find out that his son had been crushed to death six weeks before owing to the negligence of the nearby factory where he was an apprentice. It would have been his 18th birthday today, the man told me – on the verge of tears. He'd had a lot of personal problems – the break-up of a marriage, etc – and this was the last straw. He apologised for not being able to remember all the details for me, but the doctors had put him on a drug after his nervous breakdown and it left him irritatingly cloudy on memories, he said. He'd half-built a model train. Just an ordinary bloke.

Thursday, May 15th: Newcastle

On to the 125 at Darlington and various shots of The Traveller looking around him. I've long since run out of delightfully informal, spontaneous and casual gestures and am now concentrating on trying not to appear too idiotically interested every time I look out of the window.

My rosy-spectacled view of Newcastle provoked a nice comment from a local. I was raving about the wonderful easiness of the Cumberland pub in the working-class district of the Byker and someone quipped, 'Oh, yes, the Cumberland. They say there's one bar full of locals and one bar full of playgroup leaders.'

Friday, May 16th: Newcastle–Edinburgh

Wake to sunshine and clear skies and the chorus of squeaks, rumbles and soft hissing of diesel exhausts from the station below. Outside a panorama of cars and trains crossing bridges. Tyneside coming to work.

We board an HST for Edinburgh which is half an hour late. I haven't been on a single punctual train this week.

Between Berwick and Edinburgh, as the train staggers home with an out-of-action rear power car (what a bad day for this to happen to British Rail), I sit with three randomly selected 'members of the public' and we're filmed chatting. Maybe the age of television is conditioning us all, but they speak with the easy assurance of people who are interviewed daily.

My last memories of elegant Edinburgh, as serenely unflawed in its beauty as ever, are of a group of very drunken chartered surveyors milling around in the lounge of the North British at midnight, tipping each other in and out of a wheelchair. If they'd been punks they'd have been out in the gutter, but they were Chartered Surveyors of this Fine City and were in dinner jackets and had paid well for their tickets, so no-one stopped them behaving like the worst sort of hooligans. My last image was of them falling on top of each other and knocking back Napoleon brandy from the bottle.

Saturday, May 17th: Kyle of Lochalsh

Up and across the Central Highlands – shot of me reading, etc. On time at Inverness's crabbed and disappointing little station. Inverness full of yobbos, drunks and ladies with twinsets and pearls doing their Saturday shopping. We have time off. I make for the castle, but in front of it are three fairly incapable teenage Scots. One turns and spits long and high into the air. To my astonished horror another runs forward, tries to catch the gob in his own mouth and fails.

The other thing that I notice in Inverness this sunny Saturday afternoon are the number of churches. Severe, pencil-thin towers – the grey pointed fingers of disapproval. Enough to drive you to drink.

So begins the memorable nightmare of the journey to Kyle. The train has an observation car on the end, a special old coach with free-standing armchairs and tables.

Ken's idea is to fill the special coach with travellers whom I casually chat to, plus one or two specially researched guests. One of whom is a Mrs Mackenzie, a 99-year-old who I'm told remembers the railway on the day it opened in 1896. She's a wonderful, bright old lady, but not soft of hearing, and my first question – a tortuously-phrased effort to elicit information as to how old she was – is received with a stony silence. A pleasant smile, but a stony silence. I try it again, then again even louder. The crew and the rest of the compartment must be either splitting their sides or squirming in embarrassment.

For a full ten minutes I persevere, trying everything, but, like a man with an enormous fishing net and six harpoons trying to catch two small fish, I end up with very little for a lot of work. It leaves me exhausted, though still in admiration of old Mrs Mackenzie.

Tuesday, May 20th: Mallaig

At 10.30 I'm filmed boarding the Skye ferry to Kyleakin. The cameras are staying on the mainland to film exteriors from the Kyle train. I'm free until after lunch and, as I have no option but to go on to Skye, I decide on a morning's walking to compensate for much eating and drinking over the last few days.

I stride on out of town, having left my case at the Caledonian MacBrayne [ferry] office. I stop at a hotel which is a country house – red-grey stone and tall pitched roofs – set in very lush gardens with brilliantly deep pink rhododendrons and a settled air of detachment and solid comfort.

But as soon as I step inside my stomach tightens with the identification of a very early feeling of my childhood of a claustrophobia, a fear of being stifled in dark rooms with well polished doors, in which old ladies move in the shadows.

Mallaig, which we reach in the evening, is even bleaker than Kyle of Lochalsh, a fairly wretched spot to be faced with the prospect of a night in – after a day like today. But I have a room overlooking the Atlantic and the sharp points of Rum and the volcanic spur of Eigg and there is a sunset after all and it looks quite idyllic with a score of fishing boats heading for the harbour.

After the ritual of an evening meal together ('Are the "Melon Cubes" out of a tin?' one of our number enquires ingenuously. 'Oh, yes ... ' the waitress assures him quickly), Ken and I go to visit the engine driver whom we will be filming tomorrow, as his wife has called and asked us over.

They're rather a special family – with three children roughly the age of my own, and yet Ronnie McClellan must be over 20 years older then me. He married late to a very bright and articulate district nurse. Their children come down in dressing gowns to meet us (it's 9.45) and shake hands solemnly and politely. They don't have television, but they have dogs, cats and, I think, some animals in the croft. The children kiss their father obediently but warmly. I should imagine he's quite a strict and traditional father.

Back at the empty vastness of the West Highland, the two men who were drinking half and halfs (Scotch and Heavy) at six o'clock are still drinking half and halfs at twelve. Ken beats me three times at pool. Go to bed feeling inadequate.

Nylon sheets and a colour scheme which looks as though an animal's been slaughtered in the room. Read Michael Arlen's *The Green Hat* and enjoy the utter incongruity. It gives me great comfort to know that Cannes and Mallaig exist on the same planet.

Wednesday, May 21st: Mallaig–Glenfinnan

Fresh Mallaig kippers for breakfast. Later I'm told that there's no such thing as a Mallaig kipper as there's a ban on herring fishing. So it was probably a Canadian herring – which may have been kippered in Mallaig. Anyway, I ate two of them.

An especially beautiful journey down along the coast – made more civilised by the presence of a buffet bar and a couple of glasses of wine. I have to be filmed in the said buffet bar with two Danish students and a flavour chemist from Chicago who is over here on a cycling tour of Scotland. He's a great Python fan and he's honestly called Constantine Apostle.

Our hotel here – the Glenfinnan House – is situated in an almost unbeatable Highland surrounding. Pictures of Bonnie Prince Charlie's heroic failures (it was here at Glenfinnan he gathered his forces in the summer of 1745), a set of bagpipes, pieces of igneous rocks on a dark-stained mantelpiece in a passable imitation of a baronial hall.

The house is set beside a lawn surrounded by broadleaved trees and running down to Loch Shiel. Beside a wooden jetty, a couple of rowing boats bob on the water. Walk down to the jetty and look down the length of Loch Shiel, at the sheer magnificence of the spurs of epic mountainside tumbling down to the lakeside.

As we unload, a cool-looking kid of ten or eleven skids up on his bike. 'Do you live here?' I ask ... The boy, in a particularly businesslike way, nods and adds, quite naturally, 'D'you think I'm lucky?'

To bed around midnight. It seems almost a crime to close the curtains against such a view.

Monday, May 26th

A Bank Holiday again. Surfaced mid-morning. Regular phone calls and door bells ringing – mostly for the children, who have the next week off school. There was lots I wanted to do and a big pile of mail. Most of all I wanted to do nothing – to be at no-one's beck and call for a bit.

Terry Gilliam comes round soon after six. The first week of *Time Bandits* is now complete, but the shoot in Morocco was gruelling even by TG's standards.

Moroccans less good at organisation than Tunisians, which didn't help, but they managed 97 slates – some in locations only accessible by mule.

After one week in Morocco he'd come back feeling like he did after ten weeks of *Brian*. Rushes on Wednesday will show whether this almighty opening effort will spur everyone on, or be the start of the collapse.

Thursday, May 29th

A heavy day ahead. The sky is grey and lowering, but still no rain. Prepare for the arrival of the BBC unit to film outside and inside the house. Also today we're expecting Al and Claudie[1] to stay, so No. 2 has to be prepared.

As it turns out we have a most successful shoot. We block off Julia Street with a 60-foot hoist to shoot an epic 'leaving home' scene. Helen and the three children all have to do their acting bit and acquit themselves very well on all four takes. Really it's an elaborate reconstruction for the viewing public of what happens every time I leave home for filming away. Rachel, last out, hands me my toothbrush with an easy self-confidence which I hadn't expected at all.

Friday, May 30th

Helen goes out to badminton and Al, Claudie and I make a rambling feast out of quite a simple selection of soup and cold meats, ending with a liqueur tasting – Al determined to try all the bottles he brought over from Brittany. Their Jacques Brel tape played loudly – Al enthusing, as only he can, over each track. 'One of the greatest people of this century' is Al's verdict on Brel.

Claudie comes to life more when the subject turns to France, but her English is now much more confident. But I wish she would eat more and smoke less. Al wants to have a baby – they want a girl and they have a name, 'Chantelle'.

A warm and woozy evening. Much laughter.

Tuesday, June 3rd

Listen to the Python *Contractual Obligation Album*. I'm afraid it does sound rather ordinary. One or two of the songs stand out and there are some conventional sketches of Cleese and Chapman's (man enters shop, etc) which

[1] Al Levinson, an American I'd met in the seventies, and some of whose writing I'd published. His second marriage was to Claudie, a young Bretonne.

are saved by good performances. Twenty-five percent padding, fifty percent quite acceptable, twenty-five percent good new Python.

Saturday, June 7th

Drive up to T Gilliam's for a meeting. Terry is very deflated. He looks and sounds quite pummelled by the pressures of this creature he's brought into life. Filming all week, meetings with actors in the evening, all weekend looking at locations.

Now Amy wants his attention and he wants to give me his attention. So we work on rewrites and additions for next week whilst Amy piles me up with teddy bears and races round the room with a manic energy, shouting, tumbling, grimacing. The only way we can work is by me reading the script corrections as a story to one of Amy's teddies. A bizarre session.

Monday, June 9th

Work and run in the morning. Talk to a fan from Indiana on the telephone at lunchtime – she was visiting England, had seen *Grail* 17 times and *Brian* nine times and loved everything we did.

To Denis's office at two. Meet Peter Cook there. He has a very silly hat, but we have a few laughs, mainly about a pop group Peter had seen in Los Angeles called Bees Attack Victor Mature. Peter rambles on a while, then wanders off – a little concerned as to how he'll find his way out of the EuroAtlantic fortress. Denis has just done a deal for GC's *Yellowbeard* screenplay, provided that the screenplay is rewritten. So Peter Cook, whom Denis was much impressed by at Amnesty, is to rewrite the script with GC – and they have a six-million-dollar production budget. Denis does want to see us all happy.

What Denis doesn't know is that E. Idle has probably slipped the O'Brien net. A very positive letter from him in France – the 'Pirates of Penzance' now looks more likely to happen. Gary Weiss [Eric's director] is a very 'hot' property and he wants to do it. Eric now has a direct phone line in Cotignac, but asks me to promise not to give it to Denis, under threat of setting fire to my stereo.

I leave, having told Denis that the next thing I want to do is a film on my own – probably to shoot next summer.

Watch last hour of the Test Match v West Indies on the box, then Helen and I, suitably tarted up in DJs and long dresses, drive down to Kensington for the reception at the Royal Geographical Society to commemorate their founding 150 years ago.

The Queen and Prince Philip and the Duke of Kent are to be there. We've joked about going and not going, but tell Helen it's my duty as a diarist if nothing else.

Sir John and Lady Hunt are receiving the guests. He's quite frail now and totally white-haired. Lady Hunt seems very bright and on the ball.

I meet the daughter of Lord Curzon, on whose land the RGS HQ was built, and the sparkling wine with strawberries in it is going to my head quite pleasantly when we are asked to move away from the gravel terrace. Quite amiably, but firmly. Around us some people are being lined up as if for some military manoeuvre – not in a long line, but in a number of short ranks, like football teams.

Helen and I are enmeshed with a world authority on gibbons, who also happens to be an enormous *Ripping Yarn* fan and slightly more pissed than we are.

The Duke was, at one point, just beside my right shoulder and sounded to be having quite a jolly time, but entourages always deter chance encounters, so I didn't spring forward. About 10.30 he and Queenie disappeared inside.

Helen and I, quite mellow, but hungry, left about 15 minutes later, but, as we prepared to cross Kensington Gore, there was a shout from a policeman who was standing only 100 yards away from the SAS siege building – 'Stay in the middle!'[1] We froze on the traffic island in the middle of Kensington Gore and realised that the Queen had not yet left.

In fact at this moment her Daimler, with the swollen rear windows for better visibility, was sweeping away from the RGS. The light was on inside so the Queen and the Duke could be seen, and for a moment in time we on our little traffic island and the Head of the British Empire came into eyeball to eyeball contact. Helen waved. The Queen automatically waved back, the Duke grinned and the black limousine curved left and right into Hyde Park and was gone.

Thursday, June 12th: London–Llanwern

To Paddington to catch the 1.15 to Newport. There is a long wait, blamed first on signal failure, then, with what sounded like a stroke of inspiration from a tired guard, on a bomb scare. But it enables me to complete the 'Robin Hood' rewrites, losing the 'Future' sequence.

Finally arrive at the Gateway Hotel, Llanwern, at about four o'clock. Various members of *Time Bandits* crew are surfacing after the second of their week of

---

[1] Just over a month earlier the SAS had spectacularly stormed the Iranian Embassy in Prince's Gate, ending a five-day siege by Iranian separatists. Five of the gunmen and one hostage were killed.

night shoots at nearby Raglan Castle. Last night a lady on stilts 'lost her bottle', as Ian Holm put it, but the crew seem to be in good spirits.

TG and I discuss the rewrites. Then I go to my room and watch some of the England v Belgium match – some promising football and one of the great international goals by Wilkins, then fighting on the terraces and the Italian police react fiercely with riot police and tear gas.

TG's fictional recreation of the sack of Castiglione is not unlike the actual scenes I've just witnessed on the terraces in Turin. Both take place in North Italy and in each smoke is drifting everywhere and bodies are falling. But TG's pictures are much more impressive and I'm tantalised by the brief amount I've seen of this strange film that is slowly and painstakingly taking shape in the rain at a nearby castle.

Tuesday, June 24th

Midsummer's Day. And, as it turns out, the first day in the last three weeks when it hasn't rained on the *Time Bandits*.

Out in the mosquito-ridden beauty of the Epping Forest, with the pollarded trees striking wonderfully Gilliamesque poses, with lumps and gnarls and strange growths, Shelley [Duvall who's playing Pansy, one of the star-crossed lovers] and I and the mammoth unit enjoy a dry day. Not 20 miles away, there were fierce storms with hailstones scattering the players at Wimbledon and Lord's.

Wednesday, June 25th

After more shots with the dwarves passing us, Shelley and I get on to the rain sequences. I can't complain. I wrote the dreaded word 'rain', and here it is in all its dispiriting glory, courtesy of the Essex Fire Brigade, Not a terribly good take and the next 40 minutes are spent under a hair-dryer, preparing my wig for a re-take. But then it's lunch and I have to go to the pub with a plastic bag over my head.

Afterwards a fairly horrendous experience in the second rain scene, when Shelley and I are down to our mediaeval underwear. The elements of the developing shot are so various that it takes six takes before we have a satisfactory conclusion. And on each one we have hoses directed on us for about a minute and a half.

Shelley seems much more tolerant of the ordeal than any actress has a right to be. But, as she says in the car on the way home, it's better than having to cry every day for seven months with Kubrick! Nicholson had to take a six-month break after the movie [*The Shining*] was finished to get himself straight again.

Thursday, June 26th

Drive to Pentonville Road, where, on the hill from which the great Victorian painting of St Pancras was made, I find myself in the BUPA medical centre for a screening. No particular reason, I just thought I should have a complete medical check-up and where better than under the personal eye of one of the BUPA centre's leading lights – Alan Bailey.[1]

Alan reassures me on one point: that Parkinson's Disease isn't hereditary. Then he examines me, pokes, prods and fingers my genitals, after which we have a talk about houses, education, the possible break-up of ILEA [Inner London Education Authority], and he offers me a drink from his metal cupboard full of Scotch and other drugs. I have a beer and meet the doctor who is, as Alan cheerfully informs me, 'in charge of the clap clinic here'.

The clap man is neat, less of a character, and we talk about beta-blockers – pills which reduce the heartbeat. He thinks them a quite brilliant advance, and yet could talk only of the dangers of their misuse.

Alan is quite keen to show off the body scanner in the basement and the instant computer details of each patient. So far, all the results of my tests show no danger areas. I'm four pounds lighter than I was when I came seven years ago at eleven stone seven, and I'm five foot eleven inches – which is news to me and means I'm officially taller than I thought I was! Sight and hearing are 100% apart from one frequency of hearing – that of telephone bells and gunshots!

Monday, June 30th

I have something of a record in the make-up line today – four layers – my own tightly-cropped hair, a bald bladder on top of that, a wig stuck onto the sides of that and, to top the lot, a toupee. The make-up takes a couple of hours, but Elaine [Carew, my make-up artist] and I now get on so well that I hardly notice the time passing. I can't blame anyone but myself for any inconvenience either, as I wrote it.

Katherine Helmond, of *Soap* fame, who is Ruth Gordon's replacement, is

[1] Alan was one of Graham Chapman's closest friends. They had met as medical students at Bart's Hospital.

on the set for fittings, etc, together with Peter Vaughan, who plays her Ogre husband. She's delightful, Vaughan strong and quite quiet with his foxy little eyes and mouth easily cracking into a smile.

Shelley and I work all day on an impressive set of the 'Titanic'. Final shot is uncomfortable and involves me losing my toupee and causing a lot of damage. They like it on the third take and we wrap at 7.30.

Tuesday, July 1st

A stormy night as a depression, pushed by cold north winds, crosses over us. The blind flaps and bangs and it's as cold as November. Up at seven and drive through the rain to the studios [at Wembley] by eight.

Into mediaeval outfit this time. A steady morning's work on the coach interiors (Shelley and I sitting in a coach resting on inner tubes of lorry tyres – four men waving trees above our heads).

In the afternoon, as we prepare to shoot the dwarves dropping on Patsy [one of the two star-crossed lovers, played by Shelley] and myself, the director hurtles through the air towards us, strikes Shelley sharply on the left temple and knocks her almost senseless. Gilliam spends the next half-hour comforting a very shaken Shelley. Turns out he was demonstrating to one of the dwarves how safe it was to fall.

I work in my dressing room, waiting for the final call. Rain and wind outside. Quite cosy. Stodgy food and assistant director constantly coming round to ask if there's anything I want. Stardom means eating too much. After eight, Neville Thompson, the associate producer, arrives in my 'suite' to tell me that they will not be getting around to Shelley and myself this evening. The shot has been cancelled, as this was Shelley's last day on the picture.

Wednesday, July 2nd

To Park Square West by ten for a Python meeting. Eric is already there, playing the piano. I've no idea how today's meeting is going to turn out – all I know is that John has told Terry G that he's never felt less like writing Python and yet officially we have this month set aside for just such an enterprise . . .

Terry J arrives next, looking mournful – with reason, for he has his arm in a sling. Apparently he threw himself on the ground at a charity cricket match last Sunday and has a hairline fracture of a bone called the humerus.

John arrives – he's growing his Shakespearian beard back again, I think. He claims it went down very well with the ladies and shaving it off (which he did for the *Time Bandits*) only revealed what a tiny mouth he has. I advise John to have his mouth widened. He says he is considering another hair transplant.

We talk briefly about Python's general biz. Denis's call for a business meeting and a meeting to discuss his exciting new proposals for a distribution network of our own are met with almost universal lack of interest. 'Tell him we went off to sleep,' John advises Anne when she is desperately asking what reaction she should relay to DO'B about his proposals.

Then to lunch at Odin's. Cliff Richard at the next table looks permanently off the beach at Barbados. Apart from Eric, the Pythons are white, apart from TJ who's grey. After a long wait, and some white wine, I lead off perhaps provocatively by asking who wants to write the new Python film this month. Then it all comes out.

JC wants a month of leisurely talk and discussion and does not want to face the 'slog' of nine-to-five writing. I suggest that we don't yet have a very clear and positive area or identity for the subject matter of the film and that we should only write when we are really 'hungry' to write. But it's Graham who quite blandly drops the real bombshell – he's working for the next few days on a *Yellowbeard* rewrite and then he hopes to film it in Australia during the winter. This straight pinch from previously discussed Python plans is a real stunner and the well-controlled indignation of Eric and Terry J rises to the surface.

I have the increasing feeling that we are going through a period similar to the post-*Grail* days in '75, '76, when individual Pythons want to stretch their legs. Terry G led the field with *Time Bandits*, I've done the *Yarns* and the 'Railway' documentary. So I'm not too worried about proving myself.

I don't know about Eric, but he was clearly amazed when John suggested we didn't meet together till next Wednesday. At Eric's surprise JC dropped all pretences – he hung his head in his hands and became cross. 'I'm tired . . . I've done six weeks of . . . ' and so on.

This lunch and the discussions were all part of the painful process of preserving Python. We don't fit into any easy patterns, we ask each other to make enormous compromises, adjustments and U-turns, but we do produce the best comedy in the country.

Not much rest at home, for at 6.30 I'm collected by Graham in his Mercedes and we drive one and a half hours out to Associated Book Publishers in Andover for a sales-force-meet-authors binge. It all seems quite a tiresome waste of time, except that Christopher Isherwood is there, which saves the evening for me. He's 76 and looks fit and neat. His skin is weathered like an elephant's leg, in contrast to the softer, tanned brown of his friend Don Bachardy. Bachardy has bright eyes and looks terribly healthy. He's almost a carbon copy of Isherwood. Isherwood talks to Graham about a supermarket they both share in Brentwood, Los Angeles.

Isherwood talks fluently – like a man used to talking and being listened to

(GC tells me his voice has become quite 'stentorian' since doing lecture tours). I would love to spend more time with him and Don – they seem such a bright, lively pair in this drab and colourless sales conference world.

Wednesday, July 9th

To Gospel Oak School for the Infant Concert. Rachel is a sheep. She wears her clean, Persil-white T-shirt and petticoat and a cardboard mask which makes it difficult for her to see, and the sheep bang into each other. Rachel's class less imaginative than the others, but her rather morose teacher did wear black fishnet tights.

Monday, July 14th

Hurry through the rain to 2 Park Square West and a Python meeting. Eric and Denis are already there. I'm wearing a 'Leica' disposable jacket and hood which I acquired [whilst filming] at the Rainhill Trials at the end of May. Eric says I look like a red sperm.

All Pythons present except, of course, Gilliam. Denis has greatly looked forward to this meeting, for this is the first time he has aired his latest proposal to the group as a whole. The proposal is that Python should become involved in the setting-up of an independent UK film distribution company – HandMade Films.

Denis rides all interruptions as he slowly and impressively reveals his plans. But he is not a good judge of people – and of English people especially – and instead of being received with wide-eyed gratitude, his proposals are subjected to a barrage of strong scepticism.

Eric wants to know how much it all will cost us and then queries whether or not we need it, as it will mean yet another source of interminable business meetings. John C queries Denis's assumption that there will be eight 'Python-based' films at least in the next five years. He certainly isn't going to do one, and neither is Eric. Also the assumption that *Time Bandits* and *Yellowbeard* will each make at least £650,000 in the UK is received without conviction.

Denis's worst enemy is his own ingenuous enthusiasm in the face of five very complex, quite sophisticated minds, four at least of which distrust one thing more than anything else – uncritical enthusiasm. So it's left undecided.

Denis rather rapidly runs through the rest of the agenda, but he's lost us. The more he enthuses over terms, deals, percentages, controls, etc, the more John turns his mind to doing anagrams on his agenda (he had a good one for Michael Palin – i.e. Phallic Man).

To lunch at Odin's. Terry suggests the group should spend three days in Cherbourg, writing. John thinks we should do a film about the Iliad. Denis looks bewildered.

Wednesday, July 16th

Children are prepared for school – with the right clothes, shoes, music, forms for teachers, etc. At ten to nine Sam Jarvis arrives to work on painting the outside of the house and settles first of all for his cup of tea. Letters are sorted, diaries written and banks visited on the way to Cleese's for a Python session.

Only John is there at the appointed time. He's thumbing through his address book for someone to take to dinner ... 'Come on, Michael, you must know some ravishing creature ... ' and so on. He grins happily when I half-jest about the demise of Python. Eric is still unwell, TG's off ... 'I think we should disband this rapidly-crumbling comedy group for at least a year.' John grins ...

At seven leave for Tom's orchestral concert at Gospel Oak. Tom plays a clarinet solo, piano solo and a duet with Holly [Jones] and is one of the two or three stars of the show. I feel very proud, especially as his clarinet piece is quite difficult. Both Helen and I dreadfully nervous in the audience.

Sunday, July 20th

After breakfast and Sunday papers, I retire to workroom (most reluctantly) to prepare for tonight's Save the Whales concert. Various tiresome little props and costume details to sort out, but Anne H is a great help and locates such things as Gumby glasses and the like. I write a new piece – a short monologue about Saving the Plankton.

I complete my plankton piece, gather props and cossies into a big suitcase and, in a state of numbed resignation, set off under grey skies for the Venue in Victoria. I forget Gumby flowers, vase and mallet and have to drive all the way back from Regent's Park.

The Venue is a cabaret-type theatre, with audience at tables eating and drinking, so they don't seem to mind us starting nearly an hour late. From then on I begin to enjoy it. All the lethargy of a Sunday disappears and is replaced by the sharpness of performing adrenaline. 'Plankton' goes especially well and is received all the better for being obviously specially-written material.

Second half the audience are in very good form. 'Save the leopards!' someone shouts as I come on in my leopard-skin coat as the spangly compère of

'Shouting'. I reassure the audience that it *is* artificial, whereupon the rejoinder comes smartly back 'Save the artificial leopards!'

Home with huge feeling of relief and satisfaction – a 100% different from the way I felt on leaving seven hours ago. Am I a manic depressive?

Monday, July 21st

Anne rings early to say that Python has been offered four days at the Hollywood Bowl at the end of September. Two weeks in LA in late September, all together, would, I feel, do our writing chances and the group's general commitment to working together so much good that we should decide to go ahead with it as soon as possible.

Wednesday, July 23rd

TJ comes up after lunch. It's actually too hot to work upstairs at No. 4 – sticky, with bright, shining sun unremitting – so we decamp to No. 2, to the leaky double bedroom. TJ rather content here. Says it reminds him of Belsize Park![1] There complete 'Sperm Song'.

In the evening (we work on until 6.30), I ring John C to find him very disappointed with his writing progress. He claims not to have been really well since last Friday and says that he and GC have not written much and he doesn't like the family idea and could we not postpone the entire film for six months?

Thursday, July 24th

Blue skies and high summer again – the fine weather is persisting despite all forecasts. So a fresh buoyancy to my step as I come back from Mansfield Road with the papers – abruptly slowed down by the news that Peter Sellers died last night. Though not as sudden and unexpected as the news seen in a French paper on holiday in 1977 that 'Elvis est Mort!', it affected me in the same way. Sellers and Milligan were to the humour of my pre- and teenage days as Elvis was to the music.

---

[1] When Helen and I married in 1966 we lived in a flat at 82 Belsize Park Gardens.

Friday, July 25th

Duly arrive at J Cleese's at ten – bringing Eric. It's a hot day. John is upstairs recovering from taking Cynthia for an early-morning swim. We meet out in John's garden – this prospect of unbroken sunshine is so rare this last month that the sun-worshippers in the group (everyone except TJ) feel unable to ignore it.

JC proposes a moratorium on the film – period unspecified. This rather deflating proposal is perhaps made more acceptable by a general welcoming of the Hollywood Bowl show. This, after brief discussion, is received most constructively. It makes the film postponement seem less like a positive break, more of a long interruption of work in progress. We shall be together for two or three weeks in LA in late September, we will do four nights at the Bowl and it is agreed that it shall be videotaped for sale to US TV.

Our 'break-through' writing of yesterday and the days before is not even read out. John seems happy to let things drift. There's a listless feeling. EI says July is a rotten month to write anything.

No-one has yet really decided how long this 'interruption' should be. Six months is the minimum and any attempt to compromise on this meets very strong objections from John. But six months merely means an almost impossibly short period for the resolution of any alternative plans, so a year is proposed. And reluctantly accepted, as if acknowledging a measure of defeat.

We shall meet again to write the movie in September 1981.

Wednesday, July 30th

Catch the 8.55 Euston–Manchester train to see the first assembly of my 'Great Railway Journey'.

At the BBC we watch the 62-minute first cut on a Steenbeck. My impression is of endless pretty railway trains disappearing behind trees – clichés of this sort of documentary. There is little evidence of my own impact on the journey ... but more disappointingly a very ordinary, flat feeling to the camerawork and strangely the editing as well.

It was a depressing viewing – depressing because I value Ken's friendship and the working relationship between us, depressing because I had hoped that his unconventional choice of presenter indicated his intention of trying some exciting and experimental approach to the programme. Depressing because I had to fight Denis O'B so hard to come up with something so dull. I think Ken is well aware of my feelings, and there is a conspicuous lack of over-enthusiasm.

So when I dash off to catch the Manchester Pullman back to town, I know

I have a job of work on – much more than I expected to do at this stage of the programme, but there is hope and I have always in the back of my mind the memory of my first reaction to the initial cut of 'Roger of the Raj'.[1]

Thursday, July 31st

To the foot man at 9.30. He's running very late. I sit in his little surgery in Mornington Road, with a nun and a sad, rather dim, shuffling old Irishman, and write my Python album notes.

Then to EuroAtlantic for what is supposed to be a couple of hours of business and a couple of hours of thought on the content of the stage show. It turns out to be four hours of business and hardly a thought for the content.

Once again Denis pushes us towards the Telepictures video deal and the distribution company. All of us weaken on Telepictures, apart from Eric, who maintains that we should not give video rights for seven years to a company we know nothing about. At one point Eric suggests directly to Denis that he is in some way an interested party on Telepictures' side. Denis denies this. Eric will not be moved, though, and vetoes the agreement until he's thought about it more.

Monday, August 18th

Meet Ken Stephinson for lunch and we have a very productive chat about the documentary. He feels as I do that it's bland and rather dull at the moment, but we hatch plans to revive, restore and enliven it. The only thing that worries me is that I calculate I have a maximum of 12 clear writing days before Hollywood.

Thursday, August 21st: Copenhagen and Malmö

Caught British Airways' 9.25 flight to Copenhagen [for *Life of Brian* publicity] with Terry J and Anne Bennett (of CIC, our distributors) from a marvellously uncrowded Heathrow.

We lost an hour in the air and landed at Copenhagen at 12.05. A Cadillac limousine (looking very out of place) swept us and our Danish hosts through the neat, clean streets of suburban Copenhagen, with row upon row of

---

[1] A *Ripping Yarn* which I at first thought hadn't worked at all, but has since become one of my favourites, not least for Richard Vernon and Joan Sanderson's wonderfully played dining room scenes.

apartment blocks, but mainly of brick, with pitched roofs and in small units, usually angled to avoid a wilderness of long concrete vistas.

From this neat, clean, modest little capital we took a neat, clean hydrofoil across to Malmö in Sweden.

I hear from TJ (confirmed by Anne Bennett) that Python has not begun too well in Germany. Strong religious anti-reaction in Stuttgart – elsewhere sluggish. So Brianity is perhaps not to be the new world religion after all.

As we leave Malmö for the University of Lund the wind has freshened. Not much impression of Sweden on the way. An extension of Lincolnshire perhaps.

About a quarter past eight we are introduced and go into a question and answer session. Most of the questions seem to come from Englishmen or Americans. Round about nine TJ is getting rather restless and asks the audience (numbering 300 or so) if he can ask *them* a question. Much eager nodding. 'How many of you want to go to the lavatory?' Our hosts take the hint and wind up the session. For some reason we sing them the 'Lumberjack Song' and that's it. Both of us quite tired by now.

We're driven to the Students' Union and eventually find ourselves in a small, circular room where a table is laid. We each have a glass of rather weak beer – they are not allowed to serve full-strength beer to students – and nothing is happening. Outside the wind is strong and gusting and rain is lashing the panes.

Finally a large plate of Swedish crayfish arrives. They've been marinaded in beer and dill (very popular in Sweden) and are quite tasty. Then bottles of aquavit, which are drunk to the accompaniment of rather hard drinking songs. A lady called Lotta Love, said to be Sweden's foremost groupie, also comes in from somewhere.

Terry J is strongly resisting Anne's and my attempts to get us all onto the last hydrofoil to Copenhagen. I know that we must get back. We have to start early tomorrow and the drinking – already producing a noisy and rather belligerent atmosphere – will only accelerate.

With great difficulty we get TJ up and mutter our apologies. We just managed to get downstairs and into our waiting limousine, which then drives like hell into Malmö. The wind buffets the car on the motorway, causing it to veer dangerously at high speed, but we *do* reach the quay in time and to my intense relief the hydrofoil is still running, despite the storm. We are in Denmark again by one.

Friday, August 22nd: Copenhagen

Terry is terribly thankful that we didn't let him stay in Malmö, and he goes off for a walk whilst I bathe, do my morning exercise and gently test my body and brain for any damage caused by Sweden yesterday.

Outside the life of Copenhagen goes on, very unhurried, like model life in a model village. Even the workmen are clean and I don't believe that they really have the work to do anyway. They must be Play People. Eventually decide that the men engaged in raising and replacing paving stones opposite the hotel are in fact now reduced to cleaning the underneath of the Copenhagen streets.

At about ten o'clock we start interviews in our room, followed by a press conference downstairs, after which we are to give a TV interview. A Danish actor is portraying a Norwegian. The Danes and Swedes both find the Norwegians a Scandinavian joke – slow-witted, thick-headed, humourless fishing folk – and they send them up unmercifully. The fact that Python's *Life of Brian* has been banned in Norway causes our hosts great glee and the Swedes have a poster tagging the film 'So Funny it was Banned in Norway'.

We are then taken to the Tivoli Gardens for lunch and more filming. By now my head is clear, but my stomach is distinctly off-balance. I drink mineral water, eat more ham and eggs, but find to my horror after lunch that we are to be interviewed on the Big Wheel. I'm now feeling very queasy and not at all far from the point of uncontainable nausea.

Here I am, quite likely to be sick even if I just stand still, being loaded onto a big wheel compartment opposite a grinning interviewer, a cameraman and a sound man. The wheel moves up, we hang over Copenhagen then swing down, round, up again, going faster. Only desperate laughter at my plight and Terry's touching concern and huge gulps of cool air as we swing up keep my stomach contents from being vividly reproduced on Danish television.

At last the living hell comes to an end and I'm quite proud to have survived. But the interviewer hasn't finished, he wants more. High over the city we go – I really can't answer any more. Even TJ is going groggy. 'Alright,' is all I can shout. 'I give up! I give up!' At the end of the torture I'm white and wobbling, something's churning away inside. At last I can pause … No I can't … We're led away to be photographed doing funny things with the Danish comedian.

Then into the limousine, to be driven, with the dubious aid of stomach-lurching power-assisted brakes, to Danish radio. At last our Danish hosts seem to have got the message that I'm unwell, so I'm escorted carefully from the limousine and the first request is a 'toiletten' for Mr Palin.

Monday, August 25th

Work on the 'Railway' programme – looking through the video cassette and running and re-running. I'm very much encouraged, and there is enough in there to give a high-quality look to the programme – now all we need is a cohesive element of typical Palin stuff. I need to inject into the documentary what I can do best – which is not, clearly, being a straight documentary presenter.

Go out for a pizza in Hampstead, full of Bank Holiday revellers. We talk over '*TB*'. Terry is as positive about it as I've heard him since May. Highly excited by the battle scenes at the end.

I feel much encouraged by today – both on '*GRJ*' and '*TB*'. At one time I was feeling that I have fallen between so many stools this year that I can only have done myself harm, but now it looks as though all the hard work and hassle may just have been worth it.

Monday, September 1st

School starts again – Rachel and Willy to Gospel Oak today, Tom to William Ellis tomorrow. Tom has tried on his blazer, matching shirt, dark trousers, dark shoes and hates them. I must say it's a little sad to see him suddenly restricted by a uniform. Some loss of innocence somewhere.

Before I start work I have to go through the unnerving and slightly distasteful business of giving myself an enema – to clear out my bowels in preparation for a visit to the botty doctor this afternoon.

After squeezing the phosphate mixture in, I realise I'm unsure what an enema is quite supposed to do. Should I retain the fluid for a certain time? I'm downstairs looking up 'enema' in the *Shorter Oxford Dictionary* when events overtake me and I just reach the lavatory for ten or fifteen minutes' worth of quite uncomfortable straining, with nothing to read but an article on the state of the economy.

Then to the Medical Centre. Talk with Alan Bailey, then meet Mr Baker, the botty doctor. He takes various particulars, then I'm led to a room next door with various contraptions lying about. My eye flicks over them, wanting – and at the same time, not wanting – to see the sort of thing which will be going up my bum.

The doctor enters, formally, from another doorway. I'm laid down, naked and with my legs up in my chest, and the ordeal begins. His first probings are, after penetration, not too bad, quite bearable, but the higher he gets (and I can feel this tubing peering and turning and twisting and thrusting up into my stomach) the more severe the pain.

I'm told to take deep breaths and I grasp the nurse's hand tightly as he squeezes air and water into my bowels to enlarge them so he can see better. For some moments the pain is acute. I can feel sweat dripping off me. The worst thing is not knowing how long it will last.

Finally the pain eases and he begins to withdraw his instrument. Never have I been so glad to have an examination over. It turns out he's been using a sigmoidoscope and 50 centimetres of thick, black tube. 'Wonderful view,' he says, disarmingly ... 'Maybe you ought to do a postcard series,' I suggest, but he doesn't laugh.

Thursday, September 4th

Complete a rough draft of the new 'Railway' commentary by lunchtime. Then run on the Heath – it's almost a year to the day that I began regular running.

I've kept at it, apart from two or three weeks on the 'Railway' documentary and a week in Cyprus. I've run in Central Park and across Fisher's Island and pounded the lanes of Suffolk and the long hills between Abbotsley[1] and Waresley and I've run in rain and snow and 80° sunshine. In darkness and on Christmas Day.

I do always feel better after a run. It's as simple as that. And the physical well-being is very rapidly transformed into a feeling of mental well-being. Running makes me feel relaxed and gives me all the complex satisfaction of a test successfully completed, a feeling of achievement. I hope I shall still be at it in a year's time.

Then I write some extra lines for David Warner in '*TB*'. Manage to get the word 'sigmoidoscope' into the script.

Saturday, September 6th

So full of the joys of spring today that I ring George H and invite myself over for the afternoon.

Have lunch in the garden, scan *The Times*, then leave, taking Tom and Willy and open-roofed Mini. In Henley an hour later. George is mending an electric hedge-cutter which cut through its own flex. As George tinkers in homely fashion with his garden equipment ('I *was* an electrical apprentice,' he assured me. 'For three weeks.') the boys and I swam in the buff in his swimming pool, surrounded by lifelike voyeuristic models of monks and nuns.

Then George took us in a flat-bottomed boat around the lake and at one

---

[1] Abbotsley, a small village near St. Neots in Cambridgeshire, is where Helen's mother lives.

point into water-filled caves. George told me that Crisp[1] modelled one of the caves on the Blue Grotto on Capri and we went on to talk about Gracie Fields and how King Farouk [of Egypt] had been a great admirer and had come to Capri to live with her, but all his secret servicemen and bodyguards filled the swimming pool all the time and she eventually had to turn him out.

As we stood on the bridge surveying the lakes and the towers and turrets of the extraordinary house, George told me that he really wanted more space. He doesn't want to have people anywhere near him. The other weekend he'd rung up Knight, Frank and Rip-Off[2], as he calls them in friendly fashion, to enquire about a 1,600-acre farm in Gloucestershire next door to his old friend Steve Winwood. 'Do you want *all* of it ... ?' the man had enquired incredulously.

Thursday, September 11th

Basil Pao[3] comes round for a sort of farewell meal together before he returns to his native Hong Kong for a long stay – perhaps permanent. I like Basil and feel warmth and trust and friendship easily reciprocated. Basil tells how he was known as 'Slits' for five years at his English public school and the reason he was sent to the school was because at the age of twelve he was a heroin runner for the Triads!

He outlines his novel, which is epic and sounds very commercial. Put him into a taxi about 12.45. Sad to see him go, but lots of good intentions to visit.

Friday, September 19th: Los Angeles

It's ten minutes to five in the morning. I'm sitting at my desk in my suite at L'Ermitage Hotel on Burton Way in Los Angeles – Beverly Hills to be strictly accurate.

I try to sleep, but my mouth is dry from the air conditioning, so I get up and pour myself water – drink and settle down to sleep again. But my mind refuses to surrender – I notice the refrigerator as it rumbles suddenly into one of its recharging fits. It's huge, much bigger than the one we have at home for our family of five, but only contains four bottles at the moment. And I can't turn it off so I resolve not to worry about that – it's something I must learn to live with, for Suite 411 at L'Ermitage will be home for the next 15 or 16 nights.

---

[1] Sir Frank Crisp (1843–1919), a successful and eccentric solicitor, created the gardens, when he bought Friar Park in 1895.
[2] The estate agents Knight, Frank & Rutley.
[3] Basil, a Hong Kong-born designer and photographer, was introduced to me by Eric Idle in 1978, when he brought him in to work on the *Life of Brian* book.

I must also learn to live with the air conditioning, which also boosts itself noisily every 45 minutes or so. And I must learn to live with the occasional hiss of water from an invisible tap somewhere near my head, and the metallic clangs and roar of igniting truck engines from the depot outside my window.

It's a desolate time to be awake, the middle of the night. Even in America. I suppose I could watch television, but the thought of yielding to a very bad movie is worse than lying there trying to sleep.

Pour myself a glass of Calistoga mineral water – one of the four bottles in my massive refrigerator department. I tidy the room and try and improve my attitude towards it – to try to get to know it a little better.

The almost obligatory reproduction antique furniture of these hotels gives the place a sort of spray-on 'Europeanism'. It's called a Hotel de Grande Classe (which is an American phrase, not a French one, neatly translated by Neil Innes as 'a hotel of big class') and the place is carefully littered with books of matches and ashtrays. A table before the window has a basket of fruit, courtesy of the management, on it, a bowl of sweets which would set the children's eyes popping, and a rose in a thin vase, which came up with my breakfast yesterday. There are reproductions of European artworks on the wall – I have the 'Night Watch' by Rembrandt behind me as I write.

Saturday morning, September 20th: Los Angeles

At 10.30 we all assembled in the lobby of the hotel and gradually trickled in the direction of our rehearsal room for a first look at the script. Rehearsal room is a vast hangar of a place, ten minutes' walk from the hotel.

In this bleak great shed, full of Fleetwood Mac equipment in boxes with little wheels, we sit and talk through the show. A couple of short songs from the album are to go in – 'Sit On My Face' at the start of Part II and Terry's 'Never Be Rude to an Arab' (though Terry does very much want to do his Scottish poem about the otter – this doesn't impress over-much, though he auditions it courageously). John and Eric are doing 'Pope and Michelangelo' instead of 'Secret Service' and one of TG's animations – 'History of Flight' – may be cut.

Afternoon spent running words – and making ourselves laugh as we renew acquaintance with the show and material we haven't done together for over four years. In particular 'Salvation Fuzz' – perhaps the most anarchic and unruly and disorderly of all the sketches – gets us going. A very heartening afternoon.

Back to the hotel at five. Sit in the jacuzzi, talk with Neil and Richard Branson of Virgin Records, who is rather pleased with himself having this day sold off Virgin's loss-making US offshoot. Apparently no-one was interested until he doubled the price, then they came right in.

Monday, September 22nd: Los Angeles

To rehearsal at 10.30. André is there, and also Mollie Kirkland – the very efficient stage manager, who worked on the City Center[1] show. Both welcome and reassuring faces. Denis O'B looms in, beaming in such a characteristic Denisian way that we have all started doing it. He gives us all a copy of [Peter Nichols' play] *Privates on Parade*, but is mysterious as to exact reasons why.

Apart from two thoroughly enjoyable run-throughs in our rehearsal cavern, there seems to be little really good news about the shows. Ticket sales are only at 50% so far. The costs are beginning to increase and Roger Hancock is threatening to pull Neil out of the show because of haggling from Denis.

We are all trying to avoid being dragged into all this peripheral activity and are concentrating on tightening, sharpening and adding to the show. And in this we have been successful – our approach and our spirit is much less tense than it was in New York.

After the afternoon rehearsal, out to Universal City to see Paul Simon in concert at the Universal Amphitheatre. It's a spotless clean place, staffed not by bouncers, heavies, ex-army PT instructors and the general run of London concert toughs, but by endless numbers of bright-eyed college kids with red blazers.

The concert was clean and crisp too. Under a full moon with the almost unreal shadowy line of the Santa Monica Mountains in the background, Paul did his unspectacular but endearing thing, backed by a superb group of top session musicians playing with a disarming lack of big presentation.

The Jesse Dixon Singers came on and quite dwarfed Simon for a while with their polished, pumping Gospel songs. At one point I thought Paul had been literally swallowed up by one of the massive black ladies with whom he was duetting.

We ate, all of us, afterwards, and at two o'clock TJ swam.

Tuesday, September 23rd: Los Angeles

Wake at eight-ish ... snooze, worry vaguely about voice and the Bowl, then up at nine for a lounge in the jacuzzi under the cloudy morning skies.

I feel time hanging so slowly at the moment.

John said he doubted whether the group could ever agree on anything again and reiterated that he himself no longer enjoyed writing in the group and had never wanted to repeat the 13 weeks of what he considers non-productivity on

---

[1] 'Monty Python Live at City Center'. New York, 1976.

the script this year. It was history repeating itself. 1972 all over again.

A mood of determined resolution not to be brought down by John's despondency grows. TG, away from so much of the Python meetings this year, is here, and Graham joins us too and we reaffirm a basic aspect of our work together, which JC and Denis O'B and others sometimes tend to cloud, which is that it's fun.

To the Hollywood Bowl. Much standing around here and a photo-session distinguished by marked lack of enthusiasm amongst the Pythons. How old will we have to be to finally stop putting our heads through chairs, eating each other's legs and rolling our eyes? Saw an obviously posed picture of the Three Stooges going through the same ordeal the other day – and they looked about 70.

Wednesday, September·24th: Los Angeles

The air is officially described as 'unhealthful' today.

I lunch with Denis O'B. He's taking all of us away for little chats, but I think it's a sign of the good health of the group that everyone reports back to the others.

He talks of the 'family'. This is his concept of the group. A family in which we all do little creative tasks for each other. I know that he is moving around as he says this, prodding away, waiting for the opening to spring out – yet again – '*Yellowbeard*'! Yes, here it comes. I give a categoric no again. DO'B retreats.

Actually we have a good and open chat over things and he doesn't talk high finance and he restrains his bouts of Denisian 'glee' to a little outburst about all the Warner executives who are coming to the show. 'I tell you, Michael . . . there is so *much* interest . . .'

Drive myself up to the Bowl. Still the rig has not been finished. Neither of the 20-foot-high eidophor screens are up, but otherwise, with drapes now hung, the acting area is beginning to feel and look quite intimate.

We work on until midnight, then back to the hotel for a small party given for us by Martin Scorsese, who has a 'condominium' above us at the hotel. Delightful food, cooked by his chef, Dan; Dom Perignon and Korbel champagne, and Scorsese, who speaks so fast that at a recent film festival he had to have someone to repeat his English to the translator, before the translator even began.

Tells stories of *Raging Bull*, which is the picture he's just done with De Niro – who at one point had to put on 60 lbs.

Friday, September 26th: Los Angeles

Drive down to Musso and Franks for a pre-show meal. TJ declares sensationally that this is the first time he's ever eaten before a show. I remind him of last night. 'Oh ... yes ... apart from last night.'

Back at the Bowl, five thousand paying customers. Denis has had to drop the lowest price from ten dollars to seven to try and fill up the extra seats. So there are about five and a half thousand folk out there for opening night.

The show goes well. The audience is reassuringly noisy, familiar, ecstatic as they hear their favourite sketches announced – and it's as if we had never been away. A continuation of the best of our City Center shows. Thanks to the radio mikes my voice holds up.

Afterwards an extraordinary clutch of people in the hospitality room. I'm grabbed, buttonholed, introduced, re-introduced, in a swirl of faces and briefly held handshakes and abruptly-ending conversations. There's: 'I'm Joseph Kendall's nephew ... ' 'I'm Micky Dolenz's ex-wife ... ' 'We made the T-shirts you got in 1978 ... ' 'Do you remember me ...?' 'Great show ... Could you sign this for the guy in the wheelchair?'

Finally we free ourselves of the throng and into the big, black-windowed Batcar, signing as we go, then smoothly speed off to a party, given for us by Steve Martin in Beverly Hills. His house turns out to be an art gallery. Every wall is white, furniture is minimal. The rooms are doorless and quite severe in shape and design. There's a soft pile carpet and it's all quiet and rather lean and hungry. In fact just like its owner.

Martin is very courteous and straight and loves the show. He isn't trying to be funny and we don't have to respond by trying to be funny. But his girlfriend does have a tiny – as Terry J described it – 'sanforized' poodle called Rocco, which pees with both legs in the air.

This is the comedy high spot of the evening.

Sunday, September 28th: Los Angeles

Have booked back four days earlier than I'd expected – on the Tuesday night flight. Back in London on the first day of October – all being well. Helen tells me Rachel cried herself to sleep after talking on the phone to me last Sunday, and asked for a photo of me to put beside her bed!

I don't think I will go to Hugh Hefner's tonight. Graham says it's like getting into Fort Knox, but there's no gold when you get in ...

GC's book *Autobiography of a Liar* [in fact it was called *A Liar's Autobiography*] has been one of the features of this trip. Coming out at the same time as Roger Wilmut's 'History of Python' – which is straight and competent and almost depressingly like an early obituary – GC's is a sharp, funny, chaotic, wild, touching and extraordinary book. Written in great style, very lively, it's already got TJ very angry about misrepresentation and JC greatly relieved, for some reason, that it doesn't say unpleasant things about him.

Feel very much sharper and better prepared for the show tonight. Probably to do with being less tired. It was a good audience once again. Afterwards one of the scene boys said how much nicer we were to work for than pop groups!

Monday, September 29th: Los Angeles

Drive up to Hollywood Boulevard to buy toys, clothes, T-shirts, etc as presents. Everything's there, including the names of stars like Sir Cedric Hardwicke embedded in the sidewalk outside a shop selling erotic lingerie. A sign reads 'It's not expensive to look chic, but it's chic to look expensive'. Another LA motto.

Anne reckons our total BO take over the four nights will be 350,000 dollars – the total possible being 450,000. Not a crashing success, but we'll cover costs. Any revenue will come from the TV sales, which Denis says will only fetch 300,000 dollars. There are, however, the invisible earnings that it's impossible to quantify – record sales, movie re-run attendances, and just keeping the Python name up front there.

Tonight we have a film and a video camera backstage and the audience lights keep going up at strange times. But the audience stay with us and at the end a large section of them won't leave. They wait up to half an hour for an encore we don't have. There'll be outraged letters in *Rolling Stone* about that.

Behind stage, in our small and ill-appointed dressing room beneath the Bowl, we entertain G Harrison, who looks rather shell-shocked after a trip to Montreal to see a Grand Prix, then a drive across the border to New York to avoid a Canadian air-controllers' strike. It's very good to see how he lights up with the satisfaction of seeing us all performing.

Anne has organised bottles for our dressers and drinks behind stage for our rather dour American crew, of whom only a handful have tried to make any contact with us at all – my favourite being a dwarf, who carted huge weights around, generally behaved like a roadie and had an easy, warm, approachable manner.

Eventually I was driven away from the Bowl to a party flung our way by H Nilsson, who lives in a house of modern, airy design, atop a ridge of mountain above Bel Air.

Harry Nilsson, so big, all-embracing, soppily friendly and sporting a complete and refreshing lack of the obligatory LA tan, moves around with his young son on his shoulder. Not drinking, either, as far as I could see. He's terribly happy that George H has surprised him by turning up.

Saturday, October 4th

Today I'm up and out to buy the croissants and the papers. But London disappoints with its shabbiness, with the endless unswept, litter-strewn pavements and the lack of anything new and bright and lively.

A pint and a half of IPA at lunchtime with GC and John Tomiczek at the Freemasons. The remarkable thing about our meeting was that Graham had given up smoking. His most familiar landmark – the pipe with its attendant paraphernalia – proggers, matches, ashtrays and lumps of half-burnt tobacco – have, if he's to be believed, been discarded for ever . . .

He says he's not *quite* sure about what he's done, but it was an impulse when he arrived at LA Airport last Wednesday evening and was confronted with some of the worst smog he'd ever seen in the city – so he'd decided not to add to it. So he hasn't used this prop . . . that he'd had since the age of 14 . . . for almost 72 hours. 'Mind you, I've had to hit the Valium rather hard to make up for it.'

Tuesday, October 7th

Helen and I and parents and all the kids of Gospel Oak packed into All Hallows Church to give thanks for the harvest.

Rachel's class sang a 'Potato' song to Mr Muxworthy's guitar and babies cried as the vicar tried to defy the appalling acoustics of this strange Gothic Revival interior. Talked with Father Coogan afterwards – 'Very Hampsteady food,' he observed, looking down on a font with smoked salmon peeping out from behind Yugoslavian crispbreads.

Have instituted a 'read-a-Shakespeare-play-a-day' regime. More realistically, I've subtitled it 'Read Shakespeare's plays by Christmas and his sonnets by New Year'. Decide to read them through chronologically, as they were written, and completed *Love's Labour's Lost* today. Plenty of laughs and relentless wisecracking. A real Marx Brothers screenplay.

Wednesday, October 8th

Tom is twelve today. He says that 'I only woke up at 5.30 . . . that's not bad . . .' But he is now a fully-fledged adult as far as air travel goes, as I find out when booking a half-term holiday for us all in Ireland at the end of the month.

A depressing foray to Tottenham Court Road/Oxford Street to buy a new 8 mill film to show at Tom's party. Depressing because of the domination in that corner of London of the awful, blinking, hypnotising spell of video ... There is video equipment everywhere – video films, video games – and it's like a giant amusement arcade providing a sort of temporary electronic alternative to listlessness. Lights flash and disembodied voices bark out of electronic chess games and football games. There doesn't seem to be much joy around here.

Rather staid interview with the BBC at Broadcasting House. TJ does it with me.

The IBA ban on TV or radio advertising of *Monty Python's Contractual Obligation* provides the main gist of the chat.

'Do *you* think it's filth?' she asks us.

'Oh, yes,' we reply hopefully ... and I add 'and worse than that, puerile filth ... '

The nice lady interviewer doesn't know quite what to make of a comedy album called *Monty Python's Contractual Obligation* and neither do we. But all parties try hard.

After the interview TJ and I go to eat at the Gay Hussar in Greek Street. I have quite delicious quenelles of carp and then partridge and lentils. We knock back a couple of bottles of Hungarian wine and admit to each other that neither of us really thinks the album we've just been plugging is much good.

After the meal we walk through Soho to the very hub of its wheel of naughtiness – to Raymond's Revue Bar in Walker's Court. Here there is a small auditorium called the Boulevard Theatre, where a new comedy club called the Comic Strip has just opened. For a long time after the Establishment folded there have been no such clubs in London, but recently the Comedy Store opened and now this. White and Goldstone[1] are involved and this was the second night.

As we wait to collect our guest tickets, a demure voice announces 'The second part of the Festival of Erotica is starting now ... members of the audience may take drinks into the auditorium if they so desire ...' Sober-suited businessmen down drinks and shuffle off to the Festival of Erotica, whilst the rather scruffier, long-Mac brigade troop into the Comic Strip.

In a small, low room with a stage and seating for about 150, only the front two or three rows are full. There are about six or seven acts, including guests. One duo, calling themselves Twentieth Century Coyote, were excellent, with one superb performer. Targets seem to be the new establishment of the left – feminists, alternative society jargon, social workers.

---

[1] Michael White, a theatre producer, had courageously put money into *Monty Python and the Holy Grail*. It was produced by John Goldstone, who also later produced *Life of Brian* and *The Meaning of Life*.

In the intermission buy drinks in the bar and the Comic Strip trendies mingle with the Festival of Erotica straights, whilst two ladies rub and lick each other on a video film projected above the bar. TJ kept wanting to 'just pop in' to the Festival of Erotica, but we stay with the comics and talk to them afterwards. All very young. I wish them well ... but the Twentieth Century Coyotes were the only ones I would really keep my eye on.

Tuesday, October 14th

Into town to see the two and a half hour first assembly of *Time Bandits*.

The effect of the wall sliding back in the room and the first fall into the time hole are stunning, then a series of very funny sequences – Napoleon, Robin Hood, Vincent and Patsy, David Warner and the Court of Eric and the Ogres – lift the film and involve me totally.

It really is the most exciting piece of filming I have seen in ages. I want to be cautious and I want to see all the problems and not be carried away, but the sum total of my impressions leaves me only with heady enthusiasm.

Wednesday, October 15th

Graham Chapman on *Parkinson* (the first Python to be there, I think). Quiet, pipe-less, subdued, but, as an ex-alcoholic homosexual, steals the show.

Thursday, October 23rd

J Goldstone rings to say that the *Life of Brian* appears to be making great progress in Barcelona. Starting slowly, it got good reviews and after two or three days audiences began to pour in. Now didn't I always say I liked the Spaniards?

Write letters and babysit in evening as H goes off to badminton. Watch John C in *Taming of the Shrew*. John gives an excellent performance. Controlled and clear, as you'd expect, and the quiet moments work as well as the screaming. Better, in fact.

He's still not one of those actors who seem to start each new character from scratch, but he did make one listen to every word and as such did a much greater service to Shakespeare – and to J Miller, the director – than most of the other actors.

Friday, October 24th

The weather continues various. Today is bright sunshine, which makes a lunchtime visit to Shepperton all the more agreeable.[1]

First we visit the *Ragtime* lot, which has been built on the triangle of green fields below the reservoir, hired from the Thames Water Board. It's been used sensationally. There are two long New York streets of the 1900's, intersecting halfway. The J P Morgan Library and the brownstones look so solid and substantial and the cobbled streets and paved sidewalks and lampposts so painstakingly reconstructed, that after a few minutes in the middle of all this the only unreality seems to be the Friesian cows munching contentedly in the sunshine behind Madison Avenue.

Then to the newly-refurbished canteen and catering block, open now for two weeks. I feel quite elated at what has been achieved after three years of constant nagging, reaching desperation point so often that I almost gave up hope. But today what was so often a running sore on Shepperton's reputation is now bright and gleaming and freshly-painted as a set for an ad. The kitchen, through which birds used to fly and, for all I know, nest, is now compact, clean and full of new equipment.

In the bar I meet Iain Johnstone,[2] who is very surprised to hear of my directorship of Shepperton. Iain nodded to the restaurant. 'The *Gandhi* mob are here.' Richard Attenborough is indeed here, for a planning meeting for his forthcoming film on the great man.

Monday, October 27th: Ballymaloe House, Ireland

It's raining at a quarter to seven when I'm woken by Rachel talking to herself. At eight we go down to breakfast – table with bright blue and white check cloth beside a long window of gracious Georgian proportions. Free-range eggs and bacon like it used to taste before it was sealed and suffocated in cellophane packets, and home-made bread and toast too thick and generously cut to fit in any toaster. This sets us up well for the day and, to improve matters, the rain sputters to a standstill about ten.

We play a word game, trying not to listen to the party nearby talking about operations, diets and how many times they've been on the verge of death (the next morning Helen hears the same woman, pen poised over postcard, asking at the desk how to spell 'anaesthetic').

---

[1] I had been on the board of Shepperton Studios in South-west London since making *Jabberwocky* there in 1976.
[2] Journalist, critic and TV producer.

Thursday, October 30th: Ballymaloe House

On Tuesday afternoon, with the wet weather cleared away and sunlight filling the house, Mel [Calman] idly suggested that he and I collaborate on a children's story. I started work on *Small Harry and the Toothache Pills* that afternoon and completed it and another shorter tale, *Cyril and the Dinner Party* by Wednesday evening.

I've called them both 'Ballymaloe Stories' and given the scribbled pages (snatched from Rachel's drawing pad) to Mel to think about. Mel says that he isn't the right illustrator for the longer story, but will have a go on Cyril. So that's all rather exciting.

Otherwise I have done very little. I've read a rather fine little book on the history of Ireland by Sean O'Faolain, published in 1943, which makes me stop and think. The English have done some dreadful things to this country in the last four centuries. Greed, adventure, religious conviction or plain bullying have all played a part and even in this quite restrained and tolerant account there is an awful lot to shame England and the English.

I shall hate Irish jokes even more. The lovely thing about the Irish and the way the jokes arise, is their literalness. They seem not to be a guileful people, they're straight, direct, gentle, and yet very good at conversation, at describing beauty and at making strangers feel at their ease.

Our room is full of kids for most of the day, including the ubiquitous Cullin – he of the chunky thighs, who follows Rachel and is rather rough and Irish and makes her alternately excited – 'Can you see what colour my knickers are?' – and prudish – 'Go away, I hate you . . . I *do*.'

Friday, October 31st: Ballymaloe, Cork and London

Last night Mrs Allen chatted to us for a while and said goodbye, as she wouldn't be seeing us this morning. Mel tells me that when working on *The Ballymaloe Cookbook* with her, he found that she kept a little card about guests' vagaries. Some are not welcome again. Against one man she'd written 'Free with his hands in the evening'. Which all makes her sound a rather censorious, stern lady, but she's far from it. She's hardworking, capable, but very tolerant and entertaining. An excellent hostess.

I think we're probably all ready to return to England. My run last night was quite a battle after another lunch, following another solid breakfast, following a fairly unrestrained dinner.

We reach Cork about 9.30, getting lost in the traditional manner. When there are signposts at junctions they invariably have only one arm and one destination (usually where you've come from).

TG rings. Paramount are not interested in *Time Bandits*. Last Monday there was a viewing for Filmways and apparently it went amazingly well. The Filmways head of production was jumping up and down at the end, grabbing TG and calling the film all kinds of success.

The next morning Denis rang TG to say that the Filmways board has rejected it. Too long, too British. TG said he was absolutely stunned at the news after the reaction at the viewing. Denis is now fighting (which he enjoys), but is getting twitchy about his money and the long interest rate on which he's borrowed it.

Sunday, November 2nd

At 3.30 I drive down to BH for appearance with TJ on a chat programme. It's ostensibly about the new *Ripping Yarns* book [*More Ripping Yarns*] and then is to be widened into a whole exploration of the technique, limitations, causes, effects and everything else to do with 'humour'. The sort of thing I dread. A knitting machine operative from Oldham is to be on hand to ask searching questions and a man is on a telephone in Plymouth for further interrogation.

In the event the man in Plymouth never speaks and the poor man from Oldham is tongue-tied with nerves. So Jones and I rattle on and afterwards I have a glass of wine, sign some autographs and meet Kate Adie – a rather dynamic lady who tells me that she was with Princess Anne unveiling something in Darlington. It turned out to be a particularly unprepossessing plaque to 'The Spirit of New Darlington' and, as everyone applauded, Princess Anne leaned over to Kate Adie and muttered a heartfelt 'Fuck me'.

Monday, November 3rd

Attempt to go to Python writing meeting at Anne's on my bike, but the pump decides to treat me badly and sucks air *out* of the tyre. Abandon cycle for the Mini which decides, equally unhelpfully, not to start without much coaxing. So eventually arrive at this first meeting of Pythons Without John for Further Work on the New Film in an unrelaxed rush.

Anne has, I gather on Eric's instigation, kitted out the downstairs room of 2 Park Square West as a Python writing place. We have a table and our own coffee machine and some flowers thoughtfully laid out on top of a filing cabinet.

Tuesday, November 4th

The weather seems to have London in an East European grip.

Still not enough to deter me from cycling to the 'office'. There to find two bits of good news – *Life of Brian*, which, after much censorship to-ing and fro-ing, finally opened in Norway last week and has taken 100,000 dollars in the first three days. And in Australia the album has sold 25,000 copies in a couple of weeks and is now officially a gold album there.

Whether any of these pieces of good news actually strengthen our resolve to persevere with the new movie or not is debatable. But certainly our little room with its fresh flowers, fresh newspapers, fresh coffee and a ping-pong table is the nearest we've come to the Python clubhouse. But I don't remember a great deal of work being done in clubs.

I watch the Carter and Reagan election. It's very obvious that Reagan is going to win. I must confess I've never known why Carter has been so disliked in the US. Also I find it interesting how Reagan, whose initial candidacy was greeted with jeers and sniggers, is already being accepted as a sane and sensible leader of the Western World. No-one on the ITV panel really had the guts to say what they were saying about Reagan before he won. Now it's all smiles.

Tuesday, November 11th

Tonight I go to see *Babylon*, a hard, uncompromising British film set in Brixton.[1] The setting of the film and its subject make me feel very soft as a writer dealing with the Raj and with Robin Hood and railway trains. There is so much energy in the black music – so many good performances from the black actors that their repression should be seen at worst as a scandal – demanding more movies like *Babylon* – and at best a pointless waste of a national asset. For even in their most hysterical moment of frustrated rage against the white neighbours who tell them to shut up and go back to their own country, Trevor Laird yells 'This *is* my fucking country.' They're here. We need them and we need their creative energy far more than we need the energy expended in hate against them.

As I leave there's a black boy with a coloured knitted hat leaving up the stairs with me. Bouncing up with the arrogant, easy stride of the kids in the film. And I wanted to just make contact – say something about what the film had done to me. And I just didn't know how to do or say it. I smiled and that was all.

---

[1] The story of a young rapper/musician (Brinsley Forde) seeking success in the alienated black community of South London. Directed by Franco Rosso and shot by Chris Menges.

Sunday, November 16th

To lunch with John and Linda Goldstone. A couple of actors from *Shock Treatment* – the follow-up to the *Rocky Horror* film – are there. One is an actress called Jessica Harper, who is in *Stardust Memories*. When John's next guest – a bubbly, middle-ageing American who talks much about jet-lag – arrives, there occurs the following conversation:

'This is Jessica Harper.'

Man: 'Oh, I *loved* your new movie.'

Man's girlfriend: 'I loved your new movie too.'

Jessica H: 'I'm so glad you loved the movie.'

Man's girlfriend: 'Oh, we really loved the movie.'

Man: 'And you were great.'

Man and friend: 'Oh we *loved* the movie.'

The man was Henry Jaglom, who's got a movie called *Sitting Ducks* at the London Film Festival. He was very funny in a Jewish, improvisatory sort of way. I liked him a lot. His girlfriend, Patrice, was later seen by Helen taking 12 of the largest pills Helen had ever seen. Jessica Harper was a sweet, light, gentle lady who ate no meat and was of such a slight build she looked like a little doll.

And there was an actor called Cliff de Ville (or some such) who had seen us at the Hollywood Bowl and who, sadly for him, spoke and looked just like Jack Nicholson.

Thursday, November 20th

With trepidation to Owen the Feet, having vowed never to return to his shabby little Mornington Foot Clinic, with its fighting dogs in the waiting room and 100-year-old chair.

Today he seems more eccentric than usual and I wonder if he will extract some sort of vengeance upon me for shutting him up rather firmly last time. He injects my toe and gives me the electric needle cauterisation treatment. I was glad to be out of there with the toe still on. He told me that if it was painful in the next week to bear it.

Hobble into the Python meeting at 10.30.

At 12.30 J Cleese arrives to play with the Space Invaders game and watch the 60-minute video of the Hollywood Bowl stage show – which JC has been in charge of editing. All of us feel the sense of occasion is lacking. It is, after all, *Python Live at the Hollywood Bowl* and at the moment it's just Python Live Against Black Drapes. TJ's initial worry that it would look boring is borne out. I'm afraid it doesn't excite any of us.

Should there be a possible 83-minute version for theatrical viewing? TJ and

EI feel emphatically no, the rest of us would like to see one assembled. I feel that if the material is well done (and performances at the Bowl weren't bad) and the cartoon film sequences are fresh, we could quite honourably sell it in France, Scandinavia, Australia and possibly Canada at least.

Tuesday, November 25th

To EuroAtlantic.

Denis is in – having just arrived from the West Coast. Without a *Time Bandits* deal. So obviously he's subdued. He asks me what we thought of the video of the Bowl. I said no-one was that elated by it, and there were very strong feelings in the group that we should not even *attempt* to make a movie version.

Travel-crumpled Denis went off to have a haircut (saying he had to look tidy tomorrow because he's going to ask someone to lend him £2 million).

Wednesday, November 26th

Can actually feel the warmth of direct sunlight on my face this morning as I toil over post-synch lines for *Time Bandits*. Rachel sits beside me reading – she's home with a sore throat and suspected flu.

Fortunately I'm in quite good creative flow at the moment and the lines come quite easily. I even find a couple of slogans (which I'm usually rather bad at). '*Time Bandits* – it's all the dreams you've ever had. And not just the bad ones.' (This is changed after I try it out on Tom, who immediately suggests 'not just the good ones'!)

Reading *The Wheels of Chance* by H G Wells, which Jan Francis's husband, a writer called Thomas Ellice, has sent me, hoping that I might be interested in the part of Hoopdriver.

I read the story in about three hours and liked it a lot. H G Wells is a good comic writer – well in the Jerome K Jerome class and even better when he brings in the political angle – the Hampstead women with their New Way of life – and Hoopdriver becomes a full and rounded character, a nonentity who becomes a hero. I love leading characters who are introduced: 'If you had noticed anything about him, it would have been chiefly to notice how little he was noticeable.'

Thursday, November 27th

I visit the eccentric chiropodist, Owen, at 9.30. He launches into a stream of consciousness about prices, his son-in-law, the Jewish mafia who run London Zoo.

He puts on some paste to further kill the beast straddling my toe, assures me it will hurt, tells me not to run for a week and, with a gloomy nod of the head, suggests that there are chiropodists about who wouldn't have touched it at all.

George H rings. He had seen an assembly of '*TB*' and been very worried by some of the 'amateurish' stuff between the boy and the bandits – at the end especially. He felt the film should be a lot shorter and had advised Denis not to hawk it around in its present state. All of which depressed me somewhat.

At nine my episode of the *Great Railway Journeys* is aired. I was relieved how well the programme held together. Most of the potentially embarrassing spots had either been ironed out or well-padded with music and sound effects.

I expect this will not be enough for the critics. But it was enough for me – and Barry Cryer and Angela and my mother – who thought it was the best of the series, 'and not just because I'm your mother'.

Friday, November 28th

Pesky reviews. *Telegraph* generously lukewarm, *Guardian* crustily lukewarm, *Mail* happy. All stop short of personal vilification, all mention the pre-opening credits 'confession' piece as a good sign of comic delights to come and all register various degrees of disappointment that they didn't materialise.

Drive down to Coram's Fields to be present at the launching of a new 'play kit' ('kit' being a radical/progressive word for what used to be called in car showrooms 'literature'). It's being launched by Fair Play for Children, of whom I am a vice-president, to try and help teachers and play leaders with the problems of getting multi-racial kids to play together.

Neil Kinnock MP is there. He's the Labour spokesman on education and carries with him a little notebook, pages scrawled with figures and notes. Gleefully he unearths some figures he'd given to Paul Foot about Heinz beans' current ad campaign – buy Heinz products, collect the labels and you can exchange them for new equipment for your school. For 86,000 labels you can buy a video recorder and camera set. Kinnock did some quick sums, searched in his little book and came up with the triumphant result 'That's £21,000 for a video set-up.'

Glenda Jackson was also there – nice, friendly, open and quite unaffected. There's a small video film made by the organisation, which typifies all their problems. Full of good intentions, but hopelessly over-serious in presentation.

Not a smile in it. Just a dose of current sociological jargon. And this is all about play. I said I would be prepared to help their next video presentation. Glenda J agreed too – so they could have quite a cast!

Had to rush away at 12.30 to get to a Python meeting.

A successful read-through. Eric has written a classic – 'The liberal Family'. GC has made some progress and Terry is very anxious to show Graham his penis. It has some deficiency which he is worried about.

Tuesday, December 2nd

Today we sit and stare at the board on the wall on which cards bearing the names of sketches have been hopefully pinned. Graham muses rather distantly and Terry and I sputter on. But around lunchtime it dies. We only have a working lunch – sandwiches on the table – and afterwards Eric, who has been in one of his silent spells, suddenly galvanises us all into working out a story.

The end of the world, 6,000 AD, the bomber with the Ultimate Weapon, all disappear and we build on the one constant of the month – the working-class family sketch of mine, a fabric of a story about – guess what? – three brothers of the Forbes-Bayter family and the rise to fame, wealth and power of Trevor from obscure working class origins to become Prime Minister just as the final nuclear war breaks out.

It's all in place by five o'clock, but I feel quite drained of energy as the room empties. I can hardly believe that after all this work and discussion we have come around to a 'Ripping Yarn' which Terry and I could have written in a fortnight on our own.

I find curious solace in talking to a reporter from a Boston, US, radio station. Anne revives me with a scotch and I quite enjoy answering questions from this perky little guy like 'Do you think Britain's really finished?'

Wednesday, December 3rd

I have to say as we meet that I do think the family story we worked out yesterday was a soft option and that the End of the World and the 90-minute countdown remains for me a much more striking idea and a more thoughtful subject altogether. There is no disagreement here and for a while it seems that we have two films. A 'Yarn' and an 'Apocalypse'. Terry J loves the idea of making two films at the same time and showing them at cinemas on alternate nights – Monty Python's two new films.

Friday, December 5th

To EuroAtlantic for the six o'clock Python meeting. Denis O'B has stage-managed the encounter quite carefully. There is an air of calculated informality and there are delicious Indian titbits to disarm us to start with – 'No meat in *any* of them,' Denis assures us, with a significant look at Eric.

Then one by one the various members of the EuroAtlantic team give us a report – which sounds less like a report and more like a justification, at times as blatant as a sales pitch, of their own usefulness. Even though John Cleese isn't present they still sound intimidated and there is an unrelaxed air to the proceedings until Steve Abbott[1] punctures it well.

The atmosphere is very different from the unalloyed enthusiasm of the New Dawn of Python beside the swimming pool at Fisher's Island 14 months ago.

I drive Anne back at the end of the meeting and she is fuming.

I watch *Points of View* which says glowing and wonderful things about the railway programme – 'The finest programme ever' – and flatters me wonderfully. I really seem to have tapped the ageing, middle-class audience.

Saturday, December 6th

I take William over to Upton Park – not more than a 40-minute drive – to watch Sheffield Wednesday versus West Ham. The usual 10–15 minute walk from car to ground, but two tickets are waiting for us – £3.50 comps – left by the Sheffield trainer. And inside it's perfect. A cold, but dry afternoon with a wintry sun lighting up the East Stand opposite us. There's a crowd of 30,000 and an anticipation of good things to come. All the images with which the press have fed us over the last weeks and months of the danger and alienation of the football grounds are absent. I feel quite elated to be there with William and our thermos of hot chocolate and a brass band playing marching stuff over the loudspeakers and an Uncle Mac-type announcer advising the crowd to enjoy themselves judiciously – 'Let's keep the fences away from Upton Park'. And I notice for the first time the absence of the now increasingly common steel barriers to fence in the crowd.

[1] A bright young Bradford-born accountant, not long down from Cambridge and recently employed by Denis O'Brien's company, EuroAtlantic, in Cadogan Square, Knightsbridge.

Tuesday, December 9th: Southwold

At Gospel Oak Station by a quarter to nine to combine a visit to Southwold with my first opportunity to thoroughly revise the *Time Bandits* script for publication at Easter.

It's a dull and nondescript morning – the shabby, greying clouds have warmed the place up a bit, but that's all. I reach the station in good time. Holly Jones is waiting for her train to school, having just missed the one in front with all her friends on. It's she who tells me that over in New York John Lennon has been shot dead.

A plunge into unreality, or at least into the area of where comprehension slips and the world seems an orderless swirl of disconnected, arbitrary events. How does such a thing happen? How do I, on this grubby station platform in north-west London, begin to comprehend the killing of one of the Beatles? The Rolling Stones were always on the knife-edge of life and death and sudden tragedy was part of their lives, but the Beatles seemed the mortal immortals, the legend that would live and grow old with us. But now, this ordinary December morning, I learn from a schoolgirl that one of my heroes has been shot dead.

My feelings are of indefinable but deeply-felt anger at America. This is, after all, the sort of random slaying of a charismatic, much loved figure in which America has specialised in the last two decades.

Once I get to Southwold I ring George. And leave a message, because he's not answering.

I work through for a five-hour stretch and we have a drink together by the fire and watch tributes to John Lennon, clumsily put together by newsroom staff who know a good story better than they know good music. And Paul McCartney just says 'It's a drag' and, creditably I think, refuses to emote for the cameras.

What a black day for music. The killer was apparently a fan. The dark side of Beatlemania. The curse that stalks all modern heroes, but is almost unchecked in America – land of the free and the armed and the crazy.

Wednesday, December 10th

Arrive a couple of minutes early at Liverpool Street, enabling me to catch the five to six North London Line. Solemn rush hour travellers, preoccupied in themselves, until a man gets on with a watch which plays a 'digital' version of 'The Yellow Rose of Texas'. This makes many more people than I'd expect start giggling. Which is heartening.

At home pick up car and race out to a meeting with Denis O'B at

EuroAtlantic. All routine stuff, until Denis makes me a convoluted offer of 180,000 dollars to go to Sri Lanka (he shows me most alluring pictures) and take Helen and the kids for a while, early next year. I'm a little lost as to why, then suddenly the penny drops. He's trying to get me to rewrite *Yellowbeard* again!

All I commit to Denis is that I shall have a first draft script of my own movie ready by the end of June, 1981. And that's that. Denis does tell me, which I must say I find a bit surprising, that TJ has agreed to the Sri Lanka bait and will be working on *Yellowbeard*. I won't believe this till I see Terry.

Tuesday, December 16th

Watched Ken Loach's *The Gamekeeper* on TV. His lack of sensationalism and his delicate and seemingly effortless portrayal of real life amongst those people generally ignored by the commercial writers and directors is really admirable. He is, I think, the most consistently rewarding director working in Britain. But his marvellously observed celebrations of English working-class life will, it seems, never be as popular as the escapist gloss of *Dallas*. Which is a sad thing. Write 17 letters in reply to some of the 40 or 50 I've had as a result of the 'Railway Journey'. Quite a different audience from the Pythons. Mostly 70 and retired, I think. Is this the Silent Majority?

Wednesday, December 17th

At one I leave for a Shepperton Board Meeting. Fortunately *Ragtime* are about six weeks behind, keeping the studio well-used over Christmas and into January.

One of the few things on offer in early '81 is *Yellowbeard*. I'm not surprised to hear from Charles Gregson [a fellow director of the studio] that he was told that *Yellowbeard* was a Python film and that I was in it.

Thursday, December 18th

My foot is alarmingly red and a little swollen and Helen has looked in her books and is bandying words like 'toxaemia' around. I have two tickets at the Screen on the Hill for the first night of Woody Allen's *Stardust Memories*. I hope that people will mistake me for an aged, but legendary film director as I drag myself, arm round Helen's shoulder, up Haverstock Hill. Actually I feel more like a Lourdes pilgrim fighting off disease and imminent death just to reach the shrine of comedy.

The cinema is full and I like the movie very much indeed. But I can see that my appreciation of some of the scenes depicting horrific excesses of fan worship comes from having experienced this sort of thing and viewed from the other side, this could be seen as Allen kicking people in the teeth.

Though my foot still throbs angrily, I feel the worst is over. I have been cured by a Woody Allen movie!

Saturday, December 20th

The Irish hunger strikers have called off their action within 24 hours of the first expected death. This is the good news for Christmas – though how I abhor the naivety and dangerously ill-informed sensationalism of the *New Standard* billboards in Soho yesterday – 'Total Surrender'. The demise of London evening papers over the last five years is terrible to watch.

1981

Sunday, January 4th

Amongst the snippets of information buried away in the Sunday papers under endless travel articles and ads, is one that really made me feel that we live in special times – industrial output in the 1970's in the UK rose by 3%, the only decade when it hasn't reached 10% since 1810. Will this be the decade then that future historians see as the end of the Industrial Revolution?

Tom roller-skates up and down deserted streets outside. It's a chill, dull day. Willy and [his friend] Nathan do experiments – making cork tops fly out under pressure of a murky vinegar and yeast mixture and other Just Williamish pursuits.

Denis O'B calls. Says he's taken a New Year resolution not to mention *Yellowbeard* and probes a little as to my intentions. He can't really operate satisfactorily, I don't think, unless he can have all his clients neatly filed and buttonholed under 'a project'. I am trying – and intending – to be unbuttonholeable for as long as I can.

Wednesday, January 7th

To Owen the Feet at half past nine. Still having difficulty vanquishing the bugger and he re-dresses it, though I expressly forbid any of the acid which nearly burned my foot off just before Christmas. But he's quite gentle and efficient and we get on much better now that our 'political' limits have been drawn up. I learn he was a Mayfair foot man before. He is the society chiropodist I wrote into *The Weekend*.[1]

On to Wardour Street for a viewing of *The Long Good Friday*, which looks like being HandMade Distributors' first product. It's a story about gangland violence and organised crime in London.

Yes, it does glamorise violence, but any violence is glamorous to certain people and you would be irresponsible to only make films about 'nice' subjects. And Bob Hoskins' portrayal is excellent – and the whole film justifies itself by being a well-written and quite thought-provoking piece. I put it after *Babylon* and *Bloody Kids*[2] in a top ten of recent socially-provocative, English-made pictures which all deserve support and a wider audience.

---

[1] A play which I'd completed at the end of 1979. It was eventually put on in the West End in 1994 with Richard Wilson in the lead. Michael Medwin played the Foot-Man.
[2] *Bloody Kids*, made for TV in 1979, was directed by Stephen Frears, written by Stephen Poliakoff, produced by Barry Hanson and shot, as was *Babylon*, by Chris Menges.

Thursday January 8th

Jim Beach[1] rings. He wants me to write a 'Biggles' film script. Apparently they have commissioned one which was strong on adventure, but lacking in humour. Just like the 'Biggles' stories, I pointed out. Jim laughed, a little unconvincingly. 'I hear you're unbribable,' he cajoles. Depends what the bribe is, say I. 'Oh, there is a lot of money' – he mentions in rapid succession Robert Stigwood and Disney and director Lewis Gilbert, who was ecstatic when he heard I was being approached. Eric Idle had told Beryl Vertue in Barbados that Michael was *the* world's best 'Biggles' writer.

I weathered all these names and these flatteries and came out with my own individual project intact. Still free. Indeed, strengthened in my determination by these blandishments.

Bought *David O. Selznick's Hollywood*, plus a tin of praline for G Chapman's 40th birthday. We go round to Graham's for a party.

The house reflects the change in GC's living habits. Instead of boxes full of gin and tonic bottles, a rather medically-oriented bookcase. No tobacco wads lying around – the place clean, spotless almost. Graham has a flashing bow tie and is tanned from a sun machine.

Meet Ray Cooper, soft-spoken, rather spare and wispy musician who is Denis's latest client and who will be in charge of the difficult task of coordinating and arranging George H's music for *Time Bandits* He's a very unassuming, instantly likeable guy, with a bright Greek wife. Has a house in Wapping. In Narrow Street.

As Ray and wife and Helen and I talked on, we realised that most of the heterosexuals had left. Went upstairs to see Kenny Everett, who was sitting in David's room on cushions, with lights low and three or four young lads in attendance.

Everett was a little drunk. Liked the railways, said he hated television. We had a rather stilted conversation, then he asked me for lunch. I think 1981 could be the year of a thousand lunches.

Friday, January 9th

A year and a fortnight ago it seemed that the world was coming perilously close to a global punch-up when the Russians invaded Afghanistan. But it turned out that it was microphones rather than sabres which were being rattled and everything went off the boil. Looking at *The Times* and *Mirror* headlines this week, I fear we are little further forward, in fact, probably many steps back.

[1] Occasional legal adviser-turned-producer. Later became manager of Queen.

Poland, so directly involved in the start of one world war is, we learn, in danger of being occupied again. Reports resurface in the papers, rather randomly, to the effect that the recent activity of the 'free trade union' movement, Solidarity, is about to goad the Russians into another New Year invasion.

So the pressure is kept on to stand ready to defend ourselves against the still creeping tide of international communism. (This is when our own capitalist alternative is unable to give three million people in this country anything to do.)

This brings me to the heart of the fears which, in my uncharacteristically pessimistic moments, tightened my stomach one morning this week. Dr Kissinger. He's loose again. Talking about the need for more US military involvement in the Middle East and waving away the European peace initiatives. Here is the 'diplomat' of the '70's – the has-been who believes the world must be run by brute force – and it surely cannot be coincidence that his latest iron-fisted threats come only five days before Ronald Reagan becomes President.

Saturday, January 10th

Up at half past eight and taking William down to Hamley's to spend the £7.00 token he's been given by Simon A.[1]

Regent Street is delightfully free of punters. The crescents and stars of the Christmas lights looking naked and forlorn in the sunlight. We wander around, dazzled with choice, in this grubby and overrated toyshop. Willy can't decide what to buy.

But I'm less reticent. On an impulse I fork out £59.25 for my first ever electric train set – a Hornby layout with a Coronation Class Pacific. I've waited 28 years for this moment since I used to watch Anthony Jonas in Whitworth Road play with his layout – and occasionally be allowed to put a derailed cattle wagon back on the line.

So begins my 'lost weekend'. Can't wait to get the LMS set home and set it up. In the afternoon the two boys and I make a pilgrimage to Beatties of Holborn and stock up on more track and some rolling stock that's in the sales. Back home again and from then on I resent any interruption.

Monday, January 12th

Decide to make some positive moves on the *Small Harry* story. Go in to see Geoffrey Strachan as a cloudburst of hail hits London. Geoffrey's honesty is

---

[1] Simon Albury. Old friend and William's godfather.

something greatly to be valued and I keep forgetting he's the Managing Director of a publisher, so openly does he dispense it.

I left him with the story.

Build a new railway layout.

Tuesday, January 13th

This morning I waited half an hour at the Mornington Foot Clinic for Mr Owen to finish talking to the lady before me. Every word can be heard out in the 'waiting area' and I caught one memorable phrase . . . 'If there's one thing I *don't* like, it's an unshaven man.' Much agreement from the lady patient.

Wednesday, January 21st

A few thousand miles south, the American hostages[1] are flying into Algiers Airport and a few thousand miles west, Reagan is being sworn in as President. Now the enormous humiliation of the hostages is over will Reagan extract some vengeance – just how will he practically live up to his big talk of a Great, Respected America? Watch half in excitement, half in real fear.

Friday, January 23rd

After lunch I drive down to Wapping to see Chris Orr. Wapping High Street is the most unlikely high street left in Britain. Some fine houses remain, but mostly it's corrugated iron and mud and warehouses turned into wine stores.

To Chris's room at New Crane Wharf. I look at his latest etchings. The humour and the style and skill and originality are all there. Now, instead of illustrating prose he's putting words as commentary onto prints.

We walk downstairs and along cobbled streets past warehouses which other artists have moved into, but not greatly changed. Reminds me of Covent Garden just after the fruit market left. To a red-brick building opposite the Prospect of Whitby pub which announces that it was built in 1890 for The London Hydraulic Power Company.

I'm shown around by a young man and an older character, who is quite marvellous and would be a superb TV presenter – a working man's Kenneth Clark. Very articulate, tells a good story, is never lost for words, ideas and

---

[1] In November 1979, Iranian militants had taken American Embassy staff in Tehran hostage and held them for 444 days, releasing them only after Jimmy Carter's presidency ended.

references – all presented in a light and original fashion. He tells me about the use of hydraulic power in central London, pumped around a network of ten-inch cast-iron pipes below the ground which would now cost a fortune to lay. When the Hydraulic Power Co finally closed down – only four years ago – it had 3,000 subscribers, controlling the rise and fall of theatre safety curtains, lifts, the vacuum cleaners in the Savoy Hotel and, its star client, Tower Bridge.

Home to hear that *Parkinson* want me to do their show on Wednesday. I've never felt any great loss at not being on Parky – in fact Python as a group refused the dubious honour twice – but the guests with me are to be Sir Peter Parker[1] and Robert de Niro. These two, representing the best of railways and acting, are both men I admire, and out of sheer joie de vivre I accept.

I have to ring Ken Stephinson about something too and I tell him with jovial innocence that he's been scooped by *Parkinson*. There follows a chill of disappointment from the Manchester end of the phone.

I, of course, have completely and clumsily underestimated the office politics of the BBC (not being one who normally experiences such things). I had agreed to go on *Russell Harty* at the end of February and, from what Ken says, the impact of such an appearance would be lessened if I were to turn up on *Parkinson* less than a month before. The rivalry obviously matters deeply, so I retract and ring the *Parkinson* office and decline to appear.

A rather irritating little episode. All I feel is that, on looking back on it, everyone's reactions will seem ridiculously over-done and quite unnecessary. Including mine. That's enough of that molehill anyway.

Sunday, January 25th

Fine, dry, mild day. Confined to No. 2 for most of the time, varnishing the table for the railway. But the great outdoors beckoned and I felt in such a relaxed and unrushed state that on the spur of the moment, having read the Sundays and discovered what a 'structuralist' was, I decided to take Willy and Rachel into town.

We ended up at the practically deserted Tate Gallery. Both Willy and Rachel excellent company. Willy remarked on how few women artists were represented (a quite amazing disproportion – could only find Gwen John) and, as if by telepathy, just after I had the distinct feeling that the Rothko room reminded me of Stonehenge, Willy said it reminded him of a circle of stones – Stonehenge, he said. Rachel thought all the bums and titties a bit rude, but we all three had

[1] Popular, accessible Chairman of the British Railways Board from 1976 to 1983, and the only one to have a locomotive named after him. He died in 2002.

a thoroughly enjoyable time – without getting bored or feeling that we were appreciating art out of duty.

Monday, January 26th

Work on the railway again – and try and solve the sidings problem. I find I become so involved in trying to unravel the complexities of it all that it's hard to tolerate any interference. Which tonight comes in the shape of T Gilliam, who brings round some tapes of the sort of music Denis wants George to put into the film. It's average to good George Harrison quavery trillings, with some fine guitar, but seems to be quite at odds with the rather crisp, brittle, neurotic pace of the movie. Well, tomorrow we shall have all this out at a viewing and later chat with George.

I lure TG (quite easily) into playing trains.

Tuesday, January 27th

The days have become so warm, what with this balmy, recycled Florida weather washing over us, that wasps are waking up and flying into my workroom. The garden is coming alive too, eager shoots poking out in trepidation then, sensing it's spring, pushing boldly on. They're probably going to have a terrible time in February.

To Wardour Street for the *Time Bandits* viewing.

I'm very pleased with the way the film looks. The sound effects have revived my enthusiasm, which had waned a little over the last two viewings. Felt today like I did the first time I saw it – that between us we have put together an adventure story full of curiosities.

Still more music to go on, however, and afterwards I go with Terry to Ray Cooper's flat in Wapping to discuss this very matter.

24 Narrow Street, Wapping. Quite an address. We walk across the threshold and into another world. From poverty and desolation to wealth and taste. There is bare brick everywhere – much of it, I gather, the original wall sand-blasted. The brick is of mellow, autumnal gold and very restful and elegant.

Up in the lift two floors and step into a breathtaking open-plan room, with three big windows giving onto a balcony and then the Thames. Wide and impressive at this point, on the base of the U-curve between the Tower of London and the Isle of Dogs.

Everything has its place and the room is carefully and orderly set out, with coffee table books on the coffee table and a round dining table full of salads and delicately set platefuls of taramasalata and things. Crowning the whole a magnum of Château Ducru-Beaucaillou '69.

George arrives (in brand new Porsche), having driven from Cadogan Square in about 15 minutes. He brings Derek Taylor, whom I'm most pleased to see. Derek thrives on chat and good relaxed company and we're never at our best in the artificial world of meetings.

George gives, either coincidentally, but I think actually quite deliberately, the current Denis O'Brien line on *Time Bandits* – that it should be 90 minutes. There's rather a lot George doesn't like about it and I wonder if he really is the best person to be doing the music. But he seems to want to do it, though he does reveal a little petulance over the fact that Denis is constantly asking him to dip in to finance films.

'What the hell, it's only a tax-loss picture,' says George at one point. He laughs. But the laughter must grate on TG.

Wednesday, January 28th

Try to reach Richard Loncraine[1] to explain my decision not to do *Brimstone and Treacle*. Can't reach him.

To Methuen to see Marilyn Malin, the children's editor. I feel on very safe ground with her. She has the Methuen caution. Like Geoffrey. But it transpires that she really does like *Small Harry* and wants to publish it and is happy with Caroline [Holden] as designer.

It all seems to fall into place. I promise to push through the contract with minimum fuss (if terms are reasonable). Methuen undertake to print at least 15,000 copies. So I do feel rather pleased with myself as I walk out and up Holborn to the shops. Thanks to Mel Calman and Ballymaloe!

Home. Reach Loncraine. He's very disappointed, he says kindly. Fox were very interested and both Ken Trodd and Potter himself had been in favour of the casting. But it must be third on my list this year – after my film and my word to Thomas Ellice about 'Wheels of Chance'. To go to the top of my list it would have to have been something that was totally and unequivocally unmissable. And it wasn't that.

---

[1] A commercials director and inventor. I'd tried, without success, to get him to direct some of the *Ripping Yarns*. He in turn had asked me if I'd be in his film of Dennis Potter's 1976 TV play *Brimstone and Treacle*, to be produced by Ken Trodd. It was filmed in 1982 with Sting in the starring role.

Thursday, February 5th

To Charing Cross Station to catch the 10.45 to Hastings to have my portrait painted by John Bratby. I'm looking forward to it, in an intrigued sort of way.

We clatter through the labyrinth of South London. There are no non-stop trains to Hastings, which is perhaps the most indicative clue to the nature of the town itself. A seaside place without the style of Brighton or the industrial and economic usefulness of Southampton or the travelling status of Folkestone or Dover. The train approaches it with an ever-increasing number of stops. As if reluctant to ever get there.

There aren't many getting off this February morning. As I walk down the steps to the booking office and what they nowadays like to call 'the concourse', I catch sight of two figures, peering like co-conspirators in an English 'B' movie of the '50's from behind the window of the refreshment room. They collude, then start to move out.

Bratby is round, small and beaming shyly. He reminds me of Raymond Briggs's Father Christmas. He doesn't say anything or shake hands, but not in an unfriendly way. Dark-haired, dark-skinned wife with good-humoured eyes. She indicates an ordinary, untidy, red station wagon. Of English make, I think. We drive through Hastings, I making my cheerful, mundane observations about the place, their reactions not quite predictable. She doesn't like Hastings.

Their house comes up sooner than I'd expected. A rambling Georgian mansion with a tower on top linked to the house by a glass conservatory in the sky. It's set in quite unpretentious surroundings overlooking the town of Hastings and the sea.

She lets me out then discreetly drives the red car away and John Bratby takes over, showing me the way along a scruffy passage into a studio. Dominating is a big oil painting of Paul McCartney, dated 1967. Paul looks like a sad little waif – and it seems very much at odds with the capable, super-businessman I hear he is. Maybe that's why he left his portrait here.

Bratby, who seems more at ease now he's in his studio, points me to the chair where I must sit. It's like visiting the doctor's. The same relationship between myself, the object, and the professional. On my left side a window, not very clean, on my right a spotlight turned towards me. A big paraffin heater of modern design considerately set for me.

For the first half-hour he doesn't touch the three foot by two foot canvas on a stand in front of him. He compliments me on my healthiness; he is amazed that I'm 37. I find as we talk that he is much concerned with death and ageing. He is also glad to hear that I don't take life too seriously. Only when he reached the age of 50, he said, did he realise that life didn't have to be taken seriously and he wishes he'd discovered this earlier! He is quite ready to laugh and laughs rather well. He amused me too when we both were comparing notes about the fascist tendencies of Kenwood House attendants. Once they accused Bratby of having added a daub of paint to Rembrandt's nose in the self-portrait there.

Patti, his wife, keeps us well filled with coffee. He drinks it in vast mugfuls, as he squeezes more and more tubes of oil paint on to an already thick, full palette. Occasionally he stops talking, which I find disconcerting until I realise that he is concentrating so hard that he has ceased to regard me in the conventional dialogue relationship.

He likes to work in England. He loses his identity when he travels. He works very solidly. He prefers to work in his studio. He is much impressed by people like myself whom he regards as 'the last people' – individuals who stand out from the herd. He's concerned by creeping Bennite egalitarianism, stamping out all quality in life – all the odd ones who by their own great talents stand out . . . again this slightly alarming elitist theorising.

After about three and a half hours he asks if I want to see it. And there, amazingly, it is. The canvas is full, with short, thick streaks of oil paint – dozens of colours and shades – and there is me as Bratby sees me. It is done. I have to admire it, because he seems to have achieved so much with such apparent lack of effort. His painting is a complex process, yet he's achieved quite a simple image. He says that while I'm there it's difficult to let the painting speak for itself, but it will, he says, over the next week.

And then the car is ready outside and we're back into the 'B' movie. Patti drives me away to the station and onto the train back to Charing Cross.

Sunday, February 8th: Church Farm, Abbotsley

Wake, most reinvigorated. Breakfast at half past nine. Scan the *Observer*. A really encouraging report that the Minister of Transport, Norman Fowler, is giving his support to a sensible investment plan for the railways – sensible because it plans to inject twice as much government money over six years or so as it does at the moment. Sounds bold. Could all the ads and the publicity skills of P Parker, and even our series of railway documentaries have helped?

On either side of a succulent roast beef lunch I and the boys clear round the pond. Heavy, muddy, but satisfying work. Willy dredges out all sorts of old bits of rubbish – roller skates, tennis balls and bits of old pram – with his usual uncontrollable glee. He falls in eventually.

G. Chapman rings. Obviously pushed by Denis, he rather quickly blurts out that he wants me to be in *Yellowbeard*. Just as quickly I repeat my rejection of the offer. Then he talks about Telepictures. What is my attitude? Against, I say. 'Oh dear,' says the doctor, 'it's going to be a bad week for Denis.'

Monday, February 9th

To Cadogan Square to meet Denis O'B. I tell him that I'm against any Telepictures deal which involves decimation of the Python shows. This causes Denis some concern, as he says we have made a deal in good faith (though Telepictures have been granted the good faith rather than Python) and he's extremely worried about going back on his word. My suggestion is that we let Telepictures have Python product on the stipulation it isn't cut at all – and see if they want us badly enough to be able to accommodate such a demand.

Feeling I've been consistently negative thus far (in D's terms), I agree in principle to flying to Atlanta in May to speak on the *Time Bandits* book's behalf at the big publishing sales convention.

As five o'clock and my departure time closes, Denis finally gets around to *Yellowbeard* again. No, Denis, I'm not budging. It's not worth discussing. 'Wait a minute,' says Denis, 'hear me out.' So he tries to rush headfirst at the brick wall again – except from a slightly different angle this time. All he wants is one week of my writing time . . . no more . . . just one . . . and (as I stand up) . . .

'Michael . . .'

'I listened to you.'

', . . And what's more –' but at that point the Great Salesman is cut short in mid-pitch by a sharp and silly series of knocks on the door and George Harrison's head appears, beaming leerily.

George carries a sheaf of company reports and, oblivious to the urgency of D's business with me, he sits down chattily and shows me one of them – 'Sing Song Ltd' – which has a net loss of £34.

We listen to some of GH's new songs. 'All Those Years Ago' is my favourite of a number of very good tracks.

Sunday, February 15th

Take the children swimming to the Holiday Inn at Swiss Cottage. We practically have the pool to ourselves. After I've come back and am settling down to cold roast pork, the phone rings. It's 9.30 and the *Sun* newspaper wants to know if there's any truth in the rumour that John Cleese has been married today in New York. I tell the hackette that I know nothing, but think it extremely unlikely, what with John being gay and all that.

She persists in her intrusion, I persist in my fantasy – and she eventually gives up. Silly world.

Monday, February 16th

Eight-fifteen, start to drive down to London Sessions House for two weeks of jury service.

The Sessions House is a solid, impressive, neo-classical building started in 1914. It's been added to and there are now 19 courts within its 'grounds'. Park my car at a meter, then join a mass of some 200 new jurors, who are herded into Court Number 1 – a classic of the TV and film sort, full of wood panelling with a vaguely Baroque flourish. Here we sit and await a preliminary chat. A peculiar feeling – a roomful of 200 people, none of whom knows each other. Early banter tails off, and within five minutes all 200 of us are sitting in a tantalisingly breakable collective silence.

Then we're reduced to groups of 20 as our names are called and the groups are led off to one of the other courts; it's all rather like school.

My fellow jurors seem to be drawn mostly from the working classes, with a sprinkling of woolly-minded liberals like myself. There seems to be a notable absence of anyone looking rich and successful. I suppose you don't have time to do jury service and become rich and successful.

Sit for over an hour in a smoke-filled room. I try to read Sir Walter Scott's *Waverley*, but his convoluted prose and circumlocutory embellishments are not ideal for such a situation. I hear a loud voice beside me . . . 'Yeah, there's a TV personality on one of the juries. Mate of mine saw him this morning . . . Can't remember his name.'

Then, just as the day seems irretrievably lost, our room is called, again, and we are led upstairs. This time I'm called onto the jury. There are no challenges and we actually begin my first 'live' case as a juror. It's not one to enter the annals of Great British Trials, but there are satisfyingly comic complications involved.

The two accused are Indians, two young men with fashionable Western moustaches and pudgy faces, who have six charges against them arising from a fight they are said to have started in a pub in Clapton, E5, on an August Sunday in 1979. (There are very few cases ever heard here that have been waiting less than a year to be called.)

We are now actually belonging to a case – we have a purpose and, for the next two or three days, this judge, the three banisters, the clerks of the court and the two moustachioed Punjabi bandits in the dock will all be locked together in a curiously reassuring intimacy.

Wednesday, February 18th

Drive down to Newington Causeway for more life with the Singhs. Publican and two assistants gave evidence, as did an enormous policeman. Medical evidence was read out as to the seriousness of the eye injury caused by a thrown bottle to an apparently innocent old Indian watching. There is permanent damage to the eye and he has to wear contact lenses. So this is the most serious aspect of the case.

Back at home, Terry Gilliam rings. He has been on the phone to Denis in LA for one and a half hours, discussing *Time Bandits*. After their chat today, in which TG took Denis through the film cut by cut, demolishing nearly all his suggested edits, TG reported Denis to be sounding very unspirited, not to say low, not to say depressed.

I think the process of learning how difficult we all are is more painful than Denis ever in his worst dreams expected.

Thursday, February 19th

At times today as I was locked in an unmoving line of traffic on the approaches to Russell Square, I felt a surge of panic at the thought of keeping His Honour Justice Bruce Campbell QC and his entire court waiting.

But I was there on time and, after a further half-hour of Judge's summing up, our moment of glory arrived, and they had to wait for us whilst we were locked in our windowless little room to try and reach a verdict. Without much dissension we decided to acquit him of the first charge of actual bodily harm, as it was a case of one man's word against his.

The court reassembled, our foreman gave our verdicts, then the antecedents of the accused were read. Both had been in trouble with the police before. Onkar has three children and one about to be born; he's only 23, has not got much of a future either, but has just recently been taken on as a bus driver. Despite the heart-rending pleas of the counsel, our kindly, humorous judge stuck his chin out firmly and became the stern voice of punishment. Onkar Singh was to be jailed for three months, his brother three months, but suspended. And that was that.

Friday, February 20th

Split into a new jury group and assigned to Court 7.

Observed a Jamaican being sent down for eight months for illegally importing and probably dealing in cannabis. I suppose there is a danger that cannabis-dealing leads on to dealing harder drugs – but this was certainly not proven here. The man's girlfriend and mother of his two children had just gone into hospital with a blood clot on the brain, but the judge disregarded all this. Disturbing, especially when I think of the vast number of people – respectable and rich included – who smoke and trade in cannabis freely.

Then a frightened, wide-eyed black kid comes into the dock. He took a knife and threatened a shopkeeper and stole £40.00. He is sent to Borstal, despite this being his first offence and despite strong recommendations in his favour from Lambeth Borough Council, whose representative was present in court.

Monday, February 23rd

I asked at the Bailiff's Office about my chances of avoiding a long case on Thursday (my *Russell Harty* night) and they were most understanding and decided that the safest way was to discharge me from a second week's jury service altogether. This took a moment to sink in, then a great feeling of relief at this unexpected freedom. I had to wait an hour to collect my expenses, so sat in a café opposite the courts and read the paper and mulled over what to do with this free week.

Walked across Waterloo Bridge – something I hardly ever do – stopped and looked in the church of St Mary-Le-Strand, which I never, ever do, being usually far too busy roaring round it in a car. Peace and quiet and Baroque extravagance in the middle of one of London's busiest one-way traffic systems. Noted that the church was built by order of Parliament from money raised by a tax on coal!

Friday, March 6th

This morning – a march against unemployment. Can I come? But despite feeling personally more scornful of Thatcher and her solutions – Surrey Power, as I call it – I still have this aversion to making a lot of noise in a public place in direct support of any political force. Mainly because I don't easily believe in political solutions.

I think you have to work and communicate on a much more basic level than behind banners or tub-thumping on platforms – this is the showbiz side of politics. I personally feel much happier encouraging tolerance and understanding on a man to man level, or through my humour rather than telling people something which I don't believe – i.e. if you follow this leader, or endorse this system, everything will be alright.

Sunday, March 8th ·

Complete *Waverley* (which works on me like Hardy – demanding much loyalty and dogged persistence to begin with, but finally rewarding perseverance with a good tale and leaving an after-taste of affection towards the worlds he's described and the characters he's filled them with).

This very evening, begin to read Proust's *À La Recherche* . . . Feeling limbered up after *Waverley* and *Romola* and spurred on by the purchase, for £50, of a new and much-praised edition by Kilmartin.

Monday, March 9th

Unexpectedly I wake with a hint of tension, usually experienced in more extreme forms when I have to go filming, write a debate speech or appear on *Just a Minute*. But today it's anticipation of my own self-imposed project – the film script, which (in tandem with Proust) I begin today.

Sit at my desk at a quarter past nine, comfortably cocooned against steady, unbroken rain outside and realise that, despite two months of intended mental refreshment and stimulation, I'm still as riddled with incompatible alternatives for stories as I ever was.

Nothing springs instantly to my pen – no characters so all-consumingly important that I have to write about them. It's a shame really – all those people out there with burning convictions and desperate messages to the world which they can never make anyone listen to and here am I, pen poised to create entertainment for the world and not knowing what I want to say.

Wednesday, March 11th

Go up to William Ellis in the evening to hear about the curriculum, etc. Headmaster clearly pleased with progress so far on the transition from grammar to comprehensive. He does sound as though he loves his work. Turnout of parents almost all middle-class – others seem to leave the school to get on with it. (Trouble with democracy these days?)

Eric rings later to fix up a Palins/Idles theatre trip next Monday. Tells me that Graham has just been on the phone to ask him to be in *Yellowbeard*. But surely . . . ? No, says Eric, *Yellowbeard* is not dead. GC has nine million dollars of Australian money and is planning to film it off the Queensland coast. Eric is worried about how best he can say no yet again.

Thursday, March 12th

Classic writing morning. Up to the desk, clear space and open notebook at about five to ten. Estimate when I should finish. Two-thirty seems reasonable. Yawn. Stretch. Yawn. Look blankly through all I've written this week, trying desperately to summon up any belief in the purpose of these arbitrary scribblings and character snippings. Long for coffee, but it's an hour away.

The hour passes with hardly a line written. It's like insomnia, in reverse. My mind refuses to wake up.

I take the opportunity (rare this week) of a dry spell and run. As I pound up the path to Parliament Hill, a title occurs to me – 'The Missionary Position'.

Maybe, though, that's too whacky, too leading, so I settle for 'The Missionary' and the subject matter of the film swims into clear focus. An idealist, a tortured idealist in the last days of the British Empire – the missionary work would be interpreted as widely as possible, and the title has a nice touch of irony. Come back 45 minutes later muddy but feeling that I've made a breakthrough.

Cook Toulouse sausages with apples for Robert H.

Over dinner he makes what he calls, with characteristic modesty, a brilliant discovery – that the six Time Bandits are the six Pythons. He's awfully pleased at making this connection and seems quite unmoved by my own denial of any such parallel. For the record, anyway, our casting was: Randall – Cleese, Vermin – Gilliam, Og – Graham, Fidgit – Terry J, Strutter – Eric, Wally – me.

Friday, March 13th

Had a vivid dream this morning. It was set in Halifax. Very positively Halifax.

It was hazy – a mixture of Lowry and Hieronymus Bosch – but on top of the hill the walls were of rich, red stone and I walked through colonnades and arcades built in seventeenth-century classical style and met young students who told me what a wonderful place Halifax was.

At the writing desk by ten. I pursued the idea of *The Missionary*, which began to fall very nicely into place. By lunchtime I had actually sketched out a synopsis – with a beginning, middle and end – which I dared to become quite excited about. In the afternoon I tightened and typed this up. So by four, at the end of the first week's writing, I have a story. I feel, as I say, warily confident. Will see how it survives the weekend.

Tuesday, March 17th

A mighty clap of thunder as a short and violent storm passes overhead as I settle into a piece for the *New York Times* – Howard Goldberg having sent me a telegram asking for a piece on Prince Charles and Lady D. Have completed it by seven.

Ring HG in New York. He's frightfully worried that I will not, as he puts it, 'keep it clean'. 'I'm hired by Calvinists,' he explains. Dictate through to the *Times* later in the evening.

Wednesday, March 18th

Take Tom P (who's been off school today with a cold) up to St Anne's Church, Highgate, for the first night of the William Ellis opera 'Death of Baldur'. This has been the big musical event of the year for the school. It's an English premiere and the composer, David Bedford, is there with short, well-cut grey hair, looking like a natty parent. Tom is in the 'off-stage' choir and is tonight stuffed to the gills with throat sweets, etc, to help his voice.

I cannot understand a word that's being sung throughout the hour, but it's evidently to do with revenge, blindness, the gods and other gloomy Nordic specialities. Not a laugh in it. The orchestra is good, but the church swallows up voices and makes it very difficult to stage.

Very effective integration of pebble-banging – with the 'pebble-choir' ringing the church behind the audience and setting up a wave of staccato sound which had the effect of swirling stereophonic sound.

Home to hear from Howard Goldberg that he had loved my piece for the *NYT* on Prince Charles and was planning to run it on Sunday. He kept going into fits of giggles over the phone whilst checking spellings, etc. Most encouraging.

Thursday, March 19th

Estimated by lunchtime – and ten mornings' work – that I have 20 minutes of good material to start *The Missionary*, and another five or six quite strong.

Friday, March 20th

Driven out to Friar Park in stately fashion in the back of Ray Cooper's elegant and comfortable 26-year-old Bentley – all wooden panelling and a good smell of leather.

On the way Ray tells me that George had a phone call two weeks ago from some anonymous American telling George he had a gun and an air ticket to England. It all sounded like a horrible hoax, but the FBI found that a man in Baltimore had been seen in a bar making just such threats and bragging about his air ticket. George H's place was ringed by police for a week – and he had a bodyguard with him at all times. Considering all this, George met us in very relaxed style. He was up on the slopes of his Matterhorn, with the builders who are busy restoring this fine piece of eccentric garden landscaping.

Saturday, March 28th

Willy and I drive off to go to see Wednesday play at [Leyton] Orient.

It's a warm day, the ground at Brisbane Road is small, neat and feels far more of a local family atmosphere than any others we've been to this season.

It seems that a Wednesday goal has to come, but instead a scuffle at the far end and Orient have scored on one of their rare visits to the Wednesday area.

This stings Wednesday – crowd and players – into some strong retaliatory measures, but within minutes Orient have scored again and it's over – as is probably Wednesday's chance for promotion.

A satisfying incident as we walk to the car. In the long line of cars moving up to the main road are three lads, one of whom leans out of the window and shouts in delight at me ... 'Heh! It's Eric Idle!' I smile, but weakly, I expect, and walk on as they noisily discuss who I'm not.

About 15 yards further on their car approaches and they pass up the road with a chant of 'We know who you are!' This is followed almost immediately by a crunch of colliding metal and a crackle of shattering tail-light as their car thuds into the one in front and pushes that one into the one in front of him.

Monday, March 30th

Drive down to the first of a week's Python meetings at 2 Park Square West.

We appear to be very much in accord over our exasperation, frustration and consternation about Denis's role in our affairs. In Anne's painstakingly-assembled report on life with EuroAtlantic, she suggested that she and Steve [Abbott] could run our day-to-day affairs from 2 PSW.

A remarkable degree of unanimity within the group that now is the time to sort out this whole question.

To dinner with Clare [Latimer][1]. Excellent food, plenty of drink and jolly

---

[1] Caterer and next-door neighbour for many years.

company. A vicar from St John's Wood who tells me he took 50 of his most fervent worshippers to see *Life of Brian* last Good Friday – instead of moping about church 'mourning'.

Wednesday, April 1st

A dry, warm day with soft, high cloud. Everyone in a good mood. Eric suggests we all of us make a list of the pros and cons of DO'B. The lists turn out to be remarkably similar. Tax planning and tax structures are commended, but all the pro lists are much shorter than the cons – which include over-secrecy, inability to listen to or understand things he doesn't want to hear, and use of word 'philosophy'.

At lunch – Anne makes us delicious asparagus tart – we get fairly silly. Decide that the Pythons should purchase our own nuclear deterrent. We put a small ad in *The Times* – 'Nuclear Missile wanted, with warhead, London area'.

Friday, April 3rd

Denis is pleased that we have decided to go ahead with theatrical release of *Hollywood Bowl*. Which we now decide to call, simply, *Monty Python at the Hollywood Bowl*. But try as we can to drill into him that he should go for smaller distributors with more time to listen, the more Denis retreats back to the majors whom he knows.

He claims that the small distributors only handle 'exploitation' pics (violent or sexy or blatantly both, which are so bad that money is only made by a quick, sharp killing in selected theatres). His feeling is that all distributors are idiots, but he will try and find us the most benevolent idiot.

Sunday, April 5th

Denis calls me. He asks me to try and patch up the Gilliam/Harrison relationship. Not that TG has done any more than express reservations about George's music, and the last song in particular, but GH has taken it badly and feels that he no longer cares – and if TG wants to write the music he can write it himself.

I try to defend TG's position by saying that the use of GH's music was rather forced on him. Denis returns to the financial argument (does Terry realise how much money the film is costing?) which is slightly unfair. Anyway, as Denis memorably puts it, 'You just don't treat Beatles this way.'

Monday, April 6th

Collect Rachel from school, then ring George. He isn't angry in the conventional sense – I mean, no shouting or swearing – but he just is sad and a bit fed up. 'I was just a fan,' he puts it, 'who wanted to help you do things because I liked what you all did.'

But after all this comes out, we get down to discussing the end song. I tell him we both like it musically, but we've now got some new lyrics which change only the verses. Let him listen to them and sling them out if he doesn't like them. But of course he does quite like them – and is happy to do them and will send a demo later in the week. I hope all is healed, temporarily at least.

Dash off to the Python meeting.

It's quite obvious that the group as a whole trust Anne more than Denis (JC wanted it to go on record that he mistrusted Denis less than the rest of us) and Eric was the only one who signed the letter to Denis with his surname. 'Denis is the sort of person I want to be on surname terms with,' was the way he put it – and I promised to write that in my diary.

Tuesday, April 7th

To Eric's by car about seven o'clock. He has now assembled enough material for six TV programmes to be made by his company – Rutland Weekend Television – and sold to England, the US, Australia, Canada, etc. They're comedy sketch shows, basically – with music animation special effects and all set in the legendary Rutland Isles, where anything can happen.

Anyway, Eric wants me to come and play one of the three stars, along with himself and possibly Carrie Fisher. Filming would, he thinks, not take more than eight weeks and would be done in the winter on a lovely tropical island.

I'm drawn by the immediacy of doing a TV series on video and by Eric's unportentous, let's-just-get-on-with-it attitude and refusal to treat it as the most important thing ever. But it's a month, at least, accounted for and at that time I may be in pre-production of *The Missionary*.

Saturday, April 11th

Family outing to *Popeye*.[1] We ate excellent hamburgers in Covent Garden and the sun came out and shone on us as we walked through the Garden, past the

---

[1] Film version of the comic-strip. Robin Williams was Popeye and Shelley Duvall Olive Oyl. Robert Altman directed. Jules Feiffer wrote the screenplay and Harry Nilsson the songs.

escapologist, through St Paul's churchyard, where trees have been planted in memory of actors buried there. One rather undernourished little shrub was ironically plaqued 'In memory of Hattie Jacques'.

Home to hear that there was burning and looting going on in Brixton as we had wandered through the quiet bustle of the West End on this sunny Saturday afternoon.

Monday, April 13th

Help prepare for dinner with Steve Abbott and friend Laurie.

Part of my reason for asking him round is to find out more about his feelings about Denis and Euro. Basically he is concerned about divided loyalties. He cannot carry on working for the Pythons and doing what is best for the Pythons within the EuroAtlantic framework because he feels the decisions taken for the benefit of EuroAtlantic are very often contrary to the benefit of the Pythons.

Both Steve and Laurie are politically to the left, Laurie enough to have changed her bank account from Barclays (naughty South African connections) to the Co-op. Only to find that the Co-op use Barclays as their clearing bank!

Steve is I think a man of good, basic, honest convictions and if for this reason he's leaving EuroAtlantic, it makes me listen very carefully.

Tuesday, April 14th

Dry and cool. Drive down to Crawford Street to have hair cut by Don [Abaka, our family hairdresser for many years]. We talk about the Brixton riot and that Don who is, I should imagine, a very easy-going and law-abiding black – a part of the establishment if you like – still can say, as if a little surprised, 'I've not been in any trouble with the police, but I really feel worried sometimes that if there's trouble in a street they'll pick me out.'

Home to work on *The Missionary*, but for some reason, as the clouds clear and the sun shines from a blue sky, I find myself surrendering to the pleasantness of the day. Sit in the garden seat in the sun and read Bernard Levin's infectious raves about three of his favourite restaurants in Switzerland. Makes my mind drift to thoughts of holidays and sun-soaked balconies in small French towns and poplars motionless above sparkling streams and good wine and company and celebrating.

Watch the space shuttle land most skilfully. Feel, more than I ever did with the moonwalks, that the success of this first reusable spacecraft is the real start of what an American astronaut rather chillingly called 'the exploitation of space'.

Thursday, April 16th

Hardly see Helen, on this our 15th wedding anniversary morning. Am woken by Rachel at a quarter to seven, standing by my bedside, dressed and ready to go. She wakes William by tickling his feet (the only way, he claims, he can be woken up) and the three of us make for the quarter to nine North London Line train to Broad Street.

Uneventful journey to Darsham, though we found ourselves in the breakfast car next to an assured, rich-voiced, late middle-aged Englishman with half-moon glasses, sitting with a fortyish, mousy-blonde lady, with the large, bony, open features of an English upper-class gel.

He began to make notes about some speech he was to make . . . 'The recent clashes in Brixton, foreseen by Mr Enoch Powell over fifteen years ago –' His eligible companion interrupts . . . '"Clashes"? Do you think "clashes" is a strong enough word?' 'No, no, perhaps you're right . . . Battle? . . . Mm . . .'.

We left them, still composing, at Ipswich. Met by Mother at Darsham. She looked a little wearier than of late and drives a little slower and a little nearer the centre of the road.

Sunday, April 19th: Southwold, Easter Sunday

In the afternoon I read through Robert H's manuscript of the Python censorship book, which he wants me to check before I go to Crete. It's well-researched, thorough, lightly, but not uncritically, biased in our favour. The word I've written in my notes to sum up his endeavour is 'scrupulous'. Unsensational in presentation, but not necessarily in concept – it's really everything I hoped it would be.

Tuesday, April 21st

Over lunch spend a couple of hours with Steve talking about EuroAtlantic, my finances and the possible transfer of our immediate financial affairs to a Steve and Anne-run office.

Steve reveals fresh facets of his straightforward, unassuming but very independent nature. He declines a coffee because it's the Passover and he's eating only Kosher food for a week. He almost apologetically explains that he's not even a born Jew. He just began to take an interest four or five years ago, learnt Hebrew and another Judaic language and set himself certain standards of observation which he readily admits are somewhat inconsistent, but one of them is to eat nothing but Kosher food throughout the Passover period.

Saturday, May 2nd: London to The Chewton Glen Hotel

Drive down to Hampshire for the Python weekend. Collect Gilliam at 7.45, then Eric at eight and, despite some build-up of holiday weekend traffic, we are driving through the New Forest by half past nine and to the hotel, set in a rather nondescript conurbation near New Milton.

The Chewton Glen Hotel is unashamedly expensive – a soft, enveloping atmosphere of thick carpets, armchairs, soft voices, chandeliers. From the BMWs and Jaguars in the car park to the miniature of sherry with the manager's compliments, everything reflects money. Like a padded cell for the very rich. But it suits our purposes – we're here, after all, to concentrate our minds on one of the most important decisions Python has yet made.

There is remarkably little dissension from JC's opening assessment that we should tell Denis that we no longer feel we need a manager. That there should, in the interests of economy and efficiency, be one Python office to administrate the companies, and that future relationships with Denis should be on an ad hoc basis.

Within a couple of hours we've reached a heartening degree of agreement and JC is left to compose a letter. I go to the billiard room with TG for a game on a marvellous full-size table. The balls feel like lead weights after the half-size table at home. Then to lunch. The food is good – delicate and lots of things like lobster and snails and shallots.

Then a game of snooker, a game of squash with Terry J and back for more snooker and dinner. Quite like old times, with Graham leaving early to go to a gay club in Bournemouth (for the second night running, I'm told) – but even better than the old days because GC doesn't get pissed and can drive himself.

Talk, over the champagne and cream of Jerusalem artichoke soup, of Bobby Sands and his hunger strike. Eric and John think it's something you should be able to laugh at – and they do. TJ, and I agree with him, feels that the laughter must come from recognising and sensing a basic truth in what you're laughing at and you can't laugh at something you feel is dishonest – and I think it's dishonest to think of Sands as a worthless villain. And dangerous too.

To bed before midnight. How easily the 'historic' decision has been made. It's not often Python so clearly and unanimously sees the rightness of a decision and it's such a relief that it's happened like that today. It now remains to be seen how DO'B reacts. I hope he will not see it as a stab in the back, but a stab in the front. He should have seen it coming and it shouldn't prove fatal.

Sunday, May 3rd

At eight, feeling good and refreshed and bright, I walk down the drive of the Chewton Glen, taking care not to trip over the floodlighting bar which points up at the pine trees, and, taking the sign for Barton-on-Sea, make for the English Channel cliffs.

I can see the Isle of Wight in the distance. It's a dull morning with the sun only a faint lemon glow in a thickly-padded off-white sky. There are women walking poodles called Pippa and empty seaside hotels and a ravaged and collapsing shoreline which has no drama, excitement or visual splendour. Gardening and Walking the Dog Land 1981.

We assemble about 10.15. There's a re-reading of the letter to Denis and some corrections made. JC is so anxious to emphasise our inconstancy that there's a danger the cold reality of the message may not get through.

Then follows a chat about the next film – and one of the remarkable displays of the collective Python mind doing what it does best, best. Ideas, jokes, themes pour out from everyone round the table so fast that no-one wants to stop and write any of them down for fear of losing this glorious impetus. The court framework for the next movie comes up – the idea of us all being hanged for producing a film that is only a tax-dodge. It's all rich and funny and complex and very satisfying.

Tuesday, May 5th

Starts well, my 38th, with a clear and cloudless morning – the sort of day May ought to be, but hasn't been so far.

Work on the script – slowly but surely. Anne comes round at lunchtime with the letter to Denis to sign. JC has put back some of the wordiness that Eric and I took out, but it seems to be clear and bending over backwards to give us the blame!

I hear Denis will not be back until the weekend and wants a meeting with us next Monday. There's a sort of inexorability about it, like watching someone walk very, very slowly towards a concealed hole you've dug.

Wednesday, May 6th

First thing this morning, am putting out milk bottles when I encounter Peggy from No. 1 Julia Street. She's very sad because a week ago her case against her landlords was dismissed. She's got to move and No. 1 will be sold. Ring Steve and instruct him to try and buy it for me.

My *New Yorker* piece on Cinderella comes back with a rejection. Like A Coren's rejection note from *Punch* some years ago, the worst thing is the profuse apology – almost tangible embarrassment of the contact at the magazine. He's right, of course. He likes the incidental jokes which I like best and feels the whole a little too dull and conventional. A warning sign for all my writing.

Thursday, May 7th

My Bratby portrait has arrived. I hang it, not altogether seriously, but mainly to frighten Helen, above the piano. I don't like his interpretation of me particularly, but his technique of thick oil paint applied with short knife strokes in dozens of colours does make the picture very exciting. It certainly stands out, as an original should, in our houseful of rather restrained repros and prints. Quite ebullient and bright.

Friday, May 8th

Despite many comings and goings in the house (window cleaners to give estimates, recently-robbed neighbours to look at our burglar alarm system), I have the best writing morning of a bad week.

I write a sequence this morning that I know will be funny (the lost butler) and at least breaks a week in the wilderness.

Looking forward to a lazy evening in, when Denis rings. He's back and he has evidently seen the Chewton Glen letter.

He sounded calm, and in a realistic frame of mind. He was not entirely clear about what the letter proposed – could I elucidate? I elucidated as best I could, with kids clamouring for supper and Helen washing up beside me. We wanted DO'B to be an ad hoc, independent figure who we could come to for the major things he'd proved himself good at. Our essential aim was to simplify our business affairs.

DO'B was silent for a moment, but seemed to accept all this.

He talked about his 'upside' and his 'downside' and rather lost me here, but the long and the short of the call was that we should have a meeting as quickly as possible – and it needn't be a long one, he said. I promised I would ring Anne and ask her to set one up for Monday. Throughout Denis's tone was only a little injured and defensive and mainly practical and realistic – and quite friendly.

I talk to Eric later. He sounds unhelpful over the DO'B situation. He doesn't want to meet him and absolutely refuses to give DO'B any sort of preferential option on the next film at this stage. I bit my lip, and nearly my desk as well, at this.

Monday, May 11th

I drove down to BUPA to present Dr Gilkes with a long-running Palin saga – the Great Verruca, or Corn, as it once was.

He examined it and, as it has changed its shape and become less spread out, with more of a peak on it, he reckoned he could cut it out. And without much more ado, this is what he did. Using an instantaneously-acting local anaesthetic, he cut and chopped and sliced – sometimes with such great effort that I could scarcely believe it was my little toe and not some thick oak tree he was working on. Then he cauterised the edges, bandaged it all up and I hobbled out. But at least my verruca, which has been with me for nearly two years, was now in the dustbin.

I'd made Gilkes happy – 'It's been a jolly good day for the knife,' he assured me when we'd agreed on surgery. 'Some days I hardly use it at all,' he added regretfully.

I was to go straight from my verruca operation to a meeting with Denis O'B. It all seemed rather symbolic.

I hobbled in, the last to arrive (apart from Eric, who was just then landing in New York). Anne had thoughtfully provided white wine and some canapes. Denis sat looking a little careworn, but raised a smile. He had a notepad full of appointments and projects which he flipped through – films he was hoping to bring in through HandMade Distributors.

At about 7.20, after we'd been talking for an hour, John had to leave because he was taking someone to the theatre. So it was left to the four of us to decide on the next move with Denis. If we wanted to terminate – as 'I think the letter says' – Denis wanted to do it as quickly as possible.

Was there an alternative to complete and final termination? Terry J asked. Some way in which he could run a financial structure with us and liaise with the office at Park Square West? Denis didn't like this. It was all or nothing. He wanted to be free to concentrate on all the other areas EuroAtlantic could go in. He might, he said, get out of films altogether.

Graham asked if there were any 'offshore structure' which could be kept going. No, again Denis was adamant. Steve could not run a structure such as the one Denis had set up and which he still today talked about with loving pride.

So at about eight o'clock, as a dull evening was drawing to a close outside, we had to take a decision. Should we terminate? It really was the only answer. It was what the letter, signed by us all on May 5th, had said anyway. And so it was agreed and Denis left to begin to take down the structure and prepare for us a list of proposals for the ending of our relationship.

I couldn't believe it. My verruca and manager out, all within four hours.

Wednesday, May 13th

Manage the first full morning's writing this week and feel much better for it. Recently-gouged right toe is preventing me from running, so after lunch go down to Beatties and buy some LNER '30's imported teak rolling stock with the ten quid Ma gave me for my 38th. It crosses my mind that I'm 38 and still sneaking off to toyshops.

Down to Camberwell for dinner with the Joneses and, as it turns out, a rather boozed Richard Boston.[1]

He really doesn't look in good shape, which is a pity as he's such a mine of wondrous information – and knows such gems of political history as the fact that a gorilla once raped a French president's wife in the Elysée Palace, which is, of course, next to the zoo, and for many years afterwards the president was paranoid about gorillas.

And all this on the night the Pope was shot and Tom helped William Ellis swim to a 20 point victory in the schools swimming gala. And another hunger striker died in the Maze.

Saturday, May 16th

Angela and I head for Linton – our great-grandfather's parish from 1865 to 1904. I'm intrigued by Edward Palin – the man of great promise who in his early 30's was senior tutor and bursar of St John's College, Oxford, and who gave up the chance of great things to marry Brita, an Irish orphan girl – herself the subject of a great rags-to-riches story – and settle at this tiny Herefordshire village and raise seven children.

There is the grave in the churchyard where he is buried together with two of his sons who pre-deceased him – one who died at Shrewsbury aged 18, another killed in the trenches of the Somme. Next to his grave and upstaging it is the grave of Caroline Watson, the American who found Brita the orphan and brought her up.

Determined, as a result of this weekend trip, to follow up some leads on the Palins – St John's College being one of them.

---

[1] One of the first journalists to 'get' Monty Python, he was also a vigorous campaigner who, with Terry J, started an environmental magazine called the *Vole*. He gave his interests as 'soothsaying, shelling peas and embroidery'.

Friday, May 22nd

This is the day appointed for the changeover of Python affairs from EuroAtlantic at 26 Cadogan Square back to the more leisurely Nash terraces of Regent's Park. From today Steve and Lena [Granstedt, his assistant] work for Python and not EA.

I remember my embarrassment at having to tell people Python was with EuroAtlantic Ltd – an ugly name really, but I have had very good service from them. I rang Corinna [Soar – EA Company Secretary] – she was very touched by my letter and we had a quite unrecriminatory chat. She says it will be better when the changeover has actually happened. It's the transition process that's painful. I want to say to her how concerned I am about our future – that we don't see our move as a solution, just an inevitable part of the continuing development of Python, but I can't get into all that. I suggest we have lunch. Coward.

Wednesday, May 27th

Drive down to Wardour Street for a *Time Bandits* viewing.

George's single is No. 14 in the US charts and now he's under pressure to release follow-up singles – and we're under pressure to put another George song at the top of *Time Bandits*, as a potential US single. George admits with a smile that 'You grumble at them (the public) like hell when you're *not* in the charts, and then when you are in the charts you grumble at them for putting you there for the wrong reasons' (the aftermath of the Lennon shooting).

I don't like these viewings, especially when I know the room is full of people who have tried desperately to have many sections of the film cut. For the first half-hour everything seems wrong.

The laughs come for the first time on Cleese's 'Robin Hood' scene. From then on the 'audience' loosens up and I relax and George's big, bright arrangement of 'Oh Rye In Aye Ay' caps the film perfectly. At least we can talk to each other at the end. Even George, a harsh critic up to now, thinks the film is almost there, but hates the opening credits.

I must say, after today, I have a chilling feeling that we have fallen between too many stools. Not enough sustained comedy for the Python audience to be satisfied and too much adult content ('Titanic' references, etc) for the children's audience. We could just have created a dodo.

Friday, May 29th

Helen comes up to tell me that a 'For Sale' board is going up on No. 1 Julia Street. Steve A contacts Stickley and Kent, the agents. They are asking £37,500. Steve says he will get the keys.

Look at 1 Julia Street with Steve (financial) and Edward [Burd] (architectural). Damp, crumbling and filthy inside. Steve cannot believe that people were living here only a week ago and can believe even less that anyone should hope to get £37,500 for it. Edward thinks that the external walls, beneath their cracked and powdery rendering, may be stronger than they look. He reckons it would cost £30–£36,000 to renovate, and if we were able to buy the place for £25,000, despite its present state of extreme decay, it would be good value. Ed is going to find out more about the agent's hopes for the house and Steve says he can't wait to start working out how best we can pay for it!

Steve's business sense is as eager as Denis's, but his style utterly different. Denis is real estate and yachts, Steve is going to the March for Jobs rally at the weekend, three-day cricket and Springsteen.

Saturday, May 30th

Watch a clean, efficient, rather soporific goalless draw between Wales and Russia. It does one's perceptions good every now and then to see Russia – the enemy, the nation whose existence justifies enormous expenditure by Estaings, Thatchers, Carters and Reagans on weapons of destruction, the iron threat to Poland and Afghanistan, the home of Philbys and Burgesses, the cruel oppressor of Jewish minorities and cultural dissidents – playing a World Cup game at Wrexham.

Monday, June 1st

Wake to streaming, unequivocal sunshine, which looks set in for the day. Make all sorts of resolutions for the month as I sit down at my desk at a quarter to ten. I am determined to finish the first draft of *The Missionary*.

At half past six the results of my latest foray into consumerism are brought round to the house. A Sony Walkman II – an amazing miniaturised stereo set, with thin, light headphones and a cassette-sized playing machine. If they can make such sound reproduction quality so small now, what of the next ten years? A button perhaps? A pill you swallow which recreates the 8-track wonders of Beethoven's Ninth from *inside* your body?

Also I'm now the proud owner of a small colour telly with a six-inch screen which fits on the kitchen shelf and will also undoubtedly revolutionise my life, until, in due course, the wonder of these marvellous technological advances wears down into acceptance.

Moral of the tale – do not rest hopes and enjoyments on Sony products. Man cannot live by machinery alone. All technological advances bring built-in dissatisfaction.

Wednesday, June 3rd

A late, light lunch, a few minutes in the sunshine, then back up to the workroom again. But the combination of heaviness from a persistent head cold and some rumbling guts ache knocks me out and, drained of energy, I skip supper and take to my bed about the same time as Rachel.

Just stay awake long enough to catch Terry J's first programme as presenter of *Paperbacks*. Helped on by a sympathetic and very well-mixed selection of guests, Terry came across as Terry at his best – serious, but good fun, mainly sensible, but occasionally enthusiastically carried away, positive but gentle. All in all, I thought, an excellent debut and such a change from the smooth old hands of TV presentation.

And I did take in an awful lot of what was said about the books – it reminded me of how much more I took in of Shakespeare when I watched John Cleese in *Taming of the Shrew.*

And his guest, J L Carr – an ex-schoolmaster who publishes little 35p books from his home in Kettering – was a wonderful find. He is the compiler of such indispensable volumes as *Carr's Dictionary of Extraordinary English Cricketers* and *Carr's Dictionary of English Queens, King's Wives, Celebrated Paramours, Handfast Spouses and Royal Changelings.*

Friday, June 5th

A week after first being alerted to Stickley and Kent's board at 1 Julia Street, I ring Stickley's with my £25,000 cash offer. An Irish female most curtly receives the offer and, with hardly any elaboration, tells me crisply that it will not be enough, but she'll take my name. Twenty-five thousand pounds in cash for that dump and she almost puts the phone down on me. Irrational – or perhaps this time rational – anger wells up. Write a letter confirming my offer and refuse to increase it at this stage.

To lunch at Mon Plaisir with TG.

TG and I have a very good, convivial natter and excellent meal. It's as if the major pressures on the *Time Bandits* are now lessening. Our collaboration has perhaps been one of the more successful aspects of the film. There are rumours that Denis is having some success with his '*TB*' viewings in America.

Then I go off to a viewing of the film again.

There is a constant, steady level of appreciation from quite a small audience and at the end I feel so elated, so completely risen from the gloom of the showing nine days ago, that I can hardly run fast enough through sunlit Soho streets back to Neal's Yard.

Terry is upstairs, alone in the big room looking over the yard with an editola in one hand and film in the other, still trimming. 'Sensational' is the only word I can use. At last I feel that *Time Bandits* has lived up to all the work that's gone into it.

Drive up to 2 Park Square West for a Python meeting.

There is a long agenda and yet we spend the first half-hour talking about possible changes to the Hollywood Bowl film. John is quite despairing. He buries his head in his hands and summons up what appear to be his very last resources of patience. 'I crave order,' he groans, looking at the remnants of the agenda, whilst Terry J suggests we put Neil in the film and possibly a bit more animation, and JC moans inwardly that he only wants to do this 'bloody thing' to make some money (I rather agree) and Eric it is who puts the frustrating but incontrovertible arguments for protecting our reputation by putting out only what we think is the best.

Sunday, June 7th

Another eight-hour sleep – too rare these days. The swirling south-westerly winds have died down, but the sky is overcast.

As if to suit the mood of the weather, Angela rings. She says she is in a depression and has been for the last two weeks. She's decided to drop her social worker job and is looking for something 'exciting'. She keeps talking of her low self-esteem. She's not easily consolable either, but puts on a brave and cheerful front. I can offer sympathy but nothing very practical.

I wonder if she finished this Whit Sunday watching, as I did, Cassavetes' *A Women Under the Influence*. It was about madness and was rivetingly well-played, hard, depressing, uncompromising, but it aired a lot of problems and was ultimately optimistic.

I go to bed sober . . . sobered, anyway.

Monday, June 8th

A day of deck-clearing before an all-out assault on *The Missionary* script's last few scenes, which I hope to complete up in Southwold, with Suffolk countryside for inspiration and no telephones to distract.

Stickley and Kent call to tell me that my offer of £25,000 for No. 1 Julia hasn't been accepted, so I have to work out the next step. I want to make a £30,000 offer to put them on the spot, but after talking to Steve I revise this downward to £28,500 to allow bargaining room up to 30.

Wednesday, June 10th: Southwold

Wake to rich sunshine and birds chattering everywhere. Excellent conditions for a solid morning's writing at the desk presented to my grandfather from 'His grateful patients in Great and Little Ryburgh and Testerton',[1] fifty years ago this November.

Great strides made in the plot and this writing break has already justified itself completely. No phone calls, no doorbells, no carpet-layers, cleaners, carpenters, painters or television engineers, just my Silvine 'Students' Note Book – Ref 142 – Punched for filing', Grandfather's desk and the soothing, wholesome view – pheasants scurrying through a broad field of new-sown peas and a chaffinch strutting and posing on the telegraph wires outside.

Later, watch Terry J being hypnotised on *Paperbacks*. He says very little and eventually breaks into tears. Rather disturbing, I thought, for the tears don't look like tears of joy but of fear and uncertainty and loss.

Saturday, June 13th

Prepare for our sideshow(s) at the Gospel Oak School Fayre. The Palin contingent (minus H who is at badminton) troop along to the school at 1.15, armed with 'Escalado', blackboard, notices and a bottle of sweets which the nearest number guess can win. Congratulate Ron Lendon, the head, on the MBE he acquired in the honours lists published today.

For three and a half hours solid I take money and start races. 'Escalado' proves to be a compulsive hit. The races are as often as I can physically take the money, pay the winnings and start again. A cluster of a dozen kids keep coming

---

[1] Edward Watson Palin was a doctor who lived at Fakenham in Norfolk. I still correspond with a retired policeman who remembers Dr Palin taking tonsils out for free in his kitchen after church on Sundays.

back – addicted. We make 10p per race and by a quarter to six, when I'm hoarse and staggering to start the last race, we've taken about £19.20, which means nearly 200 races.

The whole fete, in warm, dry, sunny, celebratory weather, seems to have done well. Even Willy, who looked very miserable earlier on as he tried to tout custom for his 'guess the sweet' attraction, had taken over £7 by the end and had brightened considerably.

Monday, June 15th

Denis O'B rings from Los Angeles. He doesn't seem to have any ulterior motive than to be reassured that I'm still there and writing a script for him. He doesn't attempt to put pressure on in any direction. He sounds very vulnerable suddenly, as if he genuinely cannot understand how it could possibly be that five majors have already passed on *Time Bandits*.

I feel very sorry for him and if he was deliberately trying to soften me up then he succeeded. Any doubts I may have had about giving him first option on *The Missionary* faded as I put the phone down and left him to Universal.

Tuesday, June 16th

At seven o'clock, despite a last-minute volley of phone calls, I wrote the magic words 'The End' on my film – approximately two and a half working months from that run in mid-March when the title and subject suddenly clarified in my mind.

How good it is I really don't know. A cluster of scenes please me – the rest could go either way. I now have ten days of typing during which I shall tighten it up.

Thursday, June 18th

To Neal's Yard for more '*TB*' publicity – this time an interview for Granada TV's *Clapperboard*. For a simple interview on film there must be about ten people – production secretary, producer, publicity ladies, crew, etc, quite apart from Chris Kelly, who's asking the questions, TG and myself.

Terry has only just embarked on the first serious answer when he dislodges a huge can of film, which crashes to the floor noisily and spectacularly. Granada are very pleased.

Sunday, June 21st

Took Rachel to the zoo. Much activity in the bright sunshine. Baboons copulating, polar bears flat out on their backs with legs immodestly spread, scratching their belly hair slowly – like something out of Tennessee Williams, tigers crapping and penguins looking very dry and unhappy.

This evening we have to decide on how George H's song 'That Which I Have Lost' is accommodated in the opening titles. Neither Ray nor Terry feel satisfied with the song there at all. George, pushed by Denis, has done his best to make a version that works. But it was the wrong song in the first place and no-one has the courage to see that, so tonight we agree on a compromise. Part of the song under the opening names, but keep it clear of the thudding, impressive impact of TG's titles.

Wednesday, June 24th

The only event of any great significance in an otherwise unworkmanlike day is a call from Gilliam halfway through *News at Ten* to tell me that Denis has finally given up hope of selling *Time Bandits* in Hollywood. Disney, who apparently were closest to a deal, finally gave him the thumbs down. Apparently it was a case of the old guard at the top overruling the newer, younger, less conventional execs below.

Perhaps, TG and I feel, it would have been a lot better if Denis had organised a preview – like the *Brian* preview in LA which so impressed Warners. He has only tried to sell it at the top. And failed.

To bed resignedly. I feel sorry for TG. So much now depends on a big success in England. If it does badly here, or even only quite well, there is a real chance of the movie sinking without trace.

Friday, June 26th

Buy *Screen International*. The British film industry does not seem very healthy. Rank have just announced plans to cut 29 cinemas. The head of Fox (*not* an Englishman) in London gives a glib, gloomy, heartless prognosis that sounds like Dr Beeching – cinemas will only survive in about 20 major cities. The British don't go out any more. Video recorder sales are booming. Unfortunately I think he's right. It's going to be hard, if not impossible, to reverse this trend away from theatrical visits.

Wednesday, July 1st

To Gospel Oak Open Day to look at Willy and Rachel's work. Place full of doting, involved Gospel Oak parents. Impressive exhibition in the hall. Willy's dissatisfaction with his teacher this year doesn't seem to be reciprocated – she has given him a very good end of term report. But I can't imagine many circumstances in which Gospel Oak kids would receive bad reports – unless they were mass murderers, possibly. Rachel is as good as gold, I'm told by her nice teacher, Miss Evans.

Work until eleven, when I watch very good (possibly the best) edition of *Paperbacks*. TJ enthusing, as only he can, about Rupert Bear with Alfred Bestall, 86-year-old chief artist of the stories, there in the studio, complete with loose false teeth.

Monday, July 6th: London–Edinburgh

Helen takes me down to King's Cross to catch the 'Flying Scotsman' to Edinburgh to read the 'Biggles' stories [for BBC AudioBooks]. Full of Americans being roughly treated by a particularly cheeky set of waiters who execute all their tasks with a barely-controlled violence just this side of politeness. What a change from the Liverpool Street lot.

All confirms my feelings that it's the differences between human beings themselves which account for all our economic, social and political injustices and not the other way round. In short, there are plenty of shits in the world and unless we can find some wonder drug to cure them or neutralise them, I think we have to live with the fact that they will always cause trouble.

At Edinburgh by a quarter to three. Meet the team and the adaptor, George Hearten – possibly the complete antithesis of his hero, Captain W E Johns. Ex-Fleet Air Arm, so he knows how to pronounce 'altimeter', he turns out to be a reggae expert and, when we do discuss who we would all like to have been, reckons he's the Glaswegian Albert Camus.

The concentration required on the readings is quite exhausting. We do two stories and Marilyn [Ireland, the producer] sounds pleased.

Then back for story number three. This is harder and towards the end I find myself unable to say 'thousands of splinters flew' and, though we finish it, Marilyn rightly suggests that we stop for the day.

Tuesday, July 7th: Edinburgh

After breakfast walk down to the BBC and, at about eleven, we start one of the most gruelling, physically and mentally demanding day's work I can remember. Again the concentration required is greater than anything I'm prepared for, with preliminary read-throughs of each episode included. I have to speak continuously for two and a half hours, in six or seven different voices. My eyes swim out of focus when I stand up– my brain has rarely been required to work so fast – to process and redigest so much information, all the time knowing that this will be judged as a performance. We plough through five episodes by five o'clock, leaving two for tomorrow.

I feel drained – 'Biggled', I think must be the word, well and truly Biggled – as I lie back in my bath at the North British with a Carlsberg Special as a reward.

Wednesday, July 8th: Edinburgh-London

Up to meet John Gibson of the *Edinburgh Evening News* at breakfast at nine. We talk for almost an hour. He's easy company, and a dutiful journalist – he makes sure he scribbles something down about all my activities. This is primarily a *Time Bandits* piece.

From talking to him I am reinforced in this feeling that's been coming over me lately – that my reputation follows about three or four years behind what I do. Somehow, though none of the individual projects were treated with respect or reverence at the time, the cumulative effect of Python and *Ripping Yarns* and the *Life of Brian* and the 'Great Train Journey' seems to have been to raise my stock to the extent that I am now not only good copy everywhere, but also I sense a sort of respectfulness, as if I'm now an experienced hand and a permanent addition to a gallery of famous British people. It's all very worrying and offers me little comfort, for I know I am still the same bullshitter I always was.

A quick walk through Prince's Gardens – where everyone is lying out in the sun like extras in a documentary about nuclear war. Up the Mound to a restored National Trust house in the Royal Mile. Fascinating, but as soon as I enter it there is quite a stir amongst the nice, middle-class family who run it.

I'm followed from room to room by a breathless young man who finally confronts me in a bedchamber – 'Excuse me, but you are Eric Idle from Monty Python . . . ?'

Friday, July 10th

More rioting on TV tonight.[1] It's replaced sport as the summer's most talked about activity. The scenes are frightening. One can only hope lessons will be learnt fast. Whitelaw and Thatcher go out of their way to support the police, but bad policing and the effects of unemployment vie with each other as the two most oft-quoted reasons for what's happening.

Tuesday, July 14th

Settle down to read *The Missionary*, which arrived today from Alison – the first really smart copy. It read far better than I expected. It seems tight, the religious atmosphere is strong, the story and the characters develop well and, all in all, it's just what I had hoped – a strong, convincing, authentic sense of place, mood, period and a dramatic narrative providing a firm base for some very silly comedy.

I finish reading at half past eleven and, though I write these words with great trepidation, I feel the film is over 70% right – maybe even more. Now names of actors, directors, keep coming into my head.

But the chiefest decision of all is how to play Denis. I must show it to him, or I think be prepared for a final breakdown argument with him. The situation is full of uncertainties and dangers. My prestige is such that I could show it to any number of producers and get a sympathetic hearing. But I have told DO'B that I will offer it first to HandMade – so there's the rub.

Wednesday, July 15th

I call Denis in Fisher's Island [his home near New York]. It's half past eight in the morning there and Denis sounds subdued, a little cautious at first, but when he realises it isn't bad news, he begins to wind up and by the end we are both beginning to celebrate.

He asks if I have a director in mind. I mention Richard Loncraine, who I haven't spoken to for a few months, and could still be a long shot. I mention spring of '82 for shooting and he says 'We would have no problem' – 'we' being, I presume, he, EuroAtlantic, Trade Development Bank and George.

Feel relieved that I've taken a positive step forward. It would remove endless

---

[1] One of the most serious in a summer of urban riots took place at Toxteth in Liverpool. A thousand police were injured and many properties destroyed.

complications if Denis accepted the script. Should hear something by the weekend.

To Rachel's end of term concert at Gospel Oak. A rather flat affair. All the children look as though they're acting under orders. Rachel plays a lettuce.

A call from Loncraine. Good news – for me – is that the *Brimstone and Treacle* film has collapsed – Bowie having let them down very much at the last minute. He has two film projects he wants to do, but claims to be very keen to work with me, and wants to see the script as soon as possible.

Thursday, July 16th

Out of the house at a quarter to eight. Stuck in rush-hour traffic, ironically trying to get to Marylebone High Street for Radio London's live programme called *Rush Hour*.

Talk to Jackie Collins, who's also a guest. She's doing the circuits for her new book, *Chances*, which my Radio London interviewer confides to me is 'the filthiest book I've ever read'.

Out in Marylebone High Street by nine o'clock. [*Time Bandits* opened in London yesterday.] Buy all the papers and treat myself to a reviving plate of bacon and eggs and a cup of coffee at a local caff. Read the *Guardian* – 'British, if not best'. Plenty of praise, but all qualified. In the *New Statesman* our friend and *Jabberwocky* fan John Coleman said many things, but concluded that the taste left by the film at the end was not just bad, it was sour. Cheered up by an unequivocal rave in *New Musical Express*. Nothing else.

Drove on down to Terry J's. Terry is on good form. *Paperbacks* has finished and we natter happily over various things. Realise that I'm enjoying writing with an immediate sounding board again. In fact I have rather a good day and add to the 'Catholic Family' sketch rather satisfactorily, whilst Terry deals genially with a mass of phone callers.

Home soon after six. Bad review on Capital. Much praise for the film, but he blatantly calls it the new Monty Python film. If I had more time and energy I'd sue him.

Friday, July 17th

In early evening an important call – the first professional opinion on *The Missionary* – from Richard Loncraine. He liked it up to page ten, then not again until page sixty, from whence he felt it picked up.

But I was hopeful from our short chat for two reasons. One that he doesn't dislike it enough to not want to do it, and the other that all he said about the script and intentions about how to film it I felt very much in agreement with.

Now Denis and Terry J are to report! They're the only others who have copies.

Saturday, July 18th

After lunch a party of ten of us go to see *Time Bandits* at the Plaza.

The audience is responsive, consistent and picks up the jokes, but I find that, at one or two points, we stretch their goodwill by over-extending on a moment that's already been effective. The Giant is on for too long and the trolls don't add much. Heresy I know to agree on this, but the acts *do* hold up Napoleon and *don't* get a positive reaction. And, though I don't object to the parents blowing up at the end, we hold the moments afterwards for too long, as if making a significant statement, and, in doing so, overloading the gloom and killing the black humour.

So I came away feeling a little numbed. Despite three or four people seeking me out to tell me how much they'd enjoyed it, I was disappointed that I'd seen faults in it and that there wasn't a greater sense of excitement amongst the departing audience.

TG rings later. He feels this sense of doom as well.

Sunday, July 19th

Woke to yet another day of concern. I have to learn my 'Plankton' speech for a Save the Whales rally in Hyde Park. Then there's the Sunday papers – how will *Time Bandits* fare today?

A marvellous selection of qualified raves. But somehow the qualifications seem to be significant rather than the raves. I read Alan Brien, who starts wonderfully and then qualifies. Philip French in the *Observer* chunders on at length for a column and a half before one word of doubt. But then it comes in, like a trip wire 20 yards from the tape at the end of a mile race.

As I describe them to Gilliam later – they're the worst set of rave notices I've ever seen.

I feel Alan Brien's observation is the most perceptive thing anyone's said about the film – 'Where it falls below earlier Python movies, or Gilliam's own *Jabberwocky*, is in the sense it gives that once the basic idea was established the makers thought everything else would be easy.'

Still, no time to mope, as I have to take myself and rapidly-learnt script down to Hyde Park to address the Save the Whales rally – which was allowed to go ahead by [Police Commissioner] McNee despite a month-long ban on London marches following the riots, because it was termed 'educational'.

Monday, July 20th

Start of a Python writing fortnight. We tried such a session a year ago and it was not successful. Today, a year later, things feel very different.

Time Bandits is complete, so T G is back with the group. Eric is relaxed and well after France. Terry J has got *Paperbacks* out of the way and is keen to get directing again. Graham, with *Yellowbeard*, and myself, with *The Missionary*, both have projects which look like being completed by summer '82.

We decided, without any bickering or grudging, that we should now work separately until the end of the week. Everyone agreed that this film should not be extended indefinitely and if it was to become a reality it had to be next year.

So, after lunch and an amiable chat, we disperse to our separate writes.

About ten o'clock DO'B rings from Fisher's Island. He's just finished reading *The Missionary*. As I expected, the last thing he wants to do is give any artistic judgement on the script. He talks of it purely from a business point of view. He sounds to have no doubts that it's a commercial reality and he's treating it accordingly.

DO'B reckons it's an eight- or nine-week shoot, 65% studio, and will cost about one and a half million. We are looking at a March, April, early May '82 shoot.

Thursday, July 23rd

Drive over to Richard Loncraine's office in Clarendon Cross. How neat, well-preserved, paved and bollarded this little corner of Notting Hill has become. Charming, I should think is the word. Richard bounds down to answer the door, and is soon showing me his latest gadgets (he runs a toy factory employing 200 people making ridiculous things like eggs with biros in the end), pouring me some wine, raving about *Time Bandits*, which he thought absolutely wonderful, calling *Chariots of Fire* 'Chariots of Bore' and generally bubbling and enthusing like an English version of Gilliam.

Richard is going to do it and will commit to it. He repeats that he wants to work with me and he's doing it largely out of faith in what I can achieve, which is flattering and exciting at the same time, and because, although there is much in the script he thinks doesn't yet work, he thinks there's more that does.

The next step is to bring DO'B and Loncraine together next week. But I think I can say that *The Missionary* became a reality tonight.

Sunday, July 26th

Richard rings to suggest Maggie Smith for Lady Ames, which shows he's been thinking positively about it.

Monday, July 27th

To a Python meeting at 2 Park Square West, giving T Gilliam a lift. A successful day, everyone participating. John tending to chair in a barristerish way, but it's all good Python trough work. We re-read the 'bankers'. They nearly all survive and, by half past three when TJ has to go, we have a solid 50 minutes, with viable links and a sort of coherence.

Ring Terry J to find out if he has read *The Missionary*. He has, and finds it all 'unbelievable'. Not an encouraging reaction. Set off to [EuroAtlantic in] Cadogan Square. Denis, tall, tanned and looking as confidently turned out as ever, meets me and we walk through the balmy evening to the Chelsea Rendezvous.

I start by telling Denis that all three people who have read *The Missionary* haven't liked it. A little provocative, I suppose, but it's the way I read the reactions. Terry J's, strangely enough, doesn't trouble me as much as I thought. Maybe, as TJ and I just improvised over the phone this evening, it would be better for Welles to be given a mission in England – possibly the saving of fallen women. But talking to Denis I feel, obstinately perhaps, that my instincts are right and that my choice of director is right and that the film can work. Denis is not at all discouraging. Quite the opposite.

Tuesday, July 28th

I wake in the early hours in general discomfort – head and tooth aching and very hot. Just not ready for sleep, so walk about a bit. Then, from three a.m. until half past four I sit and scribble some dialogue for a new scene in *The*

Missionary – trying to take the story in a different direction, as I discussed with TJ over the phone.

Drain my cup of tea and look up finally from deep absorption in the work, to see the sky has lightened to a dark, pre-dawn blue. Feel much better. Feel I've defeated the aches and pains! Back to bed.

Later take Granny and the Herberts to *Time Bandits*.

Afterwards we all walk down Regent Street into a Mall thronged with pre-wedding [of Charles to Diana] crowds. A feeling of celebration and slightly noisy camaraderie, as if the revolution had just happened. Of course, quite the opposite; everyone here tonight was celebrating the longevity and resilience of the Establishment.

There was a mass of sleeping bags and plastic all along the edge of the pavement – rarely much class or style, except that under the trees outside the ICA a long table had been set with candles and four men in full dinner jackets and bow ties were sitting down to a meal and wine.

Saturday, August 1st

Time Bandits biz in second week is down, as Denis said, by about 20%, but then so is everyone's except James Bond and *Clash of the Titans*. We move up to No. 3 in London above *Excalibur*, now in its fourth week, and the fading *Cannonball Run*.

Marvellous review by Gavin Millar in the *Listener*. I wonder if TG had time to see it before he went off to France yesterday. The *Ham and High* and many of the rest of England papers turn in good reviews too, so that all cheers me up. But the bad news is that the figures for week one in Bristol are, by any standards, very disappointing. Cardiff is better, but certainly no signs of it being anything but an average performer outside London.

Sunday, August 2nd: Southwold

An early lunch (cheese and an apple) and drive back through Suffolk villages and down the M11, listening to another tense Test Match. Cloudless sky when I arrive in Oak Village. Australia nearly 100 with only 50 to go and seven wickets standing. But by the time I've unpacked, oiled myself and settled down for a sunbathe on the balcony they have collapsed and within an hour Botham has wiped them out and England have won.

Wednesday, August 5th

I drive into town for lunch with Neville Thompson at Mon Plaisir.

Neville is the third of the main strands of *The Missionary* project. Denis is supplying the money, Loncraine the direction and Neville could be the producer.

Like everyone else he has qualifications about the script, but has faith in the project. I try to give him as many 'outs' as possible, but he clearly feels that there is some rich vein to be tapped wherever Pythons are involved – even if he can't immediately see it in *The Missionary* as it stands. I feel a little like the Missionary myself at the moment, trying to convert the waverers to the joys and virtues of this bloody film.

Loncraine rings. He's back from New York, where he's been to see Sting – of 'Police' – for part in *Brimstone and Treacle*.

Thursday, August 6th

Over to Loncraine's for further talks on *The Missionary*. Richard has read it again and sees certain problem areas. Richard talks from the hip a bit, firing ideas out fast and in a not particularly disciplined way. Tendency to broader jokes, but, on the credit side, we come up with three very good visual additions to the script which I can immediately incorporate in the rewrites. Another heavy storm breaks – starting with an apocalyptic clap of thunder – 'Didn't like that idea, did he?' says Richard, looking out of the window respectfully.

Reagan has dismissed 13,000 of his air traffic controllers for going on an illegal strike, but Sheila [Condit, who was organising our US holiday trip] has checked with LA Airport and international flights are coming in 95% on time.

Friday, August 7th

In the evening Helen goes to badminton. I stay in to watch the news. Whilst Reagan pursues his hard line against the air traffic controllers, European air traffic controllers are quoted as advising against flying to the US. Disturbing stuff – 25 near misses reported in US air space since the strike began, the new military controllers plus non-striking controllers are working longer hours and 'safety is being endangered'. American government says rubbish, and the airlines flying to the States say so too. But not a very comforting way to have to start the holiday. I feel that, if the BA pilots are still prepared to fly with the new controllers then I'm happy – but don't go to bed elated.

We flew to California on August 9th for a family holiday, having rented a house at Point Dume, near Malibu.

Wednesday, September 2nd

Denis met with Loncraine and got on well and is anxious to sign him up. *Time Bandits* is still No. 3 in London. It will not be the blockbuster they were predicting. They'd been looking for a distributor's gross of a million, but have revised this downwards to half a million. But he has done a deal in America. Avco Embassy are to release the *Time Bandits* on November 6th with four million dollars committed to prints and advertising. Modest, by today's standards, and Avco Embassy are guaranteed against loss by Denis and George.

Thursday, September 3rd

To my desk to wrestle with the most immediate problems. One of the first calls on our return, Tuesday, was from a humbled Stickley and Kent asking if my offer of £28,500 for No. 1 Julia Street still stood. Apparently they have had some difficulty selling at £37,750. As my offer had been so summarily dismissed, I told them I would think about it.

Helen is not really keen and sees No. 1 as a lot of hard work, but on the other hand she does see the advantage of having control over the site. Edward keen to take on the job and will supervise, so on balance I stick to my first instinct and renew my interest – at the same time twisting the knife a little and giving my cash offer as £26,500. We shall see.[1]

On to viewing of *Hollywood Bowl* on screen for first time. Sixty-five minutes it runs. Sketches well performed and quite well filmed – the rest a wretched disappointment.

Back at Neal's Yard, those Pythons who saw the film – Terry J, John, Graham and myself (TG and Eric being in France) – all agree it isn't right. Main criticisms – links, atmosphere, shapelessness.

[1] We never did buy No. 1, but snapped up No. 3 years later!

I felt very proud of our little group today. In the face of much pressure to put the '*Bowl*' film out as soon as possible, to recoup our money and to have done with it, we held out for quality control first.

Tuesday, September 8th

Drive into town to join the London Library and take out, at last, some books on African missionaries – *Winning over a Primitive People*, etc – to read as background on the film.

Evening of phone calls, latest of which is Denis O'B ringing from New York. I tell him all is well, except that both Richard Loncraine and Neville Thompson think that the budget will be nearer £2 million than £1 million.

Turns out that he has sold *The Missionary* project to George on the basis of a £1.2 million cost.

Thursday, September 10th: Southwold

I watch a programme about the colossal, massive, virtually incredible madness of our world in 1981 – the designing, building and deployment of weapons of self-destruction.

It worries me that we accept now that we have to live with bombs which could kill two million people with one blast. That somewhere in the world there are men designing and manufacturing and loading and aiming and controlling and making serious considerations of policy based on the use of such weapons. Meanwhile we pay for such collective madness with unemployment, a crumbling health service, a polluted planet. It seems we know that we shall destroy ourselves somehow and the multi-megaton bombs are like the cyanide pills which will put us out of our misery instantly.

Wednesday, September 16th

A solid morning's work on *The Missionary*. Few distractions and I fall into a good rhythm.

To the airport to collect Al and Claudie. Wet roads. Repairs close the motorways, London seems empty, ghostly. At the airport soon after ten – find them waiting, the plane was early. Best flight ever, opines the bronzed and ageless poet, pulling eagerly on a cigar as they had sat in non-smoking. Claudie, just a gently convex stomach showing discreetly, looked very well and in good colour.

Friday, September 18th

Up to Burgh House at 6.00 for the Grand Launch [of Al's book of poems, called *Travelogs*]. Robert laid out a display of Signford's[1] wares on the piano of the Music Room and hardly anybody turned up. More and more I had the feel that I was in one of Richmal Crompton's 'William' situations. Involved in one of his 'grate skeems' which never quite work.

But there were enough there for me to rise to my feet and embark on the speech. No sooner had I begun than a dozen latecomers arrived in the next one and a half minutes, so the speech wasn't helped, but the party was. And in the end it was quite difficult to move everyone out.

Then out to Vasco and Piero's [Pavilion Restaurant] with Al, who had been quaffing malts during the afternoon, then much champagne at the party, but was in a big, expansive bear-like mood of delight, Claudie, and Mike Henshaw[2] and his excellent new 'companion' Penny. We all had a wonderful time and Mike paid.

For Mike and me it was a reconciliation. Having been good and close friends for 13 years, accountancy got in the way and we have not spoken or seen each other for two years. We picked up as if nothing had happened.

Wednesday, September 23rd

In mid-afternoon take advantage of dry, still, bright weather for a run across the Heath, then down to Eyre Methuen to discuss with Geoffrey S and Terry J a new edition of Fegg which we agree to call *Dr Fegg's Nasty Book*. We look through the artwork of the old – now seven years past – up in Methuen's boardroom, sipping white wine and looking out over a panorama of city buildings turning reddish-gold in the waning sunlight.

Thursday, September 24th

Work delayed this morning by arrival of T G, fresh from Hollywood, bearing such gems as a market research survey on *Time Bandits* – a wonderfully thorough and conscientious document analysing test screenings and reactions to all the various elements of the film in that earnest American way which reduces all

---

[1] Signford was an off-the-shelf name for a small publishing company I had set up, with Robert Hewison's help. Its first book was by the artist Chris Orr.
[2] Michael Henshaw, my first accountant, had been married to Anne, who had become my manager, and the Pythons' manager. She had re-married, to Jonathan James, a barrister.

things to 'product'. They confirm that the film is not for Fresno, but it could well be for bigger, more 'sophisticated' city audiences.

Interesting thing it *did* reveal is that the audience at Sherman Oaks went to the movies on average ten times a month, and in Fresno seven. Which shows the health of movies in the US is still good, whereas here the admissions level is still dropping to all-time lows.

Work on the Fermoy scene, but got involved in helping Tom with his geography homework. Then drive down to the Long Room at the Oval cricket ground for Pavilion Books launching party.

Soon was in the middle of a swirling throng – past the literary editor of the *Express*, Peter Grosvenor, on to a very persistent Scottish lady publisher who wants to have lunch and discuss some project involving Miriam Stoppard, Tom Stoppard and sex, grabbed by Molly Parkin, who's very oncoming – she says I always was her favourite – and meet Max Boyce. 'Oh I love being in a corner with two comedians,' she soothed, as we had photos taken together.

Then Bob Geldof in green lurex jacket, black skin-tight trousers and mediaeval floppy boots approached and we hailed each other like old friends, though I don't know him that well. After a brief exchange of mutual abuse, we talked about school and missionaries and he swore blind that he had been at a missionary school in Ireland where the French master was mainlining quinine, Irish was compulsory and, even if you got seven or eight 'O' Levels, none of them counted if you failed Irish.

Friday, September 25th

Drink in the Nag's Head. Aggressive podgy Cockney looms up.
'Are you Eric Idle?'
'No . . .'
'You're Eric Idle.'
'No, I'm not . . .'
'Well, it's a very good impression,' he mutters and wanders back to his mates.

Saturday, September 26th

After lunch out with the family to visit Uncle Leon in Hampton Wick, in the tiny, neat, long and narrow cottage which Leon moved into only two weeks before Helen's Aunt Peggy, wife of 38 years, died early this year. He took a long time to recover and said he couldn't bear being alone in the house in the evening. He confessed very touchingly that he's often found himself turning to talk to someone who isn't there.

A big tea with scones and home-made jam, then home under angry skies ranging from slate grey to pitch black, through the well-kept roads of Hampton and Twickenham. Perfect example of Tory middle-class orderliness. No rows of council flats with rubbish flapping around them, or grandiose public works schemes left half undone through lack of funds. This is the tidy, thrifty world of private planning, from which the poor and the underpaid seem absent. But at least personal enterprise is allowed and encouraged to flourish here, when the grey blocks of Camden seem only to have extinguished it.

Back home I watch quite brilliant first film of Bill Douglas trilogy,[1] *My Childhood*.

Tuesday, September 29th

Came near to giving up this morning. For a full hour I sat and stared. Every word I wrote seemed dull and wooden. The last three weeks of fairly solid application (well, two and a half, anyway) seemed to have produced just sludge. And tomorrow was the last day of September, when I had once optimistically estimated I would be finished with the [*Missionary*] rewrites.

But abandoning now would seem so feeble. I had to carry it through. Besides, I'd burnt my boats – turning down every other piece of work. So it was that in the hour and a half before lunch I buckled down and ideas began to flow and in fact I was well into my stride when the door bell rang at 2.30 to herald the arrival of a BBC crew to film me giving testimony in a programme about giving up smoking.

Sunday, October 4th: Southwold

Woke at 8.30. The boys already downstairs and breakfasted. Outside a steady drizzle, which increased to heavy rain and the children and I took Mrs Pratt [my mother's neighbour] to morning service at Reydon.

We leave her and drive into Southwold for more secular activities. Despite all my doubts and rational resistance to the dogma of the church, I still feel a powerful guilt at taking the children to the amusement arcade on the end of Southwold Pier on a Sunday morning. You don't notice the presence of the church in London, as you do in Southwold.

---

[1] Made in 1972, it tells the story of a boy born into poverty in Scotland and his relationship with a German POW. Douglas made only four films, all autobiographical; bleak but brilliantly observed.

Wednesday, October 7th

To the Escargot in Greek Street for meal with Terry and Al. Terry has just returned from his *Fairy Tales* promotion trip to Birmingham (which he hated) and Manchester (which he found well-heeled) and Liverpool (sad tales of the decline of the Adelphi).[1] Give the manager one of my complimentary tickets to Mel Brooks's *History of the World*, which is having a glossy preview at 11.30.

Find myself sitting next to Harold Evans, Editor of the *Times*. He seems to be very anxious to please – asking me what I'm doing, as if he knows me. Make some jokes about the SDP, then he admits that he does think they are a very sensible lot. This, together with a propensity to do the right thing by clapping whenever Mel Brooks appears on screen, makes me suspect him. Surely *Times* editors should be made of harder stuff?

The film is dreadful. Having dispensed early on with any claim to historical accuracy or authenticity and any exceptional attention to visual detail, the whole thing depends on the quality of the gags. And the quality is poor. It's like a huge, expensive, grotesquely-inflated stand-up act. A night club act with elephantiasis.

Thursday, October 8th

Tom becomes a teenager. Just writing those words makes me abruptly aware of time passing. He has lots of books about aircraft and Helen and I are to buy him a new clarinet. He goes off to school very happy.

I take him and three friends out to Century City in Mayfair – a new hamburger place, all silver-sprayed 'hi-tech' décor. Only open three weeks, but looking decidedly run down. Still, the food was good and we all sat inside a dome painted silver. At one point Alex Robertson declares, almost proudly, 'Gosh, my mum and dad wouldn't have been able to afford *this*.' Echoes from all round the table.

Saturday, October 10th

Buy presents for the evening's celebrations to mark EuroAtlantic's tenth anniversary. The celebration is to be held, somehow appropriately, aboard a boat called the Silver Barracuda.

---

[1] A once-glamorous hotel for transatlantic liner passengers. Helen is convinced our daughter Rachel was conceived there on the night of my friend Sean Duncan's wedding in 1974.

Mark Vere Nicoll [EuroAtlantic's legal wiz] makes a speech and presents Denis with a leather-covered photo album which is also a music box. Denis gives a long speech in reply. Quite fluent and informal. But he does at one point pay tribute to Peter Sellers – adding, somewhat unnecessarily, 'Who can't be with us tonight.' George, ever in touch with the other world, shouts back, 'Don't be so sure, Denis.'

Wednesday, October 14th

Helen is 39. But looks a lot younger.

Mary, Edward and Catherine Gib arrive at 8.00 and I take them all out for what turns out to be a very successful Mystery Evening. First to the Gay Hussar – good food and efficient, old-fashioned service. Then on to Ronnie Scott's to see Panama Francis and the Savoy Sultans – a Harlem Thirties jazz and swing band. Beautiful to listen to, presented stylishly and with the added poignancy that they are a dying breed. In ten years many of them won't be left. But the two hours we spent there in their soothing, infectious company were rare magic.

Thursday, October 22nd

Just after five o'clock I suddenly found myself at the end of *The Missionary* rewrites.

I've spent about five and a half solid working weeks on the rewrite and there are only about a dozen pages left intact from the 121-page first version. So I have virtually written a second film in about half the time it took to write the first.

But for the moment, at the end of this crisp and invigorating day, the feeling is just one of an onrush of freedom – of time to spare – the emergence from isolation.

Monday, October 26th: Ballymaloe House, Ireland

We landed at Cork at ten o'clock, our VW minibus was waiting and we drove without incident to Ballymaloe. The bright sunshine of London was replaced by rain in Ireland.   By early evening it's clear enough for me to go for a run – up past barking dogs and along a narrow road which grows more and more wild and directionless – giving rise in the dark corners of my mind to California-like fears of sudden mindless violence. (I was not to know that about one hour before, in the London we had just left, a bomb had exploded in a Wimpy bar in Oxford Street[1] – the IRA claimed credit.)

Thursday, October 29th: Ballymaloe

Woke about 8.00 to hear Rachel colouring industriously across the other side of the room. Then to breakfast – which now stretches from nine till ten. I love our little tableful and it's a joy and complete relaxation to sit, after children have gone, with a dependably tasty cup of coffee and gaze out of the long Georgian windows at the damp autumn countryside.

We have a packed lunch today and, on advice from an Irishman staying here, drive to Cobh and Fota Island.

Cobh, an old fishing town and fadedly elegant resort, is approached across a causeway, past an old blockhouse or pill-box on which are daubed the words 'Cobh supports the hunger strikers'. Then there are a number of small black flags on short makeshift flagpoles nailed up to telegraph poles.

Unlike anywhere else we've been in Southern Ireland, this year or last, there is a definite frisson of hostility in Cobh. It's clearly official municipal policy to support the IRA – although these initials are never mentioned. It's always 'our boys' or 'our countrymen'. Beside the station, now a fish-unloading yard, posters are stuck on the wall – clenched fists surmounted with the words 'Stand Up To Britain' and an incongruous picture of Maggie Thatcher with the words beneath 'Wanted. For The Torture Of Irish Prisoners'.

The memorial to those who died in the Lusitania has been turned into an IRA memorial, with placards hung round the necks of the 1915 sailors giving the names of the hunger strikers. Like so much in Ireland it is a rough and ready gesture – there's no style or care particularly taken. It's functional, rather ugly and very depressing.

Mary [Burd] gets fish lobbed in her direction by the unloaders and there's some laughing and sending-up. My final image of this potentially rather attractive Georgian town is of a grimy 40-foot trailer being driven at violent, shaking speed along crowded streets, blood pouring out of the back and onto the road.

Wednesday, November 4th: New York

The car horns start to blare and I know I'm in Manhattan [for the opening of *Time Bandits*]. A fine 27th storey view out over Central Park. The trees in full

[1] Killing the man who was trying to defuse it.

autumn colours, mustards, russets, yellows. Very fine, a stretch of calm on this restless island.

General atmosphere of cautious excitement improved by continuing news of fresh enthusiastic reviews. Jack Lyons [Avco-Embassy's publicity man] says he has nearly all the majors covered, but so far his spies in the *NY Times* have not been any help with leaks about the Canby review.[1] Canby's review will be out on Friday, but, if all else fails, Jack says he'll get a leak from one of the compositors on Thursday afternoon!

In the evening we have a Gala Premiere and I drink an awful lot of champagne. Jack has arranged for me to escort Eleanor Mondale, a rather classically good-looking 21-year-old blonde, who resembles, especially, with her hair-do and use of knickerbockers, a chunky Princess Diana.[2] She is quite used to the bright lights and walks with a serene sort of Scandinavian poise through all the ballyhoo. And there *is* ballyhoo.

We are driven to the theatre in limousines and disgorged before a small waiting crowd gathered good-humouredly rather than ecstatically behind wooden barriers. Then we go inside and meet the good people who have been invited along. Meet Frank Capra Jnr, the new head of Avco-Embassy, whom I quite like. James Taylor, looking like the earnest maths master in a prep school, comes up and re-introduces himself.

After the movie begins, Terry G, Nancy, Eleanor Mondale and I take off to a ceilinged, fashionable but un-chic restaurant down on 18th called Joanne's. Shelley [Duvall] joins us later with news of a complete fiasco at the Gala Premiere. It was held in a twin cinema complex and apparently the sound was very bad in the first one for ten minutes, and in the second the picture came on upside down after the first couple of reels.

Thursday, November 5th: New York

Driven by a talkative chauffeur – they don't call them chauffeurs over here, I notice, but 'drivers'. This one goes into a monologue about 'celebrities'. 'I do like celebrities. They're very nice people.' He tells me how, as a cabbie, he gave a ride to Frank Sinatra and then rushed home and rang his mother at three in the morning to tell her the news. He also has taken Gilda Radner to the dentist and tells me all sorts of intimate details about her bridge work.

I notice that the driver is totally grey – cap, trousers, jacket, shoes, hair and

---

[1] Chief film critic of the *New York Times*. He died in 2000.
[2] Walter Mondale was Jimmy Carter's Vice-President from 1976 to 1981. Eleanor, a radio presenter, was diagnosed with a brain tumour in 2005, but seemed to have successfully fought it.

face. Amazing. To the mid-West Side in sight of the big liner bays, for the *Dick Cavett Show.*

The programme progresses in uneasy fencing between comedy and seriousness. Cavett doesn't want to look like the dullard, so he indulges my subversive silliness instead of bringing it under a tight rein. The result is that some comedy works and there is nothing to fall back on when it doesn't.

The limousine takes us on to NBC and the *Robert Klein Hour.* This is a radio show I have come to enjoy greatly. Klein is relaxed, sharp, funny and good at guiding a disparate guest list – which includes Meat Loaf and Loudon Wainwright III – who remembers straight away that we met last in a massage parlour.

End up eating at Elaine's. Shelley is along with us for a while. Good Italian food, nice busy atmosphere.

TG gets his first sight of the Vincent Canby review. I'll never forget his face as he studies it, at the table beside Woody Allen and Mia Farrow, with the waiters pushing by. 'Studies' is far too mild a word for the extraordinary intensity of Terry's expression. His eyes stare fearfully like some Walter Crane drawing of an Arthurian knight confronting the face of Evil. Two years of solid commitment can be rendered quite spare in one review. At the end he lays the paper down ... 'Yes ... it's good ...'

Monday, November 9th

'*The Missionary* Mark II' arrives from the typist's, and I fall on it and read it through eagerly. It reads very well and I'm happy with the last-minute cuts and readjustments. And I laughed more, much more, than at Mk I.

Send the script round by cabs to Neville and Richard L. Watch some television. Can't keep my mind on writing. I'm half hoping the phone will ring before I go to bed and bring some breathless enthusiasm from one or other of them for the new script. This is what I need now.

At 11.30 the phone does ring. It's Rita from Los Angeles. Though it's only lunchtime Monday in LA, she tells me (in strictest confidence, she says) that *Time Bandits* took 6.2 million dollars over three days of its first weekend. This is bigger than any film ever handled by Avco (including *The Graduate*).

I'd still rather have had a phone call about *The Missionary*.

Tuesday, November 10th

Halfway through the morning Neville Thompson rings. My heart sinks utterly as he tells me that he wants to see the original script, because he feels I've lost a lot in the rewrites. I'm sure he doesn't realise what a dashing blow this is after two months' rewriting. Anything but wild enthusiasm is a dashing blow!

Denis calls in the afternoon and brightens me up with the news that *Time Bandits* has taken (officially) 6.5 million dollars in its first three days in the US. He estimates it will overtake *Life of Brian*'s total US take in two and a half weeks. Incredible news, almost as incredible as Neville not liking the new script.

Wednesday, November 11th: Belfast

Still no word from Richard L. Off to Heathrow at 11.00 to take the 12.30 shuttle to Belfast. Bag searched very thoroughly and wrapped in a cellophane cover before loading. Flight half full. Land at Aldergrove at a quarter to two.[1]

Belfast is not unlike Manchester or Liverpool. A once proud and thriving city centre suffering from the scars of industrial decline. Fine, red-brick warehouses empty. New office blocks – featureless and undistinguished. The university and its surrounding streets quite elegant; Georgian and early Victorian Gothic.

The Europa Hotel is screened at the front by a ten-foot-high mesh wire and everyone has to enter through a small hut, where my bag was searched again and my name checked on the hotel list. Then into the hotel, with its thick carpets and Madison Suites. No-one seems to find it remarkable any more that such a smart façade should be upstaged by a makeshift hut and barbed wire. Will they make the hut permanent one day? Will it be landscaped – or would that spell victory for the forces of disorder?

I have a pleasant two-room suite with an 8th floor view. Michael Barnes, tall, with long hair and sweeping beard, is very charming. 'I know we'll get on,' he said, 'because you write such good letters.' And vice-versa, I should have said, for it was something about his first approach to me by letter that brought me here.

Michael B told me that I was the second Festival attraction to sell out – two days after Yehudi Menuhin and two days ahead of Max Boyce! Anyway it was quite restorative for my ego to see a long queue of people waiting to get into the Arts Theatre.

Up tatty stairs to a small dressing room with light bulbs missing. Sort out my false noses, moustaches and at a quarter to eight I go on. The first part of

---

[1] I had been asked by Michael Barnes, director of the Belfast Festival, to go over and give a performance. It was my first one-man show. I was to do more, but only ever at Belfast. The Troubles were at their height.

the programme is what I've written and cobbled together since returning from New York. It goes well, but, after what seems an interminable and gruelling length of time, I glance at my watch between changes and, to my astonishment and despair, it's still only eight o'clock.

In fact it's just after 8.30 when I finish 'Fish in Comedy' – and I'm very hot and sweaty. For a moment the question and answer session seems doomed. Then all of a sudden it begins to happen. A steady stream of well-phrased, fairly sensible enquiries give me ample scope to talk about and enact scenes from all the favourite Python topics – censorship, the Muggeridge/Southwark interviews, etc.

There are some very enterprising audience suggestions – 'Did you know, Mr Palin, that it is a tradition for solo performers who visit the Arts Theatre, Belfast, to run round the auditorium from one side of the theatre to the other? The record is held by Groucho Marx at 45 seconds.' So I peeled off my jacket, paced out the course and went off like a rocket. 38 seconds. Whoever he was, I should have thanked him.

So I rambled on until ten to ten, just over two hours on the stage. Thoroughly enjoyable. Michael Barnes very pleased backstage.

Friday, November 13th

Gemma, a helper at the Festival and English girl, says that the worst thing about living in Northern Ireland is the way people have become used to the violence. They hardly turn a hair when a bomb goes off. Her father, who has worked here for years, will return to England when he retires. Resignation and survival rather than hope or rebuilding seem to be the watchwords.

I leave on the 10.30 shuttle. We take 55 minutes, with the help of a north-westerly tailwind, to reach Heathrow, where it's dry and sunny.

At half past two Neville Thompson arrived to talk about *The Missionary*. His doubts, which had worried me so much earlier in the week, seemed less substantial as we talked and I think I was able to persuade him that there were very funny things in the script. He in turn gave me a thought about Fortescue's character which clarified something very constructively – that Fortescue should enjoy sex. A simple, but clear observation, which gives greater point, irony and tension throughout.

Saturday, November 14th

This is one of those mornings when it's worth buying *Variety*. 'Bandits Abscond With 69G in St Lou', 'Boston's Ambitious Bandits Bag 269G', 'Bandits'

Larcenous 45G in KC', 'Bandits Looting LA. Hot 368G'. Lovely breakfast reading.

Sunday, November 15th

Work in the afternoon, watch Miles Kington's 'Great Railway Journey', which makes me want to start travelling again. But the best news of the week is that Loncraine rings with a very positive reaction to the new script. He thinks it's an easier read and much funnier. Eight out of ten, he thinks, rather than six for the first one.

Monday, November 16th

I had to bestir myself and turn out, on an evening I dreadfully wanted to be in, to run the auction for Westfield College in Hampstead. Predictably chaotic student organisation, but on the whole very nice people. They gave me a list of nearly 100 items to be individually auctioned.

The slave auction at the end *was* fun. Boys offering their services to do anything for 24 hours. Girls offering massage. I won that myself – with a bid of £23.00. Finally I had to auction my own face, on to which anyone could push a custard pie. Not once, but five times. Collected nearly 30 quid for this alone. All the pies were delivered by girls, and the last two gave me kisses through the foam!

Thursday, November 19th

At six o'clock take Willy and Tom to the Circus World Championships on a common in Parsons Green. This is a Simon Albury trip – his present to Willy on his 11th birthday.

It's mainly a TV event with cameras all over the place and a wonderful BBC floor manager squashed into a very tight-fitting evening dress with white socks on and an arse so prominent it looks like a caricature of Max Wall. Simon has secured us seats right by the ring – so we can see the sweaty armpits, the toupees and the torn tights that the viewers at home will miss.

The things I like least about circuses are animals and clowns and there are neither tonight. Instead about a dozen different varieties of balancing act. Russians holding ladies doing headstands on top of a 20-foot pole balanced on their forehead, petite Chinese ladies who throw (and catch) coffee tables from one to another with their feet. A Bulgarian boy who jumps backwards off a springboard and lands on the shoulders of a man, who is in turn on the shoulders of three other men.

The virtuosity on display is dazzling. One Polish woman can do a double backward somersault off a pole and land on the pole again. Dangerous area for punning.

In the middle of it all Willy has the evening made for him by being called out by the ringmaster as a birthday boy. There in the middle of the ring in the middle of the Circus World Championships, Willy publicly declares his support for Sheffield Wednesday! We don't get back until 11.00. Boys tired and happy and I hungry.

Saturday, November 21st

Time Bandits is No. 1 grossing film in the US almost exactly two years after *Brian* held the top spot. I still can't get over a sense of awed surprise. US new releases are falling like nine-pins. The brightest successes, apart from *Time Bandits*, are *Chariots of Fire*, still only on limited release, and *The French Lieutenant's Woman*, which is going well, but not spectacularly. Three English movies setting the pace.

George rings. He's got my *Missionary* script – but said he'd do the film just from the letter I sent with it! What *did* I say? He does express a worry as to whether *The Missionary* will interfere with the Python film and says he doesn't want to be the cause of any split in Python. As I told TG later, this didn't sound like a spontaneous George H concern. I mustn't get paranoid, but it suggested to me that someone somewhere was trying to shut down *The Missionary* for unspecified reasons.

Monday, November 23rd

Richard Loncraine rings early. He just wants to talk and make sure we are still happy. I give my usual reassurances, though I must admit I haven't had time to read the script for a week! RL's main concern seems to be making a movie that will be noticed – especially in the States. I tell him that, with *Time Bandits*, *Chariots of Fire* and *The French Lieutenant's Woman* doing good business over there, they are just ready for a beautifully photographed, sensitive portrayal of Edwardian period life, full of belters.

I hope he's convinced. I know it will be better when people are signed and the movie is an established fact, but at the moment I feel the strain of dealing with bigger egos than I became used to at the BBC – where people were just falling over themselves to get near a 'Ripping Yarn'!

Wednesday, November 25th

To Park Square West for Python writing. Very cold today. The house in which Python has been through so much now has a beleaguered air. As Anne and family have moved out to Dulwich it's now just an office, and a temporary one at that. But we are well looked after. Jackie [Parker] scurries about making us coffee, setting out biscuits and nuts and putting Tabs for Graham and Perrier for the rest of us in the fridge. The result is that we ingest steadily. Anne even ensures that a plate of sweets – Glacier mints, chewing gum and Polos – is on the table after our quiche and salad lunch.

Usual desultory chat – about *Brideshead*[1] on TV again – generally agreed it's overblown. TJ wants to talk about sex or get angry about the way Thorn-EMI have put *Brian* onto video, cropping it for TV. John will suddenly call me over: 'Mickey. Tell me what books you've read in the last four months.' Today I give him Al Levinson's *Travelogs* to read. It sends him quite apoplectic. He cannot understand how people can write modern poetry. 'It makes me quite Fawltyish,' he cries.

We proceed well on a general pattern and order of sketches. But at one point the Oxford/Cambridge split, avoided most successfully for the rest of this week, suddenly gapes. The point on which we argue is not a major one, but John rationalises his obstinacy as being the result of his grasp of 'the structure'. It's hard work, but in the end he wins his point.

I find myself telling TJ that I shall be mightily relieved when this next Python film is done and out of the way and we don't have to write together for another four years.

Monday, November 30th

Full of Monday hope and optimism, I launch into Python writing. Feel much less rushed, muddled and negative than on Friday.

To Covent Garden for a special tenth anniversary meal given by Geoffrey and Eyre Methuen for the Pythons.

All of us are there, as well as wives, except Alison Jones (who is out planning a campaign of action against school cuts). Anne and Jonathan, Nancy Lewis [our Python manager in America] and several Eyre Methuen types. A beautiful Gumby cake and indoor fireworks adorn the table in our own dining room.

Eric is in a suit, and myself too – otherwise all the Pythons look exactly the

---

[1] An 11-part adaptation of Evelyn Waugh's book had begun on Granada Television in October, and proved hugely popular. Jeremy Irons was Charles, Anthony Andrews Sebastian and Diana Quick Julia. Charles Sturridge directed.

same as they always did. Graham is there with David, and I sit next to John's new wife, Barbara. She says she desperately wants to take him back to LA for a few months, but he won't go as it gives him the creeps.

Tuesday, December 1st

Into Python meeting at 10.30. I read the large chunk that TJ and I have put together right from the start to beyond 'Middle of the Film' and into the 'randy' sequence – which goes exceptionally well. The whole lot is very well received and even applauded.

JC and GC have written some first-class stuff about an Ayatollah, but then one or two of their later scenes – especially a torture sequence – drags on and becomes a bore. Eric has written a couple of nice things and plays us a song he's recorded – 'Christmas in Heaven'.

We discuss which of the Pythons has talked the most in group activities since we began 13 years ago. John will have it that I'm the outright winner, but I think he greatly underestimates himself and, of course, Terry J. Graham happily accepts the Trappist sixth position, and when JC wants to know whether he or TJ talk most I have to say it's absolutely equal, because whatever statement one of them makes is almost automatically contradicted by the other.

Then much talk of where we go to write in January. GC wants to go to Rio for naughty reasons. I suggest a mountain chalet in cool, clear Alpine air. But swimming and associated aquatic releases are considered important. No conclusion. Except that we don't go to Rio.

Watch *Brideshead*. Halfway through, when Charles is just about to crack Julia, the doorbell rings and we're brought down to mundane earth with the news that the sun-roof on the Mini has been slashed open and the cassette/tuner has been ripped out. The police seem wholly unconcerned with the possibility of apprehending anyone. 'Be round in the next couple of days,' is their reaction.

Wednesday, December 2nd

TJ arrives at 1.30. Unfortunately only a small part of the section I'm rather proud of makes TJ laugh, so we ditch most of it and, in the two and a half hours remaining, cobble together a possible penultimate sequence, starting with the Ayatollah breaking into the sex lecture and the firing squad of menstruating women. It's mainly TJ's work.

Neville rings with the best news so far on *The Missionary*. Irene Lamb, the casting director who was so good on *Time Bandits* has read the script and likes it 'immensely'. Clearly she's had a most positive effect on Neville. Tonight he says 'You know, Michael, I think that *very* little needs changing.' John Gielgud is available, and Irene has already made the best suggestion so far on the knotty problem of Lady Ames – Anne Bancroft.

Saturday, December 5th

Buy *Variety*, *Screen International* and croissants. All are nice. *Time Bandits* still No. 1 in the US after three weeks, with *Raiders of the Lost Ark* chasing behind.

I drive over to Notting Hill for meeting on *Missionary*.

Some very good ideas come from our session and I find RL's suggestions – especially for setting each scene somewhere interesting, trains, etc – very encouraging and exciting.

At half past five Denis O'B arrives, and we have our first meeting together – DO'B, RL, Neville and myself. I've brought a bottle of champagne with which we christen the film.

Then some thoughts on casting. RL floats Laurence Olivier, with whose wife he's working at the moment. Denis throws up his eyebrows in horror. 'He's a sick man!' This rattles RL a bit and nothing is solved.

I drive Hollywood's currently most successful executive producer back to Hyde Park Corner, in my Mini with the slashed roof lining hanging down above his head.

Sunday, December 6th

Time for quick breakfast. Drive rapidly, for it's a Sunday morning, over to Clarendon Cross.

Richard is already in his office with his business partner Peter Broxton. They're looking at Loncraine-Broxton toy ideas for 1982. Boiled sweets in a box which is a moulded resin mock-up of a boiled sweet wrapper.

We begin, or rather continue, our work on the *Missionary* script at half past nine and work, very thoroughly, without interruption, until midday. Careful concentration and analysis. This is the least funny, but very necessary stage of the script. Does it convince? Do the characters fulfil a function? Is there a moral? Is the story clearly told? And so on.

Monday, December 7th

Write a grovelling letter to Sir Alec Guinness, accompanying a script, then to meeting with Denis O'B. I'm there for nearly three hours. I try to keep our thoughts on *The Missionary*, to impress upon Denis that I think he has been over-optimistic in only allowing £1.6 million budget. He in turn tells me that it is the most expensive of the three films HandMade Productions are planning for 1982. Mai Zetterling's *Scrubbers* is £525,000 and *Privates on Parade* (with J Cleese) is £1.2 million. But he won't give me final cut in the contract – says only Python get that and Gilliam didn't on *Time Bandits*.

The dynamic and shifty-eyed duo of Jeff Katzenberg and Don Simpson[1] are back in town. But this time, over a drink and inexhaustible servings of nuts amongst the green fronds of the Inn on the Park lobby, they pitch to all of us, bar John Cleese.

Basically they don't want to lose out again as they did on *Brian* and *Time Bandits*. They want us badly and sugar this with rather unjustifiable statements of the 'You're better now than you ever were' variety. Unfortunately I have to leave at 8.30 before the 'nitty-gritty' is discussed, but I can feel the incorrigibly plausible double act beginning to soften the Pythons' notorious antipathy to Hollywood majors.

Tuesday, December 8th

All quiet. Everywhere. Even at eight o'clock. Helen the first to notice the snow. Everywhere. Not a sprinkling fast turning to slush, but a 14-carat four-inch-thick blanket of snow, which is still being quietly augmented from a low, heavy, colourless sky. Lovely to see Rachel at the window of the sitting room in her long nightie, unable to take her eyes off the wonder of it all.

Wednesday, December 9th

To a viewing theatre to see *Elephant Man*. A private showing, organised by Neville so we could see the most recent performance of Anne Bancroft.

A very fine film. Admirable in its unsensational, underplaying treatment of the man. Some weird and wonderful images of London mark David Lynch out as a most original director. Almost unbearably moving for an hour, then somehow the attitudes became so clean – liberals versus working-class louts and drunks – that I lost some of the intensity of involvement which I had when [John] Hurt was a piteous, grunting creature being treated kindly for the first time.

---

[1] In 1982, Simpson was superseded as head of production at Paramount by Katzenberg. He nevertheless went on to co-produce successes like *Beverly Hills Cop* and *Top Gun*. He lived hard and died of a drug overdose in 1996.

I think Anne Bancroft could be too old and maybe too strongly dramatic. Lady A must have a skittishness ... a light, naughty side, of which, I think, youth may be a not inconsiderable part.

Friday, December 11th: Southwold

A cold grey morning. Helen rings to warn us of more heavy snowfalls in London, at least double what came down on Tuesday and it's still falling. Four people have been killed in a train accident in thick snow in Buckinghamshire and Ipswich Station has closed. So I decide to stay put.

Denis rings. He has given Loncraine the fee and percentage he asked for, but wants to defer L's last £5,000 until he's brought the picture in on budget. Loncraine refuses and won't even meet Denis until the deferment is sorted out. DO'B wants to be tough – walk away and let RL come running back to him – but fears that this will have a deleterious effect on relationships. I agree with this. I also think the money being fought over is so paltry in view of Loncraine's value to the project. So Denis reluctantly backs down.

All this over a crackly line from London, whilst next door, in my little writing room overlooking the snowswept fields, with the tiny two-bar electric fire, is my script and my scribbles, on which nearly £2 million-worth of expenditure depends.

Sunday, December 13th

As I write (7 p.m.), wind is flicking snow against my writing room windows, there are reports that blizzards have hit the South-West and the electricity has failed there too. A bomb has gone off in a car in Connaught Square, killing two, and there is a news blanket over the army take-over in Poland.

An almost apocalyptically gloomy day. The sort of day to make one question the point of writing comedy – or writing anything. Actually it also makes me feel, so far, comfortable, cosy and rather anxious to get on with work. But then I have money to afford light and heat and food and drink in abundance, and I have four other bright, lively, busy people in the house with me. I *am* one of the fortunate ones, this bleak snowswept, wind-howling evening.

Monday, December 14th

Disappointment on the faces of the children as the snow has been whittled down to brown slushy piles. I have a clear work day at home. Neville rings – says he has budgeted *Missionary*, and it comes out at £2.5 million overall – £1.3 million beyond Denis's first figure and 0.5 million beyond the Loncraine estimate. But Neville very level-headed about it, says there are trims that can be made, but this is what he will present Denis with.

Wednesday, December 16th

Below freezing again – making this Day Nine of the very cold wintry spell. But clear skies. Work well on script in the morning.

To bed at 12.30. George H rang earlier in the evening. He was anxious that I would have to give up some of my *Time Bandits* money as a result of possible renegotiations and he didn't think I ought to. He was very flattering about my role in keeping the thing together. Very touched.

Monday, December 21st

The forecasted thaw in nearly two weeks of freezing weather did not materialise and we wake to thick, swirling snow, two to three inches deep, which has once again caught everyone by surprise.

Go to see *Chariots of Fire*, as I'm dining with Puttnam tomorrow. A very fine and noble film – like a sophisticated advert for the British Way of Life. Some marvellous, memorable sequences and a riveting performance by Ben Cross as Harold Abrahams. I came out feeling as I used to when we saw films like *Dambusters* 25 years ago.

Found disturbingly similar sequences in *Chariots* and *The Missionary*, and also began to get colly-wobbles about *Missionary* casting. Ian Holm and John Gielgud merely will emphasise how similar we are to other British films. But then we haven't got Ian Holm or Gielgud yet.

Tuesday, December 22nd

Very cold and gloomy with swirls of snow. Ice in Julia Street for a fortnight now.

Have lunch appointment with David Puttnam. Just about to brave the elements when Neville rings with the news that Gielgud has turned down the Lord Ames part. What stings me more is that there was no particular reason given – he just didn't want to do it.

I gave up the attempt to drive to Odin's and slithered down traffic-packed side streets. Puttnam about 20 minutes late. He's immediately friendly, open, and he does seem to know everybody, especially amongst the 'establishment' of TV and films – Alasdair Milne, Huw Wheldon. He meets them on all his committees. Nice story that Huw Wheldon was to have been in *Chariots of Fire*, but couldn't do it and was deputised at the last minute by Lindsay Anderson.

Puttnam talks at a clipped, brisk pace, as if there's so much to say and so little time to say it. I think he's proud of his success and his work rate – a revealing cliché about being 'just a boy from a grammar school ...' He's complimentary about *Ripping Yarns* – thinks the toast scene in 'Roger of the Raj' one of the funniest things he's ever seen.

He's keen, almost over-keen, to talk business, and writes down the names of a couple of books I mention to him as filmable (*Good Man in Africa* and *Silver City*). He says Goldcrest Productions have a lot of money and promises to get one of the bosses to ring me re the financing of the next Python movie. He also sounds quite positive about *Greystoke*, with its £1 million forest set, coming to Shepperton.

Christmas Day, Friday, December 25th

And it is a White Christmas. The snow is not fresh, deep, crisp and even, but it's only a couple of days old and soon the clouds clear and give it a sparkling brightness – of the sort that is always depicted but never happens.

Tom opens his stocking at 2.30 and goes to sleep again, but we don't get jumped on until eight o'clock. A bedful of all the Palins (except Granny) as Helen and I undo our stockings.

Tuesday, December 29th

At one I have to drive into town for lunch with Ray Cooper to discuss his doing the part of the Bishop. Ray has laid on a lunch at Duke's Hotel, in a Dickensian side street off St James's and opposite 'The house from which Frédéric Chopin left to make his last public appearance at the Guildhall'.

Small, expensive, immaculately tasteful little dining room – rather in the Denis class of spending, though. A bottle of Corton Charlemagne, oeuf en gelée (rather tasteless) and some very delicious fegato alla Veneziana. We talk about casting of *The Missionary*. Ray's choices for Lady A would be Helen Mirren or Faye Dunaway – both strong on projecting sexuality. And he knows Dunaway.

Wonderful table-talk from the only other occupied table – 'I have a little Bulgarian.' 'There's quite a lot of jewellery Brenda doesn't wear all the time.' And things like this.

Up into Soho to meet Eric for a drink at the French Pub. The French is full of weird people, who seem already drunk when they come in. One man is kneeling on the bar trying to pull up the barmaid's skirt. It's all rather like being in a Chris Orr print.

Eric and I, in quite playful mood after the champagne, drive over to Claridge's where we are to meet Sherry Lansing, the studio head of Twentieth Century Fox, and the most powerful woman in American movies.

What Sherry Lansing offers us in Claridge's is much more straightforward and uncluttered by looks, whispers and double-talk than what Paramount offered us at the Inn on the Park. Twentieth Century Fox want the next Python movie and they are prepared to finance it and distribute it however and wherever we want. The board would give us complete control over its production unless they thought the script totally worthless. Tim Hampton would be Fox's representative and could be used as little or as much as we wanted. It was as clear and as positive as that. We told her she was making a big mistake and she laughed. I liked her very much. We said we didn't like *History of the World Part One* and she didn't seem to mind.

At 8.00, with a kiss on both cheeks, she left us and I took Eric back in my grubby little Mini and we decided that we should get drunk together more often.

Thursday, December 31st

Rather a miserable day on which to end the year. I feel quite a few degrees below good health. Nothing very dramatic, just aches and lethargy. This deterioration could not have come at a worse time, as I have Neville chasing me and Richard Loncraine returning from Wales, doubtless vital and restored by Christmas, to read with great anticipation the new script that I have put together. The final, very important twists and turns must be written today and tomorrow.

I set to, but lose quite a bit of time talking with Denis (from Switzerland) and Neville (about casting – he's suddenly strong on Ann-Margret).

I think I'm probably cleaning my teeth when 1982 begins. Helen and I see the New Year in without fuss – on fruit juice and Disprins, not champagne, for me. I hope the way I feel is not an augury for 1982, when, if all goes to plan, I shall need every scrap of energy.

1982

Sunday, January 3rd

Up at ten feeling fully restored and unbearably bouncy for a while. I take Rachel up to the playground on Parliament Hill. The sun's shining and it's very warm for early January. Lots of the attractions in the playground are empty or broken. It's a sadly declined place. This gentle, unambitious meandering walk up to the swings is something I haven't done much in the last three or four years, and it used to be de rigueur every weekend we spent in London, when the children were small. I forget that Rachel still is small.

We have a lovely time together, pottering, nattering, playing at trains in the Adventure Playground. It makes me sad and nostalgic – and this makes me cross, because I know I'm regretting being older – or getting older, anyway.

Monday, January 4th

To see Phoebe Nicholls, who was Cordelia in *Brideshead*, and who I'm recommended as a Deborah. Meet her in Langan's Brasserie. She's much slighter than I'd expected, with ringlets of curly dark hair, and big dark eyes, in a narrow little oval face.

I embark on a laborious explanation of the story and she watches in politely rapt attention. 'Oh, but it's lovely,' she says, as though it's a living thing. A baby or a new puppy. I instinctively feel that she will be interesting. She has a certain delicateness about her which I think will help convince the audience that she really *can* think Fallen Women are women who've hurt their knees.

Tuesday, January 5th

To EuroAtlantic Towers at 10.00 for a casting meeting re *Missionary*. Gielgud's rejection has left us with two less adequate possibilities of replacement – Donald Pleasance and Trevor Howard.

Perhaps our strongest advance in this morning's session was to eliminate any spectacular, but possibly dumb, beauties in favour of Maggie Smith – attractive, striking, skilful actress. Parts too, we hope, for Ronnie Barker and Ian Holm.

Friday, January 8th

Ominously quiet outside as we wake. Another heavy snowfall – the third already this winter and the papers are full of articles about The New Ice Age and the Frozen Eighties. It's thin powdery stuff blown all over the place by a bitter north-east wind. It's coming through the cracks in my study window and has covered Tom's homework books with a thin layer of snow.

We struggle up to William Ellis School at midday with William, for his interview with the headmaster. Have to sit in the corridor for 15 to 20 minutes with boys thundering by between lessons. Quite liked the atmosphere there. Am in my worst old jeans, sneakers and a windcheater – my father would never have entered the headmaster's study in less than a suit and spit-and-polished shoes.

Saturday, January 9th

Drive car out through snowdrifts and slither down into an agreeably empty London for a viewing of the *Hollywood Bowl* film – the first since Julian [Doyle] spent weeks trying to lick it into shape in LA. And it is greatly improved – linked far more smoothly and the sense of live occasion much stronger now there are better-chosen cut-backs to audience, etc. In short, a film which we now feel we will not be ashamed of. Performances very strong, particularly Eric.

Home by two o'clock. It really is so cold that all my systems seem to seize up. An hour in a catatonic trance before the sitting room fire improves things and I then set to with all the last-minute *Missionary* calls – to Richard and Denis (who has rung John Calley[1] in the US to ask whether he thinks Maggie Smith or Anne Bancroft would be the bigger box-office name. Calley told him neither meant a thing!) He says, as he puts it, I can have my head over Maggie Smith and he won't stand in my way.

Call George in Henley at nine o'clock. After a few rather terse exchanges he says 'You're obviously not a *Dallas* fan, then' and I realise I've interrupted a favourite viewing.

It had been decided that, as with The Life of Brian *and Barbados, we needed somewhere exotic to finalise the new film script; Jamaica had been chosen.*

---

[1] Calley, a friend of Denis's, is one of the most successful producers in the film industry. He headed Warners and was later CEO of Sony Pictures, owners of Columbia.

Sunday, January 10th: Jamaica

Touch down in Montego Bay about 8.30. Soft, stifling blanket of hot, humid air takes me by surprise.

A large black limousine is backed up outside and Brian, our driver (why is there always a Brian wherever Python goes?), squeezes us all and luggage in.

About an hour's cramped and uncomfortable drive through the night along the north coast of the island. We turn into the drive of a long, low, unadorned rectangular mansion, called 'Unity', some time after ten o'clock. A youngish black man, Winford, and a middle-aged, beaming black lady, Beryl, come out to settle us in.

Our main problem is the selection of bedrooms. Four of the rooms, all off a long passageway/landing on the first floor, are splendid – spacious and well-furnished and one has a full tester four-poster. But there are three other rather small rooms, less well-furnished and clearly intended as children's rooms, annexed on to the main bedrooms.

So we sit in the grand downstairs sitting room, with a fine selection of polished wooden cabinets and Persian carpets, and wing-backed armchairs and some attractive maritime oil paintings, and draw our bedrooms out of the hat. J Cleese has been very crafty and claims there is only one bed which he, being so tall, can fit in, and that so happens to be in one of the 'master' bedrooms, so he isn't included.

Terry G and I pick the two sub-bedrooms. At least they all look across the lawn to the sea (about 100 yards away) and mine has a bathroom. A heavily stained bathroom with rotting lino and no hot water, but a bathroom all the same – though I share it with Mr Cleese, who has the big double bedroom of which mine is the 'attachment'.

Winford advises us not to swim tonight as there are barracuda which come in from behind the reef at night-time. This puts a stop to any midnight high-jinks, though Terry J goes and sits in the sea. But it's a lovely night with a big full moon and, apart from the inequality of rooms, I think Unity will serve us well.

GC is quietly puffing away as we sit outside. He looks like any trustworthy GP. But his pipe is well-stocked with Brian's ganja.

Monday, January 11th: Unity, Runaway Bay, Jamaica

I sleep very little. Possibly three and a half to four hours. Doze and listen to the sea. I sit up, turn on the light and read our script at 5 a.m. It's light just before seven and I walk outside, having unlocked my room door and the heavy iron

With Laurel and Hardy in the garden. I bought them off a market stall on Canal Street, New York. Hardy's neck broke in the plane's luggage locker and since then I've had to look after them very carefully.

'Take Rachel on a mystery tour. By lucky chance there is a raising of the bridge as we are there. Watch from an abandoned little jetty upstream from the Tower' (October 27th 1984)

Tom with Denis the cat.

The eternal dream. By a pool, with a book, somewhere hot. Kenyan holiday, January 1983

'I've got to have fruit!' Tied to a tree with Shelley Duvall,
as Vincent and Pansy in *Time Bandits*, 1981

Shooting the *Time Bandits'* Giant on the roof of Wembley Studios.
Among those looking bored, Maggie Gilliam and Julian Doyle on camera.

Pythons in Hollywood. MP, Terry J, Eric I, Graham C, Terry G and John C.
Behind us, the Bowl. September 1980

On the set of *Time Bandits*, (from left to right) Neville C Thompson, Associate Producer,
John Cleese (Robin Hood), George Harrison and Denis O'Brien, Executive Producers.
Summer 1980

John rehearses his Silly Walk.

Dead Parrot sketch always went down well. Never more so than with the performers.

Disrobing after the judge's summing up.

The Missionary, 1982

Fortescue and his women. Caught between fiancée Deborah Fitzbanks (Phoebe Nicholls, left) and Lady Ames, benefactress, (Maggie Smith, right)

Nepotism at work. Rachel Palin, (centre), on the set at Finsbury Circus, April 24 1982

'No people, no sun-oil, no deck-chairs, no poolside bars selling over-priced drinks'. Bathing in the waterfall at Shava Lodge after the Kenya shoot, June 13 1982

'As I wait for the clouds to clear the sun, I see our two Executive Producers emerging from the orchard' Richard Loncraine, director, George H and Denis O'Brien on location, May 1 1982

John Kelleher of HandMade (centre) and myself, collect our most cherished, and only, award, from the French town of Chamrousse. 'I check in the atlas. It does exist' March 26 1985

Charles Fortescue, man with a Mission.

Missionary publicity. Judging, and participating, in a custard pie throwing contest at the Southern Methodist University, Dallas, Texas, October 7th 1982

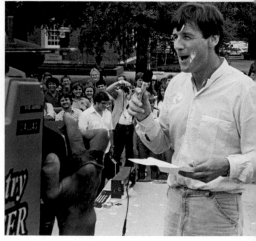

Playing a TV Presenter for *Comic Roots*. Behind me, on the left, the house in which I was born and brought up. Sheffield, July 1983

doors at the top of the stairs and then the iron and wood double doors out to the garden. Clearly this property is a target.

The house is right beside the sea, only a lawn and a few trees between us and the Caribbean – and the trees are healthy-looking and have leaves of many and rich colours. The house is kept spotless, and already the leaf-scratcher is removing the six or seven leaves that have fallen on the patio overnight. The house is not so grand as Heron Bay [the villa in Barbados where we worked on *Life of Brian*] – there are no soaring Palladian columns. Its simple shape and plain limestone construction dates, they say, two or three hundred years back, when it was the chief house on the Runaway Bay plantation. The mountains rise up behind the house and across to the west.

I sit at the table and read my script. There are one or two young black boys hanging around the beach. One of them comes over and sits down and introduces himself as Junior and offers me ganja and a trip to see Bob Marley's grave. He says he's 19 and he grows his own pot up in the mountains.

Run up the beach as far as the Runaway Bay Hotel and back. Nearly a mile. Then a swim in the limpid, lukewarm waters of the Caribbean.

Breakfast is good coffee, fresh grapefruit and eggs and bacon and toast from very boring sliced bread.

Everyone's reactions to the script are then discussed. All of us, to some extent, feel disappointed. I think the material is still very static. It could still be a radio show. The rain seems set in for the day as we sit around for a long afternoon discussion session.

It's agreed that we should proceed from the material we have and create a strong story or framework to contain it. Some silly moments in this free and fairly relaxed session – including a title from TG, 'Jesus's Revenge'. But though everyone occasionally flashes and sparkles nothing ignites.

Supper is early – about 6.30. We've bought in some wine from the super-market across the road and we have a delicious starter of fish mixed with akee fruit – a little black, olive-like fruit off one of the garden trees.

Then a group of us go up to the Club Caribbean next door. A black lady pinches Graham's bottom and GC altruistically turns her over to TJ. It turns out she is a hooker. She looks a nice, open, smiley lady, and keeps dropping her price in a determined effort to interest any of us. As TJ finally leaves, empty-handed, she asks him for two dollars.

Wednesday, January 13th: Jamaica

An early breakfast, and splitting into groups by 9.30. Terry J and Terry G, Eric and JC, myself and Graham.

GC and I, however, soon find ourselves in one of the most bizarre and distracted writing sessions of all time. Beryl, the cook, was under the impression that someone would take her up to the market, eight miles away, for all the provisions she will need for the Jamaican food we've asked her to produce. So GC and I decide to take her and work on the way.

It starts quite well as we drive up winding mountain roads for a half-hour and emerge into a busy little township with a stout stone Anglican church set in the middle of it. GC and I make a quick shopping sortie for shoes and swimming trunks then back to the car. Vegetables in the back, but no Beryl.

Still talking over our idea for a John Buchan-type story framework, we have a Red Stripe beer in a small bar. Beryl comes back and deposits fish, but then has to sally back into the market for yams.

Halfway down the perfectly named Orange Valley, beside stone walls and almost classic English parkland, is an akee-seller. We skid to a halt. When we proceed again we not only have akees, but also two black boys who want a lift. Stop at the supermarket for bully beef, and our writing session finally turns into the gates of Unity two and a half hours after we set out.

I ring Rachel and wish her a happy seventh birthday in still-frozen London.

After lunch we sit and present our ideas. I present GC's and mine. A breathtaking, marvellously choreographed musical overture all about fish – with us in spectacular fishy costumes. Then into an exciting Buchan mystery tale, involving strange disappearances, unexplained deaths, all pointing to Kashmir. The hero would have to unravel the story by various clues, which bring in our existing sketches.

John and Eric have taken the view that the film is primarily about sex and they've reinstated the Janine/girls' paradise idea that I'd gone off a year ago. Even less response to this idea.

TG and TJ have gone back to first Python principles to link it – a rag-bag of non-sequiturs and complex connections. It's full and frantic and, when TJ's finished describing it, there is silence. It's as if no-one can really cope with any more 'solutions'. As if this is the moment that this material – the best of three years' writing – finally defeated us.

I take Eric's advice and we walk up to the Runaway Bay Hotel and sit on the terrace there and have three very strong rum punches and get very silly and laugh a lot and devise the idea of a Yorkshire Heaven, in which Yorkshiremen are revealed to have been the chosen people.

Thursday, January 14th: Jamaica

Wake to sunshine and a feeling that today is make-or-break for the film. We certainly cannot continue stumbling into the darkness as we did yesterday.

TJ says that, from the timings of the sketches we all like alone, we have over

100 minutes of material. This seems to spur people into another effort. TJ suggests a trilogy. The idea of a rather pretentious Three Ages of Man comes up and a title 'Monty Python's Meaning of Life', to which Eric adds the sub-head 'See it now! Before it's out of date'.

We decide to group the material together into phoney pseudo-scientific headings – 'Birth', 'Fighting Each Other' and 'Death'. Suddenly ideas come spilling out and within an hour there seems to be a remarkable change in the film's fortunes.

Friday, January 15th: Jamaica

Writing has definitely taken a turn for the better. Eric, TJ and I in the big room make some encouraging progress on linking the 'War'/'Fighting Each Other' section. TG stands on a sea-urchin just before lunch. He's in some agony for a bit and has about nine or ten black quills in his heel. Doc Chapman ministers to him. Neville T rings from London to say the [*Missionary*] script is probably two hours long. When I tell the Pythons that Sir Laurence Olivier has never heard of us, he is heaped with abuse.

Out to dinner with Jonathan and Shelagh Routh.[1] This involves a convoy into Ocho Rios and beyond.

Rather characterful house, very different from the mansion of Unity. It's a collection of wood-framed cottages, set on the edge of a low cliff down to the sea. Foliage everywhere. About 20 people amongst the foliage. An Australian diplomat – who, at 25, seems to run their High Commission – his Texan wife, who seems bored with Australian diplomacy. There's an English artist called Graham, tall and rather aristocratic, a French/Australian who writes novels and tells me that Jamaica is a very restless society and not what it seems on the surface. Much resentment of whites.

On my way from the Rouths' a man in khaki tries to hitch a lift, but I speed on. Only later do I realise I've driven straight through an army roadblock.

Saturday, January 16th: Jamaica

Snooze a little, watch Eric doing Tai Chi on the lawn, then breakfast at 9.00, and set to with Eric and TJ to put the last section of *The Meaning of Life* into shape. Not very inspired work and we get rather bogged down on the 'Christmas in Heaven' song.

---

[1] Jonathan Routh introduced and presented the enormously popular *Candid Camera* TV series in the 1960's. He died in 2008.

At 4.30 everyone returns from various postcard-writing, T-shirt-buying trips to read through work assembled over the last three days. JC and GC and TG have come up with a tremendously good, strong opening set in a hospital during the birth of a child, and there is only one section of the film about which people have doubts.

The *Meaning of Life* theme and structure does seem to have saved the film and justified our being here. There are now tightenings and improvements to be done and songs to be written and these will occupy us for our four remaining writing days. Tomorrow we have off.

A beautiful 'zebra' butterfly flutters around us as we read. A good omen, perhaps.

Monday, January 18th: Jamaica

GC announces at breakfast, after one of his regular and interminable phone calls to London, that he is going to sue Denis O'B. This causes a few dropped jaws over the toast and marmalade. Apparently GC, having enlisted the help of Oscar Beuselinck[1] to try and buy back the *Yellowbeard* rights from Denis, who keeps increasing his demands and conditions, has just heard that Beuselinck has found enough ground for negligence in Denis, and Anne, to proceed with a lawsuit. As GC says, the shit has hit the fan in London.

All of us are concerned that Anne should not be hauled over the coals – especially as she has been doing everything to try and improve GC's financial position over the last few months by getting the rest of us to withhold payments, etc. But GC lights his pipe in determined fashion and sounds terse and unmoving.

Late lunch, and at 4.30 Jonathan and Shelagh Routh arrive to collect and lead us to a place called Round Hill, where a friend of theirs is laying on a beach party for us.

Pleasant, countrified drive, avoiding mongooses which are apt to suddenly scuttle across the road. When JC returned from his trip to Kingston and said he'd passed four dead dogs and a calf, GC speculated that journey distances in Jamaica could be categorised quite usefully as a 'two dead dog journey' or a 'three dog, one pig journey'.

Round Hill turns out to be an estate of luxurious holiday homes set on a headland with very beautiful views. We are taken to a little house higher up the hill, set amongst the trees, for a party given by 'a prominent Washington horsewoman'. She welcomes us with a bright, quick, sympathetic smile and

---

[1] Prominent and flamboyant entertainment lawyer, whom Python had consulted after Bernard Delfont and EMI had pulled out of *Life of Brian* at the last minute.

sincere handshake. Her long blonde hair is swept up on top of her head most dramatically, but giving the physical impression that her face has somehow been swept up as well and is pinned painfully somewhere in the scalp. She wears a long white dress. I am in running shorts – thinking only that we were coming to a beach party.

JC lies flat on his back on the grass at one point, worrying the hostess who thinks he's passed out drunk. He is in a wicked mood and clearly hates these sorts of people.

Thursday, January 19th: Jamaica

In the afternoon we read what has been done so far. JC and GC's 'Death' sequence is not in the same class as their marvellous 'Birth' opener of last week, so everyone becomes disconsolate again. It's too late in the afternoon to whip up much enthusiasm, so a rather important day peters out.

The two Terries and I accept Winford's invitation to go to a local birthday party celebration.

We walk about half a mile up to Bent's Bar. It's 8.30 and a four-piece Jamaican band – rhumba box (home-made and very effective), a thumping banjo, a guitar and a high-pitched, effective little singer. He looks well-stoned by 8.30 and, as the evening goes on, he becomes progressively more incoherent until he ends up clearing the tables whilst some imitator takes his place in front of the band.

The birthday is of Mr Bent, a large, paternal-looking black with greying frizzy hair, who introduces himself to Terry with a broad smile, a firm handshake, and the words 'Hello, I'm Bent'. He, like most others we've met, either has been to England or has relations there. I note that not even the most courteous Jamaicans have said anything about their relatives enjoying England.

Wednesday, January 20th: Jamaica

There isn't a lot to do but type up. It's decided to meet in London for three days in mid-February and then to take a final decision on whether to go ahead.

No-one, I think, feels we have a *Brian* on our hands, but there is a hope that we have something which we all feel we could film in the summer.

And so to bed, for the last time, in my 'servant's' quarters.

Sunday, January 24th

Late afternoon settle to read *The Missionary*. It is indeed a hefty script – 149 pages, and closely written, too. Glad to find that my own notes for cuts correspond by and large with Neville's and those suggestions of Penny Eyles[1] who timed the script. Neville rings, anxious to know when I can produce the 30-minute shorter version.

Tuesday, January 26th

There has been good news this morning – Maggie Smith likes the script and wants to meet. Apparently her comment was 'The fellers get the best lines, so I want the best frocks.'

Opening of Eric's *Pass the Butler* at the Globe. Crowd of celebrities and celebrity-spotters throng the cramped foyer as this is first night. Meet Lauren Hutton, model, actress and, as it turns out, world traveller. 'Ask me about any island,' she challenges. I catch her out with the Maldives. But she does seem to have been everywhere and is going to give us some information on Sierra Leone [which we'd chosen for a family winter break]. She advises us to have every possible injection there is.

Wednesday, January 27th

Down to the Cavendish early for the rest of my inoculations. Young male doctor this time, with vaguely jokey patter. He arranged in a line all the various syringes, then went to work. Tetanus followed typhoid and cholera into my upper left arm, then he stuck gamma globulin in my left buttock and waggled it about (the buttock, not the gamma globulin).

Back home for another two hours' work on the script, then down to the London Library. There is a two-day rail strike on as train drivers battle against BR Management's latest 'modernisation' plans. Park in St James's Square, and select some books on East African missionaries amongst the labyrinthine passageways and dark back rooms of this eccentric library. I get lost in the Topography section and can't find Uganda.

Come away at half past five armed with such gems as *In the Heart of Savagedom*.

I'm outside the Berkeley Hotel, where we're to meet Maggie Smith, a quarter of an hour early.

---

[1] One of the most sought-after script supervisors in the UK. She'd worked with me on Stephen Frears' *Three Men in a Boat* and on *Monty Python and The Holy Grail*.

I realise that this meeting with Maggie Smith is one of the most crucial on *The Missionary* so far. She is the first 'name' we seem to have a chance of securing, and her part is the most crucial in the film apart from my own. She knows nothing about me, yet is expected to help create with me the complex relationship that is at the heart of the story.

She arrives about ten minutes late. Reminds me of Angela somehow – with her neat, almost elfin features. She is dressed expensively and with a hint of flamboyance and her red hair looks as though it's just been done. Which leads me to wonder, just for a moment, if she had taken all this trouble for the meeting.

I congratulate her on her *Evening Standard* Actress of the Year Award [for *Virginia*], which she won last night. She looks rather weary but she has an instantly likeable naturalness and there is no difficulty in feeling that one's known her for ages.

She was very cross that the 'fellers get the lines, I want the frocks' line had been quoted to us, and claims she never said that. She was a mite worried about Olivier as Lord Ames – and in a polite but unambiguous way made it clear she regards him as having a 'very odd' sense of humour (i.e. none).

Richard arrived, bubbling like an excited schoolboy. His keenness seemed like over-enthusiasm at times, especially contrasted with Maggie Smith's languor. She drank vodka and tonic and we drank Löwenbräus. I settled into the sofa, also affected by her calm. She had no problems, she said, about the script, and when we left, after an hour together, she kissed me warmly and her face lit up again and she congratulated me once more on the script and was gone.

Thursday, January 28th

Take an hour and a half for a run. The Heath chilly, muddy and grey. Then down to Broadcasting House, to which I have been invited to celebrate forty years of *Desert Island Discs*.

I arrive in the Council Chamber, a semi-circular room above the main entrance, just as a group photo is being taken. About 20 cameramen, and television video cameras photographing little dapper Roy Plomley, who sold the series to the BBC the year before I was born.

Clustering around him I can see the Beverley Sisters – all dressed alike – Michael Parkinson, not a hair out of place, Frankie Howerd, Lord Hill.[1] It's like being at Madame Tussaud's. I'm hustled into the far corner of the crowd,

[1] Best known as the BBC's Radio Doctor during the Second World War, he became Chairman of the BBC, retiring in 1972. He died in 1989.

next to the tall, slightly shambling figure of Roald Dahl. 'Let's just hope they've got wide-angle lenses,' he observes unenthusiastically.

I have to go and sign a book to be presented to Mr Plomley. I see Roald Dahl sitting quite happily on his own, so I go and introduce myself and bother him with praise. He confides that a good 'standard' popular kids' book is the way to make money. A successful children's author will do a lot better in the long run than Graham Greene. We talk about children being over-protected by authors, and he tells me that he has received many letters of complaint about his books from teachers, and *Danny* [*Champion of the World*] is banned in Denmark because it 'teaches children to cheat'.

We're having a jolly conversation and have only been photographed once, when Dr Jonathan Miller looms up, being frightfully energetic and effervescent and solicitously enquiring after my future plans because he does want to get Pythons back on stage – not doing Python, but Shakespeare or whatever. (Interesting that J Cleese had come up with the idea in Jamaica of the Pythons doing a Shakespeare play together.)

Friday, January 29th

Drive up to Bishop's Stortford to talk to the school sixth form.

Questions routine and orderly until one boy rose and asked 'How difficult is it to get into the BBC if you're not gay?' I couldn't quite meet this with cool equanimity, but I got my best laugh of the afternoon by telling the boy that I was sure he'd have no problem getting in. 'That naughty boy Robertson,' as I heard him referred to quite endearingly in the staff room afterwards.

Neville rang to tell me Olivier has asked for a million dollars to play Lord Ames. Which makes a decision very easy. Not Olivier.

Thursday, February 11th

Down to the London Library to procure books on prostitutes. They are all filed under 'S' for 'Sex' and I can't for the life of me find the 'Sex' section. End up abjectly having to ask a girl attendant. 'I'm looking for Sex,' is all I can say.

In the evening Helen plays badminton. I go out to see *Arthur*. Dudley very funny – manages to make all his jokes and gags have that attractive quality of spontaneous asides. That rare thing – a comedy with laughs all the way through *and* a happy ending. Sets me to thinking about the *Missionary* ending.

Friday, February 12th

Drive down to Methuen to look over Caroline Holden's artwork for *Small Harry*. It's bright and full of life and though on occasion her attention to detail lapses and she loses a face or an expression, I'm really very pleased. Take her for a drink at the Printer's Devil in Fetter Lane. She finished the book up at her parents' house – Mum and Dad helping out. Caroline still poor and having to work in a pub to make ends meet. I do hope the book does well for her sake.

Monday, February 15th

Drive over to Clarendon Cross, arriving there at ten. Spend the day with Richard and Irene seeing 24 young ladies at 15-minute intervals to select from amongst them our Fallen Women. By 6.00 we've talked, laughed and explained ourselves almost to a standstill.

Home. Talk to Denis, who rings to find out how we got on with the prostitutes. (George H terribly keen to be there during auditions.) Terry G rings spluttering with uncontrollable laughter. He had just finished reading 'Mr Creosote' and had to tell someone how near to jelly it had reduced him.

Wednesday, February 17th

We see about 20 more actresses. A half-dozen are good enough for speaking parts – and the results of Monday's work and today's are very encouraging. But other clouds on the horizon – mainly financial. Richard thinks that the Art Department budget is impracticably small and both Richard and Neville told me yesterday that there is no way the present script can be shot in nine weeks. It'll need ten at the minimum.

All those things to think of as I drive to Anne's for an afternoon Python session. A strange feeling to sit at the table listening to other people's offerings without having had time to provide anything myself. JC/GC have put together a quite funny Grim Reaper piece. Eric has written a new opening song and a very short but effective visual before the 'Penis Apology'. Terry J has also been prolific.

At the very end of the meeting, just as I'm off to see Denis O'B, Anne tells us that Graham would like us to meet Oscar Beuselinck, the lawyer, tomorrow. Why Graham couldn't tell us I don't know. It's another bombshell from Chapman – who evidently is still going to sue Denis and wants us all to meet

Oscar tomorrow and hear the whys and wherefores. All more than a little irritating.

Thursday, February 18th

Decide I shouldn't go to Graham's meeting with Oscar Beuselinck. Lawyers on the warpath are a dangerous breed and I am concerned that attending a meeting called specifically to point out all the bad points of Denis O'B may not be the best thing to do when I'm currently trying to get an extra £500,000 out of him. And Oscar would be only too keen to say he'd 'met with the Pythons'.

I have an hour or so of the afternoon left for writing before TJ arrives. We compare notes, then he goes off to the GC meeting, whilst I carry on extending the 'Hotel Sketch'.

A meeting with Denis. DO'B clearly won't accept Neville's latest budget figure of £2.5 million, but on the other hand he is not asking us to reduce, nor even stick at £2 million. He's now talking of £2.2 million. Our whole discussion is helped by the fact that Trevor Howard has accepted the part of Lord Ames. (Neville said he was especially keen to do it when he heard *I* was in it!)

Round to Clarendon Cross and then on to Julie's [Restaurant] for supper. We go through the script – take out the dockside sequence, which has some jokes but is very expensive, and also one or two short exteriors, and we find that we can still make cuts without irreparably damaging the film. Indeed, we have one very positive new idea, which is to open on a school honours board with the name being painted out.

Tuesday, March 2nd

Best news of last week is that Michael Hordern, who was reported to have turned down the part of Slatterthwaite, has now had second thoughts, likes the script, finds it 'immensely funny' and has been signed up. So Moretonhampstead, with Maggie Smith, Trevor Howard and Michael Hordern, is looking like a quality household.

Wednesday, March 3rd

Assailed with information (Irene), opinions (Richard) and warnings (Neville) on all sides as we attempt to cast the medium and small parts. Any featured (i.e.

speaking) actor has, under a new Equity agreement, to be 'bought out' – i.e. given enough pay to make up for the actor relinquishing rights on future TV, video and other sales. It boils down to a minimum of about £157.00 per day for a 'cast' actor. So the morning is one of continuous small compromises to cut down the use of such actors – a process which surely wouldn't please Equity if they saw it.

There are still some major roles unfilled. Graham Crowden has had a hip operation and may not be well enough to play the Bishop.[1] Richard suggests Denholm Elliott, other front-runners are Nigel Hawthorne and Ian Richardson. Elliott will be twice as expensive.

Ray Cooper comes over at lunch and meets Richard for the first time. They got on well, as I knew they would. Both are artists, and indeed Ray C endears himself to Richard by remembering him as a sculptor. Ray is to be Music Co-ordinator for *The Missionary*, which fills me with great confidence.

Bombshell of lunchtime, as far as Richard is concerned, anyway, is that Freddie Jones, for whom Richard was prepared to move heaven and earth to accommodate in the picture, now says he doesn't want to do it anyway. This has plunged Richard into a bad mood performance and he rails on about faithless actors and how shitty the entire thespian profession is. I blame his diet.

Friday, March 5th

Through exceptionally slow-moving traffic to Holland Park, to talk with Ken Lintott, who made my *Brian* beard and who is head of make-up on *The Missionary*. I've lost a lot of weight, he says. He wants me to try growing a moustache again.

Wednesday, March 10th

Neville says we've no more money left. Everything is accounted for. There's no spare. But the cast we're assembling is most encouraging. Even Celia Johnson may be on again. She likes the script, but wants the name of her character changed, as one of her greatest friends is Lady Fermoy! Denholm Elliott, Graham Crowden and Peter Vaughan look certain. Fulton Mackay less so, as he has been offered five weeks by Puttnam on a new Bill Forsyth picture.

Richard rings. Denis will not agree to the test viewing clauses RL wants in his director's contract. In America it is standard in Screen Directors' Guild

[1] In the end he took the part of the Reverend Fitzbanks, Fortescue's prospective father-in-law.

contracts that, should the producer want to alter the director's delivered cut, the director has the right to insist on there being two test screenings before audiences of not less than 500 people. Anyway Denis now says that this is out of the question. It's not really my problem, but I assure RL that I'll support him. He talks of leaving the picture, which I don't think is all that likely.

Thursday, March 11th

Work and run in the morning, then to Bermans to meet Trevor Howard. Find the great man in a first-floor dressing room, standing in stockinged feet half in and half out of a hound's-tooth tweed hunting outfit, surrounded by dressers and costume designers. To my surprise Howard strikes me as a diminutive figure. His full head of fine, carroty red hair stands out.

He gives me a rich, warm smile and shakes my hand as if he's really been wanting to meet me for ages. He talks sleepily and when after the fitting we suggest taking him out for a drink he brightens visibly. Though his breath already smells of alcohol, he says emphatically, 'Yes, why not! I've been on the wagon for three weeks and I feel *so* tired.' We take him down to Odin's. He has a gin and tonic, RL and I a bottle of Muscadet.

He keeps repeating how much he's looking forward to doing the part, though curiously, in the midst of all this enthusiasm, he expresses great concern over the brief little bedroom scene between Ames and the butler. He's very unhappy about any hint of homosexuality. We agree to talk about this later, and he leaves to collect his passport for a trip to China he's making for a British film week there.

Back to Bermans at 4.30 to meet Michael Hordern. He looks older and his face redder and veinier than I'd expected. He has a straggly beard – better advanced than my moustache – which he's growing for the BBC's *King Lear*. Quite eccentric in his delivery, and sentences tend to end abruptly and be completed with a sort of distinctive hand gesture. He says he can understand about Trevor Howard – worried about a 'machismo image' as Hordern puts it. The two of them worked together on *Heart of the Matter*, but Hordern is characteristically vague about the details.

Whilst at Bermans, Neville rings and asks to meet me as urgently as possible, as a problem has arisen over the credits. It transpires that Denholm Elliott wants star billing alongside Maggie S and Trevor H. I have no objection – I always tend to think that the problems start when people read the script and *don't* want a credit. But Denis won't have it.

Neville, who is in charge of negotiations with the artists, wants me to intercede with DO'B, who is skiing in Colorado at the moment.

Home for delayed supper at eleven o'clock, followed by three-quarters of an hour on the phone to DO'B in Colorado. The process of trying to change Denis's mind is like opening doors with a battering ram. Eventually they'll give, but one has to be prepared to patiently, insistently, repeatedly run at them from exactly the same direction each time.

Saturday, March 13th

It's a very bright, clear, sunny morning. Work in the garden, then take the children down to the London Dungeon. All three love it there – the frisson of fear is very cleverly maintained throughout, yet the place is not insidious or unpleasant. The victims of the rack and the murdered Thomas à Becket and the plague rats (live) all co-exist in a rather friendly, reassuring way.

Certainly all these dreadful horrors put all the children in a very good humour and we drive back across London Bridge to see the Barbican Centre, opened last week. It's a 'culture complex' within the Barbican estate. Approach, across a piazza, as they describe cold, windswept open spaces these days, to buildings that house the theatre, cinema, library and conference hall. In front of them is another 'piazza', with fountains and lots of captive water, which looks very green and stagnant and has napkins which have blown from the outdoor restaurant soggily drifting in it.

The place is full of lost people, and men with walkie-talkies looking anxious. The children love running up and down the stairs with mirrored ceilings or sitting in the comfortable new cinema. But at the moment it feels like a giant Ideal Home Exhibit, new and half unwrapped and not at all integrated with the rest of the Barbican estate – on which one sees nobody. But then those who can afford flats in the Barbican can probably also afford second homes for the weekend.

To the BBC by 6.30 [for an appearance on *Parkinson*]. In a hospitality suite I talk to Parky and he runs through the questions. Researcher Alex accompanies me everywhere – even to the toilets. At 7.30 the recording begins. Jimmy Savile is on first, then there's a brief chat from Andrew Lloyd Webber and a song from Marti Webb, then I stand listening to my introduction on the filthy piece of backstage carpet which leads – cue applause – to the spotless piece of carpet the viewers see and a seat next to Parky.

Parky is much easier to talk to than Russell Harty – he's more relaxed and seems content to find out rather than turn fine phrases. I feel comfortable and am able to be natural – hence probably my best performance on a chat show yet.

Donald Sinden comes on third and when, in his rich, plummy RADA voice, he refers, with some pride, to meeting Lord Alfred Douglas, Jimmy Savile says ''oo?'. Sinden doesn't seem to mind being interrupted that much, but Parkinson affects mock-headmasterly gravity and banishes Savile and me to 'sit with the girls' [the backing singers for the band]. Probably to his surprise, and certainly to the surprise of most of the cameras and the floor manager, we do just that. We so upstage Sinden's interview that he is asked back on again next Wednesday.

Afterwards I chat to Andrew Lloyd Webber, who gives me his phone number as he lives right beside Highclere House, where we're filming the Fermoy scenes. He also asks if I write lyrics! Savile drops the information that he is paid more to do his ads for the railways than Sir Peter Parker is for running them.

Sunday, March 14th

Up to Abbotsley for Granny G's 69th birthday. I take Granny a life-size cardboard replica of Margaret Thatcher (whom she hates), some flowers and a bottle of Vosne Romanee '64.

Grand football match on the back lawn by the barn. Rachel, Auntie Catherine and me v the two boys. We lose on penalties. Rachel quite fearless in the tackle. Leave for home at 6.00.

Monday, March 15th

To BUPA house to have a pile injected. A not very painful, but strangely uncomfortable sensation. As I lay curled up, proffering my bum, I remembered that this was the first day of the *Romans in Britain* High Court trial.[1] How suitable.

Wednesday, March 17th

Donald Sinden appears for the second time on the *Parkinson* show, armed with blunderbuss and whip. Parky seeks to make light of Saturday's 'incidents' and Sinden says that his children thought Saturday's programme very funny – and a 'classic Parkinson'. The whole episode has achieved some notoriety, as if Jimmy Savile and I had broken some unwritten rule, that no-one should enjoy themselves on *Parkinson* when someone else is plugging their latest product.

---

[1] Howard Brenton's play, produced by the National Theatre in 1980, contained scenes of simulated anal rape. Mary Whitehouse, the morality campaigner, brought a private prosecution against the production. She later withdrew from the case.

Friday, March 19th

To Dorney Reach near Maidenhead, to look at the rectory.

Much readjusting of thoughts, but, again, after a prolonged, concentrated and wearing debate, we settle on the exact shots. Neville dictates rather tersely into his pocket recorder as RL orders lighting towers and mock walls, etc. I admire RL for his endless enthusiasm for filling frames and his refusal to scale down *his* vision of the film. Neville hints darkly that Monday, when the heads of departments put their bills in, could be a day of reckoning.

Back from Dorney to buildings around St Pancras and King's Cross. A rooftop on some condemned flats will be the Mission roof.[1] Wonderful period panoramas of Industrial Revolution Britain, but not too easy to enjoy them as steady drizzle comes down, putting a fine twist of unpleasantness on an already cold and prematurely dark evening. After recceing brothels and walking shots, we pack up about a quarter to seven.

Monday, March 22nd

A long Python film meeting.

The apportionment of parts, which took us a couple of very good-humoured hours after lunch, is such an important moment in the creation of the film; we've been writing for three and a half years, and yet the impact of the movie for audiences is probably far more affected by what happened in the 75 minutes at Park Square West this afternoon.

I don't think there are any rank sores or festering injustices, though TJ thinks Eric may have wanted to do the end song, which has gone to Graham – doing a Tony Bennett impersonation!

Universal have few qualms about giving us the money – three million dollars up front, assuring us each of over £150,000 by the end of the year, well before the movie goes out. Python has never had better terms.

Tuesday, March 23rd

Parkinson programme calls up to ask if I will present an engraved shovel to Parky at a special surprise party to mark the end of his last BBC series next Wednesday. [He's a great fan of the shovel-owning Eric Olthwaite from *Ripping Yarns*.] I must have been rehabilitated!

[1] Culross Buildings stood defiantly until the summer of 2008, when they were destroyed for the King's Cross redevelopment.

Wednesday, March 24th

To Upper Wimpole Street to see a specialist about the ache in my ear. He rather throws me by asking if I've come about my nose. I feel myself falling into a Python sketch . . .

'My nose . . . No.'

'It's just bent to the right, that's all . . .'

'Really?'

'Oh yes, but nothing serious. Let's talk about the ear . . . '

(Pause)

'You don't have any trouble with the nose . . . ?'

'No.'

'Well, I should leave it then.'

Thursday, March 25th

Only the continuing gorgeous weather keeps me going. After yet another all too brief night's sleep, I'm up to grab some breakfast and leave for a recce to Longleat[1] at eight o'clock. Somewhere on the way to look in the car I collect a large evil lump of sticky, smelly dogshit on my shoes, and I've transferred it all over the house. I resign myself with ill grace to missing breakfast and set to to clean it up, but can find no disinfectant.

At this point I crack and fly into a helpless state of rage, banging the dressing table in the bedroom so hard that Helen wakes up thinking World War III's started, tearing my shoe off and generally behaving quite hysterically. It's a combination of the pressure of work – burning the candle at both ends – the lack of time I've had to talk to Helen about everything that's happening. But it passes, I'm collected by Brian, H forgives me before I go and I feel a storm centre has passed.

Richard drives me on to Longleat and we work and talk on the way. Arrive at midday. Take the guided tour, then meet with Christopher Thynne, the second son, who runs the house. Knows me from one of Eric Idle's parties, he says.

He came with Georgie Fame who broke a table.

He shows us wonderful passages. Bedrooms that are workable but a little small (all country house bedrooms it seems are a lot smaller than one would think). He shows us into Lord Weymouth's part of the house where garish paintings of all sorts of sexual endeavour cover the walls. He shows us the first

---

[1] Longleat House, an Elizabethan stately home which has been in the same family, the Thynnes, for over four hundred years. The head of the family is the Marquess of Bath.

printed book in England, a collection of Adolf Hitler's signed watercolours, plus a paper which has Adolf's signed approval of one of three designs for the Swastika symbol.

Sunday, March 28th

Leave for Abbotsley around 11.00. Sun shining in London, but mist is still thick as we drive up into Hertfordshire. Arrive at Church Farm at 12.30 – and I go for a last run for many weeks.

As I pound up the hill beside silent ploughed fields with the mist clinging around me like a cool refreshing blanket, I feel ready for *The Missionary* and ready for Python. I know in a sense that I'm entering a tunnel from which I shall not emerge until October, at least.

I hit out at the air with my fists like a boxer, feeling ready.

Back to Abbotsley for lunch. The sun comes out. The boys play football. I teach Rachel to ride her bike, on the same stretch of road up to Pitsdean Hill on which I taught Willy, in the teeth of a storm, a few years ago.

Today in the still sunshine, Rachel's little triumph seemed to have greater significance. I sensed one of those special moments between us. We both felt so proud.

Monday, March 29th

Brian [Brookner] drives me in his red Mercedes to the National Liberal Club off Whitehall. First glimpse of the reality of *The Missionary* is a string of Lee Electric trucks parked in this quiet street. On the other side of the road Richard's Winnebago. Cables run across the pavement into the wide lobby of this once grand, marble-floored Victorian club.

The first time I appear as Charles Fortescue is in this lobby and, by almost eerie coincidence, the character is born beside a huge contemporary oil painting of Gladstone's first Cabinet, in the centre of which sits one C. Fortescue – a youngish man, not at all unlike the missionary I'm playing.

The conversion of the National Liberal Club's billiard room into a gymnasium has been stunningly successful. Opening shot is ready by ten, but the generator goes on the blink and we don't complete my entrance to the club until eleven.

As the slow pattern of waiting established itself, I nodded off twice. My cold continues to tumble out, but didn't seem to affect my mood or performance. Now that filming has begun I know I shall survive, but now it's a question of keeping standards high – and producing something better than anything I've done before (apart from the Fish Slapping Dance, of course).

Tuesday, March 30th

Lunch is a meeting with Geoffrey S, Richard, the stills photographer and myself, to discuss the book [of *The Missionary*]. Eat up in one of the vast, dusty galleries at the top of the building.

RL clearly feels GS is too cautious and GS does not react well to RL's expensive ideas for the book. I find having to conciliate the most tiring work of the day. It means no relaxation at lunch either and I have to rush down to do close-ups in the first real dialogue scene with Denholm.

Feel a surge of nerves as I wait to go on. I look round at this huge room, filled, just for me, with 30 period gymnasts. I look round at the 40 or so faces of the crew, all watching, waiting to see what I do. As if this isn't enough, I catch sight of Angela, Jeremy and Veryan up in the balcony, looking down.

I start to wobble. I have to go into this scene clutching briefcase, hat and full cup of tea. I'm convinced the tea-cup will rattle so much that I'll be asked to do it again – and that'll make it worse – and what am I doing here anyway? We do the shot, and I control the cup and the moment of blind panic passes, and I feel settled and refreshed and the rest of the day seems light and easy.

Up to Lee Studios to look at the first rushes. They look marvellous. [Peter] Hannan's lighting is of the very best – I've hardly ever seen my stuff looking so good. The various textures of the wood and tiles come across strongly and clearly. It looks interesting and gives everything in the frame a particular quality and to the whole an atmosphere you can almost smell and touch.

As to the performance – although Denholm does not do the Bishop as Graham Crowden would have done, he nevertheless comes over strongly on screen, and manages the mixture of comedy and seriousness very effectively.

I leave Lee's in great euphoria and raring to get on with the film.

Wednesday, March 31st

Picked up at the relatively civilised hour of 7.45. To Culross Buildings behind King's Cross and St Pancras. Marvellous location for trainspotters. The sky is grey and it's cold, but we start shooting without much ado amidst the flapping washing. First scenes with our prostitutes.

I have a small and rather tatty caravan, with a basin, but no running water, and a seat which shatters immediately I sit down. Denholm a little more together on his words today than yesterday at the club, but, like any actor, is bucked up tremendously by praise of any kind – and it helps him that I can enthuse so much over the rushes.

All goes ahead well until after lunch when the sun comes out, which makes the roof of the tenement buildings a much more agreeable place to be, but impossible to work on because of the light change. Go down to my caravan and sleep for an hour. After a two- or three-hour wait, RL decides to abandon shooting for the rest of the day on account of the sunshine. Denholm and I run tomorrow's scenes through.

Then off to rushes at Lee's and home for an hour before taking a taxi down to the Main Squeeze Club in King's Road, where M Parkinson's 'surprise' end of series party is to take place. I've rehearsed a little speech as Eric Olthwaite.

Arrive to find small, rather empty basement club. No-one I know. Parky arrives and is cheered, moderately, and at about 11.15 I'm asked to make the presentation. I'm shown onto a small stage, on which I'm blocked to view for half the people there. Then the microphone feeds back – whines and whistles – and I find myself having to make ad-libs with the likes of Kenny Lynch, Jimmy Tarbuck, Spike and Billy Connolly only feet away.

I survive, just, and there are laughs at the right places. Present the shovel to Michael Parkinson as 'The Second Most Boring Man in Yorkshire'.

Stay on at the club for about an hour. Talked to Michael Caine – about Maggie S mostly. 'She's brilliant,' he said, 'But watch her.' Told me I'd have to work hard to keep in the scene with her.

Then a hatchet-faced 'adviser' signalled discreetly to Caine that he should be moving on. I left soon too.

To bed about a quarter to one. Duty done. Slept like a log.

Thursday, April 1st

This morning it's raining. So for a couple of hours I sit in my caravan in Battle Bridge Road and catch up on work – e.g. reading page-proofs of *Small Harry and the Toothache Pills*.

At eleven it clears and we work steadily through the scene, finishing by six. Denholm takes a long while on his close-ups; his daughter's come to watch him. 'Amazing how difficult it is to act with one's family around,' Denholm confides, and, for a man who has made 73 films, he certainly doesn't seem to have the secret of instant relaxation.

After filming, which ends at 7.30 with a beautiful street shot with a background of the St Pancras gasholders silhouetted against a rosy dusk sky, and Peter H personally wetting the cobblestones to catch the evening light, I go with Irene in the Winnebago to talk over casting as we drive to rushes. The Winnebago has been dreadfully ill-fated this week, breaking down everywhere.

And tonight is no exception. Richard curses modern technology roundly as we lumber up the Marylebone Road with the handbrake stuck on.

To rushes at Rank's executive viewing theatre in Hill Street, Mayfair. First glimpse of my relationship with the girls. It looks relaxed and unforced. Fingers crossed we've seen nothing bad so far.

Denis claims to have finalised a deal with Columbia for *The Missionary* and the latest news is that they are preparing a 1,000 print release in the US for late October. This is exhilarating, rather terrifying news.

Friday, April 2nd

Leave home at 7.30. We are filming at the Royal Mint in Tower Hill. Abandoned ten years ago, it has a fine classical main building (used in *Elephant Man*) and workshop outbuildings. A very satisfactory set up for my scene with McEvoy (Peter Vaughan) as we can use three levels and drive a Chapman Hoist into the interior courtyard and follow the actors down. It is our Healed Leper shot, really, one long developing shot.[1] Only here it is more satisfying and better used, as the various elements of the bottling factory are introduced as we walk. It ends with us passing a fully practical steam engine – driving three belt-drive machines, and a loading bay with period vehicle, as well as a horse and cart glimpsed out in the yard.

Peter and I walk through the scene at 8.15, but the first take is not until 3.50 in the afternoon.

It is very hard work for an actor to come in for one day and shine as expected, under great pressure of time. But Peter's performance is always word perfect and, though a little tighter and tenser than I'd hoped, he's still excellent and solid. After seven takes all sides are satisfied and we finish work at seven.

To the West End for dinner with Maggie Smith. Maggie is funny, much less made-up and more attractive than when I last saw her, and quite obviously looking forward to the thing immensely. She brushes aside any apologetic concerns RL and I have for the shooting schedule – which involves her first of all appearing at 5.45 a.m. on Monday up to her knees in mud on Wapping Flats.

We go off, arms linked, past crowds clustering round a police-raided night club, the best of chums.

---

[1] Most of the 'Healed Leper' scene in *Life of Brian* was played in one shot, with camera operator John Stanier, a Steadi-Cam strapped to his body, walking backwards through 'the streets of Jerusalem' for some three minutes.

Saturday, April 3rd

I'm losing a sense of time already. I wake to my alarm and obediently swing my legs off the bed and make for the bathroom, like a battery hen. Shave, clean teeth, go downstairs to do exercises, dress up in the bedroom.

Brian arrives today at 7.50, and carts me away. Must, however awful I may feel, arrive in a jolly mood at the location – co-producer, actor and writer can't be seen to weaken. Actually, once up and about I feel fine and the only frustration of today is the length of time filming takes.

I'm at Ada's brothel, situated in the old Fish Office on the Railway Lands. From the brothel window, as I stand ready to be Charles Fortescue, I can see the trains slipping in and out of St Pancras.

A long wait whilst Peter H lights Ada's room. It has no outside light source, so he has to create this impression from scratch. Listen to the Grand National, in which a horse called Monty Python keeps up courageously before refusing at Becher's the second time around. Much more sensible than falling, I think.

At tea Angela, Veryan and Jeremy arrive. Tea in RL's Winnebago. Richard is one of the few directors who, after six consecutive, very full days of filming, can still bother to make tea for his star's family.

Sunday, April 4th

Breakfast in the garden and read, with a certain disbelief, the news that we are virtually at war with Argentina over the Falkland Islands. It seems a situation better suited to the days of *The Missionary* than 1982. It may feel unreal, but papers like the *News of the World* are howling for vengeance and Ardiles was booed every time he touched the ball for Tottenham yesterday.

Took Rachel and Louise to the swimming pool at Swiss Cottage and was just sitting down to evening 'Sunday lunch' of roast lamb and a bottle of Château Bellac, when the door bell rang and TG appeared, breathless for information on the first week of *The Missionary*. He wanted to know what had gone wrong and how far we were behind! Children behaved abominably (with the exception of Tom) at the meal as TG rabbited on. Later Willy explained that he had founded a Get Rid of Guests Club.

TG is waiting for Stoppard to finish his involvements with Solidarity before beginning work on *Brazil*, for which TG has now signed a deal with an Israeli super-financier.

Monday, April 5th

Arrive at location in Wapping at 5.15.

God is very definitely with us this morning. The sun rises into an almost clear sky – with just a hint of cloud, to add contrast and perspective. There is a little wind and the Thames has a strip of still, reflecting water across it, ruffled into the softest ripples on either side. It is a perfect dawn and, as the sun and the river rise, we film hard for three hours and a half – from 6.15 until nearly ten, when our last reaction shot of the little boy – 'Will it be a mission?' – is shot with water lapping around the camera legs.

This was Maggie Smith's first day. She uncomplainingly began work on *The Missionary* standing in a foot of muddy Thames water, pulling a ship's wheel out of the slime, and managed to smile winningly and help us push the barrow over wet and slippery rocks in take after take.

Then on to the Mission – in Lant Street, Southwark, and another tremendous boost for morale. The set – of the girls' dormitory – was quite superb. When I first walked into it, I was quite moved. Something about the pathos of the simple beds with their few possessions beside them, grafted on to a bleak industrial interior.

Lunch with Maggie S and Richard in the Winnebago. All amicable and quite easy, though I still find Maggie S and the long experience of acting she represents quite a daunting prospect.

Tuesday, April 6th

Down to the Mission in pouring rain. If our dawn shot had been today it would have been disastrous. As it is we are inside all the time, completing the scene in which Maggie leaves the Mission. I find it hard work to start with. Maggie is smooth, efficient and professional – consummately skilled at timing and delivery. Keeping up to her standard, particularly when we don't yet know each other that well, and when the fatigue of eight days' hard filming in the last nine takes the edge off one's energies, is not easy. But I survive.

I fluff a line on a take, which annoys me, as I'm usually pretty efficient at lines myself. Then Maggie mistimes a move on a later take, which makes me feel much better. Eventually the complicated master shot is in the can and I feel much relief.

Terry G comes down to watch the shooting. He's impressed by the Mission set and says of Maggie, in some surprise, 'She's really funny . . .'

A journalist called Chris Auty – jeans, leather jacket and matching tape recorder – is here from *City Limits*. I waffle between takes. Must try and work out in my own mind what this film is about – instead of relying on visiting journalists to make up my mind for me.

Thursday, April 8th

I have a more luxurious caravan today. Richard approves. Maggie S is still in one of the poky little ones. 'You could hang meat in it,' she drawls elegantly, referring to the spectacular lack of heating.

Maggie and I work on the scene where she finds me in bed with the girls – Maggie being released about five. RL thinks something was lacking in her performance today.

Then to look at rushes. Helen comes along – her first glimpse of anything to do with the film. She hasn't even read the script!

Much relieved and pleased that the first major scene between Maggie and myself makes people laugh. It looks fine and beautiful – *everything* looks fine and beautiful, but it's good to hear naked, unadorned laughter and especially as these are the last rushes before Denis returns.

Friday, April 9th: Good Friday

Feel good and virtuous and only a little cross at having to speak to a Danish journalist on the phone from Copenhagen about my 'Railway Journey', which goes out there next week. Had to explain trainspotting to him. He told me *Time Bandits* was a great success in his country, where it isn't shown to under-15s because of 'the violence'. It's also called, quite shamelessly, 'Monty Python's Time Bandits'.

Sunday, April 11th: Southwold

Strongish north wind throwing showery rain against the house. Take Ma to Southwold Church for the Easter service.

Before the service, conducted by the same vicar with the same permanent grin of redemption that he wore when Dad was put in the ground almost five years ago, we go to see the grave. It's in a small plot with several other crematees. As Mum happens upon it, she raises her voice in horror, 'They're all *dead*!'

She means the flowers.

I don't feel I can take communion with her – I just don't believe securely enough. So after the main service of rousing Easter hymns, I walk along to the front, in the teeth of a wrinkling north wind, past some of the old haunts, counting the years Southwold has been part of my life – about 25.

Home, for Granny's stew, then venture out in a still-inhospitable afternoon, though there is no rain. We walk along the beach, throw stones, push each other about, chase and generally have a very happy time.

Tuesday, April 13th

The news which dampens all our spirits is that Denis O'B, back from the States, has seen the assembly thus far and word, via Neville and Ray, is that he found the sound very difficult to hear and the pictures too dark. I suppose, because we were all so euphoric about the results, we took this news much more heavily than perhaps it was intended. But his reaction undoubtedly casts a pall over the proceedings.

Thursday, April 15th

Our first day at the Ezra Street location, where controversial amounts of the construction budget have been spent to improve the look of this East End neighbourhood. Something like £100,000, I think. Ezra Street itself has been resurrected, with a 50-yard frontage of mock houses, so well made that an old lady pointed one out as the house where she was born and another asked the council if she could be moved into it.

There are practical steam engines, piles of cobble-stones, and huge letters have transformed the local school into a Missions to Seamen Home. There are four complete streets we can use – over a quarter of a mile in all. It's the most impressive build I've seen on a film since the 'Ribat' [at Monastir for the *Life of Brian*] – and I think tops even that.

Friday, April 16th

Our day is plagued by the presence of a *Nationwide* film crew, who trap me in my caravan and suggest that I play all the locals when they interview them. I quickly abort that idea and send them off to talk to the *real* locals ... 'Oh, yes, that's quite an idea.'

A *Daily Express* lady, quite unphased, sticks stolidly to her questions as I change in my caravan. I'm in and out of costume and make-up changes all morning, which leaves me with few reserves of patience and, when at last lunch comes and my poached trout is being borne to my caravan, the very last thing I need is an interview with *Nationwide*. But that's the moment they've chosen.

The result is a very bad interview and considerable irritation. 'Oh, you were in the *Life of Brian*, were you?' asks the interviewer at one point.

In the afternoon Maggie S hides in her caravan to avoid having to talk to *Nationwide*, the *Daily Express* lady quietly and doggedly continues with her questions and I concentrate on trying to preserve sanity and remember what the hell I'm doing in Whitechapel, dressed as a clergyman.

Saturday, April 17th

Lunch with Denis to discuss my personal stuff – contracts and the like. I still do not have a signed contract, nor have I accepted any payment for *Missionary*. We walk from Cadogan Square to a pleasant, almost empty Chinese restaurant in a basement off Knightsbridge.

Denis tells me more about the Columbia deal, which, as far as I'm concerned, is the most unbelievable part of the *Missionary* saga. That we should have completed three weeks of shooting, only 13 months after the first word was written, is fantastical enough, but that we should be going out with the finished product in a thousand theatres across the US after 19 months is almost terrifying. But our little film is, give or take settlement of details, Columbia's big film for October/November.

Denis was in conciliatory mood – anxious to talk about the good things in the film. He's pleased with Richard, he was very impressed by Ezra Street and he thinks my performance has 'captured all the nuances'.

Back home I was just nodding off after lunchtime wine when TJ dropped in, having walked across the Heath. We sat in the sun and drank coffee. He had seen the assembly yesterday – chiefly to look at Peter Hannan's work with a view to using him on *Meaning of Life*. It was enormously encouraging to hear that he had liked it so much he'd kept forgetting to look at the camerawork. Not only looks was he complimentary about, but also the humour.

Thursday, April 22nd

Work out at Dorney in the morning and then nearby to a beautiful avenue of trees down by the river for a shot to out-Tess *Tess*. This is the first longish dialogue scene between myself and Phoebe. Phoebe a little apprehensive. I've written her one of my 'jargon' parts – a lot of detail about filing systems which she has to learn parrot-fashion.

I keep correcting her when she says 'Pacific sub-sections' instead of 'specific sub-sections', but it turns out she's virtually dyslexic on this particular word. A huge shire horse drawing a plough clatters past at the start of each take.

The waving green wheatfields shine in the late evening sun. Phoebe looks slim and delicate in her wasp-waisted long dress, and the jets from Heathrow bank steeply to left and right above us.

Saturday, April 24th

Up at seven. I take Rachel with me this morning, to be part of the crowd in a 'busy London street' shot, which we're shooting in Finsbury Circus. Ninety extras and a dozen vehicles, including two horse-drawn buses. Signs of our own making cover up banks and travel agencies. A big scene.

Lunch in Richard's Winnebago with a journalist lady and Maggie S. Maggie very solicitous of Rachel, who sits with unusually well-behaved taciturnity, nibbling a cheese sandwich. We chat to the journalist. Maggie S clearly not enamoured of the press and resists attempts to be photographed by the *Sunday Mirror*.

Home, collecting a McDonald's for Rachel on the way, about a quarter to eight. Ring George H, who is just back from Los Angeles. He's jet-lagged and watching the Eurovision Song Contest. I just want to communicate to him some of the end-of-the-week elation I'm feeling. He promises to come and see us next week.

Monday, April 26th

Picked up by Brian at seven. Graham Crowden in car as well. Very genial and avuncular. As we drive into Oxfordshire, on a disappointingly grey, though still dry morning, he describes how he was shot by his own Sergeant-Major during arms drill in Scotland in 1943. He said that when the rifle went off there was none of the usual histrionics that actors and writers usually put into such tragedies, just a dawning realisation and a desire to be as polite as possible about it. 'I think you've shot me, Sergeant,' was all he could say – and the Sergeant's reply was 'What is it *now*, Crowden?'

Thursday, April 29th

This ridiculous confrontation with Argentina looks more and more like sliding from bluster and bluff into killing. But the government's popularity has risen 10% overnight since the re-taking of South Georgia and Murdoch's *Sun* is writing about 'blasting the Argies out of the sky'. This episode shows the true face of the nasties. Crimson, angry, twisted, bitter faces.

Saturday, May 1st

Not used during the morning as a series of sharp and hostile showers passed over. Some hail. Whilst they filmed Deborah and the photography scene I remained in the caravan, completing various tasks like thank you letters to the actors, and writing a new introductory narration for *Jabberwocky*, which I heard from TG yesterday is to be re-released in the US during the summer. He's very excited by the improvements made by Julian in re-editing.

Give lunch in my caravan to the 'Repertory Company' – Graham, Phoebe, Tim [Spall], Anne-Marie [Marriott]. Open champagne to celebrate good work done and, sadly, our last day all together. Quite a smutty lunch with RL's description of Long Don Silver, a man with a huge dong and varicose veins, who used to be featured in a club on Sunset Strip – hung upside down.

In one of the afternoon's sunny spells we grab a shot of myself in a horse and trap arriving home. As I wait for the clouds to clear the sun I see our two executive producers emerging from the orchard. George looks like Denis's son. His hair has reverted to Hamburg style, swept backwards off the forehead. He hands me a magnum of Dom Perignon with a pink ribbon tied round the neck. I embrace him warmly, then the cue comes through and I'm swept away round the corner.

They stay around for the next shot – a small, hot bedroom scene between Deborah and myself. George squashes himself into a corner of the room behind the lights, but only a yard or so from Phoebe. She's quite clearly made nervous by his presence and her face and neck flush and we do three very unrelaxed takes. Then George gets uncomfortable and moves off and we finish the scene.

Sunday, May 2nd

J Cleese rings to hear how things are going – having read his *Sunday Times* and been reminded it's my birthday on Wednesday. He starts *Privates on Parade*[1] a week Monday. Says he can't remember what he's been doing for the past few weeks, but his pet project at the moment is the book with his psychiatrist. We wish each other well and he offers his services as a critic at the first fine cut stage of *The Missionary* in June.

[1] Peter Nichols' stage play about a British Army theatrical troupe in Malaysia in 1947 would be Denis O'Brien's next HandMade production, directed by Michael Blakemore and starring John Cleese.

T Gilliam arrives before lunch and we actually find ourselves writing together again – on the intro to *Jabberwocky*. He points out that I could be 'starring' in three separate movies in the US this summer: '*Bowl*' opens in late June, *Jabberwocky* in July and *Missionary* in October.

After he's gone, Tom beats me at snooker, I drink a beer I didn't really want and am suddenly faced with a lot of learning for the Fermoy scene and a 'surprise' party ahead of my pre-39th birthday tonight. I am at my worst – grumpy, resentful and unhelpful.

About half past eight Terry G and Maggie and the Joneses arrive and I cheer up with some champagne. Nancy [Lewis] and Ron [Devillier] are a surprise, as are Ian and Anthea [Davidson] – who I haven't seen for ages. Also the Walmsleys,[1] Ray Cooper – who brings me lead soldiers and a bottle of Roederer Cristal champagne. Robert H and Jackie – six months pregnant. Chris Miller and Bill are there and the Alburys. Twenty people in all. The Inneses are the only ones who couldn't make it.

It's a lovely party and I don't deserve it after being so surly in the p.m.

I drift – no, I plummet to sleep, thinking how nice it is to have a birthday party and wake up the next day, the same age.

Monday, May 3rd

To the Odeon Leicester Square for showing of rough assembly of *Missionary* – mainly for George H and Denis.

The projectionists are very slovenly with the focussing and as each cut comes up there is a long wait until it's sharpened up – only to go again on the next cut. But the laughter comes – especially from Denis – and the gymnasium scene (which had worried RL and myself) goes extremely well. At the end George turns and shakes my hand. Denis has been oohing and ahing at the beauty of shots and is quite genuinely and spontaneously pleased by it all.

This is just the boost we needed before starting on the last lap of the film – in Longleat and Scotland. But it pleases me most that George likes it, for it's his enthusiasm and love of the *Yarns* and the work I've done in Python that really made it all possible.

He tells me that there may soon be a settlement in the Apple business. 'Twenty years and we're just starting to get royalties for *Please, Please Me*.' As we go down in the lift he assures me that there will be no problem financing

---

[1] Nigel and Jane Walmsley. Nigel Walmsley was at Oxford with Terry Jones and myself. He went on to run, among other things, Capital Radio, Carlton TV and the television ratings organisation BARB. Jane was a journalist and TV presenter.

this film . . . 'Denis wants to keep everything tight . . . but . . . the money's there, you know . . . if you want it.'

Tuesday, May 4th

Leave home at 6.20 and drive, with Brian and Rosamund Greenwood, up the M4 to Highclere in Hampshire. The crisp, clean beauty of the countryside making the news that we have torpedoed an Argentinian battleship off the Falkland Islands seem even more unreal.

Arrive at Highclere just before eight o'clock. Already in the car I've been reassured and relieved to hear Rosamund Greenwood read the scene, with a gentle touch, but drawing every bit of comedy from it. When we 'line-up' at half past eight, I'm doubly happy to hear Roland Culver, who at 82 has an excellent combination of good acting and sparkle in the eyes. His sole line, 'Hello', brings the library down.

It's a very gruelling day, learning and retaining these long speeches, but we work on until eight o'clock, leaving three close-ups still to be done and a forbidding amount of work for tomorrow. Brian drives me to the salubrious Ladbroke Mercury Motor Inn at Aldermaston Roundabout.

A message from Terry J to ring him. As I do so, at 9.30, he's watching the news, which has just come in, of the sinking of a British destroyer in the 'non war'. The first British casualties. How crazy. Talk about TJ's rewrites on 'Every Sperm is Sacred'. He's elaborated on the sequence quite considerably.

Wednesday, May 5th: Highclere House

In the papers, 'HMS Sheffield Sunk' on the front page. It's been a cold night. Light frost on the cars outside the Mercury Motor Inn.

Drive up with Neville to the location, arrive at Highclere at eight. Quickly into close-ups of the death scene, which we complete by mid-morning. Everyone who came down on the coach this morning knows it's my birthday – they announced it on the radio!

Lord Carnarvon potters amongst us with good-humoured nods and bits of chat to the ladies. He looks like every American's idea of a belted earl – down to his velvet carpet slippers with the interlinked 'C' monogram embroidered on them.

With hard and concentrated work we finish at eight o'clock in the great hall at Highclere. It's goodbye to Phoebe, Graham Crowden (a lovely man, but a terrible worrier about his acting. As Ray C says, Crowden raises worry to an art form) and Rosamund Greenwood.

One of our unit drivers has left the picture without telling anyone, so I find myself driving in Richard's Winnebago in a pelting rainstorm past Stonehenge at half past ten. It's a stormy pitch-black night. We stop at a lay-by and RL makes toasted sandwiches for my birthday dinner.

Sunday, May 9th: Longleat House

On location by 7.45.

After a day and a half languishing unhappily at her hotel, Maggie is here, but looking rather frail. After an early shot in the hall, Michael [Hordern] is allowed off for a day's fishing, and Maggie, RL and myself rehearse lines and moves, alone, in the Chinese bedroom. The scene plays very neatly and both Maggie and I find it very funny to do. Feel quite pleased with myself – as a writer this time.

A long lighting set-up.

Maggie and I make a start on the scene, but it's late in the afternoon and jolly tiring to act on the peak of form then. The very funny run-through in the morning, before the cameras were in, now seems utterly remote. We wrap at six o'clock and Neville, in the midst of his gloom, has to laugh when he tells me the news that Trevor Howard has arrived, but passed out in the lounge of the hotel, which he thought was his bedroom.

We talk for 45 minutes – Neville, Richard and myself – while the rest of the unit stream up the road to the birthday party I'm giving for them at the Bath Arms. Neville estimates a budget overage of nearly £200,000 if we go two days over at Longleat. It's the confrontation with EuroAtlantic which he is trying desperately to avoid for he knows that once they start interfering his job will quickly become impossible.

Monday, May 10th

Quite cloudless sky today, as we drive through leafy lanes up to Longleat. I discuss with Neville my thoughts early this morning – for cuts and reschedulings to help us through the week.

In mid-morning word goes round the unit that 'Trevor is on his way'. Trevor duly arrives and is guided to his caravan. When I go to see him he grins glazedly, but welcomingly, like a great bear just hit by a tranquillising dart. We eat lunch together, then I give him script changes and he is loaded back into his car and driven off to the hotel.

Back up in the Chinese room, Maggie and I finally get into bed. The scene seems to play well and when we wrap at seven we only have two shots left to do. A showing of assembled material for all the crew has to be cancelled as we all sit expectantly in the library and the projector fails.

Tuesday, May 11th

All wait with rather bated breath, but Trevor is fine. Fortunately he's seated at a desk, writing to *The Times*, so he can virtually read his lines, which he does, writing them out carefully, with shaky hand, on the paper in front of him.

Meanwhile I wait around, unused to the inactivity. Every now and then a shout from Michael Hordern as he bangs his head yet again on some projecting part of his caravan. His head is now covered in wounds.

Wednesday, May 12th

Outside the weather is gorgeous, inside it's hot, difficult work as I do one of my few dialogue pieces with Trevor. He is sitting there trying to survive. We collect the lines on the most basic level – if he can put the words in the right order, that's a good take. I find it a strain and cannot act with any ease or comfort. Richard feels impatient and the crew have to break the brisk momentum they're into whilst lines are rehearsed.

Maggie's cool and competent delivery picks up the pace again in the afternoon and we remain on schedule when we wrap at seven.

Thursday, May 13th

Met at the location today by news from Bobby Wright, second assistant – known affectionately by Maggie as Bobby Wrong. 'Bad news, Michael. There's a neg. scratch across the bedroom scene.' Maggie and I had joked about this on Tuesday when we'd completed the scene in a fast, efficient, very hard day. But then I hear from Richard it's only on two easy shots.

Finish the sitting room scene. Trevor much better today.

At lunch we're invaded again. RL's bank manager, two children, two secretaries, as well as the 'NatWest House Magazine' photographer *and* Richard's mother and her two friends descend. There is no real relaxing over lunch today. 'When you're acting,' asks one of the secretaries of me, 'how do you know when to do all those expressions?'

Friday, May 14th

RL is shooting the entire dining room sequence on a master – dwelling longer on Maggie and myself and Hordern than on Trevor, who sits in splendid isolation at the far end of the table, a good ten yards from Maggie and myself.

About three o'clock we enter the hot, airless dining room and start to work on the scene, which has a soup-pouring slapstick joke in the middle of it, which requires quite a bit of working out. We do seven takes. RL enthusiastic about the last two. We manage close-ups on all three of us, though one long speech (six lines) defeats Trevor utterly and we have to abandon it, in close-up, anyway.

General elation at completing dead on seven o'clock. Drinks with Lord Christopher and wife, who have been very kind and accommodating, and at eight Neville, Brian Brookner and myself are in the car heading east to London.

Suddenly we are within two weeks of completion.

Sunday, May 16th

TJ rings. He says he reckons doing *Meaning of Life* will be a doddle. I gather Peter Hannan has been sent a script and is first choice for cameraman.

Open house for the rest of the day – variety of children and friends in and out. The boys, much more independent now, up to the Lido with friends. Helen and Rachel together playing some all-embracing, mysterious game. How could I want to leave all this? I do value it so much and sometimes wish I had a freeze-frame mechanism which could seal me in this present sense of contentment. But it is a fragment and soon the time comes for me to move on, collecting other fragments.

Monday, May 17th: London–Aviemore, Scotland

Wake in a Simenon novel – three in the morning, train stationary in a sodium-lamplit marshalling yard. We must be somewhere near Glasgow, where the train splits, half for Fort William, half for Inverness. To sleep again, lulled Lethe-wards by the friendly clatter of wheel on steel. Arrive at Aviemore a few minutes late at twenty past seven. We drive the 45 minutes to Ardverikie House.

Work progresses slowly as it always does with a new location and new people. We have period vehicles, including an 1899 Daimler, which prove temperamental, and the weather alternates unhelpfully between sun and cloud.

I have a room in the house, which is far less preferable to a caravan. It's like being entombed in this cold, grey temple to deer slaughter. I start the day with rowing shots and wet feet as I clamber from Loch Laggan and run towards the house. Smoke guns in the birch groves on the opposite bank complicate (but improve) the shot, and Neville is already twitchy enough by lunchtime to confer with Richard and myself about the Scottish schedule. Richard is bristly and will not compromise on rowing shots. Uneasy peace.

We are staying 45 minutes' drive away from the location in the ghetto of the Aviemore Centre. A bleak and inhospitable attempt to create a 'leisure complex' of the late '60's style, which proves once again that the more impressive the surrounding landscape, the less impressive are the powers of human design and imagination. I have a suite, but it overlooks the car park.

Go to bed feeling a bit surly, after ordering trout and champagne on room service, which arrives quite efficiently, with a flurry of autograph books.

Tuesday, May 18th: Aviemore

Drive to Ardverikie – on the way pick up a hitch-hiker with a dog, who turns out to be one of our extras, who's missed the bus. A young man with a weather-beaten face, he's a casual labourer with a wife and child. They sound like gentle people, ingenuous and idealistic. The £15 a day they are getting to do our 'Chariots of Fire' joke has, he says, 'made all the difference'.

I know Richard is uneasy about this whole section. He says he's not sure how to direct it. Both of us know it's on the thin red line between us and 'Two Ronnies'/'Carry-On'-style mannerism.

'You're glum,' says Maggie to me, in some surprise. 'You never look glum.'

After lunch we set up for a grand shot of the procession leaving the house. Two cameras, a crane, lovely sunshine between the clouds, but both the old cars refuse to function properly and we have to abandon the shot. I climb in through a window, and that's that for the day.

Back at the hotel, I eat with Maggie. Salmon is good and we sit and talk on until the place is long-empty. She does worry and things do get her down. She reminds me of Angela, bright, but brittle.

Wednesday, May 19th: Aviemore

Looming clouds after much rain in the night. Lighting and planning the interiors takes time and I feel weary and unenergetic. Still can't set my mind to anything else. Have hardly read a book since *The Missionary* began.

We work on the extra hour, until eight. Like yesterday I am only needed in the last shot – to be squashed behind a door. For various reasons the scene between Corbett [David Suchet] and Lady A does not play right, and Maggie is uncomfortable. We wrap at 8.15, but, though the scene was satisfactory, neither Richard nor I felt it was exceptional, which is why we employ Maggie.

Back at the hotel after shooting, ring home, ring Ma, and settle down to watch a Ken Loach film set in Sheffield. Have ordered a halibut and champagne from room service. But Neville comes to see me, and another crisis has to be faced. The need to re-shoot the scene with Maggie and D Suchet tonight has really only confirmed Neville's fears that we will not collect the Scottish stuff in eight days.

I have looked as clearly and constructively as I can at script and cuts, but I think back to the *Ripping Yarns* and how we always left the 'adventure' finales to the end of shooting and almost inevitably compromised. So we must get this one right.

Halfway through our gloomy discussion, the halibut arrives, ushered in by the maître d'hotel himself and two flunkeys, like some life-support machine. It's already been delivered to Maggie Smith by mistake.

Thursday, May 20th: Aviemore

Not called early today, but cannot sleep very soundly after noisy departure of unit vehicles at seven. Feel very low for various reasons. Lack of central involvement with what's going on is primary. Ring home and talk to Rachel and Helen, who says T G rang and raved about the look of what he'd seen of *Missionary*. Somewhat cheered, set out at nine for the first day on the moors location.

After parking car am driven up a steep and rutted track, along which two bridges have been built by P Verard and the construction team. On the side of a broad slope our caravans are perched, and a motley collection of minibuses, Land and Range Rovers, Weasels, Sno-Cats and other vehicles. This is base camp.

Half a mile away the picnic scene is being set up in a very picturesque bend of a stream. The champagne and the strawberries and the cut-glass set out on a table perched on a cart (a good idea of Richard's) look wonderful.

Richard maintains he doesn't ever want to direct sequences like this again. He wants to work on films of the scale of *The Last Detail* – with small locations and small casts.

George Perry of the *Sunday Times* is in attendance. He's rather well-read and has wide terms of reference and I feel very dull and boring as I talk to him about *The Missionary* in my caravan.

Afterwards we wander down to the picnic location and it's quite pleasantly warm and sunny as the unit lounges on the grass. I'm used for one shot about five o'clock, then come back to my caravan with George.

I gather that further down the track there have been ructions with Maggie as she does the last shot of the day. Can't find out what's gone on, but as she walks back to base camp she looks grim.

Friday, May 21st: Aviemore

At base camp by eleven. Most of the actors wandering around in an unused state. Apparently no shots have been done yet as the Sno-Cat, go-anywhere, do-anything Arctic exploration vehicle has stuck halfway to the location, and toppled most of the camera equipment out.

Very slowly the unit straggles across the mountainside to the butts. Maggie in full Edwardian costume and wig looks very bizarre in the creeping caterpillar vehicles. I talk to her about yesterday. 'How *is* Richard?' she asks drily. She cannot understand his rapid changes from gloom to manic enthusiasm. It was this that threw her, she claims.

By midday our little army has been moved to the location, even as rumours are confirmed that we have landed again on the Falkland Islands. I note that the 'conflict', as they are still calling the Falkland confrontation, has been running almost exactly as long as our filming. Both seem to be reaching crisis point at about the same time!

After a Perrier and pork chop lunch, I walk over the hill to the location, accompanied by Bobby Wright, who occasionally screams into his walkie-talkie. 'They want to know how many blacks Richard wants in the crowd at Liverpool? ... No, *blacks* ... Five percent? ... Chinese? ... Alright, no blacks, but five percent Chinese ... ' And so on ... It all drifts away into the silent vastness of the Scottish hills.

Sunday, May 23rd: Aviemore

The Scottish *Daily Mail* has hysterical headlines about our 5,000 heroes – the men who yesterday went ashore in the first official re-invasion of the Falkland Islands. Even the *Times* is full of diagrams with graphic explosions and hero-ically-sweeping arrows. It's real war out there now and the implication in all the reports is that it will escalate and many lives will be lost before anyone can stop it.

Drive Maggie to Ardverikie House, where we are invited to late lunch with Richard in the Winnebago. RL, with his restless energy, wants us to go and eat on the island in the middle of the loch. Maggie, with her equally strong determination not to be impressed by such mad suggestions, demurs. In the end we compromise and RL takes us out onto the loch in his little dinghy. It pours with rain – a prolonged, cold shower – we've nowhere to shelter and the only wine he's brought is a rich Sauternes.

Arrive back drenched and Richard gives us a complete change of clothes. Maggie looks lost in a huge pair of his trousers. But it's jollied us along. Peter Hannan arrives and helps barbecue the steaks – with oregano and tarragon. Very nice. The showers pass and there's a period of beautiful early evening sunshine.

Tuesday, May 25th: Aviemore

We have an important scene to play this morning – Maggie's 'dying words' in the cart. Our first scene of real, unadorned affection for each other.

The wind blows as violently as yesterday, but it's warmer and our real problem today is too much sunshine. We have to play the scene whenever a cloud comes over, and it takes two or three hours. But it plays easily and naturally, without great dramatics, which I'm sure is the right way. Maggie happier today, which helps. I fool around a bit and try to keep morale up. But the relentless battering from the wind eventually gets through to me, as we push ourselves into a series of wide shots as the sun goes down and the wind takes on a bitter, unfriendly edge. But at least the rain holds off and we finish all we need on the grouse moor.

Back to the hotel. Glorious hot bath. Then have to summon up shred of strength from somewhere to attend a unit party downstairs in the Post House. Second wind and end up dancing and talking until four o'clock. Need to let off steam.

Friday, May 28th

Wake quite early and doze. Rachel comes into our bed about 7.15 to cuddle up with me. Bright sunshine and the papers full of the Pope's first visit to Britain. Brief, illusory feeling that we have finished. Buy the paper for the first time in weeks, eat breakfast at my own table – other delusions of freedom.

Down to Tite Street in Chelsea with Brian. London looking marvellous in perfect May sunshine. We are shooting in a wonderfully cluttered old studio – a marvellous, characterful, eccentric house in a street full of marvellous, characterful, eccentric houses, mostly studios dating from the 1890s and decorated in early Art Nouveau style.

When we *do* shoot, Trevor takes a long time and has to have his words on an idiot board. Maggie says she should have seen the warning lights this morning when Trevor arrived in Tite Street with a broad smile at a quarter past ten, looked at his watch and said 'Open in a quarter of an hour.'

Tuesday, June 1st: London–Aviemore, Scotland

Awake most of the night – not troubled, just very hot and sticky and aware that I have only till 5.35 to sleep. Brian calls for me at 6.15. We pick up RL and catch the 7.40 Inverness flight from Heathrow, with the 39 others in our reduced unit.

Drive to Ardverikie House. 'Decathlon acting' this afternoon – riding horses, leaping and running onto carts and finally endless rowing shots back and forth across Loch Laggan.

Even after the sun had sunk behind Creag Meagoidh there was a soft pink glow in the sky over the loch, whilst the sharp outlines of the mountains behind us were slowly concealed by a soft mist. The water was still, the mosquitoes frequent, and it was very, very beautiful. I was still out there – a madly rowing vicar – at 9.30.

Wednesday, June 2nd: Aviemore

Work in the afternoon – running up stairs and along corridors.

RL has organised a party after shooting – there are two lambs roasted on the spit, a bonfire, candles in the trees, sangria and beers to drink.

A 'band' arrives, comprising two rather sullen young Scotsmen, who sit, slumped, on the side of the specially erected stage beside the shore, with drooping cigarettes, murdering popular ballads, and being saved only by a bagpiper and Ken Lintott and Ramon singing 'Sit On My Face'.

Towards ten o'clock RL prepared for his illuminated spoon-playing performance. As part of his 'light show', he ignited explosive on his hat, which shot a blast into the sky and made a much appreciated smoke ring eddy over the gathering before anyone realised that Richard had quite severely burnt his hand. He was taken off to a local doctor.

Thursday, June 3rd: Aviemore

For an hour or so this morning the bedroom scene, in which I try to dissuade Maggie from killing Lord A, became rather heavy work. First it lay rather flat, then RL wanted me to be more assertive, which led to me being louder and stronger, but making the lines sound suddenly melodramatic.

The scene clicked when we played it softly, listening to what each other was saying and responding accordingly – which sounds obvious, but is actually a difficult effect to achieve in a film, with marks, tight, precise movements and a clutter of camera, mikes and semi-slumbering members of the crew all around.

Saturday, June 5th: Aviemore

Another clear, still, sunny morning. Yesterday was the hottest of the year in Scotland and today seems set to cap it. Am soon put to work on ride-through shots up in the woods beside the loch. Shafts of sunlight through the trees and hordes of midges.

Rest of the day doing interiors – running up twisting staircases à la *Jabberwocky* and hanging off battlements. All in my hat and long black coat, which is very uncomfortable today.

In the garden a man plays with his children. It's all hot, still, unmoving and vaguely unreal. Reminds me of the *Grande Meaulnes* or *Picnic at Hanging Rock*. A feeling of melancholy in the back of my mind as I look out. Regret and some sadness.

Of course, it's the last day of main shooting. These people who've helped me and been a daily part of my life for the last ten weeks will be strangers again tomorrow.

About 6.30 I do my last shot up in the turret room. There's a smattering of applause. Maggie dashes off because she can't bear goodbyes. I leave the crew filming a stunt man on the battlements and head back to Aviemore. On the way I stop at Maggie's hotel to drop something off for Ramon. Meet Maggie on the way out. Her eyes start to fill with tears. Find a lovely note from her back at the Post House.

Bathe, collect some champagne and sandwiches and catch the 9.34 sleeper to Euston. A party in my compartment with the camera crew, Chuck Finch and Ken Lintott. No chance for further melancholy.

A much-reduced unit then moved out to Africa, to shoot Fortescue's days as a missionary.

Wednesday, June 9th: Samburu Lodge, Kenya

A good night's sleep, but woken by the accumulating cacophony of birdsongs and screeches and baboon roars. At breakfast hornbills and yellow weaver birds fly to the table-side and a vervet monkey makes a sudden lightning dash and removes Peter Hannan's toast. A moment or two later a vervet disappears up the tree with a sugar bowl. The waiters throw rocks after the monkeys in desultory fashion, but I should think deep down they rather enjoy the guests being made a monkey of.

About eight we set out to see the mud-walled Mission hut which Peter Verard and Norman Garwood have been here for a week constructing. It looks marvellous. Beside it is my tent – with portable writing table – and three mud huts made by Samburu ladies.

At the local school we are treated as VIPs as we arrive to listen to 'Greenland's Icy Mountains' sung in English by the Samburu kids. Proudly their teacher, Leonard, conducts them, and solemnly the children sing. A little flat in parts, but the words ring out clearly from a score of serious little black faces – 'The heathen in his wisdom bows down to wood and stone.'

Thursday, June 10th: Kenya

My first day of *Missionary* work in Africa. Alarm goes at half past five. Shave and dress and it's still dark outside. Assemble, cups of coffee and tea, and out to the location, nearby in the park, ready to cycle at first light. Pass an angry bull elephant, impala, gerenuk (the deer that never drinks) and the little black drongo bird.

At 6.30 punctually the sun comes up – so fast that there is little time for red skies and orange light – it's almost straight into a soft yellowy-green. On 'Action!' I set our vintage cycle in motion, but the pedal snaps.

Later, I'm walking past some camels with my umbrella up, when the sound camera breaks down. Lunchtime crisis. The camera, with all its sophisticated technological bowels spread open, lies on the bulrush benches in the little mud chapel. It's pronounced dead and all sorts of gloom descends. Urgent messages to London, but the nearest telephone contact is 40 miles away in Nanyuki.

We carry on with a mute Arriflex.

Friday, June 11th: Kenya

We are ready to start filming in front of the Mission hut at six o'clock. Me writing a letter home beside a roaring fire. There's a brisk wind and sometimes the flames threaten to engulf my writing desk.

We take a two-and-a-half-hour break in the middle of the day. Walk with RL (who never stops) amongst the trees and scrub, looking for insects. He finds mainly dung and scarab beetles and puts them in his jar.

Just after lunch the village kills a cow. It's a ritual slaughter carried out by the morani. The women of the village are not allowed to be a party to it, so the ceremony takes place beyond the thorn branches which mark the limits of the manyatta.

After being cruelly manhandled out of the truck, the cow is killed with a warrior's spear driven quickly and neatly into the back of the head to sever the spinal cord. I remember now the repeated dull crack of metal on bone as the spear was driven home. Then the twitching cow is lain on its side and a cup is carefully made from the loose skin on the throat. This is filled with blood, and the elders of the tribe are the first ones to stoop and drink the blood.

As I watch from the discreet shade of a thorn tree, the chief calls to me, 'Hey, Padre!' and beckons to the makeshift cup of blood. I mutter something apologetically about having to get back to acting and hurry off to the manyatta.

The other unlikely event of the afternoon was the arrival of Neville Thompson with a new synch sound camera. The message had reached him at 5.30 on Thursday evening and, with commendably quick thinking, N was in Nairobi with new equipment at nine Friday morning. Neville, white and rather haggard, appeared briefly in amongst the huts as I was trying to put together an ad-libbed argument with an aged Samburu. Then he was gone.

Saturday, June 12th: Kenya

This is the morning when we do Fortescue walking past wild animal shots.

When we sighted elephants after 30 minutes of driving, engines were cut and I walked out and past the beasts whilst Bagaboi – a Samburu ranger – covered me with a loaded rifle from behind a hedge. They all thought I was very brave. 'Hasn't he ever seen anyone trampled to death by an elephant?' Bagaboi asked, and of course that was absolutely the point. I hadn't. What appeared to them as courage was just massive ignorance.

Unsuccessfully tried to get near giraffe and crested cranes. I was told to walk slowly and deliberately through the grass 'because of the snakes'.

We shot the choir in the Mission hut in the afternoon. They had managed to learn three more verses of Bishop Heber's convoluted prose in the last two days and we were very pleased and applauded them.

Sunday, June 13th: Kenya

Today the reward of safari with no filming. Derek Barnes [our Kenya location manager] is taking myself, RL, Shuna [Harwood, costumer designer] Gary White [first assistant director] and Peter Hannan to Shava Park, near to the Samburu but, he says, much quieter. So we assemble once again around the bougainvillea-clad entrance to the lodge, just as the sun is rising. Baboons scurry after the trailer taking rubbish to the tip, like dealers at a jumble sale.

After two and a half hours we drive up to Shava Lodge. The sun shines in shafts of light through the foliage and gives the whole place a Garden of Eden-like quality. And they are well-equipped too. A full English breakfast – bacon, sausage, the lot – is cooked for us on a barbecue and served with thick-cut marmalade and toast. On an impulse I suggest Buck's Fizz and, extraordinarily enough, they have a bottle of champagne chilled.

Oohs and ahs of quiet pleasure, added to by the gentle hurrying of streams which flow from a diverted river down through the lodge gardens to the river.

Derek, armed with a panga, cuts a route down to the base of the waterfall and Hannan, Gary and myself strip off and walk beneath the waterfall itself. The hard, cooling water thuds down on us. Afterwards we sunbathe naked on a rock by the river. It's quite perfect and I could easily stay there until the end of the day – no people, no sun-oil, no deck-chairs, no pool-side bars selling over-priced drinks – just sun and water and solitude.

Out to the airport. At ten to twelve, with RL supine on a customs counter, the camera crew, Norman Garwood and myself partook of our last Tusker beers at the airport bar.

A rather crumbling, tired little group we were – with the results of our three days' intensive filming in brown boxes in an airport trolley. As someone said, this really was the end of picture party.

Thursday, June 17th

Drive up to Lee's for a viewing of the latest rough assembly of *Missionary*. Present are a half-dozen besuited young executives from Huttons. [HandMade's advertising agency].

Denis is there, looking very cheery, because even *Scrubbers* seems to be going the right way now.

We see about one and a half hours of the film. Start is sticky as usual, but once it gets going, largely helped by DO'B's infectious laughter, it works well and smoothly. No standing ovation at the end, but people clearly impressed.

Interesting reaction from Huttons was that it took them by surprise. It was nothing they had expected from either the synopsis or from previous work of mine. They all talked very positively about it – shook my hand and congratulated me.

Have to leave early to go to a Python wig-fitting.

Monday, June 21st

Halfway through one of the most hectic years of my life. That in itself is encouraging. I'm still alive and healthy. A few grey hairs showing since *The Missionary*, but I feel quite trim (11.1) and just about on top of things.

Take Rachel to school. Apparently her teacher says she has been much better this last week. I think she needs her dad and I feel very relieved that my five weeks' absence on *The Missionary* is over (longer, I suppose, if one counts the weekends and the early starts and late finishes we worked even when we were in London).

A showing of the film so far at four.

There is much good laughter and the Slatterthwaite sequence goes so well that it's impossible to follow in terms of audience reaction.

The Scottish sequence is disappointing to me in terms of performance. The last 15 minutes become very serious and very quiet and I don't enjoy them at all in the present company. I know they're wishing Michael Hordern would come on again (says he paranoically).

RL is very anxious for me to work with him on the next two weeks' editing – for we have to present a fine cut at the end of that time.

He wants me to cancel my trip to Columbia in LA. I feel it's essential to meet these faceless people before I go into Python confinement, so we compromise. I will go to the States for two days instead of three, returning Friday lunchtime and working with Richard right through the weekend.

Tuesday, June 22nd

At 9.20 a car collects me and takes me down to the US Embassy to collect my passport. There is a tube strike so the roads are packed. It's raining heavily. Into the dreadful world of visa applications – rows of faces looking anxiously to a row of faceless clerks behind desks. No-one wants to be there. I collect my passport – have to sign that I'm not a communist or a

Nazi, and several pieces of paper for fans who work in the Passport Office.

Then out to Heathrow, where I arrive at eleven. The delights of travelling First Class then take over. I have only hand baggage so check quickly through and into the BA Executive Lounge for some coffee and another long call to RL. I feel we should not show Columbia the end of *The Missionary* until it's right, but Denis has a video with everything we saw yesterday on it – so we'll have to do a re-editing job, and erase some of the tape. Get Rose Mary Woods[1] in as adviser!

The flight leaves a half-hour late. DO'B travelled Club Class with his two daughters. I visited them occasionally – taking them smoked salmon and other First Class delights. Denis's daughters sat, very well-behaved, and read and coloured books whilst DO'B immersed himself in columns of figures. Most of his deals, he says proudly, were worked out at 35,000 feet.

Wednesday, June 23rd: Beverly Wilshire Hotel, Los Angeles

Denis calls about nine o'clock to tell me that their reactions to the three video segments of the movie which they've already seen have been excellent. Everyone from Antonowsky (he's the President of Marketing) downwards filled with enthusiasm. That's a good start.

Am picked up by Denis and Inge at ten. He rents a brand new Mercedes, and we drive out to his office at Burbank. There meet Dan Polier – a thin, slowly-precise talking, late-middle-aged man with neat silver-grey hair – and David Knopf his chunky junior partner. They are Denis's sidekicks on film distribution.

'Just been working with a fan of yours,' says Polier. 'Steven Spielberg.' That doesn't spoil the morning either. Apparently they are working on *ET*, which looks set to be the biggest box-office picture ever.

At midday we walk over to Columbia Pics.

Long, low, modern office. Softly and thickly carpeted. Tall, gaunt figure of Marvin Antonowsky looming over them all. He stands like a great bird, eyes flicking around, his lean frame held back almost apologetically. He welcomes me into his office with some kind words about what he's seen, then a group of about eight or nine Columbia hacks are brought in. All seem very quiet and respectable and deferential. Young – mostly my age or less. Ken Blancato, the creative publicity head, is neat and trim and looks like a hairdresser. They don't immediately strike me as an intimidatingly forceful team. Very well-behaved in

---

[1] At the Watergate hearings in 1973 the hapless Rose Mary Woods, President Nixon's secretary, claimed she'd 'pressed the wrong button' on her tape recorder, accidentally erasing four and a half minutes of what could have been incriminating testimony.

the presence of their president, behind whose desk is a shelf full of maybe 40 screenplays. I notice *Scrubbers* is there, alongside *The Missionary*.

Antonowsky and Blancato are very confident that they have some wonderful campaign ideas and, without much ado, an artist reveals six of the most crass and dreadful drawings I've seen in my life. If I had set down on paper my worst fears of what they might produce, these would be they. A grinning, Animal House-like caricature of myself with girls dressed in 1960's Playboy Bunny-style outfits, with tits and thighs emphasised at the expense of period, beauty, truth, honesty and everything else. I have to say I find them a little obvious. 'Oh, yeah, well that's why we have another version . . .'

Ah, the subtle one. The subtle one consists of me kneeling at a long bed, with a dozen 1950's beauties lined up on either side of me in a parody of the Last Supper. I sit there, with all these expectant faces looking towards me, and I wish the floor would open and swallow me up – or swallow them up, anyway. If ever there was a moment when I wanted a Los Angeles earthquake, this was it.

But the moment passed and they proved to be not at all unadaptable. It was not a terribly easy session, though. They revealed, with a sparkling air of revelation, their slogan: 'He used his body to save their souls.' Denis sat there remarkably unmoved and I couldn't leap up and down with excitement.

Thursday, June 24th: Los Angeles

Some more writing of blurb for ads, then Denis collects me at ten. Drive to his office at Warners and I show him, Knopf and Polier my suggested ad lines and synopses. They are instantly typed up, to be presented to Columbia at our 11.30 meeting.

Also sketch out an idea for a trailer – very quick, short one-liners showing Fortescue becoming progressively more trapped. DO'B loves this and, when we file into the even more gaunt and haggard Antonowsky's office, DO'B cheerfully announces that I've solved everything – we have radio, TV and trailer advertising all sewn up. His faith in me is embarrassing, as I fumble with pieces of paper to try and bear out this hyperbolic introduction.

I read them some of the ad lines – quite a few chuckles. Outline the trailer idea, which is also met with approval. 'He had a lover, a fiancée and 28 fallen women. And he said yes to all of them' sounds the favourite, though they still cling to their 'He gave his body to save their souls' line. But Antonowsky reacts well, directs them to work on the lines I've proposed and, unless he is just flannelling me, I feel that we have progressed by leaps and bounds since yesterday – and hopefully my work yesterday evening and this morning has given me the initiative.

Taken to Hamptons – a big, noisy hamburger restaurant just beside Warners' Burbank studio – by Polier, Knopf and Denis O'B. Then a return visit to Columbia, in which I am wheeled into a conference room where about 15 PR people sit round a table. Ed Roginski, a rather calm, soft-spoken and intelligent head of publicity, chairs the meeting and all those around the table introduce themselves to me – name and position.

They ask me things like whether I have any special needs I would like catered for when I go on promotion. They are (thankfully) against a three-week cross-country whistle-stop tour (which TG underwent for *Time Bandits*). They suggest instead a week and a weekend in New York – including a 'Junket Day', when they bring key out-of-town press and radio into the city, all expenses paid, and throw me and, they hope, Maggie to them.

Polier and Knopf feel that the sooner exhibitors can see *The Missionary* the better for choice of cinemas, etc. Columbia is going through a bad time with *Annie*[1] – despite enormous amounts of publicity effort it has not brought the house down on its nationwide launch – and there really isn't any picture they can get excited about (apart from *Python Live at the Hollywood Bowl*, which opens tomorrow) until *Missionary* comes along.

A limousine picks me up at 4.30 and I'm driven back to the airport. Onto the 6.30 flight.

Sleep through *On Golden Pond* for the second time in three weeks.

Monday, June 28th

The start of Python rehearsals and writing for *Meaning of Life* coincides with the first national rail strike for 27 years and a London tube and partial bus stoppage. I drive quite easily to Regent's Park, and by great good fortune, find a parking space right outside the new office, and arrive only just after JC. He, too, is sporting a moustache. He grins delightedly at me and says I look *quite* different. Not sure how to take this.

Python Live at the Hollywood Bowl opened at 60–70 cinemas in NYC and Philadelphia to overwhelming apathy. Various reasons put forward – first weekend of excellent weather in NYC; very strong opposition from Spielberg, *Star Wars* and *Rocky*; opening too wide with too little publicity. EI very strongly blames *Secret Policeman's Ball*, which GC advertised on American TV evidently.

After a half-hour discussion it's clear that no-one has an answer. The movie collected good reviews in both the big NYC papers.

Eric wins 'The Meaning of Life' song with no declared supporters for TJ's

---

[1] A big-budget movie based on the cartoon strip Little Orphan Annie, starring Albert Finney and Carol Burnett and directed by John Huston.

version apart from myself and T G, and neither of us felt Eric's version deserving of any stick. But on 'Every Sperm is Sacred', on which TJ has done – *had* to do – so much work, there is quite a strong split. Eric takes up the position that his version is much better, musically and in every other way, than TJ's. GC bears him out quite vehemently. TJ says that his version is better, musically and in every other way, than Eric's.

Once we start discussion it's clearly crucial that JC comes down firmly in favour of TJ's version.

Tuesday, June 29th

Sandwiches at lunch and talk over the ending. Eric feels that we have cheated the audience by not having come to grips with our title. I see our title as being a statement in itself. There is no way we can tell anyone the meaning of life – it's a cliché and we are using it ironically to show how irrelevant we can be when faced with such a pretentious subject. John sees fish as the answer to our problem.

Eventually I ad-lib, with Eric's help, a very short and dismissive lady presenter winding up the film and reading the meaning of life from an envelope – this fed on from a nice idea of a Hollywood awards-type ceremony where we asked a glittery compere to come on and reveal the meaning of life. He opens a gold envelope and reads ... 'And the meaning of life is ... Colin Welland!' I think this was the best laugh of the day.[1]

We broke up about 3.30. I had a cab driver who at one point came out with the line 'Do you know how long I spent in the shower last night ...? One and a half hours ... Mind you, I felt better at the end of it.'

Saturday, July 3rd

Bowl returns even worse than Denis had led me to believe at the beginning of the week – we were 'gasping' in Philadelphia to a gross less than that of a *Bambi* reissue the week before and in N Y C only managed 125,000 dollars at 58 sites! Dreadful.

If the cliché 'you've seen one, you've seen them all' applies to any sphere of human activity, it must be school fairs – or 'fayres' as they're wont to call them. As with the Gospel Oak Fayre two weeks ago, the William Ellis version was the usual collection of bric-a-brac, shabby clothes and grubby books for sale. A few gallant sideshows run by the boys. Two tombolas run with steely-eyed

---

[1] At the 1982 Academy Awards Welland had famously brandished the Oscar for *Chariots of Fire* and shouted 'The British Are Coming!'

efficiency by the sort of parents who like running things. Some rather wet chicken tikka out in the car park, and not much else.

Helen had put together a hamper and she sat for nearly three hours beside it for about £17.00. Tom played in the wind band in the main hall at four, which was a very pleasant addition to the usual format. Took the girls back via a toyshop and bookshop in Kentish Town (I bought Mary Kingsley's *Travels in West Africa*), then home.

Am I getting more like my father in old age? I've noticed definite signs of easily roused impatience and intolerance since *The Missionary*. I put it down to the fact that co-producing, writing and acting was a giant public relations job in which I had to be all things to all men every day for eleven weeks, and the thing I need the rest from most is not acting or writing, but people.

Saturday, July 4th

Take the children for a swim. Re-read W L Warren's book about my favourite English king – John. Discover Angevins had violent tempers. Also that the twelfth century was the best-documented in English mediaeval history.

Monday, July 5th

To Python rehearsal, to find that Neil Simon had been on the phone and wants to meet me – he has some film project.

After a costume fitting I drive up to Britannia Row Studios in Islington to record 'Every Sperm' track. Ring Neil Simon. He professes himself to be a fan, says he is halfway through 'one of the best things I've written' and there's a part in it for me. Arrange to meet him on Wednesday.

The recording session is delayed while they find a piano tuner, so I sit in the big and comfortable games room and watch England start their vital match with Spain. They must win and by two goals to be certain of going into the semi-finals. Our defence is unshakeable, mid-field quite fast and controlling most of the game, but we can't score. 0–0 at half-time.

In between play I've been singing 'Sperm Song' to Trevor Jones's rather solid beat. Eventually we find a combination of takes we're comfortable with and I drive home to watch the second half. England fail to score and slide out of the World Cup. It's a hot evening.

Tuesday, July 6th

Third day of another rail strike. NUR gave in rather pathetically last week. Now it's ASLEF's turn [ASLEF was the train-drivers' union]. Reprehensible Thatcher statements likening ASLEF to the Argentinians we defeated 'so gloriously' in the Falklands.

Drive in at ten and we rehearse three or four sketches, on sofas doubling as First World War trenches, with our scripts in hand. Fizzles out about one. Costume fitting for me as a schoolboy.

Home for a run, do some work, then I have to change, bathe and go down to meet Marvin Antonowsky at Odin's. I've arranged the meal at his instigation, and he says he's very pleased that it's only the two of us, as he would just like us to get to know each other a little better.

He seems to be rather ill at ease with the food and the ordering, but talks quite fluently about his early days in advertising, his admiration for Frank Price – the President of Columbia – his stint as head of programmes at NBC, during which he claimed credit for starting *Saturday Night Live*; his move to ABC and eventual elevation to marketing head at Columbia.

He compliments me, with a sort of little head on one side smile, 'You're a good little actor ... you come over well on screen.' He clearly wants to work together again and assures me that Columbia would like to do the next thing I come up with. When I tell him I'm meeting Neil Simon to discuss a part he gets very excited. Like all Californians he uses hyperbole quite undiscriminatingly, starting with 'wonderful' for people whose guts he probably hates and working up through 'amazing' and 'marvellous' to 'absolutely incredible' human beings. Neil is 'absolutely incredible' and 'a great friend'.

Wednesday, July 7th

Over to Inn on the Park to meet Neil Simon. A man of about my height with a warm, friendly manner answers the door. He apologises for walking with a lean, but five days ago he slipped a disc, after watching Wimbledon (at Wimbledon – he's a tennis freak). Apparently he went into spasm one morning as room service called and he retold, with comedy writer's relish, how he pulled himself across the room and collapsed at the open door as he let in his breakfast. He couldn't be moved from the doorway for two hours – body half out in the passage as curious guests walked by.

After some talk and some morale-boosting admiration of my 'natural and likeable' acting persona, he told me of his project – a half-written play with a part just right for me. Apologising for being unable to précis the idea, he asked if I had time enough to read the 60 pages of his typed first draft. I agreed readily. He gave me the script, then went discreetly into his bedroom with the two *Ripping Yarns* books I'd brought as a present for him.

I recall the play was called 'Heaven and Hell' and began, with a disconcerting resemblance to *Arthur*, on a scene between an elderly butler and a very rich young man who is a miser. He's bashed on the head in a carefully organised collision in his car and taken by a gang to a warehouse which has been got up as heaven.

It looks so like the heaven that this character has come to know from the 1940's movies he always watches, that he believes in it and when they tell him he has three days to go back to earth and raise enough money to avoid them sending him to hell, he falls for it. Some very funny lines, but a disappointingly one-dimensional character.

I find my attention wandering as I read to what I'm going to say to this most famous of all American comedy writers when I've finished. Fortunately he makes it very easy for me and we talk about the character and I can express some of my feelings about him being real and understandable and Simon agrees and says he will put in more at the beginning explaining the young man's miserliness. I have to say that I can't make up my mind, that I'm very flattered, etc, etc, but being a writer myself I will probably want to write something of my own after *Missionary*.

Truth be told, I found the play lightweight in the two areas I enjoy so much – character and detail. I'm very tickled to see he has a rather insignificant character in his play called 'Antonowsky'.

Thursday, July 8th

To Claridge's to meet Ken Blancato – Columbia's VP of publicity [to organise a shoot for their poster]. Am not allowed into the cocktail lounge, as I have no tie or jacket. 'Rather silly in this weather, I know, sir ... ' agrees the porter in thick overcoat who escorts us out.

Sit in the lobby and have a couple of beers. Blancato is a New Yorker and worked in Madison Avenue. He's also a frustrated writer. When I reiterate my reservations about the roof-top shots with the girls, etc, he grins rather wearily. I feel I'm just making a nuisance of myself.

I go on from Claridge's to Neal's Yard, to try another recording of 'Every Sperm', as Monday's didn't sound entirely satisfactory. André and Trevor have rather different views of how to approach my vocal, and it's not a particularly successful session, as I'm in a rush anyway.

On to Mon Plaisir for a meal with TG. He says he'd rather like to be a monk. We talk some business. We've seen figures that show 17 million dollars returned to [Avco] Embassy [from *Time Bandits*] and none of that is owed to either of us.

Friday, July 9th

Car picks me up at 8.30 and drives me down to the Great Northern Hotel. King's Cross and St Pancras silent and deserted at the end of the first week of the rail strike.

Onto the rooftop – another hot, slightly hazy morning. Richard is there with son Joe, a bit subdued. Also he doesn't like what David Alexander [the photographer] and Camille – the bored, drawling, world-weary Columbia lady who is Blancato's number two – are doing. He's very quiet as Alexander sets up the shot and fires off reels of film like there's no tomorrow.

At lunchtime we're finished and down the contraceptive-scattered stairwells into cars and on to Lant Street, where Norman Garwood and co have rebuilt my Mission bedroom.

I have to work rather hard leaping up and down and presenting endless expressions to seemingly endless rolls of film, whilst the photographer urges me on with shouts ranging from '*Won*derful,' which means very ordinary, to 'Just the best!' when I'm trying a bit.

At one point Camille, who looks dreadfully out of place in her Beverly Hills straw hat and white strides, steps in to change a shot in which three Mission girls are in bed, and I'm below. We're not allowed to show any rude bit, or suggestion of a rude bit, so I've made sure that the girls are well-wrapped in sheets (quite unlike the way they appear in the film). But this is not enough for Camille, who fears that the very suggestion that the girls might be nude *under* the sheets could result in the ad running into trouble in the Deep South.

At this my fatigue – that intolerable fatigue of working hard on a job in which you have no confidence – causes me to crack and we have a heated exchange on the subject of *The Missionary* and the Deep South. 'It's not me ...' she keeps pleading, which makes it worse, because I want to know who it is who wants to do this to our film. That there are more than averagely narrow-minded people in the Deep South I don't doubt, but what are we all doing here today, working our asses off to try and reach down to their level?.

Monday, July 12th

Slept unsatisfactorily – woke at intervals from four o'clock onwards. The adrenaline is beginning to flow – the surge of nervous energy that I will need in the next ten weeks has to come from somewhere and the last two weeks since *Missionary* 'finished' have not really been enough to get right away from one film and into the other.

To the Royal Masonic School in Bushey, a largely red-brick amalgam of all the old public school architectural clichés. A few flying buttresses here, a clock tower and some cloisters there.

JC asks me about ASLEF and the implications of and background to their strike. I think he might be sending me up, but he's quite serious. I was quoted, somewhat misleadingly, in the *Mirror* on Saturday as saying I supported ASLEF. It's just that I can't stand to hear this self-righteous government trying to pretend it's more of a friend to the railways than the proud, independent, much-maligned and bullied train drivers' union. If the government really had the good of the railways at heart this present action would never have happened.

We're starting with a scene involving Cleese and myself and an entire chapelful of boys and masters. I play a chaplain and the similarities to March 29th continue as I don a dog collar and have my hair swept back. I even keep my *Missionary* moustache.

Thursday, July 15th

To the Masonic School again. Feeling of despondency as Brian drives me into the gates. I feel no emotional attachment to this location, as I did to those on *The Missionary*. It's a place of work. The weather doesn't help – it's overcast and looks like rain. Caravans are a good walk away from the location – so nowhere really to rest during the day.

EI cheers me up. He's in good form and we sit and make each other laugh whilst waiting for lighting set-ups in the classroom. I've brought him Signford's two Chris Orr books, which he wants for David Bowie, who has much admired Eric's Orr collection.

Keep in touch with Missionary, where Maggie S is patiently waiting for me to come in and post-synch with her. But have to keep giving them increasingly pessimistic estimates and in the end the session is abandoned and I find myself still being a schoolboy in Bushey at seven o'clock.

Sunday, July 18th

Leave at eight and drive out to Twickenham. I enjoy the sunshine and the emptiness of the roads and the little courtyard at Twickenham Studios, with flower tubs everywhere, is convivial and friendly. Richard has arrived on his bike, which he describes disarmingly, as 'Probably the best that money can buy' – and then proceeds to tell stories about how he fell off it and rode into parked cars.

Post-synch the entire 'Bottling Factory'[1] scene and we finish at one o'clock.

As I arrive back at Julia Street I find a group of kids around a cat lying in the gutter – obviously barely alive after being hit by a car. I ring the local RSPCA and they ask if I could bring the cat in. Am just loading it into the hamper I won about 30 years ago in a Fry's Chocolate competition when the Browns – the Irish family on the corner opposite – return from their Sunday lunchtime trip to the pub. Mrs Brown becomes very tearful when she identifies the cat I'm bundling rather unceremoniously into my hamper as once belonging to her granddaughter Deborah, who died tragically of appendicitis after a doctor's mix-up.

I drive to Seven Sisters Road. RSPCA man thinks there's a fair chance of its survival, which I wouldn't have expected. Cats' broken pelvises do heal quite successfully usually.

Home to the Browns to bear them this welcome news. Mr Brown, who calls me 'Palin' or 'Young Palin', insists that I stay and have a drink. A Scotch is all that's on offer – served in what looks like an Austrian wine glass. But it's very pleasant – like walking into the snug bar of a very convivial pub. No introductions or all the delicate, defensive small talk which the middle classes are plagued with – the Scotch warms me physically and mentally and I have a lovely half-hour. Mr Brown very Irish, with lilting voice, soft and very articulate, and always a quiet smile in everything he says. They couldn't be more different from the sobbing group I left half an hour before. They celebrate their happiness just as enthusiastically and openly as their grief.

Friday, July 23rd

My twelfth early start, and twelfth working day on the trot. At least this morning I am spurred on by the sight of light at the end of the tunnel – by the prospect of not only a weekend off, but then seven filming days in which I'm not involved.

But today is no easy downhill slope. For a start Eric and I have a long dialogue scene [in the hotel sequence] – four and a half minutes or so. TG has a wonderfully complex and grotesque make-up as the Arab Porter. Then there is much re-lighting and building of rostrums after TJ decides to shoot the whole scene in one. So Eric and I walk through at 8.30, then wait, in make-up and costume, until a quarter to one before they are ready.

---

[1] This scene, in which Fortescue goes to ask for money for his Mission, was shot, rather grandly, at the old Royal Mint on Tower Hill. Sadly, it held up the story and never made the final cut.

We do two or three takes at about 1.30, and in two of them I forget my lines and have to stop – which is unusual enough for me to make me rather cross and depressed when lunchtime comes. I really feel the accumulated fatigue of an eleven-week shoot and then these last twelve working days. Fortunately after lunch with EI and the strangely attired Gilliam, I feel better and, although I have to push myself physically hard, I find that I'm actually enjoying the piece.

TG, with his blind eye (as used in *Holy Grail*), nose too big for him and the wheel on his false hand broken, has created for himself his own peculiar nightmare, and he will be trapped in it again on Monday.

Sunday, July 25th

A party at Barry Cryer's in Hatch End. Roomful of comedians. R Barker, R Corbett, Eric Morecambe, Frankie Howerd, Peter Cook prominent.

Chat with Ronnie C. With a relieving sense of self-mockery, he reveals his customary interest in Python's financial affairs, business arrangements, etc. RB looks around gloomily. 'Too many comedians here,' he says. 'Not so good for character actors.' He too is obsessed with Python's wealth. 'All millionaires now?' he asks, not wholly unseriously.

Peter Cook, who wasn't exactly invited, is more forthcoming and entertaining. He's come straight from Vic Lownes's[1] house and somehow found himself at Barry's. He's very pleased with the video version of his Derek and Clive second LP. He says it's going to be shot in 2-D. He asks me in what part of Africa *The Missionary* was shot. Turns out his father was a DC in Nigeria. Cookie, in a rare moment of sentiment, clearly felt quite an admiration for his father – 'People ask me about influences on me – the Goons, Waugh, etc, etc – but in the end the person who influenced me most was my father.'

One of the King Brothers – Michael, I think – tells of a very funny stage act he used to work with – a man who wore a German First World War helmet and threw a cartwheel in the air and caught it on it as the climax of his act. The audience loved it. Only the rest of the cast (who used to flock into the wings whenever he was on) could see the acute expression of pain on his face every time he did it.

[1] Victor Lownes III was the London head of the Playboy organisation and had been the driving force behind Monty Python's first film *And Now For Something Completely Different* (1970).

Monday, July 26th

With the lighting already up and the Hendy hotel room piece already played through, I'm ready for my close-ups by a quarter to nine and have done the scene by 9.30. I feel looser and funnier and much more on top of the scene than last Friday and almost wish we could do the whole thing again.

But Eric is much quieter today. He apparently suffered a 24-hour 'flu yesterday, with hallucinations and temperature. His voice is huskier than Friday and he is clearly not happy with the performance. But he improves as we go on, and cheers up too. His son Carey comes to the set, a small, bright-eyed, scrawny little lad clutching a copy of *Rolling Stone* containing an interview with his hero – Sylvester Stallone – in *Rocky III*.

Leave the studio at two. Six shooting days off – feels like a school half-term, saying goodbye to everyone. Home for a wonderfully normal, unrushed, evening with family and a BBC programme on the chances of survival for Londoners in a nuclear attack.

Death from a nuclear blast would be short, sharp and sudden. Especially, the programme suggests, if you're living in Kentish Town!

To bed, very content.

Thursday, July 29th

I go up to CTS Music for the second day of *Missionary* music recording. I've never seen film music recorded before, so to enter this spacious modern studio, with its control room like a mighty ship's bridge, from which the eye is drawn downwards to a 60-strong orchestra, and beyond them to a screen high on the wall on which my antics appear, is stirring and a little frightening.

Everyone seems so competent and capable, from John [Richards] the mixer at his 36-track desk, to Mike Moran with his enormous score sheets, to Harry Rabinowitz (old acquaintance from *Frost on Sundays!*) looking not a day older, with headphones on and baton raised, to the orchestra of session men, who are probably from the London Symphony or the Philharmonic, but today are in jeans and T-shirts and reading newspapers in between cues. It's an epic undertaking and, when the Scottish themes thunder from the speakers to fill the control room, it's very moving.

RL and I have been discussing for the last few days an alternative photo idea for the print-ads – of Fortescue under a lamppost in the street, where normally only whores would stand. The contrast would be funny, there are three or four whores in the background to add any of the titillatory element Columbia might want. So it's resolved that there is no other way but for me to go to Denis this evening and heave some more money out of him.

Surprisingly, he accepts my point that we could do a better job here, and he likes the idea of the lamppost and the prostitutes. He will ring Columbia and tell them we want to shoot an alternative. The onus is now all on us to come up, in quite a rush, with something that lives up to our confident stand.

Tuesday, August 3rd

See assembly of 'Mr Creosote' at lunchtime (instead of lunch). Evidently 9,000 gallons of vomit were made for the sketch, which took four days to film. It's been edited rather loosely at a poor pace and dwelling too much on TJ's actual vomiting, but the costume is marvellous in its enormous surreal bulk, and Mr C's explosion is quite awful and splendid.

Wednesday, August 4th

The sticky heat continues. Oppressive, sluggish, still heaviness.

I feel quite tense from fatigue today and find myself at midday facing a long close-up take with my heart suddenly thudding, my voice thickening and my head swirling. Not a good sign of my condition, I feel. I just want to get away from films, film people and the whole process. But I am firmly stuck in it for the next few months.

As if to underline this, no sooner have I finished at Elstree than I have to go down to the Tower Hotel to prepare for an evening's shoot on the new poster. Peter Hannan comes along to help supervise the lighting of the street, we have four prostitutes and Angus Forbes is the photographer.

It's warm and still in Shad Thames where we're shooting, which helps to keep everybody happy and patient as the clock moves on to midnight, when we finish and drive back over Tower Bridge to the hotel to change. Find myself, dressed as a vicar, with Tricia George dressed as a most comely whore, in the lift with two American tourists. As they disembark at the ninth floor I gently remind them that 'London still swings'. 'Right!' was their nervous parting shot!

I'm home at 1.15.

Thursday, August 5th

Collected at 8.30 by Brian. I have a one-hour make-up as Debbie Katzenburg. Feel testy and rather low. For some reason the continuing news of the Israeli bombardment of West Beirut sickens me and I can't read the paper.

Eric, TJ and myself in drag, Cleese the Reaper, Chapman and TG the men. One of the few sketches involving all the Pythons.

The afternoon's work is slow – things like JC's beckoning bony finger taking up a lot of time, as special effects, animals and children always do.

TJ suggests we eat out together. Neither of us notice the irony that, although we've spent the whole day on a sketch in which a dinner party is poisoned by salmon mousse, I start with a delicious salmon mousse.

Friday, August 6th

A long morning around the table in a hot studio in drag. Simon Jones is playing the sixth member of the dinner party. He's a very good man with a quiet wit, well able to stand up for himself. In one morning he learnt the Python lesson in survival – over-act in your close-up, it's your only chance. Actually he did his piece modestly and very well.

Long afternoon as we have to dress in cottage walls every time we move round to do close-ups. GC and I are the last to be done. Then more special effects as we die. Eric and I blow out the candles then collapse, motionless on the table for 40 seconds. Cynthia Cleese hiccups during one of these long silences and sets us all off.

The day stretches on into evening and we sit and play games. JC hears that EI is dining out with David Bailey and, when EI has gone, expresses great incredulity that anyone should want to have dinner with David Bailey. Then he suggests we play a game – 'Not Michael, because he's far too nice about people' – to list our worst-ever dinner party.

After JC has been hauled back for yet another close-up of the Grim Reaper, Eric asides to me that it can't be much fun having dinner with John Cleese.

Saturday, August 7th

Tonight at six and eight are the first two public showings of *The Missionary* in America. Keep remembering this at odd times during the day. Moments of pleasurable anticipation.

Wolf a croissant, then up to Elstree for a tiger-skin fitting, only to find that my other half of the skin is in a pink suit doing the 'Galaxy Song' on Stage 3. Yet another breakdown in communication. Round to Stage 4 where mighty office buildings are being erected for TG's £100,000 'Accountancy/Pirate' epic.

Tucked in a corner is a tiny Yorkshire '30's cottage, filled with children who are rehearsing 'Every Sperm' for Monday. Little Arlene Phillips, with her bright, open, face and pink and maroon matching hair and tracksuit, is taking the kids through the number. We work out some movements for me to do, and then I read the build-up lines – all about 'little rubber things on the end of me cock' – some kids snigger, the younger ones smile up at me innocently

Home – and a relaxing evening in, broken only at one point by a huge series of explosions to the north. It's not the Israelis bombing possible PLO meeting houses in Kentish Town, or the IRA – the huge cracks and flashes lighting up this stodgy August evening are for the 1812 Overture, being played at Kenwood [open-air concert].

To bed after watching (and staying awake for) Hitchcock's *Notorious*. Superb performance by Ingrid Bergman. Very sexy. Put the phone right beside me in case I should get word from LA . . .

Sunday, August 8th

Richard L rings about half past two. The news is not good. He says he's confused and disappointed and just wishes I'd been at the viewings with him. He felt the audience was unsuitable – general age between 16 and 23, predominantly male – the *Stripes* and *Porky's* sort of audience. All subtitles and understated scenes went by in silence. Howls of appreciation and whoops when Maggie (or rather, Maggie's stand-in) goes down on me under the bed-clothes and the whores hop into bed.

But the figures – considering the nature of the audience – are not as discouraging when I think about them: 2% excellent, 30% very good, would recommend to friends, 40% average, quite enjoyed it, 19% only fair, and 9% thought it the worst movie they'd ever seen.

RL rings later in the evening. Says he's spoken with Denis O'B, who was, so I hear, not downhearted. They have come up with a list of proposed cuts which they want to make next week and show at a sneak preview in NYC on Saturday the 14th. Could I come? Concorde both ways. I have to say no, as Python is away on location in Scotland and Yorkshire.

Tuesday, August 10th

Arrive at Elstree 9.15. Wide shots first, with all the kids in. Mothers in attendance.

TJ is worried that there may be a walk-out if we say either my line – 'Little rubber thing on the end of my cock' – or one of the kids' lines – 'Couldn't you have your balls cut off?' – so we plan a subterfuge. I will say 'sock' instead of 'cock' (taking care not to over-emphasise the initial letter) and then the dastardly substitution will take place in the dubbing theatre. The boy's interruption will be of a quite harmless variety – 'Couldn't you sell Mother for scrap?' – when everyone is present, but we'll record the real line separately when everyone's gone.

The afternoon is very hard work. I have to go through the opening speeches, song and routine over and over and the room is warming up, and the kids, though well-behaved, have to be continually instructed and calmed down, which gets tiring. They all call me Dad, off the set.

Finish with the children (as we have to by law) at 5.30 and for a moment Ray Corbett [first assistant director], Hannan, Terry, Dewi[1] and myself slump onto chairs in the little room amongst the discarded toys – like shattered parents at the end of a two-day children's party. Nobody has the strength to say anything for a while. Then, with a supreme effort, we gird our loins and complete my tight close-ups. I end the day wild-tracking the phrase 'Little rubber thing on the end of my cock' . . . '*over* the end of my cock', and so on.

Thursday, August 12th: Glasgow

Leave the hotel at 8.30. Drive half an hour out to the north of the city, past more flattened slums, rows of shops with boards and metal frames over the windows. Then through wooded, pleasant suburbs to Strathblane, where we are quartered.

Some hanging around, talking to local press, crossword-puzzling and finally making up with mutton-chop whiskers and moustache, and squeezing into custom-made leather boots and the rather handsome navy blue uniform of a major in the Warwickshires of 1879.

Then we're driven a mile to the location – a five-minute walk up a hillside, where a British encampment has been constructed beneath a bare rock cliff, which I later gather is known in the area as Jennie's Lump.

Sudden drenching squalls of rain and cold wind cause us to abandon the planned shots and spend the day on weather-cover, with scenes inside the tent originally planned for Elstree. But it isn't only the unsettled weather which is forcing us to use weather-cover. Rumour reaches us during the morning that nearly 100 of our carefully selected and measured Glaswegian extras have walked out after a misunderstanding over costume in the local village hall.

A small group of very vocal Africans became angry when they were shown how to tie loin cloths by Jim Acheson (on the stage).[2] They had been misled,

---

[1] Dewi Humphreys, camera operator, went on to become a successful TV director (*Vicar of Dibley*, *Absolutely Fabulous* and many more).
[2] Acheson later won three Oscars for Costume Design: *The Last Emperor* (1987), *Dangerous Liaisons* (1988) and *Restoration* (1995).

they shouted. They thought they would be wearing suits. Poor Jim and his excellent wardrobe team faced a 1982 Zulu Uprising, as a group of two or three blacks shouted about being degraded, tricked ... dishonoured, etc, etc ... And 100 of them were taken back in buses to Glasgow.

We went on shooting – oblivious to all this – and completed most of the tent interiors by six o'clock. Back to the Albany. Bathe and change, looking out of my eighth-floor window across the wet streets to the grand, two-storey classical facade of Currie and Co, Building Trade Merchants. A fine, confident, assertive building, now in disrepair and white with bird shit. It looks as out of place amongst the new Glasgow horrors as a piece of Chippendale in a Wimpy Bar.

Dine with John Cleese and Simon Jones in the Albany restaurant. TJ restlessly at a nearby table with a dour Danish journalist. Simon Jones is relaxed, talkative and amusing. It turns out that he, like me, can't roll his 'r's.

Friday, August 13th: Glasgow

Cleesey very unwell this morning. We think it was the crayfish last night. At the hotel in Strathblane he looks awfully wan and up on the mountainside, as we prepare for the first Zulu attack, he is farting and belching, and at one stage actually throwing up against the barricades.

We have had to recruit white Glaswegians and brown them up as Zulus. I must say they are very patient and charge at the encampment ten times. It's a long day, heavy on extras and blood and smoke, and light on lines for the officers.

Newspapers – local and national – carry the story of the Zulus yesterday. Some very funny reports, especially in the *Glasgow Herald*. The nationals such as *The Times*, which refers to today's cast as predominantly 'unemployed youths' – note the use of the word 'youth', always pejorative – are less accurate. Still, all excellent publicity.

Try to contact Richard in New York, eventually get a rather fraught line from Strathblane to the Algonquin. Shout my instructions to some American receptionist and feel very abstracted from it all until I leave my name and the receptionist quickly returns 'As in *Ripping Yarns* ... ?' The Atlantic shrinks suddenly. But I never get to talk to Richard.

Back to the Albany. The bar is jostling with film technicians demanding of the hard-pressed barladies things like 'Two vodka tonics, two Guinness, two dry martinis, a soda water and take your knickers off.' An extra day's shooting tomorrow.

Sunday, August 15th: Bradford

To Bradford, where we eventually find the Norfolk Gardens Hotel – part of the atrocities which replaced a lot of Bradford's sturdy stone town centre with stained pre-stressed concrete. 110 of the 118 rooms are taken by our crew.

To bed 11.30. Walls wafer thin and I can hear every word from a TV blaring next door. Read half a page of Nabokov then drop off.

Woken at 2.30 by a call from RL to say that the New York preview went very well indeed with over 80% of the cards putting the film in the top three categories.

Monday, August 16th: Bradford and Malham, Yorkshire

Sixth week of Python filming – 17th week of filming since the end of March – begins with the pips from my calculator alarm slicing gently into my semi-consciousness at 6.45 a.m. It looks wet and uninviting outside.

Drive out to the location with Simon Jones, who points out to me the theatre in Bradford where Henry Irving [the great actor] collapsed, and the Midland Hotel, in whose foyer he died shortly afterwards, neglected by the hall porter who thought him a passing drunk. Sad end.

An hour and a half's drive into fine, rugged scenery up on Malham Moors.

Eric, Simon Jones and I wrap ourselves in blankets and wait in an upper room at the hostel. It's an old hunting lodge, which is now a centre for school sixth forms to come for field studies. A lot of walkers tramping around downstairs. They irritate me for some reason. Maybe it's their smug, self-satisfied preparation for all weathers.

Eric and I get into our make-up base for our Cocktail Party Ladies; outside the wind howls and the rain lashes at the windows. God knows what it must be like for Cleese, out on the moors as the Grim Reaper. Amazingly enough, in the midst of the tempest, we find that the TV set gives an excellently clear picture of a tranquil scene at Lord's, where England are fighting to save the Second Test Match v Pakistan.

JC arrives back at midday, absolutely soaked through, but in surprisingly high spirits. He takes great heart from the fact that TJ thought the shot they'd just done was second only to a day of seasickness in the Newhaven lifeboat as the most uncomfortable filming of his life.

Our appearance on the moor is put off well into the afternoon. I organise a subversive but, I feel, necessary, trip to the pub in Malham at lunchtime. As I buy pints of Theakston's, I feel I have to explain to the lady at the bar why I'm in false eye-lashes and full ladies' make-up. I tell her I'm in a film. She says apologetically, 'Oh, I never see films, I'm afraid. If anyone comes in here hoping to be recognised I'm afraid I can't help.' Eric, Tania [Eric's wife], Simon J and Graham C (with young friend) laugh a lot at this.

At a quarter to six I'm officially wrapped for the day, and England lose the Test Match by ten wickets. Back down to Malham Tarn Centre to frighten (or excite) the first batch of hearty walkers who've just filled the hallway after a 17-mile hike.

Thursday, August 19th: London–Bradford

At Twickenham I at last see the cut of *The Missionary* which they viewed in New York last weekend. It looks very beautiful. The relationship between Maggie and myself seems to come over well and is just as much what the film is about as the comedy.

Arrive at 8.55 at Leeds/Bradford Airport after leaving Twickenham at 7.15. Eat in my room and settle down to a long phone call with Denis O'B in Fisher's Island.

DO'B says Columbia are rapidly losing confidence in the movie, mainly because there weren't enough 'excellents' on the movie cards. He says they wanted to put it off till January and release it only in a couple of cities even then. He says he has pulled them back from this, what he considers suicidal, course, and reminded them that they are legally obligated to open the picture on the 22nd of October. But they've reduced the print now to between 400 and 600.

At last I feel we have some genuine response from Columbia – even if it is panic. My adrenaline is already flowing and I'm ready to fight for the film – to prove to Columbia not just what a good thing they've got, but why it's a good thing (because it's *different from*, not the *same as Porky's* and *Stripes* and *Arthur*), and to prove to Denis that I know better than he what works in a comedy film. It's difficult to do all this from a hotel room in Bradford, but I suddenly feel determined. This next week is crucial.

Friday, August 20th: Bradford

I'm driven out to Skipton at 7.30. A cold wind, occasional rain.

Terry has to ask some householders with strange, lop-sided faces if he could throw mud on the walls of their house. 'So long as you don't come *inside*,' they reply fiercely.

My shots are completed by midday. Buy a superb pork pie – North of England pies are a much underrated local delicacy. Am driven back to the Norfolk Gardens Hotel in Bradford, where I consume the pie with the remains of last night's bottle of Mercurey, then turn my room overlooking the bus station into an office for the afternoon.

Ring Marvin Antonowsky at Columbia – decide to put my head in the lion's mouth. He's brisk but amiable. Wants to have dinner with me in London on September 5th, will test our poster alongside their own and, in response to my queries about his reactions to the film, he says whilst not being 'ecstatic' about the results of the viewing, they are still behind the film nationwide on October 22nd. How many prints, I ask? 300–400, says Antonowsky. Going down!

Wednesday, August 25th

Because of poor weather this week, the 'Tiger Skin' scene has been postponed and we are doing the 'Hospital' today. Nice to see little Valerie Whittington and Judy Loe again. Valerie has all day with her legs apart as the Mother, Judy is the Nurse. I'm the Hospital Administrator. Suddenly occurs to me as I see them there that I've been to bed with both of them, on screen.[1]

A tedious day as I have a part which is not involved in the whole scene, but just important enough to keep me there all day.

I don't finish doing very little until after six and only just get down to the Preview One viewing theatre in time for the seven o'clock *Missionary* viewing.

DO'B has been on the whole quite long-suffering on *The Missionary* – has supplied the money when it's really come to the crunch and not interfered too much with the script. Tonight he sounds defensive and says things like 'Even if it's not commercial, I'm glad I've done it.'

Taxi home – back by midnight. Cab driven by a 'Silly Walks' fan. He calls it 'Crazy Walks'. Very weary.

Friday, August 27th

We attempt the 'Jungle' scene, so I have two parts to play – Pakenham-Walsh and the Rear End of the Tiger.

JC complains about performing against bright lights – quite rightly. It does reduce facial mobility by about fifty percent. JC mutters bitterly, and not for the first time, about pretty pictures at the expense of performances.

TG, who desperately wants to get this over with, so he can get back to his 'Pirate/Business' epic on Stage 4, is laboriously encased in a complete

---

[1] With Valerie Whittington in *The Missionary* and Judy Loe in the *Ripping Yarn* 'Curse of the Claw'.

latex mould of a Zulu. Then the sun goes in, and does not reappear, except for a brief glimpse, when we try the shot. But TG, who's been inside the costume for an hour, has sweated so much that one side of the Zulu sticks to him.

The 'Tiger' is eventually abandoned and instead we shoot the tracking shot of the approach through the forest. Endless takes. Constant calls over the walkie-talkie for the Test Match score.

Saturday, August 28th

Today is perhaps the most crucial in the whole history of *The Missionary* so far. We will have two showings of 60 people each – one a general audience, the other my friends and sternest critics. There can be no excuses. If the response tonight is half-hearted there really isn't much we can do.

TJ and Simon are both there and I take them round to the Ship to talk about it. Both of them thought it had worked very well, but equally both felt that the reason for my journey to Scotland was not well enough explained. After a quick Pils, I'm back to Film House.

Cleese and Gilliam and Chapman have all come along. A full house. JC asks me to sit next to him and Barbara.

Good response to the painting-out of the name pre-title sequence (which DO'B would prefer to cut) and plenty of laughter from then on. Feel more comfortable with larger numbers and there are fewer embarrassing moments. Applause at the end. Close friends all seem to have enjoyed it. John Goldstone especially happy. Cleese, surprisingly, liked it a lot.

Go to eat at Bianchi's with John and Barbara, Terry G, Helen and Ray Cooper. Over the meal JC surprisingly candid about things. He says he regards *Yellowbeard* as 'a dreadful script', but is doing it mainly because GC came to him 'and actually used the word "plead"' to try and persuade JC to come in.

JC repeats what he once told Humphrey Barclay[1] about his writing relationship with GC. 'Some days I write as much as 75%. But most days it's 95%.'

Barbara very nice. She reckons *The Missionary* could have more success in the US than *Privates on Parade* as it's a more general, less specifically British theme and it's optimistic and leaves a warm feeling in the audience.

No-one, however, felt it would be a blockbuster. A nice, likeable, gentle film.

---

[1] TV producer and colleague of JC's from Cambridge Footlights.

Wednesday, September 1st

Fakenham Press Ltd, who, to my pleasure, were responsible for *Small Harry*, have been closed down by their parent company. Three hundred out of work. Very sad. Fakenham being Father's childhood home, it seemed neat and appropriate that my first children's book should be made there.

Friday, September 3rd

The joy of not having to get up and go filming soon evaporated by the awareness that the last days of *The Missionary* are running out. It must be in final form by the end of the weekend.

Spend a couple of hours this morning agonising over how to alter the narration to accommodate various people's criticisms of plot and story confusion. Sort out the end quite satisfactorily, but it's in the middle of the last half, where TJ – backed up by Simon Albury – was vehement about making it clear that 'some inexplicable force' drew Fortescue to Scotland, that I have the trouble. Cleese, normally a great hunter and destroyer of woolly plots, had no trouble following the story or understanding why he went to Scotland as he did. Lynsey de Paul[1] went further and asked if those who couldn't follow the plot were mentally deficient.

Saturday, September 4th

See from *Variety* that *Monsignor*, a film starring Chris Reeve as a priest, is opening on the same day as *Missonary* in the US. Seeing the advertising reminds me painfully of the area we haven't yet sorted out – posters, etc. The image of *The Missionary*.

Take Willy and his friend Nicky to the Valley to see Sheffield Wednesday's second game of the season – against Charlton. Perfect afternoon for football. Sun, not a breath of wind and the pitch verdant and springy. Wednesday have a glorious and unequivocally deserved 3–0 victory.

Usual police presence outside – motorcycles, Alsatian dogs at the ready. The ever-present tension not relieved by their presence.

Up the main road, off which our car is parked, a crowd suddenly starts to run. There are shouts, ugly faces contorted with rage, bricks and bottles thrown. The police seem to do nothing.

I see a bottle tossed at the window of a house, another hurled from a van

---

[1] Lynsey, singer and songwriter, was, for some time, a neighbour of ours.

full of supporters, which lands and smashes beside a baby in a pram at a corner shop. Quite why the cruelty and hate behind the fighting can be so easily fanned, I don't know. And the urge to destroy and damage is strong. It's almost entirely the work of boys from 13–18, with one or two sinister older ones stirring it up.

Wednesday, September 8th

To Elstree at lunchtime to be Debbie yet again.

Jonathan Benson is the new first assistant and keeps us all cheered with his special Bensonian brand of dry wit, which comes out, just as does the dry ice, at the beginning of each take.

We are eventually free soon after 7.15. A quick transformation from Debbie to a freshly-scrubbed actor, then home and into a suit to become Michael Palin for the *Brimstone and Treacle* opening at the Classic, Haymarket.

Afterwards to a party given by Naim Attallah, described today in *Private Eye* as 'The Palestinian Millionaire'. He had red shoes, that's all I remember.

Not a bad party. Pursued Selena Scott, the lovely newsreader, and was about to introduce her to Sting as Selina Sutcliffe, realising only just in time that I was getting muddled up with the Yorkshire Ripper's wife.

Saturday, September 11th

With almost indecent haste, the day has arrived when I complete my second major feature in five and a half months. People tell me I look inordinately well – I blame the sunshine of April and May – and, apart from waking up some nights in cold sweats, or not even sleeping, I have just remained sane and I think I've given some good work. I do feel tired, but have been carried along on the energy of elation – occasionally dented by a poor day's work, or an average viewing. On the whole, I must say, I feel wonderful.

Today all the Pythons are together to be fish and, as this is probably the last time we shall be gathered in one place until February next, there is an added note of almost hysterical urgency around. Iain Johnstone's[1] BBC crew are filming the ABC '20–20' film crew filming us trying on our fish harnesses. I'm a goldfish, Graham a grayling, the two Terries perches and John is a carp.

It's a very weird and effective make-up, making us all look like John Tenniel's *Alice* pictures – semi-anthropomorphised.

[1] Iain was a producer and presenter of BBC's *Film Night*. He was also an author and later worked with John Cleese on the book of *A Fish Called Wanda* and the screenplay of *Fierce Creatures*.

'Shit, it's Mr Creosote' are the memorable last words of the day, nine weeks after John and I had begun the film in the chapel of the Royal Masonic School.

As if to bring everything full circle, RL rushes into the dressing room as lashings of solvent are being applied to my hair to remove the glue, with Polaroids of the day's poster session.

On the way home in the car TG and I discuss it and TG feels it's too solemn and stylish and too busy. He feels that we should be looking for a much simpler, more direct approach. Even something as corny as lipstick on a dog-collar, he says.

Sunday, September 12th

As I lie awake, some time around nine o'clock, I feel with great certainty that Richard's second attempt to produce an alternative to the Columbia poster is still not right. It lacks a sharp and clear indication that *The Missionary* is comedy – it's fun, something to be enjoyed.

TG's aside about a dog-collar with lipstick on comes into my mind. It's clear, neat and simple. As soon as she's conscious I tell H about it and she enthuses.

Tuesday, September 14th

Run in the morning. The Heath is filling up again as if summer had returned unexpectedly. Pass a group of ladies with easels in a line and five straw hats and five cotton skirts all painting next to each other.

Sit out after my run and soak up the sun – read on with Nabokov, write some letters, then collect my *Missionary* outfit from Bermans for another and final attempt to crack the poster.

Drive down – roof open, a balmy evening – to W8, to yet another photographer's studio.

As it gets dark I clamber once again into my *Missionary* robes, Sandra [Exelby – make-up] plants a thick, rich red kiss on the dog-collar – we try various angles of kiss – then I'm out in the street, where one should be on such a warm and beckoning evening, trying the silly expressions.

About nine o'clock I'm called in to take a very urgent message from Helen. She had heard from Mark Vere Nicoll, who had in turn just been rung by Antonowsky with the alarmingly sudden news that if *The Missionary* is not delivered to Columbia by this Friday they will pull out of the deal.

I call Antonowsky to try and find an explanation. He's out at lunch. Could I call back in 45 minutes?

Finally get through to Antonowsky. I ask him what's going on over the delivery dates. MA goes straight into some story about Richard Pryor involving Columbia in a damaging lawsuit because the final, fully edited version had not been shown to the blind bidding states. MA cannot let this happen over *Missionary*. 'It's us who have to pay, not you,' he garbles on. The movie must be ready to be shown within a week of this Friday or they're stuck.

'Can we deliver it by Monday?' I ask – any delay will help us.

'I'm only the middle man,' Marvin, President of Marketing and Distribution, pleads.

Tom McCarthy is the man to talk to about delivery.

At 12.30 a.m. I get through to DO'B at the Carlyle Hotel. He is in a fighting mood. MA had called him this morning and said that the movie was off, there was no deal. DO'B had argued with him for an hour and left MA in no doubt that if he pulled out he would have a major lawsuit on his hands. Anyway, DO'B has now declared war on the man who [he] said only a week ago was decent and straight. Any communications with Columbia must be noted down word for word and any agreements struck must be passed on to Denis so vital evidence is in writing.

I sense that Columbia still have some hope for the picture, but Denis firmly believes that they are now trying desperately to extract themselves. But then this is probably de rigueur in Hollywood, I comfort myself as I drive back home.

Wednesday, September 15th

Good news is that Columbia have not renewed attempts to cancel the film. Tom McCarthy is being helpful and we hang on by the skin of our teeth. But it was Richard who suddenly brought me down to earth by reminding me that the movie opens in the States five weeks from tomorrow. No wonder they are desperate for delivery.

Thursday, September 16th

Indian summer continues. Balmy, sultry sunshine – more like the South of France than South of England. Work at desk in the morning, lunch with Kathy Sykes [producer's assistant], a treat for all her hard work. Eccentric restaurant in Richmond called the Refectory, beside the church, run by a rather fine-looking man with a weathered, baggy-eyed face.

I have to let myself dwell for a moment on the vagaries of chance which end up with my sitting at lunch with Eric Sykes's daughter nearly 30 years after

Graham and I sat and watched his programmes on the telly in Sheffield and dreamed of nothing finer to do than be Eric Sykes. Now I find Kathy telling me that Eric wants a part in my next film.

Saturday, September 18th

The roads of London are so empty at 5.15 on a Saturday morning that any other vehicle glimpsed in the rear-view mirror appears as a threat.

Pick up Loncraine, who groans unhappily as we head out onto the A40. Still pitch dark when we reach Rank Labs at Denham, and their long, low modern buildings and general Hollywood aspect only increase the dreamlike quality of the experience.

To the viewing theatre to see a checkprint taken from the interpositive that leaves for the States this very day. Although there are only a handful of people watching, most of whom have seen the movie endlessly, I feel tight-stomached at the lack of reaction, until someone else enters and starts to laugh most encouragingly.

The laughing man turns out to be Mike Levy – one of the top men at Rank. 'Lovely movie,' he says and then starts to take his own lab apart for not projecting the print with the correct light intensity. Once that is corrected we can see, to our relief, that there is nothing wrong with the print itself. Peter Hannan is very unhappy about the grading in two or three places and will be going out to the States on Wednesday to make the changes in LA. This is our last line of hope.

A sour-looking man brings any further discussion to an end by pointing out that he has to take the film to the States today. So I leave Denham at eight o'clock with the sun already hot and my film being loaded into the back of a Cortina Estate.

RL and I have breakfast with Hannan at a South Ken café. We are pre-occupied with what's wrong with the film, rather than what's right. What a long way we've come from the euphoria of the early rushes, five and a half months ago.

Wednesday, September 22nd

Drive down to Knightsbridge for lunch with David Puttnam. Large numbers of police are about, closing off roads in preparation for the TUC Day of Action march. Down an almost empty Pall Mall with policemen lining my route. Can't help thinking how many police witnesses I would have if there were an accident. Probably two or three hundred.

Puttnam is already at a table in Mr Chow's – eager, voluble, enthusiastic, but a listener as well as a talker. He's been at a government-run committee this morning and is off to give a speech to Channel 4 this afternoon. *Local Hero* is coming along wonderfully and he thinks it may have as big an impact as *Chariots of Fire*. He has projects involving Rowan Atkinson, he's bought the rights to *Another Country*, he's produced a Channel 4 series, *First Love*, and has a new movie which starts shooting in Dallas in October.

We moan together about lack of time to read, be with the family (he's 41 and has a 20-year-old daughter). He asks me how I manage. I say it's quite simple, I just act as my own safety-valve. I don't have a secretary and an office set-up as he has; I take on as much as I can myself cope with, which is generally too much, but not half as much as the indefatigable Puttnam.

I hardly remember what we ate. I drank Perrier, he a bloody Mary. He told me of plans for filming the complete works of Dickens. He'd come up with the idea on holiday when, it seems, he'd read several of the books and a biography of Dickens himself. He's costed it at £50 million and is keen to find out whether Shepperton has the space for a brand new Dickensian back lot. If the project happened on the scale Puttnam was talking of today it would be a rich prize for any studio.

He's very pleased to know that I'm proposing an across-the-board percentage share-out for the crew on *Missionary*, as he did on *Chariots* and *Local Hero*. He gives me some useful advice on how to set it up. He estimates that on *Chariots* the crew will each get £1,500! His secretary, who is on something like half a percentage point, will get £75,000!

He doesn't seem anxious to get away and we chatter on for a couple of hours – about a mill he's bought in Malmesbury, where the mill-race will be used to generate electricity, about Jacqueline du Pré, in a wheelchair at a nearby table – and about the possibility of working together. He wants me to write one of the *First Love* films.

Return call to Ken Blancato in LA. They 'love the concept' of our latest poster and will be testing it at the weekend, but definitely using it for some of their smaller ads.

Friday, September 24th

Spend the afternoon reading the six children's books I have to review for the *Ham and High* [the *Hampstead and Highgate Express* – our local paper]. Very English all of them – and all printed in Italy. Alternate between moods of determination to criticise quite severely and general easy-going bonhomie. Hardest thing to write is the opening paragraph – my attitude to children's books. Am stuck on this when the time comes for us to brave a prolonged downpour and drive down to the Aldwych to see some Indian classical dancing from our ex-babysitter Asha Tanha.

Asha dances her Arangetram – a solo display of various classical South Indian dances. She's on stage for an hour and a half – and to see quiet, slight, soft, retiring little Asha dancing, miming and holding an audience of 150 for that long is a real eye-opener. She dances very gracefully and it's a difficult combination of rhythm, balance, expressions and story-telling. Very beautifully done.

I feel the frenetic pressures of London life very satisfactorily loosening and, although the music is not easy for the Western ear, I felt very much better when we left at ten than when I came in at half past seven, rushing out of the rain and the lines of stopped traffic on the approach to Waterloo Bridge.

Saturday, September 25th

Changeable, tempestuous weather. Helen collects a kitten, which we call Denis.

Sunday, September 26th

I scribble a few notes for a speech at today's cast and crew viewing of 'The Mish'.

Conventional, but not over-enthusiastic applause. I suppose many of them have seen it before, or are looking at their own work. I can't see why I should have expected this to be the best audience so far.

But almost before the 'HandMade' title has faded, Denholm is leaning over my seat, enthusing rapturously. He thinks it's 'marvellous, a little classic', and both he and his wife go on for some time in this encouraging vein. Helen still loves it and Tom, who was there with his friend Jasper, is very pleased with it too. No rush of hand-shaking fans, but a solid majority of those who think it successful.

Stay talking until five o'clock, then home. Have not eaten and feel very lumpen with the wine. Tom and Jasper are thumping out jazz improvisations on the piano, Rachel and Willy are encouraging our new cat, Denis, to hurl his little body round the kitchen, so I take to bed for a half-hour, then sit rather sleepily and read the papers.

Down to LBC for a ten o'clock programme on which I am to be the Mystery Guest. Evidently one caller susses me out within two minutes, but they don't put him through until 10.30. Meanwhile, I've been guessed as Danny La Rue, Larry Grayson, Melvin Hayes and Kenneth Williams.

Watch *Roseland*,[1] and enjoy Denis going crazy. So nice to have another Denis in my life.

Wednesday, September 29th

Columbia are postponing the opening of *Missionary* to November 6th. Reason given is that there are now four other 'major' movies opening on October 22nd.

Linda Barker from Columbia calls, presuming I'm coming out for the three weeks to October 22nd anyway. What's the point of doing promotion which climaxes two weeks prior to the film opening? She reacts like she'd never thought of this one before and promises to talk to her bosses.

Conference call around ten from Antonowsky and Roginski. MA starts by saying that all my TV appearances can be taped and used later – when I protest that I'm not going to work my ass off on a publicity tour which doesn't include the last two weeks before the movie opens. Compromise suggested – I do the college circuit as planned, starting next Monday, then return to the UK for two weeks and then come back for one week LA, one week NYC.

To bed a little grumpily with the TG/Stoppard script of *Brazil* to read.

Thursday, September 30th

Driven to Elstree. Work on some last-minute rewrites of the 'Middle of the Film'. Then into a wonderful, off-the-shoulder, 1950's style costume, supplied at the last minute by Vanessa Hopkins, which brings back all those images of my sister and *Heiress* magazine and her first smart grown-up posed photograph.

Work very solidly in a concentrated spell from eleven until two, without, I think, even leaving my armchair. As I give my final speech, I really do feel that at last it's over.

Saturday, October 2nd

TG comes round and we talk about *Brazil*. I feel that the story of Jill and Lowry takes forever to get off the ground and there is more observation of the tatty world of the future than plot development. Some repetition of good ideas, too. TG feels that Stoppard has softened it a bit, and I think he may be right. The

---

[1] 1977 movie about the Roseland Ballroom in New York City. Not a commercial hit but very touching.

characters talk without any edge. Their behaviour is observed with amused detachment rather than commitment. And the scale of *Brazil* is such that it cannot just be a gentle story like *The Missionary*. TG films for much higher stakes. Still, many good moments, effects, surreal dream sequences, which will work.

Sunday, October 3rd: London–Washington DC

Gather together my things for the first week of *Missionary* promotion, including sketches, bits of old speeches – anything that may help. Remember that Graham Chapman used to begin his US college appearances by asking the audience to shout abuse at him.

Landed in Washington in early evening. Dulles Airport, set in mellowing, wooded Virginia countryside, was unexpectedly quiet. I was paged at customs and given VIP treatment, rushed through and out into a waiting limousine by a girl called Sherry.

As we drove into Washington she showed me some of the 'merchandising'. T-shirts with 'The Missionary University Tour' unexceptionally written on them. A polo-neck with 'The Missionary' and the words 'Give Your Body To Save My Soul' on.

At eight o'clock – one o'clock a.m. my time – I go into a press conference for college students. There are about 20 people there and Marvin Antonowsky sits in as well. Many of them have seen the movie and I'm told they laughed a lot at the showing, but one black student I spoke to didn't think it would mean much to a black college audience.

Marvin seems well pleased, though, and likes what he calls 'all the additions'. Over dinner – soft-shell crabs – he fishes for what I'm doing next. Suggests a re-make of *Kind Hearts and Coronets*. Confirmed that he didn't like *Privates on Parade*. Says he finds Nichols' work too black and cynical. But we have another of our easy, friendly, convivial meals. We never seem to be at a loss for things to chat about.

Monday, October 4th: Washington DC–Toronto

An idea occurred to me for the start of my proposed University of Maryland speech. Owing perhaps a little to memories of Edna Everage's showmanship, it was that I should compose some lines of rather bad poetry in honour of the University of Maryland.

At 9.30 Sherry arrives to take me downstairs to talk to a reporter from a month-old daily newspaper *USA Today*. We have breakfast in Les Beaux

Champs – 'A French restaurant self-assured enough to serve American wines'. Grapefruit, scrambled eggs and bacon, ignore the 'Bakehouse Basket'.

The reporter saw the movie at the Washington showing last Friday. He himself liked it but did not enthuse, and he *was* worried by the big launch, multi-print treatment. He felt that Columbia will drop it like a hot potato if it doesn't perform commercially.

To the campus of Maryland University.

The students take me round back passages and up fire escapes to a theatre where I am billed to speak. 'Meet Michael Palin. Free.' say the posters.

Inside the theatre are TV crews, photographers, a stage, a dais and a full house of 750 students (with some turned away, I hear). Seeing a brown paper bag I grab it, empty out its contents and enter the auditorium with it over my head. Two besuited young students say nice things in introduction and I'm given a scroll for making the world laugh and then a floppy, big soft toy turtle.

Wednesday, October 6th: Chicago

To Northwestern University, north of Chicago on the lakeside.

A picturesque, leafy campus looking out over Lake Michigan I am to talk to a class on ... 'Acting Problems in Style-Comedy' at the Theater and Interpretation Center. It sounds pretentious, but the people involved, particularly the professor – Bud Beyer – are very warm and friendly. All nervous and sweating in the 80° humidity. Many good words about my film and the 'Great Railway Journey', which has already been shown on PBS here more times than on the Beeb in England.

The University Chaplain makes a very funny and complimentary speech about myself and the '*Mish*' and presents me with a stuffed wildcat. I read my poem and say goodbye.

To Columbia Pictures headquarters in a faceless office building in a half-completed plaza beside O'Hare Airport. I'm photographed with the girls and do my Prince Charles bit, shaking hands with everybody. I learn that they are very pleased with the exhibitor's reaction in Chicago, Minneapolis and Milwaukee. '*Mish*' will open in 14 theatres in the Chicago area – including two prime sites. Everyone seems very keen and hopeful.

Thursday, October 7th: Dallas

Alarm call at 7.15, but I've been awake since seven, trying out lines for today's poem. Southern Methodist University is not easy to rhyme.

A crowd of maybe 200 kids are gathered in the open air around a makeshift stage. I'm presented with a plaque for being 'A Missionary for British Humor in the US'. Poor PA is a curse, but my poem in response goes down well. I feel like an old-style politician at the hustings – talking off the back of a truck. The audience is receptive and appreciative and after I have finished there follows a custard pie throwing contest, which I am to judge. Taken quite seriously by beefy male students (no women contestants), including one who delivers a custard pie on a motorbike, à la mediaeval tournament.

Friday, October 8th: San Francisco

My first appointment of the day – a live interview at Station KQAK, the Quake. As I entered the limousine, Melanie [my publicity lady] chilled me to the marrow with the news that 'Really crazy things are happening down there. Robin Williams has been there since six o'clock with some other improv comics and it's just really crazy!'

Oh, God . . . Dear God, do I have to?

There was a bustle of excitement, then I was shown into the studio itself, which was densely packed with fans. They had nowhere to sit and clearly no provision had been made for their presence at all, but there they all were, like the crowd at one of Jesus's miracles, squashed into this hot and airless room, gazing at their heroes – in this case Alex Bennett, a gentle, bespectacled DJ, Robin Williams, red-faced and driven with comic improvisation like a man exorcising some spirits, and a local comic, who had a neat moustache and was also working hard, though no match for Robin.

I was cheered on entry and shown to a place midway between these high-pressure comics and two microphones. 'This is worse than the Queen's bedroom,' quipped I, helplessly . . . looking round at the sea of faces. Suddenly everyone, I realised, was staring at me, waiting for me to be witty, marvellous and funny. It was a nightmare come true – like some massive overdose of shyness aversion therapy.

Robin Williams was in his element, switching with incredible speed and dexterity into an ad-libbed playlet. Never at a loss for words, and remarkably consistent. He held the show together. Jeremy, with the moustache, and myself, shared a microphone – there was no point in my sharing Robin's. The humour was West Coast – brittle, topical, cruel, mocking, black, but with some wonderful flashes of fantasy. RW took the new film *Road Warrior* and turned it into 'Rhodes Warrior', the tale of a rogue Rhodes Scholar left alive on earth after the holocaust – 'Tough, educated, he read his way through trouble'.

The worst moment was when I was asked to describe *The Missionary*. It sounded so leaden and mundane in the midst of all this sharp, hip humour – as if it were coming from another world. I was left helplessly asserting, in the silence that followed my dull little description, 'It *is* funny . . .'

But the biggest test of the day is yet to come. My visit to the campus of San Francisco State, where Columbia, I'm later to learn, have been working very hard on my behalf.

To everyone's relief, there is a crowd – estimated at over 1,000 – clustered in the bright sunshine around a makeshift stage. It's San Francisco, though, and my 'award' this time is not to be presented by a nervous student or a well-meaning chaplain, but by – what else in SF – a comic.

My 'introducer' is Jane Dornacker, a big, busty lady, who wears her 'Give Your Body To Save My Soul' T-shirt quite spectacularly. But she docs like to talk. It's a fierce, competitive world, the world of improv, and once you're up there and it's going well, you stay. She is getting quite raunchy by now, with jokes about haemorrhoids being a pain in the ass and masturbation in San Quentin. I can see the organisers are getting twitchy because there are innumerable TV crews covering the event and there is precious little material they'll be able to use. In fact one has given up altogether. Eventually Dornacker draws to a close and has to give me my award for 'moral virtue'.

Read my poem, heavy on royal family jokes, which they love out here. Thank God for Michael Fagan.[1]

Monday, October 18th

J Goldstone had rung to tell me of a private screening of *My Favourite Year* – the Peter O'Toole film comedy which has received such good reviews in the US. I went along to the EMI Theatre in Wardour Street where, a few weeks ago, I was biting my fingernails showing *Missionary* to my friends.

Before I left I spoke to Sue Barton in New York, who cheered me no end with the news that *Cosmopolitan* had written a very good review of *The Missionary*. So it's two against one so far. (*Newsweek* good, *Time* not so good.) Not a bad start.

My Favourite Year was a lovely little film. A light piece of nostalgia for the 1950's, based on Mel Brooks's experience as a writer for Sid Caesar. For anyone's who's hosted *Saturday Night Live*, it had extra significance, being shot at NBC in 30 Rockefeller Plaza and being all about the problems of star guests on live shows.

It felt much the same weight as *The Missionary*. Gentle humour, laced with slapstick, enjoyment of characters as much as plot, and shot through with moments of pathos (beautifully handled by Peter O'Toole). Seeing it, and

[1] Fagan, an Irishman, had twice broken into Buckingham Palace. In July 1982 he got as far as the Queen's bedroom and talked to her for ten minutes before being apprehended.

bearing in mind its early success in the high-energy world of US comedy, gave me as much hope for *The Missionary* as the news about *Cosmopolitan*. I left the cinema with the feeling that I hope people will have after *The Missionary*.

Tuesday, October 19th: Southwold

Up to Suffolk. Ma meets me in the new Metro. She doesn't use first gear, as it's rather difficult, and at the moment mistrusts most of the gearbox, but seems a lot safer than in the ageing 1100.

It's warm and dry enough to sit out in the garden before lunch, and in the afternoon take Ma for a walk, in a friendly wind, out onto the cliffs beyond Covehithe.

Saturday, October 23rd

Columbia call and ask if I could find out from Maggie S if she will come to the States at any time. Not really my job, but Maggie has a way of making things difficult for anyone to get decisions out of her.

Ring Maggie. She won't say 'yes', but she does know that it helps the movie to appear in person and I think that for me she will do a couple of days in New York.

Home to start packing when TG arrives. He wants to talk about 'MOL'. He saw it at an excellent showing (he says) on Tuesday. He felt weak points were 'Hendys' (too long, but liked) and the tiger skin exchanges and Eric's Waiter and Arthur Jarrett. But his real worry is his own piece. It will be 15 minutes at least and he wants to know my feelings about its inclusion or not in the main body of the film.

All this in our bedroom, with me in underpants checking how many pairs of socks I might need and Helen in curlers about to change.

We go off to see 'A Star is Torn' – a one-woman show by an Aussie lady called Robyn Archer, which is playing to packed houses at the Wyndhams. She sweeps briskly through a repertoire of impersonations of great popular lady singers of the twentieth century, many of whose qualification for inclusion in her act seem to be that they died of drug abuse round about the age of 40. I'm sure this cheers up my 40-year-old wife no end.

Sunday, October 24th: London–Seattle

A strange feeling of unreality as I go back to *The Missionary* and its American opening. I'm sure I shall fall into the swim of things, but at the moment I just feel a deadening sense of weariness.

My scalp itches and I've forgotten to pack any toothpaste. My little kitchen and my family come to mind in sharp contrast to the world I shall inhabit for two weeks, and I know that I am coming near the end of my ability to lift up, inspire, charm, enthuse and everything else that has had to take me away from home so much this year.

Our 747 dips below Mount Rainier, tallest peak in the 'contiguous' USA, impressive and Paramount-like out of the southern windows, and we are on the ground in Seattle nearly an hour and a half late at about 3.30. The reward is a smooth, efficient, clean, empty terminal and the quickest entry ever into the US.

Monday, October 25th: Seattle–Los Angeles

At 8.30 we leave for my first appointment – an appearance on a local morning TV show – *Northwest AM*.

Back to the hotel to talk to a Jewish girl from New Jersey. Her quick, nervous speech and voluble hand gestures are definitely un-Seattlian. Talk for a half-hour over coffee, then I'm led downstairs to a group of six, mostly young and studentish scribblers, waiting for a brunch interview.

We take off an hour late and run into a heavy concentration of rain clouds.

Wonderful dialogue behind. A fat woman with a dog in a basket.

'Oh, my ears feel funny,' she exclaims as we descend into LA.

'Hold your nose and blow,' suggests a helpful neighbour.

'Blow what?' she cries, mystified.

We are bundled off briskly in LA. Almost a couple of hours late, but through the airport, or rather the half-rebuilt shell of it, in about 20 minutes. Outside a shambles of pick-up vehicles, including my enormous length of grey limousine, which is accompanied by a dapper little matching grey driver, who takes me direct to the Academy of Film and TV Arts.

At the Academy I meet Ed Roginski and Marvin, and other Columbia folk, as cocktails are being served before the showing to what seems to be a large and impressive audience, full of critics and film folk.

Grit my teeth over the sound in the pre-title sequence – how I want that hymn sound to crescendo! – and the grubby darkness of the boat sequence (one of the less successful in the movie), but the audience respond well and pick up most of the possible laugh moments, applauding occasionally. Marvin, next to me, disconcertingly keeps checking his watch.

The Longleat sequence is clearly going to become a classic, with Hordern's performance beyond criticism.

Marvin takes myself and Linda Barker, head of talent relations (!), to a meal at Trumps – all white walls and very chic. I think I ate some bass. Best news is that we have picked up another good review in *New York Magazine*.

Tuesday, October 26th: Los Angeles

A brief meeting with Marvin A and Randy Wicks to show me two alternatives for the newspaper ads – one has 'Michael Palin', the other 'Monty Python's Michael Palin'. I am against the 'Monty Python' mention and Marvin gives in to me, though he would rather use it. The small print ads are using the lipstick on the collar picture – so all that extra work was worth it.

Four interviews in my quite small suite fill the afternoon, then off to *The Merv Griffin Show*. These are the appearances I look forward to least. The movie is sacrificed to the ego and image of the host – which is what these shows are all about. Merv just makes money and grins egregiously. He has not seen the movie.

I wait in a green room, with no sign of a decent drink, together with two 'nutritionists' whose book *Life Extension* is a national best-seller in this land of instant cures. They remind me of the old quacks of the Wild West selling patent medicines. They are an extraordinary pair. He talks incessantly, she, small and wiry, shows me her arm muscles.

As I'm leaving the studio Jack Lemmon passes, with a crowd of guests. A publicist asks me if I want to meet Lemmon and before I know it I'm shaking hands with the great man, who turns out to be a Python fan – as are all his family, he says.

I tell him that he and Peter Sellers are my favourite comic actors of all time. As if he's been on chat shows so often, Lemmon quickly cues into an anecdote about Sellers writing a whole set of false reviews of a Lemmon film which completely fooled him. But he looked baggy-eyed and unfit, and a slight slurring of the words and blurring of the gaze suggested he'd been at the old liquor. But at least I'd told him how wonderful I thought he was.

I've survived the day pretty well on adrenaline, but as I relax over a meal with Polier and Knopf and their wives at the Mandarin in Beverly Hills, I begin to wilt.

I glean from them that Columbia are confident enough in *The Missionary* to have increased the prints to 500, that Polier and Knopf reckon three million dollars for the first weekend would be what they would hope for, and that they share my view that outside the big cities the film could be slow.

Thursday, October 28th: Los Angeles– New York

Alarm call at 6.30. Down to the limousine at seven. The sun is still not up as we start towards the airport. Tom, the driver, is a Romanian, and this accounts for his strange, very correct English. He works for a firm whose boss was once Elvis Presley's bodyguard and who specially asked him to tell me what a total fan of Monty Python Elvis was!

I'm at LA Airport and checked in by 7.45. 'Vicky' is our stewardess for the flight. As she goes through the ritual of checking our names, she comes to the seat next to me – a rather overweight, middle-aged American announces his name is Boyer. 'Oh, that's pretty,' she returns automatically.

Delivered about six to the Sherry Netherland. Two windows look straight down 5th Avenue into the forest of skyscrapers and the others look the length of Central Park South and out to the Hudson and the New Jersey shoreline.

Monday, November 1st: New York–Boston

Collect magazines, as this is the first day of public reviews.

Anson of *Newsweek*, we already know, liked it. *Time*, we suspected, didn't, and mercifully their totally dismissive review is short – though top of a column in which three movies are contemptuously tossed aside under the heading 'Rushes'. I find myself in company with Sean Connery and Fred Zimmerman's *Three Days Last Summer*, and the almost universally mocked *Monsignor*, with Reeve and co, as victims of Richard Schickel's contempt.

But *New York Magazine*'s David Denby runs it as his major movie story of the week, with a photo and the subhead '*The Missionary* is a satirical and naughty film – an aesthetically pleasing object that's also very funny.' Columbia's rep is very pleased and now feels we have enough to launch the movie on Friday *with* reviews.

At three Stuart from Columbia arrives with a middle-aged reporter from the *New York Post*. The trend of the *Post*'s questions reflects the newspaper. Why do we always go for religion? Do I expect shocked reactions? Surely the sight of a priest in bed with three women at *once* is going to cause some problems? (Smacking of reporter's lips.) When I point out that I am never seen in bed with three women he seems genuinely perplexed and shakes his head in disbelief. 'Well I'm *sure* I saw you in bed with three women.'

Into the traffic on what has become a hot and sultry evening, as I head out to La Guardia and catch the Eastern shuttle to Boston.

I'm no sooner there than a local TV station is clipping mikes to my shirt and sitting me down in the foyer beside the popcorn with a light glaring in my face and an earnest lady reporter who hasn't seen the movie. She asks me questions like 'Do you believe in God?' and 'Your children are very important to you, right? How are you structuring *their* future?' She actually runs out of tape on the question 'What do you believe in?'

After the session, at which I'm encouraged by this predominantly young audience's applause when I mention the names of Maggie Smith and Trevor Howard, I'm taken out to eat with Michael Bodin, the critic of the *Boston Globe*.

He thought *The Missionary* was a good film, but could have been a great one. Interestingly enough, he used the Magna Carta line in Africa as an example of the promise of greatness which he felt the first five minutes of the movie held out. This line was inserted at the very last minute of the very last dub.

We talked about movies until the waiters began to put chairs on tables at a quarter past twelve. (He it was who told me of the latest piece of linguistic butchery at the hands of the anti-sexists – in nearby Cambridge, Mass, the term 'waitress' is out, replaced by 'waitrons'.)

Tuesday, November 2nd: New York

I'm beginning to develop a phobia about American make-up artists. With very little grace they just slap on layer after layer of base and powder until I resemble Michael Palin about as much as the Madame Tussaud's waxworks resemble real people. Today a large black lady in a curiously confusing blonde wig works me over. 'I saw you on *Good Morning America* ... you looked awful ... all white ... what was the trouble?'

'Make-up,' I replied with pleasure.

Wednesday, November 3rd: New York

As the release day comes nearer, I feel myself wanting the pace to accelerate.

Variety calls the movie 'congenial but commercially uncertain'. It's a mixed review, complimenting me on my acting, liking the film, finding some 'wonderful moments' and 'exquisite photography', but managing to sound quite negative in conclusion. The script could have gone into more detail on three of the sub-plots, it said.

The doubts sown by *Variety* are encouragingly countered by *Hollywood Reporter*, which thinks the film an artistic and box-office winner for Columbia. This is the only review so far to suggest we might make money, and coming out of such a hard-nosed journal as the *Reporter* makes it doubly welcome.

Thursday, November 4th: New York

I go on to *The Letterman Show* in the last half-hour. I bring a grubby cellophane bag of things to present to Letterman but refuse to open up. He never tries to get into the act much and just lets me go on. I overact and fool about shamelessly. But he shows a clip and reaffirms that the reviews have been good and I get some laughs and applause and at 6.30 another show is over.

Back to the hotel, wash, change, then drive downtown, collecting Richard Loncraine on the way, to talk to a film class. Disconcertingly, they take a straw poll (before I've been revealed to be there) in which 40% of his audience say they didn't like the film. One woman who did like it, says 'I hate Michael Palin, but I loved this movie.' Richard nearly died at this.

We drive in search of tomorrow's *New York Times*. The excitement mounts as we find ourselves a half-hour early at the newsstands, so we head for the steamy rear of the *New York Times* building.

We wait in the car as Stu [Zakin, from Columbia] disappears into the night. He races back. Our pulses race with him. 'It's there!' he cries. 'It's there!'

'Well bring it, for God's sake ...'

'I need *change*,' Stu shouts, in a rare show of excitement. We have a rushed whip-round and he disappears again.

At about 10.10 he reappears with two copies of tomorrow's *Times*. I read one. Richard and Stu the other. I start from the top. Stu, much more practised, flips through to the end. He is the first to discover it's a good review. We have the most important critic in New York, and another daily paper to boot. That's two out of three, whatever else happens. Relief and joy.

Back on my own in the Sherry Netherland at 1.15. I spread out the *New York Times* lovingly. Better than Canby's review is the big ad for *The Missionary* which contains quotes from four good reviews, including one from *US Magazine*'s Steven Schaefer, which I didn't even know we had. 'Don't Miss The Missionary – a delight from beginning to its marvellous end.' 'Hilarious – Michael Palin is smashing' – *Cosmopolitan*. 'Michael Palin has finally left his mark' – even *Newsweek*'s backhanded compliment looks stirringly impressive in big print.

How on earth can I sleep? Who can I ring? They won't be up in England, so I try and sleep and will ring early.

There can have been few better moments when I've laid my head on the pillow than at the Sherry Netherland Hotel, New York City, as the rain finally breaks the late heatwave.

Friday, November 5th: New York

And the news continues to be optimistic. Rex Reed has given us a glowing review, which makes a clean sweep of all three New York daily papers.

Over to WCBS and Independent News Network to meet Jeff Lyons. At the end of the radio interview he asks if I will put my voice on tape for his home answering machine. Apparently he asks everyone he interviews to do this and now has an unrivalled collection of phone answerers, including David Niven, Peter Ustinov and Max von Sydow.

Then round to the crowded, noisy, dark security of the Oak Room at the Plaza for a drink with Nancy and Bruce Williamson – the *Playboy* film critic. Bruce is very good company, a droll but not pushy teller of stories and a lover of trains to boot.

During the afternoon the gilt has been slightly skimmed off the top of the critical gingerbread. I picked up a copy of the *Washington Post*, to find myself judged very harshly by one Gary Arnold, who seems to have felt the film was an unmitigated disaster for which I was almost entirely to blame.

Saturday, November 6th: New York–London

Helen and I have been apart for nearly four months this year, and when I called her yesterday, full of excitement at the news from NYC, she sounded so glum that I changed plans to leave on Sunday and decided to go back as soon as possible. I've been sustained over the past few weeks by interviews and the anticipation of reaction. Now the first wave of reaction has come and gone I want to get away from limousines and hotel rooms and do things for myself again.

On to Concorde, which leaves on time at 9.30. Only famous face I recognise is Rupert Murdoch, spectacles low down on his nose, looking like a don putting finishing touches to a thesis.

We cross the Atlantic in three hours and 15 minutes and I'm home at Julia Street six hours after leaving the Sherry Netherland. Lovely to see them all again.

I ring Neville, Maggie Smith, Norman Garwood [our art director] and Peter Hannan in a mood of great elation. Thank God it's over.

Sunday, November 7th

Denis rings from Dallas in mid-afternoon. We have apparently done well in New York and Los Angeles, but not well outside the major cities. He gives me some fairly wretched figures: 800 dollars for the first night in Boulder, Colorado; equally unimpressive in Las Vegas – just over 1,000 dollars; Phoenix 1,500 for the first night.

Denis saw a rave review in Dallas last night, but it isn't doing any business in the south as a whole. Denis's projection for the first weekend is 1.8 million dollars – a long way from Knopf and Polier's estimate given to me as we sauntered down Rodeo Drive, licking ice-creams, ten days ago.

Monday, November 8th

I decide to call Polier and Knopf in LA direct. The weekend has been by no means the failure Denis suggested. Whilst not looking like a blockbuster, the figures for three days are 'highly respectable' (Dan's quote). They are likely to reach 1.86 million for the weekend, not 1.3. But isn't this considerably short of the three million estimate? 'Oh, no, our three million forecast was for the *week.*'

'This is no hit and run picture,' is how Dan put it. Still awaiting Columbia's verdict. They won't be ecstatic, says David, but there's a fair chance they'll get behind it.

Tuesday, November 9th

A fine, clear morning. Helen says I should stay in bed, but I do enjoy breakfast time with the family. I like to wake up with them.

Cleese rings mid-morning. He asks me if I will write a letter to the Press Council supporting him in his case against the *Sun*, which published an account of the Zulus in Glasgow story quoting JC as saying to the black extras 'Which one of you bastards did a rain dance?' JC is very cross at the total inaccuracy and will not let the matter rest. The *Sun* have not been helpful. He wants TJ, myself and Ray Corbett [the first assistant director] to help out as witnesses.

Thursday, November 11th

Spent the early part of the morning writing a thank you letter to Antonowsky – something he probably doesn't receive very often, but I *do* feel that Columbia ran the campaign very competently.

Then drive down to the South Bank for the first film of the London Film Festival – *Scrubbers*.

Scrubbers turns out to be a well-made film with superb and convincing performances from the girls. Mai Zetterling has succeeded in giving flesh and blood to characters who are normally regarded as 'beyond society'.

The only problem I had is that the depiction of prison life has been done so often and so well recently in a series of documentaries. So, in *Scrubbers* there were many moments when I felt myself caught up in cliché – the stock psychiatrist, the hard governor, the keys in locks, the clang of doors. But the girls were Mai Zetterling originals, and were the heart and soul of the bleak, gloomy, violent picture.

Friday, November 12th

RL has rung to say that Warren Beatty had called from Hollywood to say how much he had enjoyed the movie (these are the little unexpected bonuses which are as much a part of the satisfaction of making a movie as any grosses).

Out for dinner to Judy Greenwood's[1] in Fulham Road. She lives in a comfortable, homely clutter above her own antique shop with a dog, a daughter and a builder husband called Eddie who has an earring and had just broken his toe. Judy is forthright, easy company – with striking Palin looks.

I defend comprehensive education and the NHS rather limply to Eddie, who has no scruples about buying a better education or buying himself out of pain ... And why not? I wonder gloomily – arguing out of form more than conviction.

Saturday, November 13th

Write to Al Levinson after reading his short story 'Nobody's Fool' – a piece of real-life drama thinly fictionalised and very revealing and moving. Al is so near to being a good writer, but just fails, sometimes – as in 'Millwork' – by the very tip of his fingernails. So I write back encouragingly, but cannot offer more

---

[1] Judy is my cousin. Youngest daughter of my father's sister Katherine.

concrete support – like an unqualified rave or an offer to publish. I still have most of *Travelogs* unsold.

Denis rings at six o'clock. As soon as I hear 'unfortunately', I know that *Missionary* has not made a solid commercial showing across the States. New York he hasn't heard from, but Chicago, even after the TV ads extolling its virtues through the reviews, is 33% down. San Francisco 27% down, Denver 31%. Even Los Angeles – where Denis says all word is that *The Missionary* is a resounding success – is 10% down.

The final overall figures will continue to be 'mediocre' and 'so-so' until Columbia pull out from 'between the mountains'. If we had opened only in NYC and LA *The Missionary* would have been hailed as a triumph. *That's* what irks me tonight.

Sunday, November 14th

A day for sitting at home with the Sunday papers and a lot of wine at lunchtime.

But I have agreed to go to the Oxford Children's Book Fair, and at half past eleven I leave, with somewhat sinking spirits, to drive out along the splashy A40.

At Oxford it's bitterly cold. I park by the new Law Library. An elderly man in a blue overcoat passes me; on his left breast a string of medals, tinkling softly. Of course, it's Remembrance Sunday – poppies and war veterans, with the added immediacy of the Falklands War this year.

Nearly all the grimy façades of my day have been cleaned, resurfaced and repointed. Oxford seems generally more opulent. The Randolph Hotel, where the Book Fair is taking place, full of well-heeled diners.

Up to the Ballroom. My presence is announced over a forbidding PA system and I'm given a chair, a table and a pile of books to sit beside. By four o'clock I've sold about ten copies of the book [*Small Harry and the Toothache Pills*]. David Ross [from Methuen] and the organiser from Blackwell's Children's Shop seem very pleased, though my presence seemed to me something of a waste of time.

Nice, silly evening at home, all of us playing a game after supper and being noisy. Then, after the children go to bed mercifully early, H and I sit by the first fire of the winter.

Monday, November 15th

Called Polier and Knopf at one o'clock and their news rather took the stuffing out of this gentle, easy day. *Missionary* is down 25–30% everywhere, including the NY and LA areas, in its second weekend. The take for the weekend was 1.4 million, as opposed to 1.86 the first weekend.

The 'good news', as Knopf puts it, is that Columbia are still supporting the movie with TV (in NYC) and press in the big cities. It's doing well in Toronto and Vancouver. Not holding up on Broadway/Times Square, where they have now sussed that it's not a sex movie! All the quality areas of cities are still reporting good figures – but David says rather ominously that the picture 'may not be long for this world'.

Thursday, November 18th

S Albury rings. He would like to do an Eric Olthwaite series for Granada, with someone like Charles Sturridge directing and himself producing. Everything about the idea, apart from being Eric Olthwaite for a year, appeals to me.

Friday, November 19th

Twelve years ago, when William was born, I was in the middle of shooting my first film *And Now For Something Completely Different*. Today my seventh film, *The Missionary*, is at No. 2 in the list of Top Grossing Films in the US.

The appearance of *The Missionary* above *ET* and the rest (for one glorious week!) was the high point of this crowded day.

Went down to the Python office and signed things and saw Lena, Steve's Swedish book-keeper, celebrate her last day at the office. Apparently she's always leaving packets of tampons around, so they presented her with a smart little case with a special plaque on it engraved with her name and the word 'Tampons' in very large letters.

Then, via shops, home to prepare for William's ambitious disco party, which is to be held tonight at No. 2.

The party runs from seven until half past ten. About 18 invited. The boys arrive earlier than the girls, but the girls, when they do appear, virtually take over the music and dancing. Some of them, in black berets with short skirts and black fishnet stockings, look about 23. The boys look younger, less self-assured, and spend most of the early party throwing and squirting things up the far end of the room. My heart sinks for a while. The girls talk, all at once and at the top of their voices, about clothes.

But gradually everyone thaws out. By the end I actually have a few boys dancing with the girls (they've been scared stiff of them for most of the evening). We have a joke-telling competition which is quite successful, and at 10.15 most of them seem unhappy to leave. Several of the girls give me a kiss for working the disco as they disappear into the night. Nobody smoked and nobody drank (probably their last year of innocence).

Tuesday, November 23rd

Halfway through the evening David Knopf returns my call. The third weekend is much as expected. Sadly no miracles have been performed. *The Missionary* has slipped 32%, below a million dollars for the weekend, and may lose up to 100 prints, which Knopf is not too unhappy about, though he is trying to persuade Columbia to keep as many prints working over the big Thanksgiving holiday weekend as possible.

'What do they feel about *The Missionary*?' I ask David, full of innocent curiosity. 'They've forgotten it,' returns David with admirable bluntness.

Wednesday, November 24th

Writing a speech for tonight's Young Publishers' meeting. Meeting takes place at the Cora Hotel in Tavistock Place, a stone's throw from Gandhi's statue. Not that anyone would want to throw stones at Gandhi's statue.

A full room – maybe 70 or 80 present. Behind the table are, left to right, Geoffrey Strachan, Sue Townsend, whose *Secret Life of Adrian Mole* has made her Methuen's newest best-seller, a very nice girl from the SPCK who is chairing the meeting, myself and Nigel Rees.

Tonight's theme is Humorous Publishing. Geoffrey is serious and efficiently informative. Sue Townsend is endearingly and honestly confused. 'I can't talk, that's why I write,' was the way she began her speech. Nigel Rees was smooth and seemingly nerveless, as befits a BBC radio personality.

I spoke last and the speech made people laugh very well for the first five minutes, then slightly less so as I warmed to the theme of 'Geoffrey Strachan – The Man Whose Life Was Changed by Humorous Publishing'.

A productive hour of question and answer. One lady who asked the quite reasonable question as to whether or not men preferred Python was told very sharply by another woman in the audience that the question was quite irrelevant! At the Spaghetti House in Sicilian Avenue I sat next to Sue Townsend, who I thought would be the most fun. She lives in Leicester and is quite happy about it. Especially as she is within stone-throwing distance of the house in which Joe Orton was born. Not that anyone . . . (That's enough – ed.).

Thursday, November 25th

To Cambridge Gate for a financial discussion with Steve and Anne. For over an hour they briefed me on the appalling problems of trying to give some of my money away – in this case five percentage points of my *Missionary* royalties to be divided amongst the crew. Because I was not the company which hired the crew in the first place I'm almost totally unable to make any agreement to reward them in a way in which I shall not be severely fiscally penalised. Infuriating and frustrating.

Saturday, November 27th

Up, earlier than I would have wished, to take Willy to William Ellis to play rugby. He says he's doing it to be the first Palin to actually play in a W Ellis school match (Tom was often selected but always avoided playing). As I left him outside the school gates on Highgate Hill at a quarter to nine on this very cold, foggy morning, I could only feel sorry for him.

Drove down to Old Compton Street. Snatched a quick look at *Variety* before driving off and saw, to my surprise and pleasure, that *Missionary* is No. 3 in the US in its second week and holding quite respectably at over 6,000 dollars per screen.

Time Bandits is No. 4 on re-issue, so yours truly is the proud author of two films out of the American top four. If only I could feel that it meant something.

Sunday, November 28th

Missionary showing at the London Film Festival. The performance is sold out. I'm taking both grannies, as well as Angela, Veryan, Camilla and friend Deirdre from Strathblane (scene of Python's 'Zulu' episode) and Marcus.

A good feeling to see everyone hurrying out of the cold night into the QEH to see my film. 1,250 people inside and throughout there is regular laughter and prolonged applause at the end. Fulsome praise from Geoffrey Strachan and family and Barry Took and family and others who I don't know. Mother bears up really well, revelling in the pleasure of not just meeting Barry Took, but hearing such praise of her son from him.

Neville had reservations, when we all went for a meal afterwards, of the production-value-swamps-the-comedy nature. He felt I could have made it funnier and more robust if I'd been let off the hook. Terry J, who loves much of it, had similar reservations and told me to stop playing such dull characters!

Thursday, November 30th: Southwold and London

The weather has settled over the weekend into a stable coolness. Last night it was two degrees below freezing. Leave home at 9.45 with Granny and reach Croft Cottage two and a half hours later. Suffolk is beautiful today in the bright, crystal-clear sunlight. Walk up the road past the sugar-beet collectors at work in the fields.

Cheered up by news from David Knopf that *The Missionary* take was up 15% at Thanksgiving weekend. The picture has now gathered in six and a half million dollars, but the best news of all is that Columbia now consider it 'playable'. (Paul Mazursky's *The Tempest* was evidently *not* playable.)

Dinner at Odin's with Marvin Antonowsky. Marvin still thinks a selective release would have worked better, but he admits that you can prove almost anything with hindsight.

He says emphatically that it has established me as a performer and advises me to get an agent for the US. I told him that my primary interest was in writing a movie –'That's fine,' chomps Marvin, drooling walnut and lettuce salad. 'Next time write it present day and not too British.'

He will play *The Missionary* until Christmas then take it off and re-play it again in February, with press, in selected markets. 'The one thing *The Missionary* has done,' affirms Marvin, 'is established your creditability outside of the group ... I shouldn't say this to you, but you are now established as a *very* good light comedy actor!'

I buy Marvin the meal and we part, with a bear hug, in Devonshire Street, soon after eleven.

Thursday, December 2nd

Largely spent assembling speech for the Society of Bookmen tonight.

Leave for the Savile Club at six o'clock. Walk across Christmas-crowded Oxford Street and arrive by 6.30. The dark-panelled lobby of the unexceptional house in Brook Street is no preparation for the prettiness of the upstairs rooms in which the Society are holding their Christmas dinner. Beautiful walls and ceilings, the dining room picked out in eggshell blue and evidently based on a room in the Nymphenburg Palace at Munich (a nice link with Python!)[1] and the anterior room equally delicate, but in autumnal colours.

No-one recognises me at first and they all look frightfully impressive, reminding me of university dons – not exactly smart and well groomed, but rather academic and a few very distinguished manes of white hair.

---

[1] We filmed there for Python's German show in 1971.

I've based the first part of my speech on the fact that Sir Hugh Walpole, the founder of the Society, is not mentioned in the *Oxford Dictionary of Quotations*. But very few of the assembled gathering seem to know or care much about their founder – so the first minute or so is received politely. Realise that they are going to be a difficult audience. Clearly they aren't going to laugh uproariously. Nothing so uncontrolled. But I persevere and adapt my pace and the level of delivery and salvage some respectable applause.

Then some questions. One particularly granite-faced old man asked me who my three favourite humorous writers were. Why three, particularly, I don't know. 'Nabokov,' I began. He clearly didn't regard this as serious, so to annoy him further I followed it up with Spike Milligan. 'Oh, he's a bore!' says this most interesting of men.

Then a squarely-built, rather rabbinical-looking figure rose momentously and I felt I was about to be publicly denounced. But instead he suggested that, as my speech had been probably the best he'd ever heard at the Savile, the restrictions on reporting be lifted, allowing the *Bookseller* to reproduce my magnificent words in full. Only a few people supported this particular line, however, and I was left with the curious sensation of having simultaneously delivered an excellent speech to half the room and a dreadful one to the rest.

The man who had so fulsomely praised me turned out to be one Tom Rosenthal, Chairman of Secker and Warburg and Heinemann. He later asked me, most respectfully, to sign his menu.

Friday, December 3rd

Collected *Variety* and saw that *The Missionary* was still in touch with the leaders in its third week – at No. 6. New York seems to be saving *The Missionary* almost single-handed.

As I draw up outside the shop in Old Compton Street to buy the paper, I hear on a newsflash that Marty Feldman has died after finishing *Yellowbeard* in Mexico [He was 47]. The *Mail* rings later for some quotes. My best memory of Marty is that he was the first person to talk to me at my first ever *Frost Report* meeting back in 1966.

Take Helen and her friend Kathryn Evans to the Lyric Theatre to see Spike Milligan's one-man show, which opened last night. Only half full, I would estimate. Rather tattily put together, with a lot of lighting and sound botch-ups.

He obviously knew I was in because he kept shouting for me . . . 'Is Michael Palin here, and has he paid?' Then in the second half he read a poem for me.

Monday, December 6th

In the evening we go out to dinner at David Puttnam's mews 'empire' in Queen's Gate, Kensington. Beautifully furnished and full of fine things, but also a lovely mixture of irregular spaces, large kitchen and small bedrooms off passageways, and a spacious upstairs sitting room with an unlikely roaring wood fire. A country farmhouse on three floors.

He's off to the States on Thursday to show the first cut of *Local Hero* to Warners. Compared to Columbia, his approach to marketing *Local Hero* in the States is very sophisticated – involving the enlistment of ecology groups and other special interest groups that can be identified and given preview showings, etc.

Puttnam confesses to loving working out grosses – sitting up long into the night with his calculator.

The Oscar for *Chariots of Fire* – Best Film 1981 – is almost casually standing on an open bookshelf. A heavy, solid, rather satisfying object. Has a Hollywood star ever been clubbed to death with an Oscar? It feels in the hand like an ideal offensive weapon.

Wednesday, December 8th

Richard has received a letter from Denis O' B, thanking him again for his work on '*The Mish*' and offering him five more percentage points on the film. 'Now I know it's officially a flop,' was RL's reaction.

Thursday, December 9th

A drunk in charge of a Volvo banged into me in Camden High Street. I tried to borrow a pen from passers-by, but they were all drunk too. It was like a dream.

James Ferman, the film censor, had seen '*Mish*' today, given it an 'AA' and said he thought it marvellous, one of the best comedies he's seen. Now why can't we put that on the poster instead of 'AA'?

Saturday, December 11th

Up through Covent Garden to Leicester Square to see *ET*.

The theatre is, of course, packed solid, and the lady next to me starts crying quite early on. It *is* a magical film, affecting and fresh and surprising and delightful despite all the prolonged build-up. I would think it almost impossible not to enjoy it if you have any sense of magic and imagination. It's pitched perfectly and, though many of the moments and situations are on the verge of being at least clichéd, at worst corny and sentimental, the picture succeeds all along with its supremely confident story-telling. Rachel is the only one of our party who comes out in tears, though I have been brought, pleasurably, to the brink on half a dozen occasions.

Later that evening Spike Milligan, in conversation on BBC2, names me as one of the few people (Norman Gunstone and Tommy Cooper are two others) who make him laugh.

Tuesday, December 14th

Set off, in a mad rush caused by a rash of ringing telephones, to meet my fellow dignitaries by Kentish Town Station.

We gather beneath a brightly painted canopy, salvaged with great imagination by a couple of local architects, BR and Camden Council from the remains of Elstree Station. Camden School for Girls sing carols behind the red ribbon, and a member of Camden's planning department struggles to make himself heard over the dual roar of Kentish Town traffic above and British Rail's trains beneath whilst being totally upstaged by an eccentric-looking old lady, with what appears to be a laundry bag, on the dais behind him.

My celebratory ode goes down extremely well and as soon as I've finished there is an instant demand for copies. I'm posed for silly photos and asked by one passer-by if I do this sort of thing professionally.

To Nigel G's[1] gallery, where I meet him and Glen Baxter, a cartoonist with Python-like tendencies, whom I greatly admire. Baxter has a thick tweed overcoat and a podgy, easily – smiling face below a knitted tall hat. He looks like a sort of Yorkshire Rastafarian.

We talk over how best Nigel and Glen B could get a film about Baxter together. He's avoiding doing too many more of his *Impending Gleam*-type pictures as he feels he's almost saturated his own market. It's not just that there are a spate of bad Baxter imitations, but what hurts him more is that some people think the worst of them are done by him.

Call David Knopf. The bottom seems to have completely fallen out of *The Missionary* on its sixth weekend. A meagre 248,000 dollars. Knopf again strongly

---

[1] My cousin Nigel Greenwood, elder brother of Judy, was much respected in the art world as a dealer and gallery owner. He spotted Gilbert and George early and Glen Baxter too. He died in April 2004.

recommends collaboration on a film with John Cleese. 'Comedy team of the '80's,' says he.

Sunday, December 26th: Abbotsley–London

Early lunch and, at 1.30, a rather hasty and precipitous departure for London, as I have to be at a Python film viewing at three o'clock. Only an hour from Abbotsley to Gospel Oak. Roads very empty until we get into London. Lots of people taking Boxing Day constitutionals on the Heath. Drop the family off, unpack the car, then down to Wardour Street.

The Bijou is packed and hot and smoky. All sorts of familiar faces there – Arlene Phillips (who's just been turned down as choreographer for the new Travolta film, she tells me), Jim Acheson (still full of excitement about the New York Marathon – he says I *must* go next year) and old acquaintances rarely seen these days like John Sims [the photographer] and C Alverson [writer and collaborator with Terry Gilliam on *Jabberwocky*]. Eric I conspicuously absent.

The film seems to go very quiet about a third of the way through, but ends very well, with 'Creosote' the high point. Afterwards I find that most people felt the first half worked very satisfactorily and if there *were* any longueurs they were either in the 'Pirate/Accountant' sequence or towards the end. But most people seemed to be quite bowled over by it.

This time five out of six Pythons have seen the film. There are no drastic differences of opinion. Everyone feels that TG's 'Pirate/Accountant' section should be in the film, not as a separate little feature on its own. And everyone feels it should be quite heavily pruned. I suggest it should be ten minutes at the most, Terry J about eight, Graham, quite firmly, seven. GC gets a round of applause from the meeting for his performance as Mr Blackitt, and TG for his 'Death' animation.

Thom Mount from Universal, who has come over to discuss release dates, etc, breaks in to announce that he thinks the film is wonderful and he would hardly change a single moment. As he's quite liked and respected by us all, this does visibly change the mood of the discussion.

Universal want some previews in the US as soon as possible to test reaction. They want to attempt a first ad campaign too.

All of which puts considerable pressure on my Indian travelling companion Mr Gilliam, who must cut his 'Pirate' piece, complete his animation and discuss ads, all before he meets me in Delhi on the 23rd of January.

1983

I was about to take on a mini world tour. A combination of a family holiday in Kenya (organised by Monty Ruben, who had sorted out our Missionary shoot in Africa), publicity for The Missionary *in Australia and a long-awaited tourist visit to India, where I was to meet up with Terry Gilliam.*

The quickest way from Kenya to Australia was via South Africa, where apartheid was still in place.

Sunday, January 9th: Nairobi–Johannesburg

Aware, as I write the heading, of the ludicrous ease of world travel today. Here I am imagining myself in the steps of Marco Polos and Vasco da Gamas and Livingstones and Stanleys – or any one of a dozen Victorian lady missionaries – and yet between 9.30 and 12.30 this morning I passed Mount Kilimanjaro and the Ngorongoro Crater, crossed the Zambezi in flood, flew over the Limpopo and reached the Transvaal – and all this with no greater discomfort than waiting for the next Buck's Fizz to arrive.

Land 20 minutes early at Jan Smuts Airport in Johannesburg. The ambivalence of the world's attitude to South Africa is apparent straight away. Here is a smart, expensive, efficient international airport and yet there are not enough airliners using it to justify the installation of jetties.

Most conspicuous absence of course is the American airlines. And one can understand it – America, for all her faults, has confronted all the problems of an open, free, multiracial society and taken its share of riots, marches and protests. South Africa has tried to avoid the issue.

My driver is a black and, as we drive in through neat and tidy suburbs, past white congregations filing out of church, it all looks so peaceful and contented and comfortable that I'm forced to ask him a few journalist's questions. His replies are not voluble, or emotional, but it's clear that he does not see things with quite such rose-tinted spectacles. 'In England it is better, I think.'

He doesn't say much for a while, but just as we are turning towards the hotel he says 'I have dignity . . . just like anyone else . . . This is what they won't let you have here . . . dignity.'

My hotel turns out to be a characterless Holiday Inn amongst a lot of equally characterless buildings that comprise the characterless centre of Jo'burg. There is a station which is about 100 years old, red brick and vaults and marble columns and elephant's head motifs and a frieze depicting, I presume, the Great Trek.

In the middle of all this I find the Blue Room Restaurant. Tables set out with solid Sheffield stainless steel, plates bearing the emblem of South African Railways on substantial wooden tables set beside polished marble pillars. Whatever the food, I have to have my lunch in the middle of this faded splendour. The meal is one of faded splendour too. I choose an Afrikaans dish, Kabeljou, which turns out to be a rather chewy piece of battered fish, which reminds one how far Johannesburg is from the sea.

Afterwards I walk into the station beneath a 'Whites Only' sign. Make my way down to the platform and, like a good trainspotter, walk up to the sunlit end where the big locomotives wait.

As I return I find myself, for convenience sake, taking the nearest stairwell, and the fact that there's a long line of blacks going up it too doesn't occur to me as at all odd until I come out at the top of the stairwell into a completely different Johannesburg from anything I've seen so far. Broken cans, discarded bottles, dirt, blowing paper, and, though it's full of people, none of them is white.

I realise, with a momentary mixture of fear and embarrassment, that I am indeed in a 'Blacks Only' world. There is no hostility, though – the blacks are just busy talking, meeting, napping, lolling – they're in their own world. What I object to most of all is that I should have been made to feel some guilt about being amongst these people.

It's this feeling of a shadow nation of blacks, which just isn't acknowledged, which is the most disturbing impression of SA.

Monday, January 10th: Johannesburg–Perth

In the First Class cabin is a family who are emigrating from SA to Australia. The father is a solicitor and avocado farmer – parents English, he was born and bred in SA. But now he's taking his family out. He points to them. 'There's no way I shall let them die fighting for an indefensible cause.'

He talks bitterly of the arrogance and inflexibility of the Afrikaans National Party. The English are treated almost as badly as the blacks by them, he said. Although he had a prosperous farm, he had no clout in politics at all. The Afrikaners are a small, self-perpetuating elite – repressive, intolerant and dogmatic – and it's they who have driven him away.

Arrive at Perth at 2.30 a.m. Met by Doug O'Brien of GUO Film Distributors, a big, friendly, gentle man, to whom I take an immediate liking. Into Perth to the Hilton Parmelia – a big, new hotel, one class up from the

President Holiday Inn, Jo'burg. Now I'm a film star and I have a suite on the eighth floor. All I can see outside are swirling freeways and lights on hills.

I've never been further from home.

Tuesday, January 11th: Perth, Western Australia

To lunch at a restaurant with a fine, indeed stunning, view over the waterfront. Arthur, the owner of an 18-cinema chain in Perth and area, and Norman, GUO's theatre owner in the city, were dining with us.

Arthur has a fine line in Aussie swearing, specially effective because the phrases come out quite naturally and without affectation from this fairly elderly gentleman. Describing a local millionaire called Bond – 'Of course, he stuck his cock in a cash register' (i.e. he married into money). A Sydney Indian restaurant is recommended with the warning that it used to be known as 'The Blazing Arsehole'.

Back to the hotel afterwards. Not welcome in the restaurant as I have no jacket. The receptionist immediately takes the side of the restaurant. 'One of the waiters had a heart attack tonight, so they may be a little tense in there' – pure Fawlty.

Friday, January 14th: Adelaide and Sydney

To ABC Adelaide for two very pleasant and easy BBC-style chats with programme hosts who were both very complimentary about 'The Mish'. Another station at which a man called Carl phones in and goes into a swingeing attack on me for being sacrilegious, etc. At one point he throws in Pamela Stephenson's name, blaming me even for her – and calling her a 'wicked Jezebel'.

At Sydney we are met by John Hartman, Managing Director of GUO.

To my room at the Regent – a 30-storey brand new hotel, from one of whose 19th-floor rooms I have a breathtakingly impressive panoramic view of the harbour, the bridge, the Opera House and the shores of North Sydney.

A surprise phone call from Basil Pao, who is in Sydney after three years' 'exile' in Hong Kong. He says he has just received a call from John Goldstone asking if he will design a *Meaning of Life* poster.

No sooner have I put the phone down than Goldstone himself rings to confirm a rumour I heard that Universal want the *Meaning of Life* to open in America at Easter.

Saturday, January 15th: Sydney

Meet Basil in North Bondi. He's at the home of a small, pretty, quite tough lady called Lydia, who is the agent of Jim Sherman [a playwright] and Philip Noyce, the director of *Newsfront*.

We drink champagne looking out over North Bondi Beach, and the scene reminds me, again with great poignancy, of my holidays at Southwold – brown, barefoot people coming home to little bungalows for supper, the toilets and bus shelters at the edge of the cliff, the sun and salt-tarnished paintwork and, above all, the feeling of lazy days. Quite, quite different from Africa *and* America. It's all so terribly . . . terribly English.

We eat at a nearby restaurant – really good food, not posh or pretentious, just very well cooked. Meet Bruce Chatwin there – he is rather sneery about things in a slightly aggressive, camp way which I don't awfully take to. There's almost an edge of cruelty somewhere there. Anyway, we bravely persevere in eating out in a force 5 gale, whilst being visited every now and then by drunken naval officers who recognise me and bring us complimentary glasses of port.

Then into the Rocks area again, where we go to see a group Basil knows. As they finish playing the room empties, leaving a lot of men without women and a crush of empty Fosters cans just dropped on the floor. 'This is the fall of Australian heterosexuality,' says Lydia.

Sunday, January 16th: Sydney

Wake about 10.30 with a cracking headache. Am extremely delicate for the rest of the morning. Bathe gingerly. Walk up to the corner of George Street to meet John Hartman, who is taking me for a drive up the coast to – I hardly dare contemplate the word – lunch.

It's a hot day – about 25 Celsius – and I'm picked up in the white Mercedes by a chauffeur complete with grey suit and peaked cap. I'm driven north along suburban roads that eventually blend into a déjà-vu Essex. I have to avoid sharp movements of the head, so when John Hartman in the back faithfully points out the (very few) objects of interest, I move like a man in an invisible neck brace.

I must be acting the interested passenger quite convincingly, as he appears determined to show me the local beaches. We stop at one and Vince, the chauffeur, parks our white Merc right up by the sand dunes and we have to pile out and walk around like a brace of property developers. How much I would rather be just lying out in the sun like everyone else. 'You've got a lot of clothes on for the beach,' comments a passing girl bather.

I'm mistaken for Eric Idle – only this time by someone who met Eric only last week, an Englishman who manages four of the England cricket team, who are now losing one-day games with the same consistency that they lost the Test Matches. He says they'll be in Sydney on Wednesday, so I promise I'll arrange seats for them at Wednesday's '*Mish*' preview.

Sunday, January 23rd: Delhi

Very quickly through the airport. I'm in the queue behind a Yorkshireman from Keighley who's just come in from Taiwan. I push my luggage trolley up a short, drab, ill-lit passageway and out – into India.

Huddled shapes spring towards me out of the darkness – men with scarves tied round their heads, as used in comic strips to denote sufferers from toothache. 'Taxi, sir?' I look vainly round for some sort of 'authorised' sign, determined to avoid falling into the clutches of the unlicensed, but I have made the fatal mistake – momentary hesitation – and within seconds my cases have been wrested from me and bundled into the back of a taxi.

There are six Indians already in the cab. The owner turns them out with much arguing and shouting and ushers me into the back. We start the engine, we stop, we argue, the boot is opened, more shadows appear from the dark, and suddenly my cabbie is gone, replaced in the driving seat by a young, unshaven desperado with an oily cloth tied bandanna-fashion round his head. He is joined in the passenger seat by another wild and mad-eyed individual. They look like archetypally dangerous men, but they drive off and out of the airport and strangely I feel quite safe and reasonably confident.

Eventually (though they miss the entrance once) we find the Imperial Hotel in Janpath. Not impressive, but at least familiar – there are even American Express signs about. A message from TG in my cubby-hole, welcoming me to India. My bags are carried up to my room.

A succession of Indians in white cotton uniforms appear, elaborately bowing and scraping, turning the bed back, turning lights on and generally doing lots of things I don't really want them to do. Then the chief bed-turner waits and asks me if there is anything I want. Because he is there, I ask for a beer, and he arrives many minutes later with a bottle of something by the name of Jasmine Parrot, which tastes sweet and is quite undrinkable.

At eight I am in the breakfast room, which is full of waiters, but not of guests. TG arrives about five minutes later. The rendezvous has worked. It had seemed quite unlikely when we parted four weeks ago, agreeing to 'See you for breakfast in Delhi'.

TG and I take an auto-rickshaw and our lives into our hands, and head towards Old Delhi.

We are dropped near the entrance to the Old City. The street is full of people, animals and every kind of activity – men being shaved on little wooden platforms, dogs with awful sores lying peacefully beneath huge cauldrons of some steaming dal, children, cows, cyclists, an old man turning a makeshift Ferris wheel made of biscuit tins or petrol cans. It's Gilliam's world completely – just what he tried to recreate in *Jabberwocky*.

We visit a Jain temple. Off with our shoes and socks. Rich smell of incense mingled with sweaty feet. The strict Jains believe that all life is sacred, even bugs and flies. On our way to the temple we passed an elderly, quite chubby, entirely naked man being led through the streets. In any other country, I suppose, the little group around him would probably be police ushering him into the nearest paddy-wagon. Here in India he's a holy man.

Continually seeing things which nothing, except fiction, has ever prepared me for. For instance, outside the Red Fort is a man selling false beards – and TG has a picture to prove it.

Monday, January 24th: Delhi and Agra

Alarm goes at six. Pack in the sepulchral gloom of my room and set off with TG into the mist of a slowly emerging Delhi dawn. A shadowy world of hooded, cloaked shapes.

Onto the Taj Express bound for Agra. We are in First Class Air-Conditioned.

We pull out on time, through this strange, atmospheric, blanketing morning mist which gradually clears to reveal the much read-about sight of Indians crouching in waste ground by the railway line and donating their night-soil. Little botties catching the morning light.

We are offered breakfast by a waiter in white cotton denims – stained and dirty. We order omelette. It arrives, accompanied by a banana, two pieces of toast and a battered Thermos of tea. The omelette is cold, thin and pinched.

For me one of the great beauties of the Taj Mahal is its setting. Not so much the well-known line of fountains which approaches from the front, but the Jumna river which flows along the back of the Taj. I sit out on the marble terrace with the shimmering iceberg-like bulk of the Taj Mahal on one side, and look out over the wide river bed, mostly dry, with its two or three bridges and, in the haze a mile away, the impressive long line of the battlements of the Agra Fort.

At the Mughal Room Restaurant. Not very good curry served whilst an impassive Indian quartet played 'My Way'.

Tuesday, January 25th: Agra–Jaipur

Refreshed and ready for the fray again. Book a taxi to Fatehpur Sikri and back.

Our taxi driver leaves us at the gates to the great palace, built during our Elizabethan period by the Emperor Akbar as the capital of the Moghul Empire, and then for some reason abandoned in favour of Agra. Towers and cupolas and columns all please the eye and lead from one to the other both literally and visually. And it's on a ridge, so there are views from the pretty turrets across the quiet landscape of green fields.

TG and I cannot believe that tourist groups are given one hour only to visit this wonderful complex. We even found a complete 'bath-house wing' which no-one else was being shown. Cool vaulted chambers, a hypocaust and several rooms all linked – presumably for the various temperatures.

We are taken then to Agra Fort Station. No 'Air-Conditioned Firsts' for us this time. We are in Hard Plastic First. An Indian gentleman, whom we come to know as our guardian angel, warns us, before he alights at the first stop, to bolt the door after him or else 'the students will try to get in'. He doesn't elaborate on this, but we follow his advice.

After a few minutes of pleasant rattling along through the outskirts of Agra the door handle rattles, then the door is banged, then the handle is wrenched more persistently. It is 'the students'.

At the next stop faces appear outside the window. 'Why will you not open the door?' TG holds them at bay through the bars, trying to explain the First Class ticket system. 'You are not right-thinking!' they shout back. Then the train starts off again and they resort to more heavy banging, laughter and jeers and then, rather more disconcertingly, leaning out of the window next to our compartment and staring in. It all helps to pass the time and after an hour or so they get bored.

We arrive in Jaipur at a quarter to eleven. Outside the station the rush of rickshaw and auto-rickshaw drivers is broken up and dispersed by bearded men with batons and sticks. There seem to be 30 or 40 auto-rickshaws lined up and no trade, so TG has little trouble in beating some poor local down from ten to four Rupees (about 75p to 20p). Our driver hurtles us through the streets of Jaipur like a man demented, his cloak billowing out in the cool night breeze.

We are staying at our first Palace hotel – Maharajahs' homes so enormous that they have been recycled as hotels. This one is called the Rambagh Palace. A long drive approach and impressively sizeable floodlit walls. TG is very rude about it and blames me for wanting such First Class travel!

To bring us even more rudely back to civilisation, there is a film crew here. They're shooting *The Far Pavilions* and have just had a party on the front lawn of the hotel. TG is recognised by the props man, who worked on *Time Bandits* with him.

Wednesday, January 26th: Jaipur

Breakfast in a cavernous dining room of immense size, furnished in a sort of European hybrid manner – a cross between Disneyland and Versailles, as my travelling companion describes it.

About nine we leave for the town. Outside the hotel Omar Sharif is learning his lines beside a row of parked cars.

We walk through the back streets of Jaipur. The Indians, unlike the Africans, don't seem to mind a bit having their photographs taken – in fact they arrange themselves in rather decorative poses and leave their names and addresses with you afterwards if it's been a particularly good one.

We return to the Rambagh Palace, who confirm that we have no rooms for the night. Indian Airlines' flights to Udaipur are booked and there is no chance of us getting on the overnight train because it comes from Delhi and is bound to be full.

We are recognised. The [*Far Pavilions*] director turns out to be Peter Duffel. He's a softer Lindsay Anderson lookalike. Amy Irving, his leading lady, asks to be introduced, though it turns out I'd met her briefly at Lee Studios when she was filming *Yentl*. She hears of TG's and my plight and offers one of the spare beds in her room for the night should we be desperate!

Then Vishnu comes into our lives. Vishnu is older and looks a little wiser than the average run of motor-rickshaw drivers and he it is who takes us to the bus station to try and book on the overnight 'de-luxe' bus.

After watching their heads shake negatively for ten minutes I begin to give up, but eventually Vishnu is summoned into a dark corner and within minutes he's back, trying to restrain a proud little smile. Money exchanges hands and we are on the de-luxe bus to Udaipur.

When we see the de-luxe bus, we are somewhat taken aback. Our seats are right at the front with a partition little more than two foot six inches in front of us. The seats don't recline and the journey time is nine hours.

Thursday, January 27th: Udaipur

Stop at 3.30. Realise, as we pile out into the clear and pleasant night air, that I'm rather enjoying the journey – it's not an ordeal at all. There's something very calming about being in India. They don't fight and fluster and bite their nails and moan and complain and it makes for a very unstressful atmosphere.

No toilets at this stop – so just a pee in the darkness and a cup of sweet tea. Enjoy the understated feeling of camaraderie amongst the passengers, of which we are the only two whites.

It's a clear, bright day and after breakfast TG and I are off up to the City Palace. Another enormous labyrinth of rooms, stairs and temples. It was lived in not long ago and has a rather sad museum with old Rolls Royces, mangy stuffed bears, many beautiful paintings of tiger and elephant hunts and life-sized cardboard cut-outs of the Maharajahs, which are quite a shock.

Sit in my room with a Herbert's lager and watch the light fading on the shore and feel very peaceful. TG and I eat at the hotel, then have a last drink out beside the pool in the courtyard which is all lit up. We're the only ones to use it.

Friday, January 28th: Udaipur–Delhi

I'm at the airport even before the staff . . . they're just unlocking the doors. So I'm first at the check-in counter. A small, rotund, self-important little man eventually surveys my ticket and pushes it aside. 'Only OK passengers now, please.' My jaw must have dropped visibly, for he continues 'You are only wait-listed, please wait until the aircraft comes in.'

Suddenly I feel how far Udaipur is from anywhere else. Times, figures, estimates click round in my head, but no comforting alternative presents itself. But hope brightens as the plane is obviously emptier than I've expected and at last, with as little emotion as he'd turned me away, he takes my ticket, scribbles across it, and hands me a boarding card.

Arrive at the Imperial, to find a telegram giving the first weekend's *Missionary* figures. Sydney outstanding, Melbourne disappointing and Adelaide very good! Late lunch at the Imperial. For the sake of *RippingYarns* and *The Missionary*, in which characters were always eating it, I choose a plate of kedgeree, which is superb, and a bottle of Golden Eagle beer.

Tuesday, February 1st

Up at 8.15. The children rush upstairs to tell us, as we are dressing briskly in freezing bedroom, that John Cleese is on TV in his pyjamas. It's true. He's the star showbiz guest on this, the first programme of TV-AM – another new TV company started by David Frost and the second supplier of breakfast programmes to have started this year.

TJ rings. He's just back from a lightning Concorde trip to the US for *Meaning of Life* previews. Two showings in Yonkers went so badly that TJ and

JG didn't even bother to look at the cards. An audience of young (15–22) cinema-goers predominantly. Eighty walk-outs.

TJ's spirits restored by a showing in Manhattan which was very well received. As often happens under pressure, some sensible cuts have been made quite quickly – 'Luther' is gone and much of the 'Hendys' too. The film sounds trimmer. Universal, as a result of these last showings, are definitely going ahead on March 25th, but with a limited release – probably even less than *The Missionary*.

At 12.30 call John Hartman in Sydney – *The Missionary* is evidently No. 3 in the country. The good news is that attendances were up everywhere in the second week.

Friday, February 4th: Southwold

On the way to Ipswich I complete the last few pages of '*Anna K*' – the book that has been my friend and guardian throughout Kenya, South Africa, Australia and India. Find the last few chapters – Levin discovers The Meaning of Life – rather comforting. I resolve to live my life better and not get angry with people any more.

Tuesday, February 8th

Very cold still – getting up is not fun. But I sleep on this morning very easily, feeling that only now have I readjusted and caught up on my sleep after the World Tour. The builders arrive and start digging foundations for the extension to No. 2.

As Cleese is coming to dinner tonight, I feel I must see *Privates on Parade*, my HandMade stablemate. It's on at the Classic Hampstead, so I go to the 3.35 showing. The 'conversion' of the Classic to a three-screen complex has been so brutal that the Screen One has been set on a new level halfway up the old auditorium. Even the old wall decorations have been left, severed, as a reminder of the modest but homely theatre it once was. A long, flat, empty space extends between audience, who number 15 this afternoon, and screen. But it's in focus and the sound is clear, so I have to be thankful for that.

The concert party numbers are well done and, as they were at the core of the stage success, are performed with panache and attractive skill by Denis Quilley and S Jones and others. Cleese and Michael Elphick are impressive at first, but gradually the film is dragged down. Relationships are hinted at, briefly consummated, then dropped just as they might have been getting interesting and Cleesey becomes saddled with the unenviable task of providing comedy as a palliative for all the floundering 'serious' realities of war at the end.

He ends up with a desperate silly walk in the closing credits – as if finally confirming that the film is supposed to be a comedy, despite the balls being shot off, etc, etc.

Thursday, February 10th

To Duke's Hotel to meet Mike Ewin – HandMade's distribution man since December. Short, stocky, homely figure with a respectable suit. He does come up with one or two classic remarks for a film distributor, particularly his cheerful admission that he hasn't seen the film ... 'But, you know, Michael, I don't think it's really necessary to see a film to know what sort of film it is.'

Walk through St James's Square and into the Haymarket to look at our launch theatre and meet the manager.

The manager, Brian Rami, is quite a character. Youngish, aggressive, Greek Cypriot I should imagine. He is a theatre success story – taking tickets in Hackney two or three years ago, he's won Classic's Manager of the Year award. He briskly goes into the attack with Ray [Cooper] and myself, asking where our posters are and where the trailer and photo displays are, as he could have been playing them for the last week. 'Good man,' I say, in response to his enthusiasm. 'Don't "good man" me,' he replies sharply, '... just give me the goods.'

Snow is beginning to fall quite thickly as Ray and I enter the scarlet and black world of The Hutton Company, but, as the *Sun* might say, we were soon seeing red of a different kind. The complications with the poster's artwork, combined with the time it will take London Transport to hang them, make it now likely that the posters will not appear until the 1st of March, two days before the film opens.

I am quite unable to control my anger and frustration. Colin MacGregor [who's in charge of our campaign], in his languid public-school manner, tries his best to calm things down, but I'm afraid there's no stopping me. Silence and heads hung everywhere.

Friday, February 11th

Today Colin MacGregor informs me that London Transport have agreed to start displaying posters on Underground and buses from February 18th – two weeks earlier than yesterday's date – and that with a bit of luck they can arrange to have poster artwork completed by the weekend. I hate to say it, but violence does seem to work – even if it's only the violence of my opinion.

Monday, February 14th

To Mel Calman's gallery at 12.30. We talk of ads, posters and the lack of good design. More positively we talk over the idea of opening a cinema in Covent Garden. It's something I've heard mentioned elsewhere, but somehow, this being a Monday lunchtime and the start of a week, Mel imbues me with great enthusiasm for the idea and, as I walk back to the car, I feel all the elation of one who has just acquired a cinema in Covent Garden.

To Bertorelli's, where a researcher for the Time Rice (Freudian slip), Tim Rice Show on Wednesday is taking me to lunch. Pre-interview interviews seem to be all the rage now. It's a very bad habit imported from America. So I talk for an hour or so to this keen, rather aggressive Scots girl, who asks me dreadful questions like 'Does comedy have a comic significance?' 'Is comedy a moral force on the world stage?' I get very twitchy about three o'clock, when she still has ten questions left to ask.

Sunday, February 20th

I drive over to Lime Grove at seven o'clock for an appearance on *Sunday Night*. Into the quaintly-termed 'hospitality room', where I'm offered some wine from a bottle they keep on the window sill outside.

We record about a quarter to eight. Eric Robson, who did one of the 'Great Railway Journeys', is the presenter – a solid, dependable, likeable man. As the credits roll and the contents of the show reveal filmed reports on how Christianity is coping in the poverty-stricken conditions of South America, *The Missionary* seems embarrassingly frivolous.

The Dean of St Paul's, another interviewee, smiles a little uncertainly at me, as the story of the film is being explained by their resident reviewer – himself a clergyman. His review of the film is not awfully good. He thinks it 'a 50-minute television programme blown up to 90 minutes', 'not very serious', 'an adolescent fantasy', etc, etc. 'My fantasies are much more grown-up,' he ends. They do drop themselves in it, these people.

The trouble is, as this is a religious programme, *The Missionary* is treated, out of perspective I think, as a carefully thought-out comment on the church. When he accuses the satire of being rather limp and safe, I counter by saying that the church gets the satire it deserves. Feel a few frissons cross the studio as I say this and hope the Dean of St Paul's doesn't mind.

Monday, February 21st

Bad news comes in early evening when Ray rings to say that the trailer has hit fresh, and quite unexpected, snags in the shape of the film censor, who has refused to grant our trailers anything less than an 'X' unless we remove mention of the word 'prostitutes' and cut a sequence in which I say 'I was just telling Emmeline how relatively unimportant sex is', despite the fact that he has given both these lines clearance for any audience over 15. The ridiculous thing is that he will allow us to replace 'prostitutes' with 'fallen women'. The mind boggles.

Thursday, February 24th

Good news of the day is that Maggie Smith has agreed to come to the press screening and may even appear on *Terry Wogan*.

But the day's excitements are not over. At home, as Helen is getting ready for another evening's badminton and the spaghetti's boiling away on the hob, Mel Calman calls to tell me that à propos our St Valentine's Day enthusiasms for a cinema in Covent Garden, he has heard of a building for sale in Neal's Yard! It's No. 2, has a salad bar on the ground floor, room for a gallery and coffee bar on the first, an acupuncturist on the second and a self-contained flat on the top. Cost £275,000. I'm very keen. Keen to buy in such a special spot as Neal's Yard and keen to help Mel C and the Workshop. Watch this space!

Stay up until 1.15 to watch the Bermondsey by-election, the culmination of a particularly vicious and intolerant campaign against Peter Tatchell. The Alliance Party are crowing. Labour *do* seem to be in quite serious trouble.

Saturday, February 26th

Arrive at TV-AM's still-unfinished studios in Camden Town. Bright, light, high-tech building decorated in the Very Silly Style, with representations of pagodas and African jungles. It's like one huge Breakfast TV set.

I'm on talking about *The Missionary*. Parky likes it. Calls it 'an important film', too, and shows a clip. They give a number on which viewers can call me with any questions. Over 200 questions come in, and they're all very excited at TV-AM as it's the largest number of phone calls for anyone they've ever had. I wish George Harrison 'Happy Birthday' on air – even though he's incommunicado in Hawaii. But I am wearing the Missoni sweater he gave me and at least ten of the calls are about this.

William and I stay for breakfast with Parky and Mrs Parky – a nice Yorkshire couple – in a rather narrow and cramped canteen which Parkinson complains about. He seems to be quite brisk with his working colleagues. I shouldn't think he suffers fools gladly.

Monday, February 28th

Off to the Classic Haymarket. The press show has run for about 75 minutes. Brian Rami is very enthusiastic about the whole thing. There is applause at the end (very rare in critics' screenings), but only he and I know that it was Rami who started it!

Walk down across Pall Mall to the Turf Club. At least it's a dry, quite pleasant day. Upstairs at the Turf, in two elegant, high-ceilinged rooms, there is a good crowd of pressmen, plus one or two of the Fallen Women and Phoebe.

Maggie S herself arrives about half past twelve. She still hasn't seen the film and I feel that she will probably continue to avoid it, as is her habit. But she looks very bright and attractive and sparkles for the press she dreads so much.

Mr Chandler, the rather icily elegant major-domo, is all smiles and very obliging today. 'All the gentlemen of the press seemed to have enjoyed the film . . .'

As I'm about to go, Mr Chandler appears up the stairs once more . . . 'Do you know Medwin?' And sure enough, Michael Medwin, looking very perky in what looks like an oleander-pink scarf, comes bounding up behind him and I find myself drinking a further couple of glasses of champagne with him at the bar downstairs.

Mr Chandler keeps saying 'He'll have to become a member, you know,' in a generous fashion. And Medwin promises to propose me and says that 'Chalky' White[1] and Albert Finney will second me. We talk over the film industry. He seems quite sanguine about 'going into the city' and getting money and most hurt that *Memoirs of a Survivor*[2] (much praised) did not receive the commercial attention it deserved.

Tuesday, March lst

To the City University to be the 'guinea pig' at one of Bob Jones's press conferences at the Department of Journalism. After an hour of this, drink with some of the tutors there. I'm listened to with far too much respect these days.

[1] Our colloquial name for Michael White, the celebrated producer and major investor in *Holy Grail*.
[2] 1981 film written & directed by David Gladwell from a Doris Lessing book. It starred Julie Christie. Michael Medwin was the producer.

I suppose it must have changed me somehow. I no longer have to look for an audience. They gather around me – even quite intelligent people – and wait for the oracle to utter.

Home to anonymity and abuse from children.

Thursday, March 3rd

Missionary opening day.

An equivocal review in the very influential *Time Out*, specifically criticising my role as being inadequate to support the film, is followed by a short, but very negative piece in *City Limits*. In the *Guardian*, Derek Malcolm has me casting the paper aside in disgust and sitting head in hands in that deep, sudden desolation that only a bad crit can bring. But when I read him again, I realise it's quite a praiseworthy review, but rather obscurely written.

Terry J rings and suggests squash and lunch, which I eagerly accept. TJ has been at Technicolor labs doing last-minute work on the *Meaning of Life* print. It's now a time panic as bad as anything that happened on *The Missionary*.

I'd forgotten about the *Standard*. Have a quick scan through Alexander Walker and it is very good – for me and the film. A big photo, lead story, headline 'Mission Accomplished', phrases like 'The *Missionary* is very, very funny' and a comprehensive relishing of the finer points of the movie which almost makes the piece look like an extension of our own advertising. This puts a new spring in my step and a quite different complexion on the day.

Drive into the West End to the Classic Haymarket. The acting manager, Ken Peacock, is in the bar. He's very pleased and reckons it could take £2,000 at the end of the day. The best Thursday for ages, he says.

Up to the projection room to say hello. My handiwork slowly unwinds from the longest spool I've ever seen. Rather exciting seeing it all through the small windows.

Friday, March 4th

A rave review of *Missionary* in the *Mirror* and the *Daily Mail* and the *Daily Express*. I only come down to earth a little with *The Times* – but even that headlines its film column 'Great Comic Acting' and only attacks the script for not being better.

Helen returns with the *Financial Times*, which also says many positive things, but in the end wanted 'a bit less caution, a little more anarchy', whereas Coleman in the *New Statesman* called *The Missionary* 'unfashionably well-written', which I don't understand but like very much.

Then after lunch there is quite suddenly a great anti-climax. The film is out and running. The radio and television shows will be looking for new celebrities and different shows next week.

At this very moment I have nothing to do – no problem to solve, no crisis to defuse, no-one to hustle . . . just a grey, wet day coming to an end and some writing which I can't settle down to. This evening Helen and three of her badminton chums are going to see my film. I shall stay at home.

Have supper with the boys and, feeling very weary, go to bed early.

Sunday, March 6th

A marvellous *Sunday Times* piece by David Hughes ending 'Here is a serious humorist trying his comedy for size. Not yet finding a visionary focus. Lacking edge. But your bones tell you that he will soon make a real beauty of a film, as exciting in achievement as this lark is in promise.'

The *Telegraph*, the *Mail on Sunday*, the *Express* and the *News of the World* are all highly complimentary. Castell in the *Sunday Telegraph* concludes 'Beautifully tailored and consistently funny, *The Missionary* is bound to convert you.'

We should publicise these reviews as quickly as possible. No time for faint hearts. We have stolen a week's march on *Local Hero*, which will be shouting about its success very soon, but it will be a similar sort of critical response and I want as many people as possible to know that *The Missionary* was there first.

Take Helen and the children to La Cirque Imaginaire, a lovely, gentle, funny circus-style entertainment performed by Victoria Chaplin, her husband and their two children. A real family circus with no animals more dangerous than a rabbit, a toucan and two ducks.

Wednesday, March 9th

To L'Escargot to meet Mike Fentiman and Robin Denselow's girlfriend Jadzia to discuss my making a half-hour documentary in their *Comic Roots* series. I liked him and they warmed to my ideas and it looks like we have ourselves a show. In June, probably.

I aim to start work on a new screenplay in April and May, break in June for *Comic Roots*, and complete at quite a leisurely pace during July and August. Rewrites in September and October, by which time ready either to begin setting up filming or to write something with TJ.

Drive down to the Classic. Traffic at a standstill in St Martin's Lane as the teachers and students are marching in protest against education cuts. Eventually reach the bottom of the Haymarket. My silly vicar looks quite striking above the marquee.

Thursday, March 10th

Nikki [from HandMade] calls to tell me that Cannon Classic will be taking an ad in *Screen International* to announce that *Missionary* has broken the house record! And a projectionist at the Barking Odeon has been arrested by the police for taking a print of *The Missionary* home with him in the boot of his car – with intent to tape it!

Tuesday, March 15th

To the Odeon Haymarket to see *Local Hero*. Apart from reservations over the Houston interiors – where both design and direction seemed less sure and the jokes, about American psychiatrists, more familiar – the film quite captivates me. Forsyth is remarkable in his ability to recreate on screen the accidental quality of humour – the way things that make you happy happen so quickly, spontaneously, that try as you can you never quite remember afterwards.

Princess Margaret is coming to see *The Missionary* at the Classic Haymarket tonight. Brian Rami is in an advanced state of excitement. 'She is one of your greatest fans,' Brian relays to me, and urges me to come down if I can.

I speed down to the West End, arriving with about five minutes to spare. Brian R is, of course, immaculate, and looks my faded jeans and windcheater up and down with alarm. In the end Princess Margaret arrives with such speedy precision that I don't have a chance to see her as she moves quickly, but haste-lessly, up the stairs behind a phalanx of very tall people. She *does* want to meet me, Brian confirms, so could I come back at a quarter to nine.

At a quarter to nine I stand clutching my signed copy of the 'Mish' – should I have written to '*Your* Royal Highness Princess Margaret' in it? – waiting for the performance to end. Martin, the projectionist tonight, is very excited, as are the predominantly Asian and African sales staff.

Down the stairs comes the little lady, almost gnomic in the relative size of head to body, and clad in black. She shakes my hand easily and talks without formality. I can't remember much apart from apologising that I should be there at all at the end of the film – waylaying cinemagoers! But she says she thoroughly enjoyed it and asks about the Scottish location, so I am able to tell her that it [Ardverikie House] was nearly the Royal Residence once. We chat quite easily and she introduces me to her very tall friends and they all laugh and endorse her opinion. Then she is taken out and past the queue – clutching my signed book.

Brian R and I drink a coffee afterwards. This film has already given him much pleasure, but tonight surpassed anything.

Tuesday, March 22nd

The telephone goes. It's Richard L. Richard has left home.

'Where shall I go? What should I do?' As if I know. Nothing in my experience quite prepares me for this. The enormity of the split he's now admitted clearly frightens him. I tell him if he needs help, or a bed, or company, that I shall be here.

Write letters and prepare stew for supper. Then, just as I've served, Richard arrives. His normal behaviour is so near to hysteria that it's difficult to tell how abnormal he is at the moment.

He eats the stew (later, when I'm trying to explain to Rachel that Richard's behaviour is because he's very, very unhappy, she philosophises 'Well, at least you got rid of the stew'). When I come downstairs from reading *The Secret Garden* to Rachel, he's asleep on our sofa.

There's not much more I can do and, feeling quite weary myself, I go to bed and to sleep at eleven.

Sunday, March 27th

A wet, dull Sunday. Helen [back from skiing in Austria] unpacks and very gradually begins to readjust to life at sea-level.

Potter around at home, unburying No. 2 from the builders' dust and debris of the last six weeks. It's quite exciting – like a new house emerging from hibernation. Tom P will move in here after Easter.

Watch and delight in *Betjeman* – the final episode. Full of gems – he's such a warm, kindly, generous but cheeky presence. On top of a cliff in Cornwall he's wheeled into shot clad in a black bomber jacket with a 'Guinness' tag inexplicably obvious over the left breast. His mouth senile and droopy from the effects of Parkinson's (that I know so well), but his eyes alive, alert and mischievous.

He's asked if there's anything in his life he really regrets ... He considers a moment, the Cornish clifftop wind untidying his hair and making him look such a little, isolated, vulnerable figure ... 'Yes ... I didn't have enough sex ...'

Monday, March 28th

We have used up most of our £80,000 launch budget, but Denis has agreed to about £5,000 extra to continue support over the upcoming Easter weekend. I hear from Ray that Stanley Kubrick wrote to Denis congratulating him on the *Missionary* campaign, which he had noticed, admired and envied. For an apparent recluse he keeps in touch, it seems.

To lunch at L'Escargot. Colin Webb of Pavilion Books is at another table. He tells me that the *Time* critic, Richard Schickel, who has given '*MOL*' such a good (and important) review, really *did* like *The Missionary*, despite his dismissive piece. He had been in a 'very depressed state' when he wrote it and has since seen it again and thinks it 'a gem of its kind'.

Home about six. The phone rings instantly. It's Tim Brooke-Taylor conveying to me an offer to direct a new Gounod opera at the Buxton Festival. We have quite a long chat and he tries his best to persuade me to do something that both of us agree is tantalisingly out of the ordinary. But I end up turning it down and inviting Tim and Christine to dinner.

Terry Gilliam appears. He looks rather careworn. America was awful, he says. He was unable to sell *Brazil* to Paramount or Universal and is extremely bitter about Hollywood studios all over again.

Tuesday, March 29th: London–New York

Exactly one year since I began filming *The Missionary* I leave the house to catch the 10.30 Concorde to New York. The flight (all £1,190 of it) to New York is being paid for by Universal Pictures for my work on behalf of the second film I made last year – *The Meaning of Life.*

A limousine takes me into New York, past the burnt-out tenements of Harlem to the discreetly comfortable Westbury Hotel at 69th and Madison. It's a fine, clear, cool day – the buildings stand out sharp against piercing blue skies.

Visit Al and Claudie on my way to the first interview. They have been through a bad four weeks – awful journey back from Paris and Claudie recently very ill and worried at one point that her bronchitis was cancer. Also a new property company have taken the block and want to make Al an offer to sell his lease, so they may contemplate a complete move to Sag Harbor in the early summer. Their little daughter Gwenola delightful, smiling, full of beans.

Drive back uptown to a bar/restaurant in the theatre district for a drink with Richard Schickel, his wife and daughter. He officially rescinds his review of *The Missionary*, saying quite sportingly that he shouldn't have dismissed it and anyway his wife had disagreed with his views right from the start. So that made me feel better and we now have quite a good relationship.

Off to Broadway Video, at Lorne's invitation. It's all looking very smart now. In a basement studio in the Brill Building Simon and Garfunkel are working on a new album, which has taken one and a half years already. They're listening to a drummer, Eddie Gatt, doing over-dubs.

Paul greets me effusively (or as effusively as Paul ever could be), then goes back to careful concentration on the track. Art Garfunkel sits behind him and nods his great beaky head every now and then – '*That's* good' – but Simon is really in control. Art passes some coke on the end of a penknife. I decline, much to Lorne's comic disapproval.

Friday, April 1st: New York–London

Down to another ABC studio to record an interview with a man whose extravagant name – Regis Philbin – denies his very regular appearance. We do ten very successful minutes. The producer of this new show is Bob Shanks – the man who six years ago was responsible for the butchering of the six Python TV shows which took us to court and eventually won us custody of the shows. He looks older and more unkempt. Quite shockingly different from the trim, smooth executive with nary a hair out of place whom we fought at the Federal Court House.

He jokes about it as we shake hands. 'We met in court . . . '. Really he's done us a lot of good in the end and it's a curious coincidence that less than 12 hours before meeting Shanks again, I heard from Ron Devillier that we have sold the Python TV shows to PBS for a fee of at least a million dollars for two years.

Sunday, April 3rd: Easter Sunday

Helen has not slept much and is groaning in pain at eight o'clock on this Easter morning.

Throughout the morning she is in great pain and discomfort. Cheerful Doctor Rea arrives at midday, quips about my appearance on the back of buses, examines Helen and takes a sample. He has no bottles, so I have to run downstairs and fetch one of Helen's marmalade jars.

The doctor takes a quick look at Helen's specimen, holds it up to the light for all Oak Village to see and pronounces it like 'a rich Madeira'. He says Helen has all the symptoms of pyelitis – an infection of the tubes leading from the kidneys to the urinary tract. He prescribes some pills, which I rush out to Belsize Park to fetch from a Welsh chemist, who's also seen me on the back of the buses.

Sunday, April 10th

Collect the Sunday papers and try to put off further rehearsal for the Stop Sizewell 'B' concert as long as possible.[1] I feel an enormous disinclination to appear on stage tonight. A wave of weariness which I feel sure is mental more than physical. I have been so much in the public eye over the last year or so – and each day, with very few exceptions, I've been required to smile brightly, chat optimistically and generally project constantly, when all I really want to do is to disappear from sight for a while.

Dinner at Mary's is a welcome break – very jolly, with Granny G declaring that she has grown cannabis in her garden ... 'And I'm growing more this year' – but I have to leave after an hour and drive down to the Apollo Victoria for the call at 3.30. The theatre is huge and it takes me half an hour to work out a way through the labyrinth of tunnels to our dressing room, which TJ and I are sharing with Neil Innes and Pete Capaldi (one of the stars of *Local Hero*).

At four o'clock the cast is summonsed to the foyer to hear the running order. Various bands – Darts, UB40, Madness – and a strong selection of comedy groups – Rik Mayall and the Young Ones, National Theatre of Brent, as well as Neil and Julie Covington and Pamela Stephenson. TJ is told that they couldn't do an explosion, so he decided to cut 'Never Be Rude to an Arab'.

Then a long, long wait whilst UB40 monopolise the stage, which is filled with a vast and forbidding array of speakers, amps, wires, leads, plugs and sockets which make Sizewell 'B' look as dangerous as the Faraway Tree. Backstage is a no-man's land of bewilderment and confusion.

Jeanette Charles – the Queen's lookalike – arrives in our dressing room about seven to add yet another bizarre element to an already lunatic situation.

The curtain doesn't go up at 7.30 as the bands are still rehearsing. Jeanette C, now totally transformed physically and mentally into the Royal Person, protests vigorously at the delay – 'I have to go to a Bar-Mitzvah ... ' she announces imperiously to some desperate and confused dis-organiser. 'When quarter to eight comes I must go like a bat out of hell to Chigwell.' Very Joe Orton.

Monday, April 18th

Begin writing new screenplay. Rather than spend days or weeks on elaborate research or agonising over a subject, I decide to ride straight in on the 'Explorers' idea which came to me about four months ago.

---

[1] Sizewell 'B' was a nuclear power plant planned for the Suffolk coast. It was built between 1988 and 1995.

To dinner with Graham and David. Was supposed to be with TJ as well, but he rang this morning, having had Creosotic eruptions during the night, to cancel. Take GC to Langan's Brasserie. He's half an hour late. Still, I enjoy sipping a malt whisky at the bar and watching caricatures of rich people entering. Feel like I'm watching a parade of the people George Grosz used to draw.

GC looks a bit drawn and haggard and, as always, has the slightly distracted air of, as TJ put it, 'someone who wants to be somewhere else'. Great praise for Peter Cook for keeping everyone happy in Mexico and Eric for being 'divine' (according to David). GC goes back to the US for *Yellowbeard* sneak previews this week. He has reached the stage of not knowing whether anything is working any more.

Friday, April 22nd

To the BBC to discuss further my *Comic Roots* piece with Tony Laryea, my director.

The headquarters of *Open Door* is, ironically, almost impossible to find. I drive past it several times and in the end have to ask directions at Lime Grove.

Talk to Tony in an office full of clutter and overflowing out-trays. Very John le Carré. I tell him my thoughts about the structure of the piece. He is a little taken aback when I suggest David Frost as someone to interview. But he was seminal to the Palin career. It's taking further shape and looks like being a very rich programme. At least an hour's worth at the moment.

Talk to a Dutch journalist for an hour. He has 38 questions.

John Goldstone makes one further attempt to persuade me to go to Cannes – using a free ticket for Helen as bait. I can't, I'm going to Newcastle. Suggest Helen goes with one of the others!

Sunday, April 24th

I embark on mass picture-hanging and clearing up in the garden until Gilliam arrives and we talk about the state of the world for an hour and a half. He *is* going to Cannes, but isn't going to wear a dinner jacket for the special evening showing. Says he'll only go if the dinner jacket very obviously has vomit all over it.

He says that he misses working in the flexible Python way and that Tom Stoppard is much more of a professional writer, wanting to be sure he's being paid before doing rewrites ... and 'Stoppard's stuff is so hard to rewrite'. But they are at the casting and location-hunting stage.

Monday, April 25th

J Cleese rings to ask us to dinner. He says he's writing his own thing and would I play a man with a stutter?

At 2.15 two young men, Edward Whitley and another whose name I forget, come to interview me for a book on Oxford. They were meant to come last Friday, but their car had broken down. They're quite pleasant, rather plummy-voiced Oxfordians. I expect from the more comfortably-off classes.

But their interviewing is less comfortable. They are aggressive and rather impatient (nothing new with students), but with an added and more sinister tone – it is as if they have made their mind up about Oxford and what it was like in my time, and nothing I say would really change what they want to think. Whitley, especially, is a clumsy, gauche questioner.

In short, what I had hoped would be a pleasant chance to recall what Oxford was to me, turns into an inquisition. I pour them coffee and try to cope with all their questions, but there is such a humourless, sour feeling emanating from Whitley that it isn't easy.

I know I have another one-hour interview to go to at 3.15, as do they, and when, at 3.20, they turn their probing eye on to *The Missionary* and begin, in rather measured, well-rounded tones to pull it to pieces, I quite simply run out of patience with their hostile cleverness and leave the house.

On to a Python '*MOL*' meeting with the two Terrys and John G and Anne. TJ and I put together a nice little 40-second radio ad and it's quite a jolly session. Goldstone says '*MOL*' is over 10 million gross in the US, but we need 40 million gross to start making money.

Tuesday, April 26th: London–Oslo

Out to Heathrow about one o'clock. Time for a coffee, then onto a Super One-Eleven to Oslo. At three o'clock UK time, four o'clock Norwegian, we're over the mainland of Norway and flying across a chill and desolate snowscape of forests and frozen lakes and finally into Oslo itself.

A man comes out to welcome the flight on a bicycle. We leave the plane and down to the terminal through holes in the tarmac. John Jacobsen,[1] thin, bearded, with his odd, ironic gaze, meets me and drives me into the centre of town and the Continental Hotel. Pleasant, local feel to it and a large room overlooking the main street of the town.

Don my suit and tie and am taken at eight o'clock to the Continental Hotel dining room (the best restaurant in Oslo, I'm told). Here I meet my hosts for

---

[1] John Jacobsen, a writer and general fixer, was Norway's greatest Python fan.

tonight, the two who run all the cinemas of Oslo – for, like alcohol retailing, cinema exhibition is here a municipal monopoly. The dark lady with a sad, Munch-like face is Ingeborg. The middle-aged, friendly, unassuming man is Eivind. 'You are not so high . . . ' begins the dark and Garbo-esque Ingeborg, 'as on the screen.'

Wednesday, April 27th: Oslo

To a restaurant overlooking the city for a late lunch with Jahn Teigen, the Norwegian comedian/singer/composer, who became even more of a national hero when he returned from the Eurovision Song Contest two years ago without a single point.

He's a tremendous Python fan, but a very intelligent one too and I like him enormously. Having a lunch together is a real relaxation from the usual round of slightly forced politenesses which these trips are all about. He's making a film about King Olaf, the tenth-century Norwegian hero. His concerts sell out all over the country and he's clearly the biggest fish in this quite lucrative pond.

Thursday, May 5th

Forty years old. Feel tempted to write some pertinent remarks about The Meaning Of It All – a mid-life, half-term report on Michael P. But there isn't much to say except I feel I'm still going – and going very hard and quite fast – and the pace of life and experience doesn't seem to show any sign of flagging.

I feel that I've entered, and am now firmly embarked on, a third 18-year 'section'. The first 18 were my childhood, the next 18 my preparation and apprenticeship and now, for better or worse, I *am* established. If I died tomorrow I would have an obituary and all those things.

The very fact that Rachel should creep round the door of our room at eight o'clock, full of excitement, to tell me that my birthday was announced, over my picture, on BBC Breakfast TV, shows what status I have had thrust upon me. I have the feeling that, as far as the public is concerned, I am now their Michael Palin and they are quite happy for me to remain their Michael Palin for the rest of my (and their) life.

So here I am. Healthy and wealthy and quite wise, but I can stay and sit comfortably or I can move on and undertake more risks as a writer and performer. Of course I *shall* go on, but, as another day of writing my 'new film' recedes and disappears, I realise that it won't be easy. And I should perhaps stop expecting it to be.

Friday, May 6th

Running on the Heath this morning, pounding away the effects of a poor, anxious night's sleep, my mind clears as my body relaxes and I resolve to extricate myself from some of the many commitments in which I have become entangled over the years.

This morning Clive Landa rang from Shepperton. Clive tells me that Lee Brothers have made a £2 million offer for the studio and two property companies are also anxious to buy it (and knock it down, of course). I feel that all my efforts over the years have counted for very little – and, to be honest, I haven't been asked to contribute a great deal of time and effort anyway. So I think I shall proffer my resignation as soon as possible.[1]

The crucial problem over the next months is whether or not I shall have time to write a screenplay by August. It's clear that *Comic Roots* will take up at least four weeks and the ever-increasing demands of publicity will devour much of the rest. Unthinkable though it might seem, I feel strongly that I must extract myself from *Comic Roots*. I shouldn't be spending four weeks on my past, when I'd rather be spending it on my future.

Saturday, May 7th

I open the Camden Institute Playgroup Fete.

I spend three-quarters of an hour 'being a celebrity' and trying to avoid a persistent mad camerawoman who wants me to do something 'goofy' for the *Camden Journal*. And all the time I'm doing this public smiling I'm inwardly trying to prepare myself for my next confrontation – with Tony Laryea over *Comic Roots*.

We talk upstairs in my workroom. I put to him, unequivocally, all the problems I foresee and ask if there is any way I can get out of doing the programme. Tony uses no moral blackmail, nor emotional entreaties either; he says that if we don't do it now we will never do it and, although there was theoretically time to find a replacement for me, he obviously doesn't want to. He is understanding of my problem and we end up going through the schedule cutting my time spent to its finest.

---

[1] Clive Landa was Managing Director of Shepperton Studios. In view of the amount of work I was doing elsewhere I sent in my letter of resignation on June 2nd after nearly seven years as a director.

Sunday, May 8th: Cannes

Am met at Nice Côte d'Azur Airport by Duncan Clark, CIC's head of publicity. I feel in good shape and the Mediterranean sunshine only improves things. As we drive through the neat and tidy streets of the outskirts of Nice and on to the road to Cannes and Monaco, I begin to feel a distinct whiff of the Scott Fitzgeralds. Terry J arrived yesterday and has already taken all his clothes off and run into the sea for a TV crew.

Our car draws up outside the Carlton, where I'm staying. One or two confused photographers put their cameras up, but it's hardly a star arrival and I notice one of them still has the lens cap on.

Meet up with the others on the terrace at the Carlton at half past eight after a bath. Graham and John T, John G and the two Terrys and wives. With them is Henry Jaglom (whose *Sitting Ducks* I enjoyed so much), so we have time for a short exchange of compliments over a beer. His new film is being shown out of competition on Wednesday evening – the same time as *The Missionary*.

Monday, May 9th: Cannes

This is Python day at Cannes. We are officially announced – each one introduced – and our answers instantly translated into French. Neither the questions nor the instant translation process make for an easy exchange of information and certainly they don't help our jokes. One woman claims to have been physically ill during 'Creosote'.

I am asked about Sheffield and I end up telling the world's press that Sheffield girls have bigger breasts because they walk up a lot of hills.

Then we are taken up on to the roof and given a photo-grilling of Charles and Di-like proportions, with cameramen fighting each other to get dull pictures of us. I've never, ever been the subject of such concentrated Nikon-ic attention. It's all very silly and years ago we would all have been persuaded to be much more outrageous.

Then, suddenly, we're free. The Terrys, Graham and Eric go back to the hotel to prepare for the splendours of the Gala Presentation of '*MOL*' tonight, and me to return to England en route for Dublin. But as long as we are here we're good publicity fodder and, as GC and I walk along the Croisette, some keen young photographer asks earnestly that we come to be photographed with Jerry Hall – 'She's on the beach, just there . . . ' he pleads.

After 'Missionary' promotion in Dublin and Newcastle, I took a short film-writing break in Canonbie, north of Carlisle.

Friday, May 13th: The Riverside Inn, Canonbie

Awake at eight. On the radio the news is all of pre-election sparring. Margaret Thatcher's transformation into Winston Churchill becomes increasingly evident as she singles out defence (i.e. wars and the Falklands) as the main issue of the election.

Down to the wondrous Riverside Inn breakfast. I'm offered a duck's egg. Very large and tasty and rather nice as I can see the duck that laid it from my window as I write. It's white. Called Persil, they tell me.

Short walk, then up to my room, with its disconcertingly sloping floor, to wrestle with the problems of a nymphomaniac drug addict accused of the ritual murder of a well-known Scottish footballer. The rain comes down gently and steadily, with sudden enormous surges – unlike my writing. I cannot reconcile myself to the 'Explorers' tale completely. There isn't enough that is new, original, different and exciting about the characters and I feel that the Polar icecap will look great for five minutes, then lose its grip on your average audience hungry for laughs.

Saturday, May 14th

TG comes round. He came back from Cannes last night. He now has his money for *Brazil* – a Universal deal for US, and Fox worldwide. Very pleased. Asks me if I'm available to play Jack Lint. I say no, of course not, but he knows I am.

Monday, May 16th

Tackle backlog of desk-work from last week. Talk to Mike Ewin who tells me that we are actually *up* by £120 in our eleventh week at the Classic H. He's also pleased with good, but not sensational, provincial figures thus far. 'The trade is pleasantly surprised,' as he puts it. And we have a second week at Weston-super-Mare, which he considers a considerable triumph!

Less good news from David Knopf, whom I phone in LA. The re-release of the '*Mish*' ran only three weeks in LA and has just opened at the Sutton in New York to little enthusiasm, leading him to rate the chances of a complete national re-issue unlikely.

And Python's '*MOL*' is fading. It did well in each area for about three weeks and that was that. It now looks as if it will take less in the US than *Brian* (nine million as against eleven).

Wednesday, May 18th

Feel rather dejected this morning. Even the news that Buckingham Palace has requested a 35 mill print of *The Missionary* to be taken aboard the Royal Yacht can't lift me from a very black gloom. Anger at everyone around, myself most of all. Feel frustrated by lack of time to write and not even sure if I want to write what I'm writing.

Watch Chas McKeown's prog on TV,[1] his first series for BBC TV. Some good jokes, nice lines, spoilt by heavy LE mugging. There ought to be something that you could put in the tea at the Beeb canteen to stop quite reasonable actors going at comedy like a bull at a gate.

Thursday, May 19th

John Goldstone phones at 8 a.m. to tell me that *Meaning of Life* has won second prize at Cannes – the Special Jury Prize.

Write up and type out my *Comic Roots* basic script. My writing time for the 'Explorers' first draft is now narrowed to six weeks, but I try hard not to think about this.

I collect the boys from the William Ellis swimming gala at Swiss Cottage. Tom has come second in two of his races and both he and William have been members of successful relay teams, so they're both in very good spirits.

Sunday, May 22nd

Read all the papers in the hope of some blinding revelation as to who to support at the election. Cannot stomach Thatcher and feel that her faceless, obedient Tebbits and Parkinsons are about to inherit the party. Labour is the only likely alternative, but they are hamstrung with doctrinaire stuff about quitting the EEC and abolishing the House of Lords and far too vulnerable to the boring constituency committee people and the intolerant, grumpy unions. I suppose I shall vote Labour in the hope of giving Thatcher as big a shock as possible.

---

[1] It was called *Pinkerton's Progress*. Set in a school, it was written by Charles and directed by Gareth Gwenlan.

Monday, May 23rd

I take a taxi down to Piccadilly – to the Royal Academy Dinner at Burlington House. The great mystery of the evening – which is why I was unable to turn down the invite – is why I am there. Who is my friend amongst the luminaries of the Royal Academy? After all, I haven't set foot in there for over a year.

Inside my coat is checked and I ascend the staircase between lofty marble pillars towards a circular chamber from which come the pleasant, rich strains of a small orchestra.

I am announced by a man in a scarlet jacket and received by Sir Hugh Casson, a diminutive, rather cheeky-looking man resembling a perky cockatoo. He is very charming, considering he doesn't know me from Adam, and he in turn introduces me to a pair of be-medalled, beaming buffers.

Then I am in amongst the central rooms of the Academy, offered what I think is champagne, but which turns out to be rather ordinary Spanish sparkling. I look at all the pictures – all ready for the Summer Exhibition – and I look at all the worthy academicians who are gathering and I suddenly think – suppose I meet no-one all evening who knows me.

I am sat next to a lady called Meg Buckenham. She has a direct, unaffected good nature which makes me glad of my luck. She made up even for the presence of Kasmin, the gallery owner, on my other side. Small, tanned and noisy. He regales everyone who will listen with stories of himself and seems very sure that he is the most desirable sexual object in the room.

Across from me is Ruskin Spear – a man who looks exactly like Father Christmas. He speaks in a deep, richly-textured, gravelly voice and seems to be gently mocking everything around him. He calls me 'Palin' in an amused schoolmasterly tone. 'I'm bored, Palin . . . ' he will suddenly say.

We have speeches from Princess Alexandra. Beautifully poised, regal and smiling winningly, but it doesn't make up for a terrible line in royally-delivered cliché. Sir Hugh Casson, sprite-like, is up and down between each speaker, jollying everyone along. It's his 73rd birthday and he's presented with a huge cake in the shape of the leaves of an opened book.

Lord Gowrie speaks for the government. He's in the Northern Ireland office. He has a thick head of hair and looks fashionably attractive in the Yves St Laurent mould, but again his looks belie his speech-making capabilities and he turns in a smooth, but vapid performance.

Sir Hugh is up again eagerly and he hands over to Lord Goodman, who replies to Sir Hugh's toast on behalf of the guests. I've never seen the notorious Lord Goodman in the flesh – only in *Private Eye* caricatures, where he is portrayed always as some vast lump topped with an elephant-like head. Although Goodman isn't quite as gargantuan as they make out, he is an extraordinary-looking creature and the prominent ears, with their dark, hairy inner recesses, are riveting. But he has the gift of the gab and scuttles through a quite unprepared speech very mellifluously. I warm to him. He is not malicious, nor cheap. He speaks intelligently and quite wittily.

Sir Hugh makes the final speech – one last attempt to butter us all up. Apparently I am present at 'one of the great banquets of the year'.

After all these toasts and some belligerent shouts of 'Rot! Absolute rot!' from Kasmin beside me, we are free to leave and mingle and take brandy from the trays carried through.

By this time several of the RA's are becoming tired and emotional and the limping figure of Ian Dury and the academician Peter Blake have joined our little group, and I'm being asked by Peter Blake to accompany him over to the Caprice for a 'nightcap'. Say farewell to Sir Hugh on the stairs. He gives Meg B a long hug. I feel like the errant young suitor in the presence of a father-in-law.

Across to the Caprice, walking slowly so Dury can keep up. He's very jokey and good value and keeps calling me Eric. At the Caprice a rather drunk young blond cruises round the tables and ends up in deep discussion with him. This is Jasper Conran. As usual on these occasions nobody really knows why anyone else is there, and it's very bad form to ask.

Sunday, May 29th

Helen packs in preparation for Newcastle trip with the children. Play snooker and try my hand at capitals of the world on the new BBC computer. I really can't wait for everyone to be gone, so I can set to work on 'Explorers' (I have a tantalisingly clear week ahead).

Another hour of halting progress brought to a rude conclusion by the appearance of TG. He's just back from working with Charles McKeown – the two of them are rewriting Tom Stoppard's script for *Brazil*. He's already setting up *Baron Munchausen* as his next film, in case *Brazil* really doesn't work! American majors have forked out 12 million dollars for rights to distribute – only thing they don't like about *Brazil* is the title.

Home to bed, in silent, empty house, by midnight.

Monday, May 30th

I make a clear start on opening scenes. But still the whole project seems arbitrary. My heart is just not in it. Staying here whilst the family is away to avoid distractions, I find myself waiting quite eagerly for distractions.

Tuesday, May 31st

Michael White's office ring – the Turf Club is still pursuing my membership and wants details of birthdate, place of education, interests. Think of lying and putting down 'horse-racing' (Alison D suggests 'horse-spotting', which I like), but settle for the dignified restraint of 'writing and travel'.

Monday, June 6th

With not very worthy feelings of guilt, reluctance and resentment, I acknowledge the fact that I could and probably should have spent more time on the '*MOL*' radio commercials which we're recording this morning.

Drive into town at 9.15, new Phil Everly tape blaring, roof open. André's just back from two weeks in California looking more successful every time I see him. JC arrives, GC doesn't.

John looks very hairy with beard and long black hair. He is in quite a skittish mood and wants to do lots of silly voices. He does an excellent Kirkegaard. He's just finished work on a book with his psychiatrist – 'Seven or eight weeks solid ... I just haven't had a moment.' Fall to talking about autobiographies. John wants to call his '24 Hours From Normal'. And for a Python biog we both like the title 'Where's Graham?'

Friday, June 10th: Southwold

After breakfast accompany Ma into Southwold. 'This is my son Michael – you've probably seen him on the television.' And if that doesn't work, it's followed by the blatant – 'He's in Monty Python, you know ... !'

Saturday, June 11th

Up at eight. Preoccupied with the NBC piece [for a new show called *The News Is The News*], and the problems of learning three and a half minutes of straight-to-camera material by half past ten. A very lordly Daimler arrives to collect me at ten. The driver wears thin and expensive-looking leather gloves.

By the time we reach Whitehall I have almost learnt the piece, though haven't been able to go right through without a fluff. The Queen is Trooping the Colour in the Mall and there are crowds everywhere. With the boldness of the blissfully ignorant, my Daimler turns into Downing Street at half past ten –

third or fourth in a line of similar limousines, except that they all carry ambassadors or diplomats on their way to fawn to the recently re-elected Leaderene.

Of course I'm turned back, having been given no clearance by NBC, and my driver dumps me unceremoniously in busy Whitehall.

A guardsman on duty asks me to sign the inside of his peaked cap. ('It's all I've got,' he says apologetically.) A rather attractive lady PC grins at me.

Producer and cameraman appear.

We retire to the pub opposite to kill the half-hour before the No. 10 Press Officer arrives. At midday it's decided that valour is the better part of discretion and all three of us march up to the police barrier. The particular constable on duty this time recognises me as no threat to the PM and we're in and walking up the narrow street – one of the most famous, if not *the* most famous narrow street in the world.

The camera is set up, alongside a permanent display of three or four video cameras and a group of pressmen drinking cans of Harp lager and not looking at all respectful of the hallowed ground they're on. Behind me the rather dull façade of No. 10. I notice all the net curtains are dirty.

With little fuss and bother we start shooting. After a while the press hacks stop talking to each other and come to listen (this in itself is very disconcerting). Some of them I can see falling about with laughter and this encourages me through to the end of an almost perfect take.

And not a moment too soon. A very senior PC looms up and looks very cross. The photographers seem delighted and snap away at him telling us off. We're asked to leave. As we do so, reporters cluster around asking if I'm the new Home Secretary, etc, etc.

Thursday, June 16th

Pick up Ray Cooper and he and I set off for a day at Henley.

George is waiting for us before the recently-scrubbed walls of Friar Park. He wears a shaggy old sports jacket which he claims has been threaded through with dental floss.

Transfer from Ray's hired black Range Rover to George's black Porsche. George drives us to Marlow as if he is at Silverstone. We dine at The Compleat Angler. It's superbly sited beside the broad weir at Marlow, looking out over a view which is the very epitome of nature tamed.

George, as usual in such places, is extremely ill at ease to start with. He resents the 'posh' service and feels that, considering he can afford to buy the restaurant several times over, the staff are unnecessarily snotty. But he loosens up over a bottle of champagne. Some excellent smoked salmon, and trout, and a second bottle – this time of Aloxe Corton '69.

We laugh a lot and talk about films and not being able to write them. I think George thinks that I've come to see him to ask for money, and offers it eagerly and generously. But when he finds out that all I have to tell him is that I can't write a film by August he sympathises and loosens up. 'I've been trying to retire for half my life,' he mourns.

Back at Friar Park, George runs through whole scenes of *The Producers* word for word – acting the parts out extremely well. Olivia has some American girlfriends who have 'dropped in' whilst touring Europe. When they've gone, Ray opens some pink Dom Perignon, which is very rare and must have cost the earth, and we sit in the little kitchen and talk about Python and things in an easy, effortlessly friendly way.

George gives me a souvenir as I leave – a baton belonging to the Chief Constable of Liverpool, which GH took off him at the Liverpool premiere of *A Hard Day's Night!*

Saturday, June 18th

The general ease and pleasure of the day added to by the fact that we only have to walk ten yards or so for our dinner tonight. To the Brazilians who are renting No. 24. Eleas, who is the husband, a psychoanalyst, cooks. He is an intellectual in the Continental sense of the word – critical, left-wing, multi-lingual, serious, a little intimidating. She is voluble, full of laughter, from a massively populous peasant family.

They are not a grumbling pair, but do criticise the English reserve – the long faces of neighbours.

He has come to study because the best of the German Jewish psychoanalysts came here before the war and it is, as a result, the best country in the world for the study of psychoanalysis. But the British immigration people are very difficult and always give him a hard time when he returns to the country. They're never violent, they never confront you with any direct accusations, he says, they just make you feel bad.

Tuesday, June 21st

Leave for Ealing at one [for *Comic Roots* filming]. The set, to represent No. 26 Whitworth Road [my birthplace in Sheffield], is at Tony Laryea's brother's house and looks quite effective.

At 2.15 Spike M arrives. As usual with him there is a brittle air of tension and unpredictability, but he and I sit down and natter for a half-hour about the Goons – the coining of words like 'sponned' [as in 'I been sponned!']. He raves about 'Eric Olthwaite'. I rave about Eccles.[1] By the time the second camera is up and ready to shoot he seems to have relaxed.

An aeroplane thunders low overhead as soon as we start. His answers to my questions about the Goons are almost identical to the answers I always give when asked about the Pythons – we did it to make ourselves laugh, to laugh at authority, we always had a love/hate relationship with the BBC, etc. Even the name 'The Goon Show' was their own and only reluctantly accepted by the BBC, who wanted 'The Crazy People Show'.

Then Spike has to leave and my mother arrives. She is very nervous, as one would expect of someone making their TV debut at the age of 79, but soon gets over it as we sit together on the couch and in the end she is utterly professional and quite unflapped. She tells her stories smoothly and says delight-fully disarming things such as (of *The Meaning of Life*) ' . . . Of course it's very rude . . . but I like that.'

Friday, June 24th

Rush away at midday to Gerry Donovan to have the temporary dental bridge he put in four years ago checked. He reminds me that 'It usually comes out about this time of year.' Last year when I ate a call-sheet on the way back from '*Mish*' filming in Liverpool and the year before in some pleasant Cretan village as I tucked into freshly spit-roasted lamb. But this year, touch wood, it remains.

Monday, July 11th

Out in the evening to a screening of *Bullshot* at the Fox Theatre. George H is there and Ray and Norman Garwood and David Wimbury [the associate producer] and various others. Twenty or thirty in all. Find the first ten minutes very ordinary, and the overplayed style rather off-putting, but the film gradually wins me over, by its sheer panache and good nature.

George opts to drive with me from Soho Square to Knightsbridge, but when I can't find where I've left my car, I feel he wishes he hadn't. A bit like an animal caught in a searchlight is our George when out on the streets and I can see him getting a little twitchy as he and I – a Beatle and a Python – parade up and down before the diners on the pavements of Charlotte Street, looking for my car.

---

[1] At one point in the interview I told Spike how I'd only seen Peter Sellers once. 'I passed him in the corridor at Wembley Studios.' To which Spike replied crisply, 'Very painful.'

Of course no-one notices and eventually I get George into the Mini and across London. He gives me a breakdown of one or two of the Indian cults currently in this country – Rajneesh I should be especially careful about. No inner discipline required – just fuck as many people as you can. Sounds interesting.

Our Chinese meal gets quite boisterous owing to the presence of a dark, slightly tubby Jewish girl who does 'improv' at the Comic Strip. I find these American 'improv' people the most difficult of companions. Most of them are perfectly nice, decent, reasonable company until they start performing – which is about every ten minutes – and you are expected to join in some whacky improv.

But we outstay most other people in the restaurant and become very noisy and jolly and all drink out of one huge glass and muck around with the straws and end up on the quiet streets of Knightsbridge being appallingly loud at a quarter to one.

Thursday, July 14th

Have been offered the part of Mother Goose in the Shaw Theatre panto and also the lead in a new Howard Brenton play – rehearsing in August. Torn on this one, it sounds the sort of heavy, non-comedic role that might be quite exciting and unusual for me. But August is hols and September/October is writing with Terry J.

Spend the afternoon being photographed by Terry O'Neill for *TV Cable Week*. Terry is a Londoner with an insatiable curiosity about everything that's going on – the Test Match, jazz (when he finds out that Tom is learning the saxophone), films (he's directing his first picture in the autumn – *Duet for One* – Faye Dunaway, his wife, in the lead). Very much one of the lads – I can remember playing football with him ten years ago. He was a good winger. He's down-to-earth and unpretentious and probably keen to be the best at everything he does.

Photos everywhere – with railway, at desk and with family. All self-conscious to some degree, except Rachel, who loves being photographed!

Sunday, July 17th

At seven, after cooking baked beans and toast for the children's supper and leaving Thomas in charge again, we drive out to Olivia's party at Friar Park.

Arrive there about 8.25 and cannot make contact through the intercom on the locked gates, so we drive round to the back gate and press more buttons. A passing horsewoman suggests we try again – 'Probably got the music on rather loud,' she explains.

When we do gain admittance, there is a very restrained group of people standing politely sipping champagne, and listening to nothing louder than a harp, in a tent at the end of the lawn. Friar Park, pristine and floodlit, looks like the venue for a *son et lumière*, up on the rise behind us.

Joe Brown arrives. Calling everyone 'gal' or 'old gal', he proceeds to rave about 'Golden Gordon', repeating all the moments – but unlike Spike getting them word for word right. He has been able to get over here because the promoter of his concert was hit by a sock filled with billiard balls and is temporarily out of business.

The champagne flows liberally and people wander about the house. In his studio George demonstrates a machine which will make any sound into music electronically.

We meet Nelson Piquet, the Brazilian driver who came second at Silverstone yesterday, and John Watson is here too.[1] Piquet a little, perky, pleasantly ambitious Brazilian. He loves his work. No doubts, no fears, from what he says.

The evening cools and the setting is quite perfect. Derek [Taylor] tells me the code used to avoid mentioning drugs specifically. 'I've got all the Charles Aznavour albums to play tonight' means an evening of the naughtiest, most illicit substances, whilst a Charles Aznavour EP may just be some cocaine . . .

And so, on this high note, we drive out of this dreamland, down the M4 back to reality.

Wednesday, July 20th: Southwold

Catch the train at Gospel Oak. Breakfast on the 8.30 from Liverpool Street. Mum collects me and drives me in her blue Metro back to Croft Cottage.

Have to do some PR with her new neighbours. At one point he takes my arm and leads me to one side . . . He apologises, hopes he's not speaking 'out of turn', but my mother is . . . 'well . . . no longer a young woman', so have I 'any contingency plans'?

Thursday, July 21st: Southwold

A restorative nine-hour sleep. Outside the best of English summer days – a clear sunlight sharply delineating the trees and cornfields. Sparrows already at dustbaths in the garden below.

Sort out some of Daddy's old papers – finally commit to the Lothingland

---

[1] Piquet was the Formula One champion that year, as he was in 1981 and 1987. John Watson, from Northern Ireland, had won the British Grand Prix in 1981.

Sanitary Department many of the school bills, school insurance bills, etc, which he had painstakingly kept. Learn from the family record that my grandfather – a Norfolk doctor – was also a very keen photographer and had exhibited in London. He was a gardener of repute and a Freemason. He and his wife sound a fiercely competent couple. Founding the local Red Cross, etc.

Home for lateish ham supper. Helen tells me about her BUPA medical screening today and of the dashing doctor Ballantine who picked her leg up and waggled it about!

The evening almost spent (and both of us weary) when Alan Bennett rings and, with much umming and aahing, asks if I would like to read a part in a new screenplay he's written. It's about a chiropodist, he says . . . oh, and pigs as well. Of course I fall eagerly on the chance and a neat man called Malcolm Mowbray – fashionably turned out – brings the script around.

Read it there and then – such is my curiosity. Slightly disappointed that the part of Gilbert Chilvers is not a) bigger, b) more difficult or different from things I've done. But he does have his moments and it's a very funny and well-observed period piece (set in 1947).

Decide to sleep on it.

Saturday, July 23rd

To the seven o'clock performance of *King of Comedy* at the Screen on the Hill. Very enjoyable – one of the less dark of Scorsese's modern parables, with much wit and many laughs and another extraordinary and skilful and concentrated and successful performance by De Niro. Jerry Lewis (one of my childhood heroes) excellent too.

Come home and, over a cold plateful and glasses of wine, think about the Bennett play. Decide that it is not a difficult or special enough part to drop either my writing with TJ, Belfast Festival commitments or semi-commitment to TG. Ring Alan in Yorkshire, but cannot get him.

Sunday, July 24th

Up to Abbotsley – driving through heavy, but very localised storms and arriving in time for a tennis knock-up before lunch. The air is heavy and damp and the sunshine breaks through only occasionally.

Hang the hammock and play more tennis – pursuits that mark the summer and for which I have literally had no time for two years. A lovely afternoon.

Alan Bennett is up in North Yorkshire and he says the lights have all just gone out. I tell him of my liking for the *Private Function* script, but of my problem with commitments until the end of the year. 'Oh, it won't be till May at least,' counters Alan. 'That's the earliest Maggie's available.' [He wants Maggie Smith to play my wife.] So there seems no point in saying I've decided over the weekend not to do it.

Sunday, August 7th

Rave preview by Jennifer Selway of the *Observer* for Friday's *Comic Roots* – Michael Palin's 'brilliant' half-hour. I can't remember this adjective ever being applied to my work *before* it's been seen – only on rare occasions many years after when affection has distorted the memory.

Sunday dinner together – watch a Scottish/Canadian writer [Robertson Davies] on the excellent series *Writers and Places*. Feel a great appetite for all things written and described. Maybe it's the relaxing break of ten days in France which has finally cleared my immediate work problems away and let other aspects of life come to the front of my mind and imagination.

Thursday, August 11th

Tom and his friend Paul Forbes leave at seven to cycle to Brighton. Helen says she can't help being worried about them.

Drop the Mini at the garage to be serviced, then Helen drops me at Alan Bennett's house on the corner of Gloucester Crescent. A camper van with what looks like carpet covering it is parked in front of the front door. Alan opens it – a little hesitant, a touch of awkwardness and an instant warmth as he shows me in to the crepuscular gloom of a sitting room which seems to have been very carefully protected against daylight. Mark Shivas and Malcolm Mowbray are on a couch against the far wall. Alan offers me a comfortable old chair and disappears to make coffee.

I long to have a good look round, but am aware of Shivas and Mowbray wanting to talk and set us all at ease. My overriding impression of the place is of elegant dusty clutter – rather like the set for Aubrey's *Brief Lives*.

Alan reappears. We talk politely of France ... holidays ... then Shivas asks me about my availability. Well, I can't go back on what I'd said to Alan ... I *do* like the piece and well ... they are all watching me ... yes, I'd love to do it.

From then on we discuss finance generally and I realise that Shivas wants someone to bankroll the entire project and so far has no definite bites. In answer to his questions about HandMade I cannot but recommend he try them – though it somewhat complicates my position, as the Bennett film will be taking away time from my own project for HandMade.

After an hour there doesn't seem much more to say. Slight feeling of reserve, which does not emanate from Alan, but more likely from Shivas. I suddenly miss Richard. Everything's a little too polite and circumspect. Walk home.

Tom rings from Brighton at 11.30. He got there in four hours. They're coming back by train.

Spend the rest of the morning writing my obit tribute to Luis Buñuel for *Rolling Stone*.

Saturday, August 13th

In the *Telegraph*, a *Comic Roots* review under the nice heading 'Chortling beamish boy', I learn 'there is something roundly Victorian about Michael Palin's face, a durable cheerfulness not to be found among other members of Monty Python's Flying Circus . . . alone of the Python team he can deflate cant without venom', but cautions 'John Cleese's angry logic is missing from his humour'.

At five o'clock Felice[1] and Richard cycle up here. RL has a film to direct now, and is into top gear, with that bristling, bubbling, provocative self-confidence which he adopts to paper over the doubts beneath.

Sunday, August 14th

To Angela and Veryan's 'Jubilation Party' at Chilton. It's to celebrate, or mark the occasion of, Angela's 50th birthday, V & A's 25th wedding anniversary, Jeremy's 22nd and his top 2nd in Politics at York. It's all been organised by the family as the caterers went bust a week ago.

So we are parked in a field by Marcus and a nice, bright-eyed girlfriend of Camilla's from Oxford, with whom she is going to Mexico and the Yucatán this holiday. I'm green with envy.

As the early cloud clears a perfect day develops. Not unpleasantly hot, but hot enough to make the ample shade from the big copper beech and lime trees on the lawn seem very welcome.

The moat is filled, now the bridge has been repaired, and is covered in a solid green veneer of duck-weed. New-born ducks skid around as on the surface of a billiard table.

---

[1] Felice Fallon, an American writer, became Richard Loncraine's second wife in September 1985.

Lots of Herbert relatives, and the slightly disturbing presence of Sir Dingle Foot's widow, Lady Dorothy. She used to be engaged to Daddy, and he called it off when she wouldn't agree to drop her political affiliations with the Liberals. Now I feel she regards Angela and me as the children she never had. 'Can't go too near people – I fall over so easily,' she warns. She invites Helen and me to one of her parties ... 'I do enjoy a good party.'

Angela in a '50's-looking dress which could have been one of the earliest she wore. And that's meant as a compliment. Can she really be 50?

Monday, August 22nd: Glasgow

To the ABC cinema complex at Sauchiehall Street. Met by the manager – neat moustachioed war veteran with Royal Signals tie. Up to one of their many 'lounges' where a 'spread' is laid out for the hungry and thirsty press at present sitting watching my film.

So I move into fifth gear and smile a lot and am completely helpful and co-operative and remember names and show a polite and hopefully completely straight face, even when a little old lady from the *Jewish Echo* asks me why I called the film *The Missionary*. Actually it is not as daft a question as it sounds, her point being that the title might put people off, which is something I've heard before, and which troubles me because I'm sure it's true.

Then entaxi to the Woodside Health Centre, where it has been arranged for me to have the second part of a typhoid vaccination. The Health Centre is set amongst a jumble of modern blocks of flats, which have largely replaced the solidly stone-built red sandstone tenements which look rather good wherever they've been renovated.

The doctor writes on my form '*The* Michael Palin', and sends me off to the Treatment Room. Can't help reflecting on the glamour of showbiz as I sit in this little roomful of the ill amongst modern tower blocks with litter blowing all around. Eventually I'm seen by a stout, warm, friendly nurse and jabbed.

Tuesday, August 23rd: Edinburgh

At breakfast in the rather appealingly dilapidated, unmodernised, Scots-Gothic country house that is the Braid Hills, the ceiling starts to leak and champagne buckets and washing-up bowls are requisitioned with great good humour by the staff.

At midday I take a taxi to the Dominion Theatre, where *The Missionary* will open on Tuesday. It's an independent cinema in the smart Morningside area of the city, run by the genial Derek Cameron with an attentiveness which befits one whose father built the place (in 1938). The bar and restaurant are run and designed as places to linger and they have a busy clientele of all ages, who come here, some of them, just to eat and meet.

Local Hero is in its 17th week and *Gregory's Girl* for a third year. Bill Forsyth's favourite cinema? I ask Derek C. Oh yes, he says, when he comes here he just raises his hands to heaven . . .

I cannot think of a pleasanter place for *The Missionary* to have its Scottish premiere.

Saturday, September 3rd

After breakfast TG drops in. I haven't even finished reading his *Brazil* and was hoping I'd have this morning to complete it, so can't give any very knowledgeable criticisms. But I like the part of Jack Lint and TG says he has kept it away from De Niro – just for me! So it's agreed that I'll do it. Filming probably some time in December.

Later in the morning Terry takes me up to the Old Hall in Highgate – his new £300,000 acquisition. Horrible things have been done to it inside, but its garden bordering on Highgate cemetery and the panorama of London from its plentiful windows are almost priceless. Of course it's enormous and rambling, but still just a town house, not a country manor. And TG needs the challenge of the space like a drug. I find the damp old smell of the wretched conversions make the house depressing, but TG says it has quite the opposite effect on him because he knows what he can do with it.

Read *Water*, the latest DO'B project from Dick Clement and Ian La Frenais, who are his latest blue-eyed boys. DO'B would like me to play the part of Baxter. First 16 pages are wonderfully funny, but it all falls apart and there isn't a laugh after that. No characters are developed, new characters are thrust in instead and the jokes become stretched and laboured.

Sunday, September 4th

Dick Clement rings re *Water*. I'm honest about my feelings and, indeed, it's refreshing to talk to someone like Dick who is intelligent and tactful and is, after all, a TV writer with an impressive record – *Likely Lads*, etc. We can understand each other's language. He professes his liking for naturalistic comedy, and yet sees *Water* as an international film. I tell him that I think 'international' comedy a very dangerous concept.

I find Dick's choice of Billy Connolly to play the black revolutionary a real commercial cop-out . . . 'Well, he'll be sort of brown,' Dick reassures.

Monday, September 5th

Hear to my great disappointment that the '*Mish*' has not opened well in Scotland. And despite my great welcome by Derek Cameron at the Dominion, and his great hopes for the picture, I hear from Mike Ewin that he's pulling it off after three weeks to put in *Tootsie* – again.

Python, on the other hand, had its best provincial figures anywhere in the UK at Edinburgh. Nearly £10,000 taken in the first week of the Festival. And '*MOL*' continues strong in the West End, where it's out-performed *Superman III* easily.

Tuesday, September 6th

Today Tom and William start the new school year. This is for Tom the start of serious work – the run-up to 'O' levels.

Helen says Tom is just like her at school, scatty, easily distracted and not really happy being taught maths and French and things. But neither of us should draw too much satisfaction from seeing neat parallels between our children's efforts and our own. They are not us, after all, they're them.

I go on down to TJ's and we read each other our starts. Both quite respectable, both start in space. Jim Henson rings, anxious for TJ to commit to directing a piece called 'Labyrinth'.

Tuesday, September 20th

I am tempted by a phone call from Ray Cooper to attend the first of a two-night concert in aid of Multiple Sclerosis, in which many great rock stars of the '60's, all friends of Ronnie Lane who has MS, will be appearing, including Ray C.

As if starved of live performance for so long, Ray tucks into the opportunity with gusto. I've never seen him live before, only heard the legendary tales. And he is a revelation. Impeccable timing and precise movements combined with a sense of high theatrical style which just avoids being camp or purely exhibitionist, is wondrous to behold.

But even Ray is upstaged by the extraordinary appearance of Jimmy Page, who weaves his way around the stage like a man who has been frozen in the last stages of drunkenness, before actually falling over. He sways, reels, totters, bends, but still manages to play superbly. The others look on anxiously and Ray tells me at the end that Page isn't well . . . 'And he lives in Aleister Crowley's house.'

But the coup of the evening is the appearance of Ronnie Lane himself. Led, painfully slowly, onto the stage by Ray (who is everywhere) and Harvey Goldsmith, he is strong enough to sing two numbers. Very moving.

And Ray, going at his gong like the demented anti-hero of some nineteenth-century Russian drama, hits it so hard that it breaks and falls clean out of its frame.

Thursday, September 22nd

Another good morning's work on 'The Man Who Was Loved'.[1] Really solid writing, not stop and start stuff, and few interruptions. Let letters pile up and just get on with it.

Terry comes up at two and we have a read-through. He has opened out the Viking saga (with a good song) and he likes what I've done on the modern, slightly more serious story. It does look as though we could have two films! Some discussion, then we swap scripts again and work on until after five o'clock. A good and productive working day – like old times.

Then TJ goes off to sign copies of *Erik the Viking* at the Royal Festival Hall and Helen and I go down to the Methuen Authors Party at Apothecaries Hall in Blackfriars.

As we go in, Frank Muir is on the way out. Some hail and farewell chat. I remember *The Complete and Utter Histories* – and his courage in putting them on. He remembers our piece about the waves of invaders in ninth- and tenth-century England being controlled by a man with a megaphone.

Only later in the evening do I find out that Frank's latest book for Methuen is called *The Complete and Utter My Word Collection*!

David Nobbs is anxious that I should read his latest novel because it's set in Sheffield. I'm afraid it's on a pile with dozens of things people have sent me to read. Even just acknowledging that they've sent them cuts my reading time down to about a book a month at the moment. This is another area of my life I must sort out.

Friday, September 23rd

Alison rings with the latest offers. BBC Bristol are doing a heritage series about Britain – would I write the one on transport? *Omnibus* want me on a programme about taste. Yet another video magazine seems to have begun, just to annoy

---

[1] Like a number of other film-writing ideas around this time, this was a Jones/Palin screenplay that remained on the drawing board.

me. Interview about *Missionary* and *Ripping Yarns*? And at last, at the grand old age of 40, the first offer to play Hamlet – at the Crucible, Sheffield.

In the evening we go down to Terry's for a meal with Ron Devillier. TJ cooks marvellous Soupe Bonne Femme, herring and roast pork, with lots of salads and bits and pieces.

TJ plays his accordion and the dog, Mitch, sings. However, Mitch will shut up instantly if anyone laughs.

Wednesday, September 28th

I read perceptive E M Forster remarks about his own fame. He says it made him idle. People were just happy for him to be who he was – to be what he had done, and there was no need for him to sully an already impeccable reputation by doing anything new.

To Shaftesbury Avenue to see *Yellowbeard*. On the plus side are likeable performances from Eric and Nigel Planer and Marty and Peter Boyle and a neat, classy, cameo from Cleese, good costumes and some fine Caribbean scenery and excellent music. Against this a very disjointed piece of direction – no-one seems to know what they are doing or why – some dreadful hamming by the likes of James Mason and Cheech and Chong[1] which kills the few good lines stone dead.

Thursday, September 29th

Nancy L rings and after weeks of dithering I say yes to the *Saturday Night Live* date for January 21st. I don't really want to do the show again, but it does make a good focal point for my mother's trip to America.

Monday, October 3rd

Am offered the lead in 'Cinders' at the Fortune Theatre when Denis Lawson leaves in January. Turn it down on grounds of incompetence – I can't sing very well and certainly can't dance.

At 12.30 Helen and I leave for Kew Gardens, to attend a launching party for Bill Stotesbury's Tarot-designed book on structural engineering. Turns out to be a marvellous relief from the traditional wine and gossip launches. For a start

[1] Richard 'Cheech' Marin and Tommy Chong were an American stand-up comedy duo. Their material drew on hippies, free-love and the drug culture generally.

we go by train, round the backs of North London. Pleasant walk to the gardens at Kew, except for the deafening noise of incoming aircraft – which means all conversations have to have Nixonian gaps in them. Helen insists on filling my pockets with conkers.

We are shown coffee and bananas (which used to be sent straight to the Queen, but aren't any longer) and a palm dating from 1775 and propped up like John Silver on long steel crutches. And trees that are now extinct, called cycads, which dinosaurs used to feed on.

Tuesday, October 4th

A very dull day. I sit in front of the Viking saga all morning with hardly more than a page filled. The trouble is not that I can't think of anything to write, but that I can't think of anything *new* to write. The historical setting with the contemporary characters has been so well explored in *Grail* and *Brian*, and when I start to write on with TJ's adventures in boats I'm into *Time Bandits* territory. The law of diminishing returns.

Wednesday, October 5th

Into black-tie for the BFI 50th Anniversary Banquet at the Guildhall. Find I'm the only Python invited – though, among the 700 guests there are many whose contribution to British films is far less obvious than TJ or TG or any of the rest of the team.

As at the Royal Academy Banquet, I am next to a lady who is excellent company – in this case Christine Oestreicher, who made a short called *A Shocking Accident*. She is funny and quite good to have a giggle with at all the pomp and circumstance around.

'Trust you to have a girl next to you,' says John Howard Davies.[1] He is rather cross, having read somewhere that there were to be no more *Ripping Yarns* because the BBC couldn't afford them. I say I thought it was the main reason and he rather curtly agrees with me, but mumbles about there being others.

There are speeches and presentations of gold medals to Marcel Carné, Orson Welles, Powell and Pressburger[2] and David Lean.

---

[1] John, a child actor who played the lead in David Lean's 1948 film of Oliver Twist, directed many top BBC shows including the first series of *Fawlty Towers* and the first four shows of *Monty Python's Flying Circus*. He was Head of Comedy at the BBC in the late 1970's, when the last of the *Ripping Yarns* were made.
[2] Michael Powell and Emeric Pressburger produced, wrote and directed some of the most stylish and inventive British films, including *A Matter of Life and Death* (1946) and *Red Shoes* (1948).

Prince Charles makes a neat, effortless speech. Surveying the gathering he says it resembled an extraordinary general meeting of Equity. Harold Wilson has to go to the lavatory during the royal speech. Orson Welles re-tells stories about John Gielgud and gets massive applause, then we all 'retire to the library' for drinks.

Barry Took is very agitated about *The Meaning of Life*. He hated it, his daughter hated it – 'she even preferred *Yellowbeard*' – and 'the daughter of one of the richest men in Hong Kong hated it'. His attack is rambling but persistent. He won't leave the thing alone. Badly shot, disgustingly unfunny – back to 'the urine-drinking' aspect of Python, he thundered. All in all, from an old friend, a strange and manic performance. But then Barry is strange, and there are more chips on his shoulder than you'd find on a Saturday night at Harry Ramsden's.

Sir Dickie Att and Tony Smith are working overtime, shovelling celebrities in front of Prince Charles, who is still here, wandering around. As I am telling Ray of the vehemence of Barry T's outburst, Prince Charles catches my eye. A moment later he steps across to me . . .

'I loved your film,' are the first words of the heir to the throne to me. Not a bad start. He was speaking of *The Missionary* . . . he loved the locations, especially Longleat. I ask him where he saw the film – 'Balmoral,' he admits, lowering his voice. Princess Margaret had recommended it, evidently.

Attenborough is a little concerned that the Prince's unscheduled chat with me is going on rather a long time. He begins to move him away. The Prince calls to me . . . 'I hope you'll make another one.' 'Yes, I will . . . if you've got any ideas.' At this the Prince returns . . . 'As a matter of fact I have got an idea.' Attenborough's face, already red with effort, goes puce and his eyes dart from side to side.

So Prince Charles tells me his idea, which is from a press cutting he'd seen about a home on the South Coast for people suffering from phobias. Every sort of phobia was catered for. He says he told Spike Milligan and he loved the idea. 'I'll write it and you can be in it,' is my parting shot. To which he responds well. A nice man, and easy to talk to.

I go to say goodbye to Sir Dickie, as most people seem to be drifting away, and he clutches my arm emotionally – 'Have you seen Orson?' I haven't seen Orson. 'You must see Orson . . . '. He finds a lackey . . . 'Take him to see Orson.' I'm not really desperate, but Sir Dickie insists. 'He's in a little room, outside on the left.'

And sure enough the Great Man (in every sense of the word) is sitting at a table in this very small, plain side-room, which looks like an interview room in a police station.

Orson comes to the end of a story, at which the adoring group of four or five young and glamorous guests laugh keenly. Then I am brought forward. 'Michael Palin from the Monty Python team.' Orson rises, massively, like the sun in India, and grasps my hand. He is clearly confused, but smiles politely. His head is very beautiful and he has a fine, full head of hair. I congratulate him on his speech.

His eyes flick to one side as another visitor is ushered into his presence, one of the Samuelsons,[1] who is telling Orson of the wonderful collection of film memorabilia he has. Orson is responding with polite interest again.

Sunday, October 9th

Take the Levinsons, who are staying with us, to the zoo. I enjoy the visit, especially seeing the delight in Gwenola's (21-month-old) eyes as she watches the prowling tigers and calls out 'Charlie!' – the name of the cat next door in Sag Harbor.

From the zoo down to Covent Garden. Take them into St Paul's – the actors' church. There on the wall of the church is an elegantly simple plaque to Noël Coward – and this the day after I read in his diaries his version of the Bible story – 'A monumental balls-up.'

We watch *Comic Roots*. Then, over Calvados, talk about the state of the world – and the soggy, comfortable, stifling affluence of the late '70's and '80's, as a contrast from the '60's, when it was exciting to write and new things *were* being said. Tell Al that I no longer feel the burning urge to write another film. I want to go to Rangoon.

Friday, October 14th

Ring Anne and express my total lack of interest in a proposal from a BBC producer to do a series called 'Monty's Boys'. Documentaries all about 'the greatest comedy group ... etc, etc ...' We really must avoid being embalmed by the media. If the BBC think we are so wonderful, marvellous, legendary, etc, why did they only repeat 13 shows in nine years?

To a fitting for *Brazil* at Morris Angel's with Jim Acheson and Gilly Hebden. Jim a bit jolly after a lunch with Robert De Niro who has agreed to do the part of Tuttle. Feel quite tangible sensation of excitement and pride at the prospect of sharing the billing with such a hero of mine. Jim says that all the talk of *Brazil* being awash with money is quite misleading. Says he hasn't much more than for *Bullshot*.

---

[1] Sydney (later Sir Sydney) Samuelson started one of the most successful film service companies in the UK. He also was one of the leading lights behind the founding of BAFTA.

Saturday, October 15th

Tom off to play rugby at Edgware. A wild day outside – the barograph plummets and as I write up in my room there are gale-force gusts which threaten to take the whole room away. And it pours. A great day to be at the work desk, but I have to leave at 12.30 to have lunch with Denis and Ray.

We talk of the 'Pig' film, as DO'B calls the Alan Bennett piece. I feel DO'B is unhappy about the Bennett/Mowbray/Shivas group. He senses that there could be another *Privates on Parade*, whose demise he now largely ascribes to arrogance on the part of Simon Relph [the producer] and Blakemore. Again I mistrust DO'B's view of history – surely he wasn't forced into doing *Privates*, it was his scheme. Also I sense that DO'B doesn't have a great sympathy for what I really like in the script – the sense of location, period detail and atmosphere.

Home and begin reading TG's latest *Brazil* script. Nod off. TG drops by. My fee demand is the big talking point. It came as quite a shock to them.

Monday, October 17th: Southwold

DO'B calls. He has had a very good meeting with Mark Shivas and is all set to go ahead in April on the 'Pig' film!

Thursday, October 20th

Anne J rings to report *Brazil*'s 'final' offer in reply to my/her request for £85,000 for my services. They've offered £33,000 and reduced the time by a day. Anne is not at all pleased. I abhor such negotiations. It's all silly money, but I find their attitude typical. Lots of bragging about the money available, then suddenly a complete tightening of the belt as reality strikes. And in a film like *Brazil* the priority is clearly being given to the sets, props and special effects. But we play the game a little – if only to establish our resentment at the treatment. So for today I'm not doing it for a penny less than £50,000!

After dinner Anne rings with the result of the day's progress on *Brazil*. They have not shifted on the £33,000, but have agreed to a percentage.

Saturday, October 22nd

To Belfast. The British Airways shuttle has improved its service no end, as a result of serious competition from British Midland, and the flight, though full, is on time and well run.

Past the roadblocks, but apart from a couple of green flak-jacketed UDR men patrolling, no overt signs of the troubles. Lunch at BBC Broadcasting House. Double security on the doors.

On the programme with me is a Belfast boxer called Barry McGuigan. He's fighting for the European middle-weight title in four weeks' time and goes to Bangor Sands to train. No sex for four weeks, he tells me. He's a completely unaffected, straightforward man. He pronounces 'guy' as 'gay', which makes for interesting complications, and refers to God as 'the Big Man'.

He and I face a panel of Belfast teenagers, some of whom look quite terrifying with either Mohican hairstyles or completely shaved heads. But the questions come easily. The best one they ask me is 'Now you've made all this money, do you still want to make people laugh?' The questioner perhaps doesn't realise what a raw nerve he's touched.

Wednesday, October 26th

To the Turf Club at lunchtime. Peter Chandler introduces me to Jimmy and Brian the barman and Edward on the door. Have a glass of champagne in the snooker room and a toasted sandwich. Rather like being back at Oxford – notice-boards and people older than me calling me 'sir'. Ask Chandler about the horse-racing connections.

The club has many owners and trainers, but, he continues without a trace of unpleasantness, 'isn't open to jockeys'.

After supper go to see a Michael Powell film, *The Small Back Room*. A war story, set in spring 1943, full of psychological insights, shadows and claustrophobia, as well as much comedy and a bomb disposal thriller ending. The theatre is disappointingly empty, but three rows in front of me are Harold Pinter and Lady Antonia.

Thursday, October 27th

At 6.30 I go to Rail House at Euston to the launch of a book on Britain's railway heritage.

Cornered by two reps from Michael Joseph. Talk turns to the US invasion of Grenada. One of them feels we shouldn't let ourselves be pushed around all the time.

I get rather irritated with his mindless jingoism and say quite bluntly that I thought us wrong to go to war over the Falklands. He reels backwards with a strangled cry and our relationship isn't the same afterwards.

Monday, October 31st

Cleese rings. Brief tirade against *Private Eye*, who call him Sir Jonathan Lyme-swold – he thinks that Ingrams is motivated largely by envy, in that he wanted to be an actor at one time. Ask JC how his time off to read books is going. Nothing has changed. JC isn't reading books all day long but deeply involved as ever with Video Arts – which swells with success daily, engulfing John's free time like a great unstoppable creature. But I ask him to lunch at the Turf next week – a chat for old times' sake – and he's pleased about that.

Wednesday, November 2nd

My writing progress reflects the weather conditions. Dull and Soggy. But as I run at lunchtime an idea breaks through the mists.

The Heath is eerily atmospheric. Closed in, the mist adding a touch of menace, making the front of Kenwood look shadowy and insubstantial. The solution to the predicament of the businessman who is lost on his way to work is that he has died. He is in Hell. Hell as the basis for the film – very strong. A clear image and one which you could describe in one sentence, but not one which in any way restricts our flights of fancy.

Ring TJ when I get back. He's enthusiastic. I feel wonderfully encouraged by this breakthrough and the more I think about it, the more levels it can work on. But no time to pursue it now, as I have to do domestic business such as buying fireworks for Saturday's party.

Then in the evening meet Michael Barnes for a chat. We meet at the Turf, but aren't able to eat there as there is some stag night. Hoyle, the night porter, is very nice to us as we are ejected ... 'We *do* have an arrangement with the Institute of Directors, sir, I'm sure they'd be pleased to see you.' I wish I had his confidence.

Friday, November 4th

Nick Lander of L'Escargot confirms that he will do my Ma's 80th birthday party lunch – even though it means opening the restaurant specially.

Have cleared a number of calls, etc, by eleven and start to elaborate on the 'Hell' idea. Become very bogged down. It could go in so many directions – can't decide which, so write very little.

Ma rings, because she's just seen the news and wanted cheering up after seeing the bucket in which Dennis Nilsen boiled boys' heads.

Monday, November 7th

To Crimpers in Hampstead for my *Brazil* hair cut – a strange-looking affair which makes me look like Alexander Walker.

Out into milky afternoon sunshine and near 60's temperatures, feeling conspicuous in my new head, to Alan Bennett's for a chat with him and Mowbray over 'The Pig Film'. They haven't a final [Pork Royale was still in the running] title yet. Make some suggestions about seeing Gilbert and Joyce arrive at the town at the beginning and one or two other comments which Alan writes down. My strongest crit with a much-improved script is the way Gilbert fades away at the end.

As we leave I notice that there is someone living in the Dormobile parked tight in his front garden. 'She's watching television,' whispers Alan . . . 'She?' 'Oh . . . I'll tell you all about it next time,' he promises . . . And I leave Malcolm, Alan and the old lady watching TV in his garden.

Thursday, November 10th

Lie in bed casting anxious thoughts about *Brazil* out of my mind. Like seeing James Fox on TV last night and realising what a finely-controlled actor he is. Why wasn't he Jack Lint? Like worrying that I should be worrying so much about something I know I can do.

At nine o'clock Jonathan [Pryce], and Terry G arrive for our read-through. Jonathan is low-key, halting and rather unconfident about the lines. Old actors' ploy – on the day he will be firing on all cylinders and I shall have to work hard to stay on the screen. Terry G would like me to smoke a pipe. I ask him to get me one, so I can practise in Ireland.

At twelve we go our separate ways – Jonathan to Hampstead to have yet more hair off, and me to lunch with John C at Duke's Hotel.

JC is delighted with Duke's and views with amused admiration this 'new side' of my life – as he calls my recently-developed St James's/Turf Club axis. We have an effortlessly pleasant wander around various subjects near and dear to our hearts.

JC shows off with a few names of the more esoteric Spanish painters. Professes an enjoyment of art galleries and a desire to go on a journey with me somewhere.

We both enjoy our lunch so much we decide to make it a regular feature. Or this is the last shouted intention as we part company in the still warm, but declining November sunshine in St James's.

Saturday, November 12th

Help Helen prepare a meal for Elias and Elizabeth – the Brazilian psychiatrists from next door. Helen makes a wonderful meal – tomato and tarragon soup, followed by gravadlax and chicken in a creamy sauce, apple pie, cheeses – Beaume de Venise.

Elias gives me a short, revealing history lesson about Brazil. A totally exploited country (by Britain and Portugal) until the late nineteenth century. Books forbidden there until 1832. No university until 1932. Didn't realise that Brazil's independent history was so short.

Elizabeth is great fun, but both are hopeless Francophiles – France is beyond criticism as far as they're concerned. To go to France or Italy, they say, after England is to go into the outside world! They think the English press are the worst in the world when it comes to analysis of foreign news.

I returned to Belfast for a second stint at the Festival. This time my one-man show was more ambitious and played for four nights at the Arts Theatre. With my debut in Brazil *imminent, it probably wasn't the wisest thing to have done.*

Sunday, November 20th: Belfast–London

A very cultured shuttle flight back, with musicians, singers and actors all anxious to be on the first plane to Heathrow. I sit next to Lizzie Spender, a publicist and part-time actress who's well connected. She is to play my wife in *Brazil* and we meet quite by coincidence.

Home by a quarter to one. Feel a desperate need for air and space before *Brazil* envelops me, so I take a Sunday run (usually something I avoid as the Heath gets busy). Feel well-stretched, but cannot run easily as have pulled a muscle in my side in last night's record-breaking round the auditorium bid. (10.07 seconds!)

Set off, with Terry G, to Wembley for a run-through on the set of our Big Scene tomorrow. The studio is bitterly cold inside, but the set's very exciting. Jonathan arrives. I always feel he is rather taut – as though something inside is finely tuned, wound up with precision to be released at just the right moments – when he's acting.

We work through the scene and I try the various props such as electronic temple-massagers – American barbershops, 1950's. We're there for about three hours, then gratefully home again for a Sunday dinner – only the second meal I've had at home in ten days.

Monday, November 21st

On the set there is the well-behaved unfamiliarity of the first day on a new picture – and a big new picture, scheduled for 25 weeks. But there are many *Missionary* faces, and my progress to the set is constantly interrupted with handshakes and reintroductions. I feel it must be making Jonathan rather fed up. It helps me, though, and the early part of the day is as agreeable and jolly filming as I can remember. TG on good form, and the camera and sound crew are excellent company.

But the character of Jack Lint is still vague in my mind and after lunch, when I'm into the three or four fast speeches of jargon, I fluff more than once.

I realise that I should have spent much more care and thought in preparing for the part – thinking more about the character, spending more time with Jonathan and more time learning difficult lines, and not going to bed so late in Belfast. But we get through it, and I'm not sure how the effect of my uneasiness will show. At the end of the day TG says he has never seen me as nervous before.

Tuesday, November 22nd

Collected at 7.15. A very cold, crisp morning. Ice on the car windows.

We start shooting in Jack's office a couple of hours later. Take the scene through to the end on my close-ups. Then we work back through it on Jonathan. We have completed the scene – eight pages of close-packed dialogue – by four o'clock.

By then the race is on to complete two other short scenes, scheduled for the day before. One involves me packing a case, fitting my bullet-proof vest, taking my jacket and leaving the office whilst talking rapidly to Jonathan. Two or three times I come completely unstuck on the lines – 'sabotaged adjacent central service systems, as a matter of fact in your block'. We complete the scene, but it's a jolt to my pride and confidence that I was not more in control.

Home to prepare supper for the children, as Helen is in UCH Private Patients' Wing, having the growth on the end of her finger removed under general anaesthetic. I have a day off tomorrow and can look forward, at last, to a night's sleep without anxiety about filming.

Friday, November 25th

I suppose I should have smelt a rat when my call was set for ten. Far too generous a call for anyone who is going to be used during the day. But I take some work in.

In between whiles walk up to the set, which is dominated by a massive 30-foot-high piece of totalitarian architecture. The lobby of the Ministry of Information. Very impressive and rich in bits of comic detail. Nuns looking with approval at little displays of military weapons.

TG has hit upon a very striking style by mixing the gadgetry of *Star Wars* with a 1940's world. He's avoided the space suit, high-tech look which everyone has done to death and replaced it with the infinitely more sinister effect of modern TV surveillance techniques being used amongst McCarthyite, G-Man figures and costumes.

Highly apologetic second and third assistants inform me that I shall not be needed for the second day running – which is a pity as I've two or three times felt just like doing it.

Saturday, November 26th

Helen, Oak Village police snoop, rang her 'Crime Prevention Officer' today to report a shady man at old Miss Clutton's house and was told, after a long delay, 'I'm sorry, your Crime Prevention Officer doesn't work weekends.'

Denis O'B calls. He's trying again with *Water*. But having re-read the script I know it's going to be only a slightly more exciting version of *Yellowbeard* and *Bullshot*.

At the same time I reassert my inclination to do Bennett's film. He sounds as though he has not yet decided on this. Was he waiting to see if I bit on *Water*? They have John Cleese already, he says. Why has John said yes? It's another ordinary, mediocre part which he will be able to do with his eyes shut ... But he's old enough to decide for himself. Or has he said 'I'll do it if Mike will do it'? I have always said no to *Water* and have said 'no' again today. It's not my thing.

Tuesday, November 29th

Collected by [my unit driver] Roy on a cold, dark morning at 7.10.

No waiting around today. A concentrated morning's work on the first encounter between Sam and Jack. I start tense – projecting and acting. But, gaining confidence from repeated successful takes, I'm able to deliver a genuine, easy-going Jack – not the college boy pin-up that TG perhaps had in mind, but an unforced, easy naturalness that I never had last week.

TG looks battered. Unshaven, dark-rimmed eyes, one of which is bloodshot. But he's clearly in seventh heaven – doing exactly what he enjoys best.

Wednesday, November 30th

Back to the TJ/MP script today after a three-week lay-off.

TJ sounds unusually relaxed about it ... he admits he no longer feels the desperate pressure to make a film as soon as possible. Our reputation is such that we must maintain a very high standard – and if this takes a while, then we are lucky to have the time to spend getting it right.

Back home, see Julian Hough[1] wandering about in Oak Village. A strange, slightly disconcerting presence. He himself admits he's spent four sessions 'inside' (a mental hospital) in the last few years, and is now putting together a one-man show, having left Patrick Barlow and the National Theatre of Brent. He has a cup of tea and, having talked of his plans, he leaves, ambling off in an amused, unrushed gangle down Oak Village.

Nancy [Lewis] rings to ask if I will speak at the wedding, as her father can't be there. I'm honoured.

Friday, December 2nd

Car picks me up at eight. To the studio where, to my amazement, I am finished and done with by eleven o'clock. The scene in which I leave the office, take the lift and leave Info Retrieval, talking to Jonathan the while, is at last complete and the bulk of my work on *Brazil* is over.

Saturday, December 3rd

To St Paul's, Covent Garden, for Nancy and Simon's wedding.

A heavily-bearded Eric Idle slips into the row next to me. What an extraordinary place for a Python reunion. A year after making our second 'blasphemous' comedy, we're in a church singing 'Love Divine All Loves Excelling'.

Cleese, alone, is two rows in front. He keeps making Dick Vosburgh laugh by singing with great emphasis words like 'next', long after everyone else has stopped. Gilliam, with family, is in the front. Terry has his duvet-like coat and, with his new, short haircut, Eric says he looks like an 'inflated monk'. Jones, also with family, has a Mac that makes him look like Jones of the Yard and, entirely suitably, Graham is late!

---

[1] Julian Hough was a strange, tormented and talented actor who appeared in one of the *Ripping Yarns* and who had hugely impressed Terry Jones and myself when he appeared with Patrick Barlow in the *Messiah*, the first production of the eccentric and funny National Theatre of Brent.

Someone has alerted the press and there is a barrage of photographers, who try to get all the Pythons to link arms with the bride and groom. John and Graham totally ignore them. But eventually, after persuasive lines like 'Two minutes and we'll leave you alone', we are snapped and can go back to reacquainting ourselves with those we haven't seen for far too long.

Then Helen and I take a taxi down to Glaziers Hall, beneath London Bridge. A man in a red coat is announcing. We give our names as 'Mr and Mrs Figgis'. The sight of Nancy in white looking like an 18-year-old in her first dress already brought tears to the eyes at St Paul's. Simon looks ineffable and timeless, but Nancy does seem to have leapt back 20 years.

Simon's best man, Philip, small, with a short beard, has asked if he can break the rules and speak before me, as he is the only non-professional to speak. Turns out he's a barrister and in fact the *only* professional to speak. A very clever, witty, slightly long speech, with hardly a glance at his notes.

I have my usual copious sheaves of longhand, but, despite sherry and champagne, I manage to read them quite spiritedly and everyone seems pleased afterwards. Jones (Terry) says they were the two best wedding speeches he'd heard.

Monday, December 5th

The morning starts at Julia Street, with an influx of kitchen-fitters, electricity meter-readers. Sam Jarvis has arrived to start decorating and is extremely worried about the whereabouts of his tea-bags.

Ring TJ, who has spent all morning on the phone and had no time to work. Put finishing touches to a peace speech, then drive down to Camberwell, via the picture-framers in Islington. Brief glimpse of the nightmare world of bottled-up traffic on the way through London. Unmoving lines of huge lorries in the drizzle. Dark, enormous, steaming, hissing, hostile and hugely out of scale with the buildings and streets they clog.

Anyway, though we didn't expect such a thing to happen, we both become fired with enthusiasm over the Viking musical idea.

We shall now go away and read about the Vikings, and not try to do a pastiche of bad Hollywood films about Vikings, but work from an informed base – as with *Missionary*, *Brian*, etc. Ideas should come from the reading.

Then I drive up to Camden Institute where I deliver my five-minute piece on peace to open Peace Week there. A small but appreciative audience of middle-aged, grey-haired intellectuals, students, slightly dog-eared supporters of the cause and people who look a little mad.

Tuesday, December 6th

Very content sitting in the sunshine reading tales of Harald 'Blue Tooth' Gormson and others. Vaguely aware of the presence of London out there – of friends to be called, lunches to be shared, books bought, projects discussed, cards sent to faraway places, but otherwise little to disturb my peace and contentment.

DO'B calls with a gloomy forecast for the survival of the 'Pig' film. His 'people' don't think it will be commercial. Very difficult to sell. Still a TV film basically, and so on and so on.

DO'B calls again at 4.30 to tell me he's had the meeting with Shivas and the project is definitely going ahead. 'The Yorkshire Mafia', as he calls Bennett and Mowbray (with Shivas an honorary member), will actually be opening an account with HandMade this week. DO'B chides me over *Water*. 'Why don't you do commercial films for once, Michael!' I want to say 'Why don't *you* do commercial films for once, Denis.'

Later in the evening I call George in Henley. Tells me that at the 'Beatle Summit' last week affairs and problems that had been dragging on unresolved were sorted in a day. Yoko had been (pause) 'very nice' (this followed by a chuckle) and the only problem had been Paul's defensiveness for the first hour until he realised that the others weren't ganging up on him after all.

André rings to tell me the good news that our *Meaning of Life* commercials have won Best Use of Comedy on a Commercial and Best Entertainment at the Radio Awards. The entire series of commercials received a commendation. André very chuffed as we beat Rhys Jones/Mel Smith's Philips ads. When I think that we threw together the scripts almost on the spot, it's even more remarkable.

Saturday, December 10th

TG arrives. Evidently Arnon Milchan has already done a 30 million dollar deal for TG's next two pictures. They are to be *Baron Munchausen* parts I and II. And Twentieth Century Fox are *very* keen. So TG's future looks very rosy. Quite rightly he has at last been appreciated as a film-maker of rare talent and accordingly he must be offered as much work as possible. I feel as I talk to Terry G that Terry J and I should both be in this same position, but we are, with the best will in the world, holding each other back.

Watch the latest American 'sensation' – *The Day After*. A TV film about the effects of nuclear war on the American Midwest.

In the hour after it finishes, Robert Kee, solemn and Solomonic, gravely adjudicates a discussion.

Most depressing of all is that, of all the David Owens, Denis Healeys and Robert McNamaras, no-one makes the simple promise that nuclear war is unthinkable and utterly appalling and therefore everything and anything that *can* be done to prevent it happening must be done and with all speed.

Go to bed profoundly depressed.

Tuesday, December 13th: Southwold

Finish [J. G. Farrell's] *Troubles* on the train, as we wait at a signal check this side of Manningtree. Excellent book. It has really caught my imagination and involved me. Reminds me of Paul Scott, but a little less heavy on the history and stronger on the symbolism. Farrell, the author, died at 46. Tragically young, as they say.

Wednesday, December 14th

Morning at the desk. No word from TJ, so after phone calls and writing of a few more cards, I have time to sit and work out strategy for the next projects. Time for some hard-headed realistic forward-planning of the sort that cheers up a neat, anally-retentive little list-keeper like myself no end.

Decide to go further with [my play] *The Weekend* – and have asked Douglas Rae[1] if he will give me an opinion. I think I know what he'll say, but I'd like a mainstream West End management opinion to see whether it's worth bestirring myself on this one.

In the evening we go round to drinks with the Goldstones.

Tracey Ullman is introduced to me by Ruby Wax – whom I met at RL's on Thanksgiving. I like Tracey U – she's funny and quite sensible and, thank God, isn't always manically funny. The TV companies wanted her to do sitcom, but she turned her nose up at that and felt she wanted to do film half-hours – 'like female *Ripping Yarns*', she says to me.

Peter Cook lurches in. His shirt tails pulled out from his trousers, his tie loosened and harbouring a neat deposit of cigarette ash on the top of the knot.

Once he has got a bead on me he teases me about my appearance on the front of the *Ham and High* this week (a report of my Peace Week opening speech at Camden Institute ten days ago, complete with rather smug photo of myself next to a peace banner). 'Wassallthis bloody peace yeronnerabout?' is directed at me from close spittle-throwing range.

---

[1] Urbane, experienced theatrical agent and friend of Denis O'Brien.

My last glimpse of him is out in the street, a shambolic shaggy figure shouting after me 'Well, if you ever get fed up with peace ... !'

Saturday, December 17th

Book-signing at the Paperback Bookshop in Oxford.

At 3.15 I can thankfully cease to be on public display and walk slowly down to the station with Geoffrey S, who's come up to escort me. We catch the 4.25 back to London. On the way I talk an awful lot about our films and specially about Paul Zimmerman's Hitler film.[1] Geoffrey is such a good sounding board.

I drive him up to Highbury and on the way back up a clogged and unfriendly Holloway Road I hear on the car radio of the news that a bomb has gone off amongst Christmas shoppers. It was outside Harrods and nine people are reported dead, scores injured.

The awful thing about such attacks is the increasing deadening, demoralising fact that there are people who take pride and pleasure in killing indiscriminately and there is nothing that can totally be done to prevent them achieving their ends. Grim stuff to come back to.

Sunday, December 18th

Leave the house at 10.15 for a Python group meeting – the first for over a year.

The meeting is good-natured. Arthur Young, McClelland Moores' accounts are not only accepted and the accountants reappointed but, at TG's suggestion, a motion is passed that a singing telegram should be sent round to tell them so.

Graham asks if he can vote by proxy and if so can he be his own proxy. John Cleese reveals that he may be Jewish. He also says his father had a nanny who had been kissed by Napoleon. I tell them that my ancestor had hidden Prince Charles in the oak tree after the battle of Worcester. To which EI came up with the 'O' Level maths question 'How many royalists does it require to hide a king in an oak tree?' Graham says he's discovered family links with George Eliot. I am complimented on my speech at the Lewis/Jones wedding and Eric is complimented on his outstandingly bushy beard.

---

[1] Paul's basic premise was that Hitler had survived the war and was living in a place called The Thousand Year Ranch in Paraguay. He contacts some American agencies to see if they might arrange a tour of the USA when he would tell his story and atone for everything. The only person who'll even consider taking him on is a New York agent desperately down on his luck. He is, of course, Jewish. Hitler becomes his client and the story rolls on – Hitler becoming a huge hit on US television. No surprise then that, in real life, no American studio was interested.

Monday, December 19th

Although a morning of recovery would have been a good thing, our house today promises to be invaded by Sam (paint), Ted (windows), Ricky (lights), Helena (vacuum cleaner), a window cleaner and Stuart (burglar alarm). Any large-scale invasion of our intimate little property always makes me twitchy – they take over, making me feel like an odd and eccentric man in the attic, who sits on a swivel chair all day booking restaurants and thoughtlessly going to the lavatory just when they're working in it, on it or around it.

Into Covent Garden to meet Eric and Tania at a pub in Drury Lane. Eric reveals that [his play] *Pass the Butler* is doing marvellous business in Stockholm, like Python. Eric and I try to analyse this phenomenon and decide it can only be that the Swedes have no sense of humour of their own and have to import it.

Tuesday, December 20th

Watch marvellous piece by Alan Plater about Orwell's visits to the Isle of Jura and his battle to complete *1984* against the advance of TB. Ronald Pickup's performance quite excellent. How he managed to keep the catarrhal rattle in the back of his throat I don't know. It was as complete a portrait of another man as any actor could hope to achieve. Comparable with Ben Kingsley's 'Gandhi'.

Sunday, December 25th: Christmas Day

Breakfast about 10.15 – can hear church bells ringing in Lismore Circus. Helen has to cook potatoes for the lunch at Mary's. As we prepare to leave at 12.45, run into John Sergeant (Anne Alison's brother and Oxford revue acquaintance), who is BBC Radio correspondent at Westminster.

He reckons that Willie Whitelaw's wonderful 'Willie-ism' over Northern Ireland – 'We must not pre-judge the past' – ranks as a great unconscious profundity, and says that Margaret Thatcher loves publicity and is becoming smoother and smoother and more frighteningly competent at it. To the press after the Harrods bombing a week ago: 'Where would you like me?' 'Would I look better here?' 'How will you be editing this?' Etc, etc. Maybe that is in fact the only way to deal with the press, but Sergeant's point is that Maggie is now becoming unduly preoccupied with presentation rather than substance.

Friday, December 30th

To the Hayward Gallery.

Dufy's work a celebration of light, colour and movement. Sea and sky and sporting ritual – regattas and race-courses figure large. Cumulative effect of his work is like opening a window onto the Mediterranean on a perfect summer's day. His fabric designs are an eye-opener – all done 50 years ago, but seem absolutely up to date.

Drop in at the Portal Gallery and see Eric Lister. Like most of Bond Street, he's empty of punters, but instantly into stories and showing me objets drôles as if we'd never stopped looking from the last time I came in. He shows me a device which incorporates a minimally inflated balloon which can be clipped onto the underneath of the shoe to give an impersonation of squeaky shoes.

Just before I leave, his friend, who has sat quietly at his desk, demonstrates a watch he's been given for Christmas, whose face can unclip from the wrist and from which arms and legs can be extended, making it into a little stubby figure which can stand on the bedside table at night.

1984

Wednesday, January 4th

Up, before Helen, and let Sam J in (he's now decorating No. 2), then go running – so feel quite perky by the time Roy arrives to take me to the studio. Am having my hair cut when De Niro appears – hot off the overnight plane from NYC, to prepare for his scene tomorrow in which he shoots me. He's very quiet and, as is the way with people you admire inordinately, there's very little to say.

De Niro goes away to practise abseiling.

The afternoon goes by and stretches into evening before I'm used. Go to the editing room and look at the first reel. My performance in the lobby is not good. Ian Holm and Jonathan impressive. Depressed for a while.

Thursday, January 5th

Quite quick run down through light, early-morning traffic to Croydon Power Station (built, I'm told by Robert De Niro later in the day, in 1948 and closed in 1980).

The Mercedes turns in off a works slip road and into a service road between 220-foot-tall cooling towers. Beside one of them stands the crane from which is suspended the steel cage from which Tuttle's raiding party will descend.

For the first hour there is coffee and nothing to do but settle in our caravans.

After an hour of desultory chatter we are called up to the set and for the first time and probably the last few times of my life, I enter a cooling tower. It's like being at the bottom of the barrel of some giant cannon.

A long, narrow walkway leads from the side to a 15-foot-diameter platform in the centre of the tower. Rehearse and work out how I shall die, so that my stunt double knows what to do.

Lunch – in my caravan. TG, Bobbie De N, Jonathan and me. TG cross at lack of progress, mutters that it should have been done with models all along. Talk turns to lavatory stories. TG recounts how he was peeing in the toilet of a smart little restaurant in France when he noticed a turd on the floor beside the bowl. Just at that moment there is a knock on the door – a queue has formed. How does our hero avoid being mistaken for the ill-aimed turd-dropper? Poor TG has no alternative but to come out looking as unconcerned as possible.

Am driven to the Selsdon Park Hotel, about 15 minutes away, where TG is overnighting as well.

Have a bath, then wander downstairs to wait for TG. The public rooms are furnished rather fussily, with heavy patterns, copper ornaments, much recent old–wood panelling – like endless Agatha Christie stage sets. Everything is expensive. My little single room (with good bathroom) is £51, a half-bottle of champagne is £10.25. And this is Croydon.

To bed at 11.30. Have fallen into a deep sleep almost as soon as I switch the light off when I'm woken by the incessant, jarring screech of a fire alarm. My room is almost vibrating with the noise.

A few minutes later the horrendous noise dies. With thudding heart I settle down to try and sleep, only to be woken by a telephone call reassuring me that it *was* a mistake. I wonder if they mean staying here in the first place.

Friday, January 6th

We progress, slowly. None of TG's camera moves are easy. A lot of high angles or low angles and complex little movements. The chill gets through to the bones, slowly but surely. There is some light drizzle after lunch which makes the narrow platform suddenly lethal and I skid twice towards the edge on one of the takes.

The day ends with my 'death' scene. A specially-prepared, remote-controlled bullet hole is fired out of my baby face mask, splashing so much blood on the camera that they can't see anything else and it has to be re-shot.

Three times I spin round to a special mark, wrench my mask off as the camera closes in and finally spin round to Jonathan, alone in his torture chair, and, grasping helplessly at him as I fall, collapse via knees to the floor.

A glass of red wine in the make-up caravan in the middle of this awesome palace of pre-stressed concrete is one of the best things of the day. One of the others was the visit of Ray Cooper, bringing a touch of style to the cooling tower. He is very excited about the Bennett film – but confirms that George H still hates the script.

Sunday, January 8th

Watch a 1973 film biog of Noël Coward on TV this afternoon. Never realised quite how prolific he was. At the age of 26 he had three or four shows running simultaneously in London – he had made a name as actor, writer and lyricist. He continued throughout his life to turn out new work with what sounds like extraordinary facility. He says in interview that he wrote *Private Lives* in four days – 'And . . .' long pause ' . . . not one word of it was changed.'

Blithe Spirit wrote itself in a week and one of his most famous songs was written in 20 minutes in a taxi stuck in a jam.

Tuesday, January 10th

Down to Devonshire Street for lunch at Langan's Bistro with David Puttnam (his invitation).

He starts straight in by offering me a *First Love*.[1] Either as writer or director, which is very nice as it's a very prestigious, well-produced series, which has been sold to the US for theatrical release. Jonathan Benson, who has now given up assistant directing, has written one of them. Puttnam says that when he asked Jonathan why he was giving up, JB told him that it was because he wanted to be able to have a shit whenever he wanted, instead of having to go through day after day holding it in until there was a long enough break.

Wednesday, January 11th

Low cloud, persistent drizzle. Glad to have a day at the desk. Become very enthusiastic about doing a *First Love* for Puttnam. The more I think of the tale of meeting Helen, Southwold, etc, the more comic possibilities I see, and also some clear ideas on locations, characters. Very liberating it is when an idea strikes and appeals so completely. Ring Puttnam immediately, but he's in a meeting, of course.

Read through Dr Fegg's work prior to meeting with Geoffrey Strachan this afternoon re re-publication.[2] In the densely-packed American edition some very funny stuff lies well concealed. Definitely worth a re-publication, for much of the book would be new in the UK anyway.

TJ has had the same reaction to the 'Fegg' material as myself, only more so. He says, without any sign of a boast, that he was in tears of laughter reading it.

General agreement on progress and some useful suggestions for what is right and wrong for the book. I suggest that it should be *Dr Fegg's Nasty Book – A Family Guide to All The World's Knowledge* – and that we should put a 'Keep Away From Children' sticker on it. TJ suggests better wording: 'Keep Out of Reach of Children'.

---

[1] This was a generic title for a series of films on a theme. Not to be confused with the US TV series of the same name.
[2] *Bert Fegg's Nasty Book for Boys and Girls* was written by Terry J and myself and originally published in 1974. We had plans for an edition with new material.

Thursday, January 12th

By taxi to Westminster and Dean Stanley Street, hard by the Victoria Tower in the mixture of very attractive Queen Anne terraces.

Into one of these I have to go to do a 45-minute chat about self and work for the British Forces Network. I feel a much closer identification with an audience than I usually do on these shows. Whatever I feel about our army being in the Falklands or Belize or Beirut, I have experienced home-sickness and I should think these radio shows are like manna from heaven to their audience.

Finish at one and wander amongst the attractive little streets like Lord North Street and the late classical flashiness of St John's, Smith Square. Then across into the Victoria Gardens. How well the Houses of Parliament and the Abbey and St Margaret's, Westminster go together. They are all inspiring, imaginative buildings in their way – built largely for the eye of the beholder. Turn 180 degrees and the heart sinks at the sight of the accountants' buildings marching grimly along from Vauxhall.

Saturday, January 14th

Prepare the house for likely visitors this afternoon. Wrap presents and write cards for Mother, who is 80 today and somewhere between Chilton Hall and Gospel Oak.

She arrives with Angela at eleven, looking quite spry and dressed in a neat claret purple two-piece with a touch of flamboyance in a ruff-like frill at the neck. She really looks excellent, as well as I've seen her at any time in the last few years. Angela too, with her hair done nicely and well cut, looks fine.

L'Escargot, which has especially opened for us, has set a buffet in the upper room, which is a perfect size for the 26 of us and full of light and airiness.

I give a short speech and mention that air travel was only three weeks old when Granny was born – the longest flight had been for 120 yards. Tomorrow she will be taken from London to New York in the time it would take my father to park the car – this is well greeted, but allows me to wish that father were here today to laugh at it himself.

Sunday, January 15th: London–New York

Sleep well. Up with the alarm at 7.45. Leave with Ma and Angela in a taxi at 8.45, just as a light snow is falling.

At the Concorde check-in I spy Steven Spielberg, Sir Lew Grade, with his white, pasty, sepulchrally-blanched head, and Tom Conti. The whole flight passes so smoothly that I don't think Mother or Angela really sense that we have crossed the Atlantic, or exchanged continents at all. Ma takes to it as easily as she might the train to Ipswich.

After unpacking and resting, we walk, along dangerously icy sidewalks, up to Avenue of the Americas, then taxi to the Tavern on the Green. Nancy has managed to book us a table in the richly-kitsch Crystal Room, only by mentioning that it was part of my mother's 80th birthday present. We are right by the window and the sun is dazzling. Outside is Central Park in the snow with a mixture of skaters, skiers, joggers, walkers and sledders passing by as a sort of continuous background entertainment.

Around the Plaza is a great throng of police – the Chinese Premier is staying there. One of the policemen on duty hails me, 'Hey! Michael', takes off his glove and shakes my hand – something no policeman in England would do with such unaffected directness. This impresses the relatives.

Then round to Nancy and Simon's for their American wedding party – or rather the party to offer a chance for their rich NYC friends to give them presents, as Simon puts it to me. I'm getting increasingly tired and find a party of all my NYC friends rather hard work on the smile button – on the first day here.

Find Granny and Angela chatting to Jeremy Irons – whose performance in Stoppard's *The Real Thing* has just been hailed as a major Broadway success. Introduce myself and we talk about all sorts of mundane things. Irons claims not to be interested in the razzmatazz and public image of a Broadway star, though he doesn't altogether convince me.

It's ten o'clock, nearly ten-thirty, when I finally get Mother away and taxi back to the hotel. To round the day off – a Python repeat ('Trim Jeans', etc) on PBS. They're still awake and laughing and enjoying it at eleven – four, UK time. Amazing.

Monday, January 16th: New York

Meet with [*Saturday Night Live* team] Dick Ebersol, Bob Tischler and a lady called Pam, whose function isn't clear. This is a sort of introductory meeting before I go to meet the rest of the writers. Ebersol, who is a big man, was mugged after the show on Saturday night at 4.30. Two black eyes and two broken ribs – and on Central Park South . . .

After an hour's chat we go over to the Rock and I meet, or in some cases renew acquaintance with, the writers.

Then I'm given my office – which is in fact Eddie Murphy's office and contains stacks of unopened fan mail as well as one or two opened letters – one from a fan (white), who wants to 'ride on your star'. The various writers in their various combinations come along and talk and try out tentative ideas on me. Without Lorne there the whole process is rather businesslike – less pleasant, lazy chat, more of an organised schedule, but this suits me well, as I have Angela and Granny waiting at the hotel.

And they're raring to go again.

Tuesday, January 17th: New York

I spend the morning in my room writing up a couple of ideas for the show. The monologue fits together neatly and is written within an hour. It involves Ma – it's too good to miss the opportunity of using her when she's in New York.

At midday she and Angela return – spirits indomitable after a hot morning at Macy's – we eat a quick snack in my room – and Ma doesn't seem too averse to appearing in the monologue. Indeed, at one o'clock when a limousine and a photographer arrive to collect us all at the hotel for the *Saturday Night Live* photo-session, Mother is carefully dressed and coiffured and ready for anything.

Then I go to the '*SNL*' office. Sell the monologue idea without much difficulty – in fact Dick Ebersol is so enthusiastic that he calls in the new publicity lady for the show and tells her to release the story that Michael is co-hosting '*SNL*' with his mother. She will not only be the first mother to co-host, but, he thinks, the oldest host ever on the show.

Wednesday, January 18th: New York

To the Rockefeller Center – snow now driving and quite thick – it looks wonderful swirling past the windows of the 17th floor.

Dick Ebersol warns me 'You're in the first nine sketches'; it also turns out I'm in the next nine. No time for shyness, just get up and throw myself into them as best I can – most of them sight unseen. It's rather enjoyable – like auditions for a college smoker.

I'm free at six and meet Angela and Granny at a recommended restaurant in the Theater District, called The Palatine. Have to crunch over a few snow-caked sidewalks to get to it, but once there I can tell I shall enjoy it. It's calm and relaxed and this marks it out as something of an oasis in New York terms.

Towards the end of the meal Father Jake, the Catholic priest who runs the restaurant, visits us at table. He sprays cards around like a computer salesman and bemoans the problems with the Vatican, who don't, he says, take kindly to a priest with a liquor licence. I am moved to write in a brand new visitors'

This photo call at a
Python video launch
seems to contradict my
diary entry, 'we all come
to the conclusion that
zaniness after 40 isn't
possible'. The Pythons,
sans Eric, and Carol
Cleveland, London
September 3 1985

Sheepish of Gospel Oak.
Supporting our local
City Farm, 1984

The Meaning Of Life, 1982

Dad in 'Every Sperm Is Sacred'.

Christmas in Heaven. (left to right) Idle, Palin, Jones and friends in foreground.
Chapman, Simon Jones and Jonathan Benson look on.

Telling the children the facts of life. 'I will say "sock" instead of "cock"…and the dastardly substitution will take place in the dubbing theatre' Elstree Studios August 10 1982

Jones, Gilliam, Palin, Cleese, Idle and Chapman emerge from the jungle. 'Endless takes. Constant calls over the walkie-talkie for the Test Match score' August 27 1982

Brazil, 1983–84

Jack Lint.
The nastiest character
I've ever played. Sadly.

Rehearsing with Terry G and Jonathan P in the lobby of Information Retrieval.

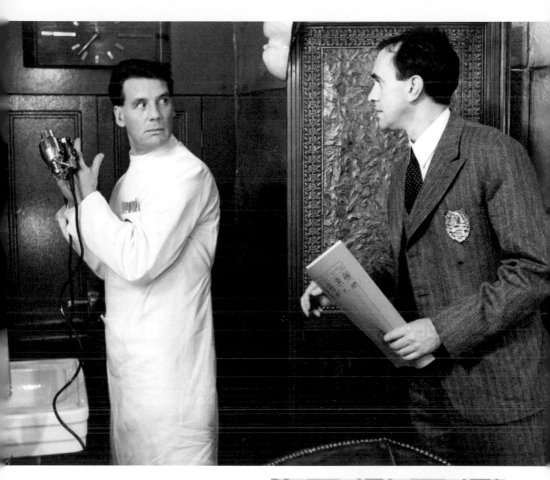

Using my heavy duty massager when Sam Lowry (Jonathan Pryce) bursts in unexpectedly. 'At the end of the day TG says he's never seen me as nervous before' November 21 1983

Gilliam the director with Ray Cooper, actor, musical director, gourmet, percussionist extraordinaire and all-round good bloke.

My mother crosses the Atlantic for the first and only time in her life, at the age of 80 years and 2 days. New York City January 1984

Mum, with Angela, at the *Saturday Night Live* after-show party. 'There is no question of Granny not wanting to go – in fact she stays there until four a.m.' January 21 1984

With my sister Angela, Nancy Lewis and Mum in Central Park.

East of Ipswich. Tristram Powell, director, in cap and Innes Lloyd, producer, worry about the weather, Southwold, Suffolk, June 1986

Wearing my Biff T-shirt at the *East of Ipswich* wrap party at the Crown Hotel, Southwold.

MP, Gilliam, David Robinson of the Times, John Cartwright of the British Council, and our Russian escort Elena, on Jabberwocky visit to Moscow and Leningrad, November 1986

My mother and her neighbour, Lily Pratt, outside Croft Cottage, near Southwold, Suffolk.

Launching a rebuilt steam-engine at the Bluebell Railway.

Mahendra "Mash" Patel, our newsagent. Such reserves of patience and good and humour that our family name for him is Mr Nice Man.

'Sam Jarvis has arrived to start decorating and is extremely worried about the whereabouts of his tea bags'

book they've been given by a guest from Texas, 'Why shouldn't God be a gourmet?'

We leave with much bowing and scraping from the priest, who has been told who I am by a waiter. One final curiosity is that the hat-check woman apparently used to run the restaurant.

Thursday, January 19th: New York

At 12.30 I walk across Fifth Avenue and into Rockefeller Plaza for a rehearsal on the 17th floor. At 2.30 down to the studio to record some promotional spots – with Mum. Any worries I've had about her performance in front of camera disappear when I see with what confidence and aplomb she mounts the stage and delivers her little rejoinders to me. She makes everyone in the gallery laugh when, after one take of the first promo, she asks, rather loudly, on camera, 'Well, what's next?'

Saturday, January 21st: New York

Mum has been given Eddie Murphy's dressing room for the day.

Dress rehearsal offers a foretaste of the sort of reception she is to get from the audience. Much greater than I had expected. She can do no wrong.

The music crescendos and at 11.35, a week after reaching 80, Mum leads me out in front of the cameras. Apart from forgetting to grab my arm at the first cue, everything she does is exactly right. She remains herself, natural and dignified, and yet displaying a winning sparkle of humour in the eyes which absolutely wins the audience over.

So Mother and I, in what must surely be one of our finest hours, are eventually taken, full of compliments, down through the lobby of 30 Rock – where Granny signs an autograph – into a waiting limousine and down to Joanna's [Restaurant on Madison Avenue] for the party. There is no question of Granny not wanting to go – in fact she stays there until four a.m., when the main lights are switched on in an attempt to flush out the most persistent revellers!

Monday, January 23rd

Mercifully, I have a day clear before *Brazil* tomorrow. And just as well. I sleep for ten hours and don't surface until 10.30.

Granny still looking well. It's as if she has gone into a sort of physical and mental overdrive in the last year. When she should have been descending the age spiral – in terms of ability, mobility, health and general comprehension – she is in fact coasting along extremely confidently and competently, as if all the excitements of *Comic Roots* and *Saturday Night Live* have actually had a rejuvenating effect.

Angela, according to Helen, is as relaxed and easy as she has seen her for a long time. Of course, what I forget is that Angela and I have hardly spent as much as a week together since I was a small boy.

Angela goes off to lunch with Veryan and at 12.15 the car I've hired to take Granny back to Southwold arrives. Momentary panic when I ask him whether he knows the route and he nods confidently and says 'It's right after Gloucester, isn't it? Sorry, sorry, *Ipswich* . . .' With some misgivings I wave goodbye to my co-star.

Tuesday, January 24th

The children are all at home as ILEA teachers are marching today in support of their employers, and against government plans to get rid of them. All the children are desperate for snow, but it seems we are the only corner of England and Scotland to escape unscathed.

TG tells me that the De Niro scene aged everyone. A minimum of twenty takes on each shot. He was nervous (of his reputation, I suppose) and forgot lines and missed business, and all this after more rehearsal time than any other actor in the film. Pryce tells me that one day De Niro just threw everything down in frustration and stomped off to lunch. I feel rather reassured – clearly geniuses are not immune from the strangely disturbing effects of the film.

Tuesday, January 31st

Ring Mark Shivas re *Private Function* [as 'the Pig Film' is now known]. As far as he's concerned it's all going ahead, but at the slightly later time of April 30th (with a week's rehearsal before). Only problem is a tight budget. DO'B at one point had even questioned the need to go to Yorkshire to film Yorkshire. Ian Holm and Ian Richardson are both being touted.

I feel completely lacking in energy and confused about plans. Not in the right mood to take decisions at all. Pick up the Noël Coward diaries and scan some entries for '50 and '51. Camp old theatrical that he was, there is an energy and a delight in his own work which rather encourages me. One has to put out in order to get anything back. Rush, stress, pressure is one side of the coin.

Success, recognition, approval and the giving and receiving of pleasure is the other.

I look again at my start on *First Love* yesterday and realise that I can't simply put a line under it and say – 'next year maybe'. Strike while the iron's hot.

Work through until about seven, steadily and quite satisfactorily. Watch Gavin Millar's 'Secrets' – second of the *First Love* tapes Puttnam sent me. Very strong, original, well sustained. A lovely oddity.

Read some of Orwell's life. I don't like him very much so far. Must always remember he went to Eton, his best teenage friends were called Jacintha and Prosper and he had a caterpillar called Savonarola.

Ring Mum. She's had a prolapse and didn't really want to tell me. Nothing serious, but it involves going to a gynaecologist in Gorleston . . . 'I've *never* been to Gorleston,' she says disapprovingly.

Thursday, February 2nd

For the first time for nearly ten years we don't have to take the children to school. Or, to put it more sentimentally, we've taken Rachel to school for the last time. As from two weeks ago she now goes off on her own. One thing the children have in common is a desire to get to school as early as possible. Tom is usually away whilst we're still dressing ('I'm going now, right?'), Willy, after tormenting Denis, goes at about 8.30, and Rachel is straining at the leash to leave as soon as the road-crossing man arrives, which is just before nine.

Drive to Oxford to give a talk to the Brasenose Arts Society. Have nothing prepared – will have to throw myself at their mercy and encourage questions. Plenty of time to think as I sit in traffic jams on the way out to the M40.

At BNC by 7.30. Met by a small welcoming committee.

I think how nice it would be to talk about my work to this very nice, bright group of six BNC undergraduates – get down to some depth, think more carefully about things, accept more probing criticism, encourage more controversial questions. As it turns out this is not to be, and my talk to the BNC Arts Society is a public performance in front of 290 people packed into the JCR. I'm ready for it and do enjoy it and we do cover quite serious matters – censorship, religious and political convictions, etc. But really they want me to make them laugh.

Their next speaker is William Golding OB, who apparently is donating his Nobel Prize medal to the college.

Friday, February 3rd

Take the *First Love* tale on for an hour, then am rudely interrupted by the arrival of a director of SieMatic. He has a black BMW (no harm in that, of course), a sheepskin suede coat, a beer gut and a pushy aggression mixed, uncomfortably, with a chummy and affected sycophancy of the 'Hello, Michael' variety. 'I'm at Michael Palin's house,' he says, loudly and pointedly when ringing his office.

He blames all the damage to the kitchen units on John Lewis and proof of the depths of his bovine insensitivity is that he does not bat an eyelid when he turns to me and says 'You don't mind if I get our PR people to come and talk to you, do you? I mean, if we can get some publicity and you're agreeable ... '. It's like Cunard ringing me to do a voice-over, the day after my family drowned on the Titanic.

Then the Complaints Manager of John Lewis appears. Neat, slim and at least having the good grace to look apologetic. Both parties try to shift the blame to each other whilst we stand rather uncomfortably in between. 'Have you seen any of John Cleese's training films, Michael? They're *very* funny ...'

Saturday, February 4th

TG has come to tell me of his decision to re-shoot the central Jack/Sam scene which I did so badly in November. He has just seen an assembly and it is one of two scenes he thinks don't work. It's not entirely my fault. TG says it's overwritten and much of the info it puts out has been superseded by scenes they've shot since. Sam's character isn't consistent either. In all he admits it was a very silly scene to shoot first. I'm relieved and pleased that we shall have another stab at it.

Tuesday, February 7th

Work on 'Fegg'. In the middle of a sea of odd ideas when someone rings asking to speak to the late Michael Palin. It's Spike. He says there's no point in asking for people who are living any more. Then he unfurls a stream of consciousness for about ten minutes – which turns out to be the outline for a play which he and [John] Antrobus are putting together for the autumn.

Set in the last war, in a vast government prune warehouse, scientists convert prunes into gas, Rudolph Hess arrives in Scotland, *The Desert Song* slowly and inexorably takes over the play, etc, etc. He compliments me at the end of these wild ramblings by saying he wants someone of 'wit and élan' to play an officer. I think he means me.

Tuesday, February 14th

Rachel very disappointed that I didn't get any Valentine cards, so she makes me one at breakfast.

At lunchtime Mr Alberts, Complaints Manager from John Lewis, arrives with a bottle of Krug champagne and a plastic display bowl of flowers which looks frighteningly like a graveside ornament.

Friday, February 17th

Work on the 'Vikings' until TJ arrives mid-morning. We read through what we have after this first week of concentrated film-writing. Very encouraging it is too. TJ has pushed on with the story and written a very macho song called 'We Don't Talk About Babies', which is marvellous. I've filled in a few holes and created a nice group of women at a devastated village.

But the best feeling of all is one of genuine and productive partnership. Both of us are contributing good material, but also both of us are enlarging and expanding on each other's ideas. Five good, forward-looking, confident days (largely because both of us were able to put in full working days without much interruption) and I now feel even more certain that we shall make this film.

Tuesday, February 21st

To Lee Studios at half past eight. Some of the numbing, negative feelings return. Why didn't the scene work in the first place? Why am I still so unsure of this character, which I was so enthusiastic to play in the first place? What am I supposed to feel – bringing the crew back onto the scene, having the set rebuilt? Was it mostly my fault? And, worst of all – will it go any better?

On the first couple of opening takes this tension – this wanting to do it exactly how I know I can do it, but having to concentrate too much on moves and props – produces the same tight, unrelaxed performance as I felt myself helplessly giving three months ago to the day. Then, as I get used to the props and the lines, I suddenly hit the note I know is right.

TG too is delighted. One take is perfect. Everything eases up, and I'm raring to go. But of course that take wasn't *technically* quite right, so we have to go again.

Holly Gilliam[1] loosens up the atmosphere and is really very good indeed – both in behaviour and her lines. She makes all our business together seem very natural.

Friday, February 24th

At the studio they are trying to shoot reverses on Holly G, who is not playing very well today. When I arrive only Terry G (operating the camera), Maggie and Holly are on the set. Every now and then TG emerges and stalks up and down rather crossly before returning for 'one last go'. Then it's time to shoot all the reverses on Jonathan. I get into costume, but not make-up and spend most of my time trying to avoid being crushed by the dollying camera, whilst Jonathan uses the lens hood as his eyeline anyway.

This is the last day of principal photography and everyone seems to think it very suitable that I should be here on the last day and the first day. We have a merry lunch and I do enjoy myself, but I see what was shot on Tuesday and, though it's better than the first attempt, I still seem to fit the part of Jack Lint like a round peg in a square hole. An odd experience. I don't think I've ever seen myself so uncertain of who I'm playing.

Saturday, February 25th

Buy Leopoldo Alas's *La Regenta*, which I've decided will be my post-Orwell literary experience. It's much bigger than I thought.

Crick's book has won me round to a great liking for Orwell – not of everything he says or the way he says it, and I'm sure I too would find the Old Shag he smoked as unpleasant as everyone else, but he thrust himself into things with an uncompromising relish for life and sustained himself with a strange mixture of anger and admiration about how this country was run and organised with which I constantly felt sympathetic. He was on the right side.

Sunday, February 26th

Sexagesima. Now there's a film title for you. Begins at seven when Helen wakes up and leaps out of bed with unusual celerity. Her alarm has been set too late

---

[1] Terry had rewritten the scene we'd shot on the first day's filming in November 1983 and among the changes had written in his daughter Holly, three at the time, to make nasty Jack Lint seem more of a family man.

and the cab is due in 15 minutes. Make the pre-skiing cup of tea and Willy, Rachel and I kiss her goodbye and wave the cab off into a dull, wet, cold morning.

William and Rachel play together, Tom finishes his homework – writing a ballad with rather a lot of help from Dad – and we end up playing Totopoly. I cook scrambled eggs which are rather hard and they all laugh. But they go to bed without any sign at all of missing Mum.

Monday, February 27th

TJ here by eleven. The preparations for the 'Erik' voyage and the start of the voyage itself are rather superficial and sound to me too like *Yellowbeard*. We've lost the contact with the reality of life in Viking times from which our early material was drawn.

TJ reads his bio-rhythms on my calculator and finds that he is going through a bad period for intellectual effort! He then goes into a mental decline for the rest of the day, constantly wandering off for a pee or some decaffeinated coffee. But we assemble the first half-hour's material and send it off to Alison to type.

I then have to drive into town to see two films [up for awards] at BAFTA – *Another Time, Another Place* for Phyllis Logan and *Sophie's Choice* for Kevin Kline.

Ben Kingsley and Don Sharp – two of my co-jurors – are there. Ben Kingsley makes rather dramatic gestures such as 'Kevin Kline!' followed by a sharp blow with his fist to his balding forehead – which I think is meant to convey a superlative. I think power has made him mad, but he's quite affable.

Wednesday, February 29th

After breakfast TJ rings. He thinks we should talk as he is not sure where to take the story on. So clean up here and drive down to Camberwell.

We have reached a sticky stage. Terry's 'What's it all about ... really?' stage. It is very important because, although I would go on writing funny scenes and characters till the cows come home, TJ cannot write until he really knows what the story and the leading characters are about.

To Lower Regent Street for a party given by the Hogarth Press to launch a new range of imprints. Meet Miles Kington, Tariq Ali – who I haven't talked to since Oxford, he says his eleven-year-old daughter is a terrific fan of mine! – and a man called Ian Hislop asks Tariq to introduce him to me. He's a round, small man with a squidgy, reassuring face. He's assistant editor of the *Eye*, writer for the new puppet show, *Spitting Image*, and I recently read and liked his *Listener* column. He says *Spitting Image* found it difficult to make a Maggie Thatcher doll unattractive enough, as she is such a wretchedly fine-looking woman!

Friday, March 2nd

Drive to Greenpeace HQ in a nondescript industrial street in Islington for a presentation ceremony. TJ and I have both donated £1,000 to help Greenpeace pay the fine they incurred whilst monitoring the nuclear pollution from Sellafield/Windscale. Spike Milligan was to have presented us with the framed certificates of shares in the Greenpeace boat, but Pamela Stephenson stands in for him – 'Spike told me to apologise, but he's got radiation sickness and shouldn't touch anybody.'

Bruce Kent of CND is there. He says the food is much better than at his office. It's all vegetarian. Outside there's a photo-call and one of the photographers calls out to Monsignor Kent 'Could you put your arm round Pamela, please?' Kent, to his credit, twinkles back at them but refuses to go along with the suggestion.

Change (Clark Kent-like) into my dinner jacket in the Python office and taxi to King's Cross and join a long and winding queue for the 3.30 Newcastle train. I'm in Durham, about 20 minutes late, to second the motion that 'This is the Age of the Train' [at a university debate].

A meal, which far surpasses anything we got at the Oxford Union. I don't really enjoy such celebrations *before* the debate as much as I would after and I have to do some polite talking and listening to the wife of one of my opposers on one side, and Tony Ridley, head of LT (trains), on the other. Ray Buckton [leader of the engine drivers' union] is making them all laugh down the other end.

Ray is the only one of us who has not observed the request to wear a dinner jacket, and he is here with one of his advisers, a nice, quiet man who lives in Savernake Road. In a very earnest tone he tells me how much like 'The Missionary' is Michael Meacher MP, his new boss-to-be. 'A cross between Michael Palin and Joyce Grenfell,' he says.

Buckton speaks largely without notes. His speech is a mixture of astute and skilful attack and a lot of revivalist, preacher-like waffle. But he has a natural warmth and humour that is very much the stock image of the trade union leader. He can laugh at himself. He suggested before the debate began that, as we were all enjoying the port after the meal so much, he should cancel the debate by calling the speakers out on strike.

Monday, March 19th

Despite feeling a degree or two under manage to write another satisfying scene for 'The Vikings', when Thangbrand becomes maudlin and sentimental with Stovold, and also invent a seer who is not good at the immediate future, but can foretell that a Viking will win Wimbledon. No-one knows what he's talking about, of course.

I am enjoying writing again and, like fresh-struck oil, the jokes, characters and dialogue are now beginning to flow freely – for the first time since we started writing in February.

TJ comes up at lunch. He hasn't hit a similar writing streak for the last couple of weeks, but is pleased with the way it's heading and we have a constructive afternoon session, despite the fact that TJ only had three hours' sleep last night. Terry did shake his head rather ruefully as he arrived and say 'Oh, *when* will I grow up?'

Wednesday, March 21st

At 3.30 Malcolm M, Mark Shivas and Alan Bennett call for me in a small Volkswagen and we head out to Broxbourne to look at the pigs. They are quartered in amongst a very sad collection of buildings, animals and 'attractions' called Paradise Park.

The pigs are very friendly and bouncy and have been hand-reared since birth, about four months ago. We all remark on their little pink, naked provocative botties. Hope the crew will not get over-excited. We're shown a Vietnamese Black Pig – a mournful creature who was in a film with John Cleese – a crow which has been on TV-AM and a lion which once worked for the Post Office.

Thursday, March 29th

Make or break day on 'The Vikings'. Down to Terry's by 9.30 and we begin to work through the script. I sit at one desk and read through and whenever we come to a character who needs a name, or a line that's superfluous or a joke that doesn't work or a plot-line that's inconsistent, we stop and go back over it. We deliberately try and avoid major rewrites, but we're continuously changing and correcting. With few interruptions we work through until 7.45.

One of the interruptions is David Frost ringing – in buoyant mood – to ask if I will appear on an April Fools' Day programme and announce some new pressure group or lobby group – he suggests 'height-watchers'. It's all to be done very straight. Ken Livingstone will be on, frightening people with plans to make Londoners drive on the right-hand side of the road.

Thursday, April 12th

Camden Council are sweeping the roads an awful lot these days. One thing Thatcher has done by introducing legal restraints on both the GLC (abolition) and Camden (rate-capping) is to stimulate both authorities into an orgy of PR. Nary a day goes by without a petition to be signed, or a new sticker to be stuck up, or a fresh slogan – Camden vehicles now carry: 'A Camden Service', 'Too Good to Lose'. Suddenly they're all on their best behaviour.

To Baker Street for a chiropody lesson in preparation for playing Gilbert Chilvers. Malcolm is there as well as a man called Graham, who is the 'chiropodial' adviser. He shows me the kit I shall have and we discuss various finer points, such as would I spread the patient's toes aside for examination (or, in Malcolm's case, a better shot!) and are the feet erogenous? The adviser is a bit cagey on this one, as if he doesn't want to commit himself.

Then we sit in on a consultation by another chiropodist, Nigel Tewkesbury. Tewkesbury anxious to show, quite convincingly, how a good chiropodist should relate to feet, by holding and touching and grasping them firmly, which gives the patient confidence. I leave with my consultant's bag – to practise at home.

Wednesday, April 18th

Have a long, slow breakfast and read (quite thoroughly for me) a *Guardian* page about the various ways in which government and police can snoop on us. I should think that my £1,000 donation to Greenpeace has not gone unnoticed.

At four o'clock to Fortnum's to have tea at the invitation of Amanda Schiff, who is Sandy Lieberson's deputy at Goldcrest.

Amanda – 'I don't eat meat and I don't eat fish' – tells me of the Goldcrest/Samuel Goldwyn scheme to make a series of small-budget contemporary comedies for a ceiling of £800,000 each in England, with British writers and stars which will hopefully be made on a continuous and regular basis like the Ealing comedies. I like the idea.

After tea back into the real world. Jermyn Street is silent, many of the shops closed, sealed off to all cars. Policemen stand at the corners diverting the pedestrians. I want to buy some shaving cream from Ivan's the barber's, but he's shut. A few feet from his door a blue polythene sheet is stretched from a rough scaffolding frame over the entrance to the street leading to St James's

Square where the Libyan Embassy is under siege after yesterday's killing of a policewoman.

At the bottom of Lower Regent Street the Great British Public crowds around hoping to see some action. The police, who seem to be the only government-supported agency with money to burn these days, are everywhere. Behind the polythene sheets are the tense faces of flak-jacketed marksmen – a far cry from the jolly, helmeted presence on Jermyn Street.

Thursday, April 19th

At a quarter to eleven I'm away down to see Maggie S in West Sussex. Through Frimley, Farnborough and Aldershot. Army and car parks. Then through Hindhead and Haslemere, in narrow, claustrophobic little valleys past houses that all have names – 'Uplands', 'Nutcombe' and the like – and a forest of Conservative local election stickers in the window. I wouldn't have thought they'd need to advertise.

We start by sitting outside sipping champagne. Toby, Maggie's second son, is there. He's been buying weights and muscle-building equipment. Maggie is a little alarmed because, as she puts it, 'their father was rather interested in that sort of thing for a while'.

I've brought Maggie and Bev[1] a pretty white vase that looks a little like a hospital specimen jar, with some blue and white everlasting flowers from Neal Street East and a pot of Gospel Oak marmalade. All the flowers have the price on them. Maggie removes the tags with great speed, skill and discretion.

She's cooked tagliatelli con carne and there's fresh bread and white wine and we have a really easy, delightful lunch.

They've just returned from holiday in Ischia with Sir Larry and Joan Plowright. Sir Larry ga-ga much of the time, says Bev. Had a habit of asking about who someone was, very loudly, right in front of them. Maggie and Joan were spotted by paparazzi in a steam bath.

Maggie throughout looks lovely. Her red hair suffuses a softly-tanned face with a glow of health and attraction. But, as ever, I feel that sometimes she is going through the motions of life – there is always a part of her – the passionate, instinctive part which makes her a great actress – which is in abeyance or being held in reserve – somewhere in there, private from us all.

At a quarter to four, after some chat about the hotels in Yorkshire (this aspect of filming always concerns Maggie) and the script itself – neither of us think the ending satisfactory – I say my goodbyes.

When I get home, I practise chiropody on Helen.

[1] Beverley Cross, a writer and librettist, married Maggie Smith in 1975.

Monday, April 23rd

At ten minutes to midday we all set off for Henley for a lunch party in Aunt Betty's honour.

Richard O'[1] makes a short and effective little speech reminding us that tonight Aunt Betty and Mother will be sleeping in their old home together for the first time for 53 years. Aunt Betty looks a little frailer than Ma, with a fine head of vividly white hair. Mum, in her 80th birthday dress, looks in good colour and full of life. Together they look like two china figures from a set; absolutely alike and quite different from anyone else there.

After lunch there is croquet and a lot of photos are taken. Clare, my goddaughter, is a great joy. She tells me with disgust how her headmistress had forbidden a videotape of *The Missionary* to be shown at the school club. I suppose I must have the attraction of the notorious.

Tuesday, April 24th

Sleep well and wake about half past seven. The sun shining from a brilliant blue sky as I gulp half a cup of tea and, armed with script and chiropody kit, set off for my first working day on 'Pork Royale' [As *Private Function* had become, for a while].

Go via the Body Centre, where I have an hour's massage – from an ex-actor who worked on Alan Bennett's *Forty Years On*.

He does come out with rather disturbing observations, viz my right leg is shorter than my left and this can 'put my whole body out'. I have small, hard deposits of crystallised fatty substances on some of my nerve ends, which are not being properly disposed of owing to tensions. I question him about this and he reveals that everyone has these deposits, adding, quite ingenuously, 'except, of course, enlightened beings'.

Arrive at St Helen's Church Hall, quite a grand and spacious place. Maggie and Liz Smith and Bill Paterson and Rachel Davies, who plays Mrs Forbes, and Richard Griffiths are there, as well as make-up, wardrobe and sundry others.

Alan gives a short intro to the effect that all this will work best if played absolutely seriously. Malcolm concentrates on the scenes between Maggie, Liz and myself. Malcolm is not keen on exaggerated Yorkshire accents; 'a hint of Yorkshire' is the order of the day for us. So into rehearsal. Alan watches some of it and occasionally guffaws loudly, but mostly sits discreetly at the other side of the hall, reading his paper.

---

[1] Richard Ovey, first cousin on my mother's side, inherited the family estate at Hernes where both my mother and her sister and Richard's father, Dick, were brought up.

I voice some of my worries about the ending, but Malcolm is gently firm and Alan doesn't bite, so we're left with it.

Wednesday, April 25th

Mark Shivas rings to warn me that there is some fighting over the budget. HandMade want £1.3 to become £1.2. Mark says they can't and, should DO'B call me about it, could I emphasise how much we're getting for so little.

Rehearse with the Smiths again, and find Gilbert much easier to play with less effort. Malcolm thinks he should be 'a bit dull'. Certainly playing him softer and gentler and more naturally seems to work. I feel much calmer after today's rehearsal. Maggie says she didn't sleep well last night – worries about the accent and, as she says, 'them all thinking what a terrible mistake they've made'.

A curious week. Adjusting to being an actor again is proving quite a roller-coaster for the nervous system. Sometimes I feel surges of nervous apprehension bordering on panic, at others I feel the delicious sense of really looking forward to showing how well I can do something. Confidence is all-important and mine veers sometimes.

Friday, April 27th

Today I have to do Alison Steadman's feet. Not an ordeal at all, and Malcolm is quite pleased by my show of professional chiropodic skill! Real progress in the characterisation of Gilbert in the Church Hall this afternoon. Malcolm is quiet, but persistent and, on the whole, accurate in his criticisms and suggestions.

Denholm is with us for the first time today. I congratulate him on his BAFTA award. He straightaway goes into a story of how he once walked out of BAFTA with Dirk Bogarde, when Denholm had won his first Oscar. Bogarde said to him as they left, 'So you've got your little piece of tin, eh?' 'Well,' says Denholm, eyebrows twisting and folding as only he knows how, 'what a ponce, I mean!'

The afternoon wears on. Maggie tries on her costumes and is instantly transformed into a thin, slight, mousy woman. I'm sure such a transformation can't please her any more than having to say the line 'I'm 38', as she looks at her reflection in the polished car.

Saturday, April 28th

Drive down to South Ken to Le Suquet Restaurant to lunch at DO'B's invitation to meet his new lady, Noelle. We have an enormous platter full of all manner of shellfish, which takes almost two and a half hours to crack, crunch, split, lick and prise our way through.

DO'B, Helen thinks, is anxious to find out about the film from me. It's as if he wants to be excited but finds an almost impenetrable barrier between him and the Mark/Malcolm/Alan triumvirate. This irks him.

We get back home about a quarter to five, just in time for the most exciting news from the BBC's teleprinter in recent memory. Sheffield Wednesday have beaten Crystal Palace 1–0 and are to be in the First Division for the first time since before William was born.

Take Helen down to the Dominion Cinema to see René Clair's *The Italian Straw Hat*, which is being performed for one night only with a full orchestra. The occasion a little better than the film. At the end of the performance, René Clair's wife, a very sprightly lady, makes a short, well-received speech of thanks in perfect English.

Monday, April 30th

Wake, by quarter-hours from six o'clock, to first day of filming on 'Pork Royale'. Roy awaits with his sparkling Mercedes, a neat, trim, RSM-like figure, on the corner of Elaine Grove.

At the location by eight o'clock. It's a 1900–20's house at the top of the hill in Ealing – a cross between mock-Tudor and Arts and Crafts.

Shown up to a bare upstairs room with so few amenities that, had it not been such a warm, outdoors day, could have ruffled the start of the shoot. Denholm Elliott, Richard Griffiths, John Normington are all in one bare room. I'm put in solitary splendour next door.

First shot is under way briskly and consists of me cycling along a hedge looking up at the house.

Then a series of shots of the three 'plotters' round the table, which takes up the bulk of the rest of the day. Talk to Alan, who tells a good story of a lady friend of his mother's who shared the same chiropodist. Having to let Mrs Bennett know of a changed appointment, but not finding her in, she'd scribbled a note and slipped it through the door: 'Foot Lady, Friday, 5.30'. Alan's father, a butcher, finding the note couldn't fathom it out and eventually decided it must he a hot tip for a horse race.

Tuesday, May 1st

Out to Ealing, for the second day of what is now officially re-christened *A Private Function*.

Denholm and his cronies work on the invitation scene and I have to find things to do to pass the time. This production cannot afford caravans to protect stars' privacy, so I sit in the patch of front garden on my chair with my name on it. I may feel the need of somewhere to hide away when the pressure goes on in Yorkshire. But by then Maggie will be with us and she won't settle for chairs in the garden!

Alan is always on hand for a chat. In reply to my asking him why he doesn't do more acting, he just says, rather forlornly, that no-one ever asks him. He kept getting offered vicars, he says. His relationship with Mowbray arose because he liked [Malcolm's] 'Days at the Beach' so much he wrote to him. Mowbray wrote and thanked and expressed admiration for A's work and later brought him the idea for the 'Pig' script. Nice when things happen organically like that. It's like doing things at university.

Thursday, May 3rd

Collected at 10.30.

Roy, stocky, bronzed from a sun-lamp, turns out to be a Buddhist chanter. Says he was introduced to it by Bill Weston, the stunt man, who always looks slightly out to lunch, but is a chanter too. I've brought an Otis Redding tape in with me today, but it seems rather insensitive to have it blaring whilst Roy is telling me how the chants have 'made things happen' and 'given me a more positive outlook on life'.

So in the end he puts on a cassette of Buddhist chants, as the Mercedes swings past Lee Studios and through Wembley to some woodland behind Perivale.

The first noise I hear as I approach the sylvan glade is the squealing of a fractious pig.

I'm used just before lunch, but the pig is very soporific and we have to try the scene again afterwards.

I have to lure the pig quite a few yards, along a plotted path with a sharp right-angled turn. No rope or halter, just with bread. The first take is slow and the pig goes off at a tangent, but it gets better and the second take is almost perfect. Suddenly realise it isn't as difficult as everyone thought it would be. Provided I brandish the bread near enough to the pig, it follows quite obediently and I can regulate its pace. This is a great relief to all.

Leave the location in very good spirits, especially as I have two days off before the four six-day-weeks of continuous working in Yorkshire. Pleased with myself at having passably succeeded at chiropody and pig-stealing.

Friday, May 4th

Up to the Rosslyn deli to buy food for lunch here with Anne J. We talk over business and dates and projects. Say no to the lead in the re-make of *Italian Straw Hat*, but yes to a limerick book. Scripts have arrived of 'Stovold the Viking'. Looks short.

Go through correspondence and play squash with TJ at five. Our first game for several weeks. I win. Afterwards a familiar pint at the Flask. TJ seems much more excited by his script for 'Labyrinth' than by 'Stovold the Viking', and from various things he says I get the feeling that he's decided his strength lies in fantasy and that our paths are more rather than less likely to divide over the next years over this difference in subject matter.

Tom is having a 'gathering' at No. 2. Constant comings and goings through the kitchen. Generally very polite and considerate, though they consume gargantuan amounts of tobacco and rifle the fridge for beer, which I don't approve of. Nor am I very pleased to spend my last hours as a 40-year-old sweeping cigarette stubs, half-eaten chicken legs and crisps off the floor of No. 2.

Saturday, May 5th

My mother rings at nine. I'm still in bed. She's sent me £50 – an unheard-of sum for a present from her. She says it's after 'all the things you've done for me'.

Helen has given me a six-foot-long giant pencil – beautifully reproduced and a very silly, but satisfying and striking piece of decoration. An AA guide to hotels and restaurants from the children gives no mention of the Troutbeck in Ilkley – which is to be my home for the next month.

Tuesday, May 8th: Ilkley, Yorkshire

Feel remarkably together and well prepared for the day. Alan is at breakfast and hadn't gone to sleep until two as he had the room over the bar. 'It was like Christmas down there,' he says, rather morosely.

He goes and I'm alone in this recently-refurbished, rather ornate dining room with 'Adam' pretensions and a giggly waitress who reports loudly my every word back to the kitchen.

I'm driven down solid, leafy roads to a cul-de-sac in Ben Rhydding and up to Briargarth, which is my home for the film. A long, detached, stone house of (probably) Edwardian vintage, with a porch and gables. Carpenters, painters, sparks swarm over it. Loud banging, shouts, and, amidst it all, actors – myself, Maggie and Liz – wandering gingerly, waiting to take possession.

Gradually the first scene creaks into action. Round the table, eating Spam. We reach around for our characters, absorbing all the clues and helps and hindrances of this brand new place in which we must act as if it were all too familiar.

Maggie, brittle and tense so often in non-acting moments, gives so much out when she plays the scene that it's exhilarating to be with her.

A hot bath and a lager. Then walk down into Ilkley – clean, ordered, respectable, with oriel windows above the shops, glass-canopied arcades and ornamental flower beds. It's like the Garden of Eden after Gospel Oak. Choose Chez François – a wine bar – for a solitary meal.

Read of Buñuel and the Surrealists in Paris in the late '20's and '30's. Similarities with Pythons. Bourgeois against the bourgeoisie. Buñuel sounds rather like TJ. Very interested in sex and the Middle Ages and blamed the media for all the world's ills.

Wednesday, May 9th: Ilkley

Drive my hired Ford Orion into Ilkley to look for a birthday present for Alan, who is 50 today. Buy him a card with a pig nestling provocatively, and a pair of nail clippers.

I've also booked a table at the Box Tree Cottage for tonight as an extra present.

Have pre-ordered a bottle of champagne and this helps Alan over his initial awe of the establishment – 'I've only walked past it' – and we have a very jolly time. The Mary Whitehouse lookalike who explains the dishes to us remembers me from Python days.

Alan and Maggie are all ears and eyes for what's happening at the other tables and there are some good characters. I think all three of us are easily moved to laughter at the most inconvenient times.

Mark S joins us. The food is original and very good, with the timbale de fraises outstanding. It's based around their home-made rose-water ice-cream and is delicate, light, aromatic and quite superb. But quite a large shard of glass in my cucumber and onions throws the Mary Whitehouse into near panic. She offers to re-cook all our meals, bring us free liqueurs, some more wine – anything short of giving us the meal free which, on reflection, would have been the only thing for a place like the Box Tree to do.

A bottle of Bollinger is thrust into my hand as we leave. And Alan, I think, was truly touched. He said he'd never been taken out to dinner on his birthday before.

Thursday, May 10th: Ilkley

We scan the papers for latest news of Honeybun, the pet rabbit of the British Ambassador in Libya, which he left behind when the embassy was closed, much to the horror of the animal-loving British public. The *Mail on Sunday* arranged to have the rabbit flown back. The *Guardian* produced a quote from the ambassador's wife to the effect that she loathed the rabbit – 'I wish we'd eaten it before we left'. The *Mail* reporter was then caught by customs at Gatwick bringing a live animal back in the passenger section and his paper now stung for about £2,000 quarantine charges. The story has kept us going all week.

The pig is brought in and for half an hour we are all banned from the surgery whilst it gets used to its paper. 'Pig's business' appears on the call sheet, but there is no need for the prop stuff as Betty trundles about depositing dark grey turds with the regularity of a train timetable every eight minutes or so.

The situation seems very bleak for a while then, with judicious use of sardine oil smeared on the floor and on the toes of my shoes, the pig turns in a series of excellent performances as the room becomes progressively smellier.

Friday, May 11th: Ilkley

Another good night's sleep and down to breakfast at ten to eight. Malcolm sounds very pleased with rushes and Alan, who comes down later, says that he found my performance 'touching', which is unexpected and rather touching.

Sunday, May 13th: Ilkley

They get round to my five-second cycling shot at five to eight at night – nearly eight hours after my call. Malcolm apologises with great concern. Alan and Maggie tell him how angry I've been about the whole thing and Maggie says she heard my caravan shaking with sobs. For a moment Malcolm believes them.

At the Troutbeck, Alan buys the meal for Maggie, Malcolm, myself and Don Estelle. We are the only diners and the food is so consistently devoid of flavour that one suspects certain special anti-cooking skills. But we laugh a lot. Alan digs gently at Malcolm, 'Buñuel would never have kept an artist waiting eight hours', and Malcolm plays up to it gracefully. But the emptiness of the dining room and the distant sound of jollity from the folk club don't raise the spirits.

Tuesday, May 15th: Ilkley

Maggie, Mark S and myself are dawdling in the car park at Ben Rhydding Station after lunch, remarking on how many trains seem to be coming through this archetypal country station which miraculously escaped the Beeching axe, when Alan B steps out of one of them. Though he never told us himself, we know that he's been up to London to collect yet another award for *Englishman Abroad*, so we greet him with a round of applause. Alan goes very pink and is delightfully embarrassed.

He says it was an awful occasion. They'd been sat next to the band, he says. He squirms as he tells us of the discomfiture he feels at having to make speeches at these occasions ... 'I feel such a twerp ... the microphone's always the wrong height ... and your voice suddenly booms out saying something quite fatuous. I haven't been given anything since 1971 ... then all this ... '. He shakes his head with bewilderment.

More slow progress in the afternoon as we wait for the pig to be coaxed up and down the stairs. The day trails away. I sit at the top of the stairs in my long underwear, kitchen knife at the ready, whilst shouts of 'Shit-bucket!' rise from below.

Thursday, May 17th: Ilkley

Today I avoid hotel breakfast and lie in bed until a quarter to eight. With Roy to the location at 8.20. Not much for me to do again. A crowded living room scene. Black drapes shroud the lower half of the house. La Nuit Américaine. Pete Postlethwaite and Jim Carter do amazing magic tricks – probably born from years of standing around at rehearsals or waiting to go on.

Denholm chain-smokes – as do most of them. Only Jim and myself of the actors don't smoke. Alan B says he has a cigarette every now and then. He says when he's trying to think of a plot – which he finds very difficult – he has a Consulate. The actors assure him that they're the worst.

The pig goes from strength to strength and received a round of applause after her first performance this morning. Maggie still very worried about her piano-playing. She scratched herself on the brass antlers of the cocktail decanter whilst rehearsing this morning and rather ruefully mutters that she'd hoped it had been worse and she'd have had an excuse for getting out of the piano-playing altogether.

They talk about their favourite Shakespeare plays. I feel dreadfully dull when the talk turns to theatre and aware of how different my world is from the rest of these thespians. Maggie dislikes *Merchant of Venice* – 'All Portia does is tell Larissa to close the curtains.' She doesn't have much time for *Taming of the Shrew* either.

Monday, May 21st: Ilkley

Up just before eight, with news on Radio 4. The miners' strike still dominates,[1] as the Falklands War did throughout *Missionary*. Local 'Day of Action' in Yorkshire has stopped mainline trains, local bus services, etc. But not the slow, steady progress of the filming.

In one of the re-shoots the pig suddenly went off ginger biscuits. Denholm said he'd noticed the precise moment the attraction of the biscuits palled ... 'Amazing,' he ruminated, 'like a Pauline conversion.'

Tuesday, May 22nd: Ilkley

After lunch a freshly-killed pig is delivered – supplied and chaperoned by a ruddy-faced little rock of a man in overalls. Everywhere there is earnest talk of where a pig is stuck in order to kill it, how long it takes to bleed it, etc, etc. We have to carry it upstairs and it feels very strange – as if still just alive.

At one point I go upstairs to the loo only to find my way barred by a huddle of people around the pig's carcass. There is a flash of staple gun from one of the chippies, a sharp click and the brown detective's hat is stapled to the pig's head. Quite the most sinister thing I've seen in a long while.

Finish Buñuel [*My Last Breath*] – a delight of a book, especially the chapter on his likes and dislikes. He lived and worked most of his life in Mexico and Spain, but had a yearning to live in Sweden or Russia. Buñuel feels like Rembrandt – a warm, direct, flawed, life-enriching character. Reading the book makes you very glad to be alive – which is what I need as the seemingly endless day draws on in Briargarth.

---

[1] The strike of 1984–5 was prompted by the threat of job losses and pit closures. Arthur Scargill's NUM (National Union of Mineworkers) confronted Margaret Thatcher's Tory government for almost a year.

Wednesday, May 23rd: Ilkley

We're on the Bolton Abbey estate in very beautiful countryside up the Wharfe Valley. The drive here this morning left everyone speechless with appreciation – the road winds through woods and undulates gently beside the river. A carpet of bluebells in amongst the trees adds the icing to a rich and almost perfect English pastoral scene.

I, alone of the thespians, have a caravan – a mousey, small affair, parked right next to the props van where the drivers gather and talk loudly about fucking. I, prissy little bourgeois, trapped in the mind-improving expectations of my class, try to read more of *La Regenta*.

Walk some way along the road. Out of sight of the vehicles all is peace and tranquillity. A soft heat. Shirts off day. Walk up into some fields on the edge of the moor.

A herd of Friesian heifers takes a liking to me. They walk – first one, then the others – slowly after me as I cross a meadow. Then they break into a run and I have to make a rushed scramble up and over the high stone wall.

Thursday, May 24th: Ilkley

Arrive at the location just about the same time as the St John's Ambulance lady. I tell her that we've got the wounded lined up against the wall, but she doesn't have much of a sense of humour.

Nor, I think, does the lady who brings the 1947 Riley. She provides Alan and me with enormous pleasure as she corners Denholm Elliott with her autograph book. The book seems to consist almost entirely of Conservative politicians, a massive haul which she got from the party conference. She points them out proudly to Denholm, who is utterly bored ... 'John Nott ... he's quite famous ... ' 'Yeees ... ' 'Selwyn Gummer, of course he's very famous now ... ' 'Yeees ...'

The weather is hot and balmy, a BBC unit from Leeds come out to film us filming and pick Alan and me off in separate interviews. They completely ignore the likes of Bill Paterson, who is likely to be very famous indeed after *Comfort and Joy*, but then these after-six programmes are never very good at spotting trends, only following them.

After a morning of what Gerry Paris [my stand-in] and I call 'we might' shots – 'Michael, we might see you in this shot' – I have a steady succession of scenes to do in the afternoon.

I do always enjoy myself when there's some playing involved, some eyeball-to-eyeball acting – some exchange of mental energies instead of cycling, waving and reacting to people who've left three hours before.

Friday, May 25th: Ilkley and Bolton Abbey Estate

Alan B shows us all a cheque from the BBC, for sales of *Englishman Abroad* in Sweden, Denmark, Norway and Belgium. £8.50!

It's time to grovel in the pig sty. The pig mixes a few long, grey turds and a pee or two with the manure that lines the stall. Myself, Tony H, Preston and Tony P-R and Derek all squashed in there.[1] Have to grab Betty's back leg, which takes some strength as she shakes it violently. But she is immensely long-suffering as I grab her in take after take, and never becomes vicious.

Annie Wingate [production manager] is hovering anxiously about the sty as we edge towards 6.30 and still three shots indoors to do. Malcolm's technique when she asks him to hurry is superb. He nods very sympathetically as she describes the situation, thinks hard and then manages to say, without a hint of sarcasm 'But ... if we don't shoot this properly ... ' (long pause) ' ... it won't work.'

But at 6.30 it's done. Wash off the shit and into the waiting Orion. At Doncaster by eight. There is a restaurant car on the train which makes the longish journey time – two hours 22 minutes – to London very bearable. A scotch, celery soup, roast lamb and cheese and a bottle of red wine as we head south, stopping everywhere. Sleep from Stevenage into London and have to be woken at King's Cross.

Sunday, May 27th: Barnoldswick

12.30: In a spacious caravan in the car park of the Civic Hall, Barnoldswick – pronounced 'Barnswick' or 'Barnslick'. The rain rattles on the roof. It's very cold. Have done some cycling and parades shots this morning, which we got in before the worst of the rain.

This town has a Rolls-Royce engine works, but from the look of the people and the number of shops 'Closing Down', it seems far from prosperous, and certainly has none of the confident comfort of Ilkley. The 'B' in RB-211 stands for Barnoldswick.

At lunch most of the unit find a local café. A lady emerges from the rain-sodden throng and corners Alan. 'I just want to shake your hand, Mr Blezzard.'

---

[1] Tony Haygarth played the farmer, Preston was the name of his son. Tony Pierce-Roberts was director of photography and Derek Suter was the clapper/loader.

Thursday, May 31st: Ilkley

It's Denholm's birthday today and he's having a lovely chin-wag with the ex-Lord Mayor of Bradford – a lady – who is a very strong, competent, articulate lady and is playing the Lord Mayor in the film.

AB has been unable to wriggle out of a proposed *South Bank Show* profile on him. He says he just can't bear the thought of shots of him driving along moorland roads with his thoughts over. But whereas on Wednesday he announced firmly that he wasn't going to do it, he's now been persuaded by personal intervention from the young producer who flew up to see him. 'Oh, I'm *such* a coward,' he admits despondently.

Today Alan has an acting role in the film. He has the part of Man Coming Out of Toilet and looks like Robert Redford as Jay Gatsby in his evening dress, and blond hair brushed back.

We are rushed into the final dance sequence, as Richard (Allardyce) has to leave first thing tomorrow to play the lead in 'Volp' (as he calls *Volpone*) over the weekend.

We go on late and, after a day of heat and crowds, the band strikes up and everyone sings 'Happy Birthday' and 'For He's a Jolly Good Fellow' to Denholm when we wrap about 9.15. Very moving as he stands in the middle of the floor acknowledging the applause.

In the car on the way back D and I fall to discussing how much time we need to get up in the morning when filming. I say 20 minutes. Denholm needs an hour. 'I have to have at least five cups of tea and I *do* like to read.' I say that all I really have to have is a good shit, but D says he can't possibly shit in the morning – he's far too nervous.

Sunday, June 3rd: Ilkley

Teeming rain this morning. Alan is in a very gloomy state about the cuts and foresees that one of today's scenes – the businessmen talking in the function room – could go in addition to the others already under sentence. No jokes from him today, just an atmosphere of near-desperation.

Malcolm elides shots and scenes in order to save time. My crucial 'blow-up' scene has to be done in one take, which is a pity, but inevitable, I suppose. Not until about five do we even get onto what was first on the schedule this morning. I stay in my caravan or sit in the sun in the car park listening to Van Morrison on my Sony – anything to avoid the gloom indoors.

Maggie and I work hard in the first part of the day. She smiles at my attempt at sarcasm over the slow progress. 'It just doesn't suit you,' and adds 'Take a tip from the acid queen.'

After five the pace suddenly speeds up and the work goes on until 11.30. Everything bar one shot (the toilet) is completed.[1] But will the crew survive late nights all week? And even if they can, will the scenes that are constantly being put on one side ever be caught up?

More time and money is still needed.

Tuesday, June 5th: Ilkley

Maggie in a very sore mood for some reason. She's tense, terse and seems to take every suggestion Malcolm makes as a personal insult. Very difficult, as her attitude affects the whole unit by degrees.

Unexpectedly, who should arrive on the lunchtime train at Ben Rhydding, but Ray Cooper, in spotty grey suit and black brogues.

Ray asks me to dinner at the Devonshire Arms at Bolton Abbey and I ask Maggie along. She accepts, to my surprise, and, apart from being very worried that she's dressed only in jeans, is sweetness and light and charm and naturalness all evening. Ray, of course, treats her well with great courtesy and flattering respect. He remembers her from when he was at the National.

We talk of film acting versus theatre acting. Talk of *Way of the World*, which she's doing at Chichester. I say that the reward of all the work must come when she steps out on stage in front of an audience. 'Oh no, I can't be bothered with that, rehearsing's the only bit I like. Getting it right, working it out.'

At eleven drive Maggie back to the hotel we've today been shunted into – the Post House at Bramhope. There is Bill Paterson in the bar. He's now like a ghost, doomed to wander round Yorkshire waiting to be used. Very bad scheduling, but he is so tolerant.

Wednesday, June 6th: Bramhope, Yorkshire

Up at eight. Papers and radio all full of D-Day's 40th anniversary. Once more the noble art of war celebrated and minds taken for a while off present discontents. Reagan the film actor is here and the D-Day remembrance is ideally suited for his and Thatcher's particular brand of ham.

This is positively our last day at Gilbert's House. On the original Hugely Optimistic Schedule this was to have been May 22nd.

---

[1] It had been difficult to find the location for the scene in which Gilbert Chilvers is confronted by the local business mafia at a urinal. Then one morning in Betty's Tea Rooms in Ilkley, Alan B appeared, full of excitement. 'We've found a toilet', he enthused, 'near Paddington Station, and it'll take ten!' Only as heads turned and the noise level dropped did we realise what this must have sounded like to the middle-aged, respectable, and largely female clientele at Betty's.

I run upstairs in my underwear pursuing the pig with a knife, then a halting unsatisfactory day of much waiting and very short bursts of activity. Around me the house is being cleared away and by the evening it has become rather sad and lifeless.

I leave the house and my dressing room with the half-peeled wallpaper hanging in strips and the little rooms we got to know so well and the book called *Instantaneous Personal Magnetism*, with only a twinge of sadness. I expect I shall miss it more as time goes on.

It's 11.15 after a dour drizzly day, the location caterer's moussaka was very strange and I had to secrete it in a black bag, and there's an extended day tomorrow. Being an optimist I'm sure it will come out all right, but I feel at the moment something is wrong in the mixture, something quite important – the ingredient of space – scale and sense of location – may be lost in this continual concertina-ing process.

Thursday, June 7th: Bramhope

It's with resignation rather than eager anticipation that I finally prepare to lead the pig into the car. The car is a meticulously preserved Wolseley Hornet. The owner, fortunately as it turns out, isn't present, but his father, an Arnold Ridley lookalike, is.

The attempt to film a single take of me leading Betty down through the groves of wild garlic and into the Wolseley founders, as Betty can in no way be persuaded to enter the car. Various methods are tried as time ebbs away and the pressure begins to rise. Huge insects, drawn by the arc lights in the woods, thud into the reflectors.

The two cameras are moved, we try again. Then suddenly the pig is in the car and, not only that, she's nuzzling at the windscreen, sitting up in the front seat. I get into the car and, moving Betty's massive bulk, am able to switch on the headlights, release the brake and slip out of shot.

But in all the attendant confusion, the first assistant has been caught in a reflection and we have to set it up again. On the next take Betty panics and lunges desperately for the driver's window. Her trotter is bearing down on my genitals and her underbelly is slimy with something or other and the smell of fresh pig shit has replaced the pleasant woody-leathery aroma of the car's interior.

I'm released and Betty's released, but the car is a pig sty – shit on the back seats mingles with old food and scraps of apple and pig saliva smears the inside of the elegant windscreen. Says our car owner ruefully: 'I could have written this better – I'd have written it without a pig in.' He indicates Alan – 'He's no Ibsen, is he?'

Roy drives me back over the dark, silent moors. I'm back at the Post House just after half past one. I tell the receptionist I've been trying to get a pig in a car. She obviously thinks I'm completely drunk. But I have witnesses.

Monday, June 11th

A depressingly run-down location in Exmouth Street, across the road from Mount Pleasant Sorting Office.

My dressing room is the small bedroom of the assistant barman of the Exmouth Arms who's away for the week. Racing cars, John Player Grand Prix of the World racetrack passes, *Sun* and 'Daily Starbird' calendars, and other pictures of sexless blondes bearing mammarial mounds as if displaying the latest racing car accessories.

'Who's in it then?' I hear asked with imperious Cockney sensitivity just behind me as I await the cue to start the scene . . .

'Michael Palin, Maggie Smith, Denholm Elliott . . .'

'Oh, no-one we've ever 'eard of then?'

Alan arrives with a crisp new paperback edition of Carlyle's selected writings (he'd found Vol. 3 of Carlyle's *Frederick the Great* in a set-dressed bookshelf in Ilkley and was quite hooked). Looking through the intro Alan finds to his concern that Carlyle had, in later life, been author of a pamphlet on 'The Nigger Problem' and, even more disconcertingly, one of Carlyle's books was discovered in Hitler's bunker.

End the day carrying a half-carcass of pork downstairs.

Tuesday, June 12th

My last chiropody scene – and the most jolly, Sue Pollett being a very good subject. Alan arrives on his bike.

He tells me that the old lady who lives in the Transit Van in the driveway of his house considers herself to have equal rights over the entire property. She complained about Alan playing his music too loud, so he tends to listen on headphones. He admits that he does sometimes sing along with the music in his phones, which must sound odd, but was not prepared to be told by her that she had heard strange sounds coming from the house, as from someone under the influence of drink!

A long day and the meat is beginning to smell. An old actor called Don Eccles, who was once directed by Bertolt Brecht and W H Auden (they hated each other), joins us. We sit on chairs in the street.

Farewells. Rather sad to leave them all. I like the crew better as we get to know each other. It does say a lot for working with a repertory of actors and crew – as Python and Woody Allen have found to their advantage.

Friday, June 15th

Cleese rings. I put to him thoughts on 'Vikings'. He isn't anxious to become involved in any more films besides a Michael Frayn script (JC as headmaster) he's been sent and the film he's been writing for many months with Charles Crichton.

About one o'clock Helen hears something in the street outside. Look out to see two men, one with black gloves, going down the street trying car doors. Helen rings police. Just slipping to sleep when police knock on door. Helen goes down – tall, dark, handsome PC to say they caught the pair. They were let off with a caution, having pleaded that they were very pissed off after seeing *Friday 13th Part II*, which they regarded as a complete waste of money.

Sunday, June 17th

TG rings to ask if I'm going to Pam Stephenson's party. I'm in that 'I will if you will' mood. So we find ourselves, at nine-fifteen, driving along unlikely back streets of Hammersmith looking for a house described as No $1\frac{1}{2}$ The Fish Factory.

Pam wears a dress made of a facsimile copy of *The Times* for March 19th '84 (when their much-publicised baby was born) and people bring her outrageous presents. The Pope's double waits at the door, a man dressed as Tarzan serves the drinks, dressed only in a loincloth and holding a plastic club with difficulty. A fully-turbaned Indian sings 'Living Doll' and other classics in front of a live band.

There is neat, trim, smiling and genuinely good-humoured Dick Lester, belligerently entertaining Peter McDougall, setting his moustache alight regularly as he fires his roll-your-own cigarettes.[1]

Talk to Billy [Connolly] as we're leaving. He's lost so much weight he looks physically much less substantial than his brawling, extrovert comedy style suggests. We talk of *Water*. He has one more week to go and is driving down to Devon for the filming after the party. I notice he's not drinking.

---

[1] Lester directed, among other things, the Beatles' films *Hard Day's Night* and *Help*. McDougall, a gritty Scots playwright who wrote for BBC's *Play For Today* and was always on the verge of delivering a screenplay for HandMade.

Saturday, June 23rd

I have a long-standing commitment at the Bluebell Railway to re-launch the only North London Line steam loco existing anywhere.

Met at the station by David Ryder and the team who have restored 58830 to service. Mostly much younger than myself. All with other jobs – electronic engineers, British Caledonian ground staff, etc.

At 2.30 the loco is steamed up the platform. Give my short speech, which is upstaged by a loud railway announcement, followed by the sweep in of the preceding train, which obliterates three-quarters of my audience. Raise three cheers for the team who worked on the loco, then I'm given a ride on the footplate up the five miles to Horsted Keynes and back, through classic English arable landscape, looking well in the sun.

There can't be many industries in which you can, or even would want to, return to your old trade well into your 80's as some of them do here. A mucky, dirty enterprise full of happy, fulfilled workers.

Wednesday, July 4th

To Don's for 9.15 haircut appointment. The extraordinary mixture of *Brazil* and *Private Function* has left my head looking like a hairstyle exhibition site. Don notices the silvery threads. I'm going grey, gently but alas irreversibly.

This evening I go to catch my first glimpse of a *Brazil* cut at the Baronet viewing theatre – a full house with 30 or so people crammed into a very small space.

The film is two and a half hours long. As expected, each frame an oil painting. A garden of visual delights. Dream sequences puzzling but unfinished.

Jonathan's central performance is masterly. He holds all the disparate pieces together. Manages to react 600 different ways to the same sort of situations and carries you along, explaining by expressions what we are required to think and feel.

Detail as usual of design, costume, props, etc, marvellous. Definitely a film for two or three viewings. Doesn't have the naive charm of *Time Bandits* – in fact has no charm at all – but is a spirited, inventive, enormously intriguing work of imagination made celluloid.

Thursday, July 5th

Jonathan Pryce rings to borrow a video machine. He still has some flying shots to complete. *Brazil* will have been a year of his life. He goes to New York in

October to do *Accidental Death of an Anarchist* on Broadway, for a nine-month contract. He says he now can't open the script without depression setting in. On the page it seems to be so awkward and yet he knows that everything happens in the performance.

He hopes to get a film part – opposite Meryl Streep – in David Hare's *Plenty*. This is why he needs the video – to copy some of the *Brazil* tapes to show the director. 'It's always the way,' he says dolefully, 'these sort of directors never really know who I am.' In his way he is as powerful as Brando or De Niro. But you have to be in the right sort of movies and you usually have to be American to be that big.

Tuesday, July 10th

To Waterloo on the Underground for a trip to the Methuen reps' conference at Andover.[1] Since yesterday LT have banned smoking on all their Underground trains. A great step forward. Smoking should only be allowed in large country houses after dinner.

Later out with Helen to see Erice's *The South*[2] – a superb, hauntingly beautiful film. Perfectly controlled and paced and shot to focus our attention on the simple elements of a very sad and touching tale. Goes above *The Servant* in my Top Ten instantly. And as a writer I am impressed again by how few histrionics are needed to make it work, how few epic visuals, grand locations and characters. It is precise and precisely satisfying.

And Helen is quite tearful afterwards as well as during. Wonderful.

Thursday, July 12th

A rather important day ahead. My first sight of *Private Function* – my life for seven weeks in May and June.

I quite enjoy Gilbert and find myself wanting to see more of him and his wife and ma-in-law. Lots of good things in 'PF'. Performances – especially Denholm E (best thing he's done) and Richard – are all strong and watchable. Much laughter.

Only drawbacks – too much sub-plot detail in the middle of the first half and a pervasive depressing feeling about most of the characters, their rela- tionships and the world they inhabit, which makes it rather an inward-looking

---

[1] Jones and Palin's *Bert Fegg's Encyclopeadia (sic) of All World Knowledge* was one of their top titles for the autumn of 1984.
[2] *El Sur* (*The South*), by Spanish director Victor Erice, was released in 1983.

piece. That's where Gilbert is important – he's honest, if plodding, and one of the only characters with whom Bennett really allows the audience to develop sympathy.

No music yet, or pig effects.

To L'Escargot with Ray and Malc and Mark and Annie.

I only have time for a smoked haddock starter before I have to rush back to [Roger] Cherrill's to post-synch 'screams and gurgles' for *Brazil*. I die horribly three or four times, then back to L'Escargot for the rest of the meal.

Friday, July 13th

Steve [Abbott] has just come back from a week in Russia. Though it didn't radically change his views about Russians, it did make him more anti-American. So much in what he saw and did contradicted the American-instigated anti-Russian propaganda. He was free to wander, he found a synagogue where Jews were free to practise their religion. He found the great buildings of the past preserved carefully and beautifully. He found an underground system in Moscow superbly clean and free of ads and litter.

Wednesday, July 18th

I pack ready for three days up in Southwold. On the way I go to a screening of *Private Function*.

The film has lost ten minutes and now runs 94. Denis looks like being proved right, for most of the trims and tucks are beneficial.

'I see you've lost me then,' says Alan in mock umbrage, referring to the ending-up on cutting-room floor of 'Man Coming Out of Lavatory'.

Friday, July 20th: Croft Cottage

As I write this, ten has just struck downstairs on the carriage clock I had restored for Mum. It's a Saturday morning. Birds sing almost constantly from various vantage points around the house. Heavy low cloud flattens out the landscape. It's cool.

Outside the window in front of me is a telegraph pole and a makeshift scarecrow of yellow polythene in a field of potatoes and clover. There is no other sign of human habitation.

The extraordinary appeal of Croft Cottage – and one that I feel sure I shall not be able to enjoy for much longer – is this momentary timelessness, this feeling of being settled in a warm and comfortable armchair from which one can survey the past easily, the present comfortably and the future hardly at all.

Sunday, July 22nd

We play a lot of tennis, for the first time this year.

Suddenly aware of time passing when Helen and I are struggling to beat Tom and William. They're both potentially very good. Tom has a fierce serve, but doesn't concentrate hard enough to produce it with consistency. William is the eye-opener. He has a very quick eye, can't serve overarm well, but always seems to be in the right place at the right time (if you're playing *with* him) or the wrong time (if you're against him). Helen and I just hold our own, but very soon we'll be out of their league.

Monday, July 23rd

A run – as I feel I need all the exercise I can get before the holiday indulgences begin on Wednesday. It's very hot and humid and the going isn't very comfortable. I note from the *Sunday Times* that Jim Fixx, whose book was the greatest single influence on my decision to start regular running five years ago, has died of a heart attack aged 52, whilst . . . running.

Halfway across Kenwood Meadow I meet Warren Mitchell. He says he's breaking in a new hip and talks of a return to Alf Garnett with Dandy Nichols in a wheelchair.

To the Zanzibar to meet Sam Goldwyn. Sam is tall, clear-eyed, silver-haired, strong-jawed. He could be an evangelist or a Republican politician or the owner of a million fast food restaurants. In fact he's a rather gentle, concerned, almost avuncular figure who has a strong liking for British comedy of the gentler kind. He's nice about what he's seen of *A Private Function* and thinks we have 'a real winner there'!

We discuss a possible remake of the 1974 TV play [*Secrets*] TJ and I wrote (coincidentally enough, with Warren Mitchell playing the lead), which Sam G likes in script form, but feels that there should be a rewrite developing a more sympathetic character.

The second idea, and more constructive still, is that if TJ and I don't feel it's fresh enough to be our next writing project, then is there anyone else we could trust? Both TJ and I quite independently suggest David Leland. Good on structure, taut and spare in his writing, convincing on the big business detail.

Tuesday, July 24th

To West Hampstead for lunch with JC. The restaurant is completely empty when I get there. I walk in, mildly put out at not even being able to find a waiter, when John's head pops up from beneath one of the tables and squeaks, mouse-like, making my heart stop momentarily.

We are almost the only diners. The waiter is a complete Manuel clone. We talk of friends and eventually of the whole area of behaviour, relationships, etc – the subject nearest to JC's heart at the moment. He does seem to spend an inordinate amount of his time thinking about himself – trying to get to the bottom of why he is what he is and is there anything he can do about it?

It's a very warm, humid afternoon. Neither of us is in a great hurry and JC drives me, at a stately pace, back to Julia Street in his Rolls. He makes strange faces as we ring the doorbell, aiming to surprise Helen, but surprises instead Sam Jarvis the painter – whose reaction as he opens the door is something well worth seeing.

Wednesday, August 8th

Ring Eric to thank him for our weekend [at his house in France]. The difference between us, I thought pithily as I plodded up to Kenwood today, is that I'm a natural agree-er and Eric is a natural disagree-er. But we are in harmony over the likely enjoyment of another collaboration – Python or Python without John. Eric says he'd been thinking of a 'Brian 2', when Bowie, with whom he was lunching, suggested we do the 'Old Testament' ... 'We could be so rude about the Jews.'

The idea of 'Python's Old Testament' attracts me more than I'd expected. I feel as though we've done the hard bit of the Bible, now we can do the fun bit – special effects, loopy characters, invasion, sacrifice, empire-building and so on. The usual Python territory, in fact. I promise I will mention it to TJ and that we should keep in touch by letter.

Thursday, August 9th

Taxi to King's Cross at half past twelve to travel with Terry J to York, for my first look at Terry's 'Chaucer' talk.[1] I'm only going as curious travelling

---

[1] Terry, fascinated by Chaucer since university days, had written the book *Chaucer's Knight*, published in 1980.

companion and am not expected to do anything myself, so it's almost another holiday excursion for me.

We eat on the train – some power-failure in the buffet results in the bizarre plight of the steward advising us that 'anything in the fridge will be warm'.

Tell TJ of the 'Old Testament' idea. He isn't as keen as I was. He feels that the 'Old Testament' is so much about the Jews and their history that goyim like ourselves are not the best-qualified people to write about it. He prefers Greek classics as a possible base. We talk about the rest of the year's work. I feel 'The Vikings' should be put in abeyance and I think TJ does too.

Two hundred or more members of the New Chaucer Society assemble to hear Terry. Derek Brewer, Master of Emmanuel, introduces TJ as 'the twentieth-century embodiment of Geoffrey Chaucer' and mentions that he and I are currently at work on a Viking musical. This raises tremendous laughter from the assembled academics, who are obviously anticipating some entertainment tonight.

Terry doesn't disappoint them. With chest bared and hair in disordered profusion, he cracks off at a pace too fast and a pitch too high for most people to immediately comprehend. But for an hour and a half he keeps me completely involved in twenty lines of 'The Knight's Tale'. Told, part as performance, with throwaways, jokey slides and well-chosen anachronisms, and part as a detective story, it's compelling stuff and throughout TJ's energy and enthusiasm keep it on a superior level of interest to most academic arguments.

Monday, August 13th

In the evening we go round to the Pryces' in Queen's Crescent. Jonathan determined to offer us the best, so we have Kir, then a bottle of Cahors they brought back from staying at T Gilliam's in France, and *then* ... a bottle of 1963 port given them by Roger Pratt. Much talk of how to open it. JP goes next door to borrow a decanter from Frank Delaney. 'Of which sort?' is Delaney's admirable reply.

I chatter on, rather enjoying myself, until after twelve. Both Jonathan and Kate look exhausted and Helen has long since stopped listening and is gazing into the decanter stopper.

Wednesday, August 15th

In the afternoon the fluffy heat turns to darkening skies and occasional rain. Enervating weather, but drag myself into town to buy office files and to take back my running shoes. At Cobra they tell me I suffer from excessive pronation as I run and they prescribe some wonderful and expensive new Nike shoes which come with a small booklet explaining everything they do for the excessively pronating runner.

As I leave the shop clutching the most sophisticated trainers I've ever bought in my life, an assistant comes up to tell me that 'rumour has it' John Cleese just visited the Westbourne Grove branch and bought exactly the same pair. Two excessive pronators in one comedy team?

Saturday, August 18th

To Friar Park. George greets me, neat and wiry in his white cotton trousers and a 'Welcome to LA' T-shirt with a comical graphic of twisted, knotted freeways.

We sit and talk and soon I mention, *have* to mention, what I've heard of his reaction to *A Private Function*. He is indeed almost completely negative about it. He hasn't been able to read more than 11 pages of the script, he doesn't think it is a story or a world that will appeal to many people. He doesn't like the pig and also says, in a kindly enough way, that it is the first thing I've done when I haven't made him laugh.

Then we walk out into the gardens, which look wonderful in the still soft, very warm sunshine. He shows me the impressive work of one Keith West – a New Zealand botanical illustrator whom George is using to illustrate another edition of his songs. Beautiful detail and precision, rich colours. Occasionally mistily mystical, but so are many of the songs he's asked to illustrate. GH says he's written over 140 songs. 'Quite a lot, really.'

Later he takes me up to the studio and rather coyly plays me a song he's written for a musical about a one-legged tap dancer (the subject came up after he and Ringo went to see *42nd Street*).

About 7.15 I start to go, but GH is buzzing with ideas for a musical. 'Hawaii ... you could use Hawaii, there's a volcano with an ash cone in the centre bigger than Centre Point.' He comes to life as it's time to go. He desperately wants to create or be involved in creation – to, as he puts it, 'blow all my money on myself for once'.

Monday, September 3rd

Today is the fifth anniversary of my decision to try and make running a habit. I don't celebrate it in great style. I have an either bruised or cracked rib (post wind-surfing), which nudges me painfully as I run. A still-unsettled stomach and rather sore Achilles tendons.

I trot rather gently round my Heath course. The grass is turning brown from lack of rain, the place cries out for a dowsing. Cloud is building up as is a strongish warm wind. The fifth anniversary run is an effort, but, as ever, having finished I'm rewarded with a glowing feeling of satisfaction.

Tuesday, September 4th

A phone call from producer Clare Downs. She prefaces a request by saying that David Puttnam had told her I quite wanted to do more serious parts. I must have sounded guarded at this, for she laughs brightly.

What she wants me to do is a short film which Paramount and the NFFC [National Film Finance Corporation] have suddenly produced the money for, with a view to having it made and screened by the end of December to qualify for the awards. It sounds an above-average number, but what really swings my interest is that Phyllis Logan has already agreed to do it. I would be her husband.

The script is sent round. It's called *The Dress*. It's quite a meaty role, lots of sexual jealousy and desire and all that, but neatly written and definitely quality. A week's filming in October. Could fit it in, I suppose.

Wednesday, September 5th

I've come to regard September as the start of the working year. New projects ahead, the pleasant, reviving, drifting summer behind.

In the spirit of such feelings, begin a new 'country house' comedy completely from scratch. Quite where it goes I'm not sure. I do like the title 'The Man Who Averted World War II'.

David Leland shares my double ticket for a preview screening of *Spinal Tap*.

Very skilful, accurate parody of musicians on tour, observed to accentuate the humour, but never at the expense of a controlled authenticity which makes it very satisfying recognition viewing. Christopher Guest and Mike McKean uncannily good as English heavy metal stars.

To dinner afterwards. Twenty-five people squashed up at table. Sit opposite Stephen Frears and beside the producer of *Spinal Tap*, a lovely, bright New York lady, who I would gladly have produce anything I do!

Drive Leland back to Highgate and he gives me the first 40 pages of his new script about Cynthia [Payne] to read. He wants some feedback before he goes on.

Thursday, September 6th

Look at The Novel ['A Bit of A Break', written in 1977] again. Frustrated by lack of progress on the film, I decide to contact John Curtis at Weidenfeld, who showed interest in reading it five years ago. He is still there and still very interested.

Ring Cleese to fix a lunch, as I am the Python appointed to try and interest him in the proposed meeting about whether we ever make a film again which Eric is trying to set up in mid-October. JC is quite brisk on the phone and with more than usual exasperation explains that he's just put his neck out, 'and a man's waiting upstairs to put it back in again'.

Friday, September 7th

To meet Clare Downs and the director, Eva Sereny, to talk about *The Dress*. They are highly embarrassed about offering me only £2,400 for the work, but this is out of a total budget of £100,000 and, as I say, I'm not doing it for the money. I hope I shan't disappoint them.

Eva Sereny I like immediately. Hungarian, married to an Italian and based in Rome, 'but never in the same bed two nights running' is how she describes her life as a photographer of international repute. This is her first venture as director. She describes the overall sepia look she wants, with the red of the dress standing out.

Sunday, September 9th

Up at half past nine. Read the Sundays and come across an interview by George Perry with *Spinal Tap* people. They liked Goons and Monty Python and saw JC and MP as 'comic geniuses'. This cheers me up, especially after a week in which the comic genius has been particularly elusive, but it nudges me suddenly in a certain positive direction – one, to write something for myself which will make people laugh rather than just smile, and two, to perhaps explore the biography – the 'life of', or the documentary.

Monday, September 10th

Lunch with Cleesie. He's waiting for me at Odin's with an incipient growth of beard. 'I hate saying I'm growing it for a film, in case people think I'm an actor,' he says, quite sincerely. He's playing an English sheriff in a Lawrence

Kasdan film to be shot in Arizona. 'Two weeks' work, Mikey . . . in a *lovely* part of America . . .'

He is very anxious to hear about everything I'm doing, but claims to be well ahead of me in days off this year. When I tell him I've had an unproductive week, he proffers some advice – that, in the same way, he says, that the creation of Basil Fawlty had been a bringing-out of Fawlty-esque frustrations in John himself, so I should try and create a character which brings something out of me, something which I feel very strongly about.

I broach Python, as prelim to asking John to October meetings, but there is nothing there.

Sunday, September 16th

Worried about my stools. The currently fashionable indication of good health is that your stools float. Mine sink like so many Titanics.

Screen International reveals that British cinema attendance has plummeted – like my stools – yet again this year. It comes home to me that there is no longer a commercial prospect in making films that will only be understood in my own country. Video deals and early TV sales could, I suppose, save a very small budget. But no room for anything ambitious. Depressing. And renders me even less consumed with energy for a new *Missionary*.

Watch the first of the *Great River Journeys*. Very good stuff from Michael Wood on the journey up the Congo to the interior of Africa. Helen worried about his theme of utter solitude and man against Africa, knowing there was a six- to eight-man production crew, but I suspend disbelief.

Tuesday, September 18th

[On my way back from a literary festival in Ilkley.] Geoffrey Boycott boards the train at Wakefield. Sunburnt face with hardly a line, he sits, chewing and reading his paper, with an enviable Zen-like detachment. He wears a lightweight pale brown windcheater with the legend 'Pierre Cardin' prominently displayed.

I am honestly too nervous to go up and introduce myself. I'm like a schoolboy again and, as a schoolboy, I always had to rely on those braver than myself to break the ice in a situation like this. At the point when I've almost plucked up courage and am right beside him, a passing middle-aged lady suddenly pulls up beside me and stares – 'Michael *Palin!*' The moment is lost.

Thursday, September 20th

It's 18 months since I sat down to write a *Missionary* follow-up.

The film script has become like a mountain. I can't yet find the best way up. Have tried three or four paths, but none lead to the top. And behind all that is my ever-returning doubt as to whether the mountain is worth climbing at all.

A run on a splashy Heath. The black paint flung across Kenwood House has now been there since Monday. 'Support the Miners' and 'No Pit Closures' scrawled across the pristine south façade. It's an ugly sight. Dispiriting in every way.

Wednesday, September 26th

Steve tells me the good news – that as from this month *Jabberwocky* is in profit. After eight years my percentage is suddenly worth something – £1.20 to be precise. But I also have an unexpected bonus of £1,500 which I evidently deferred at the time.

TG arrives hot from the *Brazil* cutting rooms. 'How can I spend so much time there without the film getting any better?'

Friday, September 28th

At ten o'clock a taxi takes me to Alwyne Road, a pretty, shady little backwater in Canonbury. No. 33 is to be the location for our house in *The Dress*. It's about to be sold, or just has been, for over £300,000. Full of conspicuous luxury – jacuzzi, double bath, sauna, electrically opening bedroom curtains and so on. The small garden borders the canal. It's a very harmonious little area, not a house or a leaf out of place.

Enjoy this morning's rehearsal. Phyllis and I try the final scene for the first time. We've discussed with Eva whether this encounter should be sexual passion or more tenderness. Decide that the latter should predominate. This morning we try an embrace or two. Eva seems very happy with the result.

Friday, October 5th

A bathroom mirror shot and I'm shocked at how puffy and grey-eyed I look. Only five weeks ago I was in peak of post-Sardinia condition, now I look as if I haven't slept for weeks. Perhaps it's the cold. Phyllis and I in bed beside an open window, half-naked. Outside the skies darken and the heavens open. Very heavy rain and flashes of lightning and splitting cracks of thunder. Then a long wait for Phyllis to change make-up.

Lunch in the pub nearby, as the rain and the turbulence continues.

Phyllis (two dark rum and peppermints) and I (one and a half pints of Young's Bitter) splash back through the rain to 33 Alwyne Road.

Another wait for make-up, then from four o'clock until about nine a period of intense and concentrated work. All the energetic après-party scene to be done, as well as the delicate and vital transition from anger to love in the bedroom.

Eva seems especially happy with one of my takes, on which I feel I bring out something a bit different, something unusual for me – without eyes and teeth – just interior feelings. Phyllis is very impressive. There seems to be nothing she can't do. She has an instinctive feel for the exactly right level at which to pitch a performance, which makes even Maggie S seem laggardly. Feel I'm seeing a very good actress indeed – all she needs now are the great parts.

Our love scene together – our lyrical, camera-twirling moment of intimacy – turns out, of course, to be as workmanlike a process as putting handles on car doors. A hot and sweaty Robin Vigeon bending around us with a hand-held Arriflex, Phyllis worried about when to get out of her shoes and how to get her dress to fall at the right moment. Me tripping over her shoes at the end [of] one lyrical, sensitive, romantic take.

To bed at midnight again. Cold still flowing copiously

Saturday, October 6th

Rachel is to play my daughter. Asked to bring toys, she refuses to bring any Sindy dolls or other paraphernalia at first, then relents and brings one doll.

Camera, on a crane, is setting up for the final sequence of the dress falling to the ground after floating away from the window. The famous dress, which neither Phyllis nor I like very much, is flapping down from an invisible wire over Alwyne Road. All this takes a long time and then there are more than two hours to kill in the cold house.

Once acting, Rachel is fine; her shyness disappears as she takes on the character. Stephen, the chatty confident boy, on the other hand, clams up when asked to act.

But about half past five, in a blacked-out taxi, we finish the shooting. Champagne is produced. Eva says thank you – she's quite drained and obviously can hardly believe that it's done – and Clare says 'It's been an easy week'. 'Easy *fucking* week!' shouts Phyllis and everyone roars with laughter in relief and sympathy.

For me it's been everything I'd hoped – an exercise in acting and in becoming involved with new and talented and pleasant people. I'm not sure about my part, the script, and how it will all eventually look, but it's been a tough and concentrated and satisfying piece of work. A kick up the arse. Rachel much complimented so we end the day a lot happier than we started. And she's £25.00 better off.

After completing The Dress *and before Fegg publicity began I visited friends in America, particularly Al and Claudie in Sag Harbor. Al had had cancer treatment quite recently.*

Friday, October 12th: New York / Sag Harbor

Amongst the rest of the news in my *Times* at breakfast today – besides the Bush/Ferraro debate and the subway fires – is a small paragraph reporting a bomb in a hotel in Brighton, where Margaret Thatcher was staying for the Conservative Party Conference.

For the next two days I devote myself to Al L. At eleven a.m. am at the *New York Times* office, to see one Ed McDowell, a writer on the world of books and publishing, whom Norman Rosten[1] has put me in touch with.

In a small room which could have been an interrogation room in a police station, I'm granted an audience with McDowell, who turns out to be much less daunting than I'd been prepared for by Norman. In fact he becomes quite intrigued by the story of my involvement with Al. Thinks my loyalty is almost unbelievable – the very fact that I've come over to see this unknown writer strikes him as very ripe.

Encouraged by this I take a cab back uptown to collect a car for the journey to Sag. A silver Buick Regal from Avis on 34th.

Al and Gwenola are at the house. Claudie is working as a lunchtime waitress. Al looks stronger and fitter and less changed for the worse than I expected. In fact the loss of 15 lbs of weight improves him. He smokes his pipe, drinks his drink and is very mobile, though obviously not able to bend, stretch, lift and carry as before. Gwenola full of energy in his stead. And interest too. 'Have you got balls?' she queries as I change my trousers upstairs.

We drive out to Mecox Beach. The sea is big. I'd forgotten how impressive and monumental is the size of the Atlantic. After several hols in the Med one gets used to a tame sea. This is ocean. The wide, straight beach is deserted, left

[1] New York-born poet, playwright and novelist. He wrote a memoir of his friendship with Marilyn Monroe, and from 1979 to his death in 1995 held the title of Poet Laureate of Brooklyn.

to the big, spray-clouded waves that steam in. Gwenola and I paddle and run up and down. I feel light and airy and happy to be out of New York for a while.

Saturday, October 13th: Sag Harbor

Wake occasionally in the night to the gratifying sound of a rising wind in the powerful Norwegian maple tree outside. Go for a walk around the neat and pretty streets by the house. It's a blustery, overcast morning, despite the forecast of sun. Generally low, timber-framed, weather-boarded houses, most detached with garden space generously distributed and many of them well over 100 years old. No-one else is walking at nine o'clock, though. Everyone slides by in their quiet, powerful cars.

Al talks quite openly and often about his new artificial defecatory system. Shows me all the bags and the tubes and seems quite happy now about having no working asshole any more. He also talks about the hospital – the horrors and the humours of which will doubtless come out in a new book.

Friday, October 19th

Wake to rain and blustery wind. A few calls, then down to Fox viewing theatre in the West End for my second look at *Brazil*. Some cuts, especially towards the end, make it easier to follow and maintain the tension well. The bombing sequences with people being pulled from the wreckage, indeed the whole terrorist/paramilitary security force there suddenly very relevant after the Brighton bombing and growing controversy over police methods in the miners' strike.

At the end Terry is surrounded by besuited distribution and marketing men. Clearly they are excited. Pass on one or two of my thoughts, then TG is swept upstairs to a distributors' 'working lunch'. Leave him to it and grab a couple of pork pies and a cup of tea and eat them as I walk back through the rain to the car park.

Wednesday, October 24th

To a launch for 'The Young Ones', book *Bachelor Boys*. It's at Ronnie Scott's and the place is already packed.

Ben Elton signs a book for me (to Rachel) and Rik Mayall (the only one of the cast there) hangs around like me at the stairs that lead into the main part of the club, largely because there's hardly an inch of open space through which to move further.

A Sphere Books rep rather anxiously asks Rik if he's going to mingle. 'Well I'm sort of mingling here,' he indicates vaguely. He's going to the National to play in *The Government Inspector*, but first is doing a tour with Ben Elton. I ask where I can see it, and he says Slough would probably be the nearest.

They're not doing any more *Young Ones*, apparently. The bus over the cliff at the end of the last episode was meant to be a final statement. There's something serious about the way he refers to this that restrains me from saying that it was only in the last series that I'd really got to know and want to see more of the dreadful characters, and that surely they shouldn't quit now.

Out into the rain and back home for Rachel's open day. Neat, very thorough work. Lots of ticks and 'excellents', but still a tendency to invert letter order in the more difficult words. But her teacher Miss Kendall is lovely and full of humour. Rachel can't wait to leave for school these mornings and can't wait to come back and play schools in the evening. But she definitely wants to be an actress.

Romaine Hart rang.[1] She raved about *Private Function*. Was only concerned that from her meetings with HandMade she caught the feeling that they were not prepared to push it as hard as she thinks it deserves.

She also said that it was the first film at the London Film Festival to sell out and has been six times over-subscribed!

Saturday, October 27th

I wake with a slowly developing near-panic at the thought of an unplanned Saturday ahead. Why should this be? Outside the sun shines from a clear sky, which unsettles me. Makes me feel I should be in the country, or somewhere with a garden into which the sun reaches for more than six months of the year.

Read in the newspaper of screenwriters meeting at the NFT for a weekend to discuss their problems. Problems I share and with which I sympathise. But I'm not there – I'm here at home, feeling aimless. I read of the CND march in Barrow to protest against the building of four submarines, each of which will carry warheads capable of delivering 7,200 times the force of the Hiroshima bomb. And I'm here at home, sitting upstairs basking in the sunshine.

I feel inadequate because I can't teach my children any practical crafts and skills, because I know so few. I feel inadequate that I have no plans to take them

---

[1] Romaine founded the very successful chain of 'Screen' cinemas in and around London.

to see this and that in London – concerts or walks or museums. But, having enjoyed a life of not having to go out at weekends amongst the crowds, I've become spoilt.

There's work to do, of course – limericks to write, film scripts to be looked at and ahead a massive programme of signings and interviews – but where to start, where to begin, what to do?

Force myself away from this slippery slope and decide to take Rachel on a mystery tour. She loves the idea and we set off after lunch. First to Tower Bridge, where, for the first time, we climb the towers and walk along the linking crossways, with views out over the city and the river down to Greenwich.

By lucky chance there is a raising of the bridge as we are there. We watch it from some abandoned jetty a little upstream from the Tower. We find ourselves beside the 'William Curtis Ecological Park', an old lorry park which two years ago was filled with soil and boulders and is now a sort of controlled wasteland.

Rachel and I talk with a girl who is working there. It will only last for two more years – that's as long as developers can keep their hands off the site – but she shows us other places in London where similar conservation experiments are going on. It's the accidental, surprise nature of this little patch with its view of the Tower of London across the river which makes both of us respond so eagerly to it.

Wednesday, October 31st

I'm at Lime Grove Studios by 6.15.

Dr Fegg's dummy has arrived and is sitting vacuously in the studio on one of the sofas. In a crowded make-up room, re-introduce myself to Frank Bough and learn for the first time that there is hot news about. Just over an hour ago word came from Delhi that Mrs Gandhi has been shot.

Apologise for being here to do something as frivolous as 'Fegg' publicity on such a day, but Bough grins reassuringly. 'I'm damn glad you're here . . . we'll need some light relief.'

Frank, ear doubtless buzzing with unconfirmed rumours that the ruler of India is dead, manfully reads 'Sawing a Lady in Half' and 'Daffodils go Ping and Oink'! Even he seems to run out of patience at the end and sums up with a broad smile 'And we're expected to buy this rubbish this Christmas?'

It's not until 7.45 that the 'unconfirmed' becomes 'confirmed' and the BBC newsmen rub their hands in glee. All systems go. Interviews, race for the first obituary, phone links with Delhi.

Meanwhile in a small back room are gathered Terry, myself, Rick Wakeman, Johnny Cash, Stan Orme MP, Ray Buckton of the TUC, two asthmatics, a man with a pumpkin and the author of a book on haunted Britain.

Cash nods courteously and introduces himself to everybody. 'Hi! John Cash.' We bask in modest glow of pride as the Great Man tells of his visit to the Python show at City Center, New York. Says he loved it. Oh God ... I can't cope. Elvis Presley a fan, now Johnny Cash ... Is nothing sacred?

Rick Wakeman is relentlessly cheery and invites us – 'if you're in the Camberley area on Thursday' – to his stag night, at which a pornographic Punch and Judy show will be the highlight. 'The crocodile does *amazing* things,' Rick enthuses.

Unexpected reaction from Weidenfeld's John Curtis – he likes the novel and wants to publish!

In the evening I drive Tom and friend to King's Cross, from where he embarks for his sixteenth birthday present – a parachute drop, after two days' training near Peterborough.

Monday, November 5th

Catch the North London train from Gospel Oak at a quarter to eight. Still feeling rather grumpy and not happy at the prospect of three more days Fegging. Encounter TJ in the bookstall at Liverpool Street. His nose is red and slightly swollen, the end of it covered in scabs and scratches. I ask him what happened. 'A woman bit it,' he explains. For some reason, I'm not as surprised as I should be.

TJ lost his temper with a difficult boy at a firework display and sharply ticked him off. Some time later a man knocked on his door and asked 'Are you the man who beat up my son?' Terry, now quite reasonable, denied that he'd 'beaten up' anybody. The man repeated his question. TJ, again sweet reasonableness, was about to ask him in to discuss the whole question, when out of the darkness sprang a woman, teeth bared, who bit Terry on the end of the nose and wouldn't let go. In her fury she tore at his hair and yelled and screamed and eventually TJ could only force her off by poking her in the eye (a form of attack much used by JC in Python sketches).

One British Rail breakfast later, he's feeling much better and quite relieved to have an excuse to be out of London. Norwich is reached at a quarter to eleven, we're met at the station. Terry is asked about his nose by the rep. We are taken straightaway to Radio Norfolk, where Terry is asked about his nose again.

Talk to local journalists, sign some stock copies, explain about TJ's nose, then we are unleashed on the public. The public are unfortunately not unleashed on us, and they come through in a very thin trickle – lots of buck-passing from shop to rep to sales department, but it's clear that a midday Monday in Norwich is not a peak book-buying time.

On 'Look East' the big story of our visit is of course . . . Terry's nose. With close-ups and everything. The nasal damage is worth more than any Fegg dummy.

The pleasantest part of the day is a half-hour break when TJ and I saunter round the cathedral. We walk the cloisters talking about the Lollards.

Tuesday, November 6th: Manchester

To the 'Stuart Hall Radio Show'. Stuart Hall is not of this world as I know it. I just can't work him out. At no point in our talk, or our interview, is there the slightest evidence that he's heard, or understood anything we're saying. He's not rude, he's not loud or aggressive, he just doesn't seem to be quite there. Only when he is talking about himself as a collector and showing us watches or magnifying glasses does he really seem to come alive. Quite curious really.

Wednesday, November 7th: Leeds

After breakfast – and confirmation that Reagan has won every state but two[1] – we begin our day's work at Radio Aire. I feel rather perky today. Is it because I know it's the last day? Is it perhaps because the Radio Aire interviewer is very grateful to me for speaking to him during *Private Function* in Bradford, when no-one else in the cast would? But it helps me through the day and I don't feel as imbecile and facetiously trivial as on previous days.

Thursday, November 8th

Time for a run this morning before a busy day of *Private Function* publicity.

The questions are friendly and generally concern the pig, though I'm asked whether or not it was difficult to play a part so obviously suited to Alan Bennett with Alan Bennett present. I'd never really thought of it like that.

On to L'Escargot for dinner with Robert H and Erica.

Robert vehement that I should not let Weidenfeld have my novel. He says that Lord W is trying to sell the company, that its heyday is over, that it's going to get terribly stung over the Jagger biog and that they are 'celebrity' publishers

---

[1] In fact, Reagan won every state except for DC and Minnesota, the home state of his Democratic challenger Walter Mondale. Reagan took 58.8% of the total vote, Mondale 40.6%.

who will publish more because of who you are than what you've done. He's very fierce. And John Curtis is his publisher.

Home after midnight.

Saturday, November 10th

As I eat breakfast I hear on the radio of the Lord Mayor's Procession and, lured by the sun, I suggest that Rachel and I go down to see it. The procession is jolly, but full of floats it's very hard to cheer – the National Clearing Banks, the Solicitors' Society, Tate and Lyle Sugar, the Stock Exchange, British Telecom, British Airways. An uneasy mixture of rich modern companies in a curiously eighteenth-century-style procession.

'Rule Britannia' precedes the Lord Mayor's coach. This is pure panto – a baroque gold-leaved extravaganza from which the Lord Mayor leans, beaming and waving as if just about to go into a song.

To cap our morning out we pass by Sir John Soane's house on our way back. It is open, so I am able to introduce Rachel to this wonderful treasure trove, with so much more atmosphere than a modern museum. The sense of the continuity of the place with its maker suffuses the house quite magically.

A McDonald's at Warren Street, then home. Make myself a smoked salmon sandwich and, with a glass of Puligny-Montrachet, settle up in my workroom to catch the last of the sunshine.

Don't respond awfully well at first to the arrival of Julian Hough. He's clearly on some downward self-destructive curve. He says he finds familiar places very comforting in his present state and claims to have visited Buckingham Palace twice already today. He fairly rapidly drinks two glasses of Puligny-Montrachet '73, then, with that strange walk of his, arms by his sides hardly moving, he launches off into the outside world again. It's like seeing someone in great pain and being powerless to help.

Monday, November 12th

Taxi to Wardour Street at nine, for post-synch on *The Dress*. Waiting at the lift in Film House when Phyllis hurries in. She looks rushed and a bit tired. She's come down from Glasgow on the sleeper.

A concentrated three and a half hours' work, ending up with re-voicing (and re-noising!) our love scene most unromantically. Kissing with one eye on the screen. Passion to picture.

Eva, Clare D, Phyllis and I have lunch at the Golden Horn – a Turkish establishment with lots of unpronounceable dishes, one of which is translated as 'brain salad'. *The Dress* is to be premiered on the last day of the London Film Festival, after Louis Malle's new film.

Tuesday, November 13th

Drive down to Camberwell for our first day's work on *Secrets*[1] with Paul Zimmerman. A long and ugly drive down in clogged traffic and as my feelings for the project itself are equivocal, I'm in rather a negative mood when Paul Z opens the door to me at five past ten.

Nor is there any chance of acclimatisation with Paul. He works from the moment he opens the door with a constant patter of quick Jewish patois. He's very funny and very sharp, but in the end the remorselessness of the stream of asides, ideas, self-deprecations, is rather like facing an endless stream of ace serves. I'm constantly retrieving balls from the back of the court.

From this frenetic display of words very few constructive ideas appear. I worry that whatever Paul does to *Secrets* he won't be able to make it English. He acknowledges this and expects that he will 'sort out the structure ... put the whole thing together', then leave us to Anglicise it.

Thursday, November 15th

I leave for Terry's at ten to nine. The fog lifts by the Thames and sunlight sparkles off St Paul's dome and the river and from a thousand windows. Ahead South London is still mist-blanketed. The contrast is very beautiful.

On the way down I hear a vintage piece of phone-iniana. Peter Stringfellow, the Sheffield steelworker's son turned millionaire London club owner, talks some good, homely nonsense but occasionally reveals alarming gaps in the otherwise almost cosmic scale of his knowledge. 'Can I ask Mr Stringfellow for his views on vivisection?' A pause, then, boldly and sincerely, 'Well, I'm not against the operation, but I certainly wouldn't like it done to me, only to find I meet a girl two weeks later who I fall in love with and want to start a family.'

After what seems like forever, Sarah Ward intervenes and sorts out the misunderstanding. There is much laughter and the questioner (who does not

[1] *Secrets*, originally broadcast in August 1973 as Jones and Palin's contribution to a Mark Shivas/Richard Broke BBC series called *Black and Blue*, now began a second life as a possible movie, spurred on by Sam Goldwyn Jr. It becomes, variously, 'Consuming Passions', 'The Chocolate Film', 'Chocolates' and 'The Chocolate Project'. And eventually it does become a movie, *Consuming Passions*, 1988, directed by Giles Foster.

laugh) puts his question again ... 'Mr Stringfellow ... what *do* you feel about vivisection?' There is quite a long pause, then, finally, 'Well, what is it for a start?'

Monday, November 19th

William 14; we buy him a Toshiba head-set with radio and cassette, plus pens, pencils, a diary and all the stationery stuff he likes. Jolly breakfast.

To lunch at Sheekey's with John Curtis and Victoria Petrie-Hay, of Weidenfeld, to hear the first publisher's reaction to my novel. Curtis is, as I'd expected, middle-aged, with a roundish, ruddy face coming to a point at the chin. He looks neat and rather old-fashioned – more like a prosperous farmer than a publisher.

He runs the lunch whilst deferring to Victoria – a younger woman with dark hair and dark-rimmed eyes and a big, defiant face – on all matters of literary criticism. She is neither sycophantic nor tentative. She feels that the first third of the book is one of the best pieces of comic writing she's come across and is not in doubt that such writing could stand on its own and I need not be defensive or bashful about it. She doesn't like the Suffolk scenes and gives quite pithy reasons why not – too melodramatic, too many deaths, another change of scene, loss of good early characters, loss of early comic tone. I agree with her.

Having come along to the lunch feeling that I must be strong with myself and hold out for a completely new book (using this one as experience), I am swayed enough by her criticisms (echoed by Al and others) to consider the advantages of rewriting two-thirds of the book and carrying on with the character of Avery, who I've become quite fond of.

John wants something signed – would a contract help? I say no. Just good to know they're very keen, and I also say I can't be pushed into a date for further work, what with 'First Love' looming, but that I will come back to them first. 'You can write,' says the dark-eyed lady with great enthusiasm, and that is the best part of the lunch.

Tuesday, November 20th

Cab down to Theatre Royal, Haymarket. 'Panto rehearsal, is it?' asks the driver solicitously. I tell him it's a press reception for a new film. He sounds vaguely disappointed ... 'Ah, well ... so long as you're busy, that's the main thing.'

At the portals of the Theatre Royal by 12.30; the daily press film critics have just seen the film. Denholm is there, with Liz Smith (faithful troopers) and the three of us are photographed with the poster – which looks very strong, perhaps Malcolm won his case after all.

Maggie arrives later, setting up a flurry of cameras and notebooks. Indicating the extraordinarily close proximity of the boxes at stage level, she says 'Olivier was there last night. A bit disconcerting. He has to be as close as possible, poor dear. Deaf as a post.' [Maggie was currently appearing at the Theatre Royal as Millamant in *The Way of the World*.]

The high point of the occasion is having Dilys Powell introduced to me. She's small and frail and moves with difficulty, but I've rarely been opposite a face with such a combination of keenness, charity and warmth. Her big eyes sparkle with life and interest and awareness and make the noise and bustle all around seem tiresome.

Wednesday, November 21st

Both the grannies now assembled in the kitchen.

At 6.40 our taxi arrives. The weather has turned against us after a very tolerable day and it's raining hard as we draw up outside the Odeon Haymarket [for the Royal Premiere of *A Private Function*].

Talk to various friends before having to go up on stage at 7.35 for that part of the evening described forbiddingly in the programme as 'Michael Palin entertains'.

After about ten or fifteen minutes I still haven't received the signal that the Royal Person has arrived, but I've run out of things to say so I thank everyone and am shepherded back up the auditorium to await with my fellow thespians. Denholm has gone to Marrakesh, Maggie and Alan are both acting, so the line consists of Liz Smith, Alison S, John Normington, Bill P, Richard Griffiths and myself.

The Princess walks down from 'Foyer 1', where she's met Malcolm and Val, his wife, and is introduced to us. I have quite a long chat about the film, acting with pigs and future plans.

Then we follow her into the auditorium of the Odeon. I don't think I shall ever make such an entry to a cinema again. Distant memories of slinking furtively into the grubby darkness of the Palace Union Street nearly 30 years ago come into my mind, but tonight I am entering the Odeon Haymarket behind Princess Anne to the sound of a fanfare.

Well-combed, expensively coiffured heads turn as we file into Row T. Princess Anne's place is denoted by a lone antimacassar carefully laid over the back of the seat. The National Anthem is played and I feel terribly important. Just in front and to the right my little mother cranes round for a better view.

Poor Princess Anne has to sit with a programme and a bouquet of flowers on her lap throughout.

The film looks and sounds very good and there is plenty of laughter, though the various royal references – 'My wife has two topics of conversation – one is the Royal Family, the other is her bowels' – take on a new frisson of significance.

At the end Princess Anne, with Helen, myself and the Mowbrays dutifully following, file out in a silent line. Then she is gone and we soon follow – to a reception at Maxim's.

As the two grannies, Angela, Veryan, Helen and myself struggle past the Comedy Theatre (scene of my first London acting appearance 20 years ago) in the wind and rain, the photographers suddenly surge forward and, pushing us to one side, direct a salvo of flashes at a long, sleek, black limousine, from which emerge Ringo Starr and Barbara Bach and Olivia Harrison.

Once the Princess has gone we move to a sit-down supper. Goulash is very ordinary and my bridge comes out in it. Neither Malcolm nor Maggie show up, which I find remarkable, but the rest of us enjoy ourselves.

Thursday, November 29th

A wonderful review in the *Guardian* – 'nothing would give me greater pleasure than to see this film in the top box-office earners next week' – but the expected dampener from *Time Out*. Richard Rayner takes the same view as the *Melody Maker* – the acting is fine, but the film is a mess. A Bennett taken to task for not facing 'the realities' of the rationing period. It's a slipshod review, praising, in the cast, one 'Richardson', which shows how accurately they have faced up to the realities of the film.

Work on 'First Love' in the morning and limericks in the afternoon. Teatime greatly improved by a rave Alexander Walker review in the *Standard*. 'I'm glad I lived long enough to see it!'

Ring Mother who sounds a bit low. She's 'coping', but I'm a little worried. Probably suffering post-Royal Premiere depression.

Friday, November 30th

To lunch with Richard Loncraine at L'Étoile. Tells a good story of actor Lou Gossett, with whom RL worked, for a while, on *Enemy Mine*. RL once asked him, in one of their rare moments of philosophical intimacy, what was the one thing Lou really enjoyed. 'I'll tell you, Richard – it's fucking and sushi.' 'That's two, Lou,' suggested RL ... 'Hell, it's the same thing to me,' replied the megastar cryptically.

A night at home. Evening ends with me becoming rather hooked on a snooker semi-final between Higgins and Thorburn – both of whom have a marvellous, battered, dissolute charisma which is so much more refreshing than the boring, bland healthiness of the Coes and Steve Davises, the Torvills and Deans. Long live Alex Higgins and his fags and beer. Though, the way he goes on, he probably won't!

Sunday, December 2nd

In the Sundays – 'Fegg's' first appearance in the best-seller lists, at No. 6 on the 'General' chart, and a nice review of 'Fegg' by Russell Davies in the *Observer*, opposite the Philip French rave for *Private Function*. A nice feeling for a Sunday morning. The brief, illusory satisfaction of being wanted.

Then down to the Lumiere for the world premiere of *The Dress*. Lumiere full – six to seven hundred people. A Louis Malle film, *Crackers*, on first, and before that Derek Malcolm 'informally' introduces Eva S, Phyllis and myself to the throng.

I really don't like going to the cinema like this. Miss the dark anonymity – here are Phyllis and I now, marked men and women. *Crackers* is not very good Heavily played comedy. Louis Malle crying out for a Woody Allen to show him how to direct a comedy of charm and wit.

Then it's over and almost without pause we're into *The Dress* I think that this is a mistake, and does not help distance *The Dress* from comedy, which, with me in it, the audience clearly expects. They begin to titter early on.

I found my performance difficult to judge as I was not required to play for laughs – so none of my conventional yardsticks of success applied. 'Serious' acting of the sort I do in *The Dress* seems to be dangerously easy to do and my feeling at the end is one of confusion. I sense that in Helen who thought it very funny to be watching me being so serious.

Wednesday, December 5th: London–Southwold

At Liverpool Street the big expensive, automatic destination board is still only half-working. The lead story in my newspaper is of another fatal rail accident – the sixth in as many months. It looks to me as if the railway system is very near breaking point.

I take deep breaths and try to control my bitter feelings about what Margaret Thatcher's war against organised labour is costing this country. I feel these are darker days even than in the early '70's when Heath took on the miners. This time people are paying for 'strong government' with their lives.

But all these awfulnesses seem less immediate as I reach Suffolk and eventually step off the train at Darsham to find my exiguous mater, stooped and thinner in the legs, scouring the incoming train with a frown.

The field behind the house is full of potato-pickers. They're aided by a mechanical plough, a tractor-trailer and a fork-lift truck, but the picking of the potatoes from the cloggy earth is done by hand. There are a dozen figures, well wrapped in thick coats, scrabbling the potatoes into old fertiliser bags. Bent over the job. Old-fashioned, unskilled agricultural labour in the wind and the rain, a hundred yards away from where I sit at my desk trying to pick the right words out of the equally cloggy soil of my imagination.

Thursday, December 6th: Southwold

Wake at half past eight. Low cloud and rain. No potato-pickers. Work until one. Weather clears and temperature drops sharply without cloud cover.

Mother said quite categorically that she doesn't like driving the car any more, and, as nearly categorically as she's ever been, that she can't foresee another winter at Croft Cottage.

Reckon I've spent about ten hours this week on *East of Ipswich* (as I'm provisionally calling 'First Love') – the progress has all been forward and quite exciting.

Sunday, December 9th

At the London Palladium for something in the nature of a good turn to J Cleese, who was committed but is filming in the US. We're supporting the Oncology Club – oncology being the study of tumours – and it's a big house to fill.

Terry and I look like the oldest members of the cast – which I realise with a shock we probably are. Neil [Innes] is there to cheer us up. He's given up smoking, on his 40th birthday.

I open the show – almost on time at 7.30 – with the 'Politician's Speech', which goes well, but not ecstatically.

Alexei Sayle begins the assault on the audience with a display of manic energy and lots of 'fucking' and 'cunting'. Chris Langham has a lot of wanking jokes and Rik Mayall does a piece about an elephant giving someone a blow-job in an Italian restaurant. This last marvellous.

It's over by 10.30 and we go to a small party at which Neil is given a birthday cake in the shape of a piano. All the foul-mouthed 'alternative' comedians sit quietly with their wives or girlfriends.

Wednesday, December 12th

Am settling down to watch *Oxbridge Blues* when the door bell rings and there is the red face and sad apologetic smile of Julian Hough. He spent last night in the cells, he claims. He's no money and has resorted to stealing – rather proud of the fact that he took a bottle of white wine and a jar of caviar from a shop in Hampstead – and then went back for some carrots.

Sunday, December 16th

M Mowbray tells me that Mr Gorbachev – the Soviet No. 2[1] visiting the UK at the moment – has requested a print of *A Private Function* to be delivered to the Soviet Embassy! Alan apparently very pleased.

Monday, December 17th

To Duke's Hotel for a Python meal.

GC and EI discuss the relative merits of cocaine – 'A killer . . . keep off it,' counsels Eric fiercely – and acid, which both agree taken in the right circumstances with the right people can be marvellous. Graham says he played snooker under acid and 'couldn't do anything wrong. Potted every one'.

EI has been doing Lampoon's '*Vacation* II'. He said that at least he was keeping up his record of having appeared 'only in flops' apart from the Python films.

At the end of a very good meal, I, a little playfully, ask of the gathering when we might all work together again.

A Python History of America emerges as front runner. A totally fabricated history using facts as and when we want them – rather on the lines of GC's *Liar's Autobiography*.

Best feeling about our little reunion was the reaffirmation that when we are all in accord there is no more satisfying group to work with. The shorthand that exists between us all cannot be replicated outside. This bond is stronger than it ever was – a bond of people of roughly the same age who have shared a unique experience. I hope we can be something more than a luncheon club.

---

[1] Konstantin Chernenko was the President of the USSR until his death in March 1985 when Gorbachev succeeded him.

Wednesday, December 19th

Across the West End to St James's Park on my way to a lunch given by the Chancellor of the Duchy of Lancaster *and* Minister of the Arts, Lord Gowrie.

I approach behind a seedy figure in a dull brown overcoat who turns out to be Alan Bennett. So pleased to see him I give him a big hug. The security man has my name in the book, but not Alan's. 'Oh well, up you go anyway,' he says to him.

Room 622 is the office of Lord Gowrie. A small collection of mixed artistes – Ronnie Scott is sitting already talking, there's Cleo Laine and Melvyn Bragg and Stephen Frears. Why are we all here? seems to be the general theme of most of the conversations.

Bob Geldof, definitely the man of the moment for writing and organising the Band Aid Christmas record for Ethiopia, arrives bristling over the government's decision to collect VAT money on the record – which everyone had made for nothing. The Minister of Arts, sensing this, seems to spend a lot of time grinning at whatever the unshaven Boomtown Rat says.

Jeremy Isaacs – who has done an excellent job with Channel 4, I feel – comes across to tell me that the IBA have refused clearance to put the *Life of Brian* on TV – even at 11.15 at night. It might offend 'Christian sensibilities' they say. Isaacs is hopping mad and looking forward to a fight.

Monday, December 31st

Visited Beatties [the model railway shop]. Collected various accessories, including trees and a lot of people – 'army personnel', 'commuters', etc – all in little bags. Ian Davidson later suggests they should have little models of well-known people – like 'Sir Harold Nicolson'.

On the way back I stopped at Alan Alan's Magic Shop in Southampton Row, where I was served by a small, neat, be-suited gentleman with an arrow through his head. Quickly and efficiently he demonstrated an extraordinary variety of bangs, squirts, farts and electric shocks as if he were selling nothing more exciting than a coal scuttle. Little children watched in awe as their fathers idly toyed with a pack of sexy playing cards only to receive a sharp electric shock from the pack. I bought a variety of revolving and lighting-up bow ties, an exploding pen, dribbling glass, etc, etc, to give as presents at our New Year's Eve party.

For me a curious year. *Private Function* the unexpected highlight. *Brazil*, hard and salutary experience, looks like distinguishing itself in 1985. But I'd not found in 1984 a new and successful vein of creative writing. The limericks are slight, the 'Vikings' unsatisfactory, 'Fegg' fun and frivolity.

Best moment of the year is in the picture beside me as I write. Mother, hardly bigger than the railings behind her, standing, with a broad smile, on the snowy sidewalk of Brooklyn Heights, with the buildings of Southern Manhattan mushrooming behind her. Journey of the year, undoubtedly.

1985

Thursday, January 3rd

The papers are full of news of the *Life of Brian* ban by the IBA. *Guardian* reports/describes the film as 'parodying the life of Christ'. This misrepresentation irritates me and I spend the first working hour composing a letter to the paper.

Turn down four days' work on a P&O Ferries ad and a training film for a company called Interlink. Wash the Mini, take our old video recorder round to Alison Davies and meet her dog called Burglar. She says she does find calling him in at night quite silly.

Monday, January 7th

In the evening Rachel and I go to BAFTA for a special screening of *The Dress*. An overflowing house, with more than a dozen standing at the back.

Flurries of laughter at moments when I feel the film is taking itself too seriously, but apart from those and the fact that my shirt collar doesn't look as though it fits properly, I quite like the piece, or at least I don't cringe with embarrassment as I did at the Lumiere showing.

Rachel is quite pleased with herself too, and probably will never be as excited again by seeing her name on the credits.

Eva tells me that it will be going out in this country with *Beverly Hills Cop*, the Eddie Murphy film which is currently one of the biggest successes ever in the US.

David Leland rings with words of praise. 'Is there another side of Michael Palin I don't know about?' he'd asked himself. He thinks 'reaction' acting is the hardest of all to do. I still think it's the easiest.

Saturday, January 12th

After early shopping, take Rachel on a little birthday trip to the Bethnal Green Museum.

Then I take her to Islington to pick up a key for the Art Deco clock I bought for TG's birthday, then lunch together at the Pizza Express there. We do enjoy ourselves and, on Rachel's last day in single figures, I can't help but feel glad that I'm enjoying her growing up — that I don't have a romantic, nostalgic, escapist longing for her to be five or six again.

A rather ordinary evening, enlivened a little by Tom arriving home about ten with 'some friends', five out of six of whom are women. They process through the house to No. 2. I feel like one of the exhibits at the Bethnal Green Museum, sitting by the fire reading my *New Statesman* as they peer curiously through the glass door at me.

Sunday, January 13th

Watch a very impressive programme on Alan Bleasdale. I envy his street wit, and his delight in writing and, in Bleasdale's case, the seriousness and urgency and fluency with which he seems to be able to write about now. Working-class writers seem to have much more to say about the present state of things. But will he be hoiked up by his talents into a sort of honorary middle-class writer? Watching the programme made me want to buckle down to my own writing. To produce something with some edge, some guts . . .

Wednesday, January 16th

No fresh snow, but bitter cold. I hear that this is likely to be the coldest day in London for 20 years. Wrap up well, in double-sweater order, and once again get to grips with *East of Ipswich*. Pleased with the morning's progress. Am very strict about not answering the phone until one o'clock and it helps.

Phone my mother, who is resigned to her 'imprisonment' and re-plan my visit to Southwold for next Tuesday. Angela phones — Chilton without water despite being surrounded by a moat, which is frozen enough to skate on.

Some masochistic streak in me has me pulling on my tracksuit at two and off for a run. I've met most conditions in the five years I've been a Heath regular, but never cold as intense as this, and I feel I have to try it — one, because I feel I need exercise, and two, because it's there.

Monday, January 21st

Afternoon curtailed by an interview at the Python office with Michael Owen of the *Standard*. He's a card. A wry, gossipy, ruddy-faced little man. Sardonic and quite bitchy. He'd seen *Brazil* (although he doesn't admit so to start with) and couldn't make head or tail of it. I say I'm glad he isn't the cinema critic and ask where Mr Walker is these days . . . 'Oh, in Hong Kong,' says Owen, 'doing something or other for the CIA.' Alexander Walker and the CIA, that's a new one.

Our chat, based on his viewing of *The Dress*, which he liked, is a little defensive – testing each other's tolerance towards teasing. He is one of the few journalists whom Maggie S gets on with. He describes her as a very rare and delicate thoroughbred, but admits that this is not the kind of thing he could say to her face ... 'You make me sound like a bloody horse,' he mimics, quite accurately.

Maggie is to get the *Standard* award for Millamant, he confides, indiscreetly.

Thursday, January 24th: Southwold

Put Mother's house once again on estate agents' lists, but this time with the serious intention of moving her within the year. The man I speak to says he has a house on the Common which is being converted into four flats. It sounds interesting. He suggests I move as quickly as possible as they are under offer already.

A light snow-shower swirls round the Common as we look at the architect's plans for the ironically-named Sunset House. The rooms look of reasonable size and, though the two ground-floor flats are already gone (to single, elderly ladies), there are two more, on the first and second floors, with two bedrooms. One of these is already being chased.

Home in good spirits, but no Helen, the fire won't light and the first stage BAFTA awards show nominations for *Private Function* as Best Film and in most categories except Best Actor. For an hour this hits me very hard, but looking at those who have been nominated (including, of course, the obligatory pair for *Killing Fields*), I realise how little chance an easy, natural, light comedy performance stands.

Monday, January 28th

To Odette's to meet Jonathan P.

He tells me that Liz Smith went all the way up to Leeds for the *Private Function* premiere last Thursday, a week early. He's getting quite a steady flow of job offers, including eight weeks in Samoa and Australia playing Robert Louis Stevenson. 'If only it weren't so bloody far away,' he mutters, rather gloomily.

Tuesday, January 29th

Best news of the day comes from John Kelleher at HandMade. *The Missionary* has finally been sold to a French distributor. They've had good reactions to their screenings and are spending 200,000 Francs on the launch!!! Les peanuts, mais c'est quelque chose.

Kelleher also tells me that *Private Function* is to open the LA Film Festival – Filmex – in March (as I think *Holy Grail* did about ten years ago). And *Private Function* has been selected for the Un Certain Regard category of the Cannes Film Festival – 'the second most prestigious category' as JK describes it.

See Maggie collect an *Evening Standard* award for Best Theatre Actress of '84. Maggie accepts it nervously and yet still has time to complain about the lack of heating in the Haymarket dressing rooms.

Monday, February 4th

I take a taxi to the Inn on the Park to meet Marvin Antonowsky, who called me yesterday. He hugs me to his bosom and then we have a drink and a chat.

He loves *Brazil* and likes to see himself as Terry's supporter against Sid Sheinberg. Sid S wants to cut the picture with Terry. Marvin thinks Terry should cut it without Sid, make ten minutes' difference, and then Sid S would be happy. Trouble stems from the contractual requirement to supply a 125-minute film, no more. TG has supplied a 140-minute film.

To Fitzroy Square to meet Tony Ross, who is to illustrate the limericks. He is a boyish, middle-aged man. He's soft-spoken, enthusiastic and went to art school with John Lennon. At one time he knew more guitar chords than John and claims to be the only man who was asked to join the Beatles but turned it down!

Wednesday, February 13th

Richard Benjamin[1] has rung Anne re a film part he wants me to do (via Spielberg's Amblin Entertainment). He's in town and would like to meet. The script is sent over. It's called *The Money Pit* (heart falls at the title) and it's by David Giler. There are hundreds of relentlessly funny New York Jewish one-liners, but the whole lacks any real warmth, depth of character or indeed charm of any kind.

---

[1] Actor, (*Goodbye Columbus*, 1969) producer and director. *The Money Pit* was eventually made with Tom Hanks, Shelley Long and Alexander Godunov in the lead roles and released in 1986.

I am to play the part of a successful, sexually irresistible orchestra conductor. Well . . . I ask you.

Sunday, March 10th

To collect papers at ten. Mr Nice Man[1] has been attacked in his shop. Three days ago at four o'clock a boy of 15 or 16, wearing a mask and holding a gun, came into the shop with a bag which he laid on the counter and asked Mr N to fill with the money. He struck Mr N and as he fell down behind the counter he grabbed at something beneath it to break his fall. The 'gunboy' thought he was going to a weapon or an alarm and rushed off.

What can this intelligent, polite, hard-working Asian make of this country? I notice a greater contrast than usual between the US and the UK on my return [from *Private Function* publicity in New York & LA]. There seems to be a weariness here, a lack of direction, a lack of unity, a low national morale (the defeat of the miners is only seen as a great victory by the Thatcherites) and a feeling, quite unlike the States, that the bad news can only get worse.

Monday, March 11th

To the family dentist – Mr Lewis – in Camden Town. I no longer have enough confidence in Gerry Donovan to replace the constantly ejecting bridge. Quite a break, after 20 years with Gerry, whom I liked very much, except as a dentist.

Lewis's surgery is busy, unglamorous and informal. He is a very direct, no-nonsense Northerner, and impressed by the state of my mouth. 'Quite a battlefield in there,' he mutters in some awe. But he sounds much more businesslike than Gerry and clearly relishes sorting it all out.

I ring Susan Richards [at Enigma] for her reaction to *East of Ipswich*. She likes it and, more encouragingly, says she feels it is much nearer a finished product than a first draft. Puttnam and Goldcrest sound like parting company over the *First Love* series, which hasn't been a financial success, and Susan R has a Machiavellian plan to try and get them to drop *East of Ipswich* so it can then be taken to Anglia TV, who she thinks will absolutely leap at it.

---

[1] Our family name for Mahendra 'Mash' Patel, who ran, and still runs, our local newsagents. He has a wonderful temperament and apparently limitless reserves of patience and tolerance.

Saturday, March 16th

Helen's taxi arrives at 4.30, which must be a record for early starts.[1] She looks almost unfairly bright and breezy considering the hour. Bid her goodbye from the top of the stairs, then back to bed and sleep through without difficulty for another three and a half hours.

I go up to Pizza Express with the Pryces. JP very funny about the 'celebrity' screening of *Brazil* at which no-one recognised him. He didn't mind so much before the film, but when, after two hours 22 minutes constantly on the screen, very often in searing close-up, the first person to come up to him afterwards said 'Are you Patrick?' he could take it no longer.

Tuesday, March 19th

Trying to keep up my resolution to catch up on movies while Helen is away, I drive down to Cinecenta to see *1984*. It impresses me a lot, though I can see why [Michael] Radford got annoyed with the grafting on of the Eurythmics soundtrack. He keeps very tight control of the picture and it's only when the modern music comes in that it begins to sound like a pop video.

Struck by the similarities with *Brazil*. The police state, the dreadful grubbiness of the city, the love story which is at the heart of the action, the tiling in the torturer's cell, the design of [Richard] Burton's office, even the chair in Room 101 itself and the eventual destruction of the central character. It's all there in both films.

But whereas Radford keeps his nasty tale tightly under control, TG fires off in all directions. Difference between the two people, I suppose. But Radford's careful, wordy approach to his adaptation of the Orwell tale produces considerable yawns and restlessness, which I've never heard in a *Brazil* screening. Mind you, you can never hear anything in a *Brazil* screening apart from the film.

Monday, March 25th

To see Mr Lewis for preparation work on my new bridge.

Lewis is the complete renaissance dentist. He rambles on – no, ramble is not the word to describe his delivery, it's more abrasive, views expressed challengingly, inviting confrontation, which it's hard to provide with a mouth

---

[1] She was leaving for what had become annual skiing excursions with friends from her badminton class. This one was to Val d'Isère.

half full of mould-making gunge. Anyway, in an hour and a half he covers a wide ground from dentistry (which he loves), psychoanalysts (whom he doesn't like), nineteenth-century English watercolourists (who he not only likes, but collects and knows a lot about), to Russian drama (which he goes to see regularly with his wife, who is a Russian) and to holidays in a camper in Southern Turkey. Turkey he likes very much because it is as he remembered Greece (now spoilt) 25 years ago.

He enjoys playing to a captive audience, but does his job skilfully and carefully and with a pride in the result which dear Gerry never seemed to convey.

Tuesday, March 26th

The Missionary has won top prize at a festival of 'humorous films' at the French Alpine town of Chamrousse (which I check in the atlas. It *does* exist; it's near Grenoble).

A Private Function increased its take in NYC this weekend and went up in its second week in Boston. In the UK it will have grossed a million pounds by the end of the month and hopefully one and a half million pounds by mid-May. So over a third of the initial production cost could be cleared in the UK alone.

Wednesday, March 27th

Shivas sends over Canby's latest from the *New York Times*. He has written a long piece criticising the tendency to 'cynical' comedy – the Hollywood genre of *Ghostbusters, Porky's, Risky Business*, etc – and contrasting with 'sceptical' comedies exemplified by *Purple Rose of Cairo* and 'the delightful new British import *A Private Function*'. 'Performed with dazzling assurance by Miss Smith, Mr Palin, Denholm Elliott . . . *A Private Function* is a comedy of the first order . . .'.

To lunch at Odette's with Walmsley to give him the Glen Baxter entitled 'Walmsley seemed to be experiencing some difficulty with the seafood salad' – at which our waiter laughs so much he is unable to describe the vegetables and another, more serious waiter has to come and replace him.

Monday, April 1st: Glasgow

To Glasgow for *Private Function* publicity. A photo with the Lord Provost and two pigs in a pen outside the Odeon. The Lord Provost is a game little Scotsman who reluctantly enters the pen where two hairy pigs – one of which I'm assured is a boar – snuffle violently for food in a bucket, which I hold. The photographers shout at him as if he were some witless object – 'Lord Provost! Look up!'

Then into the theatre to talk to the audience after the screening. The film seems to have been appreciated. Sign autographs and generally receive good feedback from the young in the audience.

Then more photos with the pigs and the Lord Provost outside in the street. One of the pigs is snapping greedily – just like the photographers – and despite my warning that the food has run out they keep me in there until it bites my finger quite sharply, draws blood and at last they believe me.

Thursday, April 4th

Up to Hampstead to address the Hampstead Gay Community. The organiser apologised in advance for some recent poor attendances. He said that a well-known writer 'who shall be nameless' refused to speak until ten people arrived. They never did and he somewhat reluctantly spoke to nine. Last time they had an MP – Matthew Parris – who gave a complete, self-contained party political speech and no-one knew what to say afterwards.

So I am flattered to find 30 people at the Citizens' Advice Bureau – none of them looking anything other than completely respectable and demonstrating the shallowness of the archetypal 'gay' look. I respond to their general laughter and appreciation and thoroughly enjoy talking and answering questions for an hour and a half.

Friday, April 5th

After breakfast and settling and clearing my desk of immediate business, I settle down to read Paul Zimmerman's 'A Consuming Passion' as *Secrets* has now become. Full of expectations. But after a bright, but roughly-written opening, it gets stuck for page after page on a broad exploration of all the jokes about collecting human bodies, making it a heavy black farce rather than the sharp satire I'd hoped it could be.

At four I go to the Body Centre to play squash with TJ. We discuss our reactions. They're both the same. Disappointment.

Saturday, April 6th

Talk to Paul Z. He says TJ called him last night whilst 'well oiled' and was therefore able to be very frank. PZ sounds resilient, but clearly unhappy at our reaction. But Goldcrest and Goldwyn have reacted well and he (Paul) is so pleased with it, that he makes me feel rather a spoilsport. 'The ball's in your court now,' is Paul's view. 'Tell me what you want me to do.'

Tuesday, April 9th

A harassed Mr Jones arrives at half past ten. Settle down with a cup of tea. Then we begin to compare notes on the Zimmerman script, prior to meeting Paul at lunchtime.

As we talk it's clear that Terry and myself are in general agreement that what is wrong is that Paul has gone for a much too stylised, full-frontal, 'schlock' approach, emphasising the acquisition of meat and the procurement of human bodies much too directly. The tension of the concealment attempt has gone and the believability which to me seemed the raison d'être of the whole piece is shot to pieces.

It's clear that we cannot expect Paul to rewrite it on the lines we want, nor can we co-write it with Paul. Either we find a new writer altogether, or we abandon the project or Terry and I take it on.

Now, whether it's the effect of a beautiful spring morning, or sheer relief that there is a solution, or a real burst of new thoughts stimulated by Paul's work, or a combination of all three, Terry and I have not only decided that we shall write the next draft ourselves, but we've also set aside the rest of this week and dates in May and June to work on it.

Paul arrives here at one. He's as nervous as we are about 'the confrontation', but over lunch at a chic but quite deserted Belsize Village restaurant called The Orchard, all three of us discuss quite amicably and agreeably the proposed solution. Paul would like not to be 'dismissed from the case' completely, but to be there to advise and criticise. 'Use me, I'm quite good really.'

Sunday, April 14th

The *Sunday Times* echoes the prevalent optimism about London with a colour supplement devoted to the revival of the city. Periodically London is rediscovered, it blossoms then fades back into its elusive ordinariness whilst somewhere else is discovered. But if the '60's were Swinging London, the mid-'80's are Smart London. The 'revival' is based on money. On the ability of businessmen to do business with the Far East in the morning and New York in the afternoon of the same day. Thank God for the Greenwich Meridian.

Monday, April 15th

Cannot find the right book to read at the moment and feel very exercised about this. Decide on Arnold Bennett – because he describes 'ordinary people interestingly', it says on the blurb.

Saturday, May 18th: Southwold

A long night's sleep enlivened by some wonderful dreams, including Maggie Smith singing a song called 'Lobster Time'. A fine morning.

After breakfast we go to view progress at Sunset House. Shape of the rooms now clear, so we can make some early decisions about furniture, etc, which is really why Angela and I are up here together. One thing which slightly disappoints is the height of the bay window, which is such that when you sit you lose most of the view.

Monday, May 20th

I go to the French pub and there are Bernard McKenna and writer Colin Bostock-Smith, sharing a bottle of wine after the successful read-through of one of their scripts. Bernard has severed relations with GC after *Yellowbeard* disagreements. We retell good tales of Tunisia, including the time Bernard and Andrew MacLachlan got an entire Arab crowd to chant 'Scotland!' (when GC walked on as Biggus Dickus).

Wednesday, May 22nd

Woken by a loud crash outside the window. It's five a.m. In deepest sleep the sound seemed almost unreal, a jarring, violent impact with a high, almost metallic top note. Helen it is who discovers a pane of the downstairs window smashed, apparently with the end of a stout, five-foot-long wooden post which lies outside the window. No sign of an attempt to break in. Back to bed after clearing it up. Slightly shaken, but I feel that it's one of those random, irrational acts of destruction which occasionally occur round here – plants pulled up, aerials bent. Neither of us can think of any reason someone would do it on purpose. Back to sleep. Helen dreams of massive disasters.

Thursday, May 23rd

At BAFTA at four to meet Tristram Powell, to talk about *East of Ipswich*. He is a lean, open-faced, relaxed man, anywhere between three and ten years older than me I would think.

He, it turns out, is a director, not a producer as I'd assumed, and I think would make a very good job of it. I feel quite a bond with him by the end of our chat. And I have a feeling he's Anthony Powell's son, but I never dared ask because it would have involved me having to admit I never made much headway with *Music of Time* Vol I. Now I'm determined to try again.

It would be very neat if all worked out and *East of Ipswich* could be made by Powell some time next year. Certainly our meeting today seems to have solved the major problem of director.

Collect Granny's clock from Camerer Cuss – always struck with curiosity as to how the clock expert there manages to reconcile such precision work with his very shaky hands.

Friday, May 24th

To Mayfair to meet TJ and then Sam Goldwyn re the 'Chocolate Project'. Meet TJ at a pub in Shepherd's Market. He's on good form – having just had a 'breakthrough' over the ending of *Erik the Viking*.

To Sam Goldwyn's flat in nearby Hertford Street. Shepherd's Market feels very much like Soho is always thought to be but never is. Here there are still ladies in doorways who say 'Hello' as you pass. Sam settles us both down with voluminous scotches and watches us talk about the film.

At one point find his wife standing at the open window of the bedroom and smoking out of it. When I asked her for the loo, she spun round like a 'B' movie actress playing guilt.

After a morale-boosting chat we share a taxi back to Cavendish Square, feeling rather jolly. The sky has cleared and left London looking fresh and sparkling.

Tuesday, May 28th: Abbotsley–London

Tom Maschler [of Jonathan Cape] rings in ebullient, heavy-sell mood to ask if I will write a children's story for a new book which will be 'a very big seller indeed'. He won't tell me why, but eventually he makes the secret sound so attractive to himself that he has to tell me. Holography is the key. A new process which can apply holographs to the illustrated page – he compares it to the pop-up book, or Kit Williams' *Masquerade* in potential appeal. Maschler exudes self-confidence, power, excitement, fame, success, but basically it's all a sales pitch. As Michael Foreman is the artist and as it only has 2,000 words, I express interest in a meeting later in June.

Wednesday, May 29th

Write to Al L and settle to watch the much looked-forward to European Cup Final.[1] Instead find myself watching sickeningly familiar scenes of drunken fans fighting. This time, though, it is even worse – a wall has collapsed, killing 25. No-one seems to know what is going on. Fans are throwing missiles at each other; police with riot shields seem to wander about the ground to no particular plan or purpose, occasionally hitting people as hard as they can. The fences look flimsy, the barriers between the rival sets of supporters virtually non-existent. What were they expecting?

The death toll from the wall collapse mounts, but the crowd, on the verge of hysteria anyway, are not told. Jimmy Hill and Terry Venables trade solutions – national service (Venables), withdrawal of passports, more Thatcherite toughness (Hill), and Bobby Charlton chips in with a plea for the restoration of corporal punishment.

But it is the lack of any controlling hand over the activities at the stadium that is most frightening. Fortunately most of the crowd wait patiently and sensibly, but the 'minority' still hurl anything they can lay their hands on. At one end a group of Italian boys posture and swagger with sticks and iron piping, whilst the Brussels police just watch.

[1] The match, between Juventus and Liverpool, took place at Heysel Stadium in Brussels. Thirty-six Juventus supporters died when Liverpool fans charged at them and a wall collapsed. The game went ahead, Juventus winning 1–0. English clubs were banned from all European football competitions for the next five years.

Thursday, May 30th

To the Royal Academy to look at the Summer Exhibition. Somewhere inside me I just want to enjoy the good things of Britain after the awful shame of Brussels. The events last night were a national humiliation and there's a sense of sobering shock today, mixed with an almost eerie frisson of fear. I think the actuality TV coverage has made the difference, causing millions of people to experience the violence as if they were actually there.

Crowds mill around the elegant rooms of Burlington House. See one small painting I fancy for £200, but it is snapped up just ahead of me. Come away with only a confused swirl of images in my mind – landscapes, Bonnard-esque views from interiors out through windows, occasional nudes and comfortable portraits of successful middle-aged men.

Some shopping, then home by cab.

Julian Hough has dropped in. He's just out of the Scrubs, and Helen says he went on about how nice they all were inside, reading Camus and Shakespeare.

Friday, May 31st: Hull

To King's Cross to catch the train up to Hull for my 'celebrity lecture'. [Part of a series of appearances outside London, which I, and others, had agreed to give for British Film Year.]

No seats are booked in a crowded Edinburgh express and one of the HST cars fails, so we arrive at Doncaster 40 minutes late and have to take a taxi on to Hull. We arrive at the party to launch the Hull Film Festival somewhat rushed. I'm shown straight to the Disabled toilet.

Then into a room full of local worthies. Have to remember that the *Life of Brian* is still banned in Hull! Some sweet German wine, a bite at a buffet and a chat with two very nice people who won a competition for seats at the lecture (which sold out two weeks ago) by answering questions such as 'What was the name of the leading pig in *Animal Farm*?'

Who should then stroll onto the scene but J Cleese, who begins work on a Frayn script, *Clockwise*, in Hull on Sunday.

John had hoped to get into the lecture unannounced and ask rude questions from the back. As it is, I find him all too near – in the second row, just below the stage on which Iain [Johnstone] and myself recline in rather grand, high-backed winged armchairs.

Q and A with the audience is successful and we go on for 90 minutes before Ian asks John if he has any words to sum up Michael Palin. Poor JC. He tells the audience that I am the most genuinely silly person he knows. 'He doesn't have to work at it. It's straight from the heart.' I counter by thanking JC for teaching me everything I know.

Discuss mothers with JC, who says with feeling 'My mother is dreadfully stupid, completely neurotic, but I do like her.' Later JC thaws out enough to say 'You know, the other day I suddenly thought how nice it would be to do another Python TV series.' Here he pauses, very effectively. 'I thought that for about six hours.'

Saturday, June 1st: Hull

Driven by the organiser of the Festival, together with two friends, out to Beverley, a very attractive little town. The Minster dominates the skyline rather like the church at Haarlem in seventeenth-century Dutch landscapes. Honey-coloured stonework, very beautiful decoration around the west front, a fine building.

A thriving market place in which stands our destination – the Playhouse Theatre. Built as the Corn Exchange, it has been a cinema for over 50 years. Now run by a largely volunteer force and saved from closure by a fire-eater and his wife. It doesn't make much money, but they count *Private Function* as a great success an average of 99 a night, says the manager.

Up a ladder through the projection room to the manager's office, where I am treated to some of his grapefruit wine. More photographs. Local paper not there, which seems a poor piece of organisation.

From the Picture Playhouse to a Sam Smith's pub known colloquially as 'Nellies' – run until a few years ago by two 80-year-olds who insisted it should not be substantially altered. So, aside from bare wood everywhere, there is also gas light and in the evenings a folk band plays by candlelight.

Back to Hull, pausing to look at 29 Victoria Avenue, where the parents lived in 1932/33. A small, characterful Edwardian semi, with a big mock-Tudor gable and some quite elegant stained glass. It stands in a modest, leafy avenue, built as part of a 'development' with wholly surprising baroque fountains at two of the crossroads.

Home by four. Helen in the garden. Join her and am quite lazy until it's time to go next door to Eliz and Eleas' for dinner. Five psychoanalysts there. Two Americans, two Brazilians, two Argentinians. The conversation tends to the serious and there is much post-mortemising of the Brussels riots.

Eleas thinks that part of the problem is that the English bottle their feelings and passions up – there isn't much on-street or café debate and discussion. Emotions too are kept tightly under control, so that when they snap they snap more fiercely and a lot more repression is poured out than in Brazil. The Argentine thinks that the British lack of volatility does have its advantages.

Wednesday, June 5th

Michael Barnes rings at breakfast time to discuss Belfast Festival dates.

More thunder forecast today. As I run over Parliament Hill I look out over London and it lies swathed in a soggy mist, as if it's raining upwards from the ground.

Tom is in school doing his second exam paper of the day – 'O' Level French – William is off school for four days during this fortnight because of teachers' 'industrial action'.

Some more writing, then drive into London, park at the Chinatown car park – near whose entrance gather a group of winos, who sit amongst the litter, occasionally hugging each other, their red blotchy faces the doors they've shut against the rest of the world. If they were rich they'd be in clinics in Hertfordshire.

Tuesday, June 11th

Osborne of Adnams rings to tell me that a new offer of £44,000 for Croft Cottage has been received from the single lady, Mrs Marshall. Should he go back to the couple? I made it clear that I and Ma and Angela all would like the house to go to someone who will live there. This apparently counts out the couple, who want it as a second home, until their retirement. So after some to-ing and fro-ing I agree on Ma's behalf to start negotiations for the sale of the house for £44,000.

Wednesday, June 12th

I work through the work I've done in the last two weeks on 'Chocolates'. Then at 12.30 down to TJ's. He has been suffering a 'low-grade headache' for the past two weeks and this finally laid him low over the weekend.

He does perk up, though, enough to get angry about Mary Whitehouse's remarks re the Brussels tragedy in the *Guardian*. She sees it as an indictment of the permissive liberalism of the last 30 years!

Despite his low state of health he comes up with some good and incisive comments. I leave my notebook with him and at 4.30 set off to drive across London to the TV Centre.

Arrive at White City about five minutes late for a meeting with Innes Lloyd and Tristram P re *East of Ipswich*. Innes Lloyd [Alan Bennett's favourite producer] has the reassuring look of a much-loved schoolmaster and the bearing of a naval commander. Tall, upright, of good colour and gentlemanly amiability, I find it hard to immediately connect him with Alan's caustic Northern observations, but easy to like and trust him.

He says he loved the script and we talk for less than half an hour before deciding that it should be approached primarily as a TV film – and who better to do it than the Beeb? Innes L will put it to [Peter] Goodchild, who's head of drama. Leave the BBC feeling very hopeful. Like Ma's house, this project seems to be fitting together suspiciously easily.

Sunday, June 16th

About to rush to squash with Richard when George H calls from Australia. He's in a Sydney hotel room (it's 2.30) and for some reason announces himself as Jane Asher. He sounds at first rather sleepy and, as the call goes on, rather drunk. I'm reminded of GC's inexplicable midnight calls, except there is no invective here, just a rather sad GH reflecting on the joys of chewing 'Nicorette' gum, and anxious to tell me that he's given up smoking, and drugs, and his only vice is Carlton Lager, three of which he's just consumed. He wants to know if I will come to China with him and his acupuncturist next year.

Monday, June 24th

At six I am at Tom Maschler's office at Jonathan Cape. A huge, at present characterless room, dominated by a carefully restored Adam ceiling (all Robert Adam's specifications, including choice of colour, were found in the British Museum).

Tom, lean and brown and smoking roll-ups, presides over a cautious little group, including Mike Foreman and a man whose name I never really catch. He is the hologram expert, a big man with the look of an early 1970's rock drummer.

The book, as Maschler assured me, could make us all *very* rich, and the early 1970's rock drummer [Richard Seymour] emphasises that it must be of the finest quality, using holograms integrated into the text and into M Foreman's illustrations. It sounds exciting and, as they all turn and look at me hopefully, I say yes and promise to write a new, two-to three-thousand word children's ghost story by the time we leave for the Seychelles (about five weeks away).

Back home I hear from Tristram Powell that Peter Goodchild likes *East of Ipswich* very much and wants to go ahead with it – probably next April.

Sunday, June 30th: Southwold

Helen drives me down to Liverpool Street. They have begun work on the demolition of Broad Street, which is a sad sight – its façade is one of the finest and most unusual of all London's main terminals.

At Ipswich Station, I'm buying a cup of coffee when a 'youth' on roller skates rockets into the station, grabs hold of me to steady himself and shouts 'Get the police'. He's followed by a very thin, weedy, unhealthy-looking man who proceeds to attack the roller-skater and heap curses at him. Then a very angry lady arrives and screams abuse – 'You fucking pervert', that sort of thing. A burly American keeps them apart and does a fine job, but the ferocity of the woman's anger – 'You insulted my father-in-law last night ... you faggot!' – takes quite a while to subside.

Saturday, July 13th

To the desk for an hour, lunch and flop out again, periodically watching the Live Aid concert and the Test Match. First quite upstages the second. Wembley packed and from the air looking like an open sardine can, but no menace in the presence of this huge crowd (well, I suppose they've all paid £25 minimum). It looks like a day out for the white and well-off. But the music is good, the spontaneity of a live event exciting and, because it is a Giant Global Good Deed, everyone feels united in a most unusual way. If I were a rock promoter I'd feel vaguely uneasy about the happiness which is engendered when people know that no-one is making a profit.

Thursday, July 18th

At two o'clock I'm at BUPA for a screening (medical, that is). Two years since I was last here and feel that I should keep up regular inspections. Everything seems to be fine. On the computer questionnaire I print in that my libido has decreased – mainly because I'm bored with my own lack of any interesting medical history but the doctor doesn't seem interested. My favourite this time is 'Have your stools changed colour recently?'

With my body well serviced, I return home, make some calls, then go to put on my DJ for a black-tie invitation to *The Life and Death of Colonel Blimp* at the Screen on the Hill, in celebration of 50 years of the National Film Archive. No DJ. Remember Ed B borrowed it for Glyndebourne. Race round to Albert Street with half an hour to spare and collect it. Then find that I can't remember how to tie my bow properly. Eventually it comes back to me after a fashion.

Arrive at the cinema with 15 minutes to spare. Have my photo taken with Romaine and then TG and Maggie arrive. Both TG and myself have made an attempt at black-tie. Jonathan Miller and Jack Gold and Gavin Millar have neither tie nor black.

Michael Powell and Pressburger come onto the stage at the beginning. Powell, arms stiffly at his sides, looking like a well-disciplined doorman in his plum-coloured tuxedo, beams wickedly. Emeric Pressburger is close by his side, but is old and can't move much and looks a bit like Powell's dummy.

Powell starts by telling us what a very British film this is – 'Shot by a Frenchman, produced by a Hungarian, designed by a Prussian, scored by a Czech . . .' He reflects a moment, then continues, 'In fact about fifty percent of the crew were enemy aliens at the time.' He gently but firmly debunks the notion of film-makers making a grand decision to work for a particular country – films were made 'where they fell'.

Pressburger comments rather acidly on the need for an intermission because the projection at the Screen isn't able to show 160 minutes non-stop. 'I was quite pleased when I heard that there was an intermission, as it showed that 1940's film-making was ahead of 1980's technology.'

Then they trot off and the epic begins. As a piece of comedy it has its ups and downs – some gross over-playing in minor roles (of the Germans, of course), and some long, laboured comedy scenes – but always surprises – the beauty of the sets, the superb colour, the lovely performances, especially of Anton Walbrook. In the end a feeling of having seen a warts and all tribute to Britishness – its heroism, naivety, bumbling incompetence, luck and charm.

Friday, July 19th

Lunch with Puttnam.

The Mission is responsible for him losing a stone in weight. The food in Colombia was dreadful. They're now on their way (by overland convoy) to Argentina to finish shooting. He's confident it will work, but is tight-lipped about 'Revolution', which he says has been very badly organised and is four million over on below the line costs.

He says straightway that he's happy for me to take *East of Ipswich* to the BBC. But 'get in there quick', he confides and advises that I keep foreign rights and access to negative (to blow it up from 16 to 35 if necessary) and outtakes. Try a 50/50 split with the Beeb on all foreign proceeds.

Now he's lost some fleshiness around his face, his big eyes look out through his trim beard, at which he tugs when he's not running his fingers along the inside of his collar.

As usual I am drawn by his liveliness, good sense and charm to overlook the relentlessness of the hustle, the continual selling and the breathless pace of the man's life. But as a gossip, he's second to none. The Royal Family detest Thatcher, but Prince Charles has a lot of time for Ken Livingstone – as does his mother!

Monday, July 22nd

At midday begin the ghost story [for the hologram book]. I don't feel in a very good frame of mind about it. I feel that I've accepted an unnecessary pressure – to come up with a story merely so that Maschler can sell it at Frankfurt. Would it not be better to take time to find the *best* story, then sell it?

Perhaps sensing a mixed enthusiasm, my system rebels and I find myself with the worst sort of literary lassitude.

Despite the hostile weather outside – fierce gusting winds bringing dark clouds over low and fast from the west – I decide running is the only way to break out of this slumberland. Hard to stand at the top of Parliament Hill, so strong is the westerly gale, but after that it improves and at one point I'm running in sunshine and looking out over a thin, black-clouded belt of rain drifting right across Central London.

Once back I find myself much fresher and sharper and, carrying on through the evening until 10.45, I complete a ghost story. Not, I feel, *the* ghost story, but at least something to show I've tried.

Thursday, July 25th

Only with meticulous plans and copious lists will I be able to survive today. So many projects have to be attended to, cosseted, completed and confronted, as tomorrow I intend to put up the shutters until September.

Various calls to bring the Croft Cottage/Sunset House situation up to date. Brian D [Duncan, builder] promises me that September 30th will be a sensible date to aim to have moved in by. Ring Ma. She worries, despite all my assurances. 'I've never done anything quite like this in my life,' she tells me. There's a first time for everything, even at 81, and I try and set her mind at rest and give a generally reassuring morale boost. She's trying so hard not to be a burden, but has to reiterate how she finds it such a lot of money and almost implying she's not worth it. She has the good, solid Christian virtues that money and wealth mean not a thing – but spends all her life worrying about them.

Monday, August 12th

To a meeting re 'A Consuming Passion' at Goldcrest.

The sumptuous luxury of their new Wardour Street HQ is something of an irony in view of their recent, well-publicised financial troubles and boardroom struggles. But at the moment they're still in business and, in amongst the carpets, the mirrors, the high-tech decor and internal gardens, we set to discussing our low-budget comedy!

Goldwyn is there, Amanda [Schiff] and Sandy [Lieberson], who joins us later. Goldwyn is the most concerned. He doesn't like Watney killing Rose, Kingsley and Irons. He feels that this will be a shock for the audience. Terry J accepts this, but thinks that the audience need to be shocked. Well, we're not prepared, says Sam, for a character we've grown very fond of to kill another character we've grown very fond of. Both TJ and myself are unable to press home our disagreement with total conviction, as neither of us have read the script for two weeks.

Sandy L breezes in. He's been trout-fishing with Puttnam in Wiltshire. He takes a back seat to Sam when discussing the script. Various suggestions for adopting, adapting and improving come up and TJ and myself agree to rewrite in mid-September. Sam G is trying to push the film in November, which is clearly going to be a rush, but reveals that he doesn't consider his criticisms basic enough to hold up the making of the picture.

Talk turns to directors. TJ won't say he can't do it, so that door is still left ajar. Loncraine's name comes up. Sam G roots for Malcolm M.

We break up about six, with rough agreement on rewrites, no decision on director or shooting date and no further meetings planned until September.

Wednesday, August 14th

TG appears.

The *Brazil* battle is hotting up. Arnon [Milchan], who TG says now has the bit between his teeth, is showing the uncut print to as many influential people as he can in New York. Alan Hirschfield [at Twentieth Century Fox] rang Sid Sheinberg and offered to buy the film. Universal declined and are threatening legal action to stop Arnon showing the original version to critics, etc.

TG leaves after doing a very funny mime of chimpanzees mating, which he saw on some TV nature film.

Friday, August 16th: Oslo–Haugesund, Norway

[On a train across Norway, on way to British Film event.] The driver is called John, he's younger than me and wears a constant half-smile.

As we pass placid, glassy-calm lakes I mutter the usual appreciations. Not for a moment relaxing his quiet smile, he reminds me that there is 'no life' in these picturesque lakes, thanks to pollution from Britain and, to a lesser extent, Germany and Poland. The Norwegians are not at all happy about the British attitude (which is to do bugger all and stop others from doing anything) and I cannot defend it and am quite embarrassed. He's proud, though not crowingly so, that Norway has the second highest standard of living in Europe and the second lowest unemployment rate (in both cases after Switzerland). But there are only four million of them.

No restaurant car at all on this six and a half hour journey and on the trolley only rolls and no alcohol, except for a special low-strength beer, which has all the adverse effects of making you flatulent with none of the benefits of either taste or mild euphoria.

The Norwegians control alcohol sales very carefully. Only government monopoly shops can sell liquor at all and then only at certain times of day. Consequently, JJ [John Jacobsen, my host] confirms, there is a lot of drunkenness and moonshining.

We climb to a summit of 4,300 feet above the tree line and above the cloud into a brightly-lit no-man's-land of grey rocks and dirty snow.

We reach Bergen at 2.05 and walk rather aimlessly from the station towards the quayside – the Brygge – where are the tall, thin houses of the Hanseatic merchants, before queuing for the hydrofoil in rapidly-deteriorating weather.

A three-hour journey. Both of us sleep for a time and I read some of A Powell, which feels very incongruous. We stop four or five times at various islands and reach Haugesund about five minutes late.

JJ is quite anxious by now, evidently hotel bookings have been confused and we are expected by the Mayor at dinner within ten minutes. Both of us change in my room.

I can't find the bathroom light or get the key out of the door. JJ can't find the lavatory flush. Fifteen minutes of pure Keystone Cops before we emerge, only slightly less crumpled than before, but at least besuited.

A long table, set with British flags amongst the flower arrangements. Myself and JJ, whose attitude to things I quite like, are sat at the end like naughty schoolboys. In the middle are the likes of Roger Moore, Liv Ullman and the Mayor and British Ambassador.

Speeches at the end. The Mayor of Haugesund is very smooth and fluent and uses references to Andy Capp – 'We're passing one of the oldest pubs in London. Capp: Why?' – and manages to be politely flattering about the James

Bond movie *View to a Kill*, with which the festival has just opened.

The British Ambassador murmurs a vague and wet 'Hello' as he passes. Clearly not the slightest clue who I am. JJ feels that we've been upstaged by Bond. Frankly I was much happier at the naughty boys' end of the table.

Saturday, August 17th: Haugesund, Norway

We visit the world's largest herring table, which stretches for a couple of hundred yards up the main street in an attempt to break the Guinness world record for serving the greatest variety of herrings! Pickled herring in pineapple – that sort of thing.

The *Private Function* press conference has been moved from the hotel to the YMCA. Here, in a gloomy, inhospitable hall, about 30 journalists gather. A quick and nervous man takes it upon himself to introduce me and act as interlocutor. To add to the absurdity, two heavy mikes are on the desk top in front of us.

This overkill produces one of the most uninformative and pointless press conferences I've ever attended. But I have to maintain calm and composure through silly photos outside and two more interviews, even though I'm hot, tousled, sweaty and smell of crab and shrimp.

Nor is there any let-up. Before I can go back to the hotel I have to go to rehearsals for the Amanda Awards, Norway's first ever film and TV awards ceremony. I have the unlikely honour of presenting the first Amanda of all time.

Norway's leading theatre actress introduces herself enthusiastically to me. She's called Winky and as far as I can tell the show's producer is called Bent.

Leave the hotel at 9.45 for the awards. These go off quite well and I just about get away with my Norwegian pronunciation. At the end all the presenters have to reassemble on stage and simulate the spontaneous joy, happiness, warmth and wonderfulness of the occasion. It's during this ordeal that friendly Liv Ullman shakes my hand and introduces herself and says she hopes I'm going to the party afterwards. We all stand there with bunches of carnations whilst the press snap away.

At last, when it's time to go, Roger Moore suggests I come with him and his party back to the Park Hotel – he hints mysteriously at the chance of crayfish. But I have to find JJ and hope I'll get a chance to talk to Liv Ullman so, unlike Roger M, I give the official party a try.

Crowds of people, but no Liv Ullman.

When at last I reach the Park Hotel it must be around three o'clock. Whom should I encounter on entering, but Roger Moore. 'Michael! You *missed* the crayfish!'

He welcomes me profusely, and brings from his room a bottle of Chivas Regal and a bottle of Glenfiddich and sets them on the table.

He really wants to say how much he wants to work with us, how he loved everything I'd ever done and watched me on the *Cavett Show* (why this comes up particularly, I don't know) and so on. He is especially keen to know what Gilliam is like to work with.

At one point a hotel guest comes up to Moore for his autograph. As he signs, Moore points at me and asks the poor petitioner if he knows who I am. The man nods and reveals that he saw *Private Function* this morning. 'Did you like it?' asks Moore. He nods. 'Which did you like most, his film or mine?' Bravely the man considers, then, with a shriek from Roger Moore, indicates me.

As we set off for bed, Moore reiterates his desire to do something – indeed anything – with the Pythons. 'I work cheap.'

It is a quarter to five.

Tuesday, August 20th

Lunch with Basil and Pat [Pao].

Basil spent two weeks in Cotignac working on 'The Rutland Isles' script with EI. Basil suggested a change in approach which was evidently too drastic for Eric, so the collaboration sounds only fifty percent successful. He seems now much more certain that he will get the job of assistant art director on the Bertolucci China movie [*The Last Emperor*] if and when the finance is finalised.

Into Covent Garden for some shopping, to Peter Lewis in Parkway for a check on my new bridges. He took his family in a minivan up the east coast, then up through Lancashire. 'Depressed towns really interest me.' He went to Rochdale, on his holiday.

Thursday, August 22nd: Southwold

Outside it begins to rain heavily and I hear the clock strike one downstairs well before I slip off to sleep. I wake about six hours later and lie for a while wondering why I was able to sleep for nine hours night after night in the Seychelles. I conclude that I am suffering from a condition which expands even small anxieties into a general level of tension which it's hard to evade at night and which awaits me first thing in the morning. Not that today threatens any major worries, but maybe Tom's imminent 'O' Level results are there at the back of it all.

Hear Mother coughing. She 'wakes' me at 8.15. There's been another air crash, she says, pushing aside the curtains to reveal the clear blue sky of a perfect East Anglia morning, something at Manchester . . .

Phone rings at ten. It's Tom. He sounds worried, says Mother, holding out the phone and looking thoroughly confused. Talk to him. He's passed in six out of seven subjects so far, with chemistry a disaster and English still to come. This is right at the top end of his (and my) expectations and I'm terribly pleased for him.

Talk on the phone to Tom Maschler. Bad news, he says, Michael Foreman has decided he hasn't time to be involved. 'He's probably heading for a nervous breakdown,' confides Tom. Maschler, I fear, is one of those manically energetic souls who never get nervous breakdowns, only give them to others.

Monday, September 2nd

Lunch with Geoffrey Strachan. We meet at 1.15 in Fleet Street Rugantino's and talk about GS's idea for a Palin travel book. Decide that it should take the form of a diary, should be unashamedly personal and subjective and based on my notes taken over the years, as well as trips to come. GS likes my plain title 'Going Abroad', and I quite like 'Travelling to Work'. Agree it should be a project for at least two years hence. Both of us become very enthusiastic.

After lunch I walk to the Turf Club for my annual visit.

The club is open, but deserted. I sit myself at one of the dull, brown leather armchairs on the dull, green carpet beside the huge windows overlooking the dull drizzle over St James's Park.

On the way out I at last hear sounds of life from the billiard room, but on looking in find the barman playing on his own. By the door there is a neatly-typed notice reminding members that denim jeans are not considered permissible apparel. I leave and cross the road in the rain. Looking back I have the melancholy feeling I've just visited a benevolent old uncle in hospital. And he hasn't long to live.

Tuesday, September 3rd

TG comes round and we proceed together to the BBC for a photo-session and lunch/reception to mark the release of the Python videos.

On the way TG brings me up to date with the *Brazil* saga. Sheinberg is refusing to make up his mind, but has it put about that he will not be releasing the picture this year, and that there is still work to do on it.

But Arnon M has artfully revealed to an LA journalist that several of the national critics, including Bruce Williamson and Joel Segal, have seen the film in its original version and raved about it. The story, published in an LA paper recently, has added fuel to the controversy and hopefully will force Sheinberg into a more positive attitude. A decision is expected this weekend.

We assemble in a bunker-like room beneath the BBC in Langham Place. Terry J is back from France and looks slightly dazed. Graham, rather pale and thin-faced, is benign, amused and, as always, not quite there, and John, sporting a blue pin-stripe suit with dead parrot tie, is his usual lordly self. Eric is not present.

We have our photos taken with rather dog-eared cut-outs of Michelangelo's 'David' in a small garden in Cavendish Place. It's all rather low-key, as none of us can think of anything interesting to do, and we all come to the conclusion that zaniness after 40 isn't possible.

Back to the basement, where food has been laid out (including dressed crab, which is definitely a step up in BBC's catering style) and a Python video replays 'Piranha Brothers' and 'The Spanish Inquisition' in the background.

After what seems like an hour of talking, one of the organisers notices I haven't had a spare breath for any food. Gulp down some crab and pâté and then am dragged back to answering why the Pythons don't get together any more, when all I want to do is get together with the other Pythons.

Wednesday, September 4th: London–Southwold

Talk with Richard Seymour – the hologram man. They now have secured the services of Alan Lee to replace Mike Foreman. According to Seymour he is the finest illustrator working in the country today – as was Mike Foreman, when he was on the project.

I feel more and more like the world-weary, worldly-wise old owl these days.

As the rain and wind spread yet again from the west, I go to bed with *Adrian Mole*, which I'm discovering for the first time, and find it makes me laugh very much and, I think, for all the right reasons.

Friday, September 6th: Southwold

Sleep well and wake in good spirits to a bright, cloudless sky. To work by 9.30 after a bloater breakfast. Quite a successful morning on 'Cyril', considering this is my first day devoted entirely to the new project. *Cyril and the House of Commons* comes together quite nicely.

After lunch I concentrate on the clearing of Croft Cottage. Already we've filled a black bag with old bills and accounts and other minutiae which my father would never throw away. Go through a lot of photographs from the halcyon days of my father's life. Full of smiles on the liner 'Arcania' coming back from the USA in the mid-twenties. Lots of pictures of him dressing up and fooling about, then some more suave portraits. His nose and prominent, rather sensuous eyes and lips remind me closely of Tom P. He was a very pretty boy and doubtless had to fight off a few at Shrewsbury!

The clearing is at once a revelation and an irksome, rather depressing job. My mother keeps finding fresh bags of letters, or old ties, or other objects, which appear, unannounced, on my bed, on the desk where I'm working, or in the middle of a room we've just cleared.

In late afternoon I revisit Sunset House and find two or three things still to be done. Drop in on Brian Duncan who is, as usual, gaily reassuring about everything.

Back to Croft Cottage for what I suppose may be my last run along these lanes.

It couldn't be a more perfect evening to remember them by. A big, burning, golden sun slowly descending behind Reydon Church, brushing the deep golden brown of the corn with a tinge of red. A harvester, with visored driver, is cutting the corner field.

Sunday, September 8th

In mid-afternoon I drive down to the V&A to see the watercolours of Bonington, Prout and others of the early nineteenth century. This at the behest of Lewis the Dentist, who collects nineteenth-century watercolours.

Find an artist called William Wyld, who excites greater admiration than either the neat, methodical Prout or the elusive, but exceptional, Bonington.

Then up to the top floor of the Harvey Cole Wing to look at the Constables – very appropriate as I did homage to Dedham Vale yesterday. Realise for the first time that the A12 dual carriageway runs clean across the middle of Constable's favourite view.

Monday, September 9th

Back to 'A Consuming Passion'. TJ reads me, over the phone, a letter from Paul Z – 'Seriously, I hope you won't fault me if this letter doesn't overflow with enthusiasm for a draft that virtually obliterates my previous work.' His letter is like Paul – funny, articulate and bracing. But his reaction, together with Amanda's two-page critique, combine to reduce our energy and enthusiasm. Suddenly it's an uphill task again.

After lunch TJ suggests we avoid Grove Park for working as they have a pneumatic drill in action. So we go instead to his boat in St Katharine's Dock. Here, two huge cranes swing round on a nearby building site, helicopters rattle overhead every 15 minutes and there's the constant distraction of various other members of the boat-owning community arriving back unsteadily from lunches.

The dock should be a charming, attractive haven, but I feel uneasy there. Uneasy at the scale of development, building and demolition which marks the 'regeneration' of Dockland. It's being largely undertaken by the big construction companies and will, I fear, come out as a grotesque parody of Olde London – neither excitingly modern nor convincingly historic. I think it'll be buggered up in the way the City of London has buggered up its Thames shoreline (though perhaps nothing could be as bad as that).

Wednesday, September 11th

Have been dipping into V Woolf's extraordinary diaries over the last few days and found a neat phrase – to 'rout the drowse'. Sounds like street talk, in fact it describes what a good walk does for her creative energy. So, as I feel increasingly addled, I eventually go for a run, which routs the drowse most successfully.

We seem unable to clinch a screenplay and I think it's because we have different preferences which it's hard to reconcile – TJ for fantasy and more overt moralising, myself for the fine detail of life, without necessarily having to make a judgement. TJ wants to be engaged in the issues. He wants to tackle injustice, incompetence, bigotry or whatever head on. I am more the spectator. More detached, therefore perhaps more able to go in close without getting stung.

TJ carries an emotional involvement into everything he does, finding it difficult not to say everything he wants to say about the world in each script, which is why he isn't so good on characters. He won't stand back and allow them to have a life of their own.

Friday, September 13th

Feel somewhat lethargic and lacking in clear-headed energy for today's vital decisions on 'A Consuming Passion'

Clearly TJ doesn't want to have anything more to do with the rewrites as he has pressing problems of his own – 'Erik' and 'Nicobobinus' [his children's story] foremost – so I suggest that I write a third draft, aiming to complete in relatively unrushed time – by Christmas or late November if possible. This decision lightens both our minds. The only factor which could affect it is quite a surprise – Amanda Schiff rings to say she's being made redundant by Goldcrest. Sandy L will ring. Where all this leaves us I don't know.

Tuesday, September 17th

Meet Sandy L at the Flask. The meeting becomes like a Python sketch when a very chatty young man in a suit becomes irrevocably involved in our discussions after recognising me and then TJ.

So, whilst Sandy explains, lengthily and frankly, the politics at Goldcrest which have led to his resignation, he has occasionally to answer questions like 'What do you do?', 'What *is* a producer?', and so on. Sandy is marvellous and plays it most courteously and unpatronisingly and patiently. But it is rather like having one of our own creations – a Pither or a Charlie Legs – incarnated before our very eyes.

Wednesday, September 18th

To Chelsea by cab to be witnesses at Richard and Felice's nuptials.

The Chelsea Register Office is decorated rather like one of those 'no questions asked' hotels where you go when you're not married. There's a lot of Indian restaurant flock wallpaper and cheap chandeliers. As far as I can see there are no fresh flowers. You probably have to order those yourself. The short speech from the Registrar binds Richard and Felice to eternal faithfulness, which Richard thinks is 'a bit much'.

We drive back to their house and kill time for a couple of hours, which is an odd way to carry on on a precious weekday working morning, but a rather satisfactory change of pace. Time to take in all the wonders of Richard's interior decoration – his kettle which makes the noise of an American train whistle when it boils, his compact disc set-up, his several thousand pounds' worth of bicycle. He asks me if I'll come on a cycling and railway trip through Java in November. Apart from my Belfast commitments, I think I wouldn't know how to work his bicycles.

Thursday, September 19th

At eight walk up to William Ellis for a meeting to hear the local MP for the school, Geoffrey Finsberg, talk about the eight-month-old dispute between teachers and Sir Keith Joseph. Finsberg talks for a half-hour with the soulless precision of a politician who has been too well briefed. He concentrates almost entirely on the teachers' rejection of a new pay and promotion package three days ago and their refusal to go to arbitration.

No-one makes the pithy point that if this package is so wonderful, why wasn't it offered eight months ago? The questions from the floor come, for the first half-hour, from articulate, organised opposition, whether Labour Party members or teachers, and Finsberg quite happily deals with them. They're his own breed after all.

Driven by fear that he will go away with the impression (that he so wants to go away with) that we parents are being innocently led to the slaughter by a militant, unionised minority, I stand up at the end and ask him why he thinks Sir Keith Joseph is so generally and universally disliked and mistrusted by teachers of all shades of opinion. He slips out of the question as smoothly as he slips out of the meeting five minutes later.

Saturday, September 28th: Southwold

The day of the Great Move. Everything is on schedule. Angela has been up there for a day already.

The weather has made everything much more like a celebration, less like a departure. The sun is warm and bright and generous and makes the spreading panorama from the windows of Flat 2, Sunset House, a very adequate replacement for the cosier, more reassuring cornfields on either side of Croft Cottage.

The Herberts moon about until about half past eight or nine, then Veryan, who has been hanging mirrors, screwing in toilet rolls and coat hooks, Marcus, who's been telling me all about his recent trip to Burma and Thailand and Malaysia, as I stack books and shelves, and Camilla all embark for Sudbury, after we've christened the neat home with Mumm Cordon Rouge.

After Ma goes to bed I walk out for a bit to get a feel of the location of the new home. The night air is moist and still and vaporous. I follow a bright arc light and the sound of rhythmic thuds to a wall bordering the Common. Sounds like night filming. I peer over a flint wall to see, beyond a smouldering bonfire, a group playing floodlit croquet on a trimly-kept lawn. A good enough image on which to retire.

Retrace my steps through the wet grass to my mother's new home. Angela and I share a room. She reads. I fall asleep.

Sunday, September 29th: Sunset House, Southwold

Sleep very soundly – a good omen for the future. Wake about 8.30. Find Granny downstairs amidst the debris of the half-unpacked kitchen. Apart from her early morning coughs, she seems remarkably unruffled by the whole thing – she's faring much better than her children.

Spend the morning unpacking and positioning furniture. Mrs Haythornthwaite asks us across the landing to No. 3 for a drink. Despite a plummy accent and the confident bearing of one long used to the company of 'professional' people, she is bright and amusing and down-to-earth and very long-suffering, but without a trace of self-pity.

Married three years ago, for the second time, to an old soldier turned farmer who suddenly had a stroke and is at present confined to chair and stick and moves stiffly.

But he is alert and funny and likes a midday drink – legacy of the army, she says. Mother becomes quite flirty with the old man, despite being about 15 years his senior.

Angela and I drive over to Croft Cottage. The wine has wrought its usual havoc upon my energies and vacuuming the whole house is quite a push.

After an hour or so of cleaning, we leave Croft Cottage for the last time. I still cannot feel sentimental about it – but it was only the second house my mother lived in, in nearly 50 years. It looks good today, I feel we're passing on something quite special, not really losing it.

Thursday, October 3rd

Up to Highgate for lunch with Graham C. He and David and John T and Towser and Harry[1] are all moving down to Maidstone next week to a new house in the country. It's a seventeenth-century house with additions including an indoor swimming pool. Graham seems continually hard-up and paying out huge bills to builders – but he does drive Aston Martins and likes his house to have a pool and a gym.

Graham is a bit twitchy and unrelaxed to start with, but expands during the meal. We talk diet. He's very keen on the low-cholesterol, low-fat diet, and takes it far more seriously than me – with regular blood tests, etc. I suppose this is the price you pay for being a doctor and knowing so much more about what's happening inside you.

He seems to have no immediate work lined up. Still looking for alternative

---

[1] Towser and Harry were their two dogs. Harry was named after Graham and David's great friend, musician Harry Nilsson.

funds for [his film project] 'Ditto' after Paramount backed out.

Bid goodbye to GC and to his association with Highgate, the Angel pub, dinner parties with amazing food and eccentric service, the house where I first met Ray Cooper, and so on . . .

Sunday, October 6th

Packed up both cars, then up to Abbotsley for lunch.

Its conker time and I went with Rachel into the church graveyard and we soon filled a small bag full. Sign of the times is that the boys, who used to love to collect conkers, hardly appeared all afternoon. Both were working away at homework.

Looked into St Margaret's Church which had been decorated for the harvest festival. On the altar was a loaf of bread, a glass of water and a pint of red-top. The Redundant Churches Fund, who saved this church from rotting the last ten years, have done a very careful job of preservation and restoration. Took Rachel in and for once I could show her what the church almost looked like when we were married. If it decayed so rapidly in the 15 years after our wedding, how on earth has it survived since the thirteenth century?

Tuesday, October 8th

Sam Goldwyn rings to find out what's going on with 'A Consuming Passion'. I have to trot out the same tale of disillusion which I've already given Sandy (twice) and Amanda Schiff, but no-one seems to tell anybody else, which leads me to have some fears over who is actually claiming the project.

Sam G is very keen. He would fly over tomorrow if it would help strengthen our resolve. He reiterates his point about the dearth of good comedy. I tell him that we'll decide one way or other by the end of October.

Wednesday, October 9th

A day (almost) to myself. Run at lunchtime and then complete my second 'Cyril' story, in the process of which I come up with a nice idea of a man whose moustache has a life of its own.

Thursday, October 10th

Wake at twenty past five. Feel quite rested, despite less than five hours' sleep. Arrive at the BBC about an hour later. Usual disorienting walk along anonymous and labyrinthine corridors. Last time I was here Mrs Gandhi died. This morning it's Yul Brynner (and will, later in the day, be Orson Welles), whose demise doesn't disrupt the programme as drastically as the late Indira.

Frank Bough reads limericks to a bleary audience at seven o'clock, and reads them very well. I make various appearances throughout, the last being with Lance Percival and the man who runs Battersea Dogs' Home (either he or one of his dogs farts silently but fiercely on air while sitting next to me) and Tony Ross, who is doing some on-the-spot illustrations. I can't think how Bough survives – I feel I've done a day's work by 9.15.

Friday, October 11th: Birmingham and Leeds

To Pebble Mill. A 25-minute radio interview, then preparation for the one o'clock TV show.

I appear first of all in a kilt with my foot in a bucket, reciting a limerick about [Bob] Langley [the presenter]. Ben Kingsley is the other main guest – hot from *Othello* at Stratford. I sign a book for his son Edmund – 'as in Kean'.

Then to Leeds.

Appear live on *Calendar*. The autocue has one of my limericks printed up wrong – instead of a lady from Louth with a lisp they've put up 'A lady from Louth with a limp'.

On to the Hyde Park Picture House – the characterful little pre-First War cinema on the corner which is running a Michael Palin week. *The Missionary* and *The Dress* tonight, as well as two personal appearances by me. Jeff Thompson, the manager, who runs the place for love rather than money, says he could have sold the house three times over tonight, which is good for the ego.

Saturday, October 19th: Shrewsbury

To Shrewsbury and park near the Kingsland Bridge (now a 5p toll) beside St Chad's and walk into the Quarry and look up at the schools sat on the hill. The long, red-brick rectangle in early Victorian workhouse style unchanged, as is the steep slope below it whose zig-zag path I know so well from rowing days.

I go to see Rigg's Hall. Much of the freedom which I had to wait until university for is now available here – single-occupancy study/bedrooms for the sixth-formers, girl visitors, a much more tolerant attitude to the school dress.

I walk upstairs, on my own, and look into the bedroom I first occupied in May 1957. The room is almost the same, the iron bed-frame is almost certainly the same. Duvets are the only sign of the times. Try to remember the complicated feelings I had in that same room on my fourteenth birthday – my third or fourth day at Shrewsbury. Pride and loneliness, anticipation and expectation and aching home-sickness. A formative room, and now enshrined in *East of Ipswich*! The power of the writer! Or perhaps the scourge of the writer – to have to remember, to have to note and identify and record every damn thing.

At 5.15 I pay a last call to the school buildings, say my farewells and walk out of the Moss gates. It's beginning to get dark and there is a still, misty, mustiness over the site. It was on evenings like these that I would, in my last term, October '61, make my way to a secluded spot and there light up a Capstan and feel, at last, truly grown up.

Wednesday, October 23rd

To a meal at the Gay Hussar with Barry Cryer and Alan Bennett. A sort of 'Three Yorkshiremen' sketch. We're an oddly-matched little trio, but the effect of three keen senses of humour keeps us going. A lot of BBC reminiscences, at which Barry excels.

He always attributes the source of a story most generously. He tells of Dennis Main Wilson once rounding on John Wells in the BBC bar, pint of beer clutched in the crook of his arm, and firing at him 'Christianity . . . bum steer?'

Alan is acting in a Nigel Williams play for the BBC. I ask him about the part . . . 'Oh, the usual,' he says. 'I went in for a costume fitting and they took one look at what I was wearing and said "That'll do".'

I drive Barry C back to Finchley Road Tube. He thinks Graham Chapman has become duller since he gave up strong drink.

Friday, October 25th

Clean the house in preparation for Sandy Lieberson and the Gilliams.

TG has only just returned from the US, where his battle with Sid Sheinberg is coming along nicely. He was invited to show *Brazil* (in the UK, European version) at USC [University of Southern California], but Sheinberg himself phoned USC to put pressure on them not to show the film, and in the end only clips could be used. A great rabble-rousing speech from Terry won over the students, but the Dean remained unmoving and refused to let the film be shown! DO'B, for the record, thinks that TG can never win and is doomed as far as any future work in Hollywood goes.

Sandy is a great supporter. I tell him that I want to direct. He seems to think this is a very good idea, but suggests I should do some small film or at least some directing exercise before taking on a major film. He will put me in contact with Colin Young at the National Film School.

Saturday, October 26th

Cast around for a 46th birthday present for John. But the magic shop's closed, so I give him a bottle of '61 Lynch Bages and a copy of *Rogue Herries* in memory of the 'Cheese Shop'.[1]

At 7.30 to Rue St Jacques in Charlotte Street. JC, looking as relaxed and expansive in company as I've ever seen him, greets me. He's tieless and this is the first time I've out-formalised him!

About 20 guests. Peter Cook is not drinking and very funny, but still one of those people who like to take the floor when they talk. His eyes have a way of moving fractionally slower than his head.

Saturday, November 2nd

We are invited to a party before the Primrose Hill firework display. We cram into Clare's shop and drink the first mulled wine of the winter, then up to Primrose Hill, where there is a spectacular gathering – reminiscent, in heads silhouetted against bright light, of the closing scenes of *Close Encounters*.

At the top of the hill is a bonfire which sends huge sheets of flame swirling upwards. As that begins to die down, heads turn to the bottom of the hill where the firework display begins. The Telecom Tower winks in the background, like a giant firework which won't go off. 'Oohs' and 'Ahhs' and orgasmic shrieks of delight fill the air.

Everyone in very good spirits, hot dogs are sold, but it's the sheer size of the crowd which is impressive – 20,000 at least, I should imagine.

Back to Clare's shop, where Mary and myself fall into conversation with the cookery editor of *Options*, who happens to be one of James Ferman's team of film assessors (she won't use the word 'censor'). She says that they have had to enrol new staff to deal with all the videos – especially the Indian videos, which

---

[1] John as Mr Mousebender: 'Good morning, I was sitting in the public library in Thurmond Street just now, skimming through *Rogue Herries* by Horace (sic) Walpole, when I came over all peckish.'

cannot show a kiss, but are incredibly violent. I ask her why Python TV shows and *Ripping Yarns* are both '15'. She promises to find out. 'Is there a "fuck"?' she asks.

Sunday, November 3rd

The sun, low, clear and brilliant, encourages me out of the house again, this time to take Rachel to the zoo. The tigers pace disturbingly and continually. The ostriches and emus and cassowaries are in poor housing and look rather seedy. The penguins remain my favourite entertainment.

Then we walk up Primrose Hill together. Though it is very cold, the leaves are still on the trees and the great glowing gold sun picks out the fading colours with breathtaking richness. We pause at the top of the hill and marvel. With Rachel beside me, in her fashionable and elegant navy blue coat, it's one of those moments when you wish you could freeze time.

Wednesday, November 6th

Read Malcolm Mowbray's long synopsis of 'Watching the Detectives' – a very 'Private Functionesque' tale set in '30's Exeter. Small-town hypocrisy and deceit, but this time for sex rather than meat.

Mowbray, rather like Terry G, counsels me against trying to 'learn directing'. He says Colin Young will not be able to give much help and that the best preparation for directing is just the 'burning desire' to direct. A good lighting cameraman will do the rest.

Friday, November 15th

Sleep fitfully. Apprehensive on waking of how I will cope with a foodless day. [A 24-hour fast for an Oxfam publicity campaign.] Answer is to get to work and a brisk morning follows of Belfast [Festival] preparation.

To the Old Hall at one to borrow some moustaches from Maggie. At the moment the interior puts me in mind of some mediaeval ducal palace with a half-dozen workmen (at least) going about their business – carpenting, sawing, joining, painting. The top floor is beginning to take impressive shape. Terry G has such flair for design and an enviable knowledge of how to achieve the effects he's after. It's all quality stuff, too, and must be costing a fortune. I could never spend money this way. Not that I wouldn't want to, but I just wouldn't know how to. I would have panicked long ago.

Lunch and its temptations past, I drive to Bedford Square for a meeting at Jonathan Cape. Present are Richard Seymour, 'Gauleiter' of the project, Alan Lee, quiet, intense illustrator, and four people from Cape. Maschler apparently threw a wobbly some weeks ago and has been 'resting'.

On the table is a typed schedule which tells me the book is called 'Toby' and that I have to have the finished text by the 29th of November. As this is the first positive information about the project I've had since early September, I'm not immediately helpful. But am disarmed by Alan Lee's gentleness, enthusiasm and the beauty of his drawings and the first of the holograms (of the boy looking in the mirror), which is exciting.

Try to avoid the kitchen. Drive up to the Everyman and a new print of Clouzot's *Wages of Fear* gets me through the evening. By the time I'm home it's 11.15. No visions, no heightened senses, just weakness.

At two minutes past twelve I tuck into broccoli and cheese. The whole exercise a bit of a fraud. I think that to know real hunger is to not know where your next meal might come from.

Tuesday, November 19th: London–Belfast

Had forgotten how far Gate 47 – the Belfast gate at Heathrow – is from everything else. Sort of symbolic of the UK's arm's-length attitude to the 'province'. The Hillsborough Agreement between Thatcher and Garret FitzGerald [the Irish Prime Minister], signed last Friday, has resulted in cries of outrage from the Prots and much-increased security at Gate 47. Intensive searches, unpacking my bag item by item. Clusters of police behind uniformed security staff and, even after one's been through this, I notice a parked car at the bottom of the aircraft steps, watching us all as we embark.

Wednesday, November 20th: Belfast

An 'Ulster breakfast' in the Carriage Room. Can't quite see what is so quintessentially Ulsterish about bacon, egg and sausage, but there is some fried soda bread lurking. Break all my dietary rules and tuck into the lot.

At 6.15 we begin a run-through. Topping and tailing and only just time to try the changes. We don't finish until a quarter to eight.

By 8.05 I am ready for action. But news gradually filters backstage that there are problems. In fact the sound system has completely broken down. There's no sound 'box' at the Arts. It's all done from an old-fashioned tape-recorder on some packing crates. Someone in the audience complained that they couldn't see for the tape-recorder, and nice, helpful David took one of the packing crates away.

We have to take quick, alternative action and I decide to do the second half (Q and A), first. At least I have something to talk to the audience about. So I go out 15 minutes late and the audience response is so immediate, responsive and fulsome that I really begin to enjoy myself. From somewhere come a host of ideas, improvisations, one-liners, bits of repartee, that I'm sure I should never think of in 'real life'.

Thursday, November 21st: Belfast

Wake feeling quite pleased with myself after last night. Take my time and get to breakfast just after ten. The Ulster breakfast, I am informed, stopped at ten. But I could have an Ulster grill. This turns out to be exactly the same as the Ulster breakfast.

Friday, November 22nd: Belfast

Bobby Charlton is sat at one of the tables at breakfast. Freddie Starr at another. Freddie asks me to join him, but I've just scanned through an irritating review in the *Irish News* and want to have another look at it.

'Frequently not funny' is the phrase that really sticks. There is lots of credit for the way I carried on on Wednesday, but he makes it sound as if the material was weak. Funny how stupid things like that can cut through – despite the raves in the *Telegraph* and in the *Newsletter*.

I'm rung just before I leave for the theatre by the BBC to ask if I'll appear as a 'guest celebrity' on a Children in Need appeal which is to be done as an inter-Britain link-up.

So I find myself at midnight, halfway through my first square meal of the day, locked in interview with Sean Rafferty and a man who calls himself Fearless Frank (though Sean calls him Fearless Fred for a while), who once hung upside down for a record time to raise money for charity.

Saturday, November 23rd: Belfast

To a book-signing at eleven. The shop looks as dead as the city centre. Not my fault – it's all because of the rally called by Paisley and Co to protest against the Anglo-Irish Agreement. Within two or three days of the Agreement being signed, the city was covered with 'Ulster Says No' stickers. Still, our cultural oasis – the University Bookshop – moves about 100 books of *Limericks* in one and a half hours.

Then I'm whisked away to a school fund-raising to present prizes. But this again is in the centre and is half-empty. The master in charge is very sad. They've made several thousand pounds less because of Paisley's action and he thinks the Unionists should make up the difference! But the children who are there are the usual bright, lively, cheeky alert kids who give the lie to the idea of a city gripped by depression and apathy. I enjoy meeting them. Sign autographs.

On my way back to the Forum I find my path blocked. The police don't recommend me trying to get through. An army of marchers is heading straight for me. Group after group, band after band, fifes, drums (struck very loudly), red and white and blue uniforms, bowler hats, sashes. A solemn and quite impressive sight, until you look at the faces. Unattractive most of them – hard, blotchily red, unsmiling.

Wait for a while, then notice some children joining the procession and nip smartly in amongst them. A few steps later, having been briefly part of the biggest Protestant rally in Belfast since 1912, I'm across the road and into the Forum.

Tuesday, November 26th: London to Dulverton

At last, a completely selfish journey.

Rush around getting my things together. Can't decide between Proust and *La Regenta*, so take both. These two, plus a *Good Food, Good Hotel* and *AA Road Guide* make the case weigh a ton.

At Paddington board what they call 'The Torbay Express'. It's full of South-woldy people. Well spoken, elderly and quite eccentric. 'They used to start the train with a great whistle from the engine and now they just glide orf without you hardly knowing,' says a very old, white-bearded character behind me, ruminatively.

We leave late, but catch up time and as we reach Taunton the sun comes out. Collect my car.

Drive to Dulverton, which is a neat, quite charming little village of no great architectural merit, enclosed by steep, wooded slopes. The Ashwick Country House Hotel is a couple of miles outside the town, almost on the edge of the moor.

Lots of calligraphed signs around. One says that the wallpaper in the hall is a 1901 William Morris original. Another announces, as I enter my large bedroom, 'Complimentary drink'. I sip it, it's French vermouth. A card reads 'Welcome to Ashwick House – Mr Pabin'.

Inside, the hotel is almost as silent as outside. As I go down to dinner I notice for the first time that my room is called 'Larch'! The other two guests are in Chestnut.

Wednesday, November 27th: Dulverton

Eat sausage and bacon in solitary splendour looking out at the lawn, the tall fir trees and the ponds.

Into Dulverton to buy a newspaper and a waterproof. Then, rather than drive a long way, I go as far as Tam Steps and head off up the valley of the River Barle.

The path is difficult. Slippery, muddy and winding a contorted route through woods and over roots ready to take advantage of any lapse of concentration. So it's a bit of a scramble, beside a river alternately calm, clear and stately and then rushing over stones. The clouds thicken and I'm caught in a couple of hail showers.

All goes well for a while, but with hills to climb and rivers to ford and bog to extricate myself from, I'm still walking as darkness is falling. As I wait on the Dulverton Road for a flock of sheep to pass by, a motorist offers me a lift. Takes me to the Tam Steps turn-off, so I've another 25 minutes' half-running, half-walking, past a group of farmers outside an EHS – an Experimental Husbandry Station. Men in paramilitary green jackets and Land Rovers – snorting with laughter at something.

Very relieved to be back at Ashwick. Estimate I must have covered 16 miles or thereabouts today. That's about 20 with yesterday. One other couple at dinner.

They take some pride in what's called their 'Presidential Suite', which can be completely separate from the rest of the hotel – own cooking, own bar, own entrance. Mr S [the proprietor], a gentle, kindly man, says there *are* people who want this service – but not what sort of people they are. The mystery thickens – especially as in amongst all the delightfully calligraphed notes on the hotel is one reading 'We regret we are unable to accommodate armed security guards on the premises'!

Friday, December 6th

Waiting for the hologram story, which I've decided to call *The Mirrorstone*, to come back from Alison.

She likes it more than the first draft, which is always a good sign. Feels it's more direct, less obscure, aimed more clearly at a younger age group. I check it through and make various alterations and edits, which Alison puts onto the processor, and copies should reach Alan L and Richard S by the weekend.

About five, as I have just finished the story, Michael Owen from the *Standard* rings and, in his flat, almost sinister, tones tells me that the judging panel for the '85 awards have given me the Peter Sellers Comedy Award for *Private Function*. Now there's a nice thing. The awards will be doled out, at the Savoy, on the 26th of January, which is the date I've held in my diary for more than a year as the New York Critics' Circle awards. I'd promised to present. But in this case, as I say to Michael O, it's better to receive than to give.

Sunday, December 8th

Read *The Mirrorstone*. I'm quite pleased, but there are moments when the story content seems perilously arbitrary and I wouldn't say that this project is one which fits me like a glove.

In my prescient moments I do worry that, such will be the fuss made of the book, there will be little chance of my avoiding responsibility, so I should be sure not to make it something I'll be embarrassed about. But then it isn't a project with any precedent – not in my experience. A story to fit a technique.

Meal with Terry J. He's casting away on *Personal Services*, which he keeps referring to as 'Personal Functions'.

Monday, December 9th

To Richard Seymour's studio in Fulham.

They read the new draft then and there. On the whole they seem pleased, but not ecstatic. The discussion then becomes wider, with Richard S having a number of proposals and Alan, much more quietly but equally persistently, putting in his criticism as well. Our talks last for nearly four hours.

For some reason Jonathan Miller's son is there to take photographs of the three of us for the publishers. Is this some legal precaution on their part? Why waste valuable time taking publicity photos when we still don't have the book?

Am not home until 9.15 and I know that I'm now under pressure. I have tomorrow to co-ordinate all the new ideas into a third draft. Will have to cancel my National Film School visit.

Tuesday, December 10th

At 1.15 I scribble the last lines, but am not at our rendezvous – the Pontevecchio Restaurant in Old Brompton Road – until ten to two. Apologies, then read through the new material as best I can with waiters interjecting things like 'Spinach?', 'Who is the gamberetti?' and so on.

Wednesday, December 11th

At 8.30 I'm at my desk looking over *Mirrorstone* again. Final, final amendments, then it's off to Valerie Kettley at Cape by lunchtime.

I celebrate my relief at the work accomplished by sitting and reading Al L's 'Roommates' at one go. Though I feel dozy and below par, my condition is as nothing to the awfulness Al describes in this 'novelised' account of his cancer op.

At one point he finds Python on hospital TV and gratefully switches over to his favourite show, only to find it's the 'Brutal Hospital' sequence – with TJ staggering towards him, blood pouring from his stomach. Al, for perhaps the first time in his life, can't take Python and flicks the switch.

Thursday, December 12th

Lunch at the Gay Hussar with Richard Faulkner, the man I met by chance at Leeds Station whilst on the rounds with *Limericks*, and a lady called Susan Hoyle, from Islington. A brisk, earnest, forceful but not overbearing woman.

They ask me to become Chairman of Transport 2000. This I am completely unprepared for, but they are persistent and persuasive. An architect was Chairman, but he now wants to move on. I should need to attend a monthly board meeting, write occasional letters and make appearances occasionally on TV and radio. Susan H would supply me with the facts and figures.

I leave the Gay Hussar and cross Soho Square with my mind racing. At last a chance to become involved on more than just a nominal level with one of the issues I feel most strongly about.

Friday, December 13th

In to my copy-editing appointment at Cape.

Flat, moist, drab, very mild weather as I drive down there. Valerie [Kettley], very motherly, and deceptively soft, then begins to go through their suggestions for improving grammar, etc. This is on a much more comprehensive scale than I've ever been used to before. I'm just inordinately glad that the text is only 4,000 words.

Before I leave I'm shown into Tom M's office. He's lost weight and looks rather wild-eyed and jumpy. Not a man who is completely better. He refers to the 'time off' and admits that he'd reached the stage where he could no longer read a simple letter. Here he motions to his desk, which looks as chaotic and disordered as Tom himself. 'Well, I'd been working 18 hours a day for 25 years' and so on.

I feel a bit sorry for him. This huge, high-ceilinged office suddenly feels like a mausoleum and I have the feeling that Tom knows and everyone else in Cape knows that his best days are over. That he is now almost a revered relic in the company he's done so much for.

Sunday, December 15th

Yesterday the LA critics chose *Brazil* as their Best Film of the year, TG as Best Director and the script as Best Screenplay. This, over *Color Purple* and *Out of Africa*, was an enormous surprise to everybody, but now puts *Brazil* in as a potential Oscar-winner. And it's not yet been shown.

TG and Arnon are off to the States in the next couple of days to try and negotiate the requisite one week's playing time it will need, before December 31st, to be eligible for the '86 Oscars. In ten days the NY critics will be selecting their winners and *Brazil* is now bound to be taken a lot more seriously. Amazing scenes, as they say.

Dinner with the Alburys. SA's octopus soup sensational. Then osso bucco. Talk to him about the Transport 2000 proposal. He advises acceptance.

Tuesday, December 17th

Drive over to J Goldstone's Christmas cocktail party. Not that there are cocktails. No-one in our line seems to offer them.

Al Clark [the editor and film producer] confesses that he has nominated me for a best supporting performance award for *Brazil*. He says he's quite concerned as to where such a convincing streak of nastiness lies hidden! Ruby Wax says she spent three years trying to learn how to pronounce my name.

Outside as we leave the rain pelts down. Makes for a difficult drive on to our next venue – the Elton John concert (featuring Ray Cooper) at Wembley Arena. Ushered by walkie-talkie-wielding promoter's men to the 'guest enclosure'.

All we can see is the back of Elton's head.

Ray gets an enormous ovation when Elton introduces the band. I can see why Elton may be nervous of having him there. He is so much more charismatic than dear old Elton – described so well by John Peel in the *Observer* as giving the impression of not so much a rock singer, more an amiable mini-cab driver.

Afterwards Elton, who seems very aware that we are Ray's pals and that Ray is very highly thought of, is almost defensive to start with. Shakes hands with his left hand and seems to only want to talk about the *Meaning of Life* and the 'Grim Reaper' scene, which he regards as a work of pure genius.

We talk of Watford and Sheffield Wednesday and he says the football chairmen and managers who run the FA are, en masse, a depressing bunch.

Friday, December 20th

A wet and miserable morning. Low, gloomy, damp skies. To Euston to catch the 9.35 to Birmingham with Hettie, who's organising *Limericks* publicity. We talk about Transport 2000, on which I still haven't taken a decision. I feel myself that if I had really thought it the right thing to do, I would have said yes a week ago. This indecision, I sense, is a way of saying no. Hettie sensibly makes the point that whatever decision I take I'll regret at some time.

The buffet crew are in a mellow, pre-Christmas mood and strains of 'Always Look on the Bright Side of Life' fill the train – hummed, rather badly, over the intercom!

Monday, December 23rd

Valerie Kettley of Cape calls to hear my reactions to their latest changes. It takes more than an hour to talk through the latest draft.

Tom M wants the front part reduced even further. Valerie is paid to do Tom's bidding and tries desperately to make every line, every word cut she can. We end up friends, though, after I bridle to begin with.

The unusually inviting weather lures me to a run after we've finished our exhaustive talk. As I run I talk through with myself the Transport 2000 offer. I feel that I must make up my mind and resolve to do it as soon as I get home.

For two or three miles most of my thoughts are negative. I'm an entertainer, a comedian – I've no business launching into things I know so little about. I haven't the time, I shall be dragged into all sorts of activities above and beyond running meetings – and I may not be able to do that anyway.

Against this is a feeling that here is a rare chance to do something sensible.

To help a good cause. Is it not my public duty to become involved, if it will help them? The public and private sectors of my life are locked in struggle.

I really cannot make a decision. But as I run down from Parliament Hill I'm pretty much decided to say no. When, after a bath, I pick up the phone to Sue Hoyle, I'm pretty much decided to say no. When she answers I say yes. On the condition that it's a year only.

Christmas Day

Wake at nine from a deep sleep. Children already dressed. All of them clamber on our bed as we undo our stockings. All I hear from Rachel is 'Dad! You've left the price on!' A very good feeling of being together, sharing the day.

I read out bits of *A Christmas Carol*, as I do whenever we have Christmas here. Note the use of the word 'good' eight times in one sentence and think of Tom Maschler's endless notes on my *Mirrorstone* copy – 'repetition'! He'd have had a field day with Dickens.

Sunday, December 29th

Most of the day I have that restless, slightly unfulfilled feeling which hits on a Sunday. I suppose I miss religion – which throughout childhood used to take care of most of the day. In its most negative form – a guilt about doing anything too weekday-ish – its effect is still with me.

Watch a review of '85. Full of ugly images. Football hooligans, South African police, striking miners and police striking back. And the West, like the weather today, in the frozen grip of the forces of conservatism. Not a year I shall miss.

Tuesday, December 31st

A little nervously up to the Royal Free at 9.15 for an appointment with Morgan, the urologist. Freudenberg has suggested I see him after passing blood a few weeks ago – and once before in Sierra Leone.

Nearly all the ancillary staff seem to be West Indians, rather in the way that most of those who keep Heathrow Airport clean are Indians – it can't be just coincidence. I'm carrying with me a sample of urine in a jar that once contained apple sauce.

I see Dr Morgan at a quarter to ten. A man of about my age. He asks me a lot of questions, then examines me. After this he tells me he would like to run some tests, just to 'eliminate possibilities', though he hints that it could be something minor and quite safe, like a blood vessel in the bladder temporarily rupturing.

I am to have my blood tested and to come in for an X-ray on Thursday morning. He would then like to do a cystoscopy – which is a bladder examination up the urinal tract. He thinks he can get me in on Thursday afternoon. This is all rather sudden (and causes a part of my mind to entertain paranoid imaginings).

I set off on a late run across the Heath.

Of course there's probably nothing much wrong, but clearly the tests will be looking for signs of cancer and I feel a twinge of panic, which isn't helped by the encroaching darkness and the sound of a bell being dolefully rung outside Kenwood House by one of the park staff.

1986

Friday, January 3rd: Royal Free Hospital, Hampstead

Read some of Ackroyd's *Hawksmoor* until at 8.30 two nurses arrive with my pre-med. This is injected in the bum and is called Omnipon. Delightful feeling of drowsiness without fatigue.

Listen to Haydn's string quartets and some of Bruce Springsteen. Try to read, but the lines roll in front of my eyes. They're running late on the op before me, I'm told, so I have another three hours on Omnipon.

Then it's time to take a journey to the theatre which exactly recreates the speed, the door-banging, but not the discourtesy of the start of *Meaning of Life*. I'm asked for my autograph at the end of the journey. Someone says 'No, not now', but I find myself surprised that I can still write.

In the ante-room I'm in the middle of telling some story to the anaesthetist, who is pumping something into the back of my left hand, and then I'm in a recovery room and hear my nurses saying 'He looks better than when he went in'. I'm so pleased to see them all I just start talking again. I think I'm the only one in the recovery room who's conscious.

I doze on and off, but am reading a book within three hours of the op. Helen comes in at about 3.30 and says that Morgan has rung up to tell her everything was OK. I knew it would be.

I have a disconcerting and painful pee. Burning sensation, then blood – quite thick – and a sort of urinary cough – air spluttering out through the penis.

Sunday, January 5th

Not sure whether or why the two-day exploration of my urinary system should be responsible, but I have a good night of qualitatively quite different dreams than usual. Clear physical images, some nice erotic moments. Maybe something still lingering in the system.

Down to the South Bank. Rachel comes along with me. The 'Ten Day Wonder' event is a GLC booking, so I have to sign an assurance that I won't perform in South Africa or Namibia. I resent this – it's as if I can't be trusted to make my own moral decisions.

I go on at 2.30. The house is about two-thirds full and there are a lot of under-sixes.

Small Harry and *Cyril* read the best, *Limericks* the worst. Not much response to Belloc or A A Milne, or Just William. End up making up limericks on the spot. Find I've done one and a half hours without a break – no wonder I feel a surge of weariness.

Tuesday, January 7th

By taxi to Golden Square for a showing of JC's new film, *Clockwise*. Starts promisingly, even though many of the jokes are sub-Fawlty – including, amazingly enough, kicking and hitting a car that won't go.

Eventually the level of laughs begins to drop as the situation becomes more familiar and some LE casting, music and direction fail to lift it to the level that JC's performance merits. He comes in well ahead of the field with Frayn second and Morahan plodding along way back. Too safe by half.

Sit with Eric and Tania and Terry J and Steve and Iain Johnstone. John is relaxed and eventually sits with us and we have the sort of chat which shows the best side of the Pythons. Sensible, generous, but critical. John, far from being put off, listens intently and agrees wholeheartedly that the ending does peter out – with no satisfactory resolution.

Just before I leave, JC takes me on one side and asks, almost apologetically, if I mind him writing a part for me in his next film. He says it's a four-hander. Me, Kevin Kline, John, Jamie Lee Curtis!

Wednesday, January 8th

A dark, gloomy morning. To work, but phone calls dominate the morning. *The Mirrorstone* comes back from J Cape with lots of 'as's' and 'buts' queried, but basically almost there. Read through and ring Valerie K back and by early afternoon the copy is agreed, finished and I can forget that for a while.

To the dentist at five. Kieser opens a bottle of champagne afterwards to celebrate New Year – funny drinking with five other people all in white coats.

Thursday, January 9th

I'm rung by the British Council to ask if I will go to Czechoslovakia with *Private Function* at the end of the month. I'm very keen to see Prague – one of the few European capitals I still haven't visited, so say yes, providing it can be a weekend.

TJ says EMI have today withdrawn their offer for foreign rights to *Personal Services*. Michael Hordern turned down the part of the Wing Commander who, at one point, TJ admits, does have to be masturbated by one of the ladies. Apparently Alec McCowen is happy to do it.

Monday, January 13th

Into taxi for one of the more important meetings of my life – the Transport 2000 introductory party and board meeting at which the fate of my chairmanship will be sealed. No turning back after today.

The organisation's offices are in a drab, low, sixties building beside Euston Station. They're the HQ of TSSA, the railway white-collar union. (I am moving into a world riddled with initials.)

Susan Hoyle, who is humorous in a rather deadpan, busy way, takes me across the Euston Road, pointing out one of the most dangerous pedestrian crossings in London, to meet Jimmy Knapp and Ray Buckton[1] at the NUR HQ. This is an '80's block and more like Madison Avenue or a TV company than a railway union. But amongst all the smoked glass and tastefully-designed wooden furniture, there is a tell-tale British touch. On the desk at reception is a ledger headed in scribbled biro 'Air Conditioning Complaints'.

Up in the lift to a floor where all is soft carpet and silence. No-one seems to have much work to do. After a short wait, Susan and I are shown into a spacious, smart, though not intimidating office.

Jimmy Knapp, taller than I expected, a big, genial man with an almost albino-pink complexion and a jolly thatch of white curls which spill down onto his upper cheek, rises to meet me. Ray Buckton is on the other side of the table.

Knapp is easy, friendly, unforced. He flicks through my CV, but clearly knows nothing of my past work (perhaps a good thing).

Buckton just goes on about my speech at Durham. Flatteringly, he seems to have remembered more of it than I ever could. He says it was one of the best he's ever heard.

After 20 minutes or so, we take our leave. Jimmy Knapp assures me that if we ever want any help or support from him or Ray B it will be forthcoming.

Back perilously across the Euston Road and by this time about a dozen people are in Richard Faulkner's office for the buffet lunch to meet Michael Palin. The older members – representing Wales and Devon, for instance – are very gentlemanly and courteous.

A number of people arrive by bike, and the big, bearded, Northern

---

[1] These were the two most powerful men in the railway unions. Jimmy Knapp was General Secretary of the NUR (National Union of Railwaymen) and Ray Buckton was General Secretary of ASLEF (Associated Society of Locomotive Engineers and Firemen).

CAMRA Mafiosi – who, I am to find out, virtually run the board meetings – are a little guarded, perhaps feeling their power threatened. I don't know.

Harley Sherlock, the outgoing Chairman, is enormously nice. Affable, straightforward and competent, with lashings of the best sort of disarming charm.

I have prepared a short statement of my qualifications and disqualifications – emphasising that I don't regard my appointment to the chair as a fait accompli – and until it's put to the vote later this afternoon Harley is still Chairman. He's obviously held in great affection and I am most envious of his fluency and patience and diplomacy.

At 4.15 I make my apologies and, with a well-received 'May the best man win', I leave them to the 'election'. Out in the windy streets I seek out a 24 bus to take me home in preference to a taxi. Symbolic gesture!

An hour or so later Susan H phones me at home to tell me that I have been unanimously elected Chairman of Transport 2000.

Tuesday, January 14th

Ring Ma on her 82nd birthday. (If I live as long as her I'll see 2025!)

At quarter to twelve drive out, through a fierce hailstorm and some fine celestial lighting, to the Film and TV School at Beaconsfield. I have an appointment with Colin Young – the head of the school.

Colour photos, well taken and expressive, of all the students and teachers are stuck on a notice-board and this companionable feeling – of an enlightened university campus – is quickly evident.

After showing me two studios, Colin gets hold of a lean, intense man with big eyes and high cheekbones called Paul. He is the No. 2 here and Colin asks him to lunch with us. We talk, Paul and I, for a while about what has to be learnt about directing.

Colin takes us into 'New' Beaconsfield to an almost deserted Chinese restaurant of very good quality, where he orders authoritatively. 'The only thing you need to be a director is confidence,' he asserts confidently.

Then they ask me about my film (the one that I want to direct). I feel apologetic and faintly embarrassed as I take up their time waffling about my inability to start writing.

At the end of the meal, as we sit in the car, Colin (like Jimmy Knapp yesterday) insists that I should call him if there are any problems and that I should consider coming for a one-week session at the school in the summer, but the last thing he says, of my desire to direct, is 'We do think you should do it'. Well, this is the year of trying new things, I think, as I head out onto the M40.

Thursday, January 16th: Southwold

Fancy the Crown for an evening meal, but Ma is quite shocked by the £10 price for a three-course meal and dismisses it.

A diplomatic call upon the Haythornthwaites, mainly to thank her for all her work on the hallway. Have a scotch and a chat.

He was in the Parachute Regiment. She is the daughter of a Jewish father who worked in the film business for a while. She went to work on *Vogue* – hence the good taste of the decorations. Very complimentary about my mother, 'Very game', 'Out in all weathers'.

Wednesday, January 22nd

To the T2000 office. Meet Susan H.

Over a very good Indian meal, we talk a bit about each other and backgrounds. She's twice married, a first in PPE from Somerville, has a son called Tom who's a year younger than Tom. She's persuasive, talkative, sharp, restless and enjoys gossip. I like her. I feel rather dull and soggy but hope it doesn't show.

On to transport business. Do we want to supply a judge for *Motor Transport*'s awards for the most environmentally-sound lorry? We shouldn't be endorsing lorries at all, but we should be aiding any belated recognition that they damage the environment. Susan is in favour of agreeing.

Then she talks at length about personalities in the office. I still feel like a prospective fiancé coming to meet his new family, so I listen and avoid too much judgement.

Home via Belsize Park with a feeling of slight unreality. Can I really fulfil all the functions (to quote the Bank Manager in 'Eric Olthwaite')? I know here and now that I shall not be able to take on the workload when I'm making/selling the next film. Next year something will have to change.

Friday, January 24th

David Leland calls and offers me the part of Eric in *Heartbreakers*, which he's directing for Channel 4 in the autumn. Eric is a 'totally charmless' character and David L is interested to see how I could do something which doesn't rely on charm.

He also says something about wanting to push my acting a bit further out. I know what he means. Take a few risks. Well, again, it all fits in with Putting Myself on the Line Year. Agree to read the script.

Sunday, January 26th

Not since *Private Function*'s Royal Premiere 14 months ago have we dressed up together like this. [For the *Evening Standard* Film Awards.] After one unsuccessful attempt and a whole day's shopping last week, Helen has assembled a very stylish, elegant outfit. She's bought long earrings to go with it at Camden Lock today, and new evening bag, shoes, etc.

Arrive at the 'river entrance' of the Savoy Hotel about seven.

There are only about eight awards. Alan and Malcolm win the first – Best Screenplay for *Private Function*. Alan's speech is short and to the point – 'It just shows you can't go wrong with incontinence.' Norman Garwood wins the next award – Technical Achievement for *Brazil*.

Joanna Lumley gives a very generous, clear and humorous intro to my award, which is number four.

Stephen Frears collects the Best Film award for *My Beautiful Launderette* from Rod Steiger, who looks as if he is in a catatonic trance. But his ringing inspirational clichés bring a nice touch of Hollywood to this rather low-key, 'British' evening.

George, exceedingly nervous, and Denis, even more so, go up to collect the last award of the evening, one given to HandMade Films by the Duchess of Kent. George describes her as 'Your Majesty', inadvertently. She counters that that is 'one or two up from me', to which George, quick as a flash, replies 'Nothing's too good for you, ma'am.'

Monday, January 27th

Arrive at TV-AM just after dawn. A more comfortable, relaxed, expansive feeling to the place now it's comfortably ahead of BBC's *Breakfast Time* and expanding its advertising revenue. Roy Hattersley and Nicholas Ridley are sitting in the foyer. Not talking to each other.

I chat to Hattersley briefly about Sheffield. He asks me where I am from. When I say 'Ranmoor/Crosspool borders' he gestures with his forefinger under his nose ... 'Oh, the posh end.'

He goes in and scraps with Ridley over the upcoming Commons emergency debate on the Westland leaks.[1] Ridley is dismissive, patronising, and can't have done himself any good.

---

[1] Two weeks earlier, Michael Heseltine, the Defence Secretary, walked out of the Cabinet after his plan to save Westland, the British helicopter company, by merging it with European companies was overruled by Thatcher. She questioned the MOD's independence and insisted Westland be merged with the American company Sikorsky.

Nick Owen, one of the presenters, reveals that I was his house captain of football. He was at Shrewsbury for one term with me, and I had written about him in the house football annals. All this poured out onto a million breakfast tables.

Also Jimmy Greaves, quite out of the blue, declares his love of *Ripping Yarns* and especially 'Golden Gordon'.

Home and an interrupted morning's work. Phone calls from Maggie S ('Darling, you looked about 12, as usual') and an interesting job offer from *Jackanory* to read *Charlie and the Chocolate Factory*.

Evening at home, fairly quietly, with the TV. Thatcher chews up Kinnock. She sounds like some pre-historic bird swooping, shrieking about her nest. News item of the day – 'The remains of a Polish tax-collector have been found in two suitcases.'

Tuesday, January 28th

At seven Angela comes round for supper and a natter. It's a pity so much of her brightness and energy is unexploited. She is still quite brittle and castigates herself for everything. She feels she hasn't lived and has had her eyes tested today and been told that she'll have to wear glasses when driving. All this depresses her more than if she were a placid, easy-going type like her brother.

Wednesday, January 29th

Terry seems remarkably unruffled by the fact that Zenith have now withdrawn their money from *Personal Services* and the project looks doomed. Most backers can't see the humour, only see the outspoken sex.

Mum rings to say Mr Haythornthwaite across the way has died. I liked him, glad I knew him.

Read Kundera's *Joke* for most of the evening – as a sort of preparation for Czechoslovakia, where the book and the author are banned.

Friday, January 31st: Prague

Not much to see of Czechoslovakia until we break out of the clouds and head in over one of the most enormous factories I've ever seen. Note from my reading that it was a Czech (Čapek) who coined the word 'robot'.

At Praha Airport are planes from China, Cuba and Algeria. We are the only capitalist airline. Met by a slightly harassed, chatty, humorous Englishman called

John Green. He's the cultural attaché and looks like Alec Guinness playing Alec Guinness. He wears a sheepskin coat which has seen better days and looks less smart than most of the Czechs.

He moves me briskly through the formalities ('You never get much trouble if you come in from the West, it's the East Europeans they give a rotten time to'). John Green is the first of many people over the weekend who emphasises that the Czechs do not think of themselves as East Europeans, but as Central Europeans (we are, after all, further west than Vienna). They hate the Russians (in common with nearly every other Soviet satellite). They were the fifth most prosperous economy in Europe before WW2 and had close cultural links with Great Britain.

To Wenceslas Square, which is in fact a gently-sloping rectangle, with wide road and sidewalks. Hotel Jalta, in heavy National Socialist style, but comfortable inside with mini-bar, bathroom and radio and TV. The breakfast menu offers 'grey bread – any chosen sort'.

Much waiting around whilst the various delegations sort out my future. Am introduced to my interpreter Irena, a slightly nervous, greying-haired lady in mid-50's with a sensitive and kind face. When we are out walking she emphasises 'everything I say is only my own point of view and shouldn't go further'.

On to a special showing of the film [*A Private Function*] for university and embassy people. I introduce the film in English. As soon as it begins I go off on my own for a walk into the old town, across the Charles Bridge. Quite magical.

Back at the screening, I'm buttonholed by a red-eyed English teacher from the university. He warns me darkly against getting too involved with the 'embassy crowd' and that 'You'll never meet any real Czechs, 'cos they don't know any'. I arrange to meet him tomorrow.

Irena and her husband Dick take me to eat. Dumplings and red meat seem to be a Czech speciality. Then I'm taken to a 'Theatre of Small Spaces' – in effect an intimate cabaret-style club. A group called Ypsilon sit about on stage . . . loosely structured, talk, discussion, maybe leading to a sketch. Place is packed. In the second half I'm called up on stage. Perform a little and then sit there grinning idiotically whilst the Czech banter swirls around me.

They know all about irony and apparently they put across a lot of criticism, cleverly veiled so the authorities won't see it. A sort of intellectual second economy.

Saturday, February 1st: Prague

Sleep seven hours despite great heat from air conditioning. As I sit on the lav wrestling with the unperforated toilet paper, I try to sort out a few thoughts for my various public appearances today. Scrambled egg, good strong coffee, then meet Dick, who is going to walk me round this morning.

His wife and two children wanted to visit friends in York in 1977, but she had to apply to the Ministry for permission and was at first given the stock reply 'apply again in seven years'. But she knew the wife of a top official and the whole process was speeded up. As Dick tells me such things he drops his voice – as if the streets themselves might be bugged. From habit probably. I shouldn't think he is aware of how odd this behaviour looks to me.

We pass Kafka's house. He shrugs and smiles a little bleakly when I ask if Kafka is still read in Czechoslovakia . . . 'Oh, he's read . . . but he's not published.'

He takes me into a wine bar – a Vinerana – a small, smoky, whitewashed room, with plain wooden tables and counters. We have a couple of glasses of excellent, fruity Moravian white. He tells me that Jan Schmidt of Ypsilon apologised after the show last night for not talking to me more on stage, but as the house lights went up to welcome me he noticed two men from the Ministry of the Interior sitting at the back. These are the shadowy government 'cultural officials' who can close their show at any time, so he decided to play safe.

We talk about Britain. Dick says that the Czechs think of Britain as a golden land of freedom and cannot believe things are bad there. The football riots made the worst impression, everything else bad they regard as government propaganda and discount it. Dick says that the Czechs are very racially prejudiced and would agree with Enoch Powell.

Then we walk up the hill to the splendidly-sited British Embassy, to which Her Britannic Majesty's ambassador has summoned us for lunch. Very formal, lots of servants and polite introductions to a number of Czech theatrical folk who have been rounded up to meet me.

Then whisked away to a screening of *Private Function*.

Another speech, translated this time, more flowers, champagne, and, at last, driven back to the Jalta by Mr Green. By now it's six and within ten minutes the phone rings to announce the arrival of my teacher friend and his colleague – studying Czech, from Lancaster University. Both fairly classic types. Anti-London, anti-privilege, beer-drinking in quantity. But not lost for a word and soon we are in a long, old, vaulted room, simply, almost austerely, appointed, full of all manner of Czech – man, woman and child – drinking beer.

Then up the hill to another pub – this is the Black Cat. Some Czech ladies at the table next to us in a merry state. Czechs have very bright, humorous eyes when they want to use them. Have long since forgotten what the teachers and myself have been earnestly talking about, but we agree to repair to the hotel as all the pubs have, quite sensibly, closed.

Sunday, February 2nd: Prague

Wake after eleven o'clock. Feel a heavy pain in my right hand. Head not too bad, stomach queasy. Lie there as if hit by a bulldozer, then ease myself out of bed, cursing myself for missing my looked-forward-to morning walk round Prague, and a little concerned that I've probably missed breakfast and within an hour I shall have to get myself across town to Sunday lunch with my interpreter.

Only then do I become aware that things are not too good. There is a line of bloodstains on the pillow and sheet and duvet. My hand is quite grossly misshapen and, though I have no usual feelings of hangover, my face is uncommonly sallow. I wash and shave and clean my teeth with difficulty. Usual exercises out of the question. Just getting dressed is an athletic feat. But with my hair washed and a fresh shirt and a set of clothes on, I feel that I can at least venture out. A cup of coffee and a glass of fruit juice washed down with mineral water, then out into the town. I vaguely remember trying to have a bath, falling . . . but not much else . . . Oh, dear . . .

After my lunch I find myself in the southern part of town, pushing open a door of a grubby apartment block and walking into a lobby which smells of old meat. Upstairs to the flat above the butcher where the cultural attaché and his wife lives.

They were burgled two days ago and the police could not have been more thorough until they suddenly broke off the inquiry, leading Green to suspect an inside job. But he's like the best and worst of the English . . . quite stoical and unemotional about the whole thing. Takes it with a pinch of humour. At one point he leans forward, and without a change in his tone of voice, warns breezily . . . 'By the way, this place is almost certainly bugged . . . I don't know if they're listening at the moment, but it's best not to mention any Czech names of people you've met.'

After supper we go into the centre to a concert in a grand, excellently-restored, neo-classical hall. The government gives an awful lot of money to the arts . . . but of course they must be officially approved.

We end up drinking Czech liqueur and talking about the various celebs who've passed through Prague. The actors he liked, the musicians, especially orchestras, he found rather loud and apt to behave in Millwall-ish fashion at airports.

Monday, February 3rd: Prague

To lunch with two men from the Czech film organisation. Officials, probably Party members. The older man asks me to describe Margaret Thatcher's policy. Monetary control, tight legal restraints on opponents, intolerance of debate and discussion, strong defence capability ... as Irena says afterwards, I could have been describing the Czech Communist Party.

She puts me on the 4.45 plane home. I give her a four-day-old *Guardian* and any other English literature I can find – a *Listener*, a copy of Larkin's 'Whit Sunday' poems and Anita Brookner's *Hotel Du Lac*. She slips them quickly, discreetly into a brown cotton bag.

Tuesday, February 4th

Up to the Royal Free by 10.45 to see Mr Morgan. A Lowryesque collection of the old, infirm, squat, bent and shuffling gather around the desk at Clinic 4. A man next to me talks of his brother-in-law ... 'We put him away last Friday. He was a great racing man, lived for the horses, so you know that bit of the funeral service where they throw earth on top of the coffin? Well, I threw in a betting slip, along with the earth.'

After a wait of 40 minutes or so I am called in. Today Mr Morgan is surrounded by seven or eight students. He grasps my hand effusively and I let out a yelp of pain. He looks at my still-swollen right hand and I tell him what happened in the bathroom in Prague (grins from the reverential students) and he says he will get someone to look at it right away.

Within a half-hour I'm down at Orthopaedic, signing an autograph for a porter, chatting to a boy who'd broken his leg acting, and being shown into Mr Wilson's room. He looks, squeezes, has me X-rayed (long chat with radiographer about *Brazil*, and then shows me that I did indeed cause myself more than a bruise in Prague. I can see clearly a fracture in a bone on the side of my hand – the metacarpal, he tells me. He puts the side of my right hand and little finger in an aluminium-backed splint, which I shall have to wear for three weeks. It will be six weeks before it completely heals.

Feel on remarkably good form, but writing isn't easy and I shall have to take to the typewriter. Ah, well, it all fits in with this year of doing things I've never done before. Like breaking a bone.

Sunday, February 9th

On returning from the Mansfield Road grocery store with a bottle of milk in either hand, I hurried across Elaine Grove to avoid an oncoming car and felt my trusty 15 quid shoes, which have been my mainstay for seven or eight years, slipping on the hard-packed snow and I was upended.

Instinct made me protect my be-splinted right hand, which threw me off-balance, and I ended up lying on the ground with the broken glass of a milk bottle sticking from the base of my left thumb. (The other bottle, I'm pleased to say, was safe and sound in the three fingers of my broken right hand.) I remember staring for far too long at the chunk of glass which had inserted itself into my flesh like a wafer stuck into soft ice-cream. Then I picked the glass out, and I was aware quite coolly that I had hurt myself rather badly. Still managing to carry the other bottle, I squeezed my hand over the wound and walked home. The driver of the car rolled down his window. 'You alright?' 'No,' I said. He grinned and drove on.

I was then driven to the Royal Free. Even as queasy as I was, I did appreciate the regularity of my visits there so far this year. I was stitched up and Diana [wife of my friend Sean Duncan, and a doctor] stayed with me for the hour and a half I was in there. Apart from the 'freezing' injection into the wounds before they were stitched, I felt remarkably little pain, nor had I lost much blood, nor, thankfully, and according to Diana very luckily, had I cut any tendons.

Monday, February 10th

At Walkden House [T2000 office] I begin the first of many explanations. Susan H thinks the sight [of two bandaged hands] almost uncontrollably funny. A lot of gasps and 'Oh, no's'.

We walk across Melton Street to the grey marble slab of Rail House [British Rail headquarters]. Up to the meeting, which is in Room 101 – though no-one alludes to the significance. Grant Woodruff, British Rail's Director of Public Affairs – grey-haired with a young face – opens the meeting briskly.

We have a briefing on the Channel Tunnel[1] and we're asked to help put pressure on the customs and excise to make checks on trains which they at present refuse to do, and to cause a fuss over Section 8 (grants for freight transport) at the DTP [Department of Transport].

Lunch is up on the seventh floor. There are about 15 of us altogether, including three out of the four past executive directors of T2000. I feel that the

---

[1] The Bill to approve its construction had just been given a third reading. It became law in July.

BR attitude throughout is brisk, a little patronising, as if we're seen quite clearly as a bunch of weirdos, as you get in all societies of the world, and are really only there to make good, honest businessmen's work that much harder. They're the do-ers, we're the talkers.

Wednesday, February 12th

The side-effects of my two accidents seem almost entirely beneficial. I'm improving the speed of my typing, I get washed in the bath by Helen and I've slept long and well for the last three nights.

Thursday, February 13th

At half past twelve a brown, plain-clothes police car, grubby inside and smelling of stale cigarette smoke, picks me up to take me to Kentish Town nick, where I (with my Curse of the Mummy's Tomb hands) am to be guest of honour at a lunch. The topics of conversation are predictable. Camdenspeak – the name given to the attempts by our council to purge the language of any words with sexual or racial connotations – is high on the list. So onto the scrapheap of progress go such words as 'chairman', 'ladies', 'midget' and, of course, 'black'. Officers are completely bemused that Accident Black Spots cannot be called that any longer.

All present, and there must be 20 senior detectives in the annexe room with brick wallpaper, agree that things are 'getting worse'. Nearly all are against the decision to put armed police into Heathrow ... indeed every one is against arming the police force any more than at present. They don't like political duties – either in Nottinghamshire or Wapping. There are few obvious heavies, but equally few who can make intelligent conversation. An air of benevolent philistinism.

One stands head and shoulders above the rest – a man called Blair, who has written a seminal (dare one use the word in this context?) textbook on rape and is sharp, soft-spoken and acute. Either he will rise like a rocket or else he'll resign.[1]

About three and a half hours later I'm driven in an official police Rover through Kentish Town. 'What a dump,' says the driver. 'I wouldn't bring kids of mine up here.'

---

[1] In 2003 the 'man called Blair' became Sir Ian Blair and two years later Commissioner of the Metropolitan Police. He resigned in 2008.

Friday, February 14th

Yet another visit to the doctor's starts the day. This time to have my wound looked at. Nurse says it's healed well and removes the stitches. Back home to write copy for the *Limericks* book, then take Rachel by Underground to County Hall, where she is to receive a prize for being one of the six winners out of 10,000 entries in an ILEA poetry competition.

County Hall is enormous – built with such pretension and high expectation, and now beleaguered and rather sad, a cross between a school, a hospital and a parliament house in the Third World. No colour, no pictures on the walls – it feels like something that has been stripped to its bare essentials, robbed of any respect it might once have had. Across the river from its windows can be seen the Gothic pretensions of the Houses of Parliament, where the fate of County Hall was sealed last year [When the Greater London Council was abolished].

Rachel and the five other winners read their poems bravely in front of the barrage of photographers and TV lights, and tears fill my eyes as Rachel finishes her poem about Tom. A moment of real pride.

Wednesday, February 26th

A check through my speech in the taxi and a long, slow journey to St Katharine's Dock. With some difficulty I find my way to the 'Jock', a stout, broad-beamed sailing barge. A small, quiet handful of journalists. Harley Sherlock looming above them all; the thin, heroic Gallic face is Pierre Bermond – Chairman of Transport 2000 International, who has come over for the press conference [called to introduce me to the media].

I start well with a couple of ad-libs, then dig into my speech, which I deliver as well as I could have hoped, but it seems to fall into a vacuum. I have some ringing phrases, which receive no reaction, and some jokes, which receive no reaction. Maybe it's like this at press conferences. To someone brought up on the need for audience response it is a little disconcerting. I introduce Pierre Bermond, who also is received in this polite vacuum.

A cycling magazine want a picture of me on my bike, an anti-road-widening campaigner wants me to come to the first day of a public enquiry. *The Civic Engineer* wants to take me to lunch and Capital Radio interview me on the round bed in the captain's cabin. The owner of the 'Jock' is a very smooth fish, who clearly thinks that my involvement with such people is quite inexplicable.

From there by cab to *London Plus*, the BBC's evening programme. Stuck in the worst traffic jam for years, and arrive breathless and am rushed straight onto the show. At least I have first-hand experience of the problems T2000 wants tackled. Home by cab at nine.

Phone rings immediately – it's BBC *Breakfast Time* wanting me for tomorrow.

Monday, March 3rd

A fine day and sniff of a change to more generous weather in the air. To the Television Centre for 10.30. There are about 20 people in the studio involved in putting [my reading of] *Charlie and the Chocolate Factory* on the air.

For an hour and a half they check captions and I sit reading in make-up beside a make-up lady who looks exhausted, hardly exchanges a word with me and occasionally slumps forward onto the worktop, all in.

I'm aware, during the day, of the sad fact that for many people in the studio this is a dull job. The girl at the teleprompter reads her Ken Follett paperback at every available moment. A caption man, whose job is to put five caption cards in order every two hours, falls fast asleep as we begin to record.

The work required from so many people is so minimal, so unfulfilling, that I see with the force of a blinding clear light that any new technology which could replace some of these jobs would be relieving people not of noble struggle but of extreme monotony and boredom.

Tuesday, March 4th

To the BBC for the third day running, this time to meet Innes Lloyd and mark the 'official' existence of *East of Ipswich*. Nat Crosby seems still to be the main choice of cameraman. Innes is extremely helpful and responsive over casting – and accepts that Tristram and myself are thinking away from big names.

Meet 'the girls', as Innes refers to the three ladies of varying ages who are the basis of the team – Thelma Hornsby, who was on *Three Men in a Boat*, is one of them. They seem very efficient and I have a confident feeling that the production will be well looked after. It will need to be. The shooting schedule is now only 23 days.

Friday, March 7th

Up to Hampstead for lunch at La Cage Imaginaire with a reporter and photographer of *New Civil Engineer*.

Then to Julia Street to be photographed with a bike giving views on cycling in London. Cannot pose with my own bike as the saddle's missing. Halfway through the photo-session Mrs Brown on the corner arrives back boisterously drunk and insists on being snapped with me. Later she confides 'We've just been to a funeral.'

Thursday, March 20th

For some unknown reason Denis [our cat, not our producer] has chosen one of the busiest days of the week to pee on the sitting room sofa – for no apparent reason. Scrub down the offending parts of sofa, then out into a grey and wet street for the paper, only to find our bag of litter upturned. Stuff all that back, collect the *Guardian*, find that a dog has evacuated right outside the front door.

By taxi to Kensington Town Hall for a conference organised by T2000 with some money from the GLC.

I creep into the room, expecting a handful of keenies, but find that the place is full – 70 or 80 people – with their little tables and writing pads in front of them.

Listen to two platform speeches. Both much more critical than my own. Mayer Hillman of the Policy Research Institute is uncompromisingly in favour of immediate legislation to regulate private motoring.

I take the stage at two o'clock and feel loose and in control as soon as I get going. Deliver another mixture of laughs and, hopefully, serious scoring points. Over in about ten minutes, apologies and leave.

Have the feeling I may have rather overdone the ham.

Monday, March 24th

John explains to me his new film 'A Goldfish Called Wanda'. I am to play a man with a stammer who kills Kevin Kline by running him over with a steamroller. John bemoans the fact that he's written himself another 'boring, uptight authority figure', but otherwise sounds very enthusiastic and is anxious to plan ahead so it can fit in with my dates.

My 'dates' depend on a conclusion to 'Explorers', to which I attend later this morning, for the first time in several weeks. Can make little headway. Suddenly free from weeks of tight deadlines, I'm momentarily lost, and cannot work out my priorities.

At seven I drive into London for a 'reception' at the Reform Club given by Richard Faulkner and Will Camp.[1] (Faulkner's 40th birthday, Camp's 60th.)

---

[1] Will Camp knew everyone in the political world. In one of his obituaries in 2002 he was described as 'Writer and corporate and political adviser'. In 1999, Richard Faulkner was made a Labour peer, Baron Faulkner of Worcester.

The Reform Club seems to embody the twilight of Empire better than any building I've been in. Apart from telex machines, there is little inside this time capsule to suggest that the Boer War is not still in progress. Huge Corinthian columns dominate the interior spaces, which are grand and dusty and faded. Leather armchairs, a few people scattered about drinking and talking.

Upstairs and round a gallery to the immense and gloomy library. Here, a gathering of about 100–150 is swallowed up in the vastnesses of shelves ten stories high, more Corinthian columns and a soothing old brown ceiling with panels and stucco.

And quite a gathering – Michael Foot, Peter Shore and one or two less well-known Labour front-benchers. Bob Hughes and Prescott and others. Norman Lamont and a smattering of Tories. I feel like a new boy at school. People keep asking me who I want to meet. I really just want to meet someone who isn't powerful or famous, just good company. But these gatherings are clearly lobbying occasions.

I talk to Peter Snape, MP for West Bromwich and an ex-railwayman. He's concerned about the effect on railways of the abolition of the Metropolitan Counties who gave much help to local lines. Bob Reid of BR is there, a thin, aquiline, rather interesting man physically. He would look just right in a monk's cowl or on a cross.

Wednesday, March 26th

Sitting at the desk a fresh approach to the new film occurs to me, forcefully and with the instant attraction of having solved an increasingly encumbrous problem – where to go with 'Explorers'. A simple two-hander, a love story, a sort of 'Long Encounter'.

A curious week, thus far. Charitably it's part of a recovery and re-stocking after the last few hectic weeks, at its worst a reaffirmation that I really don't know what to say next.

Down to the Python office to move this impasse momentarily with a T2000 interview. Michael Williams from *Fleet News* – a freight-oriented periodical – waits patiently, as from the room where the interview is to take place comes Arnon Milchan. Warm embraces, face against his stubbly chin – his shrewd, playful eyes close into a smile. Commiserations over lack of Hollywood Oscars, agree to meet for lunch in London soon, then back to *Fleet News*. Wonderful collision of two worlds.

Watch the *20/20* TV programme about *Brazil* – Terry as the little man who took on Hollywood . . . and won. Now officially enshrined in US mythology. Terry's supporters (especially amongst journalists) are impressive. The programme, aired two weeks ago, apparently added 20% to the box-office.

Tuesday, April 1st

No more GLC.[1] As much as anything about their passing, I shall miss their radical and stimulating attempt to shift the centres of power and influence in this country from big institutions run by middle-class, public-school-educated men to everybody else normally excluded from power. And they've been open and extrovert and consultative.

I see from yesterday's *Telegraph* that the lorry ban is to be ended immediately on 69 miles of road which the DTP has now taken over. Sensitivity, tolerance, understanding and conciliation – it's a spirit utterly alien to the Thatcher-inspired politics of the '80's. Irony is that it should take a woman to combine all the worst of the new male middle-class attitudes.

Some brighter news is the arrival in the post of Caroline H's two 'Cyril' covers, which look bright and eye-catching and colourful. My hope is that they'll be taken for Adrian Mole books and sell millions! These two, combined with the first sight of Alan Lee's *Mirrorstone* cover, bode quite well for next Christmas and make me feel I've done some work after all!

Sunday, April 6th

Up and across the Heath just after nine. A cold east wind, but good for running. Pad past Michael Foot, who lurches from side to side as he walks, like a rather overloaded cart. He occasionally shouts for Diz [his dog, Disraeli].

Home for a long, leisurely levée. Ring TJ to wish him well for tomorrow's start of *Personal Services*.

Down to the Shaftesbury Theatre. Rory Bremner, encountering me at yet another charity show, asks me if I work professionally any more.

I'm on at the end of the first hour, reading 'Biggles'.[2] At the difficult stage of knowing it just well enough to look away from the book long enough to lose my place. So one or two fluffs, which irritate me. Neil Kinnock and Glenys are down there in the front row.

Our 'Custard Pie' routine[3] does not disgrace us, but Graham ballses up the lines on a couple of occasions – and, as TG points out, 'He's the one with the script!' All of us aware that it's timid stuff compared to the quite frenetic energy of the Mayalls and Henrys and Edmondsons.

[1] The Greater London Council, London's administrative body since 1965, the year I came to live in the capital.
[2] A piece written in the style of Captain W E Johns, about Biggles, Algy and Ginger trying to get tickets for a Bruce Springsteen concert.
[3] An academic lecture on slapstick comedy.

We're all behind Geldof at about 11.30 singing 'Feed the World' and the show ends just on the four-hour mark.

Collect our carrier bags as Rik packs up his dead chicken, which he'd previously stuffed down his trousers, Frank Bruno, who's been playing Juliet to Lenny Henry's Romeo, removes his mediaeval bodice, and we all repair to the Marlboro' Crest Hotel, where a party is provided.

Ade Edmondson tells the awful tale of how Bob Geldof, who had been playing the Cliff Richard part in the Young Ones hit, took it upon himself to smash Edmondson's guitar live on stage, presumably thinking it was a prop. It was in fact a Fender something-or-other, Edmondson's most prized possession.

Rik, talking of his disgusting act, says he was very worried about his parents seeing it, but his father had quite approved – 'Just how they used to talk in the navy!'

Monday, April 7th

Lunch with Tristram and Innes. Innes, in his bluff and hearty way, is quite a canny operator. He's always nibbling away at the script in an effort to cut down on cost and time. The word 'crowd' in a script still terrifies the BBC.

Tuesday, April 8th

Lunch with JC at Cage Imaginaire.

John looms in from Flask Walk looking like one of the steelworkers from *The Deer Hunter*, in a woolly hat and a chunky, inelegant windcheater. When he's taken off his jacket he still has several layers of sports jackets and sweaters underneath.

He's had bad 'flu for about a week, he says, and over the last few days it's induced 'the sort of depression I haven't felt for ten years'. The root of the depression is the recurring Cleese bogey of feeling trapped – trapped by success, by work responsibilities like Video Arts, trapped even by the film he's writing for me, Kevin Kline and Jamie Lee Curtis, with Charles Crichton ... 'Quite honestly, Mikey, if Charlie Crichton dropped dead tomorrow I probably would abandon it.'

What he does want to do ... 'I've reached a time in my life ... ' is learn, read, travel and not have any work responsibilities at all unless, for instance, 'Louis Malle asks me to go to Greece for a few weeks'.

Thursday, April 10th

Taxi to the BBC for the first auditions at 10.15. Then finalise script with Tristram and spend the afternoon dictating the corrections to Innes's secretary.

The office opposite is occupied by Ken Trodd – an intense and slightly disconcerting presence. His office is full of junk. His clothes are everywhere and in the middle of it all a TV shows DBS programmes from Ted Turner's US channel.[1]

To outward appearance there is an air of precarious improvisation, but undoubtedly this shabbily-appointed fifth floor at TV Centre is where the British Film Industry exists. Chris Morahan, Gavin Millar, Alan Clarke, all have current projects under discussion. Richard Eyre is in production. Fifteen or so films are made here in a year, on a rolling programme which the 'Wardour Street' film industry never seems able to achieve.

Monday, April 14th

Talk to Tom about his continuing inability to concentrate on his 'A' Level maths course. I just want to keep the lines of communication open with him. His friends are largely a street crowd and in many cases his academic inferiors, but he has a strong loyalty to them, which sometimes gets in the way of his work. I feel it's very hard for me to advise him not to spend so much time with these people.

Tuesday, April 15th

Feeling in one of my late-afternoon lethargies, I walk for a while around Covent Garden, looking for a present suitable for tomorrow's 20th wedding anniversary. Eventually settle on a book called *Fatigue and How to Beat It* – mainly because I'm too tired to keep looking.

Simon and Phillida round. We go out to *After Aida* at the Old Vic. A rather heavy piece to start with, but the second half is especially effective – with light and energetic playing from Ian Charleson and big Arnold Bennett-*Clayhanger*-like prickly authority from Richard Griffiths.

The restoration of the Old Vic is magnificent. One of the finest theatre interiors in town since 'Honest' Ed Mirvish spent two million quid on it. Pity it is only half-full. Later go backstage. Actors in their underpants – always a bit of magic destroyed.

R G berates us for being the worst audience they've had.

[1] Direct Broadcast Satellite. Satellite TV was not yet available in private homes.

Wednesday, April 16th

The day after Reagan bombed Tripoli, and after the shock the gradual realisation that not only has Reagan set in train the dreadful prospect of more and more warlike actions, of further reprisals by Libyan fanatics in Europe, and of a generally much less safe world, but that 90% of Americans are behind him! My feelings of revulsion against this dark side of America – the clumsy, ugly face of power without intelligence, the world bully – have quite put me off going over there next week.

Happily 70% of Brits polled oppose Thatcher's decision to let our bases be used, but that's about the only good news.

Write a nice piece called 'Biggles and the Groupies' which gives me more pleasure than I've had at the typewriter in a long while.

Friday, April 18th: Sheffield

Gather myself together for my third transport meeting in two days – this one up in Sheffield.

At Midland Station I meet Jo Guiver, the Buswatch co-ordinator, who turns out to be a bright, likeable, jolly sort with a huge backpack, as if she's walking the country. Hint of difficulties ahead when I'm introduced to Layna, who is of Polish stock, with a punky haircut and a Vegan.

I rise to speak, a little despondently, to about 30 faces. Susan follows me, then a smooth, but quite plausible man from the South Yorkshire Passenger Transport Executive.

Then Layna's two friends, one called Jesus and the other Mark, speak inaudibly, though quite sensibly, from the back, but it is clear that they are not at all grateful for having had three years of the lowest fares in the country and instead want to have a go about travelcards, etc.

We close about 9.35 with my rather waffly summing-up. Must learn to do this better. A hotel has been booked for Jo, Susan and myself, but we have to be in by 10.30. Susan hasn't eaten since three, so this is out of the question and we ring the hotel to ask for dispensation. No-one answers.

Thanks to a friendly member of the audience we are driven to the hotel. The door is locked and no-one answers the bell. Our driver sees people in one of the rooms apparently watching TV. After much banging on the window, one of them is persuaded to open the door for us. A card beside a bell reads 'Reception and Emergencies'. We ring the bell but no-one appears. The guest shrugs, 'They live in the basement.'

We leave after ringing the bell yet again and I end up buying all three of us rooms at the much more pricey Rutland Hotel nearby.

Sunday, April 20th: Southwold

Mum meets me at the door, anxious, no doubt, that I wasn't here earlier. Quite sharply aware of her frailty. She's thinner than ever – especially her arms and legs – and moves with greater difficulty than usual. Quite a change and for a while it worries me.

I've brought lunch and afterwards I'm just happy to sit and talk. Her alertness and humour and liveliness are unimpaired, I'm glad to say. Julie next door has had a man in all night. 'It *could* be her brother. Of course, it's no business of mine,' and she rounds it off with a laugh at herself.

After supper we watch *Heimat*.[1] My first view of it and I'm very impressed. Late night walk and contemplate writing a Palin-style British *Heimat* – extended version of the memoir-style of *East of Ipswich*.

Wednesday April 30th: Paris–London

The plane arrives in London three hours late after a further fault is found as we taxi out for take-off. So tempers are already frayed when we arrive at Terminal 4 (recently opened and subject of a big ad campaign and much media attention).

One man checking all UK and EEC passports. A very angry and vocal little Scotsman, who turns out to be an MP (wearing his House of Commons tie!) finally approaches one of the officials and indignantly puts the case for more than 400 travellers who are in the middle of the nightmare. The official, without a word, gets up and walks away.

The MP turns to us and, arm upraised in the manner of Lenin or Robespierre, shouts 'Come on, everybody through! Everybody through!' Some reluctance, then a few start to move. The officials turn in horror and make to apprehend one of the passengers but they're simply brushed aside. The frightened look that so quickly replaced the smug look of power will remain imprinted on my mind. Not to put too fine a point on it, I saw through power for a moment.

Thursday, May 1st

In the evening go to the William Ellis summer concert. The headmaster is waiting anxiously on the steps bemoaning the lack of parental interest – 'Where *are* they all?'

---

[1] An 11-part German series directed and co-written by Edgar Reitz, which follows the fortunes of a family in a Rhineland village from 1919 to 1982. There were two further series in the 1990's and the 2000's.

Inside there is some excellent music and the attendance does swell quite quickly. Tom plays both saxophone and clarinet. He still does his Cheshire Cat grin a lot and looks bashful, but plays well.

Talk to Rachel's headmaster – Nicholas Harris – afterwards. Teachers starting industrial action again and Rachel likely to lose her school journey for the second year running. The effects of the government's attitude to public-sector schools continue to worsen.

The hope that I had for state education has dwindled to the point where I'm beginning to seriously question whether we made the right decision for our children. The answer certainly is that we did, at the time, but should we not take another decision now – to remove them from state education before the whole thing collapses? I feel that we must keep the faith. The ideal of equal opportunity in education cannot be seen to fail. Maybe I should be more vocal. Maybe I should organise a school journey together with other parents.

But, being the lazy non-activist I am, I end up at home watching the *Heimat* episodes I missed whilst away.

Friday, May 2nd

A balmy warm smell rises up to my room as I sit with a solicitor and answer his various questions on the origins of the 'Lumberjack Song', what it means and why it's sufficiently important to us to want to proceed against United Biscuits and their agents for using it as the basis for a commercial.

Silly situation, really. 'Lumberjack Song' is just a bit of nonsense, but in order to establish the principle that we've been wronged, we have to pretend it's of great significance – a piece of modern culture. But I do resent the way it's been used without permission, especially as I would have given an emphatic 'no' if we had been asked.

Friday, May 9th

I read David Leland's *Heartbreakers* script. The character of Eric tantalises me. He's a marked difference from the characters I usually play. I talk a lot about my freedom to do 'what I want', and yet my acting roles in recent years have been very similar and, with the exception of *Brazil* and *The Dress*, nice and safe. Eric is neither nice nor safe and the part is better than *Brazil* or *The Dress*. So I'm tempted, despite the fact it looks like cutting into my writing time.

To the office and an interview with *Labour Herald* about T2000.

Of course they're all very elated by last night's local government and by-election results in which the Tories were roundly trounced. In Camden, depicted by Thatcher and the government as wasteful, over-spending and dangerously left-wing, there are now even more Labour councillors.

Go on from the office to see the Jamie Lee Curtis film *Love Letters*. A low-budget, serious and quite strong US picture. Jamie is good. It's interesting to see her playing a woman not a glamour girl. The small Cannon Theatre is cramped and full of smoke. Not a great environment to see a movie.

Monday, May 12th

Read a deposition on the 'Lumberjack Song' from a solicitor, based on our talk last week. Very rough, ungrammatical and badly-phrased – and rather depressing. Trying to assert 'rightness' seems to involve entering a world where patience, stamina and self-belief have first to be tested by irritation and frustration. And it rains outside. A filthy May thus far.

To Chalk Farm Station, thence to Euston – litter, pervading shabbiness – and to the Great Nepalese Restaurant in Eversholt Street – inviting, comfortable, spacious, friendly. There to meet and talk with Susan and Jo Guiver prior to the board meeting.

'The Future of Transport 2000' comes up about four and clearly cannot be fully debated in this meeting. Peter Horton [one of our local group representatives] stokes the fire a bit here, 'Important document', 'We put it off last time', etc, etc. Quite unhelpful, but maintains his own position as guardian of the heart and soul of Transport against the wily and untrustworthy Londoners.

Massive relief at another board meeting completed. I have a worrying feeling that I didn't enjoy it as much as the first. Is this the familiar Palin pattern? Attracted by something new, accepting an unusual challenge and then, once the challenge is overcome, being rapidly disillusioned by the usualness.

Tuesday, May 13th

Walk across into Tavistock Square. Sit beside Gandhi and the tulips, as a brisk cool breeze dilutes the warmth of a, so far, clear, sunny morning.

Try to focus my mind for the next hour on *Mirrorstone*, for I have to jolly along the Cape sales conference on the same subject within half an hour. I remember so little about it, except Cape's prodigious editorial interference. Look at Gandhi for inspiration, a hunched bronze figure over there in the centre of the flower bed. He doesn't look at all like Ben Kingsley.

Summoning up all my powers of positiveness, I head for the conference venue at the Drury Lane Hotel. A modern, concrete infill hotel, which doesn't improve the north end of Drury Lane. Silent foyers, signs, conference suites. Up to the fourth floor. Am on the phone to the office when Tom M emerges, greets me warmly and says 'You're on!'

Without further ado I'm ushered into a room packed with expectant people. Most of them sit round a table which must be thirty yards long, but many others sit behind them. It's like an over-stocked peace conference. I'm told Roald Dahl is to be there later in the morning. God knows what that rather shy and reclusive author will make of it.

Tom announces me and I waffle on as best I can for a few minutes. Jokes go well, general good reception, but occasionally I catch the hardened, cynical faces who recognise a Maschler hype when they see one. Tom says a quick word, leads me out, cries 'Thank you, you were wonderful!' and shuts the door. I'm left quite alone in a small ante-room. Search for my coat and leave.

Taxi takes me across to Acton, to the BBC Rehearsal Room for the *East of Ipswich* read-through.

John Nettleton and Pat Heywood are wonderful as the Burrells. Nettleton misses not a single line or a single moment of humour. I don't think I've heard anything of mine read as well first time.

After playing Mrs Wilbraham in the read-through and seeing the crew and cast together, I begin to feel broody for acting.

Thursday, May 15th

This morning a letter from someone who had never forgotten the image of me having breakfast in the Lochalsh Hotel looking out over Skye and had eventually made a pilgrimage to the same breakfast table. Not only was it all he'd ever hoped, but he took a friend and they fell in love and 'have been in love ever since'.

Gilliam rings. We talk over *Munchausen*. He's off to LA next week, though, to talk to Fox about the production. Once again he chides me about not being able to write any more – about being busy with everything but the main thing, and so on.

Friday, May 16th

To Martin Lewis's party.[1]

Ever since reading the Rachel Roberts book [*No Bells On Sunday*, published

---

[1] Martin is a comedy entrepreneur and party-giver, now living in the USA. He had worked on some of the Amnesty shows and was a friend of Lindsay Anderson.

1984]¹ I've thought of Lindsay Anderson and how I could use some of his acute and down-to-earth good sense. But I couldn't really think of any reason why our paths might cross again. And there, on the lawn outside Martin's basement flat off the Finchley Road, is the man himself. A little larger in the belly than I remember, but his fine hawk nose still the distinctive feature.

I am so pleased to see him, I don't have time to think what to say, so out comes my spontaneous pleasure. We have a very good, too short, natter. Lindsay, who stands so close that I feel myself being edged into a flower bed, is, he says, going to start a campaign against the use of the words 'rather', 'slightly' and 'quite'. He would cut this diary at a stroke.

He hasn't yet seen *Private Function*. He confesses that he thinks he might not like it, but clearly doesn't like himself much for saying so. And he couldn't go to *Room With a View* because he's fed up with films 'in which Maggie Smith and Denholm Elliott are *so good!*'.

He also is the first person I've come across who didn't like *Englishman Abroad*. His brow creases painfully at the mention. 'Oh, too facile ... all those *camp* Englishmen.' The only film he's liked recently is *Crazy Family*.² 'The violence is so *productive*'!

Then across London to dinner with Richard Seymour and his wife at his little terraced cottage on the main road at Richmond. The smell of the trees and the countryside and the glimpse of the river's bend are wonderful and remind me how rough our part of north London is.

Look through the *Mirrorstone* dummy – see most of Alan's drawings for the first time. The holograms are much smaller than I expected and not really as comprehensive a part of the book as I'd imagined.

Foresee the dangers of the Maschler approach. He has so sold the book on the new techniques that I think there is a distinct danger that the hype could rebound on him.

Saturday, May 17th

A sour, gusty morning of continuous rain. Shop for food, read the papers, then across the road to the Oak Village residents' 'Spring Lunch'.

I meet the new people from No. 1 Julia Street. He's called Denis, which must have given him a few uncomfortable moments when Helen's been out at night shouting for the cat!

---

¹ Rachel Roberts won a BAFTA for her performance in *This Sporting Life*, directed by Lindsay Anderson in 1963. Married to Rex Harrison from 1962 to 1971, she died in 1980.
² A Japanese film, released in 1984. Directed and co-scripted by Sogo Ishii.

Tuesday, May 20th: Southwold

Find the [*East of Ipswich*] unit in Walberswick rehearsing the gents scene, with the car. Tendency of John Nettleton to huff and puff in comic fashion. Suggest to Tristram that John deliver the line with less effort. This he does on the third take and it sounds much better.

A local, with rich, upper-class accent, cycles by – 'Out of the way, you *bloody* people!'

Thursday, May 22nd: Southwold

I am at the location, right in front of Glan-Y-Don,[1] at eight o'clock.

Elinor [our production manager] and her local team are deploying extras along the beach. Occasionally they have to be moved back as the tide reaches its height. But someone seems to have boobed and the tide, which is supposed to turn at nine, rises remorselessly and seems to delight in hurling the odd wave at any extra we place, and at every camera position we set up.

We keep retreating, then re-setting, and the sea calms, then out of nowhere a line of salt-white foam hurtles across the beach, forcing everyone to leap out of the way – with varying degrees of success.

Saturday, May 24th: Southwold–London

Various shots around the house with Edward Rawle-Hicks – who is daily becoming more secure and solid in the part. Rather a poignant moment as I pass Glan-Y-Don this morning on my way to its film equivalent and there are the Palins of the 1980's having breakfast.

Send a Stanley Spencer postcard of Southwold beach 50 years ago to Puttnam to tell him that our lunch plans of two and a half years ago are becoming film!

The catering truck is parked behind the toilets at the far side of the pier – one of the least salubrious spots in all of Southwold. Here the unit spreads itself beside the dog-shit, the oil and the remains of scattered dry bread crusts which even the seagulls ignore.

At home William greets me with news of 94% in his chemistry mocks – best in the year – and Rachel has one of the leads in the Gospel Oak fourth-year play. Tom has been learning how to defend himself with a short stick and is covered in bruises.

[1] The guest-house on the corner of Pier Avenue and North Parade where my parents and I stayed on our summer holidays from 1959 to 1964, and on which 'Tregarron' in *East of Ipswich* was based.

Open one or two of my pile of letters. Someone wants me to do *The Missionary* as a stage musical.

Wednesday, May 28th: Southwold

After lunch, in an upstairs room amongst the narrow bedrooms of the Crown [Hotel], Ken Pearce [the editor] shows the first rushes I've seen. Very encouraging. Every beach shot is highlighted for me by the wind, which blows at the hair and the ladies' dresses and tugs at the windbreak and seems to epitomise east-coast holidays.

Sunday, June 8th: London–Southwold

Bundle things together and set off about midday. I feel tired and not particularly happy, as if some dark cloud is temporarily settled over me. Very curious feeling. Vestiges of shyness. Or is it just that a film unit is a potent and demanding entity and you're either part of it completely or just a visitor? I'm uneasily in between.

They're at The Mount.

Inside 'Treganon', the combined efforts of Sally's design team, the costume, actors and actions are very satisfying to behold. It's the 'white soups' scene, with the room silent save for the joyless scraping of soup bowls. We've put one of the ladies – Miss Chatty or Miss Oliphant – in a neck brace, after seeing so many of them around Southwold.

Tuesday, June 10th: Southwold

To the location early.

Innes is quietly putting pressure on me to write 'another version' of Graham Crowden's sex-talk speech, omitting words like 'penis' and 'vagina'. He is worried about 'losing some of our audience too early on'. I refuse to write an alternative because, as I say to Innes, 'I know that's the one you'll use'.

Quick look at rushes. Leave Tristram to go to Aldeburgh for Dame Janet Baker and dress and drive out to Tinker Patterson's house on the marshes. Tinker, Norman Parkinson's favourite male model, had encountered me in The Mount, which he now owns, grasped my hand warmly and said how delighted he was to find another Old Salopian and would I come round to dinner so he could tell me stories of School House in 1944?

Margot, Tinker's dynamic German wife, has just returned from the Continent – stealing menus for her new patisserie/coffee house on North Parade.

An act of purest optimism, but she says there are a number of new, young professional people coming to Southwold who will patronise it.

Tinker tells me of a prep school master who used to come around and check the boys' hand positions before they went to bed. 'Hands Up North' he would say, which meant that they should point their hands palm upward and lay them on the pillow. 'Hands Down South' meant only depravity.

We have a simple supper – 'You're talking about school, so I'm afraid it's school food,' says Margot, modestly.

Tinker gets out school photos and tells me of boys like Spurway and Cameron and how he'd once been asked to eat food off the floor. He clearly loved his Salopian days and wants to know how much it had changed in the 13 years between his leaving and my arriving.

Then we get on to talking about East and West Germany and how the Baltic Coast is like Suffolk and how soap-powder is still considered a luxury item for Margot's cousins in the East. Tinker tells how Margot's father – a Stuka pilot in the war – wore an Iron Cross at a recent posh dinner at Fishmongers' Hall – much to Tinker's amusement.

A beautiful and tranquil sky as I leave.

Saturday, June 14th: Southwold

We finish at 6.35 beside the lighthouse in Stradbroke Road. Nineteen days and four nights, 23 shooting days altogether.

Celebrate the end in the Sole Bay Inn with a pint of Adnams with Nat [Crosby, the cameraman] and Innes and Tristram and others. A moment to savour. The relief, the feeling of achievement and the sympathetic surroundings, the bond of the team, all combine in a low-key but incredibly satisfying moment. Eventually Tristram and I are left talking as everyone leaves, as if in a curtain call at the theatre.

I have my reservations still about some of the sequences, one or two moments of performance and amount of cover left un-shot, but, all in all, I've never felt something done as close to the way I wanted it done as this.

At eight we repair – Tristram to the Crown, myself to Sunset House – for a bath and brush-up before the end-of-filming party at nine.

We're in the Upper Room [at the Crown Hotel] and music is already blaring out – 50's hits. Innes makes a short speech and thanks me for 'introducing us all to Southwold'. Granny sits happily in the midst of it all, attracting, as if by some perverse magic, all the tallest men in the room, who have to bend double or sometimes even treble to listen.

Monday, June 16th

Go to see the latest possible Python property purchase. This is a collection of buildings off Delancey Street in Camden Town.

The layout of the odd assortment of buildings around a central 'courtyard' feels just right for our purposes. There's a very good space for André, promising surroundings for Anne and Steve and the office, as well as small, low buildings ideal for viewing theatres, production offices and editing rooms.

TG scrambles, burrows, prowls, plans, elaborates. He responds so unfailingly positively to life that all I can do is watch and marvel. TJ has a black eye. He went to the help of a black man who had been nearly run down by a car in South London and was punched in the eye by one of the assailants – who were white.

We have tea and citron pressés in the Delancey Street Café and discuss next moves. Very positive feelings all round, but the asking price of £420,000 is considered excessive. TJ counsels an offer of £300,000. Anne feels she can start no lower than £360,000.

Have officially left Barclays Bank after 25 years. First Coutts cheque signed today.

Friday, June 20th

Start the day with a huge surge of optimism for the great-grandfather, Brita Gallagher story, encouraged by a *Listener* book review of *The Tender Passion*, a survey of Victorian attitudes to love, sex, attraction, infatuation, etc.

For an hour or so I'm convinced that at last this is the answer to screenplay problems. But, as I run in late morning in order to think over the idea, various difficulties cloud my previous optimism. Chiefest of these is that, were I to play the main man, I should be casting myself as a straightforward, sexually-involved clergyman, and that has a familiar ring to it. So I return, dripping sweat in this high humidity, with only the frustration of another clear path ahead blocked.

Anne rings to discuss how she should approach purchase of the Delancey Street complex. She thinks the seller will definitely *not* budge below £400,000 (he's shifted already from 420G, I point out). The more I think about the place, the more positive I become. It *is* right, somehow, and I would hate to lose it. Anne decides to go back (she feels much as I do), with a 'final' of £380,000.

Saturday, June 21st

Our offer for 68a Delancey Street (£395,000) has been accepted!

Chilly, windy, overcast morning for the tenth Oak Village Street Party. Miss the lunch as I have to go to Harrods for a book-signing. Read some limericks to a polite, but bewildered group of shoppers in the children's book department, then sign for an hour and a half and shift 120 books.

Last week someone sold seven in two hours, so I feel I've earned my champagne and smoked salmon sandwiches in an office looking out over Knightsbridge. Harrods, like the transatlantic airlines, has suffered considerably from Americans' fear of Europe since the Libyan bombing.

Back to the street party. Dance, flinging myself into some R&R with Helen. To bed at half past two for the second night running, after enjoying late-night chat with Mr Brown on the corner, who told me that I 'should have been born an Irishman'. High compliment indeed!

Monday, June 23rd

The morning not a good one. As time drifts by, I resort to all the writer's time-wasting devices walking downstairs, making phone calls that aren't vital, pottering, reading snippets of other works – and all the time hoping that, like Maradona's 'Hand of God' last night,[1] something would strike and show me the future.

I read some of *The Tender Passion* and also some more of great-grandfather's notebooks (he did mention young women, or just women, an awful lot), but by the time one o'clock comes I am not much further on with a decision.

Relieved to be temporarily released from my frustration, I go to Odette's for lunch with Eric I. He gives me some encouragement, partly by telling me that he's been writing very badly recently, and partly by a very sympathetic response to the Victorian idea.

By 6.30 I'm at the Commons to meet David Mitchell, the Transport Minister (Railways). He takes me to the Commons Bar. No-one else I know there except Roy Jenkins at a table by the window. Amidst the almost suffocating leather and oak panelling, have a beer – the Minister a tomato juice.

He advises me to feel free at any time to ask him or his department for any help with facts and figures and he assures me that he keeps telling the DTP that we are not 'dangerous'.

---

[1] Maradona's disputed first goal, in which he appeared to put the ball in the net with his hand, was the first of two he scored for Argentina in the quarter-finals to put England out of the Mexico World Cup 2–1.

Tuesday, June 24th

Drive over to the Riverside Studios by Hammersmith Bridge to see Max Wall (now 78) in *Krapp's Last Tape* with TG, Helen and Maggie. Max is marvellous. He moves carefully and precisely, his timing and eye for detail are exact and delightful. Maybe it's because, as TG says later, Max *is* Krapp. Audience predominantly young.

Afterwards we stay for a drink with him. It's as if no years have passed since Pembroke Castle and the rain in summer '76. Max still drinks a pint of Guinness, slowly. He remembers *Jabberwocky* line for line and we talk nostalgically of John Le Mesurier and others he remembers with generous enjoyment, and how he used to keep his teeth in a little bag at his belt. He talks quite cheerfully about his various 'conditions'. 'Fallen arsehole,' he confides, out of the girls' earshot.

Wednesday, June 25th

JC rings from a hospital bed where he's having a cartilage operation. The goldfish film seems set for May/June '87.

Robert H comes round for dinner. Talk over Robert's plans for various theatre groups he's trying to help, but I resist his pressure to commit Gumby funds. It's not so much the money as the fact that I have too many fingers in too many pies. I must reduce my involvements or they will at worst swamp me and at best become a blur of half-participation.

Tell him about the Victorian film. His advice is that I should write the Edward Palin character for another actor than myself, someone physically different – only then will I break away from the good old *Missionary* types.

Thursday, June 26th

At 2.30 to Rachel's classroom for the last progress report on any of our children at Gospel Oak. Mrs Deadman says Rachel combines the best of Tom and William, that she has great potential – she was one of two girls who did not drop a point in her maths test – she is sensitive and easily bruised, but has developed a toughness and determination which will carry her through.

The girls run the class, says Mrs Deadman, and Rachel's table are far and away the most talented. And – some of them – very difficult. Rachel's problem is that everyone wants to be friends with her, and she is nice to them all. If she was able to be as sharp to them as some of them are to her she'd be less hassled.

Monday, June 30th

Hot night, morning starts cloudy. Am reading *Tender Passion* and making notes when it occurs to me that what I need is some up-front money to tide me through the period of research – in short, I need what I've avoided taking on my 'new film' for years: a good, old-fashioned commission.

Look at the calendar and apportion time for three projects up to the end of '87 – the Victorian film, a short film, possibly to be done at the National Film School as a prelude to directing the Victorian film, and some time in summer next year provisionally set aside for JC's film.

An evening phone call from D Leland awakens my interest in the part of Eric in *Heartbreakers*. It would ruin all the plans made earlier today, but would give me a new direction in acting, to complement the 'new direction' in writing to which I've now committed myself. Can I do both?

Wednesday, July 2nd

To the House of Commons with T2000 team.

Searching procedures at the door take a while. A man is trying to hand in a small gift-wrapped box with a ribbon around it, which he says is a present for the visiting German Chancellor. The lady at security wants to know what's in it. He doesn't know.

We pass through and into the Gothic world of Parliament, winding up back stairs to what could be the maids' quarters or the room of some demented sister who's not talked about, but turns out to be Committee Room 17. Inside a panel of ten MPs sit in a semi-circle around a secretary who takes shorthand of the proceedings. Opposite the semi-circle is a table at which currently are sitting four men from the Transport Users' Consultative Committee. They're all Major-Generals and look most impressive from behind. We slip in at the back, where a half-dozen people are listening.

I, who have been quite looking forward to the experience, find it one of the least pleasant of my T2000 outings thus far. The courtroom atmosphere, the ritual, the respectful 'grown-up' procedure, the 'sirs' and the 'I beg, Mr Chairman' – in fact all the quasi-legalistic panoply – make me uncomfortable. I feel as if I want to speak but can't. Or is it just that I don't know what they're talking about?

Monday, July 7th

Rachel is having her tea today when she asks 'Are you unemployed?' Expostulate as I do, there is a grain of truth in her question which rankles. Of course I have hardly a spare moment, but much of the time is spent holding on – to friends, obligations, duties such as T2000 – and comparatively little, at the moment, in the creation of new work.

Tuesday, July 15th

Taxi to L' Escargot and lunch with Sandy L. I had this morning sent round to Sandy the Victorian film idea, merely for reference. He thinks it has great potential, feels I should go to someone like the National Film Development Fund for first-stage writing money and that I should make up my mind whether to direct or act. More or less decide then to direct. It seems such a short and logical step on from writing and anything that might prevent me playing a sympathetic clergyman again must be a good thing.

To St James's Square. Slowly because of the heat. All the flowers around the 'shrine' for the policewoman shot by the Libyans are dried up and dead as I cross the square and into the time-warp that is the London Library.

Nervous, bookish, soft-spoken assistants with mad clothing direct you to the various areas of human experience. 'Domestic Servants, next to Dogs.' Takes a while to familiarise myself with the layout, but soon I'm getting into the swim of turning the lights on and off and encountering strange figures in between Ireland and the Gambia.

Leave with seven books, taxi back home. Driver's a great fan and I have to talk a lot and sign his book.

Not much time to unpack before Angela H arrives in preparation for Rachel's appearance in the Gospel Oak musical 'Carrots' tonight. Give her a glass of champagne. Helen rushing in and out, house not very restful.

To the school.

Rachel gives her cheeky Cockney character – Carrots – a hint of timidity and uncertainty which she shouldn't really have. But she delivers her lines with good expression, clarity and assurance, and once she's free of the stageful of unmoving people and into one-to-one acting she's excellent. She sings two solos falteringly and a third very promisingly and robustly.

Wednesday, July 16th

A very sultry night, through which I sleep with considerable ease, until eight. At 9.15 I am at Acland Burghley School to discuss Tom's progress with Mr Trafford, his D&T [Design and Technology] teacher.

We talk for almost an hour about the poor funding of the course. Officially he has about £12 allotted per pupil per year for equipment! He manages to augment this ludicrous amount by various devious means – but fund-raising and PR are taking up far too much of his teaching time. Without whingeing, he paints a sad picture of neglect and obstinacy in the education system. He's not against some form of assessment, but first of all wages and resources need to be improved – morale is very low.

Thursday, July 17th

A cool and refreshing day – sun without the sweat. Reach my goal of four hours' research and reading. Helen rushes around all day buying food for the Gospel Oak school leavers' party which we go along to in the evening.

Rachel and a few friends produced an end of term magazine today which seems to sum up all the creative brightness of Gospel Oak School. All the children have been happy there and have made good friends. I shall miss it.

Wednesday, July 23rd

The Royal Wedding [of Prince Andrew to Sarah Ferguson] is everywhere. Thirty-one countries have pulled out of the Commonwealth Games. Reagan has outdone Thatcher in trying to clothe economic expediency in moral respectability, calling sanctions against South Africa 'repugnant'.

Saturday, July 26th

A leisurely start to the day, then embark on a clear-up of my workroom, sorting out the piles of books, letters, scripts, papers, many of them sparking flashes of guilt at work not dealt with, an opinion unexpressed, a cause unaided, but I have done so little work of my own these past few weeks that I really cannot feel any great qualms over my inability to respond to everyone else's demands.

Lie awake and talk to Helen, which I don't do often enough, of my worries about the Victorian film (am I desperately chasing a red herring?), about

T2000 and my doubts which are fast developing into certainties – I'm not an institutional man, a committee man, a board man. I'm a writer, an actor, an occasional visitor – a flea who can sting and bite occasionally. I'm not cut out for Head of House.

Thursday, July 31st

To the Zanzibar to meet Michael Barnes, who is taking me as his guest to the Bolshoi Ballet at the Royal Opera House. As I've seen neither, this is a double first.

Before the opening of the ballet an announcement is made to try and forestall those 'who may try to use this occasion to make some sort of protest'. In a very English way the manager asks them not to disrupt the performance but to come and have a word with him at the interval. Obviously he's referring to those already protesting across the road, outside Bow Street Police Station, on behalf of Soviet Jewry.

The ballet is *The Golden Age*, and an unlikely, but entertainingly odd piece. Not grand or historical, it takes place, almost in the present day, at a seaside resort on the Black Sea and involves healthy undefiled workers' co-ops and a 'sleazy', but rather attractive night club called the Golden Age, where, dressed in dramatic blacks and golds, the bourgeois dance the tango.

Indeed, and most bizarrely, there's, at the start of the second act, a marvellous Shostakovich arrangement of 'Tea for Two'. Lots of echoes of American musicals – including *West Side Story* and *Sweet Charity*. I begin to be carried away and from then on the sheer skill, energy and excitement of the music and dancing are completely riveting.

Friday, August 8th

Drive to Oxford by ten and into St John's. Through two quiet, dignified quads to the library. I arrive at the same time as a bearded American scholar who is there to look at a thirteenth-century illuminated manuscript. Am reminded of the quiet wealth of the colleges – not in their buildings, beautiful though they are, but in cellars, archives, cupboards and chests.

I easily pass three hours at a desk with copies of the Oxford Calendar for 1843–62, and make copies of a number of pages and also of some good contemporary sources. Up above me is a marvellous long chamber with plaster and wood vaulted roof and Archbishop Laud's bust.

By the time I leave Oxford seems to have woken up and the spell is broken. The college buildings swarm with beefy Americans in Bermuda shorts, all here for some summer study course. One thing these colleges are getting very good at is making money.

Back to London by five.

Just enough time to say hello to Al L who arrived from Brittany yesterday, then off to an hour's tennis coaching.

Saturday, August 9th

Take Al to the bookstores of Charing Cross Road to satisfy his craving for Stevie Smith. Am struck by how rich London now is in bookshops. Despite the cinema revival, four-channel TV, cable, video, booming theatre, a lot more people seem to have a lot more time to read.

Have a half of bitter at the Crown in Seven Dials. Al so full of fears and worries – mainly centring on Gwenola and the effect on her when he goes. He has had two scares over the last two or three years and precious little has gone right, apart from the fact that he has survived, where many wouldn't, and Claudie, with her plain, philosophical Breton good sense has been a tower of strength.

I take him on an 'East London' tour. To satisfy both our curiosities. First to Leadenhall Street to see the Lloyds Building. I like it more this time, perhaps because Al's so enthusiastic. For him it's a work of genius. I appreciate today the way it fits in and complements the buildings around. It's big but light and its lines continuously broken, giving vistas through, across and round it, so at times it gives the impression of translucence – not a quality associated usually with the intimidating and imperious City buildings.

We drive on to the east and find ourselves amongst the glossy, high-tech of the renewed, revived Isle of Dogs, where enormous investment has transformed Docklands, to the benefit of businessmen and to the detriment of the local people who have found themselves largely unwanted, their neighbourhood swiftly, comprehensively, unapologetically re-ordered by outsiders.

Wednesday, August 13th

On the Victorian film news is that all goes ahead well. Steve has met with Sandy L and got on well. We decide not to go for an advance from the Film Development Fund. It's not money I need, and the submission will require synopsis and waiting for processing, all of which will take time away from my vital priority – to produce a script or other evidence by the end of October that we are not all barking up the wrong tree.

Back to Camden Town for a visit to Peter Lewis. He pronounces my teeth in good shape and talks about his Prussian grandfather who broke two ribs putting up a deck chair. Hear on the radio that 63% of callers in an LBC poll want British troops out of Ulster.

Monday, September 1st

Begin work on the Victorian screenplay.

Unsure about the sound of the dialogue – the period flavour – the detail – Latin verse, etc – but once I'm going it doesn't hold me up and I experience the pleasure of creating characters, lives, incidents; enough this morning to leave me optimistic.

Rachel has gone off for her first day at Parliament Hill, with her new Cahors black satchel, black earrings, white shirt and black skirt.

Ring Ma and Angela. Angela says she's in the middle of quite a serious depression. She's decided to be forthright about it and not cover up. Is there anything genetically responsible, she wonders. Perhaps Daddy suffered from depression as well. He certainly took things very seriously, was underpaid and had a stammer, but could this be genetically transmitted?

Cleese calls to say his script is finished. Tony Jay evidently approved greatly – which John is cross about as he'd hoped Tony would suggest the 20-minute cut it needs. I suggest John sends the script to someone he knows really hates his stuff. John finds this very funny. Top of his list is Richard Ingrams, with Peter Ackroyd a close second.

Wednesday, September 3rd

To the Python office to have my photo taken – to help out a student who's doing a portfolio of writers 'because they're most likely to be at home'. Can't get used to the intrusion of the lens poking towards me. Then an hour's chat with two very young, keen Python fans, who run a mysterious magazine which, they assure me, comes out about every four years.

After a couple of hours of being famous and unpaid, I meet with Anne and Steve. Their latest reservations concern the extra money needed – over and above buying studio equipment and the freehold to the buildings – for the creation of Redwood Delancey. Costs now up from 48 to 101G.

Rather a gloomy chat. I have the money, but it clearly irks Steve to advance yet more of my money to the project – interest-free. These are nervous times for Redwood. I think we have no option but to be bold and resolute and hope that in ten years' time (for it won't be before) it's all been an amazing success and a nest-egg for old age.

Thursday, September 4th

Angela and Veryan round in the evening for Angela's birthday present – a home-cooked meal. Champagne, tomato soup, chicken and mango, cheese, fresh berries and '79 claret, all very nicely cooked and served and Angela cheerful for most of the time. She responds to our house like someone warming themselves at a fire.

Friday, September 5th

To lunch at Odette's with TG. Voluble, boisterous, endlessly full of ideas and opinions. He wants to create some sort of 'corporate identity' to embrace Python and post-Python and ex-Python solo efforts. He's so restless – like a rubber band has been wound up in his formative years and has now been let go.

From Gilliam to the quieter dynamism of Richard Faulkner. I'd hoped to mention my feelings about retirement. More and more I'm becoming convinced that chairing is not me, but as soon as I bring it up Richard skilfully side-steps it, referring to my 'leave of absence' next year. It will be more permanent than that, and one of these days I shall have to tell him and he'll have to listen.

Back home – ring Tristram. London Film Festival have passed on *East of Ipswich*. Snobs. Bias against comedy? I just feel it's a backward push after both '*Mish*' and *Private Function* were at the Festival.

Sunday, September 7th

A sunny day in prospect. Late rising. Read Sundays. Martin Amis in the *Observer* reviewing *Speed* is fairly certain that being a nice guy is a positive disadvantage to a writer. This puts the wind up me. Perhaps I recognise a truth. My main problem is that I'm a lazy writer. Line of least resistance. There's another title for my autobiography: 'Lines of Least Resistance'!

Sit out in the unbroken sunshine over lunchtime and Helen and I work our way through stacks of old photos – ordering, albuming and ditching. They do present a view of a placid, gregarious, well-travelled, spirited and close-knit family of which I'm proud and for which I'm grateful. Dare I say a family with less than its fair share of troubles.

Tuesday, September 9th

Steady, but unspectacular morning on the Victorian film, which I would like to call *American Friends*, though the Wim Wenders *The American Friend* niggles.

Reading a *Guardian* article on Eton College's shabby treatment of their properties in London, when a very clear idea for a TV play occurs to me. The efforts to move a rather dignified and well-bred old lady from a house which the powers of commerce want to develop. Plenty of scope for little ironies, social comment and on a subject dear to my heart – greed versus dignity, coercion against consideration. Spend an hour writing the first couple of scenes, which flow easily.

The prospect of writing two new scripts before Christmas becomes a reality and an attractive one at that. After all the hopes and half-starts and *Limericks* and *Mirrorstones* and *Cyrils* of the last 18 months, I feel now solidly employed, stretching myself and enjoying a simple and satisfying return of writing appetite.

Thursday, September 11th

Tom is back from school and by his face and general uncommunicativeness I can tell all is not well. We talk for some time about his aversion to maths, his feeling of inferiority compared to the others in his class, and it's obvious by the intensity of his feeling that he is finding it difficult. Is this because he's faced with the realities of very hard mental study and concentration for the first time, or is it that he's genuinely unable to understand the work? I think the former.

Out to have dinner with Jonathan and Kate, prior to his disappearing up to Stratford for *Macbeth*.

We eat at Zen in Hampstead, or Zen W3 as it's cleverly called. The décor is chic black and white. It could be Beverly Hills or New York. An incredibly noisy table of Chinese businessmen passing Chivas Regal round the table with the speed of a Catherine wheel, turn out to be the management and owners.

No wonder they're celebrating – the place is packed. It's so self-consciously designed to attract the young, rich and successful that it's acted like a magnet to the new Hampstead money – not money which lives in the village, but, I suspect, in the new villas of Finchley Road and Golders Green.

There are no traditional materials, London brick or timber. The wood has been removed and replaced by a giant weeping fig tree which stands two floors high. The food is delicate, beautiful and incredibly tasty; unlike the atmosphere.

Late to bed after we ask for the bill from six different waiters.

Friday, September 12th

Receive photos from Mick Powell taken a week or so ago. I think I may be in for a W H Auden face – or at best a Michael Parkinson. A lot of lines appearing. The sight of them mentally ages me several years. Have noticed other signs recently – I hardly listen to pop music on the radio now – it's talk or classical.

To Clare Latimer's 35th birthday party at her shop in Chalcot Road. Slip over as I'm going in and crack my hip on the pavement. Not too seriously, but feel very foolish as a group of lads are passing the shop and mockingly surveying the noisy, middle-class guests clutching wine glasses within.

But there are some pleasant ladies there – always a much better prospect for small talk than men – and excellent food. I thaw out, but feel old and leave with the elderly and those who have babies.

Tuesday, September 16th: Southwold

I apply myself to the Victorian film, which has become *American Friends*. Writing, sometimes a little meanderingly, but writing all the same, and quite pleased with progress.

After lunch some letters and another short spell on the film, then across the Common for a run.

When I return a notice has been stuck across the windscreen of my Sierra – 'Please move your car so we can park outside our house. Public car parks are provided.'

A visit to Julie Haythornthwaite (such a spectacularly different neighbour from Mrs Pratt). She pours me a scotch and ice and we talk. She's most concerned about Angela, who was in to see her recently, and was, she thought, not at all well. We discuss some whys and wherefores and as Angela obviously finds it easier to open up to Julie than to Mother, then I don't feel I'm betraying anyone. Julie has a number of friends in the same boat.

Wednesday, September 17th: Southwold

For no reason at all, other than there being no reason at all, I find myself unable to sleep, despite being too sleepy to read.

I'm at the desk by nine, though. There then follows a sort of re-run of the previous night, except that instead of sleep eluding me, this time it's a story eluding me. Sense of the same helplessness, close to despair, as the minutes turn into hours and nothing comes. The little room and the cramped table, which once seemed so friendly, now conspire against me, as does the east wind moaning around the roofs and wires outside.

But I persevere with my four hours. Nothing to show at the end of it except frustration at the impasse into which I've lead the characters.

Back to some letters and then my great stand-by – a run. Running can never be anything but positive – that's the joy of it.

Thursday, September 18th

Down to Bedford Square to collect *The Mirrorstone* from Tom Maschler. My first sight of the finished work. Tom gushes uncontrollably, unstoppably about its brilliance and genius and beauty and I grope around, like someone having a very bright light shone in their face, to try and find the source of this dazzling hyperbole.

Momentarily a squeezing of the stomach. The holograms are tiny and none of them work in the dull early evening light. Tom rushes to put on his old Habitat standard lamp. It doesn't work at first. Then, with the help of the spotlights, some of the holograms come quite impressively out of the book.

I flip the pages. All sorts of negative thoughts. Brilliant draughtsmanship but blank faces. The whole book takes itself too seriously.

Thursday, September 25th

Complete four hours of good, steady progress on *American Friends*. Then a run and some calls – including one from the British Council asking me if I would like to go with TG, David Robinson of *The Times* and John Cartwright of the Council to the Moscow Film Festival. *Jabberwocky*, *Brazil* and *Private Function* are all represented. Very excited – another November possibility, if I can clear the book publicity dates.

To Visconti's *Ossessione* at the Renoir. Few people there and, as it shakes into black and white life with dramatic music and the title large across the screen, I hear a voice behind observe in some surprise – 'Oh, it's Italian.'

Saturday, September 27th: London–Southwold–Norwich

I'm away by ten and, after a slow slog along busy roads, at Granny's by one.

She potters out to see where I'm parked. I've brought lunch – some smoked salmon and peaches. Conscious of having to make an effort every time I hear 'Are you looking for something, dear?' when I open a drawer or cupboard.

All I want to do after lunch is sleep in an armchair over the newspapers. I settle instead for sitting outside on the balcony. The light breeze and the grunts and imprecations of rugby players on the Common keep me awake. The sun is soothing and we have a natter over all Granny's worries – damp patches in the bedroom, bathroom window opening, income tax – nothing too serious.

It's almost a year since she moved from Reydon, and as I kiss her goodbye at four and leave her waving from between the parked cars that concern her so, I feel very relieved with the way she has coped with the whole upheaval. And proud of her too.

To Norwich.

I'm welcomed by Kingsley Canham – slight, bearded administrator of the regional film theatre, Cinema City.

Even before a cup of tea or an introduction, I'm being talked at by two 'young people' from a group called Snowball. They want to use law against the bomb. Their aim is to get so many people to commit the 'minimum' crime at a nuclear base – cutting a strand of wire, etc – that they will clog the courts and eventually their view that a small crime committed to prevent a bigger crime is not illegal will be examined. The boy tells me proudly he's been inside for 40 days. 'But the police are getting wise – they're not arresting us any more . . . we have to go and give ourselves up.' Promise I'll read their literature.

Tuesday, September 30th

Collect Eric I and Tania by cab at Carlton Hill and we are deposited at the Royal Court Theatre at a quarter to eight. An audience of quality packs every seat for Bennett's *Kafka's Dick*. One feels that there are at least six reserve casts amongst us.

The play is based on the rather neat premise of a writer (Kafka) being magicked forward in time to the house of one of his greatest fans (an A. Bennett household complete with Alison Steadman as the unfulfilled, sexy wife, and an old father who is about to be put in a home – Alan plagiarizing *Private Function* surprisingly shamelessly). A lot said about the artist's right to privacy and the grasping, twisting manipulation of money-grabbing agents, publishers and other lesser talents.

'Woody Alan Bennett' is how Eric sums up our views of the evening.

Tuesday, October 7th

Like the mild and gentle weather, my writing goes on mildly and gently and my days fall into a settled and unchanging pattern.

A run, and then shopping for Tom's birthday present. A couple of hours around Jermyn and Sackville Street. Buy him a rather fine razor, slim, black and beautifully weighted. When I get home I find it's been used and I kick the cat and generally throw a fit, seeing as it comes from Oggetti and was not cheap. But it's hard to complain to these new and fashionable 'gift' shops. Like their goods they feel themselves out of reach of the general public.

Taxi down to the Coliseum to see Eric in *The Mikado*. A splendid theatre inside, voluminous and impressive, with marbled columns and huge, gilded statues of lions and charging horses. A full house and curtain goes up on an imaginative and striking set – which has the effect of making the characters look like the occupants of a decaying white dolls' house.

Very unsatisfied by the staging of the first half. Why is it in the '30's and why is so much of the comedy played like the Marx Bros? Eric keeps his end up well, but comes into his own in the second half and steals the show from under the noses of the fine, trained singers, because he, almost alone, is able to exploit the comic potential.

Wednesday, October 8th

At work by half past seven. Quite a good morning. Tom is 18. We give him £84 towards a 'boogie box' (ghetto-blaster, Brixton briefcase) and a desk tidy (hopefully), his razor and a Chris Bonington climbing book.

Tom's lifestyle and his expectations are so different from mine at 18 that I find it hard to empathise with him as he sits at the breakfast table surrounded by his cards and gifts. But the famous Tom grin is much in evidence, so I feel perhaps all's well and we ease off our pressure on him to be a bit more like us.

His martial arts training shows in a fit, good-looking, lean body. Reading and writing don't seem to appeal.

Meeting with Steve. He wants to tell me about the latest plans to protect all the other Pythons from the effects of Graham C's impending bankruptcy. (Having said that, it's been impending for at least a year.)

Anne and Steve propose a buy-out of GC's share of Python – his directorships and everything else. Then, if he does go under, we shall not have his advisers on our boards, nor his liabilities either. It seems a more significant emotional moment (the first Python to go under, the first 'legal' break-up of the group) than financial.

Friday, October 10th

Am conscious of letting the average slip back this week. The less time I spend, the less easy it is to maintain my commitment. Have lost sight of the whole work this week in a mad dash for the end. Now I am relying heavily on my three days in Yorkshire next week to get back in touch with the script, leaving me two weeks to trim, edit, order and make it presentable for November typing.

Monday, October 20th

To the Fox preview theatre in Soho Square to meet John C, and for the first time the various people involved in 'Goldfish Called Wanda'. Charles Crichton does seem to have some difficulty with speech and movement, but has a wicked smile and I get to like him more and more as the evening goes on.

We're seeing an American film called *Ruthless People*[1] which has taken a lot of money out there.

It's a West Coast film and I suppose is as far from the intelligent, perceptive, graceful world of Woody Allen as it's possible to be. But the fact that it has been so successful accords with my reading in the paper that 40% of students in a poll at the California State University hadn't heard of Mikhail Gorbachev.

On afterwards to a meal at the White Tower. Jonathan Benson, who is now with Shirley Russell,[2] immensely good company and it's so good to see him again. Later Kevin Kline and Phoebe Cates arrive, though no sign as yet of Jamie Lee.

Kevin K, quite unmaliciously, recounts tales of Sir Dickie calling African extras 'Darling' to their obvious bewilderment. They've been filming 'Biko' [later, *Cry Freedom*] in Harare, which he found incredibly dull and uninteresting and says he feels they got out just in time.

Wednesday, October 22nd

To the Great Western Hotel for lunch with David Mitchell.

The Minister, plus two private secretaries, arrives at one. The three of them immediately go to the toilet.

---

[1] Released in 1986, it was directed by Jim Abrahams and David Zucker and starred Bette Midler and Danny de Vito.
[2] Shirley Russell, costume designer, ex-wife of film director Ken. She designed costumes for most of his hits, including *Women in Love*, *Tommy* and *The Boy Friend*.

A pleasantry or two. He was at the House until 4.31 this morning. Then I begin by mentioning the topic that cannot be ignored – the report in the papers of this very morning that the government is to cut BR's grant by 25% next year.

He tries to lecture me (agreeably enough) on the link between funding and performance, on not solving a problem by 'throwing money at it'. I declare my readiness, as a taxpayer, to see my taxes used for the creation of the best possible rail system, and so we go on.

He seems almost frustrated by BRB's [British Railways Board – the management] willingness to accept these cuts. He suggests that they don't need to. If they feel unable to keep up quality of service on the money they are getting, then they should say so.

Friday, October 24th

We leave at eight for JC's birthday party at 82 Ladbroke Grove, whose interior glitters and drips pictures and opulence. It's been once again redesigned, and has a lush, soft, rich creamy feel to it.

Michael Frayn is there – nice, ironic, soft-spoken with a gentle, permanently amused look. Reminds me of his contemporary, Bennett, in his undemonstrative self-possession.

Talk to JC's mother, who sits in a corner and talks quite cheerfully about how she's been stuck in the corner. Keeps saying 'John would think I'm silly' or 'John would tell me to stop being a nuisance'. She's 87 and seems extraordinarily fit. Am able to tell her how the recent *Fawlty* repeats keep my mother from total gloom!

Sunday, October 26th

Jonathan P calls by with [his son] Patrick. Hear about Jonathan's battle with the sponsors. He refused to play Macbeth (the day before rehearsals began) when he saw that Barclays Bank [who had invested heavily in South Africa;s apartheid regime] were sponsoring. Barclays' £60,000 was returned and JP kept on. But he's been suffering from considerable criticism, especially from the theatre staff, who resent his interference. He says he's had notes stuck under the windscreen wiper of his Mercedes giving last year's Mercedes sales figures in South Africa. But he's weathering the storm. His hair is growing long and his beard looks more like Lear than Macbeth.

Monday, October 27th

A Russian visa application arrives by motorbike. William has to be taken to an architect's practice in Camden Town where he is starting a week's 'job experience'.

To King's Cross and the sigmoidoscopy clinic. There are seats outside it now where you can wait. An elderly man next to me reads his M M Kaye whilst from within there are some stomach-chilling shrieks of pain.

Friday, October 31st

At my desk at 9.30. Down to page-numbering, but still noticing bad lines, overwritten, unnecessary dialogue and plot discrepancies. Change as much as I can, and by half past twelve the completed screenplay – eight weeks, roughly 300 hours of writing – is ready for its first delivery. Only as far as Alison and the word processor this time, but it feels satisfyingly weighty and, whatever its deficiencies may be, I feel a sense of relief that I have persevered and have completed the process. If I'd left it half done, or even three-quarters done, feel it might have joined many other uncompleted screenplays in the 'One Day Perhaps' file.

Monday, November 3rd

Drive down to the Imperial War Museum for a party to launch Spike's latest and last volume of war memoirs.

Spike is in a three-piece striped suit, the suit he uses, so he says, to visit his bank manager. At his most benevolent and easy. I tell him how I read an extract to a fourth-year class at William Ellis of his *Hitler – My Part* and suddenly found myself describing the 'semen-stained underpants' of Sergeant Harris. Spike thinks my discomfiture hilarious. I leave him to his various admirers. He sits down for most of the party and people come to him.

Tuesday, November 4th

To Ealing for a look at *East of Ipswich*. My first sight of it for three months and first sight of the finished product (give or take some grading adjustments). Enormously pleased. George Fenton's music adds a touch of class and life to the piece wherever its pace slackens. The sound-mixing is confident and all in all it seems to work most gratifyingly. The comedy and the pathos, the atmosphere and the oddness all seem to balance and Edward R-H's performance grows in stature every time I see it.

Afterwards have a drink with Tristram P in the Fuller's pub across the road where we so often used to end Python filming days. It's half past five, dark already, but clear and cold and I feel an unequivocal glow of achievement as I drive home.

Friday, November 7th

1.30 Python lunch. I'm the first there. Eric, with a little trilby hat on which reminds me of his unforgettable portrayal of the Duke of Kent, steps down from a taxi. Sign a *Life of Python* book for his mum, then Terry J, Terry G (encased in thick Donegal tweed coat) and Anne and Steve all arrive. Terry J has got everyone kissing everyone else these days, but I pass on TG and Steve.

TG is soon to announce *Munchausen* and would like to announce a sort of post-Python production company, based in Delancey, etc, like Enigma or HandMade. Eric suggests Enema – motto 'bums on seats'.

At five o'clock to squash with TJ. I just win the battle of the business lunch.

Then I have to hurry across a wet and windswept London to 82 Ladbroke for a reading of 'Goldfish Called Wanda'. My first acquaintance with this project, which is already as far as having chosen the caterers.

Inside the warm, soft-pile comfort of JC's home, Jamie Lee Curtis awaits. Physically much more delicate and waif-like than one expects from her screen presence and her face somehow darker and slimmer. She has a softness guarded by a sharp-eyed, defiant exterior. Kevin Kline arrives half an hour later, from almost his last day on 'Biko'.

After Chinese take-away supper, we settle, around an artificially roaring log fire, and the windows slightly open as it is such a warm night, to read the 'Goldfish'. We don't finish until twenty to twelve, and this is the problem. This quick-fire farce should have been over in half the time, but Kevin finds it difficult to sort out his various voices and the Anglicanisms such as 'loot' and 'doing the job'. John has to explain the stage directions at some length, so it all drags on a bit.

I enjoy playing Ken and see potential for a much more eccentric, physical and unusual character than I usually play. JC is quite straight. There just aren't enough laughs. Maybe they are all there, but this evening compares unfavourably to the readings of Cleese/Chapman sketches which were nearly always a treat.

Sunday, November 16th

Jolted to hear that Angela has been no longer able to cope with her depression and has been taken into the West Suffolk Hospital for two weeks. This hits me hard.

Wednesday, November 19th: Moscow

It's half past four, USSR time, as we touch down. A queue at the passport control. Another Englishman next to me warns of at least one and a half hours of queuing, here and at baggage control. Gloom descends, which isn't helped by standing for four or five minutes in the glow of a prison-search-style striplight, with an angled mirror beyond so they can check the back of my head. But I'm cleared through.

A very reassuring, British figure steps forward to meet me. 'Are you Mr Battersby?' Then I'm alone again. Notice a pretty, befurred Russian lady eyeing me. She introduces herself as Helen and hands me a business card on which her name is printed as 'Elena'. Call her Elena from then on.

She whisks me briskly through baggage clearance. A huge Seagull (Chaika) black limousine is waiting. Looks like a '50's Chevrolet. Russian pop music blares out. Elena asks the driver to turn it down, but the control isn't working. Eventually he tugs at some connection and the whole system gives up.

Cannot take in much of what we're passing as we speed along a broad, straight, featureless, empty road towards the centre of Moscow. I am to be driven directly to the Archive Theatre, where *Jabberwocky* is to be shown at seven o'clock.

Enormously wide, straight roads, bulky solid buildings, wide, empty spaces, soaring walls. Feel like Tom Thumb.

The Archive Theatre has Russian and British flags up outside and heads turn as I emerge from the Seagull. Hands are shaken and I'm taken into a back room where coffee cups are laid out, alongside cakes, pastries and orange and mineral water. No sign of a vodka anywhere. (Apparently Gorbachev has decided to try and confront the problem of drunkenness and officially frowned upon alcoholic entertainment. No public places are allowed to serve alcohol until after two o'clock.)

Terry and John Cartwright of the British Council and David Robinson of *The Times* arrive.

Terry G comes in, rumbling in American and with his video camera turning. He even takes it into the auditorium, where 300 Muscovites are assembled to watch the film we made together ten years ago. As part of his speech he turns the camera onto the audience. Most laugh. Some do their hair.

We're presented with carnations and the film begins. Watch 15 minutes or so. Rather depressing reminder of how much my face has aged in ten years.

Then I'm driven to the Sovietskaya Hotel to wash and brush up before catching the 11.45 night train to Leningrad. (I later hear it on good authority that most Intourist trains run at night so that foreigners won't be able to see 'sensitive' installations.)

Talk for a while. David Robinson tells of the way Murdoch bussed his journalists into Wapping.[1] He had certain phone numbers to ring to find out where the bus would be leaving from, and always an Australian voice answered! His review of *Rosa Luxemburg* was criticised for taking up too much space when there was an English film also on release. 'We are a conservative paper,' he was told.

Thursday, November 20th: Leningrad

Outside all is grey sub-light. A line of tanker wagons silhouette against the sky as we move slowly into Leningrad.

Magnificent view of the Neva from my dispiriting little room. Everything functional – one tiny picture, three empty beer cans in a cupboard, water too dirty to drink, bedside light switch doesn't work.

Monday, November 24th: Moscow–London

When the pilot announced we were leaving Russian air space there was a ghoulish cheer from Americans on board but one American student I just spoke to claimed his Moscow trip had been the 'high-point of my year'.

Like the American I found the visit an extraordinary and unusual one. A glimpse into a world about which we talk so often and yet know so little. The beauty of Moscow was a surprise – the number of churches on the Kremlin, with their twirly domes quite the antithesis of the monumental architecture I'd expected. The warmth and friendliness of most of those we met was reassuring and surprising.

The early comfort-shocks – poor lighting, poor food, absence of small restaurants and bars, joinery that didn't join, almost empty shop counters,

---

[1] Rupert Murdoch, with the support of the Thatcher government, had moved production of his newspapers (*The Times*, *The Sunday Times*, the *Sun*) out to custom-built non-unionised premises in Wapping. After a vicious dispute lasting almost a year the power of the print unions was broken in the same way that union power in the mining industry had been broken two years previously.

cheap and grubby curtain and furnishing materials, exasperatingly impenetrable bureaucracy, compounded by the gloomy weather and gloomy faces – were depressing and almost frightening after the West.

However, as the days went by I adjusted. I no longer kept making comparisons with what I'd left, but with what was there, and though my material expectations may have lowered, I was able to enjoy and appreciate other values – an absence of the bombardment of advertising, a lack of anger, violence and pressure, the pleasure of discussing basic issues of freedom, responsibility, social organisation and the like in a country where all these issues really matter.

The knowledge that the Workers' Revolution has only produced a different kind of privileged elite who *can* travel abroad, who *can* book tables in restaurants and who *do* get food from private sources without having to queue, gives one the impression that this is not a particularly happy country. But the genuine warmth and emotion from Elena when we kissed goodbye today at the airport makes it impossible for me not to want to return.

My last memories are of the airport building, which was clean, spacious and almost empty. And T G and his four-hour video film of delegates to the first British film week for seven years, slung round his shoulder as he scuttled off to the flight to Rome and discussions with the *Munchausen* designer.

Tuesday, November 25th

Wake at six, i.e. nine Moscow, then sleep for two more hours – filled with Muscovite dreams of wide streets, looming buildings and silent, slow-moving lines of people.

Talk with Steve about *American Friends*. A cautious, even faintly embarrassed reaction. I really must finish reading it and see what's wrong!

Then by Underground to Stockwell to present certificates to local school children who've drawn variations on the 'Red Bus' theme for a local public transport pressure group. The children's pictures are marvellous. Bright and imaginative and full of little jokes and bits of detail, and all very different. Nearly all the winners are either West Indian or Asian.

To the Bijou for the cast and crew screening of *East of Ipswich*. All four 'juveniles' there. Three of them currently have no acting work at all.

I love the film. Nothing I've done gives me as much unqualified pleasure. So glad to be able to transmit my elation to those responsible, especially Edward, John, Oona and Pippa[1] – with whom I end up drinking in the

---

[1] Edward Rawle-Hicks, John Wagland, Oona Kirsch and Pippa Hinchley were the four main younger-generation actors in *East of Ipswich*.

Intrepid Fox. 'You weren't in *Crossroads*, were you?' asks an aggressive gay at the bar.

Thursday, November 27th

To the T2000 office for a pre-AGM briefing with Susan H. None of them seem to be lit up at the thought of, as Susan puts it, 'spending what looks like the last good weekend of the year in the Oldway Centre at Paignton'.

Spend two more hours on my speech, then set to my other task for the week, reading both *Erik the Viking* and finishing *American Friends*.

A very bright sunlight glows around my workroom as I begin to read Terry's jokey adventure of sunless Iceland. Some dynamism missing at the centre of the film and also the balance between anachronistic comedy and gritty Norse/Bergmanesque realism not struck quite right. By comparison *American Friends* is wordy, but I'm encouraged by its richness and the potential of all the characters.

Leave for squash at four feeling very optimistic and quite excited that we have two Prominent Features here.[1] Find myself quite eloquent about *Erik the Viking* – and hopefully offer Terry some good advice. He seems very happy at my reactions, and in turn I'm going to make some instant changes to *American Friends* and let him read it whilst I'm away.

Saturday, November 29th: Paignton

Walk to the Oldway Mansion, a huge house, built on the proceeds of sewing machine sales by the Singer family and set incongruously amid the nylon and print semis and just up the road from the ex-cinema. It is completely out of character for T2000, but Cyril Perry, our organiser, fixer, and member of the NUR Executive Committee, has set us up in the ballroom, and orchestral music plays over speakers in the marbled hall.

I'm a little thrown by the scale but, before I can settle, a squat, mediaeval-looking figure is introduced to me as the Mayor's assistant. Cyril Perry has evidently secured the services of his worship to open our proceedings.

I am marched away by the Beadle – and addressed familiarly from the start as 'Mike' – to meet the Mayor.

The Beadle treats the Mayor like a dog or a ventriloquist's dummy. 'At 9.30 sharp we proceed around the gallery, and I bring the Mayor into the ballroom.

---

[1] Prominent Features was the name of our new Python-based film production company. A name dreamt up, as I remember it, by Alison Davies at the Python office.

Everyone stands. We go to the podium, you will say a few words of introduction, his worship will declare the conference open, you may reply, then I have to take him out again.'

Sunday, November 30th: Paignton–London

The morning session begins at 9.30. Kerry Hamilton, who made a TV series called *Losing Track* – one of the few to have something to say about public transport – is a guarded feminist, with a hard and daunting Irish exterior, which melts away somewhat when she's not under threat. She says that when Channel 4 first commissioned her series they repeatedly insisted it must be 'controversial'. When it was finished and done (with a five million viewing slot for one of the programmes), their judgement was that it was too controversial! She shows excerpts, which liven up the talk.

At midday I wind up the conference, final speeches of thanks abound, and I'm quite touched when John Gregg – the white-haired, kindly Devonian member, who has spent the entire proceedings with a hand cupped behind his ear – rises to propose a vote of thanks to me. He calls my chairing 'genial'. They all seem very happy and content and, though I was steering blind through much of the weekend, I think that I found my way through all the pitfalls, kept control and maybe managed to stamp some of my character on the proceedings.

All back together in the train – and a jolly crowd we are. In fact my hope that the experience of the AGM would be the final straw that made up my mind to resign, is unfounded. Still, no time to reflect now, as I have to unpack, repack and set off on my travels again tomorrow to promote *Ripping Yarns* in America.

Tuesday, December 2nd: New York

Live at Five call to say that owing to the President's announcement of the appointment of a special prosecutor,[1] there won't be room for me on the show. They need a seven-minute 'window'. As I was set for a ten-minute interview, this is quite a blow for the CBS/Fox machine.

Feeling unadventurous and low on energy I remain in my room, occasionally

---

[1] The announcement that Lawrence Walsh was to be appointed as a special independent counsel marked the latest step in the murky Iran-Contra affair, the biggest scandal of Reagan's presidency. The US was accused of illegally selling arms to Iran in order to raise funds to help anti-Communist 'Contras' overthrow Nicaragua's left-wing Sandinista government.

going to the window to watch fierce rain lashing the home-going crowds ten floors below. I watch extensive coverage of the Iran arms deal crisis. Call some friends, then order supper. Drink a half-bottle of red wine and then have to fight against sleep. So in a most unsatisfactory state when Judi Marie and the limousine call at 9.15 to take me to a live TV interview.

The interview is quite hard work. Get through it on nervous hysteria. Thick greasy coating of make-up and nothing to drink but cold coffee, whilst all around, like flies, the crew do their Python impersonations. I'm afraid I'm just not in synch with them tonight.

Wednesday, December 3rd: New York

Paul [Wagner, in charge of publicity for CBS/Fox] rang and was quietly and politely critical of my CNN interview last night. He felt that I let the interviewer guide me and didn't push *Ripping Yarns* enough.

Then on to a very badly-run new TV show called *Made in New York*. The make-up man hasn't turned up and I'm made-up by the other 'guest' – a lovely, pregnant singer.

To the *Letterman* show. Julia Child on before me, cooking hamburger. Her electric ring doesn't work, and she improvises marvellously. Lovely, big, slightly shambolic lady who looks like John in drag and is a wonderful breath of fresh air after the coiffured Leona Helmsley clones of the past two days.

Swept away from NBC to drive uptown for another TV chat show – *Nightlife*, with David Brenner. Water has flooded their control room after recent storms and recording is delayed by an hour. I never feel at my best between four and six anyway, and after the day and *Letterman* I have to work very hard at being happy to be there. Brenner is a good host, if a little less playful than Letterman. I'm on for half an hour.

Still no let-up as Paul wants me to 'work the room a little' at a big video dinner-dance at the Marriott Marquis.

On the stage a man called Ken Kai is exhorting free enterprise on to further challenges. Hardly a word he says can be understood owing to a thick Oriental accent, but at one point I plainly hear him say 'Get up off your asses!'

Thursday, December 4th: New York–Los Angeles

Breakfast arrives late, packing and bill-paying all in a rush, then sit in slow traffic through the mid-town tunnel, arriving at JFK 45 minutes before the American Airlines flight to the West Coast.

I'm driven to the 'Carson' studios. Someone called Jay Leno is hosting.[1]

Am shown a dark and wretched dressing room with my name on it and a tray of food in the middle of the floor. All eaten. Lot of hanging around, omens not good. But as air-time nears things brighten up.

Amy Irving is one of the guests. A bevy of 'friends' cluster round her in the make-up room, but she remembers very well our encounter in India nearly four years ago, when she and a friend offered Terry G and me use of their room at the Rambagh Palace, and we chose the overnight bus to Udaipur!

Am last on. Amy I is lovely – a little nervous and formal, but very beautiful. Eva Marie Saint – older, and more relaxed – looking back on working with Brando, etc. Dignified and very funny.

Then me last. For some reason the scales fall from my lips and I'm blessed with the gift of tongues, going into a very silly improv about my mother being a sword-swallower, being the oldest high-wire act in England – the wire having to be 18 inches wide – and my father having a dental comedy act. Taking his teeth out and impersonating great world leaders (the Yalta Conference comes to me from somewhere).

Could not have done this with Carson. I think everyone feels the difference – Leno is much more like Letterman.

Thursday, December 11th: New York

Meet Paul Zimmerman at the very Jewish Carnegie Deli.

Already at midday every table is taken – everyone squashes in next to everyone else. It's friendly and fast. Businessmen on one side, mother and child on the other.

My pastrami sandwich is ridiculous. About 25 layers of pastrami strain the rye to breaking point. A wooden nail pierces the whole lot in a vain attempt to hold it together. I ask Paul why on earth they make anything this big. 'Guilt,' he says. 'It's an expiation of 2,000 years of history, a desperate attempt to make up for everything that's gone wrong.'

Paul's fortunes are improving. He's been paid – or promised – 100 G's for writing a film called 'Digby' for Denis O'Brien.

Makes up for a complete falling-out with Goldwyn over 'A Consuming Passion'. This is now being rewritten by one Andrew Davies. I get an odd feeling when I hear this. A twinge of jealousy? Like hearing that one's ex-wife has yet another new man!

[1] *The Tonight Show*, an American institution, had been hosted by Johnny Carson since 1962. This particular night he handed it over to a comedian called Jay Leno. Six years later, when Carson retired, Leno took over *The Tonight Show* full-time.

It begins to snow; quite pretty for a while, then it turns to rain. I buy a copy of *Mirrorstone* at B. Dalton's for the Zimmerman family. Paul insists the assistant knows that I'm the author of the book. She takes some convincing. 'They like to know things like that,' Paul assures me as we spill out into the crowds.

Friday, December 12th: New York–Dayton, Ohio

Land on time at Dayton – at a quarter past one [to see Simon Jones in a touring production of *My Fair Lady*]. Clean, clear, still, a complete change from the freneticism of New York.

To the theatre. Simon's dressing room is more like a service closet. Pipes across the ceiling, a very small mirror and worktop and that's about all. Various people have signed the wall, including Steve Lawrence,[1] who has signed 'I'll be right out' on the door of the lavatory.

They've sold out. 2,800 seats. Apparently Richard Harris came here with *Camelot* and sold out a week, making 380,000 dollars, of which Harris took 10%. Now I understand why people do these gruelling US tours.

Have never seen the stage version of *My Fair Lady*, and am impressed by the literacy of it all, and the part of Higgins especially is full of wonderful lines. Simon plays him at a brisk, belting, no-nonsense level – projecting at a volume well above most of the others. The part is admirably suited to Simon's skill at the testy, quizzical and dryly down-putting. And he sings with confidence too.

Saturday, December 13th: Dayton–Sag Harbor

Breakfast together with Nancy and Simon (who sounds seriously croaky). We drive to a Dr Feelgood who has been suggested to Simon for his vocal problem. Leave him in a smart surgery at a spotless, low-slung, modern building among a lot of similar, comfortably affluent erections in a road called Corporate Way. The doctor is called Boyles.

Nancy then takes me to the airport.

At La Guardia I pick up a Buick Skylark – with digital display panel – and, with only one brief wrong turning, find myself in three full lanes of moving traffic along the LI Expressway, passing turn-offs to Babylon and Jericho.

Al is cooking when I bang the glass of the sliding door on his porch. Embraces, greetings (the pattern of the last week). He looks thinner and moves more slowly. Yes, he has aged. Tea and a bagel as a late lunch.

Presents are exchanged and opened. Then I take a short walk along the

---

[1] American singer, born Sidney Liebowitz, best known for duets with wife, Eydie Gormé.

darkened streets – Division, Madison, Rogers and Jermain. The houses all different, all interesting, yet something missing – I think it's people.

After a delicious fish stew (cooked by Al) and cheese and Far Breton [a prune flan] and a lot of wine and calvados, Al and I walk together down to Main Street.

Al sounds discouraged. Morale low. He writes, he says, but with great difficulty and . . . who for? Sometimes he says he feels like a 'bull elephant, just waiting for the end'.

To bed soon after eleven, on a put-you-up in the sitting room. It's so cold I have to sleep in my sweater.

I get up to pee. It's 1.30. Al is in the kitchen reading E F Benson. He raises his big, impressive head and gives me one of his most heavy-lidded looks. In a tone of great weariness he says 'I'm waiting for the irrigation system to work.'

I bid him not to strain his eyes, and return to the sitting room. I'm quickly asleep.

Sunday, December 14th: Sag Harbor–New York

The sun streams in. The comforting sound of a home coming to life. Occasional patter of feet, a pause. I'm being looked at. Then back to the kitchen, footsteps slapping on the exposed floorboards. Sound of shushing.

About a quarter to nine I give up further sleep. I've had seven hours on this makeshift bed. Feel on good form. Al, in dressing-gown and *Missionary* sweatshirt, is at his 'irrigation' again. He's also begun reading *American Friends*.

We talk about the screenplay. I know as I descend the steep steps into his writing bunker that the news will not be good. And for some reason it all seems to fit Al's mood at the moment. There's hardly a glimmer of light in the picture. His criticism is pretty comprehensive. There seems nothing, at first, that he likes about it.

We go for a walk, round a wildlife reserve which is deserted by all wildlife on this bitterly cold morning, except for black-headed chickadees tame enough to take crumbs from the hands of three parka-ed humans.

After the gloom of the 'hold', we talk constructively. I realise where I've gone wrong. It's too wordy (I knew that), too much reported speech, and the 'incidents', such as death of his mother, blackmail, Symes's seduction, are perhaps too strong, too dangerously melodramatic. A simpler telling of the tale seems the solution.

At two I leave for New York. For the first few miles drive in a melancholy mood. But I put the radio on and soon the patter of music, ads and the endless traffic flow anaesthetises all but the most basic senses.

Thursday, December 18th

TJ tells me he's read *American Friends*. 'Tell me the worst' is my (post-Levinson) reaction, but it turns out most gratifyingly that he enjoyed most of it, and once or twice was moved to tears. He has criticisms, such as predictability, therefore tediousness, in the early setting-up of the stuffiness/priggishness of Ashby, but he is the first who's started his criticism by saying he liked it.

We repair to the Flask. Squally showers whip across Rosslyn Hill as we walk up past a well-advertised *Mirrorstone* window at the High Hill. Heard from Don at the Belsize Bookshop that he had sold all his copies – 'And we took a lot' – so something is happening.

Over a pint we talk further on *American Friends*, then turn to *Erik*. TJ now feels that there is nothing much in the way of making the picture. Lisa Henson and Warners are very keen and quite anxious to close a deal.

Talk about casting, and to my honest surprise TJ names me as one of the two or three names for Erik. The others being Harrison Ford and Michael York. But, as TJ is very keen for the film to be primarily a comedy, it does suddenly seem very plausible that I should play the lead.

Encouraged by TJ's comments I'm resolved to treat *American Friends* as a working project, but there are rewrites to be done and there is a time problem in shooting the Alps in summer, when I'm officially committed to John's *Wanda* project. So it seems quite attractive to set aside autumn and winter '87 for *Erik* and have my film ready to roll in early summer of 1988. If JC's works out too – a nice continuity of work.

Saturday, December 20th

By taxi to Harrods. Meet Richard Seymour and Rachel Kerr, Jonathan Cape publicist, in the book department. There follows a disappointing *Mirrorstone* signing session from twelve until 1.30. If the Harrods staff hadn't rallied round it would have been near disaster.

Then home and almost straight out, despite misgivings, to a misbegotten Camden Council cock-up called 'Citizen Cane's Christmas Cracker'. This involves me standing in Father Christmas outfit in a cold, draughty, empty warehouse as it is getting dark, rattling my money box and trying to solicit funds for homeless children from charity-battered punters. Abused by most people 'Where's your beard?' (it was worn this morning by Ken Livingstone, but wouldn't fit me).

I am one of a number of 'celebrity' Santas. Monsignor Bruce Kent is to do a stint after me. There is no publicity as to who the Santas are, or a hint that there might be anything special about them. In fact the whole occasion makes

one's heart bleed for our borough – and for substantial amounts of our money –
that both should be in the hands of such basically decent, incompetent folk.

Christmas Day: Abbotsley

At nine o'clock Cathy G, Granny P and myself drive round to Abbotsley
Church for the Christmas Service. We would have walked, but for the problem
of getting Granny P over the stile. The service is held in the chancel only. A
number of rough-looking lads seem to be officiating, together with a myopic
organist with Brylcreemed hair combed sparingly away from a low brow. The
priest is of that waxy-hued, rather baby-faced complexion – as if he'd been
brought out of cotton wool only very recently.

But there are 35 souls there, and I feel it a very satisfying continuity with
the past to be standing next to my mother. She complains about the modern
language in the service.

Full of virtue we file out, after taking communion, at a quarter to ten. I tell
the waxy-faced vicar that I was married in this same church 20 years ago . . .
and am still married . . . 'To the same woman,' I add, which Cath thinks very
funny.

Friday, December 26th: Abbotsley

I have an idea to take Tom P for a driving practice to Ely, with a visit to the
cathedral my reward for sitting with him. The idea spreads rapidly and is soon
a full-fledged expedition, involving all of us except Rachel, who watches *Chitty
Chitty Bang Bang* on her own.

Veryan rings. Angela is back in hospital. She took an overdose of pills, but
is now back and her condition is satisfactory. Veryan tentatively suggests that
perhaps the hospital was irresponsible in sending her home at the most dangerous
time of the year. They sound to me almost sue-ably negligent. But it's a measure
of how desperate she is.

Sunday, December 28th: Southwold

Enjoy the drive across to Stowmarket, very easy on the eye. Then onto the
new, improved A45 to Bury and find myself tensing in preparation for what
I will find at the West Suffolk hospital. Long, low, modern building, quite
carefully and thoughtfully landscaped.

Park and walk in through the main entrance to find myself completely alone. No-one at Enquiries, no-one anywhere, and no plan of the hospital or indication of where I can find Ward F8. Eventually, at a chocolate slot-machine beside an AIDS warning display, I find another visitor who knows the hospital better than me. She directs me upstairs.

Ward F8 is the medical ward where Angela has been put temporarily after her overdose on Saturday. This afternoon she is to be moved back to the psychiatric ward, where she has spent most of the last five weeks. I'm directed vaguely and find Angela, a slight slip of a figure, apparently asleep in a chair beside her bed. The bed has been stripped and on the mattress is her case.

Angela isn't deeply asleep and opens her eyes quite quickly. Her hands are hot, her eyes dead and limpid. She talks slowly in a monotone. At first it's as bad as I feared, but gradually she revives and the blanket covering of negativity lifts every now and then. She knows that hospitals don't particularly like 'overdosers' – thinking of them as people who abuse drugs – but the nurses and staff seem kind and cheerful enough. She's brought some lunch whilst I'm there, which she eats with enthusiasm.

I stay for an hour or more. Have never hugged my sister as much as I do in the ten minutes or so before I leave. But my reward is to see her smile, make some quite bright small talk about my coat, etcetera, ask about my plans.

I leave her, a frail figure waving at the end of a hospital corridor. Have to walk very slowly to let my emotions sort themselves out. When I do start back for London, I drive straight back without stopping for lunch. As I drive I feel sure I did some good to Angela, feel encouraged by the spark still glowing at the back of a fire that at times seems to have completely gone out, guilty that I didn't stay longer and determined to do all I can to get her away from the hospital.

Monday, December 29th

I decide to call Richard F and Susan H together before the year's out, hopefully, and tell them that I cannot continue as Chairman for much longer.

The chairmanship of T2000 was good and worthwhile as an experiment, and an experiment which could only take place in the deliberately time-marking, low-profile two years I've just been through. There really is no place for these experiments if I am to make films as well. And one thing I am sure of, after tasting various alternatives in the last couple of years, is that I want to make films.

1987

Monday January 5th: Southwold

Within 15 minutes of arriving at Sunset House I have rung Angela at the hospital and arranged visiting times.

An hour and ten minutes' drive; the hospital car park is packed, but then public transport is almost completely absent in Suffolk. Am parking when we see Angela waving vigorously from a ground-floor room opposite, a completely different person from the drowsy, slurred, almost helpless figure I left here eight days ago.

She meets us at reception and writes her name in chalk on a board – 'Angela Herbert – out with family'. Hers is the most elegant and controlled script.

Then we walk to the car, drive into Bury, walk some way to a wholefood coffee shop, where we have tea and a talk. Be positive, don't raise anything complicated, keep cheerful, burble on.

But with Angela today it is hardly necessary. She is much more aware and alert. She has had four ECT sessions this week and they seem to have pulled her sharply out of the depression in a way in which the drugs never did. She laughs quite easily. But I can see that the limits of her composure are still narrow.

She tells me, when Granny is in the loo, of how she nearly killed herself twice. Her tone is alarming – it's almost one of pride, as if to say 'Now, that's something I *can* do.'

But she is responsive and good company throughout. A cold walk down to the car, dropping in at an antique shop on the way she notes down details of some library steps for Veryan. Her hand is steady, but her memory has suffered. She doesn't remember me going to see her last Sunday week at all. And I was there for one and a quarter hours.

We drive back, Mother and me, twisting along the friendly 1120. I'm optimistic in the short term, very concerned in the long term. Mum just feels that we must get her out of 'that place' as soon as possible.

Wednesday, January 7th

The snow, ice and chaos forecast have not materialised. A cold, but benign morning with weak sunshine. I'm offered the lead in *Bulldog Drummond* – a new Stephen Fry treatment for Chichester, and *Me and My Girl* in the West End . . . !

457

To lunch at Langan's Bistro to tell Susan and Richard that I can't continue as Chairman of Transport 2000.

Richard, shrugs off the problem and immediately suggests that we should appoint another Vice-Chairman, besides himself, possibly Harley Sherlock, and that the two of them should run things for a year until I can come back.

He and Susan both feel a departure would do unnecessary damage to T2000 at the moment and that the members are so pleased to have me as Chairman that they would rather do anything than see me resign.

Thursday, January 8th

Up at eight and after breakfast begin work on a transport article. Susan Hoyle rings to tell me that she has been shortlisted for a new job, and would I be prepared to give references? Pleased for her, but can't help feeling that this news hard on the heels of yesterday's pleading for me to stay cannot be coincidental. They must have both been aware of the considerable extra pressure which will have to be borne by a Chairman when the Executive Director resigns. Feel a distant twinge of righteous anger.

To Cambridge Gate. Meeting re Prominent Features. John C is happy to put his film through PF, but doesn't want to be a director or have anything to do with the running of the company. Eric is brisk, organising and pays for this by being voted Chairman. Terry J is uncharacteristically quiet, TG the most visionary.

Many questions raised. How big should we be? How big should the launch be? Who should we employ? How will the launch be run?

Monday, January 12th

Off by taxi to Walkden House. Today is the first of our new, extended board meeting days – another measure of the extra work the organisation has taken upon itself in the last twelve months.

Steer them as best I can towards finance, etc, but have to end at 12.30 for our 'celebrity lunch'.

A big, amiable-looking man with very fair hair and pinkish skin stands awkwardly in our little office. This is John Palmer, Deputy Secretary at the Department of Transport and our first 'informal' lunch guest. First impressions lead me to think we have chosen well, but once we have collected our sandwiches and our glasses (I stick to orange juice) and begun talking I realise otherwise.

He maintains, I think, an almost scornfully Mandarin vagueness which I feel is an insult to the generally good and balanced questions that come from our members. He talks slowly (maybe this is deliberate) and everything is approached with a caution that could be taken for ignorance, except that he has been the man in charge of surface transport planning at the Department for ten years.

Back to our board meeting at 2.20 after seeing Mr Palmer off. 'Do you want any more of our chaps?' he asked.

Thursday, January 15th

The 'Winter of Misery' (LBC this morning) is into its fifth day. Snow remains uncleared in Oak Village and there is no rubbish collection again.

Don the gloves and woolly hat and run into the bitter wind. Plenty of children on Parliament Hill sledging on everything from proper sledges (very rare) to plastic red and white striped barriers pinched from road-works abandoned during the bad weather. Arrive home glowing.

Monday, January 19th

Rendezvous with our T2000 delegation. Susan has been unsuccessful in her application for a new job, but is taking it philosophically. We walk through Euston to the new British Rail HQ in Eversholt Street. Two of our members manage to lose themselves in the Euston concourse for five minutes.

Small, plain meeting room. No concession to art or decoration. Chris Green from Network South-East is our first speaker. Greying hair growing tight across the head, a broad head, like a ram or a rugby player, which puts me in mind of Al. Like his head, his approach is solid, factual, no nonsense, no frills, no rhetoric. He is forcefully impressive. A touch of impatience establishes his superiority comfortably. He knows the facts, we don't. He runs railways, whilst we talk about it, sort of attitude.

Bluntly honest that he has a problem with staff recruitment. Many of his drivers (the majority) are over 50 and it takes five years to train them. Blunt about the unions, overmanning – messianic about one-man operations. But he does talk more than just containment – he talks of expansion, he talks of new lines – to London Airport, to Stansted – and hints at the prospect of a new NE SW Underground line for London.

Up to the Forth Room for a lunch of tough meat, but some good talk. Will Camp is there in lieu of Richard Faulkner. He has a wonderful nineteenth-century face, with twinkling eyes and a fuzz of dark hair garlanding his baldness. He has a languid manner – talks softly, but persistently.

He reminds me that the Labour government's attitude to railways, in the days when Tony Crosland was in charge, was unhelpful. They regarded railway users as pampered and subsidised and Conservatives were much more pro-rail. Quite glad to hear this, as I have just written in my 'On the Move' article that we should not presume that a change of government will put things right automatically.

Thursday, January 22nd

Veryan rings to say that the pipes are leaking at Chilton, but that Angela is out of hospital and could she come to us at the weekend?

Angela comes on and my heart falls. She sounds very low – quite different to her perky self of two weeks ago. The hospital didn't work out well, but she has taken the blame for that herself – 'a failed patient'.

I am shaken and affected in a way which surprises me. I think it's because I have been confronted with the fact that Angela is not cured, that the hospital has been ineffectual. And, with Angela in the state she sounds to be in at the moment, I fear that anything we can do will be ineffectual too.

I keep my worst fears from Mother, when she calls, and Helen when she gets back, and when we eventually do talk about it together it is constructively and reassuringly. Angela will be with us on Sunday.

Friday, January 23rd

Into a rush of a day. To BAFTA to be present at the press show for *East of Ipswich*.

Arrive a little late owing to inane cab driver. 'Not your lucky day, is it?' he remarks cheerfully as he takes me on some unerringly disastrous detour. Then, out of the blue ... 'Did you know diesel fuel isn't inflammable?' He is full of observations on the nature of diesel fuel ... 'If you inhale diesel ...' (pause) '... it makes you violently sick.'

I scurry away from him, across Piccadilly and up the gloomy stairs to BAFTA.

I tell Tristram the outline of 'No. 27', the story of the lady being evicted by Eton College.

Home by 5.30. Adrenaline buzzing. The prospect of completing 'No. 27' after the second draft of *American Friends* suddenly seems the best option for the rest of the year. Less well paid, but infinitely more rewarding in other ways than doing a 'cameo' for some American film.

We are about to go to bed when the telephone rings. It's 11.25. The rather apologetic, frightened voice at the other end is from the *Daily Mail* and wants me to give him Terry Jones's number. Of course I refuse. But that is not the end of it. The hack calls again, fifteen minutes past midnight. This time he asks if I will ring Terry Jones and ask him to call them. I refuse with a little more asperity.

Saturday, January 24th

On the *Sun*'s front cover . . . beside the bold, black headline 'TV Python Comic At Sex Orgies' is a rather camp photo of my writing partner and bosom friend of 22 years! 'Jones, 44, is said . . . ' (wait for it) 'to have chatted to . . . Cynthia Payne – who faces charges . . . at the foot of the stairs.'

It is an astonishing piece of comedy come true. The sort of headline Python and *Private Eye* have been making fun of for years. Now, as ever, the paper has the last word. The full report of the police 'stool-pigeon's' evidence is within. And very high-farce it is too, with tattooed ladies from Leamington Spa and transvestite bottoms being pinched.

To Chipping Barnet for André J's wedding. An old church, Victorianised.

Terry J slips into our pew with Alison at the last minute. I think it's quite something to know someone who's appeared on the front cover of the *Sun*. To have shared a pew in church with them on the same day is beyond the realms of the hoped-for.

Much standing around outside. Trevor Jones, alias John Du Prez, cheerfully refers to TJ as the Sex Beast, and Terry, who seems to have taken it all with equanimity, is resigned to the fact that nothing he can say will make any difference to what they print. He is now resigned to trial by innuendo. (I must say, it does seem a bit weedy, Anne and Steve being quoted as saying he went to the sex parties for 'research'.)

Sunday, January 25th

Another anonymous day of cloudy skies. A windless, unshifting Eastern European blankness. Grim stories of Wapping riots. Both sides blaming the other for violence.

Thatcher will not talk, listen, understand or concern herself in any way with those individuals who do not entirely submit to her way of regenerating Britain. In the end, if their protests continue, they are 'marginalised' (vogue word of the mid-80's) by her, her ministers and most of all by her greedy, subservient press, and then, quite simply, roughed up.

Jeremy delivers Angela about five. She looks well; slim figure and well-cut, thick, dark hair, and a woollen two-piece tracksuit sort of thing.

We watch *Screen 2* on the BBC. A very funny Simon Gray play, 'After Pilkington', but – good old BBC – it ends up with a disturbing portrayal of a mad woman who sticks scissors into men's necks. Just when we wanted something uncomplicated and jolly.

As she goes to bed, Angela voices the desperation that is frighteningly close to the surface. 'What's it all *for*?' The unanswerable question. Leaves Helen and me to go to bed in a sober mood.

Monday, January 26th

Pleasant evening – supper with Rachel and Angela, then a game of Trivial Pursuit by the fire. Angela as bright and convivial as I remember her at the best of times.

The evening, though, ends splendidly, with me reading some of Wordsworth's *Prelude* and Angela really appreciating it – whereas the family always disappear when I start to recite. Quite spontaneous silliness – I put on an accompanying record of train noises and read John Betjeman, then Angela reads Joan Hunter Dunn and we all go to bed.

Tuesday, January 27th

Bad news of the Maudsley Hospital is the only cloud on the horizon. Mrs W, whom Angela was seeing last year, will not be able to see her until next week and Veryan, ringing this morning, could not improve on this. Rather a nuisance, as renewal of contact with the Maudsley was to be the focal point and purpose of this week.

There follows a gloomy lunch and repeated declarations of worthlessness. Physical manifestations like shaking and sweating make both of us alarmed. Helen goes off to her piano lesson, I determine to talk to someone on Angela's behalf and try and break this deadlock of inaction. She desperately wants to be taken into the Maudsley.

I arrive ten minutes late at squash and TJ says I look white. I suppose it is shock.

Wednesday, January 28th

Collected by car at six to go to the *Wogan Show.* Jeffrey Archer is just being ushered in as I arrive. The black-uniformed commissionaires greet him effusively, then turn to me looking blank. I explain who I am and why I'm here. They look confused. Whilst they're ringing for clearance, Wogan, looking relaxed and tanned, appears, greets us both warmly. Archer, like a sort of gusher of ingratiating enthusiasm, grasps both our hands and lays into the familiarity straight away.

As we walk upstairs he tells us how he'd been seeing 'Alasdair' (Milne) only this morning and noticed the letter E was missing from the words 'Director General' on his door, and 'D'you know what?' (pause to allow audience to appreciate story-telling technique), 'I went straight round to the nearest Woolworth's and bought him 'one of those awful, mock silver letters you see on the front of people's houses, and sent it round to him!'

Archer is awfully pleased with the story. We pass Donald Soper, modest in his cassock and looking quite incongruous in this company; Jeffrey cannot but be the first to grasp the great Methodist's hand.

Pass into make-up, then up to the Green Room. Jeffrey Archer is re-telling his Alasdair Milne's door story.

Soper is on first and is, as usual, fluent, balanced, articulate and provocative.

Archer is next and straight away there is bristle and drama. Wogan nudges him into a remark about 'the scandal'.[1] Archer, to his great credit, doesn't side-step. But he begins to warm up and soon is clearly displeasing our Terry by embarking on long, hectoring monologues about the virtues of free enterprise and the Western way.

Archer, to be fair, plays the game well. I talk about Mr Heeley's[2] sex talks and Lord Soper has the impeccable last word when he says that when he was given a sex talk at the age of 14 he had the distinct impression that he knew more about the subject than did his teacher.

Wogan, amiable as ever, is the only host who seems to actually want to stay and have a drink with his guests afterwards. While he and I are talking about TJ and Cynthia Payne, Jeffrey Archer comes up and tells us both the Alasdair Milne story again!

Back home. Am about to settle down to stew and dumplings with Angela when Charles Sturridge calls. I suppose it wouldn't be too dramatic to say that it's the call I've been hoping for, but virtually given up expecting, ever since I knew that he had taken over the *Troubles* screenplay, or, indeed, ever since I read the book during my second stint at Belfast in 1983.

Over a long phone call it transpires that he has always had me in mind as a

[1] Archer had been accused by two newspapers of paying hush-up money to a prostitute called Monica Coghlan, with whom the *Daily Star* alleged he had had 'relations'. Archer successfully sued the *Star*, and though he was cleared of charges, the scandal forced him to resign as Deputy Chairman of the Conservative Party. He was found guilty of perjury in 2001.
[2] Howard Heeley was the Headmaster of my prep school in Sheffield. Boys about to leave the school, mostly aged 12 or 13, were required to attend one of his 'sex talks' which took place in his study and involved desk items, such as paper-clips and ink-pots, as props. Most of us came away deeply confused.

possible Major, but the crucial factor is now the age of the actress to play Sarah. After six months of auditioning Irish actresses he has only two front runners. One is 27, the other ... 'Well, I hardly dare tell you how old she is.' Fifteen, coming on 16, but like a young Helen Mirren.

So, Charles is not yet decided which way to go; if it's the 27-year-old then I could be the Major, if it's the 16-year-old the age gap would be too obvious. Would I like to see the script? It is sent round to me within the hour. Two fat two-hour episodes.

With Denis [the cat] and shots of Armagnac for company, I sit down and read the entire four-hour adaptation, finishing by 2.30.

Thursday, January 29th

Up in time for the eight o'clock news. Still don't feel tired. Too much going on. *Time Out* has a very favourable piece on *East of Ipswich* – 'a considerable delight'.

I sit down and write captions for *Happy Holidays*.[1] In the middle of dictating to Alison, Sturridge rings on the other line. Maybe *because* the call is so important, I press the wrong button and Alison stays, but Sturridge disappears and I have no number for him.

Sit there feeling foolish for about three minutes. Then he rings back, I tell him that I have liked the adaptation and, subject to a few date difficulties, am happy to do it. I warn him I can't play the piano or dance, and he laughs. Says he is delighted and, though he's still cautious, he sounds genuinely pleased – or is it relieved? He has to see the actresses again, though, and will ring me tomorrow to talk further about the part.

Friday, January 30th

To Kenwood with Angela. Pleasant walk inside and outside. Put it to her as gently as I can that she should find somewhere else to stay from next weekend. She understands. But she is still enclosed and tense – even at a time like this when place and company should be congenial and conducive to unwinding.

Later in the afternoon she packs, then drives the car down to Veryan's office (no mean achievement for someone feeling terminally depressed). She is to spend the weekend at Chilton.

---

[1] Encouraged by Colin Webb at Pavilion Books, I'd written text for a collection of vintage British railway posters. It was published in 1987 under the title *Happy Holidays*. It was one of the most enjoyable things I ever did.

Sandy L rings from Atlanta. His reaction to *American Friends* is one of wary admiration for my bravery in going for a story and treatment so far away from what he'd expected from me. On detail he wants Brita to be warmer and more sympathetic and Ashby to be less one-dimensional. I know that both will be in the playing, but it obviously isn't coming across from this script.

Sunday, February 1st

Leave for TJ's – Rachel, Helen and myself – at eleven. As ever, 9 Grove Park is already full of people. There's always a foreigner or two, and twice as many children as Al and Terry have. TJ breathlessly scurries about, muttering genially about the number of people expected vis-à-vis amount of food available. Somewhere a telephone is always ringing.

A meal appears. Sancerre flows. TJ goes round the table embracing. He introduces Jill Tweedie as the woman 'whose book changed my life'.[1] There is so much noise, chatter, occasional howlings of attacked children that I'm almost relieved when 3.30 comes round and I have to hurry back for a four o'clock meeting with Charles Sturridge.

Charles arrives in dirt-encrusted black Citroën as we are unloading. I make coffee for both of us and we adjourn to my workroom. Two hours of discussion later, as the sun sets and I reluctantly switch on the light, anxious not to interrupt a cogitative atmosphere, it's clear that I have the part of Major Archer in 'Troubles' if I want it.

What a commitment – on both our parts. I hope I can deliver his high expectations.

Monday, February 2nd

[*East of Ipswich*] Reviews ranging from complete ecstasy (the *Daily Mail*, invoking Wilde and Noël Coward as my peers!) to virtual dismissal – Nancy Banks-Smith.

Angela arrives back from Chilton in seemingly good form, but I have little time to chat as have to get myself down to Transport 2000.

We walk over to Unity House to meet (after many cancellations) Jimmy Knapp to talk over salaries. Jimmy remarks on *East of Ipswich*. Yes they both watched it and 'it was greatly appreciated by my wife'. Nuff said.

---

[1] The book was *In the Name of Love*, published in 1979, and later described in the *Guardian* (for whom Jill Tweedie wrote her columns) as 'a dazzling set of observations about love, sex, men and women'.

We have a good session. There is no chance of getting the full amount we have asked for, but we come away with half and a few other promised benefits. I think he is straight and he's certainly convivial enough today. We shall see if he can deliver.

At home brief time to talk with Angela. She seems very much more positive.

Tuesday, February 3rd

Lunch at Grimes in Garrick Street with Charles Sturridge, Michael Colgan and James Mitchell – the lawyer who I wrote to three years ago to express my interest in 'Troubles'.

I put my point about dates and don't get much sympathy back from the producers, but Charles is concerned and will try and do some readjustments to save perhaps a couple of days of my Mürren [family skiing] trip. I so much want to see Mürren again, but it seems unlikely.

The producers asked me, as a writer, if I was happy with the title. They are worried that the Americans will not understand it. But so far their only suggested alternative is 'The Major and the Fisheater'!

Wednesday, February 4th

Michael Colgan from 'Troubles' rings. He's the amiable, artistic one of the production duo, I sense. Apologising for 'being a bad producer by telling you this', he goes on to say how delighted the three of them were after our lunch at Grimes yesterday. I *was* the Major, he says, and they were 'walking on air' after meeting me. Then he alludes to the unsavoury business of the contract and how they had asked LWT to go to the limit. Also bad news on the skiing holiday, which doesn't seem negotiable.

Thursday, February 5th

Nothing is heard from 'Troubles', so I continue in this limbo-land, unable to confirm, cancel or plan anything from March to May.

Clear my room and spend an excellent evening with Angela at the Caravanserai Afghan restaurant in Marylebone and then at the screen on Baker Street seeing *Heavenly Pursuits*. Angela is well disposed to her Maudsley lady and prefers her technique of P and M to a full-blooded Freudian analysis. P is for pleasure and M for something not necessarily pleasurable but achieved –

hence the M for mastery. Angela has to keep a weekly record of P and M moments.

This evening definitely P.

Friday, February 6th

Angela leaves at five. Her two weeks' stay with us is over and I'm quite sad in a way. When on form she's very good company. I know she depended on us and was warm in her appreciation of what we did for her. I hope she'll be able to continue moving forward as she has done over the last few days.

About half past five Anne rings with the final terms of 'Troubles'. They're acceptable. Now I have no longer any reason not to do it. The die is cast. I'm spoken for until the end of May.

Michael Colgan rings. He assures me that he will try his best to make sure the little things are provided for me — such as somewhere to write. Then Charles rings. It's been a long week since our talk in the gathering twilight last Sunday when my destiny began to be firmly linked to his.

So by seven o'clock all is done. Barring some dreadful accident I am to embark on the longest and largest single acting job I've ever done.

Wednesday, February 11th

Start the day with a reassuringly approving bunch of letters re *East of Ipswich*, sent over from the BBC. Tristram rings to say that we had a viewing figure of 6.5 million and were top of BBC2 for the week. For a programme starting after ten on a Sunday evening this is considered good.

Thursday, February 12th

Talk with Anne over contract details on 'Troubles'. LWT are not being helpful. Their contracts lady prefaces most of her calls to Anne with the advice that she's worked there 23 years.

But there are certain specific conditions which will make my life more pleasant over the next 14 weeks, like sole use of room or caravan to work in, a car in the morning which doesn't cruise the whole neighbourhood picking up the rest of the cast, and some policy on stand-ins. The more I think of them during the day, the more I'm convinced they're not petty details.

Saturday, February 14th: Southwold

Up by nine. The rain from the west hangs low and mistily over the Common. An odd 'friend' of Ma's rings to say how much she hated *East of Ipswich*. She tells her that she loved God, she loved her (my mother) and she (had) loved my father, but she hated the film. It was the sex again that was the problem. And this from someone who has had five husbands! Ma takes it all very well, but is clearly quite shaken. Fortunately I have brought up a sheaf of letters and reviews from people who thought otherwise.

Mr Hurran (Ma's protector) comes in as I'm reading a story in the *Daily Telegraph* about a cricket team which is destroying all its boxes because of fear of AIDS. He takes the Sierra and has the cassette-player mended.

I have promised Angela I shall drop in at Chilton on the way back, even though it adds well over an hour to the journey. She and Veryan are there. Angela reading 'Troubles' with one of the cats pinning her down to the kitchen chair. She seems enormously better. At the edges there are glimpses of frustration and fear and sometimes she is almost too bright (as if making a great effort), but a transformation from the Angela who came to us at the end of January.

Monday, February 16th

I sleep well and take a cold, early morning run before my car arrives at a quarter to ten to drive me to the read-through. My driver, John, is young and has a habit of blowing air out in a sort of silent laugh.

We cross the river and head ever further into the wastelands of Rotherhithe. It's rather as if I'm being purposely disoriented. We could be in Novosibirsk. At an ill-converted, light industrial building we find one of LWT's 'colonies' and I'm led through into a smoky room with protective grilles on all the windows, rather as I imagine border police stations in Ireland.

I'm taken round by Charles to meet the cast. Rosamund Greenwood, Rachel Kempson, with a glowing, handsome face and a bright slash of lipstick. Patience Collier, who has a special reclining chair and sits amidst us all most incongruously. Gwen Nelson, who's 86 and reads her script, with a huge magnifying glass.

Ian Richardson, I note with some dismay, is a smoker. He looks surprisingly rubicund, an agricultural tan. Colin Blakely is suffering the effects of some skin disease which has left him completely bald and his skin looks pale, exposed and very fragile. He smiles and shakes my hand with such open warmth that I know I shall like him. Same too for Tim Spall.

I'm introduced to Fiona Victory. High cheekbones, defiant eyes, long, dark hair – she was aptly described by Charles as an Irish Charlotte Rampling.

After all the introductions, Charles makes a short speech and the read-through begins. I suppose, to be honest, I am not quite comfortable; as my first line (which somehow seems the real psychological moment of commitment!) approaches, I feel my heart thumping more than it should and my body tensing up in preparation. But quite quickly the moment is over and I've not made a complete fool of myself.

The rest of the read-through is easier, though strange to be reading such intimate scenes in public with a Sarah I can't even see beyond the cluster of heads. I think the scenes with Ian and myself will be fine. We read until after one o'clock. Tomorrow Charles will split us up for rehearsal.

Good phone chat with Eric I, who loved *East of Ipswich* and also has some very pithy remarks about *American Friends*. He says it reminded him of a Hardy story and when he read the script he felt that it must have been adapted from a novel! Both agree that speeches in Latin will be hard to sell to Hollywood.

Tuesday, February 17th

Taxi to Grimes Restaurant, this time to meet with Ian R, Fiona and Charles. Warm to Ian. He is very Actorish in delivery and self-dramatising style, but regards it quite unashamedly as his trade. He says, without any immodesty, that he's a very easy person to work with, but then catches my arm and adds 'But I'm very easily hurt.'

Fiona and Charles and I are driven to London Weekend, here to rehearse in a long, narrow, un-cared-for office with an absolutely wonderful view out across the river.

Someone is editing *South Bank Show* theme music interminably from next door, which makes it difficult for us to maintain the intensity of concentration that listening to Charles demands.

About 5.30 Charles has to go to a production meeting. Both Mitchell and Colgan look nervous. Clearly things are still in a very restless state.

I walk over Waterloo Bridge, because I like doing it, but a north-easterly wind makes the cold as intense and unbearable as any this winter. En-taxi for a private view of Virginia Powell's paintings and pastels in Motcomb Street.

Introduced to Harold Pinter ... 'Do you know the population of China?' he asks. (He has a suave blue coat and neat tie.) Evidently it's over one billion now. But my evening is made when I at last manage to tell him that I did McCann in *The Birthday Party* at Oxford and it was the high point of my Oxford acting career! To which Pinter replies 'Oh, I *know* all about that ... I know all about your McCann.'

Off into the Belgravian night, fortified by a glass of white wine, feeling marvellously relaxed and comfortable. Home to a glass of champagne, some salmon and a steak. Watch a man having an artificial hip fitted (on TV).

Wednesday, February 18th

At 5.30 I'm taken to Penge to the Peggy Spencer Dance School [for 'Troubles'] to relive the horrors of dancing class which I had tried to exorcise in *East of Ipswich*. I have to learn the rudiments of a foxtrot with the twins.

Peggy Spencer is a tall, erect, but kindly lady. I jab her once or twice with my feet, which she says do stick out. But the hour-long session, watched with irreverent amusement by the drivers, is not as hair-raising as I expected, in fact it's quite successful. The twins are wonderful. Very natural and un-actorish.

Thursday, February 19th

To Morris Angel by ten for fittings. These take an hour and a half and the suit looks very dapper. Then, clutching two pairs of leather shoes which I have to 'break-in' by Monday, I find a cab.

To the Great Nepalese for a lunch with Susan. Amongst our general chat we touch on (or rather, I force into the conversation!) my worries about the future of my chairmanship. Even before 'Troubles' the prospect of JC's film and my own seemed to preclude my continuing; now I shall have to miss the next two or three meetings.

I suggest some sort of honorary or presidential (how the word jars) role and by the time we finish our mughlais I realise I've as good as resigned.

From the Great Nepalese I'm swept away in [my driver] Billy's Mercedes for a haircut. Christine, a close-cropped peroxide-blonde Scot who will be 'looking after me', does the job well and without fuss. The process of Majoring goes on, and I'm taken to an upper room to practise playing, or looking convincingly as if I *am* playing, 'Eine Kleine Nacht Musik' with Fiona.

Friday, February 20th

Meet Tristram for lunch. Have chosen La Bastide in Greek Street. Its chintzy, bourgeois, salon-style interior is at first disturbingly, then refreshingly un-designed. Naff in fact. But the food is excellent. I have boudin and apple and it tastes authentically Froggie.

Tristram helps the atmosphere with a marvellously positive reaction to *American Friends*.

If I don't direct *American Friends*, I promise Tristram (on the corner of Greek and Old Compton) that he shall be top of my list. Definitely the best reaction thus far. The only one that made me want to rush straight back and read the thing.

Steve has positive news of the JC film. It looks like a July 13th start and some ridiculous amount like 300,000 dollars in the kitty – per person. None of the stars to get more than any other (which is kind to me, I think).

Home by 11.30. If I had wanted just one restful day this last week of 'freedom', this wasn't it.

Helen packing and preparing for Switzerland [the family skiing holiday I'm missing because of 'Troubles'] means we don't get to sleep until half past one.

Saturday, February 21st

The withdrawal of all the human sights and sounds and feelings seems to strip the house bare for a moment. It's as if the carpets had gone or the water had been cut off. Something essential has disappeared. Despite a shortage of sleep, I don my tracksuit and head for Parliament Hill and Kenwood. My solution to everything!

Back at nine and breakfast and organise myself for an overnight to Southwold. Thank goodness for my mother and for a lovely and appreciative card re *East of Ipswich* from Maggie Smith.

Have just relaxed pleasantly by the time I reach Sunset House, when Ma imparts the news that Angela has rung only an hour before to say that things are 'so dreary' at Chilton that she's coming over to stay the night.

Sunday, February 22nd: Southwold

Lunch together then time to go. Angela tests me on my lines.

I head back to all the whopping challenges of the next 14 weeks at a quarter to three. Home by five. It's cold and empty and darkness is falling at 4 Julia Street and Denis is waiting for me.

So is another Denis – for within ten minutes of my arrival the telephone rings and the cheery voice of Denis's namesake resounds. DO'B has, he claims, been trying to contact me all weekend to say how much he liked *American Friends*. His reaction even caps that of Tristram. DO'B gives a complete, unqualified rave and concludes that there may be two weeks of rewriting, but that's all. Wary of his praise as of his criticism, but there is no doubt that this is heartfelt and what is more exciting is that he can and will finance it next year. He says as much.

Practise piano and tying ties and putting on collars.

Monday, February 23rd

It should be a very significant sort of day. Lightning and thunder and some stirring music should accompany its dawn, for this is the First Day of Filming.

Actually, it's A First Day of Filming. I reckon it's my tenth – if you include *Three Men in a Boat*, but not *Time Bandits*. The tenth time I've been through all this. But it's two years and four months since I spent much time in front of a film camera and that's the most significant.

That's why I've lain awake most of the night – my body ready much too early. The signals hurtling from the brain to the four corners, waking nerve ends that should have been left to curl up and relax.

Into the Mercedes and down to the Isaac Newton Junior School off Portobello Road, where the vehicles are drawn up. It's a cold, bright morning. Good conditions to start anything.

Charles S is a careful, quiet, but thorough director. I feel he's watching everything and he won't let me be loose or lazy. As I want this to be an exceptionally good and consistent performance I'm pleased, but when my confidence in my ability and stamina sags I find his persistence hard to cope with. But the day's work is done. And by 4.30 at that.

I feel rather like someone who, for the last two weeks, has been running alongside a rapidly-moving vehicle and not really able to get on board. I think I'm aboard now, but I'm pretty breathless still.

Tuesday, February 24th

We have moved today to the Linley Sambourne House in Stafford Terrace, behind Kensington High Street. Sambourne was a *Punch* cartoonist and the house is now preserved as a museum of late-Victorian interior design and decoration. Dark and gloomy with heavy drapes, some intricate but rather well-hidden William Morris wallpaper, stuffed animals in glass cases and every inch of wall covered with an eclectic selection of his cartoons, and various etchings on all sorts of subjects – classical, French eighteenth-century stories, and so on. Presumably various leaves from books he'd illustrated.

My first scene with Rachel Kempson plays quite sweetly. Rachel is a lovely, very easy-going partner and I think Charles is quite pleased.

I realise that this is to be unlike anything else I've done. There can be no question of getting by on the first couple of takes with an accurate caricature, as we do so often in comedy – Sturridge is very fussy, very concerned to get things right and quite happy to go to seven or eight takes if necessary – and it always seems to be necessary.

Poor Rachel K hopes to have finished with our bedroom scene by lunchtime,

Will and Eric in France. Summer 1984. I'd had a Geoffrey Boycott T-shirt made for Eric as we were both slightly obsessed with the Greatest Living Yorkshireman.

My friend Al Levinson (left) with Norman Rosten, poet laureate of Brooklyn, and like me, a champion of Al's work.

A Private Function

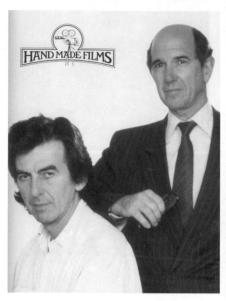

ABOVE *A Private Function* was the last of five films I made with George Harrison and Denis O'Brien as Executive Producers. The HandMade logo was a Gilliam design.

ABOVE RIGHT Advertising bicycle clips with Alan Bennett, North Yorkshire, May 1984

RIGHT 'Kill it, Gilbert !'. MP, Betty and Maggie Smith.

BELOW With Maggie, enjoying a break from porcicide in the garden at Briargarth, May 1984

With Alan and Maggie and
the foot from my chiropodist's
surgery, on the set of the
dance sequence after the
Mayor's dinner, June 1984

Anne Gibbins, Helen's
mother, with my mother
and Helen at the *Private
Function* Royal Premiere,
November 21st 1984

Toilet of the Stars (left to right)
Denholm Elliott, Jim Carter, MP,
Pete Postlethwaite, John Normington
and Richard Griffiths in the gents at
The Great Western Hotel Paddington,
June 1984

Will, Tom, Rachel and Helen on holiday in Majorca, August 1986

'Photographed with a bike giving views on cycling in London. Cannot pose with my own bike as the saddle's missing' March 7 1986

12 Feb 1987

Dear Michael

Thank you again for appearing on my show. I'm so sorry for the delay, but I just today received the enclosed photograph back from the corner drugstore. (Unfortunately, it was the corner drugstore in Fairbanks, Alaska.)

I hope you'll think of this photograph as a remembrance of your appearance. Let it also serve as a small token of my appreciation.

thankyou, God.

5746 SUNSET BOULEVARD LOS ANGELES CA

All-American look for the Joan Rivers show. She was the only American host who ever wrote me a thank-you letter.

Comrades in arms.
(Clockwise from top left): With Charles Crichton, director; Gerry Paris (the best stand-in in the world); Kevin Kline, chip abuser and friend.

John C (Archie Leach) trying some unsuccessful information retrieval.

Ken Pile. Fan Photo.

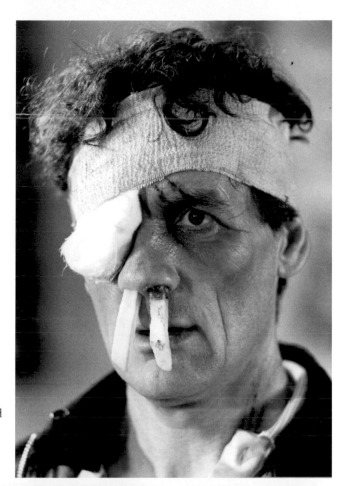

'Start the day being kissed
repeatedly by Jamie on
the bathroom floor. Very
pleasant form of acting'
July 17 1987

Tom, Will, Helen, Granny and Rachel brave an east coast gale outside Sunset House, Southwold. 1987

With 90 year-old Joyce Carey, friend and muse of Nöel Coward, on the set of *Number 27* 'Apparently her skirt fell down as she stood in the rose garden. "Normally I would have laughed, but this time I was a little cross"'
June 23 1988

for her 'stays' are killing her. She eats little at the catering van and tells me that the worst thing about the costume is that it encourages strange wind effects in her stomach.

We complete the scene and I make use of the Michael Palin Room (supplied as per contract) at the top of the house. Alan Polly, of props, is most solicitous and has provided me with Perrier and even a Thermos of coffee. So I sit squashed into a springless armchair, coat pulled round me against the cold, and a pile of books about Victorian life, which I thumb through, an eye open for suitable information for *American Friends*.

Thursday, February 26th

A difficult day ahead – perhaps the most difficult of the week. First scenes with Sarah, including our piano duet and some more emotional stuff around the fireside.

Charles takes me to one side and swells my confidence with genuine enthusiasm for my performance. The scene that made him feel so 'buoyant' was the Major's bedroom scene with Rachel, which he says was very moving and suggested the sort of depth which he was hoping for in choosing me for the Major.

The afternoon spent largely on a very complicated lighting for the 'war reminiscences' scene. By the time we get to do our bit, it's nearly 5.30.

But it is done. There are eleven or twelve takes. I try to imagine I'm seeing the horrors of war, when in fact I'm seeing 25 people, all standing ten feet away, directing all sorts of equipment at me. Fiona is easy to work with. A serious girl, but with an attractive Irish sense of madness just below the carefully controlled, non-smoking, non-drinking, body-exercising exterior.

The last scene set for the day has to be abandoned. This is the first time we've fallen behind. But I'm quite elated at the work done and pleased that I've survived a tough couple of days.

Friday, February 27th

Collected at 7.30 and down to Banstead to a sprawling, but handsome collection of Victorian buildings which comprised, until only a few months ago, Banstead Mental Hospital. Today it is to be a hospital again – of 1918 vintage – and I am recovering from a gas attack.

Complete change of temperature after the tightness of the first few days – it's now almost balmy. Breakfasts are sorely tempting. Black pudding has been my downfall this week and with it scrambled eggs – fresh and irresistible – and two rashers of bacon. It helps to pass the time, I suppose.

Talk to CS at one point. It's as difficult to get things out of him as it was with Frears; it just isn't his nature to gush or headline his feelings. But he has two problems. Colin Blakely, who is undergoing chemotherapy, and still appearing in the West End, has collapsed and will at the very least be unavailable for his first appearance on Monday.

More serious is that some of the scenes we shot earlier in the week may be unusable. I can't elicit exactly where the blame lies, but it seems the lighting is not everything that CS wants. Something to do with exposure. CS, however, refuses to see the setback as a negative thing, and hopes to win something out of it – more time, presumably.

This is less than good news in view of the effort put in this week, but you have to be prepared for everything and this is just another frustration to be absorbed.

The bed scene is not shot until quite late. We all wait around with our variously gruesome facial injuries. I listen to the *True Stories* soundtrack on the headphones.

Then a mad rush to shoot the last sequence of the week – the bathroom. All I have to do is sit in a hot bath with my eyes bandaged and not play with myself. Finish, with much shouting and wafting of steam, at seven o'clock.

Saturday, February 28th

Sunshine spills into the garden and it's generous and unseasonable enough for me to be able to sit outside and read the papers and feel its warmth. My feeling of well-being is augmented by the lack of phone calls, the ability to potter round the house, the pleasurable anticipation of seeing the family again, and a quite different attitude to the 13 weeks' work ahead than I had last weekend. Quite a lot of my uncertainty and anxiety has been laid to rest and replaced by glimmerings of control and confidence. And, dare I say, enjoyment.

Cleese rings and we talk a little about the part of Ken. I swallow for the moment my reservations about the film itself – well, I can't say I don't like it, that I find it everything I wouldn't write myself: hard, uncompassionate, leering. I have a feeling this is the one I shall do for money, rather than love.

All the family back about 7.30. No fierce tans, but all looking well and full of praise for Mürren. For a moment I feel rather like Helen must do when I come home. My neat world invaded. How different from this time last week when I missed them all so much!

Sunday, March 1st

Buy two magnums of '62 Leoville Lascases for Barry and Terry Cryer, whose 25th wedding anniversary we are invited to tonight.

Just as we are about to leave, Charles S calls. 'Good news and bad news,' he begins, with characteristic enigmatism. The good news is that all the heads of London Weekend's various departments who've seen the film think my performance is wonderful. The bad news is that it's so difficult to see the performance that they are suspending filming for a week.

Helen and I reflect on this stunning news as we drive out to nice, ordinary, uncomplicated Hatch End. A wonderful reunion evening with Ronnie Barker, Tim [Brooke-Taylor], Graham C, Eric, David Nobbs, Roy Castle, Kenny Everett and others.

Barry's speech involves going round the room and thanking us all individually. Quite a brave feat. Once you've set out there's no going back. But his 'speech' is capped by a very funny and composed series of one-liners from his 13-year-old son, Bob.

Not much time to talk to Barry, whose hair resembles more and more that of a Regency footman. Ronnie Barker, in striped blazer as if he's just come off the beach, helps hustle me away after midnight from the clutches of a well-oiled K Everett.

Monday, March 2nd

Examine possibilities of a three-day break in the latter half of the week, if I'm really not required. Narrow down possibilities to Venice (most exotic, but familiar), Paris, the Lake District (have been enjoying W's *Prelude* and fancy some contemplation).

See the evening off by a log fire, trying to make up my mind about early casting possibilities on *American Friends*. Anne Bancroft seems way ahead as Miss H; Brita has to be a new 'star'. Ian Holm or Bob Hoskins would make a splendid Weeks, and D Day Lewis is quite a possibility for Syme. Difficult not to put Denholm or Maggie in as a matter of course.

To sleep easily. An hour later a mad lady bangs at the door and rings the bell. I panic. Helen quite sensibly calls the police.

Tuesday, March 3rd

Charles rings as I'm at my desk, about ten. The news on 'Troubles' is that there is likely to be a fight between union and management.

Apparently management are strongly and unanimously on our side and Nick Elliott [LWT's Head of Drama] has very forcibly warned the union about the consequences of trying to force their own lighting cameraman back. As CS puts it, a dance now has to be played out with its own elaborate moves. The union will meet today and decide, on principle, to back their man. Later the management will, in response, cancel the project. Then the union's employees who stand to lose a great amount of money from such a step will put pressure on and by Friday a compromise will have been reached.[1]

Apparently John Birt[2] is in fighting mood and not mincing words. If the union prevails it will be the end of filming at LWT, so he says. Words, threats, poses – it's all going to be very sour and probably quite childish. Equity are not supporting the ACTT.

CS didn't think it a good idea for me to go as far as Venice, so I book up a Lake District hotel.

At 6.40, in my DJ, set out to address the Chelsea Clinical Society at the Berkeley Hotel. For various reasons, mainly 'Troubles', I have not had time to write them one of my prepared speeches, and, with unusually blithe confidence, haven't worried.

Met by Stanley Rivlin, enthusiastic, very Jewish, like an unkempt bear. I'm told he only does one operation, that's varicose veins, and he's made a fortune. In even lower voice I'm told he did Mrs Thatcher.

Talk about my film career, de-glamorise, pig stories, etc. Amazed that these high-powered professionals not only listen but listen most appreciatively.

But the day is not over. After midnight Michael Colgan rings to tell me that 'Troubles' is now officially cancelled. John Birt gave his decision at eight o'clock.

Unlike CS this morning, Colgan is emotional and far less positive about a satisfactory outcome with LWT. He reiterates ('It's been said behind your back and now it should be said to your face') that everyone is delighted with my performance, but his tone about the affair is quite different to Charles, more on the lines of 'I want you to know that whenever this gets done you'll be our Major . . .'

Colgan sounds weary both in the short and long term. He sounds like a man who wants to get as far away as possible from LWT and to make a fresh start with 'Troubles' as an independent feature.

[1] In short, we were caught in a variation of the many employer versus union struggles of the 80's. LWT were taking on an in-house, unionised labour force.
[2] Director of Programmes at London Weekend Television since 1982. He left to join the BBC as Deputy Director General in 1987.

Friday, March 6th: Applethwaite, Keswick

Breakfast at 8.30, and drive east and south along Ullswater. Start walking at 10.15, along Martindale, realising that I've unthinkingly chosen a path straight into the wind, which flaps and tears at me in gusty assaults, threatening to remove the hat I bought this morning in Keswick.

After 15 minutes come to a small church, really just a simple rectangular building without tower or arches or any adornment – just grey stone walls and a slate roof. Set by the river, with a farmhouse a hundred yards away, otherwise quite isolated. Go inside and find an interior of such simplicity and dignity that it brings tears to the eyes. A plain stone floor, with some wooden movable pews, an ancient stone font, a table as an altar, and at the back a pulpit, carved, seventeenth-century. Nothing unnecessary, no show, no spiritual fireworks, but very affecting, especially as the wind batters at it. To me a much more profound and successful religious building than St Peter's in Rome.

Walk along the road up the dale. A collection of deserted farm buildings, substantial stone constructions with broken roofs and holes in the walls. But all carpeted with snowdrops – in and out of the buildings.

Pass through farms full of free-range animals – chickens clucking, cockerels patting about with self-satisfaction, bulls in straw-floored stone barns. Good smells. Then the road ends and a track pulls up towards the ridge. The rain turns to sleet, which then turns to snow. A horse on its own, black and slightly-built, shelters behind a wall and yet comes out to walk with me for a while, as if pleased to see a friend.

I push on up, the snow gets heavier, the wind now blows all the time and drives the sleety-snow stinging onto my face. I'm not quite sure where I am, except that below me the gently protective dale recedes and a sweeping amphitheatre of rock curves away to the south.

At the top at last, I feel now completely alone and cut off from the world. The snow here is six inches deep at least and conditions seem to be worsening. Turn right and walk along the ridge between Martindale and Boredale. But the constant fierce presence of the wind persuades me that I must abandon the path and, in a long, controlled sideways slip, I descend into Boredale, sending a deer darting away round the edge of the hillside.

Sunday, March 8th

Papers full of horrific details of the ferry that capsized outside Zeebrugge, 'Herald of Free Enterprise'. It sounds much more like the victim of free enterprise. All sorts of safety corners cut in order to be 'competitive'.

It looks very much as if the 'suspension' of filming is going into a second week. LWT and the unions are locked in their own internal struggle, which involves issues far greater than just this programme. Meanwhile, in order to have some alternative to this stasis, Mitchell is beavering away to try and set up some independent deal. Decision will have to be taken by the end of this week.

Monday, March 9th

So begins my second week in limbo. Like a soldier who has seen action briefly, been superficially wounded and then unexpectedly withdrawn from the lines, I don't quite fit in anywhere. What makes it worse is that I spend much of the time, on the phone, having to explain to people why I'm not away at war, after I'd kissed them all goodbye.

Angela comes by for tea and to collect the two tickets for *King Lear* that I had thought I should never be able to use, but now of course could. She seems much more confident and in control of things. Did we over-react that first week she was here?

Tuesday, March 10th

Anne has been talking to Colgan; a re-start date of March 30th is mentioned. Quick calculation suggests this is impossible, as it would not free me until the end of the first week in July, a week before *Wanda* and no time for rehearsal.

Terry J arrives. He is not happy with lack of progress on 'Erik'. Eleven Hollywood studios have passed. Orion are the only hope and they want young American stars in it. TJ wants more ingenuity from John G and Prominent Features in suggesting alternatives. So he is in a sort of limbo himself.

Susan Hoyle rings to report on yesterday's [T2000] board meeting. The idea of elevating me to a presidential position has been well received, and so long as I can stay on as Chairman to the end of this year, will be implemented. Relief.

Wednesday, March 11th

In the afternoon Colgan rings and spins me a wonderful Irish yarn about the 'Troubles' reserve package, involving clandestine support from London Weekend management, who have already gone to the lengths of 'smuggling' scenery out of the building at 4 a.m. to get it out of the union's hands. The union has threatened to burn any sets already made if it goes ahead without them.

The cancellation cost to LWT will be £1.16 million, but they can get some of that back if the new 'Troubles' production can use sets, costumes, drawings, etc, already acquired. Equity is being completely co-operative, a designer from *Out of Africa* will come in to help – even Hugh Leonard, who wrote a screenplay for 'Troubles' which wasn't used, has sent them a good luck telegram.

Colgan slips into romanticism ... 'They all want to see this little Irish company taking on the big boys ... and showing they can win.'

I promise to find out the exact end dates from *Wanda* to see what my availability in the autumn might be. JC's approach to the *Wanda* film is the exact opposite to 'Troubles' – careful, considered, full of dates and detail supplied almost a year in advance.

So I shuttle between the hysteria of 'Troubles' and the icy calm of *Wanda*. The best I [can] do is to offer myself to 'Troubles' immediately after *Wanda* and right up to my pre-production period on *American Friends*. This gives him October to February. Not the best filming dates.

As I explain all this I feel I am talking myself out of the Major, probably permanently.

Thursday, March 12th

The phone is ringing as I get back – it's Michael Colgan. He puts the problem to me quite starkly – either they go in late March and re-cast, or they postpone until the autumn and hope to keep me. Could I meet them to discuss this second alternative? Fix a meeting at the Python office (before we meet, Colgan asks me not to reveal to anyone, even Charles, that the bulk of the 'rescue' money is coming from LWT).

The meeting hovers between dream and reality. They seem very anxious to do all they can to accommodate me, but the *Wanda* schedule spreads itself, languorously, over the summer, and Anne thinks that my contract will demand an extra two weeks on top of the ten I'm already booked for.

They will investigate the feasibility of postponement until the autumn, I will do my best to reduce the *Wanda* 'insurance weeks' in September.

Home, feeling much better about things. A real chance of saving my part. Touched also by their loyalty to me.

Friday, March 13th

My Major's moustache is five weeks and two days old. Helen said I ought to shave it off, but somehow I still pathetically hold out hope. Shaving it off severs my last, fragile hold on the character of Brendan Archer!

Nancy [Lewis] calls, at eight o'clock, thinking she'll get me before I start on the last day of my third week of filming. I have to pour out the story all over again. (The *London Daily News* seems to have been the only paper to run the story, with three reports, each progressively more accurate.)

Nancy has a five-week film part with Bill Cosby, in San Francisco from April 13th, for me. Just to complicate matters.

Saturday, March 14th

Night's sleep broken by awareness of Helen's early departure. She's gone by a quarter to eight, off to Saas Fee.

A fine, dry, sunny day. Shopping, and at one o'clock over to Islington to have a drink with Ken [Cranham] and Fiona [Victory]. Airy first and second floor of a handsome, though externally grubby, villa in Thornhill Road. Well-polished bare boards, big hand-made carpets, a chunky, rough-hewn table which probably cost an earth or two. Ken, hair all swept back, has aged interestingly. Curious mixture of naughty boy and careworn middle-aged man. Both flash across his features in seconds.

We walk down past well-kept, gentrified town houses, which remind me of what Gospel Oak might have been but for the comprehensive redevelopment plan. Thornhill Road, Islington, is the sort of place where people who devise comprehensive redevelopment plans live.

To a pub called the Albion. Ken is a great teller of theatrical tales – he really has acted with almost anybody. Tells a touching story of playing Beckett with Max Wall. Wall, very tired before they went on, rested his head on Ken's shoulders in the wings, Ken gently massaged his co-star's temples. Max after a while perked up enough to say gloomily ... 'That's the trouble with this business, you're only as good as your last performance.' Then, just as the lights came up and they made their entrance ... 'Like marriage, really.'

Fiona laughs at my thought that filming in Ireland would be less complicated than dealing with LWT unions and their persistent demands ... 'You don't know Ireland,' she chuckles.

Sunday, March 15th

After breakfast William and Rachel express interest in a trip out. Rachel has become interested in the Great Fire, so I suggest we go to where the fire began and look for Fish Street and Pudding Lane and Farina's the baker where it actually started.

The City is now littered with awful, unimaginative, dispiriting modern buildings. The complete boringness of the tallest of them – the NatWest

Tower – seems to have set the tone. And the site of the Royal Bakers where the fire began has suffered particularly ignominiously, with a long, low, concrete façade (for Lloyds Bank), which makes a Second World War bunker look sensitive.

Rachel takes some photos. At least the Monument can't be redeveloped for offices. There is a solid wedge of traffic through the heart of the City and across London Bridge. Into the middle of it all comes a stream of beautifully-kept Morris Minors with anxious owners consulting bits of paper. A vintage rally gone hopelessly wrong.

Monday, March 16th

The script of the Bill Cosby film arrives; read it in the cab on the way to a *Wanda* get-together at the Meridiana Restaurant.

At least with Python we had an eccentric, understated surrealism which kept things fresh and unpredictable; here the sledge-hammer of zaniness has been wielded mercilessly. It's cruel, corny, clumsy stuff, and I feel that I'm not yet ready to do *anything* for money – even be Bill Cosby's butler, with some good lines.

At the Meridiana are gathered Charlie Crichton, Roger Murray Leach [the art director], Greg Dark, Jonathan Benson, Sophie [Clarke-Jervoise, John's assistant], Steve and JC. A pleasant group, and I begin to feel very warm towards this film, which up till now I've rather underestimated. The bungling incompetence of 'Troubles' has increased my admiration for *Wanda*'s single-minded efficiency. JC makes much of the relaxed, wonderful, easy time we're going to have.

Thursday, March 19th

Anne has spoken to Michael Colgan and all seems set for an October 5th start on the new, improved 'Troubles'. Only myself and Ian Richardson know this, according to Anne. Until I hear more I can't quite be sure, but it's the best possible solution.

Wednesday, March 25th

I have been invited to an Author of the Year reception by Hatchards. The reception is on the top floor of New Zealand House, from which there is a fantastic panorama of London.

I see Roald Dahl across the room with Jane Asher and Gerald Scarfe and realise that I'm too shy to barge in there. I still have the mentality of an outsider looking in. I don't share their lifestyle, I don't easily have their apparent cool poise and urbanity – well, not in these circles. They circulate because they know people will want to speak to them.

Anyway, Bob Geldof brings me out of my shell, hailing me warmly. He's just come from doing a commercial for shaving which he's rather pleased with. I hint at disapproval and he snaps at the bait. 'My morality is absolutely clear. I just want to make lots and lots of money' – classic Cleesian position.

Friday, March 27th

A morning of desk-clearing is eclipsed by trouble at 'Troubles'. Anne rings with report of negotiations. The money being offered for the new 'Troubles' is not much more than the old. She spent three hours with Colgan even to get this far. Colgan wants me to sign a letter today committing myself to the part in October, for 16 weeks and almost all in Ireland. As he has not yet got Charles's signature, this seems like putting the cart before the horse, but when Colgan calls a few minutes later I agree to his request for a meeting and hie myself to the neutral Mountbatten Hotel.

Ferociously strong gusts of late-March wind strike from time to time, reminding us comfortable city-dwellers how fragile a place we live in. For a moment a whole street goes out of control. People, caught unawares, stagger at the force of it, lose their belongings. People help others retrieve their hats, wild newspaper spreads spiral high over buildings to dive-bomb the innocent in neighbouring streets.

At the Mountbatten all is calm. They even serve herbal tea . . . orange flavour. Colgan is a teetotaller, which he says is almost unacceptable in Ireland. The only way he can not drink and maintain a shred of respect is to say he's on the wagon. That at least conjures up feats of heroic consumption at some time in the past.

The gist of our hour-long armchair discussion is that there is money available to re-mount the film. 'Don't ask me who it is . . . I can't tell anybody. I haven't *even* told my wife.' (Helen, when I tell her this afterwards, is the first to mention the IRA.) The money needs written commitments – signatures. Evidently he is asking for mine and Ian Richardson's. These will satisfy them.

But what of Charles – who seems to be the artistic driving force?

Colgan, who is a humane, tolerant and sensitive man, looks pained as he describes Charles's reaction to the autumn re-start. Evidently Charles felt that this was a chance for a whole 'new' look at the way they might do it. This could involve a different sort of location, and he is very keen to get Peter

O'Toole as Edward. Colgan is an admirer of O'Toole, but says he is impossible to tie down and will be a destabilising factor. Colgan, in short, has run out of patience with Charles and wants a deal to be struck which would then be presented to Charles. October 5th or not at all.

I am most concerned not to stitch up the one person who involved me in the project, nor am I willing to sign my autumn and winter away to another director.

Tuesday, March 31st

Gallop on with 'No, 27' [as the play about property developers had become]. The flow seems so easy that I worry it will all be junk when I put it together, but it's a wonderful feeling, wanting to write.

With Helen to the 'Gala Preview' of *Personal Services*. A red carpet has been laid across the pavement in Jermyn Street, but the only illustrious names I see are Jones, Leland and Gilliam. Then Cynthia is amongst us and we are all roped in for a photo. Cynthia sparkles, figuratively and literally, in a tight-fitting diamante sort of number. 'One, two, three se ... x!' she choruses for the cameras. There's a big, red lipstick mark on her left cheek.

Afterwards to a 'reception'. Wine is free, but Helen has to pay £2.00 for a non-alcoholic drink. I meet Bert Kwouk, so I feel I achieve something.

Thursday, April 2nd

My invitation to attend a special preview of LWT's *Scoop* arrives in the post. In the form of a mock telegram, it talks of 'delightful LWT onlaying drinks'. It just stirs in my mind a now-receding, but still potent resentment of the company, none of whose representatives have given me one word of solace, or explanation, let alone apology, since cancelling 'Troubles' five weeks ago.

Work through the afternoon, trying hard to keep to one side the desperate cries from various charities that have come in today's post. People *are* starving in Mozambique, young children *do* have cystic fibrosis, AIDS *is* dreadful, and all these causes lie balefully staring out at me from my letter tray. Cover them up with a request to write an introduction to another railway book!

Monday, April 6th

Lunch at Odettes with Steve and Michael Shamberg [*Wanda*'s American co-producer]. Shamberg looks and sounds East Coast, in fact he's from Chicago and now works in LA. He has an aristocratic drawl and a pleasant, laid-back approach, which is easy, quite intelligible and relaxing.

Shamberg thinks we should have a theme song for *Wanda*. Suggests someone like Phil Collins, who is popular in the US but British. Groans from Steve. Apparently it was suggested to JC, who didn't know who Phil Collins was. Mind you, he also thought Sting was called String, and Boy George George Boy, so not much hope of guidance there.

Write a letter to the Bishop of Birmingham re chairmanship of T2000. Checking a hunch, I find from Robert Hewison's *Python – The Case Against* that he was indeed one of the bishops who spoke out against *The Life of Brian*.

Tuesday, April 7th

Start the day with a lot of energy. Organise a family party here for Granny next week. This involves ringing Angela at Chilton. A small, unhappy voice answers. She's feeling awful again. At least she doesn't disguise it with me. She feels guilty about Granny – not seeing her enough, not being able to tell her what she's going through. She's doing her tap-dancing and working at the Quay Theatre [in Sudbury], etc, but she says they're only temporary diversions and 'the blackness', as she calls it, always returns.

Monday, April 13th

Wake to a dull morning. Am to launch a public transport initiative called 'Freeway' in Trafalgar Square mid-morning, only to hear that the launch has been cancelled, as the special bus broke down.

Good news on the transport front is a letter from Hugh Montefiore, ex-bishop, confirming his interest in the T2000 chairmanship, and requesting me to phone him after Easter.

Take Ma, by taxi, to the Clore Turner gallery [at the Tate]. She manages well, despite a swell of visitors. I manoeuvre her tiny, increasingly gnome-like bulk into gaps beside pictures wherever we can find them.

Then to the restaurant for lunch. Hard to hear each other and the waitress calls Granny 'the young lady with you'. But Mum has a wonderful way of filtering out angst in such situations. I quite envy her cheerful smile.

Home and help prepare for a big night at Julia Street – the arrival of all the Herberts for a family dinner. Angela has driven down from Chilton. She arrives first at a quarter to seven. She tries to be cheerful and on top of it all, but clearly is not comfortable.

A noisy and merry occasion, except for Angela's unease. 'Find me a job with witty people' is her last (despairing) attempt at a smile and a lifting of the spirits.

Tuesday, April 14th

To an un-looked-forward-to task at Highbury Magistrates' Court, to which I'm called as a witness in the case of the owner of the cab that hit our car last November.

No-one either welcomes me or even tells me what to do or where to go. Ian, big Scot from across the road, who took the cab's number, is already waiting. We sit for half an hour completely unattended.

Then a police officer, there to give evidence, recognises me. He moans about the Crown Prosecution Service, which is only a few months old, and replaces the police's own prosecution service.

A little later, after we've been sat there for 50 minutes, another helpful policeman comes to tell us that the case is on at the moment, but has just been adjourned owing to non-appearance of a witness.

He suggests we sit in the back of the court and wait to talk to the prosecutor. We do so, and are eventually told that the witness who didn't appear was Mr Palin. At which point I spring up and tell them I've been outside for the past hour. Magistrates full of apologies and very pissed off with a hopelessly confused, over-worked prosecutor, who hasn't even looked our way, let alone consulted with us.

Thursday, April 16th

Twenty-first wedding anniversary. A very warm day in prospect.

A call from the production office of a film which Chris Menges is directing.[1] Would I come out for a week in June to Zimbabwe to play 'the nicest man in the world'? Unfortunately it's the second week of *Wanda* rehearsals. Also a call from *Animals' Roadshow* – would I like to be interviewed, with Denis, by Desmond Morris?

From the ridiculous to the sublime!

Back at home catching up with the diary before going out yet again when a call is put through to me by Rachel. A voice, of no particular class or distinction, says 'Prince Edward here'. I play my reactions cautiously, my mind flicking at double-speed through a card-index of possible Prince Edward impersonators, but it transpires it really is Prince Edward.

---

[1] *A World Apart*. It won the Jury Prize at the Cannes Film Festival in 1987 and BAFTA Best Screenplay in 1988. The 'nicest man in the world' was played by Jeroen Krabbé.

He wants me to join a giant *It's a Knockout* competition to be held for charity at Alton Towers in ... of course, June. It's on the day we're rehearsing, and the day when I would like to be in Zimbabwe with Chris Menges. Explain my problems, but he deals with the first one by saying that JC will take part if all the *Wanda* cast agree.

At seven by cab to the Latchmere to see Bernard Padden's potato plays. Padden rang earlier in the week to make sure I came along. Have roped in Terry as well.

The theatre is casually run by very tall, wafer-thin, young students. 'Are you unemployed?' TJ and I are asked at the ticket office ... We joke – something about only for tonight. This cuts no ice at all with the young man who rather curtly elaborates, as if talking to very stupid people, 'Are you currently in acting work?'

Good Friday, April 17th

Call Alan Bennett to pass on my favourable reaction to last night's Padden play. He will try to go to it. He confesses that the heavily gay ambience would worry him. I tell him to take a butch friend with him – 'a hulking heterosexual' as Alan puts it.

He's trying to write another stage play – 'I'm always trying to write a stage play, but I just can't come up with the plots.' He says he has no difficulty writing the monologues currently being made by Innes for the Beeb.

Then I call Cleese, who disarms me with very generous observations about *East of Ipswich*, which he has at last got around to seeing. He's the third to mention it this morning.

He and I laugh as loudly as I have for a long while over John's revelation that the first thing he knew of the recent discoveries about the Queen Mother's relations was a headline on Teletext 'Three more Royal relations found in Surrey mental home'. It was the 'more' which really broke him up.

Sunday, April 19th

Up to Church Farm by lunchtime. Tom drives some of the way and Rachel shows me her diary. She gives days marks out of ten. Hasn't had less than six and a half this year!

Do some garden clearing and weeding for Granny. Often think I would make a good gardener. Solitary, contemplative, open-air sort of life has an attraction for me. Yesterday, skimming the papers for hints of places to go for a break at the end of May, I lighted with interest upon an article about Mount

Athos. You can spend 96 hours with the monks evidently – living very simply in a splendid location – olives and bread and hard beds. Strikes me as perhaps the sort of 'new' experience I should be looking to sample.

Wednesday, April 22nd

To the Minister of Transport. His office is located in the HQ of the Department of the Environment in Marsham Street. It is one of the drabbest, shabbiest, most utterly dispiriting of all the drab, shabby, dispiriting buildings put up in the 1960's and '70's. The fact that it houses the ministry responsible for the environment is richly ironic.

Three men sit ranged at one side of the table; the Minister at one end, his private secretary, who transcribes all we say, in laborious longhand, into a big book – rather like the old Boots' scribbling pads. We are not encouraged to shake hands with the advisers – two on buses, one on rail tunnel – and they sit there, either frozen with fear or with boredom.

Mitchell is very welcoming and easy, though, and only gets at all disturbed when revealing that he has been sent a broadsheet from the GLC in Exile along with our [magazine] *Transport Retort*. He cannot disguise his distaste for the GLC in Exile and becomes quite headmasterly, as if warning a boy from associating with 'townies'. They are '*intensely* political' he warns us.

Thursday, April 23rd

Fine spring morning. Amongst other things, a script arrives from Susie Figgis on behalf of Chris Menges, bearing a short, but memorable note on the part offered – 'it is in fact Joe Slovo, who is one of the most important figures in the struggle for the liberation of South Africa . . . '. It certainly makes a change from the camp butler or the zany transvestite English hairdresser.

Read it through, sitting in copious bright sunshine. Very moving. It's written by Shawn Slovo, who is, I assume, son of Joe. [Shawn is, in fact, his daughter.] Straight to the heart of a family directly affected by the cruelty of the SA regime. Makes all the stuff we're doing here seem suddenly trivial – window-dressing. This is spare, tightly-written, unsophisticated but enormously inspiring. It's literally about life and death.

So ring back and express my enthusiasm. They will not be able to get back to me until Monday – so Prince Edward will have to wait!

Friday, April 24th

JC has committed us to the Prince Edward charity weekend (good publicity for the film, he's been told) and so it looks as if I shall be wearing huge mouse masks and falling into water rather than playing one of the most important figures in the struggle for South African liberation.

By Underground to a lunchtime meeting with Nick Elliott and James Mitchell at L'Etoile.

Elliott says that LWT are definitely intending to go ahead on October 5th. They see no problem with the unions as IBA are to stipulate that in future 25% of programme content must be independent. Their 'Irish' agreement will ensure that 'Troubles' comes under this category. They do not want to make many changes from the previous set-up, but will have to look for another director, as Charles S wanted 'too many new conditions – including reappraisal of the part of Edward'.

No pressure is put on me to sign on the dotted line, and we leave on good terms at a little after half past two.

Wednesday, April 29th

TG rings. He's somewhere between Rome and Spain. He calls with criticism of 'No. 27' – very similar to TJ's thoughts. He feels, as I do, that it could be expanded, but is still basically a TV film.

He offers me the part of the Prime Minister in *Munchausen*, and has Max Wall in mind for the Sea Captain. He is now after Peter O'Toole again for Munchausen himself.

Then a whole series of calls. The Menges film must start on the 15th of June and won't change its dates for me. So I have to ring the royal office and accept, rather equivocally, the *Knockout* invitation.

(TG and I speculated earlier that it is an indication of the way things are that knighthoods, CBEs and the like are more likely now to be won by wearing ten-foot-high rabbit heads on the fields of Alton Towers, than in little boats squeezed between the North-West Passage, or for heroic encounters with the French fleet!)

Friday, May 1st

A delightful evening, apart from calls to Granny and Angela, which give a depressing picture of some of Angela's visit last week. Angela had been quite open with Granny about her state of mind. Angela says she sees in Granny all that lies ahead for her – loneliness and confusion. I point out that Granny is 83 and remarkably bright and undemanding compared to many much younger mothers and mothers-in-law. But through Angela's desperately distorted view of life, everything around her can be interpreted at its worst.

But then the delightful bit – Rachel cooks, serves and clears away a meal for Helen and myself. It's for our anniversary.

Wednesday, May 6th

Up at a quarter to eight for a few minutes of what, at present, I laughingly call 'meditation'. It is quite a soothing bridge between night and day, but as soon as I close my eyes Gospel Oak sounds like an international traffic hub.

To Tony Stratton-Smith's[1] memorial service at St Martin-in-the-Fields. Keith Emerson plays a somewhat laboured piano piece, 'Lament to Tony Stratton-Smith' (sic), which sounds like a prolonged Elton John intro. Michael Wale talks from the enormously high pulpit about Stratt's fondness for public houses, though, of course, no-one mentions that it was 'the lotion' (as I heard Robbie Coltrane put it on TV later) that did him in.

Graham does a rather perfunctory introduction to 'Always Look on the Bright Side'. They play the whole lot – even the verse about life being a piece of shit and always looking on the bright side of death. But, as they say, Tony would have approved. I am the only other Python representative there and very glad I went as we have three wonderfully stirring old-fashioned hymns – including 'Jerusalem'.

Graham and I walk back to the Marquee, where some hospitality is laid on. GC doesn't seem very relaxed, but then he never has since he gave up the lotion. He's been working very hard, doing his lecture tour of the US, and is now rewriting 'Ditto' yet again.

At six o'clock Helen and I set out in the blue Mini for Buckingham Palace.

There is something quietly satisfying about driving up the Mall knowing that, unlike everyone else, you are going into the house at the end. Smiling policemen direct us past the camera-wielding public, across an outer courtyard and through an arch between two scarlet-coated guardsmen.

There is a rather gloomy courtyard at the back which could do with some greenery. Have to open the bonnet and boot of the Mini, and the underneath is searched with a mirror.

---

[1] Tony Stratton-Smith, a successful indie music manager, started Charisma Records, for whom most of the Python albums were made, along with those of Genesis and John Betjeman. He also helped finance *Monty Python and the Holy Grail*. Tony owned a racehorse called Monty Python, somewhat less successful than the comedy group of the same name.

Then in through the porte-cochère, familiar from Royal Weddings, into a hallway, with a raised area straight ahead. We are shown by the ubiquitous footmen up a red-carpeted, silent staircase and eventually, to the accompaniment of a low and respectful hum of conversation, we find ourselves in a long room with a curved glass ceiling. This is the Picture Gallery.

Prince Edward, all informality, comes across and talks to us quite chattily. He's got this thing together himself, and I feel quite touched by his ingenuous resolve and complete innocence in the face of many hardened fund-raising wheeler-dealers, some of whom are represented here.

The Prince makes a short speech and attempts to explain the proceedings on June 15th. It sounds either like a complete nightmare of embarrassment and potential humiliation or a surreal experience of hallucinatory bizarreness, according to how much you've had to drink.

Monday, May 25th: Southwold

I get my head down over 'AF' at nine, emerge for an hour's lunch at one, then a more or less uninterrupted run-through until half past six.

By evening the curious east-coast micro-climate has produced low, sweeping trails of mist, only as high as the water-tower some of them, which reduce Southwold to a shrouded silence, like something out of the 'Ancient Mariner'. Potter forth with my little mother into the vaporous evening. Welcome at the Crown almost better than the food, which is oddly tasteless tonight.

Celebrity for the evening is Maureen Lipman, looking wonderful and expensive in a big black and white patterned number with nice, crumpled hubby Jack Rosenthal and two children in tow.

Maureen's *Wonderful Town* has finished (early, I would think), but she says the pleasures of being thrown in the air by six Brazilians every night were finite – especially when two or three didn't turn up.

Tuesday, May 26th

To dinner with Barry Cryer and Alan Bennett. Organised by Barry again – and at the same venue, the Gay Hussar. Alan arrives clutching his back and front bike lights, which he secretes beneath the table. He drinks only Perrier; Barry and I have wine.

We catch up on the news. Alan waxes lyrical about 'My Life as a Dog'.[1]

[1] A touching and at times very funny Swedish film, directed by Lasse Hallstrom and released in 1985.

Barry has become friends with Ben Elton. He says Elton commented once on how much Barry smiled. 'None of our lot smile much,' he'd said. Elton thinks that we've lost the art of story-telling – this clearly is why he likes Barry!

Alan is still in trouble with his plots, he tells us, as he unchains his bike from the railings before cycling back to Camden Town.

I'm home by half past eleven. Angela is staying with us until the end of the week. Notice that her hair is greyer than I remember, but she looks as neat and petite and tidy as ever. Tomorrow she has some work at the BBC.

Wednesday, May 27th

Angela left for the BBC this morning in quite a funk, but survived in the Duty Office until half past seven. But she doesn't think that she is confident and composed enough to work there yet.

Thursday, May 28th

Helen and Angela go to play tennis at Parliament Hill. When they get back I hear from an admiringly disbelieving Helen that Angela has defeated her. She ran everywhere and quite took Helen, who has been getting cocky recently, down a peg.

By seven o'clock I have assembled the new 'AF' script. What it needs now is another dispassionate read through. But cannot do any more good to it tonight, so let it be and have stew with Angela, Rachel and Will and then out to see a film with Angela.

To the Classic Tottenham Court Road to see *Desert Bloom*.[1] I like it a lot. A family saga of quality and sensitivity with an attractive re-creation of Las Vegas in 1950. It is about madness, fear and families, but the happy ending makes me feel less anxious about Angela's reaction.

She enjoys it too.

Friday, May 29th

I am up at seven o'clock. A lovely morning helps. Sun rising visibly and generously. Have read the new 'AF' through yet again and found a couple of scenes to take out; so a very productive last read-through. By half past ten my

---

[1] Released in August 1986, it was directed by Eugene Corr and starred Annabeth Gish, Jon Voight, JoBeth Williams and Ellen Barkin.

two years of writing are over and the year of acting lies ahead.

Then say goodbye to Angela, who disappears up the street in her hired Volvo about 11.15. She never seems well in the morning and, once again, before she leaves, makes it clear that we can never understand how awful she feels.

Helen tells me that she sounded an even more chilling warning than usual and, as I drive down to some shopping and the Python office, a real fear passes through me. Still, she is on the way to her psychiatrist and she has shown a remarkable ability to function perfectly well this week. I like having her to stay, though she does have to be pushed away from a tendency to want to just 'lie and curl up'.

To Holloway Road to find some clothes for Ken Pile [my character in *Wanda*]. A wonderful Jewish men's outfitter called Garman. The manager and owner serves in the shop and chews a cigar. It's all very Broadway. Quite like old times with Hazel [Pethig] – very jokey and relaxed.

Am in my study making my lists when Helen calls me downstairs. It's between 9.30 and a quarter to ten. 'It's Angela ... she's done it,' is all I need to hear. Then I speak on the phone to Veryan, who confirms that Angela has killed herself. She went to the psychiatrist, then saw Veryan at lunchtime, and seemed on good form, telling him all about her week with us. She returned to Chilton, and there, at about the time Terry and I were chasing around a squash court, decided to go to the garage and asphyxiate herself.

Helen, very composed, though her eyes stare helplessly. I ask her to ring my mother. I've never asked her to do anything as important in the whole of our life together and she copes with it unquestioningly. I decide that I must go to Southwold straight away. As I leave, all I ask for is a couple of the green apples that I like to see me through the journey. But Helen had given Angela the last two.

I am up at Sunset House by ten past twelve. As I drove I was not taking much in. I knew I didn't want music or to hear anyone else's happy world still going on. I suppose I wanted to be sorry and that's what I was doing.

Ma in very good shape, considering. A little shaken, but it seems not to have caught her emotionally. She had seen it coming too. There is not much to be done tonight. I ring Aunt Betty in Australia. Hear myself saying (because there is a real danger using equivocation to an aged lady 18,000 miles away) 'Angela is dead. She took her own life this afternoon.'

As I settle into bed soon after one o'clock, in the same air of unreality, I pick up the bedside book – a collection of *Spectator* competition pieces selected by Joanna Lumley. Inside it reads 'To my brother Michael from sister Angela, Happy Birthday 1986'.

Saturday, May 30th: Southwold

After a broken, unrefreshing night's sleep, am up at 8.30 to face the practicalities of the day which will, I'm sure, keep all of us from digesting the full impact of what has happened. Mum seems still to be in complete control. The tendency to incomprehension which Angela found so irritating in her, is in fact a strength. I don't think it is lack of comprehension anyway. I think it is an ordering of priorities which comes from an instinctive awareness that survival is the most important thing. No wonder Angela could not respond.

Phone calls come in and the vicar calls. A short, well-meaning little man with a seraphic smile and an arrangement of very fragrant white flowers, cut by his wife.

He brings his particular brand of soft-spoken solace which seems quite at odds with the business-as-usual atmosphere of the flat. He holds my mother's hand solicitously (she won't even let *me* do that for long) and stares at a photo of Angela.

After this well-intentioned little charade is over, I get on with the more painful part of the day − to ring Veryan and then to break the news to various relations − Hernes, the Greenwoods. The task is made easier by the fact that everyone knew she was ill, so there is no sudden complete shock to confront.

Lunch with Ma and at two o'clock I leave her. She does not want to change her life or routine. Sticking to it is her best way of managing. And the old ladies downstairs have both been assiduous in offering her company and sympathy. In fact she's been completely dry-eyed about the whole thing.

Then the journey I'm really not looking forward to − from Southwold to Sudbury. It's a beautiful afternoon, softly warm, and the Suffolk fields and woods and ochre-washed houses look their best.

First to greet me at Chilton is Camilla, then the two boys. All of us on the edge of tears, but controlling them. Great comfort in being with people who you know are feeling the loss as intensely as you are. Veryan is mowing the lawn. Tomorrow there was to be a local walk, meeting for refreshment at Chilton. They have decided not to postpone it.

The children make some tea and we sit in the small yard at the back of the kitchen and for two hours chat about everything but Angela. Jeremy's Jane arrives. I think it helps them all having outsiders there to distract from their grief. I feel very close to them, which is a warm and satisfying feeling, an unexpected bonus of the tragedy.

Drive back to London, still numbed, and by the time I'm home am able to sit and talk about it, over a glass of wine, matter-of-factly.

Nor do I feel any need to cancel our dinner with Terry and Al. Quite the opposite. I want to see people. I want to talk about Angela. I don't want to sweep it aside or under any carpets. And of course Terry is just the right person to be with.

We eat at 192 – a bright, trendy, new place in Notting Hill. TJ anxious and full of touching sympathy, but articulate and sensitive. Al too, though at one point she breaks into the sort of tears I've kept at bay all day. An excellent evening altogether, and I shall never be as grateful for the Joneses' company as I am tonight. And for Helen's strength and common sense, too.

Refuse to accept complete desolation. As she was unable to.

Sunday, May 31st

Still some more phone calls to be made. Betsy-Ann [cousin on my mother's side] says, apologising in advance for saying it, that she thought it 'a very brave thing' that Angela had done.

After the phone calls, another side of me cries out for satisfaction, for a dose of revitalising normality. The day at Abbotsley proves to be just that.

And what a day – warm in a gentle way, soft and summery – the garden full. The hammock is slung, football and cricket and rounders played. Gardening done and a copious lunch. The best of days.

Tuesday, June 9th

At Chilton for lunchtime. Helen, I think, more tense than I am. This is the first time she's been to Chilton since Angela's death, and she and Angela had become much closer in the last few months – talking in the kitchen, shopping at M&S, tennis, etc. I think Helen saw herself as a lifeline and in a way she feels more affected by Angela's death than I do.

Piers [Veryan's brother, a barrister] is there, with stories of his chaotic but busy life. His three-piece-suit – originally well chosen and quite stylish, is turned up at the edges and a little creased from over-use.

We set out for Colchester Crematorium – Marcus, Veryan and, in our car, Piers, Helen and myself. The crematorium is within shouting distance of Colchester Barracks, where, in the autumn of '82, I was screaming at a squad of recruits and actors for *The Meaning of Life*.

The innocuous collection of buildings where the cremation is to take place make no special impression. Somehow I don't want to remember the place. One or two other people – I remember a woman in a flowery hat – walk by, otherwise we are left very much alone.

The efficient and discreet funeral director, who seems to have one eye missing, checks we are all ready and then we make our way to the door.

At that moment, Angela's coffin, on the shoulders of four men in dark raincoats, is carried past us.

We then form up behind the coffin and make our way into a small chapel, whilst pre-recorded organ music sounds, tastefully, from somewhere. It's all quite strange and disorienting to think it's used all the time – rewound and used again. It's like sleeping in someone else's sheets.

The presence of Peter Hollis, a priest and friend of the family, a sane and sensible man of no pomposity and a tough CND pedigree, makes the whole tawdry occasion special. He asks us to be silent for a while and remember Angela in our own ways. Then he reads some simple prayers – never over-sentimental or over-emotional, but one felt he shared with us all something of Angela.

Then, with the words, 'She is at rest', the curtains draw across (I find myself fascinated by who causes this to happen – someone listening somewhere pressing a button – are they automatically triggered in some way?) and the coffin slides away. I am dry-eyed, mainly because I don't look at the coffin, nor do I want to let my grief out in such an anonymous place.

We shake hands with Peter Hollis and then an awkward moment of not much to say in the car park before Helen and I leave for London.

We talked there and back about Angela.

Wednesday, June 10th

Park by the Serpentine Gallery and walk down to the Polish Club in Exhibition Road.

Always struck at this time of year by the sheer weight of greenery – the thickness of the crowns on the trees, the lushness of bushes and shrubs, the deep, thick pile of grass cover. It's June, it's raining, and England puts on its own impression of a Continental rainforest.

At the Polish Club I sit with a Perrier and wait for Tristram. Dark, smiling eyes of the girls at the bar – friendly, curious. It is like being in a very benevolent foreign country.

Hardly anyone else dining there, except for a few very smart, grey-suited Polish men, well preserved, with interestingly aged faces. Tristram tells me that they're the Polish Government in Exile.

Excellent borscht and then dumplings/meatballs and sauerkraut. Some good talk on 'No. 27' and *American Friends*.

In the evening to a PEN club function at the Zoo restaurant. Myself and Charles Sturridge and Dorothy Tutin have been invited as special guests to thank us for our help in last year's fund-raising effort 'The Sentence is Silence'.

I find myself temporarily next to a fierce lady called Sybille Bedford. Neither she nor most of her friends know who I am.

Unfortunately, once Michael Holroyd makes his opening speech welcoming self, and others, I make a grab for the bottle of red wine on the table, magnanimously and enthusiastically offering it to all the old ladies. A chorus of disapproval and very odd looks. Sybille protectively clutches the bottle. It turns out to be her own and not, as I thought, a complimentary. Many apologies. My confusion compounded by the fact that I'm discovered to be on the wrong table – I should be at high table, next to Dorothy Tutin.

Thursday, June 11th

Wake to rain. Election day.

Vote, and spend most of the late evening watching the results come in. The exit polls are complete spoilsports, quashing any real chance of surprise. Like reading the last page of a thriller first.

Nod off in my chair and finally to bed at two with the Tories well set for a third term. A depressing sense of inevitability and, to be honest, a hint of relief. The opposition just don't seem to have got themselves together yet.[1]

Sunday, June 14th

Drive, unhurriedly, across Derbyshire to the Peveril of the Peak Hotel, where Helen and I are staying in company with many other celebs [for 'It's A Royal Knockout']. An unpretentious, low group of buildings set amidst trees and fields.

Time to sit downstairs and read the papers and have coffee before setting out in a bus for Alton Towers.

At Alton Towers the security operation is elaborate, with police, private security and young PAs all armed with radios. We're taken to see the set – a wooden sixteenth-century castle-cum-manor house façade facing the slightly less real ruin of Alton Towers across the lake.

After a talk from Prince Edward, who seems to be completely in his element, we are all settled in the stands to watch a run-through of all the games by a special squad – who, we find out later, are largely from the army. Then to try on costumes, and eventually back in a bus to the hotel.

Assemble for a coach to the dinner at Alton Towers, at which four royals

[1] The Conservatives won with a majority of 102. It was Margaret Thatcher's third consecutive victory. Labour, whose share of the vote increased by 1%, was led by Neil Kinnock.

will be present. They are all staying at the Izaak Walton Hotel and I'm told no four royals have ever stayed together in one hotel before. Hence the security.

Our coach is late leaving because Princess Anne (created Princess Royal yesterday) is late arriving. We are jammed in. As we sit waiting we are treated to the sight of security men in a field chasing cows away from Nigel Mansell's helicopter.

Eventually we move off, and all the way from the hotel to Alton Towers the route is lined with police and, on the odd occasions when we pass a house, by waving citizens. We pass regally through the town of Ashbourne, then out, up and over the quiet hills, and ride into Alton Towers between cheering – well, waving – crowds until we're drawn up outside Bagshaw's Restaurant. The weather is still fickle and umbrellas are provided for us as we scurry into the hostelry.

First glimpse of the 'other' royals. Andrew, thick-set, with a wide neck and big, piercing eyes. Fergie, eyes always looking about, smaller and slighter than I thought.

We're at tables. Next door but one to me is Margot Kidder, less irrepressible than usual, as she is jet lagged and flu-ey, but still great company. Beside her, looking distinctly unhappy, is Nick Lowe, her current man. He turns out to be a kindred soul, articulate and full of the same sort of childhood memories I have. We get on well, though later Margot tells me this is exceptional, as Nick is not happy at this sort of do and fears for his street cred.

Prince Edward makes a speech, peppered with well-told jokes. I congratulate him on the one about the Scottish lady discovered in the snow by a relief helicopter which yells down 'Red Cross!', to which she shouts back 'No thanks, I've given already.'

Prince Andrew and Fergie are by this time throwing bread rolls about and as we leave we all have to crunch over a layer of sugar crystals which Andrew emptied over Michael Brandon's head.

Then back into the coach and off into the night. All the staff of the restaurant watching us, noses pressed against the window.

Monday, June 15th: Peveril of the Peak Hotel, Derbyshire

Into our costumes for a dress rehearsal. The rain stops, but it's dreadfully muddy underfoot. Still, Python filming and pop festivals prepared me for all this. I'm in the first game, which involves winding a cannon uphill on a capstan and having to jump over the taut rope at every revolution. We're dressed in four-foot-wide rubber rings with skirts hanging round them. It's absolutely killing.

Then I have to try the 'Mini-Marathon', which involves attempting to cross a revolving pole whilst having food thrown at me by Viv Richards. I fall in twice. George [Layton] is very good and John Travolta refuses to take part in two of the games in case he gets his hair wet.

At lunch the indefatigable Pamela Stephenson, who doesn't seem to be living if she isn't performing, coaches her team in a chant and we decide to call ourselves the Pandas.

After quite a wait, Prince Andrew appears to give us a team talk. Normally he would be considered intolerably bossy, but as he's third in line to the throne, it seems excusable. Then we're all sent off to change.

At four o'clock, after team photos, we line up behind our various royals and their banners. I'm at the back of our team and next to Fergie. She it is who starts the chorus of 'Why Are We Waiting'.

The crowd fills the stands, whipped by a cool, but mercifully dry wind, as we parade in after the fanfare.

First game is disastrous for us. Working savagely hard, we are in the lead when Gary Lineker and George Lazenby catch their skirts in the coiled rope. Not only do we come third, but Lineker has to suffer the indignity of being pulled out of his skirt by the Duke of York and others.

My turn on the pole in the Mini-Marathon ends in predictable ignominy as I join Mel Smith, Sunil Gavaskar, Barry McGuigan and others unable to make the crossing. Lazenby once again distinguishes himself and wins three points for us.

We don't come to the final game until nearly seven o'clock.

At the end Andrew becomes the army officer again and barks 'Everyone on the stage!' at us. 'Sounds as though he's won it,' I mutter to Princess Anne (who indeed *has* won). 'Oh, no,' she says, in that wonderfully lugubrious tone she uses to great effect, 'he's always like that.'

We have come second, which, after our early failures, is quite a relief. Everyone begins to peel off their mediaeval frocks and goodbyes are fondly exchanged. Prince Edward thanks every one of us and presents us with a Wedgwood commemorative bowl. I shake Andrew's hand and say goodbye.

At the hotel, goodbyes to such as Steve Cram, quiet, self-contained, and Meat Loaf, who tells me with some embarrassment that Fergie has taken to calling him 'Meaty' and says she wants to visit him in New York.

At last into our car and back to being the Normals. No police escort, but cordial waves from the detectives as we pull away from the Peveril of the Peak. It's as though all of us know that we have been part of a very peculiar, but almost magical occasion, the like of which will never be seen again.

Tuesday, June 16th

Scan the papers – the more popular of which carry a story about Prince Edward swearing at the press at a post-event press conference. His question as to whether they'd enjoyed themselves had been met by stony silence from the hacks – none of whom had been allowed in the arena or near the contestants.

In fact Edward had done wonderfully well in keeping them away and undoubtedly making the whole occasion relaxed and informal and enjoyable – 30 hours out of real life.

To JC's for the first day's rehearsal on *Wanda*. Jamie opens the door and gives me a big hug and a kiss, which is not a bad way to start the film. We spend most of the day reading through. The clash of styles – Cleese/Palin revue-based instinctive efficiency, Kevin Kline's New York method and Jamie Lee's West Coast directness – makes for an interesting day.

Kline is up and about with the script, touching, grabbing, shouting, always exploring every bit of the part. He has a disconcerting habit of dropping into the double lotus position with the same ease with which I would bend down.

Michael Shamberg is there, his sigh and mournful tone very recognisable. He makes up an American threesome; Charlie Crichton makes the third of the Brits.

There are many cultural clashes. The Americans can swear and motherfucker this and that, but are squeamish about a word like 'penetration'. They like things to be worked out, explained through in a way which makes even John seem wildly spontaneous.

But there is strength there – in technique and in physical presence and in sheer control and range with Kevin, in a bright and lively physicality from Jamie L. The scenes between John and Jamie are well played and very moving, JC having early on echoed Alan B's remarks at the first rehearsal of *Private Function* – make the characters real and the comedy will follow.

By the end of the day we are not even through the script. Hazel arrives and we try costumes, etc. Mine is approved of. Throughout John has been alert and guiding and never once irascible. The sun shines on and off in the garden outside and the house is comfortable, though the chairs are almost too big, like small rooms.

Wednesday, June 17th

We carry on reading through. Kevin prowls and pounces, but always with a strange softness of touch, which makes his behaviour entertaining and stimulating rather than dominating. JC hisses and wheezes with laughter and occasionally thumps the table and breaks into uncontrollable coughing. Charlie C listens wryly, interspersing intelligent observations, always with a twinkle in the eye and a generally well-calculated aggrieved air about the way John treats him.

Jamie is straight off a movie (which she hadn't much enjoyed) and into this set-up, with three people of whom she clearly is in some awe, and all of whom have quite different approaches to the acting.

We have a much freer approach than she has been used to and she is beginning to expand into it. At the moment she is as jerky and brittle as Kevin is broad and relaxed.

Friday, June 19th

Down to Park Lane to test drive a Mercedes 190 which I am toying with as a replacement for the Sierra.

We splash through the rain, which allows the salesman to show off the 86-degree wiper action and deliver some predictable abuse towards a march which has been holding up the traffic. There are red banners, Arabic writing and students, and he goes into a 'why do we allow them in the country' bit, but back-pedals like a true salesman when I respond with some liberal waffle about freedom to protest being better than revolution.

I shouldn't imagine Mercedes drivers are a left-wing bunch, and herein lies my concern about becoming one. Like it or not, it does rub people's noses in it. It is an expensive thing and, like travelling First Class, you are *seen* to afford it. On the other hand it is silent, strong and feels safer and much more strain-resistant than most cars I've ever driven.

To Upper Brook Street and Le Gavroche. JC, whose generosity has been well displayed this week, is hosting a dinner, ostensibly for Cynthia's end of exams, but with Shamberg, Kevin, Jamie and husband Chris, Helen and a girlfriend of JC's all there as well.

Occasionally JC looks paternally over to Kevin and myself as we talk, and he beams broadly and mutters some aside to Helen. He gets on well with Helen and at one point asks me across the table 'Is she as rude to everyone as she is to me?' I tell John he's privileged.

Saturday, June 20th

Rehearsal at JC's. The Americans have problems with the beginning – over how Otto is discovered, how their relationship is established, etc, etc. Kevin does most of the asking, but Jamie, who went running in Battersea Park at a quarter to seven this morning, takes a dynamic lead in suggesting answers.

JC is tired and not taking it in too well. I concur with Charlie C that there is no good reason for jettisoning the start we have, and that it should be made to work better with the injection of some of the ideas that Jamie has come up with.

Jamie makes us all a salad lunch and the atmosphere remains friendly and cordial, but for the first time I sense that JC's patience is being sorely tried by Kevin – for whom the present opening was written after they were in Jamaica together.

I haven't been home long when JC rings to apologise to me for what he feels might have been a bit of a wasted day for me. But I can honestly say it wasn't. The time we're spending together being very useful and instructive.

Later in the evening our new neighbour [Jonas Gwangwa] comes to our house after he's locked himself out. He's a tubby South African black with a kindly, well-used face and it turns out he's currently musical director of the 'Biko' film, in which Kevin has a lead role. The other musical director is George Fenton, who wrote the *East of Ipswich* score.

Tuesday, June 23rd

I have had the bright idea of having my character's hair curly, and Barry the hairdresser goes over my scalp with the curling tongs. Much too hot to start with, and a puff of smoke and violent smell of burning hair don't exactly bode well. But Barry has 'done' Ann-Margret and others, so not to worry. The result is quite effective. It certainly changes my usual 'boyish' look and the usual line of my haircut too. Show it to John, Charlie and others and, apart from Kevin, who reacts against instant decisions anyway, it finds general approval.

Wednesday, June 24th

We rehearse the various sequences that will occupy me for all but a day of the first two weeks. John tends to concentrate on the performances, whilst Charlie, walking-stick in hand, looks for the shots.

At lunchtime JC disappears to his office for a salad and a lie-down. Charlie adjourns to the bar, reminding me as he does so that the genesis of *Wanda* came from JC telling him what a good stutter I could do.

Kevin has now settled for a small, black cap, which tapers the top of his head, making him look a little ridiculous, sinister and fashionable at the same time. He wears a flowing black coat with blue stripes and the stagey flamboyance reminds me of Marlon Brando's outlandish outfit in *Missouri Breaks*.[1]

---

[1] 1976 movie, directed by Arthur Penn and starring Marlon Brando, Jack Nicholson and Randy Quaid.

Thursday, June 25th

Into rehearsal. Jamie, projecting energy at an almost reckless rate, stares, frowns, worries, opines, suggests. At one point she comes up to me a little awkwardly and kisses me juicily on the lips. She apologises, but says she did it because she's going to have to do it in the scene coming up. Wonderful, but very American.

Lunch with Kevin and Donald Woods, whom Kevin plays in 'Biko'. Woods is a very lively, instantly warm man with a twinkle in his eye. We talk about the 'Biko' film. He says how careful they had to be in the script and in the making of the film to give 'equal air time' to all the various African resistance groups.

He also tells of how our new neighbour Jonas and George did the final music section. Apparently Jonas came into the session completely arseholed and played every single instrument to great effect. For a newspaperman Woods is infectiously indiscreet.

Friday, June 26th

JC is playing and re-playing what he calls the 'renunciation' scene with Jamie. Iain Johnstone is prowling around, recce-ing for a film about the filming. Jamie is very cross that she cannot seem to play the scene the way JC wrote it.

Then we have a read-through. Problem seems to be that it's still too long. Despite her glumness, Jamie still comes in with acute suggestions for cuts. Later in the afternoon we're talking and she tells me that the only way her father [Tony Curtis] could get a date with her mother [Janet Leigh] was by pretending to be Cary Grant.

'Biko' has been completed today and I go for a couple of lagers with Donald Woods and his wife Wendy in the bar. They live now in Surbiton. They seem to detect no irony in ending up in Surbiton after such an exciting and dangerous life, wading across the Zambesi, etc.

Monday, June 29th

Board the 8.55 to Birmingham International, where we begin the first day's filming on the 'Eco' programme on Transport 2000.

A small crew and an efficient day's filming. We start almost the moment I arrive, in the airport, then on the MAGLEV, and later at the main entrance to the National Exhibition Centre.

The end of the day's filming is of my returning, as the 'ideal' business traveller, to be met by a loving wife at home. Hazel, the lady they have secured to play the loving wife, is quite a surprise. She sits sipping wine in the garden.

She is the complete antithesis of a wife. Her whole appearance, from the bouffant, tinted hair to the ankle bracelet, via the voracious pink lipstick, is of one who threatens the whole institution of marriage.

On the third take, when the director has suggested that we hold 'a beat longer' on the kiss, her tongue is exploring my mouth (which is quite taken aback) in no time.

Being devoured by Hazel on a Solihull housing estate on a tropical June day is, I have to admit, the least expected perk of chairing an environmental organisation.

Saturday, July 4th

We arrive at Chilton at 11.15.

I walk Mother slowly along the path to Chilton Church, across the fields, where the ripening corn is half her height. We move slowly, meeting people on the way – their first reaction is to smile at the fineness of the day. It's extrovert weather. At one point, looking behind me, I see my own family following along behind, surrounded by cornstalks.

A wait at the church before everyone is in – and Peter Hollis starts the service at 12.15. Beside me is Granny, then Helen, Rachel, Will and Tom. In front of me is Veryan and then the children. An organ plays. Across the aisle and through the vestry I catch a glimpse of golden sunshine and green grass framed in a doorway.

The first hymn is 'Breathe on Me, Breath of God'. Chris Bell[1] gives a short address and, as he says later, 'I only just got through it'. Very brief, unflowery and he sums the tragedy of my poor sister up so well when he says 'If only she could have seen herself as we all saw her'. I read a lesson from One Corinthians – 'Faith, Hope . . . Love' (not charity). I would have preferred something more immediately relevant, but it's beautiful language, though I still don't understand quite what I was saying.

At the end of the service we walk to the tiny graveyard where a hole has been dug to receive Angela's ashes, which stood on the altar during the service.

A short prayer by the admirable Peter Hollis at the graveside and then, for a moment, all the grief flows out. Every one of her children lets the tears come, and I embrace each one of them.

From this moment on Angela's life and the memory of her will recede slowly but gently into the past and into memory. The tears will flow less easily (though they are pouring down my face as I write) and the lives of those she knew so well will readjust to being without her. But in the middle of this hot

---

[1] He and his wife Carys were long-time friends of the family.

summer day, amongst the fields beneath which lie old Chilton Village, the precise moment of loss is marked amongst us all.

Then, as happens, real life resumes. There's Terry J and Al to be welcomed. Everyone to be talked to. I walk back with Derek Taylor.

There is Pimm's and orange juice at a table beneath the copper beech, as we walk over the bridge. A wonderful party develops – full of memories of the last one here.

Everyone who had seen her recently seems almost to have expected what happened to happen. Everyone thinks it an awful, tragic waste. As Sepha points out, Angela looked ten years younger than most of her contemporaries here today.[1] She was so good at bringing the family together, says Joan Herbert, Veryan's cousin.

This last thought leaves me with the only real sadness at the end of an afternoon far, far happier than I'd expected, and that is whether such an occasion will ever happen again. Angela was the common friend of all these people. Now, as her memory fades, will we all see each other again?

Wednesday, July 8th

Drive over to Hackney. At the Assembly Room I find a crowd of maybe 100– 130 people listening to Dinah Morley – a local politician. Dave Wetzel, transport head of the GLC and in my book a Good Man, speaks before me. Very disappointing – list of all the good things the GLC did, then, rather than apply the lessons to the current subject – which is transport in Hackney – he ends with a long Labour rant. Purely political and quite unconstructive, especially as the Tories have just been voted in by a resounding majority for the third time.

Before I speak, the Mayor of Hackney, who is chairing, has to announce some business, but at the same time a large, black lady is announcing something at the back of the audience. The Mayor plods doggedly on, the lady's voice rises, people's tolerance for their brothers and sisters begins to wear thin and she's asked to shut up. '*You* shut up!' she returns lustily, and continues barracking.

The Mayor seems unable to control her and she's still ranting on when I'm introduced. I stop and sit down until she subsides, but when I do go on it isn't very comfortable.

At the end a distracted middle-aged lady with wild hair comes up to me, 'You don't mind me asking, do you, but are you left-wing?' 'Moderately so, yes,' I reply judiciously. 'Oh, thank you. In that case could you sign my book?'

---

[1] Sepha Wood is one of Angela's closest friends from Sheffield days.

Thursday, July 9th

Taken down to Daniel Galvin in George Street to have my hair permed. This is the most drastic change to my appearance I ever let myself in for. As it was my suggestion to play Ken curly, I've only myself to blame. The process of perming is all quite soothing. It's a nice place and I'm fussed over. Some foul lotion, smelling of ammonia (it is in fact sulphur) is poured over my curlers.

My first real test of the new head is, incongruously enough, at a small party given by Sir Robert Reid of BR to his 'good friends'. So the first time I actually get to meet the most powerful man in the railways is six hours after I've had my hair permed.

Friday, July 10th

Picked up at nine and to the studio for rehearsal.

My dressing room is quite spacious. It's separated from Kevin's by a sliding wall. Kevin has an extraordinary quality of making himself look big and impressive, when he isn't a lot taller than me, in fact. His room is full of costumes, back-exercising equipment, books, etc. Mine is almost empty.

The day's rehearsal ends at six. In the course of which dogs are auditioned. One of the terriers has to resist. 'The Resisting Dog', it becomes known as, and will as such go down in my list of possible public house names.

Saturday, July 11th

To Harrow Driving Centre at half past ten for a second session of motorbike tuition. It doesn't all come back to me at first and I become dispirited. But I persevere and, with the patient help of Phil, improve and by the end am able to drive with a passenger on the back and manoeuvre through a slalom of cones without knocking any over. Like learning any skill one has to pass through the barrier of complete clumsiness.

Monday, July 13th

The usual, slightly over-hearty buzz of a first day's filming. Whilst I am in make-up Cleese arrives and as a present gives me a poster from the LMS in 1954, which announces the re-opening of the refurbished Gospel Oak Station – complete with wonderfully idealised picture!

Kevin gives me a gay book by one Phil Andros, published by the Perineum

Press, called *My Brother Myself*. In it he's written 'Dear Michael, Happy Wanda. I love working with you. Herewith a book I found which could be developed into a project for the two of us.'

I am alone with the goldfish in the first shot – 'Hello Wanda' – and it's disposed of quickly and efficiently and we then embark on a roughly chronological sequence of scenes in George's flat. The speed of Alan Hume's crew and the understanding between us after two weeks of rehearsal, combined with John's unflagging enthusiasm and advice and delight in what he's seeing, make for a very productive morning.

Wednesday, July 15th

Experience the first real hints of how unsettling it can be acting a scene with Kevin. We're playing the scene in which I discover him on the lavatory (or pretending to be on the lavatory). The first barrier to sharing the scene is that Kevin is retreating into himself to discover whatever he can bring out of the lines and the action. I feel, perhaps wrongly, that this is not a process to whose depths I can be admitted. I feel a little like the magician's assistant.

Then, as we run it through, I'm aware of Kevin's reaction against direction, against marks, against restriction of any kind. Like a pacing lion he has to work out his own parameters. Charles Crichton tells of how when he worked with Alec Guinness they could never be seen to use marks. One evening he and the camera had plotted out where the great man should stand and a mark had been, inadvertently, left there.

When Guinness saw it in the morning he deliberately ignored it and played with his move for an hour before eventually coming to rest on exactly the same position as the mark.

By the end of the day, even JC is getting a little impatient with Kevin's habitual look at the end of every take, which is deep gloom.

Our last scene together for the day – his proposition to me on the stairs – feels very good. JC applauds generously at the end of a particular take and says that I won't do anything much better than that ever again!

Thursday, July 16th

Up at 6.45. Pick-up at 7.15. Complete the scene on the stairs with Kevin, then a long hiatus as they shoot Tom Georgeson and the police arresting him.

There is no sunshine about either – just a melancholy-inducing low cloud. At last, in mid-afternoon, I'm required, and work on, concentratedly, until six. Then a look at the rushes.

After they're over, Charlie, who is congenitally averse to showbiz hype, wobbles a bit and casts his soft, dog-like eyes up at me ... 'You're bloody marvellous, you really are.' I'm quite taken aback and hopelessly unable to handle the thoroughness of his compliment, but it sends me home mentally beaming from ear to ear and I hardly remember the soggy, lethargic evening, and the long lines of blocked traffic almost every way we turn.

Friday, July 17th

Start the day being kissed repeatedly by Jamie on the bathroom floor. Very pleasant form of acting. We move on very fast and I'm in nearly all the set-ups, and in a variety of different make-ups, combinations of bandages and cuts and bruises.

Am immensely relieved and rather proud of the fact that I have been the heaviest used of all the characters this week, and that I've not just survived, but flourished, despite fatigue. I think performance has always brought me to life, and I feel more confident, more quickly in Ken's persona than I ever thought I would.

Life's little ironies, No. 32: Christopher Morahan is at the studios, casting for 'Troubles'!

Monday, July 20th

Begin work on the fish-eating sequence, for which I have my head bandaged, one eye covered, a bruise and scratches, and am tied to a most uncomfortable chair. Later I have chips inserted into my nose by Kevin. Not difficult to show expression of distress, and Charlie's decision for me to play the scene (and the rest of the film) with one eye covered doesn't seem to affect the degree of laughter from the crew.

The day wears on, as filming days do; all the days, weeks, months, even years of preparation for a scene are finally whittled down into a few hours. It's all businesslike. Charlie bangs his stick and laughs at himself ... 'I can't remember what the hell's going on.'

Kevin spends most of the day racked by doubt – even when he's done the most brilliantly inventive take he stands, shrugs, and looks like a man who's just been given a tin of contaminated beef.

Tuesday, July 21st

More of the fish-torture scene. Good word on the rushes of yesterday. I am subdued during the morning – the part is so uncomfortable – but in the afternoon we begin the slapstick, stammering scene with myself and JC.

John, who has found even his generous policy of praise and encouragement is not always a match for Kevin's mood of gloomy reappraisal, beams with real happiness as we start to play the scene together. By the end of the afternoon he is corpsing regularly and suggesting we write a film together.

Finish at six. A physically very hard day for me – perhaps the most demanding so far – but on the rushes I can see that my one-eyed reactions are funny and, as Dave drives me home about seven, I feel, despite a 12-hour day, that I am really enjoying this return to uninhibited comedy. A chance to expand and experiment – a world away from the 'heroes' of '*Mish*' and *Private Function*.

Wednesday, July 22nd

Shamberg feels that there should be closer footage of the fish being eaten by Kevin. Charlie stoutly resists, saying that any more specific shots would spoil the 'beauty' of the piece and make it 'vulgar and coarse'.

I carry on after lunch and it's not until half past four that I'm released from eight successive days of heavy filming. Say my farewells until late Friday.

JC rings about 8.30 to tell me he thinks that the shot of me with the chips up my nose and the pear in my mouth – still desperately berating Kevin – is the funniest thing he's ever seen me do.

Thursday, July 23rd

The office phones. Someone who has seen me in *The Dress* wants me to play in Pinter's *Betrayal* at the New End Theatre – a 'major' actress is lined up to play opposite me. More tempting is increased interest from Steve Woolley and Nik Powell at Palace in my availability for a new Neil Jordan film. They will send the script to me.

Looking with half interest at what the Everyman may offer for a night out, I see that Charlie's *Lavender Hill Mob* is on at six. This must be a sign. I drive up there. Unfortunately the accumulated fatigue of the last two weeks decides to hit me as the film begins. Almost as soon as a succession of nostalgic images – the old censor's certificate, the Rank gong and the leaves of Ealing Studios' logo have come and gone – I'm fighting against a fierce desire for unconsciousness.

The film is a delight – played with great humour by basically rather nice characters. Its strengths are amiability and a good pace. I hope that Charlie will be able to inject the same into JC's film.

Friday, July 24th

Read Neil Jordan's *High Spirits* halfway through and am considerably intrigued. It's Irish-American hokum, but my part is quite interestingly manic and as I run over the Heath I feel a great surge of enthusiasm for the project.

My head clears, too, on *American Friends*. Decide to confirm Tristram as director, with the possibility of the now freelance Nat Crosby as photographer, and to try and make it as cheaply as possible. So the *Missionary* gloss would go and we should concentrate on the characters rather than the crowds of costumed extras. Ingenuity will be the key.

The second half of *High Spirits* is a bit of a come-down. The comedy becomes more desperate and the laughs cruder and the last page is dreadful. In fact the script bears all the hallmarks of Hollywood's corrosive influence. Suddenly, it doesn't seem like a good idea.

Wednesday, July 29th

Heavy rain as we start the day's filming. I am bent double in the back of a van with wet, sticky, grubby floor, trying to control a Doberman with a pair of pink knickers in its collar.

Back in my caravan I try to cat-nap. Overhead a gigantic flash of lightning and almost simultaneous clap of thunder.

Dog shots in the early afternoon and I end up back in the van with the Doberman, which is a very amiable, if somewhat confused, dog clearly not given to the level of ferocity required. 'Give his bollocks a squeeze,' someone suggests. Then he becomes realistically angry. His eyes stare and strain, his teeth are bared and I'm damn glad there's a muzzle. I'm dismissed at a quarter to six.

Back home, Neil Jordan calls from LA and before he can do any extra persuasion, I tell him I've decided, for time reasons, not to do *High Spirits* . . . well, it's almost true. Unlike producers, he doesn't put up much of a fight and seems resigned.

Thursday, July 30th

After lunch I experience the odd sensation of nervousness and uncertainty as I approach a fairly simple shot. Despite rave notices from all sides for my work in the film so far, I still have only myself and my own gut feelings to trust and to deal with.

In the scene I have to discover that not only has a dog been killed, but that Mrs Coady has died of a heart attack. Gloom and remorse must turn to smiles and laughter. I do it, but formularistically, with tight representation of laughter, instead of laughing because I want to. Charlie is very happy, though, and moves quickly on to the next shot.

For the first time I feel rushed and confused. I felt critical of my performance, even if he didn't. I talk to Charlie. 'If ever you want to do it again, you just have to say,' he replies magnanimously, before adding 'and I'll say "Bloody actors"!'

Friday, July 31st

A frenetic day. A new location by Clerkenwell Green.

Two filming crews filming us being filmed, or, worse still, filming us off-camera, 'relaxing'. Feel like a caged animal being prodded through the bars to be animated, amusing – to do tricks – when really all I want to do is sit as quietly as possible and harness my energies to complete the day.

Charles Althorp[1] interviews me for NBC's Today programme. I manage to be lively, but unimaginative. He is quite sensible, softly-spoken and easy to talk to. Then the prying eyes of Iain Johnstone's crew pick me up and I improvise with John and everyone laughs, till we run dry.

Jamie is back with us. She's edgy and, as I'm beginning to realise, covers her edginess with a manic display of extrovert energy. As John is in the middle of being interviewed by NBC, interminably, Jamie grabs a policeman and leads him to arrest John. It works very well and the policeman goes all pink.

But when Jamie does the same thing on Kevin, who is giving an equally interminable interview to Iain Johnstone, it backfires; Kevin is not much amused, and poor Jamie sits down again, deflated. She is like a bright child, very up or very down. Open, eager, energetic, but always demanding a response; thriving on attention, but frequently finding it's the wrong sort.

The afternoon is even more like a circus. We are crowded into narrow streets, hemmed in by dour old council housing, filming a car exchange on a

[1] Princess Diana's brother. He became 9th Earl Spencer after his father's death in 1992.

getaway (the police obligingly tell us that this location has been used for just this purpose by real crooks, twice in the last six months).

Jamie is practising the line 'Shut up!' when a group of Scots winos stagger past. One turns on her – 'You fuckin' shut up!'

David Byrne, whose *True Stories* was one of the most interesting films this year, and whose 'People Like Us' tape has brightened many journeys to Southwold, appears with Michael Shamberg (who carries his mobile phone like a sinister black detonator). A thin man, with big, soft, dark eyes, hair in a pony-tail and a rather nervous, apologetic manner, which is belied by sudden bursts of lusty laughter.

The motorbike has to be ridden for the first time. I have to ride it whilst holding the black bag of clothes, which is something I never practised. Charlie decides on no rehearsal. 'Either he'll do it, or he won't.'

As it happens I do it, and they're happy with the take, and the Lowry-esque crowd begins to disperse as the unit moves off for the last shot. For me it's the end of week three, the end of my 13th full filming day out of the first 15.

Wednesday, August 5th

We're up early – seven o'clock – to see William off on his cycling trip to Holland; he's going with friend Nathan for two weeks. Everything squashed into two pannier bags on his new Muddy Fox mountain bike. Brightly-coloured Bermuda shorts and his recently-acquired Pizza Express baseball cap give him quite a jaunty look as he heads off up Elaine Grove, on a soft, quite cool, autumnal morning.

To the Curzon Mayfair to catch the first performance of the highly-praised *Jean de Florette*.[1]

Enjoy the film – my attention constantly engaged by absorbing wide-screen photography and a small group of characters giving riveting performances.

Turn it over in my mind as I drive north, to see if I can winkle out any lessons for *American Friends*. Keep it simple, is as far as I get.

Monday, August 10th

Today we are filming at one of the maintenance areas at Heathrow.

British Airways have, extraordinarily, given us a 747 to play with for the week and it's tugged into position at the back of our shot. Only the tyres are

---

[1] Directed by Claude Berri and starring Gérard Depardieu, Yves Montand and Daniel Auteuil.

of human scale – the rest towers above us, comparable only to some huge cathedral or fortress.

Special effects are responsible for the false concrete with which the area is being surfaced, and into which Kevin must fall and die. It's made from a base of porridge and Camp coffee, and smells a bit like pig swill.

I have a steamroller to drive, which looks formidable and belches out black diesel smoke. Quite easy to operate, though not for racing, and I enjoy bearing down on Kevin very, very slowly.

Wednesday, August 12th

A stunt man is squashed into the porridge first thing, as Brian (special effects) drives the front wheel of the roller over him. All executed with skill and admirable lack of fuss and bother; everyone applauds.

More steamroller-driving in the afternoon takes us almost to the end of the sequence, a day early. My last lines are screamed out above the noise of steel on porridge.

A pleasant, but humid evening. Tom enthuses to me about climbing, in which he clearly finds success and confidence.

Thursday, August 13th

At the airport soon after eight. A low, damp morning with drifting drizzle. Melvin [the second assistant director] greets me with the news that they have reversed the day's shooting and will first be doing the final sequence inside the Jumbo.

So, a morning in the caravan. Dip into a 1920's travel book about 'Undiscovered France', which Jonathan Benson has brought in for me. Jonathan loves France and all things French, and is very interested in my imminent departure for our summer visit to the Lot. He remembers reading a card stuck up amongst others offering 'Cane-chair saleslady' and 'French lessons', which read simply 'Phone 487 3294 for the Lot'.

Friday, August 14th

A mild and benevolent morning, and there is a cautious air of celebration about the unit. Can't be just the sunshine, or because it's Friday, I think that a general air of confidence is seeping into us all. This is the end of five weeks' filming, in which there has not been one day which hasn't produced something remarkable, and Michael Shamberg's only worry is that it may be too long.

Jamie, to whom I have given a copy of *American Friends* earlier this morning, retired to her trailer and read it all at a sitting. She is tremendously enthusiastic. 'I get so many scripts, I have to tell you, if something like that came along I would ring my agent and say "Get me the job" . . .'

Saturday, August 22nd

David [Dodd] and Andaye and sons Alex and Jehan are round at Simon Albury's. We talk about the '60's, about the change that has happened since then, and the Conservative '80's. Nothing in the US has really changed deep down, Andaye feels. Reagan has managed to divert attention away from the problems of hunger, poverty and prejudice by concentrating his time and his efforts on those who are successful, tough, patriotic.

We are deep in a conservative cycle, I wonder if when there is a return to restlessness, and questioning, radical attitudes, the conditions for their dissemination will be the same. In '68 quite a lot of people, journalists, editors, media folk, went along with the celebration of change; now, as the Murdochs tighten a stranglehold on the press and international money markets are so sophisticated that a crisis of confidence in a radical government could be quite quickly implemented, one wonders how open or democratic any display of dissatisfaction will be.

Back home at four to see Patrick Cassavetti[1] as the next stage in pulling 'AF' together. We talk for an hour. Patrick impresses with his seriousness, his knowledge of what's going on in films, attitude to the crew and the team and lack of interest in big money film-making. Leave him with the script. If he says he wants to produce, then I shall be flattered and encouraged.

Monday, August 31st

Work through letters in the morning. Jo Lustig,[2] an amiable and even historic figure of our times, calls to tell me that Anne Bancroft would love to hear from me on 'AF'. Al L sits in No. 2 and reads 'No. 27'. A lovely day, warm and sunny and breezy. Lunch together in the garden.

---

[1] Among other things, he'd produced *Mona Lisa* for HandMade, co-produced Terry Gilliam's *Brazil*, been associate producer on *Made in Britain*, David Leland's powerful TV series about the state of modern education, and location manager on Gilliam's *Time Bandits*.
[2] Press agent and manager whose clients included John Cassavetes and Jack Kerouac. In 1986 he co-produced the film *84 Charing Cross Road* with Anthony Hopkins and Anne Bancroft.

Later I run and afterwards ring Anne B. Response is heartening. She begins by gushing her praises for my work and the Pythons – though what she's seen of my solo efforts I cannot establish. She is admirably direct and funny and sounds quite irresistible.

She says she's touched that I've written a part for her and yet doesn't waffle or flood the phone with insincerity. Our brief contact is very exciting and hopeful. But will the script justify the approach?

Wednesday, September 2nd

The location is a church school hall in Roehampton, which is doubling as a prison visiting room.

Kevin, Jamie and Tom Georgeson are playing a scene. Phoebe, Kevin's trim, dark-haired lady, looks on. She chuckles . . . 'Kevin will always try to steal the scene some way or other.' I am able to grin agreement. 'Did he do his zipper up in that last take?' she asks.

Kevin and Jamie are finished by lunchtime. Lunch with JC, who has reduced his waist by four inches since he started his pre-film diet, Robin Skynner, his straight-backed psychiatrist and fellow author, and two comedy writers – Renwick and Marshall. Having been one of a comedy duo, I recognise the identification problems. One automatically thinks they're one interchangeable entity. Renshall and Marwick. They seem very amiable.

After lunch a couple of scenes with Tom Georgeson. At one point he seems very troubled by how to deliver the line 'Un-be-fucking-lievable!'

At that point Charlie gives one of his occasional extraordinary performances which reveal a natural clown, or ham, whichever way you want it. He leaps up, flings his sticks to one side and bellows the line at top volume and with ferocious energy. Spontaneous applause breaks out in our smoky, crepuscular hall. Tom admits he can't follow that.

Thursday, September 3rd

For most of the afternoon I'm in black – balaclava and tracksuit and shoes – robbing safes of jewels. The set has an end-of-term feel to it, marooned as it is in the almost empty Studio 3.

Kevin arrives later, to see the rushes. He says he would like to direct. My view is that I wouldn't like to perform and direct. Kevin says that's what Laurence Olivier did, to which Charlie replies that Olivier could do it because he was a dictator on set.

Home, but not much time to relax, for Al is bubbling after reading *The*

Weekend, which he thinks is absolutely marvellous, and does cause me to re-examine it. He also gives me a half-hour's wisdom on 'No. 27', which he feels has more errors.

To Vasco and Piero's for another splendid meal and a more gentle and thorough continuation of all we've talked about during the week. What is so agreeable about Al's company is that he does care about people and how they are and how we depict them and, well, the struggle of the artist to find the truth, and all this makes me so glad to be with him rather than at the table across the gangway where they seem to manage to talk about the Spanish air controllers' strike throughout a three-course meal.

Friday, September 4th

To 68a Delancey Street which, from September 1st, is now the Python, Mayday, Prominent address. It is Prominent Studios.

Amongst all the plaster and sawdust and stacks of gypsum board, and pipes and the sound of generators, hammers and drills, can be found various office staff – already quite cosily installed, though the walls need painting and the stairs are still under construction.

New additions to the staff include Liz Lehmans, Steve's assistant, and John Roebuck, who looks even less like an accountant than Steve or Ian. I've brought them a plant in a rather handsome glazed pot. Just to add to the chaos.

Saturday, September 5th

At last, after two or three days of lines crossing, make contact with Patrick Cassavetti. He has read '*AF*'. Felt the first half rather laboured – 'stodgy' is the word he uses – but as he read on he became involved and, finally, moved. As we talk it is clear that he is interested, would like to work on it with me, but is carefully and strategically hedging his bets.

He sees difficulties in attracting finance, as the film is not easy to target at an audience. I agree. It's an act of faith, in a way. If we believe enough we'll make it work. He is heavily committed at the moment to a David Hare film, which if it goes will keep him solidly involved until after Christmas. We agree to consult in three or four weeks. So ... no producer yet.

Dinner with Jonathan B and Shirley at Strand on the Green. The approach to their house – or rather their complex, for it contains Shirley's frock business as well – is very spectacular. An alleyway leads off the mundane side street to reveal the river and a darkly wooded island in the middle, the lights of Kew Bridge off to the right, a newly-painted iron railway bridge to the left, and towers and chimneys standing in sharp silhouette against a honey-coloured evening sky. Inside, wide, open-plan rooms.

Jonathan reveals that he shouted at Charlie yesterday for only the second time on the picture. Charlie then became extremely docile and repentant, leading Jonathan to think perhaps he'd over-reacted. 'God, the man can drink though.' Jonathan recounts that during the half-hour they spent together in the pub after Friday's filming, Charlie downed eight scotches. 'He's like a pickled walnut,' Jonathan declares, but agrees that he has survived amazingly well on a long shoot.

Monday, September 7th

Ring Camden over the rubbish levels in God-forsaken Lismore Circus. Then write a long letter to Anne Bancroft.

To Seven Dials Restaurant in Covent Garden for lunch with Terry J.

The restaurant is, surprisingly, half-empty. Thierry, the maître d', who used to be at Mon Plaisir, runs it now and greets me warmly. TJ is celebrating not only *Personal Services'* first prize at a Swiss comedy festival! but also *Nicobobinus* being No. 1 in children's paperbacks. He has had a 'marvellous' hols in Corsica and admits that he is feeling much more confident these days.

TJ's lack of confidence may not have been evident, cloaked as it was by Welsh directness, bonhomie and strong opinions. But I think TJ means creatively and here we tangle a bit. We talk about collaboration – or rather Terry talks about collaboration, for I have nothing to offer at the moment. Whether he wants me to rewrite or addend *Erik the Viking* or not, I don't know. Anyway, the discussion turns into quite a minefield.

TJ telling me how he felt *The Missionary* should have been written. Fortescue as a very highly-sexed man – not a man avoiding sex. I *do* accept TJ's point and think he's right, but TJ plants yet another mine, very close to where I might tread, suggesting that the 'wrong' course the film took was the result of my personal approach to life.

Whether I like it or not, I do regard TJ as a bit of a conscience and this hits home. Perhaps I am too tight, controlled, careful.

As usual we drink too much, and end up being treated to 1942 Armagnac by Thierry, who's having his dinner on the other side of the restaurant. I leave with a vague sense of dissatisfaction. We haven't quarrelled, but we've bristled at each other.

I have a two-hour briefing with Susan H at the T2000 office. Find it very hard to keep awake. But cups of tea help and am much sobered when the time comes to drive to the BBC.

Will Wyatt, head of documentaries, looks like an airline pilot, as do the other two whom he calls in to talk to me. Their offer is for me to write and present a recreation of Phileas Fogg's journey *Around the World in 80 Days* for the BBC. Would try and travel round the world, on surface transport only, in the allotted time, accompanied by two film crews – one filming me, the other everything around me. Six 50-minute programmes would come out of it (hopefully). Drink Perrier and play it very cool. Must put my own film first, but as an autumn/winter '88 job it's very tempting.

Tuesday, September 8th

Woken at 7.15 by a phone call from the London *Evening News* to say they have a news item that Jonathan Ross is planning the first all-nude chat show and that myself and Simon Callow would be stripping off. Could I comment?

Thursday, September 10th

Drive down to Marylebone Road to Radio London for another interview re the AIDS show.

With me on the interview is a young man called Nick who has AIDS. Like Princess Di I shake his hand and feel no threat. He has been a PWA (Person With AIDS), as they like to call themselves, since June. He doesn't look ill. He is pink-skinned, short-haired and very sensible and straightforward. Almost impossible to fully comprehend that he will die soon.

Buy some gifts for people on *Wanda* – including some old travel maps of France which I've decided to give to Jonathan B because I can't think of anyone – myself included – who'll get more out of them.

Friday, September 11th

Alarm at 6.15. At 6.45 collected, with Hazel.

Chin-wag as we proceed across London heading for a pet cemetery in Cobham.

My last 'official' day of filming is in amongst graves with marble tablets beneath which lie 'Spotty', 'Susie, Naughty But Nice' and, ironically, the one I have as my opening mark, 'Monty, 1970–1981'!

Charlie says 'As this is your last day, I'm going to show you how to act' and he clambers over the gravestones with complete disregard for their occupants and the little plastic fencing that surrounds them.

My last shot is me looking terribly unhappy behind a tree. In fact, apart from a nagging feeling of inadequate sleep, I feel the opposite. The crew give me a little round of applause, Charlie says, with quite palpable sincerity, 'I think you're quite a good actor'. Joe Steeples interviews me for the *Sunday Times*, who take photos of me, scratched and bandaged, amongst the graves, various of the crew want autographs and, to cap it all, Iain Johnstone's camera crew hover for a last interview.

Jonathan Benson is very delighted with his maps, but apprehensive of his invitation tomorrow to Kevin and Shamberg's – when 'charades' are to be performed. JB hates charades. 'That's what we spend the whole week doing,' he mutters, rather grumpily.

Sunday, September 13th

At half past five I leave for a charity show for Frontliners at the Piccadilly.[1] A cluster of thin, ill-looking men determined to be brave sit in the front seats at rehearsal. Drag queens abound. Funny that homosexual men should go to such lengths to imitate the female – like vegetarians making cutlets, I suppose. In the line-up Liz Smith, Graham Chapman and Sheila Steafel and Paul Gambaccini.

I'm first on. I read 'Biggles'. Audience receptive, but not ecstatic. In the second half I do the 'Martyrdom of Brian', which goes well and I do smoothly. We all sing 'You'll Never Walk Alone' at the end. Sea of male faces in the front rows lighting up with pleasure at being part of it all. Really quite moving.

Wednesday, September 16th

Back at my desk – call comes from Colin Brough of Akela Productions, who has read *The Weekend*, as have his two assistants. They all like it very much and feel that, apart from some updating, it is in very good shape and they would like to produce it. I agree to look through and make immediate changes and meet them at the beginning of October.

Thursday, September 17th

Go for a run, and reflect on work. One thing does clearly stand out in my mind, and that is that the *80 Days* documentary would be a chance of a

---

[1] Frontliners was a pioneering self-help organisation for HIV/AIDS sufferers. It was disbanded in 1991 following fraud and nepotism investigations by the Charity Commissioners.

lifetime. It will give me a combination of acting and writing and could be fitted in with *American Friends* if they were prepared to shoot late in '88. By the time I pad sweatily (for there's high humidity) through the traffic on Mansfield Road, I have 90% made up my mind to say yes to the project.

Sunday, September 20th

Terry G calls from Highgate. He starts filming tomorrow on *Munchausen*. A first week of night shoots! Bill Paterson is in the cast. Terry is delighted with him. Sean Connery is to play the King of the Moon, and I, as Prime Minister, shall therefore be working with him in December. Max Wall has turned down the part of the Sea Captain.

The film is already suffering bizarre strokes of fate. The Italian stunt-co-ordinator died, of old age. The horses they had specially trained cannot be used on the Spanish locations owing to some African Horse Disease, and the two performing dogs have a rare liver condition.

Monday, September 21st

At last! Word from Anne Bancroft. A spirited note, but judiciously worded to give no assumption of commitment to '*AF*'. She says my accompanying note was ' spot on' and diagnosed 'the weakness of the screenplay'. She urges me to start re-writing straight away, 'don't wait for October or November', 'then send it to me'. 'It would be wonderful to work together.'

Tuesday, September 22nd

By 7.30, when I get up, the skies are clear and it's a strikingly good day for positively the last of *Wanda*.

My first scene is a shortened version of the bathroom scene in which Jamie seduces me. Jamie has an idea for it, JC has an idea and I have an idea. Jamie's is the best. She envelops my mouth in mid-catatonic stammer with such a generous kiss that afterwards, almost in a trance, I give her the information as if healed of my stammer.

So Jamie kisses me about eleven times (including rehearsal and close-ups). Then she is applauded, for it's her last shot. She cries as a huge bouquet of flowers is presented.

Jamie and Kevin both write me fulsome and emotional notes which just underline how undemonstrative we Brits are. Jamie gives something to *every* member of the crew.

Amidst all the present-giving there is still work to do and, as JC and I prepare for a shortener for the 'stammering scene' – or at least the slapstick part of it – Charlie makes an announcement. 'I'm very happy to be able to tell you that this is the *last* acting shot.' Fun to be doing it with JC.

More applause at the end. My last shot of all, ten weeks and a day after my first, is a close-up of me writing 'Cathcart Towers'.

Linda in make-up and Claire the nurse tell me I've been voted by the women on the crew as the man on the crew that they'd most like to spend a weekend in Paris with. Jonathan Benson is second, and very put out. He mutters about 'the euphemism – a weekend in Paris'!

Out to the Meridiana in Fulham Road.

Jamie very emotional again. Her high spirits are so fierce, in a way, that the sheer effort of keeping up with her own enthusiasms must tire her out. JC is presented, by Shamberg, with the Emmy he's just won in the US for his appearance on *Cheers*.

Some bond has been forged between us all, but I'm not yet sure how strong it really is, after the hype. Maybe much stronger than I think.

Saturday, September 26th

Take Rachel down to Marshall Street Baths in Soho for a swim. She loves swimming and doesn't do enough of it and I'm very much happier with a weekend if I work some exercise into it.

The baths are impressive. Custom-built – maybe 50 or 60 years ago. Stone fittings and marble surrounds to the pool. A sort of Art Deco curved ceiling, restored in the last year, and a good-size, almost empty expanse of water – and all this within spitting distance of the London Palladium. I think we may have made a find here.

On the way home drop off at 68a Delancey Street to find an army of builders spending my money. The building is now moving forward at a reassuring pace. Talk to a contract painter down from Wolverhampton – 'They won't work weekends in London.'

Monday, September 28th

Dying to begin work on the '*AF*' rewrite, but T2000 still hangs onto me and my time. The process of parting company with them is a slow and lingering one, and though I took the decision to resign in the 'Troubled' days of February,

I still find myself, not writing my film, but taking the Underground to Euston for another BRB [British Railways Board] meeting.

Then we are treated to a most depressingly impenetrable hour's disquisition on railway marketing, scattered with American business jargon rather proudly, as if the dynamism of the words will somehow miraculously interact with the business itself to make it as efficient. As it is, the words are a smokescreen, and we learn almost nothing, except how to make an interesting and very relevant subject deeply boring.

Wednesday, September 30th

To TV-AM to record a story for Children's Book Week. I read the last chapter of Spike Milligan's *Badjelly the Witch*. Rather pleased with myself, as no fluffs and plenty of spirit – 'We didn't expect *acting*,' says the floor manager afterwards.

To lunch at Odette's with Clem Vallance[1] – for the next step towards my *80 Days* project. He has a background in travel and anthropological ventures – he once took Gavin Young to do a programme on the Marsh Arabs.

We get on well together, but the most dramatic thing about the lunch, apart from getting on well together, is that a date for departure is fixed – September 13th 1988. Almost a year from now, at the tender age of 45, providing Michael Grade [Controller, BBC 1] likes the idea and I have no second thoughts, I shall be embarking on the longest journey of my life.

Friday, October 2nd

In Oxford with Tristram. We travel up to John's together to talk to Dr Boyce, the Bursar, about the possibility of using the college for filming next summer.

Boyce is a pleasant, approachable man, anxious to know that we shan't be 'lampooning the college' or giving it 'the "Brideshead" treatment'. He walks us around. We leave him a script and assurances that we are interested in a serious re-creation of the college life in the 1860's. He smiles, not altogether convinced, I feel. Maybe it's my haircut.

To lunch at Brown's in St Giles. A 'fern restaurant' as Tristram advises me such places are called, owing to the profusion of rather dull, potted Filices.

Home to be de-Kenned by Don. My curls, or most of them, removed after

---

[1] Clem came up with the original idea of the television series *Around the World in 80 Days* and asked for me as presenter, after Alan Whicker and Clive James declined. I later learned that journalist Miles Kington and Noel Edmonds had also been offered the job by the BBC.

two months and three weeks of looking like Gaddafi, Malcolm McLaren, Simon Rattle and 'a thin Dylan Thomas' (TJ).

Monday, October 5th

By Underground to Leicester Square and a short walk to the austere and temporary looking suite of rooms above St Martin's Lane that pass for Akela's offices. Colin Brough has almost nothing to say about the rewrites of *The Weekend*. He's more enthusiastic about the clutch of new titles I've slung together on the train between Chalk Farm and Leicester Square.

He, and I, quite like 'Listen', but I also have a fondness for 'Putting the Cat Out, and Other Things to Do at the Weekend'. Brough looks horrified at this – do I realise how much it will cost in small ads?

He has some interesting ideas on casting and direction (I notice a very elegant rejection slip from Michael Caine on a side-table) and seems to want to expedite the project by sending a copy ASAP to Paul Scofield. It would be ironic if he accepted, for he was Angela's idol when she was a teenager, and we used to tease her about him! On directors he suggests Alan Bennett and Ron Eyre. Both excellent choices and a reassuring indication that he's thinking in the right sort of direction.

Thursday, October 8th

To a six o'clock drink with Robert to mark the publication of his new book – 'Now this one you *must* read,'[1] Robert insists, and I feel guilty. It's quite slim, but a little polemical for my leisurely tastes – about our museum policy and how we live in the past too much.

Geoffrey Strachan is there. He looks wary as he tells me of the imminent likelihood of the disappearance of Methuen London. The Thomson group, ex-owners of *The Times*, have bought Associated Book Publishers, but are not interested in keeping on general books or Methuen Children's Books. Geoffrey and co-directors think they can raise ten million for a management buy-out, but, gloomily, he reckons Thomson's could hold out for £20 million.

Whatever happens, things will never be quite the same again and Geoffrey

---

[1] This, Robert Hewison's fifth book, was *The Heritage Industry*, published by Methuen, with illustrations by Chris Orr and photos by Allan Titmuss. It argued that 'instead of manufacturing goods, we are manufacturing *heritage*, a commodity which nobody seems able to define'. As it happens, I have read it and it holds up very well.

and Methuen – our greatest publishing friends for the last 15 years or more – may be parted in the next few months.

Friday, October 9th

Clem Vallance rings from the BBC, much aggrieved that Will Wyatt has told him he cannot direct *80 Days*. A director, Richard Denton, will accompany me round the world, and Vallance will do all the setting-up. He is most indignant, especially as Denton has no particular qualifications for 'travel' filming, which is Vallance's speciality. The first reversal for what seemed like such a simple, effective idea.

Wednesday, October 14th

Still no word from A Bancroft on availability in LA in November. Getting a little tight as I have to book my Round the World First Class Apex at least two weeks before leaving.

Business to do in the morning. What do we want our credit to be on *Consuming Passions* [aka 'The Chocolate Project' etc] and do we want a credit at all? Decide that to take our names off completely sounds very significant – and I'm not sure what it would be significant of. They want 'From a story by . . .', but TJ and I prefer the accuracy and greater detachment of 'Based on the television play *Secrets* by . . .' I'm sure this will involve Anne in much faxing with the West Coast!

To a wet and windy Soho for another Spike Milligan book launch, in an upper room at Kettners.

Michael Foot and his wife pass on the way out. 'Spike's looking awfully smart these days,' observes Footie, in his surprisingly strong and ringing tones.

I leave at eight and, hurrying through the rain, holding aloft the purple umbrella which Angela bought for us, make my way along the pitted pavements of Greek Street to the Gay Hussar, where JC is waiting for me.

A good meal and a comfortable and loquacious session – mainly about *Wanda*. JC surprised that within five days of finishing the film he'd totally forgotten it. He doesn't want to direct (actually, he's like me – he'd quite like to, but is worried about the technical side) and is 'quite honestly' not desperate to do another film. 'The difference between us, Mikey, is that you seem to be able to enjoy things.'

I think he'd rather be a philosopher – if only it paid better.

Thursday, October 15th

I watch *84 Charing Cross Road*, Anne Bancroft's latest film. One or two thoughts go through my head. The only negative one is whether or not she's too old for the character I'm writing (Connie Booth appears briefly in the movie and I'm struck by how good she might be as a 'younger' Miss Hartley).

But Bancroft's superb ability to fill characters with life without becoming fussy or exasperatingly hyperactive, and her ability to move me (to tears by the end of the movie) are breathtaking. She is a strong, big, major actress and would give '*AF*' an enormously firm centre.

Friday, October 16th

In the depths of the night we're woken by the telephone. Not ringing, but dying. Lights flash and strange, helpless gurgling sounds emit from the receiver. Then it falls silent. Notice that the light outside the bathroom has gone out.

Downstairs to the hall to fix the trip-switch and at last pin down what is odd — the house is in complete darkness only because the street is also in complete darkness. Up to my workroom. A tempest is raging and bits and pieces of leaves and twigs and God-knows what rubbish are being forced under the glass and scattering over my desk. No lights anywhere, except for the stairwells of the flats and the reassuring yellow ring at the top of the Post Office Tower.

Back to bed. It's by now about 4.25. Helen decides she's hungry and gets up. The unusualness of a power-cut makes me switch on the radio, but can pick up neither LBC nor BBC, only the emergency services — police, ambulance, etc.

The lines crackle out stories of 'Trees blocking the eastbound carriageway of the A12', 'Lorry and trailer blown over blocking the M20', 'Borough Surveyor urgently requested to go to Erskine Road W12 where four-storey block of flats in state of partial collapse', and the most dramatic thing about it all is the calmness of the voices, the ordered, efficient lack of emotion in lines like 'There has been a major power failure'. Exciting stuff.

Try to go back to sleep, then snapped into wakefulness by the sound of some heavy metal object cracking against walls and cars.

Power is restored to us by 7.30, but still news is coming in of continued blackouts. Winds of 94 miles an hour were measured on the ground and a gust of 110 mph on the Post Office Tower, after which the gauge broke.

The phones ring — grannies are both safe. Up at Lismore Circus a huge tree has fallen and several smaller ones are leaning crazily. Boughs and leaves and branches provide an unbroken carpet around the shops. Mr Nice Man and his papers are there – except for the *Independent*. Everyone's talking to each other, as if it's the war.

I have an appointment with press cameras at the zoo at eleven, to publicise Oxfam's Fast Week.

I'm the only one of the 'celebrities' who've made it. Tom Baker and the manager of QPR have cried off and a lady from *Eastenders* will be late. The press are consulted and word comes back that they will probably only print a picture of me and the *Eastenders* lady together, or possibly just the *Eastenders* lady, but certainly not me alone!

Later in the afternoon I go for a run. The sun has gone and been replaced by a very cold, light rain.

Six or seven huge trees are flattened, with disks of earth and roots measuring 20 feet by 15 feet suddenly wrenched up and standing where the tree itself used to be.

In the grounds of Kenwood House, there is devastation. Paths are almost impassable and an avenue of limes which forms one picturesque approach to the terrace in front of Kenwood has been almost totally uprooted. There is no-one else around now, and being in the middle of this dreadful damage is quite eerie. One thing's for certain – the reassuring landscape I've run through for eight years has been drastically changed. It'll never be the same again.

On the news I hear that Kew Gardens have suffered enormous losses, which cannot be made good within a lifetime.

To dinner at Terry J's. The impressive avenue of Camberwell Grove is a shambles, with two cars completely crushed.

The assembled company is somewhat muted, almost as if a party is indecent after what has happened. Ken Branagh and Emma Thompson are there. Emma, with her short, cropped, red hair, looks so different from her *Fortunes of War* character that, despite having stared at her for 50 minutes last Sunday night, Helen still doesn't recognise her!

She is of the Phyllis Logan school, easy, well adjusted, direct, funny, unaffected and great company. Ken is nice, modest, similarly approachable and unshow-bizzy. They are obviously very fond of each other, and a couple, though not living together.

Terry has salmon and crudités and bags of Sancerre and four mighty crabs which just happened to have caught his eye, and then the confit de canard, with lots of red wine.

Terry is like a man with a starting-handle, working with enormous energy, emotional and physical, to give us a really happy, 'different' evening, and then, I sense, vaguely disappointed that the vehicle he's started hasn't gone forward as fast as he'd like. Personally, it's one of the nicest, happiest, jolliest, least Dinner-Party-ish evenings I've spent for ages.

Home, past the remainders of what the radio is at long last admitting was a hurricane. Britain's worst since 1703.

Friday, October 23rd

Will Wyatt from the BBC wants to come and put his (i.e. the BBC's) view of the Vallance affair to me next week. Now this is one of those times when I can gauge how exalted I have become, when the BBC Head of Documentaries is prepared to come to me.

Drive in state to JC's 48th birthday do. Peter Cook is there this year and we spend a lot of time on talk. JC still intrigued at why Ingrams hates him so much. He thinks it's envy. Peter thinks not. Definitely not. Peter will not hear a word against Hislop or Ingrams.

Peter seems very easy-going at the moment, happy writing bits and pieces for *Private Eye*, doing an HBO special [Home Box Office, founded 1972, the pioneer of cable television]. At one point he asks me if I find it hard to 'do' any more. Meaning write and perform comedy. We both agree that we miss the quick turnover to write and perform. Long, slow-burn projects like *American Friends* are all very well, but they lack opportunities for what I think Peter and I can do well, which is rabbit endlessly on and make people roar with laughter while doing same.

Talk with Jack Rosenthal, who is sitting next to Helen. He is a very amiable and sympathetic fellow and his high praise for *East of Ipswich* means a lot, for he is one of the finest practitioners of recollective comedy.

Monday, October 26th

My first sight of *Wanda*, cut together.

And very good it is too. As I had expected, uncluttered, competent direction, no artistic gimmicks, and a pretty tight edit by John Jympson. John C has made Archie work completely – his best all-round performance since Basil Fawlty. Kevin and Jamie are immaculate.

I find myself a little disappointed with myself. God knows why – maybe it's just because so many people have built up what I've done: 'star of the film' nonsense. I think it's not that I do what I do badly, it's just that I'm not really called on to do much more than react to other people's bullying. What I can do best of all is the subtler shading of character and perhaps that's what I missed in Ken, except for a few lovely moments – two of the best being those I did on the very last day of filming.

Afterwards John has us all in for a session of thoughts and reactions. Thorough to the end.

Wednesday, October 28th

Decide that I can wait no longer for messages from Jo Lustig, and I ring Anne Bancroft direct. Once again I find her good sense and clarity very attractive. She suggests I get the script to her via Mel (Brooks, her husband), who is travelling to the US on Concorde on Friday. She will read it as quickly as possible and will call the office – Anne or Alison – early next week with a reaction.

She thinks that the only reason for not wanting to talk in LA would be if there was *nothing* constructive she had to say. Even if she had criticisms, suggestions, etc, would it be worth my while coming? Yes, I agree readily.

Thursday, October 29th

With Anne to a screening of *Consuming Passions*. Perhaps because our expectations had been so low, we both react with relief to the first few scenes which are well played by Tyler Butterworth and full of well-executed slapstick jokes.

After that Jonathan Pryce and Freddie Jones and Vanessa Redgrave show that they had been given free rein and that it had worked. Though it all goes rather adrift at the end – 'pantomimey' as TJ put it – it is hugely enjoyable along the way. A real curiosity.

Back at Prominent Studios I have my first piece of luck for the day – Mel Brooks is at his hotel, before leaving for a dinner. Yes, of course he will take the script. 'Love your work,' he barks, by way of signing off.

Home by eight. Send off the script and at last I can afford to spend time thinking seriously about going round the world. [To see Thailand with Simon Albury, then home via Los Angeles and Anne Bancroft.]

Friday, October 30th: London–Bangkok

I set to reading *American Friends* with greater care than yesterday's enforced rush. This time I have 13 hours and 45 minutes' flying time ahead of me. I can luxuriate over every full-stop and comma.

At the end of my read I have to admit that it begs as many questions as it answers. Structurally it's more confident and it has an interesting shape now that it's seen through Miss W's eyes. And yet expanding the Bancroft role has also put the spotlight on the other two main parts. It's become a little more of a psychodrama than a nice, period, comedy-adventure drama and, now I have embarked on the course of examining the leading characters in more depth, I think I have gone forward, but into uncharted territory.

So I cannot lie back and enjoy the hoped-for luxury of knowing I had cracked *American Friends*. It will remain to nag me, to pull at the fringes of my attention all the time.

My night on the plane begins too early, and is interrupted with a stop at Bahrain, so I do not sleep, and by the time we ease down over the rice fields of Southern Thailand I've been awake for 22 hours.

Tuesday, November 10th: Bangkok

4.25 a.m: Am about to shave, ready for a five o'clock departure to the airport and on to LA, when Anne J calls. Bancroft has rung. She has not been well – laryngitis or something worse. She does not see much interest in the character. Anne's feeling is that she doesn't want to do it.

Standing naked in a Bangkok hotel bathroom I receive the news philosophically. I shall have to speak to Bancroft at some stage. I am booked on a plane that leaves in two and a half hours and I have very little chance at this time of the morning to check out alternatives.

Financially I might, with a quick withdrawal to London, save on a few US hotel bills, but I would have cancellation fees and the possibility of no flights to London today and extra expense in Bangkok. Keep going forward, I feel.

At 5.45 in Bangkok Airport. When I ask if there is a First Class lounge, the girl replies 'In February'.

Midnight, and we're approaching the Bay Area. Have crossed over the Date Line, so it's Tuesday again, and it's already nine o'clock in the morning. Can see the Golden Gate Bridge and can understand why Americans like coming home.

7.20: At the Beverly Wilshire.

The year of Living Dangerously continues: after 'Troubles', it's clear that '*AF*' will not go. Talked to Anne Bancroft, who sounds nicer and more sympathetic each time we speak. She says she doesn't think I've yet made my mind up what it's about. The latest draft showed I could write – the writing even better than the second draft. But it's like a fine suit of clothes, without 'the nakedness', as she describes it, beneath. She says she's a perfectionist, but it's that sort of criticism which is worthwhile.

Read in the *LA Times* that TG's *Munchausen* has stopped filming for two weeks and the completion guarantors want to replace TG. Will my December *Munchausen* work fall through as well?

Tuesday, November 11th: Los Angeles

Woken about 9.30, by a dreadful banging on the door, which turns out to be the air-conditioning having a trauma. Outside a very bright, clear, perfect day, a real advert for life in the Pacific South-west. Warm, dry air blowing out from the desert. Skies a deep blue, no smog.

Walk up Beverly Hills Drive, buy a paper, breakfast at Il Fornaio. The girl at reception is a 'big fan'.

Ease slowly, luxuriating in this glorious weather, temperatures in the upper 80's, back to the Beverly Wilshire. I take some sunshine, swim, then Michael Shamberg sends a slim young Virginian called Karen to collect and take me to Fox Studios.

Note: LA people always sit *by* the pool. Only foreigners seem to go in!

Shamberg looks mournfully delighted to see me. Takes me to lunch at the commissary.

First person we meet is Mel Brooks. Chunky, rack-like, barrel chest, with a firm, no-nonsense light paunch, he grabs my hand a lot – shakes it probably five or six times. 'I forgive you guys everything ... I want you to know ... you're so good, I forgive you for all those ideas you used.' Is he joking? 'Spanish Inquisition?' he digs me knowingly. Not sure what's going on.

(Chris Guest[1] later tells me that Brooks has an almost pathological inability to accept competition – it's all a reduction of his own world. Apparently he said, after seeing one of Allen's early movies, 'When Woody Allen was born, I died'.)

Saturday, November 14th

T Gilliam rings.

He's home for a weekend before returning to Rome to take up the cudgels again. He thought two days ago that it was all over and he would walk away from it, but apparently Charles [McKeown] pulled him round and gave him a talking to and together they came up with a formula for cutting the script which could ensure survival. McK is in Rome rewriting at the moment.

---

[1] Chris Guest, Jamie Lee Curtis' husband. Actor, writer, musician – *This is Spinal Tap* (1984), and later director too – *Best in Show* (2000), *A Mighty Wind* (2003) and others. In 1996 he inherited his father's title and became 5th Baron Haden-Guest.

Jake Eberts[1] has emerged as TG's latest hero. He has moved mountains to keep the film alive and apparently told TG that 'Whatever happens, let me do your next two films'. So there are silver linings, but TG is not looking forward to returning. Whatever happens, he says gloomily, the next 12 weeks will be hell.

The personal postscript to all this is that it looks as if my part will be a victim of the cuts. Terry says he will have to give me something else – he can't have a Gilliam film without me – but he sounds as though this is just another addition to his growing multitude of problems.

Sunday, November 15th

Stay homebound. JC calls in the evening. The film is down to 117 minutes. Larry Kasdan, 'one of the brightest Americans I know' saw it last week and raved – so JC is very pleased about that.

I ask him how *he* is. 'I'll tell you something that'll really make you laugh,' is the way he leads into it ... 'Are you ready for a laugh? I've moved out.' He says it hasn't been working for two years, and he's only leaving now because he feels confident enough of his relationship with his daughter that she'll 'understand that I'm not sleeping there, but can still see her each day'.

Thursday, November 19th

The King's Cross Tube disaster is another nail in a dreadful year for the country.[2] 'Herald of Free Enterprise' tragedy, the storm of October 16th, a series of fatal motorway pile-ups – quite a battering.

Friday, November 20th

Down to the T2000 office.

Susan has been much in demand by the media over the last 36 hours. She bemoans the fact that it takes a major accident for the press to show any interest

---

[1] Eberts, a Canadian film financier and producer, was, with David Puttnam, the founder of Goldcrest, the most successful British film production company of the 1980's. They made the successful *Chariots of Fire*, *The Killing Fields* and *Local Hero*, and the less successful *Revolution* and *The Mission*. Eberts left Goldcrest and set up another British-based film company, Allied Filmmakers, in 1985.

[2] A fire which began in uncleared rubbish at the bottom of a wooden escalator left 31 dead and 60 injured.

in transport. Jonathan [Roberts] has been the man of the hour, for he issued a report on the Underground for some users' group after the Oxford Circus fire of '85. Full of suggestions for safety improvements (which were not taken up) and prophetic words about only luck that there has not been a major disaster ' ... and luck has a habit of running out'.

We talk over tomorrow's AGM, at which I will officially step down as Chair after 21 months – or 22 if you count my pre-press-launch work.

Saturday, November 21st

To Brixton for the AGM and conference of T2000 – my last day as Chairman. The *Independent* has front-page coverage of Earl's Court Underground – damning photos of rubbish, inflammable grease, empty fire-buckets, and fire equipment locked in cupboards.

The Brixton Recreation Centre is a brand new building which looks committee-designed. A cluttered interior with escalators, lifts and staircases everywhere. Impossible to find one's way around. Eventually, having asked a cleaner, I'm directed to the 'Social Rooms'.

The AGM goes briskly along, with no problems, unlike last year. I am presented with *Jane's Urban Transport Systems* by John Gregg, who makes a short and kind speech, referring specifically to the fact that throughout my chairmanship meetings ended on time!

Then Hugh [Bishop Montefiore] makes a crisp, funny speech – wondering at one point whether he had been chosen for his knowledge of 'vertical rather than horizontal transport'. I reply.

As I reach the climax of my speech – and one of the few serious bits – a booming metallic voice comes over the Tannoy: 'Julian to the poolside please ... Julian to the poolside.' A fitting climax to my two odd years as Chairman!

The rest of the day is taken up with a T2000-organised conference on disability and transport.

A blind, or partially-blind, man from Sheffield – John Roberts – is quite excellent. Funny, clear and compelling. He it is who makes a plea for the Swedish attitude to public transport – that it should be designed and run so that it is accessible to everybody, including the ten percent of all travellers who are, in effect, disabled. He wants no special buses, specially-adapted trains – just the awareness in the first stages of design that 99.9% of the country's travellers must be able to use transport, not 90%.

Sunday, November 22nd

Terry G rings from Rome to confirm that my part as Prime Minister of the Moon is no more, but offers me the consolation part of a man who is discovered in a corner singing a mournful song, prior to falling dead from his seat. 'It was going to be my part,' he admits. Being a great admirer of Terry's parts and conscious of the fact that De Niro wanted Jack Lint and TG stuck by me, I assure him that I'm happy to sit this one out.

Wednesday, November 25th: London–Belfast

Tom has had his injured finger diagnosed as a fracture (a Hap-Ki-Do injury) and the surgeon wants to put a pin in it. He's booked Tom into the Royal Free today. So Helen and Tom are preoccupied with getting him to the hospital and I'm preoccupied with packing for Belfast. Three bulging bags – T-shirts, costumes and my own stuff.

Leave home at midday.

In the Arts meet Jimmy and Paddy again – my faithful stage staff. Paddy has lost weight and seems to be very short of breath. We all look older. It's getting dark now and I notice people lined up at the windows looking down into the street. There's rumour of a security scare.

I carry on running through the sound cues with Joe, who is a new man. Young. He apologetically tells me that he broke his arm three weeks ago and still isn't quite himself. He is in charge of all the lighting and sound cues! Very Irish.

Malcolm, the general-technical manager comes up to us. 'We've been asked to leave the theatre.'

Outside in the street a couple of the grim, colourless army Land Rovers are parked. White ribbon is being unwound across the pavement and Malcolm hurries us as far away as possible. We walk to College Gardens and wait at the office. I desperately need some rehearsal time tonight, but it becomes clear that I'm unlikely to be going back.

The general impression from reports and rumours is that the whole of central Belfast has been sealed off. Then we hear that the M1 motorway has been closed.

The Europa Hotel is evacuated. Michael [Barnes] reacts calmly, puffing a little more fiercely on his cigarette and forgetting that he has one already smouldering in the ashtray. It looks as if the security alert is big one, though there are no reports of any explosions.

Michael has to take some decisions and cancels the Lyric's production of *The Hypochondriac* [Molière's *Malade Imaginaire*] – 'A lot of money wasted there,' he shakes his head resignedly, rather than angrily. He then opens a bottle of champagne and we begin to get a little drunk.

The Europa will not be cleared until two o'clock. There have been so many alerts all over Belfast that the bomb disposal teams cannot cope.

I end up being offered a bed on the floor at Robert Agnew's house.[1] Thus I find myself in the unreal calm of a suburban house in Myrtlewood Road, finally getting my head down in Robert's front room at a quarter to one.

Thursday, November 26th: Belfast

I wake in the middle of the night. Not immediately sure where I am. I look up and there, staring down at me, is Rowan Atkinson. The walls of the room are covered with Opera House playbills.

Doze some more, then lie awake thinking of my own show. Completely unrehearsed, yet by the time this day is over it will have played to 500 people, and possibly been telerecorded. The script isn't even complete. Try to go to sleep and forget about it. Only partially successful.

Last night 21 different bombs and suspect vehicles were dotted around the city by the IRA in an attempt to show they still have formidable ability to stretch the Security Forces. Two vehicles were detonated and the rest were hijacked vehicles with no bombs in them.

At the theatre Ulster TV cameras are installing themselves. They are anxious not to disrupt at all, and they won't need extra lighting, but I feel exposed suddenly. The show has always been so private.

We go up at 8.10. I'm discovered standing on the podium for the 'Olympic' opening and rewarded with a good round of applause. Everything hangs together. I'm pleased with my delivery. Most of the cues work. Very few laughs dropped.

Tuesday, December 1st

To Goodge Street and Heal's Restaurant, where I am to meet Clem Vallance (at his invitation).

Clem V tells me of an embarrassing lunch that the BBC laid on a year ago to try and tempt Alan Whicker to be the presenter of *80 Days*. As soon as Whicker heard that not only could he not bring 'the little woman' along, but

---

[1] Robert was the business manager of the Belfast Festival.

that he might have to spend several days and nights on an Arab dhow, not much more was heard.

Clem says I was always top of *his* list, with Clive James second. He floats the possibility of approaching Michael Grade to make it independently,[1] but really there is little we can do until the BBC make the next move.

Wednesday, December 2nd

Denis is in very bad shape. Apparently he started shaking this morning and Helen took him again to the vet. But now he's breathing only with difficulty and in short, gravelly intakes. Every now and then he retches violently, bringing up very little but bile, but clearly causing himself great discomfort. Helen is out. I ring the emergency vet, who counsels me to keep him warm.

Thursday, December 3rd

Denis is at the top of the stairs, but very weak, still breathing in dry, rasping gasps occasionally accompanied by fierce twitching of the head. I drive him to the vet at Islington with Helen. I wait in Cross Street, noting a run-down but elegant Georgian terrace of town houses opposite me.

We drive home. The vet will call us again at five o'clock with news. A day of phone calls clouded by the chance that one of them may announce the end of our Denis.

Friday, December 4th

A script by Jonny Lynn called *Nuns on the Run* has arrived with Eric's blessing.

Then by taxi to Soho to do an LBC interview with Michael Aspel re the Python album. I like Aspel. He's straight and amiable and likes a laugh and our piece is as relaxed and comfortable as any I've done for a while.

The day begins to gather momentum as Helen prepares not only for a dinner party tonight, but also for a TV interview she's to do for the BBC on 'Motherhood'. I take out the car and go to collect fuel, booze, food, etc.

When I get back at about half past three, Helen greets me with the news that Denis is dead. The vet and Helen took the decision about ten minutes before she had to go into the interview. Sally Doganis, producer, seems pleased by the piece. 'There won't be a dry eye in the house after they've heard Helen,'

---

[1] He had just joined Channel 4 as the new Chief Executive.

she tells me. I imagine that it must all be to do with the loss of Denis, but in fact she is referring to Helen's contributions on motherhood.

Not only is the news of Denis's death communicated to me before an entire BBC film crew, but as they are clearing up, the children arrive back and have to be told. With Rachel it's unbearable. She's at the front door having said goodbye to her friends. I'm unloading logs. I call to her. She turns and pre-empts the careful phrases . . . 'Is Denis dead?'

Tears well up in both of us and I put my arm round her. If only the film had been on 'Loss' or 'Grief' they'd have had a real scoop.

Sunday, December 6th

After breakfast Rachel and Helen go off to Islington to collect Denis's basket from the vet and I am hoovering the stair-carpet an hour or so later when they return, with another cat peeping out like a rejuvenated Denis. Rachel was so taken with this five-month-old tabby which the vet had been looking after for some time that she and Helen decided then and there that they should bring her home. She's a spayed female. No name. Helen will look out for a neutered male to be company for her.

I must say at first I am a little shocked by the speed of the arrival of the replacement for Denis. I feel I haven't had enough time to accept his absence. But she is a perky, curious, friendly little cat. Permanently wide-eyed of course, especially at the to-ing and fro-ing in our house, the glass, lights, mirrors and so on.

A very good roast beef Sunday dinner and we debate names for the cat. Nancy, Lucy, but Tom finally cracks it with Betty. So Betty, with her colouring which is, as Will says, a negative of Denis – smoky black where Denis was white – comes to be part of Julia St life.

Wednesday, December 9th

Steve A arrives. An update on all our activities.

He tells me of the *Wanda* screening in NYC. Seventy-eight percent of the cards filled in (243) put the movie in the top two of five categories.

Anyway, MGM are now pleased, though by mutual agreement they and the producers will alter certain things which the screening seemed to tell them. The audience didn't like to see blood when the dog's crushed, and felt the fish torture too hard to take. And these are the audiences that flocked to the cheerful slaughter of *Beverly Hills Cop*.

Ring Camilla to find out if her friend saw the Belfast show and catch her in a tearful state. She's been dealing with a suicide at work and had been affected by the news of the churchman who committed suicide yesterday in a fume-filled car in a garage, and just had no-one to talk to. So we have a long talk about Angela.

Camilla finds that the men in the family don't talk easily. Friends just don't mention it. I feel the same and it's a great relief to both of us to break the silence.

Thursday, December 10th

At lunchtime to Twickenham – a near-two-hour journey to re-dub one line. Charlie is there, as benignly grumpy as ever ... 'I don't like *people* very much, you see,' he confides cheerfully as we go upstairs to the dubbing theatre. He also tells me that the audiences in New York liked me very much, and that's why he's had to cut the torture scene!

Sunday, December 13th

When I return home I find another cat there. This is Albert, a male tabby – younger than Betty by three or four months. I can't see much of him as he won't come out of his basket, from which he blinks at me without moving.

Betty's first reaction is not reassuring. When not actually hissing at Albert, she growls and hisses at the basket.

Against the background of this delicate relationship, and indeed of their relationship with us and our house, the afternoon passes with occasional glimpses at the paper, lots of phone calls and some Christmas card writing.

Tuesday, December 15th

Jonathan Ross calls to tell me that the 'nude chat show' idea is off for Friday. None of the women would agree to do it, except for Janet Street-Porter.

To the new Waterstone's in Hampstead. Wonderful. A New York-style bookstore within walking distance of my house!

Wednesday, December 16th

Hassled by a phone call from the 'organisers' of the King's Cross Disaster Fund photo-call which I've agreed to attend, suddenly making it all sound far more elaborate – with carols to sing and Dickensian costumes, etc.

I drive to Chalk Farm. Announcements on the platform of delays due to shortage of staff – if only there were video information screens at station entrances, one could decide on bus, foot or an alternative before being stuck on the platform.

To Leicester Square Theatre at which a selection of notables is assembling.

Most of us have baulked at being asked to wear Dickensian outfits. Carols are sung, we all do 'Hark the Herald', then photos are taken, from which peripheral celebrities are ruthlessly excluded – 'Mr Davenport, could you step out, please!' 'Good expressions, now!' TJ quite amused and thinks this could be a new, instant form of directing. 'King Lear ... look sad ... this way please ... good!'

Bill Paterson appears, as he often does, from nowhere. He's late for the call, but no-one knows who he is anyway. We go for a coffee – myself, TJ, Bill, Marcia Warren and Anna Carteret. On the way I'm buttonholed by the Thames TV crew. 'Michael, could you give us a piece straight from the heart, all right?'

Friday, December 18th

Am collected for the Jonathan Ross *Last Resort* show at seven.

The show is all set up as a beach party and I'm given some long shorts, a loud shirt, sweater and '50's sunglasses.

Janet Street-Porter is on the show and doesn't impress. She evidently rates herself rather highly – arrives at the last minute, cars collect her immediately afterwards – but what really pisses me off is that she eats in her dressing room, then puts the half-eaten, mucky tray-ful of mutilated food out in the corridor. She then pushes it along to my door. 'I can't stand having trays outside my dressing room.'

A run-through. I'm to appear on a donkey. Seems to work well. At the end everyone is delighted. 'If in doubt, get in a Python,' Jonathan enthuses.

Saturday, December 19th

First inkling that the Ross interview might not have been as riotous as it had seemed, comes from Rachel's very muted response. 'You were very silly, Dad,' is about all she will say as we drive into Soho for our Saturday morning swim.

Sunday, December 20th

Up the road to a lunchtime drinks party with a new resident. I feel all should be done to keep the reality of the community spirit to which we all pay lip-service. In a very small room full of women (mainly), I meet a paediatrician in Kentish Town – a New Zealand lady, both voluble and opinionated, who writes children's books and [long-time residents] Miss Clutton and Miss Goodman.

Little old Miss Goodman greets me with 'How did you like China?'

Impressed that she even knew I was travelling at all, I correct her good-naturedly . . . 'Thailand'.

'The china I gave Mrs Palin.'

Miss Clutton is on excellent form. Wafer-thin and neat to the point of severity, she has great spirit. The extrovert New Zealander talks about what hell it's been having her house converted and being without a bathroom. Miss Clutton grins cheerfully, 'I'm *still* waiting for mine.' This slightly throws the conversation off its middle-class path, bringing it to a total stop when she adds 'I haven't had a bath for 75 years.'

Tuesday, December 22nd

Some local shopping – am told to 'Piss off' by a grubby shopkeeper with a Mediterranean accent, just because I want to buy one clementine and one lychee for Helen's stocking. And I was in such a good mood.

Back home, find a *huge* hamper of fruit from George Harrison.

Out to dinner at ZenW3 with Terry G and Maggie, during Terry's brief break from *Munchausen*. 'What's the latest?' I ask him, adding hastily '*briefly*'. 'Thirty-six million dollars,' is his reply. He wants to talk about doing a different sort of film, a small, funny film made with people he likes. He's fed up with being called 'Maestro' and having all these sycophantic and highly-paid Italians with incredibly fragile temperaments waiting on his every word. He saw an hour's footage this afternoon. 'The money just isn't on the screen . . . it's OK, but no way should that have cost 20 million.'

Because it's been so long since I last heard it, even his grumbling seems fresh. Maggie is to have another baby. God knows when he had time for that.

Friday, December 25th: Christmas Day

Granny sits on the sofa listening to Lord Denning's *With Great Pleasure* (Denning has a way of sounding exactly as one would expect a wise old lawyer to have spoken 500 years ago). Helen is peeling potatoes and watching *White Christmas* on TV in the kitchen. Tom and Will are ringing friends. Rachel's piling the presents into bags. We've been blessed with a sunny morning.

Round to 100 Albert Street.

Christmas lunch never fails to be jolly and the presents then virtually swamp the upstairs room, leading Edward to mutter that the house is too small. An aircraft hanger would probably be too small to accommodate a Full Gibbins Christmas.

Granny Burd, the oldest of the grannies present, sits erect as ever, and at one point leans over to Catherine B to ask if she knows she has a bit of silver on the side of her nose. As Catherine had her nose pierced about two years ago, this produces some mirth. Granny B thought it was a Christmas decoration.

1988

Sunday, January 3rd

Wild, wet weather for most of the morning. No temptation to do much outside. Clear my room in preparation for a re-start on '*AF*' tomorrow. Write to Sepha and Chris and Carys Bell to invite them to some sort of get-together, because I feel Angela is in danger of becoming a non-person, the memory of the good times in her life trapped by the nature of her death.

Monday, January 4th

Violet, Jonas's wife, is round from next door to ask Helen's advice on schools. She doesn't think she can go back to her home in Botswana, let alone South Africa. I cannot conceive of what threat someone like Violet poses to prompt the South Africans to bomb her house, which they did in Botswana, sending bits of Jonas's piano flying everywhere.

    I ask her if they feel safe here. Violet nods her head emphatically ... 'Oh, yes ...'

Tuesday, January 5th

Carys Bell responds immediately to my letter about Angela. She's also at her writing desk, putting finishing touches to her second Welsh-language novel. Even on the phone the memories spill out. Angela was very practical. Yes, I'd forgotten that.

    Ring Alan [Bennett], whom I feel I must now approach head-on over *The Weekend*. Just before Christmas Brough called to say he had had a rejection from Scofield. His second preference is to approach Alan B as director. I don't think Alan would be interested. The play isn't delicate or oblique enough, too clumsy I think he'll think. Arrange to go and see him on Friday. For tea. He's not a lunch person. Quite ascetic that way.

Wednesday, January 6th

Lunch with Peter Luff.[1] He is an enthusiastic European. I didn't know his mother was Belgian. He sees 1992, the end of customs barriers in Europe, as a Great Day, and is working for a movement to raise the awareness of the Brits in advance of the changes in '92. Thatcher is aggressively anti-Europe, which doesn't help.

Watch a 100-minute tape assembly of material for [a documentary called] *From Fringe to Flying Circus*. There is a revealing moment in an interview with Jonathan [Miller] and Alan [Bennett] in which they're asked about satire.

Jonathan feels that, apart from Alan, none of them were particularly concerned about attacking anything.

Thursday, January 7th

In the afternoon begin work transcribing Edward Palin's diaries. Much of it is slow and lacking in great eventfulness, but I find his handwritten, notebook descriptions very compelling, even when he's off on one of his obsessions, such as the state of Catholic churches.

Perhaps because I know so few people have ever seen these notes, perhaps because I feel close to the spirit of them, being a notebook-er myself, the words seem very direct, the communication immediate, as if he'd been in Ragaz only last week and, what's more, that I'd been with him. He does sound a cheery, uncomplicated, gregarious character. This slightly complicates my decision on how to present him in the film.

Friday, January 8th

Using the breakdown of scenes I worked out late last night, I transfer *American Friends* to cards, *Saturday Night Live*/Lorne Michaels style, which I pin up on the board in my room beneath the framed brass title-plate of *The Missionary*.

Phone off the hook, I sit and talk myself through the scenes, making adjustments here and there and scribbling thoughts in a notebook. A growing feeling of exhilaration as the storyline becomes clearer and the characters sharper.

The odd tension I've felt all week lifts and, although I would like to sit down

---

[1] Peter had produced 'The Secret Policeman's Ball', the first of the Amnesty fund-raising concerts back in 1976. He had also proposed me (successfully) for Fellowship of the Royal Geographical Society.

and write my way through the whole film here and now, I am due at Alan Bennett's for tea.

Alan makes a mug of Earl Grey. 'I write all the time,' he confesses, waving his hand helplessly towards a pile of papers . . . 'I'm like Tolstoy, but I just don't know what to do with it all.'

Alan, as ever, gives the air of being unambitious, unplanned, unstructured, but of course that's not the reality. He's clearly quite buoyed by his appearance in *Fortunes of War*[1] and admits he'd like to do more acting.

I explain to Alan about *The Weekend*. When I tell him about Paul Scofield, he laughs – 'Every one of my plays has been sent to Paul Scofield.'

Alan gives me the latest bulletin on his van-lady. 'If you see a red light on, don't worry . . . it's her rheumatism light.' I ask what a rheumatism light is. 'I don't know . . . she exposes herself to it.'

Monday, January 11th

An hour's drive out to Twickenham Studios for some more *Wanda* post-synching, much of it in an attempt to make my reactions in the fish-torturing scene less pained and more aggressive.

Up on the screen, on relentless loops of film, are shards of my performance – a performance into which an enormous amount of pain, effort and energy was poured. Now, quite clinically, on a chilly January evening, we're banging a few nails in, shoring it up there, making good here and leaving it to the sound mixer to paint over the cracks.

To an acting purist the process must look like sacrilege, but it's all part of making a product, part of the composite mish-mash to which all individual egos and identities have to bow. Next month the TV version is to be recorded, a shaming little exercise in which all 'rude' words from 'bastard' upwards must be removed.

Wednesday, January 13th

Woken by Rachel coming into our room to open her birthday presents. A mini-Christmas.

To work at nine and a very productive day follows – all sorts of surprises as I try to get Ashby, Brita (as I've decided to call her again) and Miss Hartley

---

[1] Seven-part BBC TV adaptation of Olivia Manning's novels set in Bucharest at the time of the Second World War. Kenneth Branagh and Emma Thompson starred. Alan Bennett played Lord Pinkrose.

more involved with each other. They *all* have much more to say for each other now. They're fuller characters and I like being with them.

I work through until five o'clock when it's time to light the candles on Rachel's cake and, with Helen [Guedalla] as her sole guest, sing 'Happy Birthday' at her party.

It's raining persistently, but not heavily, as I park the Mini in Bedford Square at a quarter to seven and cross briskly, via Tottenham Court Road and Oxford Street, to Wardour Street and another screening of *Wanda*.

John has asked along a 'panel' of friends, so we are going to have one of those 'think-tank' sessions afterwards. Charlie C abhors them, preferring to rely on professional instinct.

The trouble is we are being asked to judge why an imperfect film (the sound unmixed, lines and music missing) might offend certain Americans. It's all wallowingly hypothetical and, though clever souls like Jonathan Benson and André slope off afterwards, I am lured into a session at a table at Groucho's.

I experience a form of intellectual claustrophobia. My mental processes will not apply themselves to the problems of *Wanda* in the way John expects. John, as usually, dissects the film with the icy and impressive precision of a Mercedes mechanic stripping an engine. Fay Weldon comes across with an opinion which sounds confident and starts the ball rolling.

Michael Frayn has some good 'farceurs' ideas, but they involve bringing in another character at the end, which seems quite wrong to me. I think the best suggestion for beefing up the ending is that Otto should appear, cement-clad, at the window after the plane's taken off. That's my idea, so perhaps that's why I like it.

Friday, January 15th

Though tantalisingly close to the end of my rewrite, I shall do no more this week as I have agreed to go to Wakefield to 'unveil' a 130-foot-long sculpture on the station.

The taxi doesn't turn up, so Helen, who is on her way to take Albert to be castrated, gives me a lift on to King's Cross. I end up running for the train.

We are about ten minutes late in Wakefield, having lost the southern fog somewhere north of Newark, and a crowd of photographers, reporters and at least two television crews converge on me as soon as I step off the train.

A defunct siding has been attractively converted to take the sculpture, which consists of five, fan-like constructions of painted timbers, arranged in a graceful rise and fall effect, which Susan Hoyle rather unfairly described as looking like a fence that had been recently blown over.

A short speech and I unveil a plaque, at the end of which is my name. For some reason seeing my name up there on a plaque fills me with intimations of mortality.

To the town hall for a reception. Speeches from the Chairman of Leisure Services – an unrepentant leftist. When he hears that Wakefield Station is to be restored in its old colours, he cannot resist some dire remark about hoping it isn't blue, for Wakefield has always and *will* always be red! This flourish seems to embarrass most people.

Tuesday, January 19th

Letter from JC with his various proposals for rewrites on *Wanda*.

Phone Sophie with my reactions, only to hear that the great man, far from hanging on the end of the line for my pearls of wisdom, is in Kent for three days shooting a 30-second commercial. 'He's being paid billions,' says Sophie, reassuringly.

Outside the cloud is thick and the light dim, but it's still not cold, as I put finishing touches to the fourth draft of '*AF*'. By eleven it's done. The last two and a half weeks have been the fastest, most concentrated and most satisfying work I've done for a long time. If it is a good omen that the script has had a happy birth, then the chances of this one surviving are very high.

Alan B rings, he sounds to have 'flu ... 'I'm in bed ... I'm reduced to watching a programme on the beaches of Rimini.' We agree to put off our *Weekend* meeting this evening.

A friendly-sounding man rings from LA. He is producing David Leland's film and wants to give him a surprise on first day of shooting by having the entire crew turn up in long shorts of the sort worn by David in [the *Ripping Yarn*] 'Golden Gordon'. Wants to know a bit of dialogue to have embroidered on the shorts. Suggest 'Shorts don't matter, it's what's inside them that counts.' I feel a warm breeze from the past.

Friday, January 22nd

Prepare for Chris and Carys Bell, who are coming to dinner in response to my letter about Angela, and keeping memories of her alive, as it were.

Talking to them, I become aware of how little I knew about Angela's history of depression and how far back it stretched. Chris says that Veryan virtually brought up Jeremy for the first few months.

Carys goes back even further, to when Angela was in Brownies, and tells of a friend who knew Angela then and who said that when she took over from someone in a Brownies play, having understudied her proudly, she 'went to bits', as Carys put it.

I've a lot to learn about my family. It seems that they have to die before I can really find anything out.

Saturday, January 23rd

Drive to Gloucester Crescent around five. The 'rheumatism light' is on in the caravan as I open the gate, but is switched off by the time I'm at the front door.

We fall to talking of *The Weekend*. Alan seems very positive. He read it three times. He has some helpful thoughts about the end and we laugh a lot. Halfway through our chat the phone rings. 'Oh, how nice of you ... oh ... well, writers don't usually get noticed ... ' and so on. He is clearly being praised.

Muttering that he'll get a pencil, he mouths to me in mock horror 'Ian McKellen!' McKellen has heard that Alan is to be given an award for *Prick Up Your Ears* at the *Evening Standard* bash tomorrow and wants Alan to mention the 'homosexual' Clause 28 which the government are trying to introduce in the Local Government Bill, making it illegal to 'promote homosexuality ... in a pretended family relationship'. Terry J wrote a good, outraged piece in the *Guardian* on Wednesday.

He advises me to send the play to Ron Eyre.

Sunday, January 24th

To the *Evening Standard* Awards at the Savoy.

There is a royal in attendance – the Duchess of Kent – and Helen and I are taken from anonymity in a jolly throng of film celebs to a brightly-lit corner of the room, where we stand rather awkwardly with other 'royal fodder', such as Bob Hoskins and wife and Jane Asher and Gerald Scarfe and Deborah Kerr. The latter seems frail and rather confused by the whole thing. A crush of cameramen accompany the royal personage, elbowing anyone else out of the way.

At last it's our turn and the whole circus focusses on the three of us – Helen, me and the Duchess of Kent. The Duchess (and, as with Princess Anne, I can't help noticing how enviably cool and unflustered she remains) goes immediately into a soothing routine which does not betray for a moment whether she likes my work or not, whether she's actually seen it or not, or indeed if she knows who I am or not. After a warm wash with the royal lather, I throw in a few observations of my own on life, work and writing comedy and immediately wish I hadn't.

Then the camera crowd and their royal leader move on and we are left in the no-man's land of après royalty.

The awards go smoothly. Alan B very effectively alludes to Clause 28 as requested – he talks of the thin line between 'promoting' and portraying homosexuality.

Monday, January 25th

A day largely taken up with writing a piece on 'something I feel strongly about' for *Family Circle* magazine. Try to marshal all my indignation about poor transport provision into a cogent argument and bore myself stiff in the process.

Terry G calls me in the evening to offer me the part of the King of the Moon. The *Sunday Times* was right yesterday – Connery has turned the part down.

The dates on which TG would like me are the 22nd to 26th February. Exactly the weeks of our skiing holiday. It seems I'm doomed never to ski at Mürren. But I tell him categorically that I have to take the holiday, especially as it may well be my last chance for a while, if '*AF*' goes ahead. He'll make sure the script is sent to me tomorrow.

Wednesday, January 27th

TG rings from Rome. The latest is that I cannot be the King of the Moon as I am not bankable enough. Film Finances have drawn up a list of Connery substitutes and my name isn't on it. Gene Wilder is the current favourite. and then Walter Matthau.

Thursday, January 28th

At seven o'clock by cab to Gloucester Crescent to pick up Alan, with whom I am to see *Lettice and Lovage*.[1] News that the appeal on behalf of the Birmingham pub bombers has been flatly turned down worries Alan.[2] He feels it's not just that it's been turned down, but that the uncompromising and complete rejection of any fresh evidence sounds like a show-trial.

Maggie is effortlessly brilliant and keeps me smiling – sometimes weeping

---

[1] A play by Peter Shaffer, who also wrote *Equus*. Maggie Smith won a Tony for Best Actress in 1990 for her role as Lettice Douffet.

[2] In November 1974 bombs exploded in two Birmingham pubs: 21 people were killed and 182 injured. The Provisional IRA were blamed and in 1975 six Irishmen were found guilty and sentenced to life imprisonment. After a campaign led by the MP Chris Mullin, their sentences were overthrown by the Court of Appeal. In 1991, after spending sixteen years in prison the 'Birmingham Six' were declared innocent and released.

with laughter – throughout the first act. Alan has doubts at the interval. 'What do you think the play would be like without her?' He says that the lines in *The Weekend* are much funnier than those he's heard tonight.

The second act leaves Maggie on hold and brings Margaret Tyzack to the fore. She's a good actress, but the role is full of tired old lines and attitudes and her conversion to Maggie's theatrical games doesn't begin to convince. Both of us are rather silent in the third act and, as we get up at the curtain to go backstage, Alan breathes 'This is where the acting comes in.'

Saturday, January 30th

Jonas Gwangwa comes in for a glass of wine. Talk over things in South Africa. Jonas says morale of the black people is very high. Hints at strikes against foreign company bases in South Africa. On a lighter note he says that the one thing the government can't understand about the ANC and the African resistance is that they laugh a lot.

Jonas says that some of the apartheid laws are so silly they should be laughed at. Blacks and whites can marry in some places, but they cannot live together in the same township. But there are one or two de-segregated coaches on the railways now. The only place that those enjoying a mixed marriage can actually procreate is in certain coaches on the 7.15 to Johannesburg!

Monday, February 1st

Up at eight. Tired. Dragging myself into another important week. Fierce weather outside. Wind, sometimes very strong, and occasional deluges. Look again at '*AF*' in light of Tristram's recent comments. Bolstered by a call from Irene Lamb, who finds the script delightful. She thinks Ellen Burstyn a good choice and will send videos over.

Will Wyatt calls with 'the good news'. All is to go ahead on the *80 Days* trip. I must disappoint him with my reaction, for he asks 'Do I detect a note of caution, or is this your natural state?'

Thursday, February 4th

To an Eric Clapton concert at the Albert Hall, for which Ray has secured us [tickets]. He has two spares, so Will and his friend Raffi, who cannot believe their luck, come along too.

The concert is well received. Ray, of course, mesmerising. He doesn't just

play, he performs; an extraordinary ritualistic, stylised, eye-catching performance it is too. Just a tap on a bongo drum from Ray is a piece of
consummate showmanship.

After the concert, a wallow, in the Elgar Room, with the celebs.

Bob Hoskins says he would love to do a film with 'you lot', as he calls us.

Phil Collins also very keen. Says that after doing *Buster* his appetite for acting
came right back.

William and Raffi, having shaken the hands of the likes of Clapton, Starr,
Collins and Bill Wyman, say they're going to cut their hands off and keep them.

Friday, February 5th

Put down some ideas for my appearance on a Comic Relief eight-hour bonanza
this evening. Think I'll play my Manager – chance to re-do Dino Vercotti.[1] As
I write I have the feeling that Dino's world-view is quite a good vein of
humour. Rather like Edna Everage – once the character is there the material is
inexhaustible.

My head is thick, my nose streams, but I take a couple of Honduran lagers
and a taxi to the BBC.

Then upstairs to the sixth-floor hospitality, where the new men of the
BBC – Jonathan Powell and John Birt – are hosting a night-long 'reception'.
Yentob of Two is there, and much the jolliest and most approachable of the
three wise men.

Talk to Jennifer Saunders and Dawn French and Adrian Edmondson, and
I can't help noticing how nicely they're treated by the BBC, these enfants
terribles of alternative comedy. They stand comfortably and confidently at the
centre of things, the new establishment. Still, there could be much worse
establishments.

In the 'Most Popular Sketch' section, 'Parrot Shop' is voted No. 1 and
'Lumberjack' No. 3. So not a bad night for an ailing comedian.

Monday, February 8th: Southwold

Irene comes back with the first intelligence on Ellen Burstyn (born Ena May
Gilooly!). She's free in the summer. But she's with heavy agents CAA.[2] A

---

[1] Dino Vercotti and his brother (played by myself and Terry Jones) were two hopeless Italian
Mafiosi who appeared in Monty Python offering 'protection' to the British Army (played by
Graham Chapman).
[2] Best known, probably, for her performance in *Alice Doesn't Live Here Anymore* (1974), she is a
prolific stage and screen actor and the first woman President of American Actors' Equity.

fellow casting director in New York gives her bad word of mouth – not much sense of humour, self-centred, fussy. Irene dismisses all this as the sort of talk which always surrounds very good actors or actresses who are difficult when doing run-of-the-mill work because they want to make it right. We decide to send her the script ASAP.

Wednesday, February 10th

Meet with Ron Eyre to discuss his thoughts on *The Weekend*. He lives up the modest end of Ladbroke Road, if there is a modest end, in a sensibly-sized terraced family house. Ron has no family and has just let off various flats in the house.

Our hour or so ends inconclusively with Ron saying that there's not much to do, but there's a lot, and hedging further on whether he would be interested in directing it. He reminds me that he turned down the chance to direct the early Michael Frayns *and* the early Ayckbourns. Is this to demonstrate the frailty of his own taste or just to let me down gently? But I leave with a clutch of very good suggestions for further work to be done.

To lunch at Hilaire to meet the putative second director of *80 Days*, Roger Mills.[1] I like him and feel comfortable with him straight away. Maybe it's because he is drinking gin, which he then spills over the menu, but he reminds me, in spirit, of Ian MacNaughton.

He further endears himself to me by telling me that *East of Ipswich* has won a BAFTA nomination for Best Single Drama. This couldn't have come at a better time for the Palin-Powell partnership.

We discuss attitudes to the journey, the programme and the BBC and reach near-unanimity on all of them. I do feel we have to be seen to take the rough with the smooth in this – the days in dingy hotels in Djibouti will add immeasurably to the audience's cathartic appreciation of the Taj in Bombay.

Out to dinner at Meridiana with John C, Jamie and Kevin.

Paul Simon arrives; Kevin has asked him along. He glides softly to the table, he smiles softly, he speaks softly; a well-modulated man. Easy and amusing company, though one feels that there is part of him kept carefully hidden.

Later Kevin is very complimentary about my performance – 'In the scene with me I was watching *you*,' he admits incredulously.

---

[1] He was one of the most successful and experienced of BBC documentary producer/directors. He had created the *Forty Minutes* format, which won him two BAFTA Awards for Best Documentary series. Rather than take a job as Executive in charge of BBC1 documentaries, he had opted to go out on the road. *80 Days* was his first job as a freelance.

Thursday, February 11th

Patrick C [Cassavetti] arrives at nine. He has some reservations about the script, but they don't seem substantial. His feeling for the spirit of the piece is much the same as mine. I like his enthusiasm for film and he has a distinct preference for the tightly-budgeted quality picture than for anything big and expensive.

He still has *Paris by Night* to see through post-production and is still not sure if he can commit to '*AF*'. Rather as with Ron Eyre yesterday morning, I'm left with the impression of cordiality and sympathy and evasion.

Car collects me at 2.30 to go down to Roger Cherrill for some more *Wanda* post-synch. This time it's for the US TV version! I have to say 'flaming' instead of 'fucking', but draw the line at 'bashing' instead of 'buggering' and change it to 'brutalising', which still has some bite to it. Kevin C has re-voiced about 40 lines! John is there. I thank him for his uncontrollable hospitality in funding meals for us all. He gives me the old twinkle. 'You should do commercials, Mickey.'

To the Bush Theatre to see Dervla Kirwan's play [Dervla was Charles Sturridge's recommendation for Brita in *American Friends*].

Dervla is nervous. I hope I've not made her so. She's intriguing. A face that it's impossible to sum up in a word. She can look different from every angle. She has long, dark hair and would be perfect in period costume. I find her interesting and appealing and she reveals clearly in this play that she's a natural actress. At times her maturity shows well beyond her 16 years.

We shake hands afterwards. She's obliging, friendly and with just enough shyness. Don't stay long as have a full day tomorrow and shall be meeting her again. But am excited and know that we're on to something good.

Monday, February 15th

Begin the morning in good heart, but gradually the lack of reaction to '*AF*' grinds me down. The last call I had from Steve's office was on Friday late afternoon to tell me that none of the MGM heads would be in London or New York in the next few weeks. So to see them I must go to LA. *The Weekend* – silence on all fronts, apart from a good chat with Irene Lamb, who has been enthusiastic throughout.

I try to tinker with the script. But I feel I am working in a vacuum and inspiration dries to a thin trickle. Worse still, because I'm expecting 'significant' phone calls, every one that comes in and isn't about the film hits a raw nerve of expectation and jars it into irritation.

Thursday, February 18th

Hear from Steve that he's read in the trades that Burstyn is on the Berlin Film Festival jury which is sitting at the moment. The fact that her agents (CAA) allowed us to go ahead and courier the script to her in LA has inexplicably lost us at least a week.

To a BAFTA screening of Tarkovsky's *The Sacrifice*. It's one of the four nominations for Best Foreign Film and I've agreed to be on the judging panel.

A scattered audience of about a dozen people, none of whom I know. They all look frightfully serious, knowledgeable and intellectual. Bump into Mark Shivas in the lavatory. He's very pleased to hear I'm a juror – 'Brighten it up a bit.'

The Sacrifice is not a bright film. It's a carefully-paced, Bergmanesque piece about a man who's so intelligent he has nowhere to go but insane. Solemn and serious, full of marvellous images and brilliant lighting by [Sven] Nykvist, but ultimately I find it a rather tiresome muddle. It ends, suitably I think, with two men in white coats coming to carry off Erland Josephson, who's taken two and a half hours to go barking mad.

Taking advantage of a Wanda *screening there, I had decided to go to LA and try and drum up interest in* American Friends. *Alan Ladd Jr, CEO of MGM, who had made* Wanda, *had shown interest in my project.*

Sunday, February 28th: London–Los Angeles

Wake and worry about the LA trip. The film can no longer be just 'a project', a chance to prove myself or any indulgence like that. I shall be going to sell it. I shall be looking for a commitment. Is it really, absolutely, what I want to do? I lie there and occasionally the scale of it all washes me with fear.

Steve and JC are at the new TWA check-in, being brown-nosed by the VIP staff. Lots of jokes, broad smiles and we're even taken from the lounge to the gate on a sort of motorised golf buggy. Whilst seated on this silly vehicle, JC solemnly gives an interview to a lone press hack, whilst three cameramen snap him from all angles. 'Yes . . . the separation is amicable'[1] and so on.

---

[1] This was from his second wife Barbara.

Monday, February 29th: Westwood Marquis Hotel, Los Angeles

About one o'clock a minor triumph – I actually prize out of the agent Burstyn's number in Paris and at last we talk. She likes the script – finds it 'very well written' and 'charming' – but feels that she and I should meet 'before you cast me'. This is the call I had hoped would come before I left London, but at least it's encouraging.

To an enormous new polished marble skyscraper to meet our lawyer who is doing the MGM deal – David Nochimson. His law firm also represents clients such as Michael Jackson.

On our way in we meet a short, combative man called Tom Hoberman, who is Eric's lawyer. He talks to us for a while in his office, which is fashionably anti-corporate. For such as Tom – men at the top – informality is the order of the day and the office is full of old wood high-backed chairs, Persian carpets and a general anti-institutional arts and crafty feel. I'm reminded of how we used to decorate our studies at school.

Hoberman clearly loves all the competition, the fight, the struggle, the deal (America's fastest-selling book at the moment is called *Making the Deal* by Donald Trump, the property billionaire from NYC). When he hears of Ellen Burstyn his reaction brings all our delusions down to earth ... 'She is a good actress, but she wouldn't open up a picture any more ... you could pull her in for around 300 (thousand dollars) ... '.

Back to the hotel and dinner with JC, Michael Shamberg and his wife Megan. JC, fresh from his masseuse, is sharp, funny and marvellous on things like American inability to appreciate cricket, 'or any game not directly based on greed'.

Tuesday, March 1st: Los Angeles

Steve and I repair in our little Toyota Tercel to Island Pics, to meet Russell Schwarz. He indicates that there are changes afoot in the financing of Island Pictures[1] and makes it fairly clear that we would not be in their price range.

Back to the hotel for calls to England. Also speak to Ellen B in Paris. I will take her to dinner, at the Pharamond, Friday night and Tristram will fly over on Saturday to talk. If decision taken, Steve can do the deal with her agent before he leaves the US.

A half-hour massage and a swim before leaving for the MGM meeting.

Our meeting is with Alan Ladd Jr. Small, erect, striped blue shirt and hair, which needs a trim at the back, brushed tight down over his skull. Dark hair

[1] Island Pictures had released *A Private Function* in America.

and dark eyes. He also favours traditional wooden furniture in his office, quite at odds with the modernity of the building. Big, squishy, comfortable armchairs and sofas.

I like Ladd but, as we leave, I honestly cannot gauge what might be the prospects for a pick-up of *American Friends*. But I don't think Steve and I could have put our case better. The formal submission will be made next week.

Drive back to the Westwood. Charlie [Crichton] arrives in the bar after his flight from London. When he wants a drink he hoists his walking-stick in the air.

Wednesday, March 2nd: Los Angeles

Down below me white-clad Hispanics are already attending to the pool area at which white-bodied Caucasians will later lounge. In Beverly Hills other dark people will be out clipping the lawns around the 'Armed Response' signs.

To breakfast with Steve – coffee, fruit, two eggs, bacon, hash browns and a croissant. Usual sprinkling of film people. Shirley MacLaine scuttles out of the elevator looking serious.

We have run out of meetings for a while, so have time to sit in my room and catch up. Then walk out to the shops in Westwood. A beautiful warmth in the air, the neat beds of pansies outside the hotel sparkle.

The unlikely figure of Charlie Crichton approaches, preceded by the walking-stick. He's perspiring slightly but has already walked up through the Botanical Gardens and halfway round the UCLA campus from what I can tell.

Talk of Sandy – Alexander Mackendrick[1] – who lives in LA but not for much longer, according to Charlie. He is anxious to get JC and Mackendrick together while there's still time.

A white limousine transfers JC, Charlie C, myself and Steve to Lorimar (the old MGM studio) for a screening of the latest version of *Wanda*.

Watching the pic in the US for the first time I notice how much easier they are with Kevin than in the UK. He brings out laughs easily. The JC/Jamie rewrites at the end are smoother, but just compound the immorality, rather than solving it, and Kevin reappearing at the window seems a crude mistake. But enormous buzz of appreciation at the end. Frank Oz[2] shakes his head in admiring disbelief – notes with pleasure the intensity of the performances.

---

[1] Along with Charlie Crichton (*The Lavender Hill Mob*), Mackendrick had directed some of the classic Ealing comedies of the 1950's and early '60s including *The Ladykillers* and *The Man in the White Suit*. Since emigrating to Hollywood he had made, among others, *The Sweet Smell of Success* with Burt Lancaster. He died in 1993.

[2] Frank Oz, puppeteer, actor, director, created and voiced many of the famous Muppets before moving on to direct feature films, including *Dark Crystal* and *The Little Shop of Horrors* (1986).

Friday, March 4th: London–Paris

Take the 2.30 flight to Paris. Am staying at L'Hôtel. It used to be the Hôtel D'Alsace and Oscar Wilde died here in 1900. The year my father was born.

Inside everything is very small – rooms, lifts tightly packed in a curve around a central gallery which runs uninterrupted to the top of the building. It's like being in an extremely chic lighthouse.

My first sight of Ellen B is of a shadowy figure in the back of a taxi which slides up outside the hotel about 20 minutes later. I launch into brisk and well-rehearsed instructions, in French, for the cab driver, after which Ellen touches my arm gently and advises . . . 'It's alright, he's from Cambodia.'

The driver is indeed Cambodian, came over to Paris in 1975 and has never heard of his family since. This starts our evening off in a fairly serious vein, and when we are installed at Le Pharamond she continues to talk rather intensely about her worries for the world – especially what's happening in Israel at the moment.

In between apologising for the cold blasts of air from the street which send shivers along our row of tables every time someone opens the door, and trying to be attentive and concerned when I really wish the conversation were on a less demanding level, I'm aware that she has a broad face with a pretty mouth, soft skin and a good complexion, a slightly bloodshot eye, and she brushes golden hair back with a hand in plaster after a fall from a horse in LA two and a half weeks ago.

She has her idiosyncrasies, some of which are a little worrying, such as the fact that D H Lawrence came to her in a dream and she's now reading his poems – in public.

Halfway through our meal I had a little twinge of fear that we were barking up the wrong tree, but as we taxi home I'm a little more reassured. Maybe I'm too tired to think.

Drop her off, then, despite not having a coat suitable for the sharply cool weather, I walk, for an hour and a half, around the Left Bank, stopping at a couple of bars, enjoying what only certain great cities can provide – a marvellous set against which to invent and play your part. Like Venice, Paris dramatises everything.

Saturday, March 5th: Paris–London

Tristram arrives from London at 12.15. Cannot raise Ellen B – her phone is always engaged. TP and I set off to walk to her apartment, but when we arrive there is no name on the bell.

As a last resort, perhaps thinking what a Truffaut hero would do under similar circumstances, I try a loud, crisp shout of 'Ellen!', which echoes between the high walls of the narrow street. Sure enough shutters open several floors above us and the day is saved. It could turn out to be one of the more significant shouts of my life, for she had not known her phone was out of order and was feeling rejected and finally rather cross.

All is put to right over an expensive but delicious lunch at La Perouse – an ornate, old-fashioned restaurant on the Quai des Grands Augustins. Snow flurries sweep over the Seine. We sip champagne (her suggestion) and Meursault and eat angler fish and wild mushrooms and are about the last to leave (though no-one hurries us).

Ellen much more relaxed and afterwards Tristram remarks on how much humour she has – more than he'd expected. He finds her more soft, attractive and vulnerable than he'd seen Miss Hartley.

Wednesday, March 9th

Ring Ellen B, as have heard the good news this morning that a deal has been done with her agent. She must have insisted on a quick settlement, because he evidently agreed to our price – 300,000 plus 40,000 deferment and ten percentage points. She sounds happy and anxious to meet, so I have to arrange a visit this week which will fit in with my plans and her language lessons. We go for Friday morning.

Then to BAFTA for the jury deliberations on Best Foreign Film. Clear from the start that Nigel Andrews, Carole Myer and Philip Strick all regard Tarkovsky as God, and I think they're just trying to be polite to the rest of us in not being completely dismissive of the alternatives.

No-one fights for *Jean de Florette* or *Manon*, but Peter Greenaway's film editor – John Wilson – and I put up persistent arguments for *My Life as a Dog*. The trouble is that we are up against those who feel that even a difficult, confused, occasionally very dull film with a risible ending is, if it's by Tarkovsky, intrinsically more worthwhile than an accessible, moving, entirely successful picture by someone else.

In fact, the more we say we like *My Life as a Dog*, the more the Intellectuals seem to shift impatiently. It's not about enjoyment, it's not about accessibility. The more people who like a film, they seem to be saying, the more suspect must be its artistic credentials. We lose.

Thursday, March 10th

Tristram here about half past ten. He went to see *Handful of Stars*[1] – Dervla's play – last night, and did not like her much.

Over to the BBC to have a drink and chat with Clem, Roger Mills and Will Wyatt. All is amicable and in fact this is the best *80 Days* meeting so far.

It's decided that we shall make the journey in January 1989. Much clearer for everybody. Also I'm quite articulate on my feelings about the style of the programme. The rough with the smooth – a documentary unlike any other . . .

Friday, March 11th: Paris

Walk around, past the ever-present security forces along the Rue de Varennes to Ellen's apartment. Arrive there at nine o'clock – give or take a few minutes – to find that she has breakfast neatly set out and coffee brewing.

She has a view of the Eiffel Tower and over the wall into Rodin's Garden, with a group of burghers in a permanent huddle just below the wall. She also overlooks a small hotel with cobbled courtyard. An elegant and discreetly quiet corner of Paris. Her flat is small, brightly decorated and full of light.

During our conversation about the script, Ellen comes up with a very pertinent suggestion about her relationship to Brita – basically that she should at first be encouraging Brita towards Ashby, then she falls herself. Several nice ideas for new scenes or for adding to existing scenes stem from this. An excellent and productive session.

I leave her about half past eleven, as she prepares for her afternoon classes. She says she's making very little headway with the French language. I find we talk very easily and that she has an attractive wit and modesty – she is very concerned to know the dates of filming – 'I need a month before to lose weight . . . I tend to expand between work.'

To Charles de Gaulle. A South African team of some sort – speaking Afrikaans – are waiting for our flight – they 'can't wait to get back to Jo'burg and the sun'. A tough-looking lot with vacant red faces. One is so hirsute that his chest hair erupts from beneath his collar and tie and emerges as a kind of jet-black ruff around his neck.

Briefly touch base at home, then to the Bijou Theatre to see *Temptation of Eileen Hughes* – Tristram's latest film for the BBC. Bijou projection doesn't help what is a gloomy, unhappy little tale which I don't much warm to.

Afterwards talk to Nigel Walters, the lighting cameraman. He has been approached to go round the world with me and is most enthusiastic. He tells

---

[1] A play by Billy Roche. One of his Wexford Trilogy.

me the original *80 Days* idea was to be on video, with live reports and with Noel Edmonds as the traveller.

Saturday, March 12th

In late afternoon go with Rachel and Tom to Latchmere Leisure Centre, where Tom is taking part in a Martial Arts Display.

He and his class, under Gavin, are the best item on the programme. Well drilled and presented, they take us through from simple exercises to routines, throws, fights and leaps, to Gavin breaking six roofing tiles with one blow of his forehead. Tom, the youngest of his group, is very lithe and crisp in his movements. Rachel and I are both impressed. At the moment he is a Green Belt, second rung on the ten-rung ladder to Black Belt, but he clearly will do well, and fast, if he sticks to it.

Monday, March 14th

Lousy weather, cold and wet. Donald Woods calls – just for a chat. Reception of *Cry Freedom* not as good as hoped in the US, but excellent in Europe. He's been travelling everywhere with it, even Iceland. Says he nearly phoned me from Portland, Oregon, where he found himself in the house of friends for whom Python was the greatest show ever aired. Donald wanted to show off that he knew me!

Tristram here at 10.30. Work on through the script. Had been to M&S to buy sandwiches for our lunch, but the shelves were bare – no delivery yet. Writers with withdrawal symptoms looked dazed and disbelieving – saw Denis Norden heading helplessly for the chicken tikka.

A meeting re Prominent Studios, with Anne, Steve, the trustee in a suit and tie who's rather nice, Eric I, Ian [Miles, our accountant] and Terry G, is not as fraught as expected. We are only £175,000 over the estimate of £1.2 million which we were given in January last year. But, as Anne says, at one time it was to cost £200,000 to refit. Malcolm Ballisat, the 'outside' trustee, is very reassuring – we have a wonderful building and it's a credit to our pension funds.

The next step, however, is to equip the viewing theatre, sound transfer and editing rooms as best we can. So far they are shells. If we want them we must find £300,000 more.

Tom [currently on the staff] is back at Redwood at midnight to lock up. They are working him savage hours at the moment and he shows signs of demoralisation.

Friday, March 18th

Steve rings to tell me that MGM do not want to do *American Friends*. This is a bit more of a blow than I had expected. For a couple of hours I have to work very hard to be cheerful.

Decide must take the bull by the horns and ring Burstyn, Tristram and Irene with the news. When all this is over and I am about to settle to work, Terry J rings, so I have to tell him the saga.

Find it very hard to concentrate on the rewrites. The sun shines happily outside, but in my room I am assailed with doubts – why continue writing a film that will never be done? Has my bluff finally been called? Is this the beginning of the end for '*AF*'? Has reality intervened? And so on.

In the absence of any word of hope from Steve on '*AF*', I call Ray and begin the delicate process of re-opening links with Denis O'B. Ray promises to call him ASAP.

Saturday, March 19th

No time for brooding – to Marshall Street for a swim, which sets the world to rights, then home for breakfast and at midday a call from Ray Cooper. He's contacted Denis. Denis is very happy to look at the script, but he sounded one or two dark words of warning about hawking it around, disinclination to co-production and so on.

I feel that the approach to Denis is necessary, but regrettable in a way. Steve will surely suffer in some way, but I checked with him yesterday on the HandMade initiative and he agreed it should be made.

Sunday, March 20th

It's raining as Helen and I, in our 'awards' gear – Helen in her very sexy purple sequinned top and black skirt – step into a taxi for the Grosvenor House and BAFTA. Park Lane is a sodden jam as taxis and limousines disgorge some of the 1,000 or more guests.

We talk to Jonas and Violet – Jonas here for the *Cry Freedom* score. Peter Sissons is chatty – his Channel 4 news by far the best thing on TV. Ben Elton is much confused at walking down the grand staircase to the accompaniment of a fanfare from Royal Marine trumpeters.

The fate of *East of Ipswich* is over very quickly. *Lifestory* wins in that category – music, applause, one minute of glory for the producer/director, then on to . . .

the best adapted children's documentary in a foreign language. End of our, admittedly slim, hopes.

Johnny Goodman reads a hugely verbose tribute to Bergman off autocue and at the end of the massive build-up fluffs his name – Iggimar Bergman. Enrico Morricone provides widespread unintentional laughter by referring to Princess Anne as 'His Royal Highness'. His award – for the *Untouchables* music – is extraordinary, when Jonas was overlooked. Was Sean Connery really the best actor of the year in *Name of the Rose*? Was David Jason really better than the incomparable Coltrane as TV actor?

Jean de Florette was outvoted as Best Foreign Film, but voted Best Film.

Thursday, March 24th

To Prominent Studios for a meeting with Tristram and a reading with Dervla.

We read three scenes with Dervla in the eight-track studio at Redwood. She still imbues everything with this odd and precocious air of sophistication. What is beneath it, I don't know. TP clearly thinks very little. So it's inconclusive, and I leave to play squash with TJ feeling that we have no Brita and, as yet, no film.

We talk of '*AF*' and it's clear that TJ didn't much like the January rewrite. I thought I'd solved it, TJ thinks I've lost sight of what the story essentially was.

I've deliberately tried to widen it – to make it less like *The Missionary*, to give the three main characters equal weight – as TJ says, I've approached it like a novel. I still think this is the way to go, but TJ gives enough good criticism for me to walk back down Hampstead High Street to my car, with mind almost made up to accept a postponement and to concentrate on a 'No. 27' and *80 Days* year.

Friday, March 25th

Wake early. About half past six. Doze and mull over the matter of '*AF*'. From every way I look at it, the case for a postponement seems solid. The recent work on the script only emphasises how far it is from being just right (as Helen said last night, the best things you do are clear in your head before you start).

TJ's words of last night echo Anne Bancroft's of last December: 'Why do you want to do the film?'

By eight o'clock, when Rachel brings Betty up to snuggle down beside Helen in the bed, my mind is virtually made up. But first this newest draft must be completed, and I do this in a couple of hours. Talk to Tristram and Patrick, who both feel I'm being sensible.

Sunday, March 27th: Southwold

Wake about eight, still tired. Take Ma to church. It's Palm Sunday. We have to leave in plenty of time so she can ensure her usual pew. We have almost the entire nave to choose from when we get there.

Her friends gather, generally single ladies, who I assume have outlasted husbands. They all have something wrong with them. Every snippet of talk is of 'bad nights' and people being '*much* worse'.

A last walk to the sea and, as the sun spills out of the mess of rain clouds, I leave for London, and am in Covent Garden by a quarter to seven.

To the Albery Theatre for an ILEA support concert. To raise money for a parents' ballot before the government can destroy ILEA. Rachel told me only last week of the effects that the cutbacks on education in the wake of ILEA dismemberment are having – larger classes, some subjects withdrawn.

Helen tells me that yesterday she had the *News of the World* and the *Sunday People* checking on a story that Graham C might have AIDS. They were preparing this solely on the basis of how he looked at BAFTA. GC had already been contacted and had told them, with his customary reticence on such matters, that he had not indulged in penetrative sex for ten years! What more could I have said?

Friday, April 1st

Settle into a long evening's TV with the first part of *The Sorrow and the Pity*. Absorbing and provocative. How much history is propaganda? How many of the contemporary images we have of the period are distorted by bias? Ophuls' film is an attempt to look at German-occupied France in as truthful and balanced a way as possible.

As Paris is falling the phone rings twice in rapid succession. First it's Ellen B's agent, Todd Smith. I tell him I've been trying to contact her all week. All he wants to know is that we'll come back to Ellen first next year. All I really want is the chance to speak personally to her, thank her and assure her that this is so.

In a couple of minutes I'm in the Burstyn position, fielding a proposition from Frank Oz that I should co-star as a smooth English conman, with Steve Martin as an incompetent American conman, in a film he's making on the Riviera this summer. Says he's keen and Steve's keen to have me.

Tuesday, April 5th

My copy of 'King of the Mountain', the Steve Martin/Frank Oz film, has arrived from Mike Medavoy's[1] office. I read it at one go before we leave for dinner. Though the part is written for an American, it reads quite well as an elegant Englishman, and, though there is dancing and water-skiing with one arm to cope with, I read the part with mounting interest.

Different for me – I'm not the victim, or the shopkeeper, but the dominant instigator of most of the events – and a meaty role which would place considerable demands on my acting, but that it is what I need.

A message from the office to tell me that Innes Lloyd has a definite go-ahead on 'No. 27', shooting in June. Suddenly I'm in demand and the year looks like being acting, writing and documentary.

How fitting that this Dies Mirabilis should end with Granny G's 73rd birthday party at L'Escargot – Mary, Ed, Cathy, Helen and I – and that Princess Diana should be at the table next door.

She holds her head and shoulders in a hunched, protective curve, as if not wanting to draw attention to herself. Her generally downcast, but big and beautiful eyes and pink cheeks very attractive. What she can be making of the bulbous man next to her, shouting about 'lesbian co-operatives in the Balls Pond Road' and other jeering anti-leftist clichés, I can't imagine.

We all get up around the same time to leave. She drives off, herself at the wheel, from a car parked right outside. Elena, of course, has dealt with the whole thing *most* discreetly.[2]

Wednesday, April 6th

Various phone calls re 'King of the Mountain'. Steve reveals JC turned down the part, but most reluctantly apparently.

Drive to Twickenham to make noises of myself sliding down a baggage chute. Charlie and John Jympson tell of a rather unpleasant meeting in LA after I'd left with a music supremo called Newman who was very rude about everything and asked John C if he'd ever done comedy before. I *do* laugh at this.

Frank Oz rings. He admits to being very embarrassed. Another actor is involved who had been sent the script and who had not responded and who suddenly wants to do it. I'm about to reassure Frank that I know who the actor is, when he tells me it's Richard Dreyfuss.

---

[1] Mike Medavoy was the co-founder of Orion Pictures Corporation.
[2] Elena Salvoni, legendary maîtresse d', at Bianchi's and then L'Escargot in Soho, and now at L'Etoile in Charlotte Street. In 2005 she celebrated 60 years in the business.

Just as well I do not have a great ego over these things. Yet my part in 'King of the Mountain' is someone with a huge ego, so I'm assertive for half an hour. Oz very sympathetic, says it's not entirely his decision. Producers, money boys, etc.

Work on the script until half past eleven. Only in bed do I allow myself to ride a wave or two of self-pity. It feels as though I'm doomed not to act again – already this year *Munchausen, American Friends* and now this have slipped from me. Add all these to 'Troubles' and a pattern emerges that could be attractive to a paranoiac.

Mind you, I sleep much better than when I thought I *had* the part.

Tuesday, April 12th

Frank Oz calls. Dreyfuss read for my character, Lawrence, and couldn't get it. Too much energy, he couldn't play the laid-back characters, he wanted to be Freddy. So I'm back on the list and he would like me to fly over to New York before the end of the week.

He calls back at ten minutes to midnight to ask if I can fly on Concorde on Friday.

Wednesday, April 13th

Up at 8.30, and by ten heading off with William towards Winchester. He wants to see the cathedral and the library in pursuit of his Malory enthusiasm.[1]

Winchester, an hour and a half from home down the M3, is a good-looking, well-kept little city. A pleasure to walk around.

On the way back we discuss Thatcher and what's happening in the country. For the first time I feel that sense of helplessness before the weight of the Thatcher machine. It's changing everything that I've believed in in the years since I left Shrewsbury, and there seems no way of stopping it. I feel too old to change things, but William understands what's happening and knows it's up to him and his generation to carry the torch of concern, compassion, co-operation and conscience. (That's enough alliteration – Ed.)

[1] A collection of stories and legends about King Arthur was collated by Sir Thomas Malory under the title *Le Morte D'Arthur* and published by William Caxton in 1485. An earlier version known as the Winchester Manuscript was discovered in Winchester College Library in 1934. It's now in the British Library.

Friday, April 15th: London–New York

I'm bouncing in a limousine through the shattered landscape of 2nd Avenue, Harlem. Buildings either burnt-out, bricked up or covered from head to foot in graffiti. Here in Harlem the security is quite overt, bent iron grilles, padlocks hanging onto rusty metal.

Then into the nineties and regeneration begins. Instead of decay there is cautious conversion. Once into the eighties we're among some of the most expensive apartments in the world. It's all New York. Like an eccentric friend – it's impossible to understand but has to be constantly talked about.

I set my bags down at the Parker Meridien. I notice my computer-printed check-in slip is headed 'Star of Monty Python's Flying Circus'. If this gets me a room with a view then it's fine.

I'm 31 floors up and looking out towards the greening park and amongst the towers around me is the famous Essex House, or Excess House, as it would be renamed in my autobiography. From here I can appreciate how gigantic the letters are atop the hotel and I should imagine in a storm there must be considerable likelihood of being struck by a falling 'S' 'E' or 'X', or possibly all three at the same time.

At a quarter to twelve US time, a quarter to five my own bodily time, I'm deposited at 50 Riverside Drive on the West Side, where Frank Oz's apartment is located. Steve is already there.

We talk, have coffee. I sense that Steve has been through this before. I can't help being affected by the knowledge that I am a name on a list. Not *the* name. We read some scenes. Frank O shows me photos of the villa where they're shooting. He's anxious that I should have as much material as possible on which to base the character.

Well, I find I'm not giving Frank quite what he wants. He wants it light and debonair and elegant and stylish and I am not delivering. I'm suddenly tight, heavy, plodding and predictable. I have to face it that I'm out of practice and it isn't coming nearly as easy as I expected.

After an hour and a half we go for lunch at a Japanese round the corner. Across the road Irving Berlin lived as a recluse for many years; at the corner is a hookers' hotel. There's a welfare hostel across the street from one of the most expensive private schools in the city.

At lunch I learn more about the film. They've changed the title to 'Dirty Rotten Criminals'.[1] When I also hear that the mystery writer is Dale Launer, who wrote the ugly *Ruthless People*, I begin to feel that my lustreless reading earlier may have saved me.

Walk back across Central Park. Magnolia, azaleas and hawthorn in blossom,

---

[1] And it was to be changed again to *Dirty Rotten Scoundrels*.

but at the same time the number of odd, mad and sinister and threatening individuals wandering by seems to have increased and I feel a little jumpy. Brought out of my reverie as a woman passes, stops, turns back and gasps . . . 'Oh God, I have just passed a myth.'

Monday, April 18th

Cannot shake off persistent feeling of the blues this morning, and a nagging feeling of slipping backwards, of projects aborting left, right and centre.

All this tinged with a common enough gloom ingredient – am I doing the right things with my life? Should I have stayed in grubby Gospel Oak? Should the children have gone to beleaguered local state schools, instead of gaining the enviable confidence that private school children seem to have?

These last considerations all come under the heading of envy, which I know to be one of the Deadly Sins, and one which would be present at any level, so I refuse to take them too seriously. But they niggle, as a lot of other things niggle, this morning.

Friday, April 22nd

Happily listening to 'How to Write a Screenplay' on *Kaleidoscope* when Oz calls, 'just to keep you in the picture'. Now Dreyfuss is re-interested and also onto the scene has strolled M Caine; 'It's between you three,' a rather harassed-sounding Oz assures me.

More and more I don't want to do it, but, just as much, I *do* want to be chosen. I think Caine is probably the nearest he will get in an English actor to the effortless charisma of Niven.

Tuesday, April 26th

Am bought lunch by Hilary Neville-Towle of BBC Books. Rather of the class and style of most publishing ladies, but very nice, un-pushy and interesting.

She reawakens my enthusiasm for the *80 Days* trip and I try to forget that the contract cannot be signed because of the ridiculously low fee which the BBC have offered. Good progress on the book, which *must* look more exciting than the *Great River Journeys* she brought along. Poor photos, dull format.

With Helen, to dinner at the Garrick with Mel [Calman] and Debbie [Moggach, a novelist and Mel's partner]. Like all these old clubs it's on a grand scale – with huge windows and high ceilings – but everything, from the armchairs to the doorman, is slightly shabby.

This is an element of the English way of doing things that the Americans just couldn't understand. They would make everything shiny. A coat of paint, unless applied with a liberal mixture of dust, would ruin this place.

Wednesday, April 27th

I check through my *Number 27* rewrites as they come hot off the presses. Tristram rings to say he has found the complete Miss Barwick – Joyce Carey, who actually *is* 90!

William arrives back from a week's biology swotting in Pembrokeshire full of heroic tales of William Ellis's effortless superiority over the other schools. He hears later in the evening that his 'A' Level history teacher has just quit, on the verge of a nervous breakdown. Will thought him a good teacher who knew his subject; still, no match for the Thatcher/Baker steamroller under which all London teachers are being squashed.

Sunday, May 1st

A significant coincidence. As the first part of 'Troubles' begins on LWT, Frank Oz rings to tell me that they've decided to go with Michael Caine!

The latter doesn't hurt nearly as much as the former.

In fact, now I can contemplate a more leisurely summer, richer in everything, I hope, except, of course, money!

Wednesday, May 4th

Set off for a poetry-reading at the Chelsea Arts Club in honour of Robert Graves. The Club is in an odd and characterful white building on Old Church Street; the bell must be pressed before you can enter (so the sound of the bell ringing marks the entire evening).

As I arrive, a very elderly lady is being assisted towards the low Beatrix Potter-like doorway.

I have a pint of beer. Out in the garden, which is very green and airy and protected, George Melly sits alone.

Spike is late, so the poetry-reading is postponed for an hour. I'm taken to meet the old lady I held the door open for. She is Ros Hooper, Robert Graves's sister, and she's 94. Quite easy to talk to once one ceases to be apologetic and sycophantic and behaves naturally. She clutches a book of Georgian poetry. She's clear-eyed and says she can still read quite unaided. She also hears and digests info in the middle of this noisy throng with great ease.

She's most concerned about the food and she enquires of every admirer who is brought to meet her when the food may be provided.

Spike arrives, looking very well, smooth of complexion and with a ruddy pink glow, either from fresh scrubbing or from the country life he now enjoys in Kent. He was quite a friend of Robert Graves and talks to Ros for a while.

Spike and I have an exchange of jokes. 'Why are you so nice to me?' he suddenly asks. 'Because I like you.' When Spike is on good form I can hardly imagine anyone better to be with – the combination of silliness, huge generosity and emotion makes him at times irresistible.

Eventually the delayed homage to Graves takes place.

Laurie Lee reads so well that I and the audience hang on every syllable and I'm made aware of how important it is to read poetry aloud. Ros Hooper reads beautifully too.

I shake a few hands and slip away from this sardine-like dining room and into the street. It's a cool, but pleasant evening. The whole thing quite surreal and dreamlike. But somehow suitable that I should be there to remember a writer whose *Goodbye to All That* was one of the seminal books of my early teens, turning me towards other war writings.

Friday, May 6th

'*AF*' is such an elusive number. Every time I read it, questions arise. Now why didn't I ask them earlier? I feel like someone trying desperately to fill a suitcase, from which bits keep popping out. Even when it's shut there are lumps which you know you must sort out before you go anywhere. But I feel as I read through today that I am at least editing from strength.

To Delancey Street for a meeting about '*AF*' with Patrick C, Tristram and Steve A. I take the initiative and suggest that we tuck our horns in a little, trim the budget and head for UK or European money first, largely because of my gut feeling that this will be a difficult one to sell to the US and that MGM's reluctance will likely be matched elsewhere.

Saturday, May 21st

To William Ellis to see their production of *Midsummer Night's Dream*. A great success. That one could spend three hours on those small, hard chairs, in that acoustically suspect hall and hardly notice physical discomfort says a lot for them. Always good to hear Shakespeare interpreted by good people discovering it for the first time. Will Palin, as he is in the programme, did the lighting, and I am proud of him.

Sunday, May 29th

Wake about seven. Cannot forget that Angela took her life a year ago. Everyone seems to have coped with it, though my hopes of talking about her, her life and death and the whys and wherefores with the family haven't materialised.

Though it doesn't haunt my life, when I stop and think of Angela, I cannot believe she isn't there, and that's when the pain begins.

Wednesday, June 1st

To Eaton Place, where Joyce [Carey] lives in a ground-floor flat. She has warned us that there is some building work going on nearby, and would we mind drinks instead of tea.

An erect and handsome woman with slow-moving eyes comes to the door. She behaves towards me like a 16-year-old, flattering and flirting quite shamelessly. Is the chair comfortable enough? Would I like some taramasalata with my whisky?

She's effusively complimentary about the script. Tristram uses a phrase of Jonathan Miller's to describe the process – 'a Niagara of praise'. She tells stories of Noël [Coward] and has several photographs of him – in fact those days, presumably between the wars, seem to have been her happiest.

At one point she asks Tristram if he's a bully.

We leave after an hour or so, leaving her in her tiny room, with her dark Maitland oils of London parks and her Corot miniature, and her signed photos of Noël – he wasn't a bully, but 'he knew what he wanted'.

Monday, June 6th

Take Ma to the Hayward Gallery, where 85 pictures from the Phillips Collection in Washington are on show. Mum astute enough to loathe the grim, concrete approaches to the gallery and the extraordinary two-floor gap between one half of the exhibition and the other, but the pictures are all interesting and some are amongst the best of that particular artist's work – notably an atmospheric empty city and railway tunnel of Edward Hopper, the complete contrast of Renoir's party after the regatta, a big Bonnard panorama, and Van Gogh's entrance to the gardens at Arles.

How they can put a coffee shop at the top of the Hayward Gallery and build windows too high to see out over the river is just another on a quite limitless list of questions I should like to put to Denys Lasdun on behalf of the despairing punter.

We walk by the river. Notice a new passenger boat service in operation – the Thames Line, sponsored, as most endeavours in the country are nowadays. This time it's Barclays Bank who get their ugly logo across the stern. Lovely walk, high, puffy white clouds. A Dufy day over London.

Saturday, June 11th

Decide only to do the 'Politician's Speech' at Wembley. The concert [Free Nelson Mandela] has already attracted controversy – the South African government condemning the BBC for televising it at all – but there it is on my TV at midday, the stadium packed out and nothing heavily political besides a large backcloth showing Mandela behind bars which says everything that needs to be said.

My car arrives for me at three. It's been arranged for me to bring William and three friends, but the driver will not take more than four people, so Tom brings Will in the brown Mini, trailing us through the back streets of Harlesden.

A dark, cavernous hospitality/reception area is filled with the sound of the music and there are monitors and a huge screen to accompany the pounding beat. And nowhere to get away from it.

On the whole it's run unintimidatingly, with much of the work being done by smiling young women. Rather as one might imagine behind the lines in the First War.

All of a sudden I'm buttonholed and led up towards the stage. Catch my first glimpse of the 70,000 crowd. Mainly young and white, whereas backstage was mainly middle-aged and black.

They want me on early as Stevie Wonder's organ has been stolen and everything is being rearranged. Then they ask if I can do more than I've planned. Say three minutes – as long as possible. It's been bad enough being dressed as a Tory MP throughout the afternoon, and now to be asked to incorporate another piece. Decide on 'Plankton', though I don't have the gear.

Miriam Makeba is coming to the end of her set on the big stage. I am to be on immediately she finishes. Rehearse the words and think of links furiously. Makeba finishes. I am poised. Makeba begins again. Finishes. Jubilation. On I go ... Makeba launches into one more number.

Not only has Wonder's equipment gone missing, Lenny Henry's mike has gone down, so I will not be introduced. Irony that I, who have come here to make an introduction, miss the honour myself.

Walk out. It's very strange. A feeling of slow motion, as if performing to a drunk. The huge crowd swings slowly, heaving, rippling and lurching, in my direction. A strange lack of connection between us.

Decide that I best just plunge in, hoping I have the attention of a few thousand.

Monday, June 13th

To the Everyman with TG to see *La Grande Bouffe*. This is rarely revived and I am interested to see if it is as good as I remember it.

Despite it being a very scratched print, and a little too long, it is. The audacity and outrageousness of it, with the sexy and the scatological so stylishly combined, are an object lesson.

Bad taste served up with good taste. Ugo's death, being spoonfed till he's stuffed at one end and gently masturbated by a schoolteacher at the other, is one of the greatest and most bizarre deaths in cinema – closely followed by Piccoli experiencing a terminal fart.

We eat a small amount afterwards at the Pizza Express.

Friday, June 17th

An urgent message to call JC reveals that MGM have changed the release date for *Wanda* yet again. It's now to open in selected theatres in New York, LA and Toronto to gather word of mouth in time for the big release two weeks later. My dates are all now in upheaval.

To lunch with Tristram. 'I need rather a lot of wine,' he confesses. We laugh a lot.

Maybe our laughter is just pre-filming hysteria. I know that there will be more problems with this than with *East of Ipswich*, and the finished product will not be as special or as much loved. Awful to feel that way.

But for now on, with slightly hysterical cheerfulness, we talk about the British attitude to sex and 'all that sort of thing', as his mother puts it. According to Tristram his father has become much more outspoken on the subject than he used to be. Apparently he's now quite likely to refer to someone as a 'silly cunt'.

Home about six, then out to a Hap Kido demonstration with Tom's class, in a Catholic premises behind the Royal Free. Odd to see them breaking breeze-blocks with their hands beneath a huge mural of Christ displaying juicy stigmata.

Thursday, June 23rd

To the Disabled Ex-Servicemen's home in Ealing, where 'No. 27' is filming. There have been problems since Monday. Five hairs in the gate – an unforeseeable chance at any time, but all this afternoon and all involving Joyce, whose first day it is. They have fallen behind despite working until nearly ten o'clock last night.

But the sunlight, filtered through the trees, is very pleasant and the location comfortable, if one can get used to the presence of limbless servicemen in wheelchairs dotted about.

I am able to make a few suggestions and entertain Joyce – who does seem to have taken quite a shine to me. Apparently her skirt fell down as she stood in a rose garden earlier. 'Normally I would have laughed, but this time I was a little cross,' she confesses.

Tuesday, June 28th

Drive to Epsom College which has become Melford School for the day. A slow journey – one and a half hours for about 20 miles. Cool and drizzling when I arrive on the site which is spacious and well endowed with cricket nets, fives and tennis courts and various pitches.

Afternoon spent in the still rather horrible conditions, shooting the scene we nearly cut – the aborted royal arrival at the end. Three hundred boys in suits and the school band. It looks impressive and is completed by 4.15. Early wrap, so everyone euphoric.

I had to be available to sign autographs (apparently they got a cheaper filming rate because of this!). About 120 boys availed themselves of the offer. I wrote a different message every time, knowing they'd compare them. Humour very strained by the end.

Back home, crossing the river at the fourth attempt – all usual routes blocked – I have a message to ring Shamberg. I know it bodes ill, and it does. Shamberg, not even deigning to break his monotone in sympathy, tells me that there are 'awareness problems' with the picture and that the release date has been changed again.

Wednesday, June 29th: Southwold

Whilst running an idea occurs to me for the 'Articles for Sale' drama series to which I have been asked to contribute by Jack Rosenthal. It's to do with Hemingway – the object being a seat which one fits to the deck of a boat for deep-sea fishing – as in the famous photo of Hemingway. From this I work out a story involving a post office clerk and Hemingway fantasies.

Back at Sunset House scribble my ideas down while waiting to cool down. The lines, characters and odd ideas spill out quite fluently.

Thursday, June 30th

As I leave Granny sounds rather a pathetic note, saying that she feels so 'bereft' when I'm away. I'm afraid I scold her a bit for using such emotional blackmail, but it does show that she is not as composed as she appears. Money matters of all kinds are a perennial source of anxiety and I drive myself to the limits of frustration reassuring her that she need have no worries.

Park my car near Blackhorse Road Station and a very easy Victoria/Piccadilly Line ride to Knightsbridge. At Wheelers 'Carafe' restaurant in Lowndes Street almost exactly five minutes late for my lunch date with Joyce C.

She is sitting amongst a sea of empty tables, down in the basement. Her neat appearance, erect bearing and eyes with their characteristic imploring look. She's wearing a very well-chosen azure blue dress with a pattern of white flower petals. She advises me to have the sole. 'Dover, of course, not lemon.' She chooses gravadlax to start with. 'Very sustaining.'

She politely asks me a little about myself, but I hurry on to talk about her and all her experiences. She confesses 'I'm a bit of a mixed bag, you know. My father was Jewish, but he didn't know he was Jewish for quite a while ... he'd say terrible things about Jew boys and then suddenly remember ... '.

Talk turns to Noël. Her mother – Lilian Braithwaite – was in Noël's very first play – *The Vortex* at Hampstead Everyman. She tells me, with some hesitation, of something Noël said to her once in a taxi – the gist of which was that he liked Joyce because 'Though you're the most feminine of women, you have the code of a man.' 'Well, I think it just meant I wasn't silly,' she says modestly. But it says a lot about her, and about Coward.

She was with him in Portmeirion and discussed *Blithe Spirit*, which he then went off and wrote in five days. For a time she and Noël C used to, as Coward put it, 'mystify people' at parties. They did a sort of improvisation based on characters suggested by the audience and 'many people tried to make a fool out of him, but no-one ever succeeded'.

The beans arrive, 'Fashionably undercooked,' comments Joyce with a twinkle. Rather as with my mother this morning, the only thing that ruffles Joyce's composure is the financing. She asks several times if she's paid the bill (she insists on taking *me* out) and the Oriental waiter smiles very tolerantly and reassures her gently.

I walk her back to her flat in Eaton Place, slowly, crossing many roads. She shows me a garden she likes on the way. At the flat she insists on giving me a brandy and then shows me some more of her pictures – including a graphically very bold painting of Coward's, of a Jamaican standing amidst palm leaves with the blue mountains and dark skies behind. She's very proud, too, of the portrait of her mother. A pre-Raphaelite beauty.

Saturday, July 2nd

At 12.30 to go to Camden Lock to cut a cake celebrating 40 years of the NHS. Frank Dobson, our local MP, is one of the other participants and I'm quite keen to meet him as he's one of the livelier and more effective Labour performers. Meet him in a café opposite the tatty, run-down Camden Labour Party HQ. He's a very jolly, hustling figure, full of jokes about poofters in the Durham Labour Party.

We walk to our spot, which turns out to be a small trestle table which is the Labour Party presence at the Lock. Frank has a megaphone with which he harangues the largely apathetic shoppers. Lots of ill-looking people come by – old with shrunken faces and eyes cast down, their faces dull and many resentful of our being in the way.

Frank is heckled by a surly and humourless cluster of *Socialist Worker* and other left-wing pamphlet-sellers, who are virtually falling over each other in Inverness Street today. I only hope they have better luck with the proletariat than we do.

Sunday, July 3rd

Bathe and shave and then talk over the phone to Benedict Nightingale, who's writing a piece for the *NY Times* on *Wanda*. He was at Cambridge with JC and remembers him as a quiet, rather self-effacing figure.

TJ then rings. Nicholas Cage sounds like a possible Erik and TJ is going to NYC tomorrow to talk to him. By coincidence staying at the Parker Meridien, as am I.

On the 6.30 news we hear of an Iranian airliner shot down by the Americans by mistake. Nearly 300 killed. Talk of reprisals will hardly reassure my mother!

Monday, July 4th: London–New York

Buy M Shamberg's cigars and have a glass of orange before boarding Concorde. I've become blasé about travelling supersonic now, which is sad. It used to give me such pleasure. Now it's like a commuter service. Full of Americans who came over for the Wimbledon final, which was rained off yesterday. 'If the rain stays like this, we could be home in time to catch it live on TV.' None of them mentions the shooting down of the Iranian airliner.

We leave London in rain and low cloud and land in hot sunshine in NYC.

My cab driver, a thin-faced, sallow-skinned, unhealthy-looking white man, talks compulsively – repeating endlessly a story of blacks at Penn Station who've taken to robbing car drivers ... 'There's a fucking precinct house two blocks away! I tell you, if this was New Orleans they'd have sorted those guys out. They'd have broken their fuckin' legs by now.'

Tuesday, July 5th: New York

Call Al L only to hear that he has some problem with his spinal nerve and can hardly walk. He can't come to the screening on Thursday. I suggest that I could go to see him on my return from LA, but his sister has 'decided to choose that weekend to get married again'. He is mortified and convinced that 'the big foot', as he calls it, is coming lower.

Picked up at 12.15 by Sue Barton, whom I remember with pleasure from the *Missionary* publicity days. She tells me Ed Roginski, who was Antonowsky's right hand and a very good man indeed, is dying of AIDS. She was in California with him yesterday.

Wednesday, July 6th: New York

It concerns me that I have trouble focussing in on small print. Taking out the diary this morning at the Parker Meridien, reading the menu last night at the Museum Café, remind me that my eyesight is becoming fallible. Also the odd crackle (the only way I can describe it) on the left side of my chest has had me wildly fearing that my system is about to seriously rebel against the demands put on it.

Picked up by limousine and taken down to the Gramercy Park end of town for a series of satellite interviews ahead of the *Wanda* opening. These consist of myself and Jamie on a sofa, John in a leather wing-backed armchair, with some funereal flower arrangement on a table in front of us, being interviewed about the movie by largely invisible interrogators, whose name and destination we only know from cards stuck across the bottom of the camera – e.g. 'Wilmington, Harry Brubaker', then 'Des Moines, Jack Phibbs'. We sometimes hear their voices in our ear-pieces before the interview begins. 'Michael *who*?' I hear from Linda in Washington.

Out to see *Much Ado* in the Park. Our limousine intrudes us almost up to the auditorium itself. We disembark in the middle of a wide-eyed mill of 'ordinary people' and for the rest of the evening are on display.

Being one who prefers to watch rather than be watched, I find it all faintly uncomfortable. John cruises along with it, but then he never really does notice people. Jamie is a little brittle, on edge, wanting the fame, because she's American, but feeling uneasy with it because she's intelligent.

I've never been to the Free Theater before. No-one pays, except for refreshment, so it's a much less formal, more relaxed crowd than you usually find in a West End or Broadway theatre.

A marvellous production. Full of life and energy and humour. Kevin [Kline] is on great form as Benedick and Blythe Danner matches him. As night falls, the stage and the lights of the village set focus our attention more clearly, as the play is drawing us in at the same time.

Thursday, July 7th: New York

My lunchtime radio interviewer has postponed until tomorrow as her husband was held up at gunpoint by two kids in Brooklyn and forced to drive around for much of the night before being robbed.

New York seems a lot crazier than I remember it. Perhaps it's the heat. Temperatures are up into the low 90's and it's humid and cloudy. Thanks to the wonders of air-conditioning I don't notice the extreme weather – except for the occasional soft blast of air between lobby and limousine.

Friday, July 8th: New York

To the Bay Hotel (formerly the Taft), where we are to talk to the out-of-town press. It's a most luxuriously appointed hotel on Broadway and 61st. Absurdly expensive touches such as a small silver display tree with a truffle chocolate perched on the edge of each branch.

JC arrives with advance copies of the *People Magazine* review. It's a rave – especially for John, but nice words for everybody. I'm called a 'deadpan delight'.

Then we are all distributed to various rooms, and there, like whores in Amsterdam, we sit waiting to be talked to.

Saturday, July 9th: New York–Los Angeles

We are travelling (Shamberg, Cleese and myself) on MGM Grand Air to Los Angeles. Small, luxuriously appointed airliners (727s) with a convenient and rather cosy little terminal building. The plane itself is decorated like Caesar's Palace; thick pile carpets, velour seats, deep, artificial and violently unmatched colours, mirrors, frills of one kind and another.

To the Four Seasons Hotel. Both of us so pleased to see unequivocal sunshine after the hazy mugginess of the East Coast that we repair straight away to the pool, which is crowded with rather uncommunicative LA types.

As we sit there, JC opines that he would rather like to do a Python stage show – provided we could do 'Cheese Shop'. I'm of the opinion that if we do it we should do it in a smaller theatre – 1,000 seat max and well equipped. JC would most like to do it in LA. I favour Sydney.

Talk about GC. John thinks that Marty F[Feldman]'s opinion that GC was in love with JC is not far off the mark.

We swim and sunbathe and then both feel the effects of the NYC week and collapse rather in the evening.

Sunday, July 10th: Los Angeles

Breakfast at the Sidewalk Café. My first cooked breakfast of a disciplined week. A bookshop adjoins the very busy restaurant and there I buy two or three more Hemingways – so impressed was I by The Garden of Eden, and encouraged too by a favourable reaction from Shamberg and Cleese when I told them of the 'Tea and Hemingway' script yesterday.

Gilliam is with us. He and Cleese haven't met for months. Here in the relaxed, neutral and unthreatening territory of Venice Beach, they both unwind. JC chides TG for having to have an enemy, be it a Denis O'Brien or a Sid Sheinberg.

TJ is still looking for an Erik. He sounds dispirited.

I sit by the pool for an hour with JC, who is very chatty. We swim and JC puts down some intense psychology work with a very boring title and poaches my Hemingway, The Sun Also Rises.

TJ and Carrie Fisher pick me up to drive down to the Ivy at the Shore Restaurant, where are gathered, Jamie, Rob Reiner[1] and Cleese.

Jamie and Carrie immediately fall into conversation – their lives are so similar. Both offspring of star parents, beautiful mothers and promiscuous

---

[1] Reiner had directed Princess Bride and Stand by Me but was perhaps best known for directing, and appearing as the director, in the seminally wonderful This is Spinal Tap.

fathers. Both hardly knew their fathers, both of whom later became dependent on drugs. Both mothers too went through difficult periods. The thought of Debbie Reynolds too stoned to work is, to my 1950's British view of her, quite unthinkable. Now these two tough children have reversed the roles. They are looking after parents who seem driven to childishness.

Friday, July 15th: San Francisco–Los Angeles

Not an easy start for the day. I am at Alex Bennett's radio show on – with live studio audience. Alex I like – he's benign, amusing, with a long moustache, a long history and an engaging, elder-statesmanlike aura – but this early exposure to the fans is gruelling. Grins, handshakes, autographs, how-dees, how-are-yers, how-you-doin's and inane replies to inane questions take their toll, and by the time I'm at the mike in a studio filled with the faithful I'm feeling the pressure.

But Alex seems entirely happy with my presence and schedules me for a further half-hour. 'When guys like Michael Palin come along, I just want to say hang the news, but we have to have it . . . so let's make it quick . . .'

Back to the Portman for breakfast and the reviews. The first shock is that Canby, such a loyal friend in the past, hates it. But Sheila Benson in the *LA Times* gives a much more comprehensive and better-written rave. Still, Canby rankles and stands as a stern warning against over-confidence.

Saturday, July 16th: Los Angeles

To breakfast with Tom Jacobson and John Hughes to talk over the 'Larry Meister' project.[1] I like them. Jacobson is quiet, trim-bearded and soft-spoken. He's from Kansas. Hughes is chubbier, pale-faced, bespectacled, like the clever boy in the class. Articulate, humorous. They're both younger than I expected. As so often happens, they know my work more thoroughly than I know theirs.

John C comes down to breakfast, sits at the other side of the dining room and starts to make 'yak-yak' gestures out of their view, but not out of mine. Later he is stricken by one of his lung-wrenching bronchial spasms, which usually result from him finding something incredibly funny. In this case it turns out to be the Vincent Canby *New York Times* review. Introductions are made.

---

[1] Tom Jacobson was a producer and John Hughes a writer, producer and director (*National Lampoon's Vacation*, 1983, *Ferris Bueller's Day Off*, 1986, *Planes and Trains and Automobiles* with Steve Martin, 1987). They had sent me a script to consider called 'Larry Meister Late for Life'. It was, as far as I know, never made.

Jacobson cannot quite get over the fact that we get on so well after twenty years together.

Tuesday, July 19th: New York

Over to NBC to appear with Jamie and John and Kevin on Phil Donahue's show. Donahue, an agreeable man of the people, is a show for Middle America, but has big ratings and it is a great coup that he should be spending a whole hour with *A Fish Called Wanda*.

Kevin, whose vanity did not go unremarked in the *New Yorker*, is already in make-up. He's careful and attentive and gives them advice as to how to darken his moustache. Jamie and John are live by satellite from Los Angeles. Jamie, with her fringe and glasses making her look like someone deliberately not wanting to look attractive (and failing) looks wan beside John, who's clearly been at the poolside a bit more, so much so that when he smiles he looks like one of the Black and White Minstrels.

Facing Kevin and me on the platform is an audience of some 200 New Yorkers. They ask questions like ... 'I really like you and are you married?' 'You look great with hair like that, will you keep it that way?' Nothing profound and the average IQ of the entire audience would probably equal that of A J Ayer's earlobe, but it's a nice, genial show.

Monday, July 25th

First off today is an *80 Days* meeting with Clem, Angela [Elbourne – production manager] and Anne J at Ken House.[1] They now have a bigger office and one wall is covered with a whiteboard chart. Only the first day is filled: 'September 25 – 11.00 Depart Victoria, Orient Express'.

It's undoubtedly exciting to be in the office now the project is official, contracted and under way. They are putting onto the bare bones of the route the flesh of actual trains and vessels. The Orient Express and Venice will be an exotic start. From Singapore to Hong Kong they have us aboard Ben Avon – one of the three largest ships afloat.

A drink in the bar, then drive over to Brecknock Primary School in York Way to present books to the leavers. The school is on the run-down border of Camden and Islington, on an island of houses and shops, triangled by busy

---

[1] Kensington House in Shepherd's Bush was the hub of the dynamic BBC Documentary Features output. It's now been turned into a chic hotel called K West.

roads. Old, stout building of pre-First World War vintage. Inside a good spirit. It's full of children's work and drawings and clutter.

As the rest of the school sing a couple of songs the leavers, all of 11 years old, wait maturely and with a right sense of responsibility to collect a book each and shake my hand. After which I'm required to say a few words on the subject of 'moving on'. Produce a sheaf of notes, then tell them I can't read my writing and throw it away. This seems to cheer them up.

Wednesday, August 10th

Breakfast enlivened by some San Francisco cuttings re *Wanda* sent, generously, by Don Novello.[1] I have already heard via Steve at the weekend that John was extremely concerned as to how I had engineered such a rave review for myself in the *San Francisco Chronicle* – what sexual favours had I granted the critic? How much money had changed hands? It is rather a gushing piece – 'The comic performance of a lifetime. He's up there with Sellers, Guinness and Mastroianni'! And that's even before he's mentioned John.

To White City to see 'No. 27' on the Steenbeck. My first glimpse of any cut footage.

First impression of great pleasure in the lighting and art direction – both nice and carried off with a sure touch, as is most of Tristram's interesting direction. Seems a little slow at the start, but strong performances, especially from Alun A and Robin Bailey, draw one in and the story-telling is quite exciting.

Really very pleased, and apparently Goodchild is too.

Thursday, August 11th

I finally see Hemingway's life through to its double-barrelled conclusion. Lynn's book leaves a bad taste.[2] Why was Lynn's work as highly praised as the cover quotes imply? A word-processor job with a few theories about Hem's mother nailed in there. All seems, like his subject's life, to have been ended in a hurry.

---

[1] I had worked with Don on *Saturday Night Live* in the 1970's. His best-loved character was Father Guido Sarducci, a Vatican spokesman. In 1977 he produced a very funny book of fake letters by a creation of his called Lazlo Toth, and their genuine replies from politicians and others in authority. *The Lazlo Letters* were the inspiration (unacknowledged) for *The Henry Root Letters* by William Donaldson, published in the UK in 1980.
[2] My own view, of course. *The New York Review of Books* called Kenneth S. Lynn's *Hemingway* (1987) 'One of the most brilliant and provocative literary biographies in recent memory'.

Friday, August 12th

To a Redwood meeting with Bob and André. Profits around 25,000 this year. Next year a bigger rent and rates bill and we shall need to increase turnover by about 30% just to break even. At the moment it seems alarmingly quiet.

Chris Pearce [the Manager of Delancey Studios] is so prickly – forever shouting at people, even arguing with clients – that Bob and André at one time seriously thought of moving to get away from him. Apparently Tom P burnt some toast this morning and set the fire alarm off. Chris went off as well and began shouting and screaming. I'm glad to hear that TP shouted and screamed back.

Tracey Ullman rings halfway through the meeting. She very much wants me to be on the show. As she puts it, 'I've got four lovely Jewish writers who are just waiting for me to get some English man on the programme.'

Finish our meeting. It's agreed Tom will be asked to stay on for a second year, which is a relief. André says he's very good at picking up information, but *as* good at forgetting it the next morning.

Saturday, August 13th

Wake Rachel about nine and together we go down to the Marshall Street Baths. The baths, run at present by Westminster Council, are to be taken over by an outfit called Civic Leisure from August 28th. Present staff will have to go. Socialism rolled back a little bit more.

At the end of the evening Helen and I are flopped in the kitchen when the doorbell goes. Helen urges me to look very carefully through the spyhole before opening it. I look through the spyhole. There, beside the scaffolding, clutching an envelope, is one of the Beatles. It's George, with the Wilburys' sleeve notes he wants me to have a look at.[1] Dhani and Olivia are in the car and Dominic Taylor [son of Derek and Joan] and his girlfriend.

I invite them all in. After all the years of embarrassment about inviting George and him not being able to come at the last minute, this spontaneous visitation is a wonderful relief – despite the fact that the house is in a dreadful mess. But Dhani loves it all and wanders around, occasionally checking with me about details of Python shows. He specially likes the foot on top of the TV [which Denis O'B had given me after *A Private Function*].

Turns out it's Dominic's 21st, so we open a bottle of champagne.

---

[1] A couple of months earlier George had asked Eric Idle, David Leland and myself if we'd help make a spoof publicity film for a group consisting of himself, Tom Petty, Roy Orbison, Bob Dylan and Jeff Lynne. They called themselves The Travelling Wilburys. We never made the film but I wrote sleeve notes for the first of their two classic albums. And I'm quite proud of that.

Tuesday, August 16th: Southwold

Sleep well. Woken by the sound of St Edmund's clock striking eight. A perfect summer morning, sunshine in profusion, hardly a breath of wind and the outline of the horizon on the North Sea razor-sharp.

After breakfast sally forth to the town – buy home-cured smoked haddock and fresh-dressed crabs and brown bread – called a cobbler – home-baked at the back of the shop.

Return, ready for half a morning's work, only to find Ma ready to go out to the vicarage coffee morning and surprisingly adamant that I should accompany her. So I do, and it's worth it. Mum quite a celebrity and much twittered over by various local ladies. 'We look after her, you know,' they proclaim over her head, as if talking about a prize vegetable.

Delicious crab for lunch. Sit out on the balcony. Some desultory sports training is going on below us on the Common.

Mum tells me more openly than she ever has before of the circumstances of my conception. She remembers the day exactly, she says. For some reason she knew that she had to do the deed. After years of vacillation Daddy would do nothing. She remembers it well, the summer day in 1942. 'The vicar and his wife had been round for tea – we'd had tea on the back lawn.'

That night, as if, she hints, at some divine bidding, she tricked Daddy into impregnating her by leaving out her pessaries. There is no doubt in her mind that that was the night and that she knew what she was doing; she remembers every detail of the event, she says, even what was on top of the cupboard! She also knew I would be a boy, though Daddy, to the bitter end, thought otherwise and already had me down as Elaine!

Wednesday, August 17th: Southwold

At breakfast Ma says she feels 'unsettled'. I ask her about what and she dithers a while, as if worried that she has already over-dramatised her feelings. 'Well, everything, you know ... Southwold just isn't the same ...' Not quite sure if she's trying to say more. I can't read the signal.

But she seems happy enough and her sangfroid recovers as I carry my bags down to the car. A letter has been delivered by hand, addressed to me. Quite unsolicited, from the local Tory councillor, quite ingratiating and asking me if I will be the 'Famous International Celebrity' they've promised will judge some photo competition. I realise that the days of quiet inconspicuousness at Southwold are numbered and I resent that.

Thursday, August 18th

To Notting Hill, then Holland Park and lunch with John, just back from the US. He's relishing having his house back – Barbara having now moved out to a place nearby. Inside there are empty walls (Barbara's huge canvases having gone) and dusty rings on the carpet where pots and vases have been removed. He drives me the short distance to the Hiroko in his new Bentley. 'It's not *new!*' he insists.

A light, clean Japanese lunch with gossip and the latest figures. They are estimating a 50 million gross and this, together with 20 mill for TV rights and a conservative forecast for non-US rentals, should make my points worth 350,000 dollars.

Our lunch is awfully pleasant and friendly and relaxed and we gently remind each other of the things that have made us laugh together. I am able to tell him that Helen and Rachel saw *Wanda* on Tuesday and raved.

Back home via shops for two more interviews – the first is with Anthea Hewison. She's interviewing me for *Here's Health*, but has just trapped her sciatic nerve and has to conduct the entire interview from a prone position.

Tuesday, August 30th

To the BBC for an *80 Days* meeting with Clem and Roger and Anne and Angela. Roger makes one or two suggestions with his stolid, commonsensical approach, symbolised by his pipe. He is worried that we may be top-heavy in the early interviews and that some of them may bite the dust. He also has an idea for me to check out garbage disposal whilst in Venice! (Apparently it's quite spectacular and certainly a different view of the canal life.)

Then to the London Library, where I enrol Will as a member and show him the quiet, woody time-warp of the Reading Room where he will write his extended essay.

In a burst of opportunism, I end up buying, in Jermyn Street, a bag which I hope will be sufficient to take my things round the world. It's made of a strong canvas and leather and when I get it home Helen's immediate reaction is that it's too small. Well, I shall have to practise with it. It's certainly easy to carry about on the shoulder – as Clem advised.

Sunday, September 4th

The *Sunday Times* carries a piece headed 'The Wonder of Wanda', an apparently unsolicited gem of a story about how successful the film is in the US.

Spend much of the morning working through the *80 Days* schedule. Play tennis with Helen later in the afternoon, and win rather competently. Back home for gardening and family phone calls to Ma and the Herberts. We plan on a get-together in London before I leave for my circumnavigation.

Tuesday, September 6th

Reassuringly good night's sleep and feel quite calm as the first day proper of the project that is to occupy almost my entire next year comes round.

Taxi to Stanford's, where I meet my *80* Days film crew. Nigel Meakin, cameraman, short, friendly, straight, agreeable and unpeculiar.

Ron Brown, the sound man, is tubby. He seems most concerned about the plans for accommodation in the boats and the hotels and who's sharing with whom. But he does listen and in between the banter is a considerate and deceptively gentle character.

As we prepare to shoot, a phone call comes through for Ron – 'The Pope wants you for Friday'. He has indeed been asked to Rome, for he is the Pope's favourite sound man and has accompanied the great man on many travels.

What with Roger Mills having just returned from Vietnam and Ron Brown talking of the cookery programme they've just completed in Hanoi, I'm made clearly aware of my own parochialism. Documentaries are like a club, travel documentaries a club within that club.

Thursday, September 8th

Ring Joyce C early to confirm our lunch arrangement for tomorrow. I tell her that I'm enjoying the sunshine. 'Yes, it's a great comfort, isn't it?' she replies with the impeccable delivery of a great tragic actress.

Friday, September 9th

Tristram P arrives to talk over the future of *American Friends*. Innes has read it and, as he puts it, wants to 'pick it up and run with it', which sounds encouraging.

We take Joyce to lunch at Bibendum. I help her up about 20 stairs to the restaurant only to find out there's a lift. The restaurant itself is of striking design. Very big windows, two of them stained glass. Conran furniture – clean, crisp and fairly soulless.

Rex Harrison is dining at another table. He looks like an old dog, his head nodding slightly forwards, food and drink held close to his eyes. An aged man. Ask Joyce if she knows him and she does. In fact she's been to see his show in London – *The Admirable Crichton* – at the Haymarket.

We effect an introduction between Rex and Joyce and as soon as he's with people he animates and transforms from being merely an old man to a charming, humorous and enormously attractive old man.

His wife, a Swiss woman, younger by far than him, is brisk but friendly . . . 'Come on, Harrison!' she orders. 'They're just about to order their lunch.' 'We're just holding hands,' says he, gazing down at Joyce, who leans back, smiling up at him. He shakes hands with Tristram and me. 'This is the writer,' says the umpteenth Mrs Harrison. Rex smiles at me warmly. 'She enjoyed it so much, you know.'

Joyce reveals that Rex H was in the American production of her play *Sweet Aloes* and it was a disaster. She wrote under the pseudonym Jay Mallory – professionally it was better to be androgynous at that time. A reviewer in Scotland said of the play . . . 'Mr Mallory is a most impertinent young man'. She enjoyed that.

Tuesday, September 13th

Drive to BUPA HQ, where I'm to be filmed having a medical check-up.

The crew have to sit amongst men in dressing gowns and I sense mutiny rumbling. Ron keeps asking why we're filming so much pre-journey material, and especially why we're talking to Alan Whicker.

I'm whisked off into a dressing gown and given the tests. Results similar to last time, except that vision in my right eye is less good. The dread word 'optician' is mentioned – and for the first time in my life not in a sketch!

Friday, September 16th

Out of bed about ten past eight. Feel more relaxed about things now the filming's begun, though big questions like how good will I be at the job, how will we all get on together, and how long will three months seem, remain.

By 10.30 I'm at the Royal Geographical Society in Kensington. It's a pleasant late-summer day and the park looks quietly green and tempting from the windows of the Society.

John Hemming is very welcoming and helpful and enthusiastic. He has been on expeditions to Brazil and has been among the first men ever to make contact with primitive Amazon tribes. He's lost many friends – ironically more killed in road accidents than by man-eating tigers or poison darts.

We film in the library, which is wonderful, well stocked and makes me feel colossally under-prepared. Leave with a big book on Oman under my arm.[1]

Rest of the afternoon at the Health Centre, receiving jabs. Then to the producer Jackie Stoller's fine, eighteenth-century office in Bedford Square, for a get-together with the writers of 'Article For Sale'.

Alan Bennett and Posy Simmonds and Jack R are already there. Alan, with white-socked Hockney-like legs thrust characteristically straight out in front of him. Jack is looking strained and poorly and not surprisingly, as he is going into hospital within a month for a hip replacement.

Carla Lane arrives. She talks about a pigeon she's befriended and about meeting in the vet a man who had brought along his snails.

Posy, slim, white, in a simple black top, is instantly disarming and tells me how when she was a bridesmaid at a wedding at the age of ten she put a tortoise on her head and it peed all over her.

We ask, over smoked salmon and cucumber sandwiches, about things like deadlines and special requirements. 'Will rogering be allowed?' asks Posy, in the tone of a Jane Austen heroine.

Monday, September 19th

To a house in Hambledon, near Marlow, a quite beautifully situated Thames Valley village, enclosed by wooded hills and bordered by misty green meadows. Here I am to do an interview, along with George H, for a programme on ten years of HandMade Films.

The house, largely shuttered, belongs to Harry Hambledon, who owns the village.

George is not at ease and feels that it would have been much better for me to be interviewed alone, then I could say what I really feel about HandMade. This is D O'B's idea and George evidently likes it no more than having to wear black-tie at next Friday's party.

When at last we're through, George tries to persuade me to come over to Friar Park. I tell him I can't as I'm meeting Alan and Barry C for one of our 'Three Yorkshiremen' meals. George tells me to bring them all up to Friar Park ... 'We'll get drunk together'. For a moment the idea of adding George and Friar Park to our threesome is tantalisingly bizarre.

Am whisked back to Vasco and Piero's rapidly enough for me to be first there.

---

[1] Oman was to be a key location in *Around the World in 80 Days*. It was to be the place we picked up a dhow to cross the Arabian Sea to India. In the event all plans fell through in Saudi Arabia, and we ended up having to make a considerably longer dhow journey from Dubai.

Noël Coward is talked of. Alan recalls Coward commenting at a party at which Dudley [Moore] had had the temerity to play the piano ... 'Oh, how clever, he uses the black notes as well.' But Alan found Coward very helpful and charming. They first met when Coward came backstage after *Beyond the Fringe* in New York.

Alan drives us all home in his new Audi. At a traffic light in Kentish Town, a fussy little middle-aged man comes up to the car and demands a lift to Highgate. Alan, momentarily confused, but, ever the good Samaritan, agrees to take him part of the way.

So in gets this red-faced, rather truculent man, who sits there like a character in a bad play or, more to the point, a Python sketch. His presence rather silences our bonhomie and, when Alan drops me at Lamble Street and I see him drive away with Barry and the man in the raincoat sat in the back, I laugh all the way to the front door.

Tuesday, September 20th

A day of considerable pressure on the *80 Days* front.

More gruelling London traffic, then into Lloyd's of London for an interview with the man who, among other things, writes the names of all the shipwrecks in the book. The building is like a huge toy, with the escalators looking like a clockwork motor up the centre. No-one that I talk to likes it very much.

The human inhabitants are at first glance all men, all comfortably covered and impeccably dressed. 2,000 of the well-off classes beavering away. It's like a giant public school at prep.

The analogy is confirmed by a steady stream of bits of paper darts, pellets and rubber-band catapults that drop from the galleries during the interview. 'Oh, you've got off lightly ... it's usually much worse than this,' says my interviewee.

Wednesday, September 21st

To interview Alan Whicker at the Dorchester Hotel. Will life on the voyage be as hectic as this? I hope not.

Whicker's room is approached through a series of valets and PR persons. One would think we were visiting royalty. There is a positive, almost religious, build-up of reverence as we approach the door of his suite. In the first of many coups de théâtre the door is actually only leading to a flight of stairs, off which there is another door at which the great man, greyer in moustache than I expected, welcomes us.

Whicker is fascinated with *Wanda*'s earnings and, by extraordinary coincidence, CNN-TV, which rabbits on from a corner of the room, suddenly shows a familiar face. It's me and my perm, illustrating the movie charts of the week – which show *Wanda* still number three in America.

All this serves to keep my end up, which is what you feel you have to do with Whicker. He is very much the Godfather. The way he tells his stories, knowing he's keeping everyone waiting, indicates that he's used to having things his own way. The suite, with the view over the park, must be one of the most expensive in London, and it's coming off our production budget.

Whicker is sharp, alert, dapper – competitive – generous with advice and with his time. Oozing charm as we leave. Before we go he talks about Roger M – 'a strange man', 'a man of ferocious intellect'. Whicker's tie and blazer are as important to him as Roger's lack of them are to Roger.

Thursday, September 22nd: Southwold

Listen to the BBC's 'Get By in Italian' tapes in the car. Whicker was quite adamant about what to do in an emergency – 'Don't try and speak the language, you probably won't be able to anyway. I just use Britishness, it never fails.'

Feel weighed down by all the work I've to do and after lunch set myself up at the kitchen table with the telephone. The oppressiveness of the phone calls and the interviews for 'No. 27' and so on seem worse as I see my mother looking very much frailer than before.

She cannot sit up on a dining chair for long as her coccyx aches. She says the doctor does nothing. I ask her what she wants to be done – 'Oh, you can't *do* anything . . . it's arthritis.' The skin on her thin little arms hangs down in folds. I suppose I've never seen anyone of nearly 85 so closely before, but her body, bowed over by her spinal curve, seems to be so inadequate for the job. But she remains cheerful and is determined to be good company and she potters around and cooks and reads and looks at the photos I've brought.

After supper I have to work again – honing the HandMade speech.

Later walk through deserted Southwold to the North Sea. I shall have been on such an unimaginable adventure by the time I next see it again. Walk to the edge of the waves, which are building up noisily in anticipation of a windy night.

Friday, September 23rd: Southwold–London

I feel happier and more confident about Ma's condition as we eat our lunch. She has rationalised my absence on the trip and there is no longer a hint of a moan. As we part she says 'It's a school term, that's all . . . just a school term.'

The still-blustery wind keeps her from coming into the street to say goodbye. She waves from the door. Make a mental note that at some time I shall have to get angry with the builder over the door and the rapidly crumbling window sill.

So little Ma recedes and I set myself to the hurdles that remain today. To the doctor's for a double gamma globulin jab and home at five.

Then back to the speech. Feel hot and rushed – the paraphernalia of the journey lies on the floor of my room. Lists of things to do lie accusingly on the desk. A scotch and ice calms the racing system and at seven I'm at last finished with the speech.

The dinner [celebrating ten years of HandMade films] is at the Old House at Shepperton and is like a much jollier, friendlier version of the BAFTA Awards.

I find myself on the programme under Master of Ceremonies, and beside 'Music: Carl Perkins and his band'.

Just before I go up, Michael White cautions 'Take it slowly'. The opening jokes about this being HandMade's latest film are well received – the talk of Denis not being able to do co-production because the lift at Cadogan Square is too small, hits home, and from then on I know I shall have a good ride.

At the end everyone is very complimentary. Denis tells a long and only moderately funny dirty joke in reply and George heckles him unmercifully.

George presents me with a gift for mastering the ceremonies – it's one of his old Oscars with my name scribbled on a luggage label and stuck across the base.

Much fun later on and a lot of jawing. Had meant to get home early, but it's four o'clock before head hits pillow.

Saturday, September 24th

A wet, warm day – straggly low storm cloud and strong winds. In *Variety Wanda* is the No. 1 grosser for the first time.

Gradually assemble a workroom full of bits and pieces needed on voyage. Find, after all the preparation, that I've forgotten simple things like toothpaste.

Mary, Ed, Helen and I escape to L'Escargot for a last meal.

Lots of last minute hitches, including the small accompanying bag being rather small and it has to be substituted, but considering I have less to set off with for 80 days round the world than I normally take for two weeks in the States, I'm quite pleased.

To bed about two o'clock and to sleep an hour or so before dawn. There's no turning back now.

Index

Index

Anderson, Lindsay, 132, 422
Andrews, Anthony, 126n
Andrews, Nigel, 585
Andros, Phil: *My Brother Myself*, 505–6
Angel, Morris, 276, 470
Ann-Margret, 133, 501
Anna K, 239
Anne, Princess Royal
  at BAFTA awards, 21, 559
  in Darlington, 60
  at premiere of *Private Function*, 345–6
  in *It's A Royal Knockout*, 497–8
Annie (film), 180
Another Time, Another Place (film), 303
Antonowsky, Marvin
  and publicity for *The Missionary*, 179–80,
    184, 198, 202–3, 207–8, 213–14
  praises MP's acting, 225
  and release of *The Missionary*, 225
  MP meets in London, 355
Antrobus, John, 300
Apocalypse Now (film), 6
Apostle, Constantine, 32
Apple (company), 164
Applethwaite, Keswick, 477
Archer, Jeffrey, 462–3
Archer, Robyn: 'A Star is Torn' show, 212
Argentina: and Falklands War, 157, 162, 165
Arista/Charisma, 24
Arlen, Michael: *The Green Hat*, 32
Armstrong, Alun, 578
Arnold, Gary, 218
Around the World in 80 Days (BBC TV series)
  MP asked to recreate for BBC, 517, 518,
    521–2
  MP books tickets, 523
  preparations, 547, 555, 557, 559, 564, 577,
    582, 585–6
  Roger Mills and, 549, 581
Arthur (film), 144, 185
Arthur Young McClelland Moores, 288
Articles for Sale (series), 571, 583
Asher, Jane, 482, 545
Aspel, Michael, 534
Astaire, Jarvis, 9
Atkinson, Ron, 334
Atkinson, Rowan, 205, 533
Attallah, Naim, 201
Attenborough, Sir Richard, 58, 275, 441
Auden, W.H., 322
Australia
  MP visits, 230–3

The Missionary shown in, 234, 238–9
Auty, Chris, 158
Avco Embassy, 112, 185
Aviemore, Scotland, 168–74
Aykroyd, Dan, 19, 120

B

Babylon (film), 61, 70
Bach, Barbara, 346
Bachardy, Don, 39–40
BAFTA
  awards (1980), 21
  Denholm Elliott wins award, 309
  screens *The Dress*, 352
  nominates *Private Function* as Best Film,
    354
  Tristram Powell at, 362
  screens *East of Ipswich*, 461
  MP serves on jury for Best Foreign Film,
    551, 585
  awards (1988), 558–9
Bailey, Alan, 37, 47
Bailey, David, 192
Bailey, Robin, 578
Baker, Dr, 47
Baker, Dame Janet, 444
Baker, Tom, 525
Ballisat, Malcolm, 557
Ballymaloe House, Ireland, 58–9, 76, 118–22
Bancroft, Anne
  in film of *84 Charing Cross Road*, 53, 514n
  proposed for *The Missionary*, 128, 130, 135
  proposed for *American Friends*, 475,
    513–14, 519, 523, 528
  declines *American Friends*, 528, 559
Band Aid concert, 350
Bangkok, 528
Banks-Smith, Nancy, 465, 479–80
Barbican Centre, London, 150
Barclay, Humphrey, 199 & n
Barker, Linda, 207, 214
Barker, Ronnie, 134, 189, 475
Barkin, Ellen, 491n
Barlow, Patrick, 284
Barnes, Derek, 177
Barnes, Michael, 122–3, 279, 366, 432, 532–3
Barnoldswick, 319
Barrett, Alex, 210
Barton, Sue, 211, 573
Bavaria, 4
Baxter, Glen, 228, 358
Beach, Jim, 71

Index